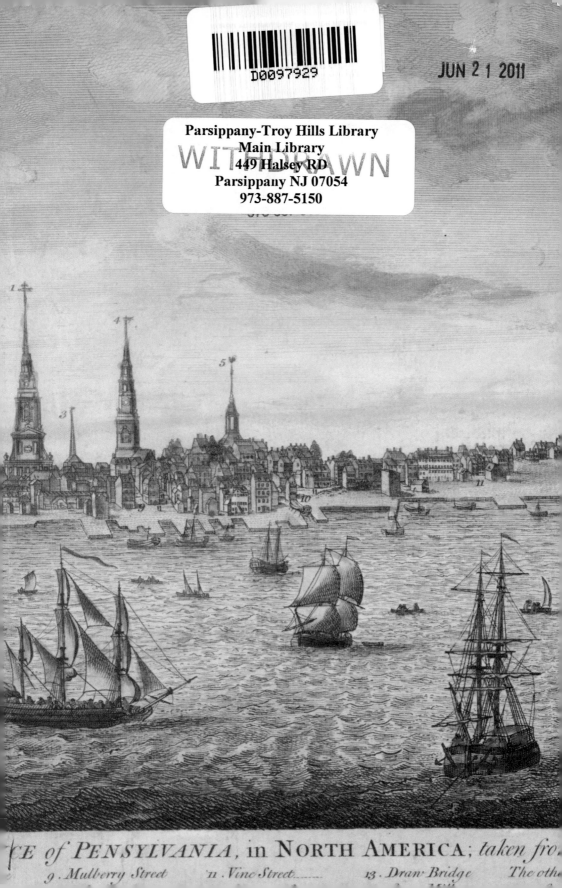

E of PENSYLVANIA, *in* NORTH AMERICA; *taken fro*

9. *Mulberry Street*   '11 *Vine Street*   13. *Draw Bridge*   *The oth*

INDEPENDENCE

*The Ascent of George Washington: The Hidden Political
Genius of an American Icon*
Almost a Miracle: The American Victory in the War of Independence
A Leap in the Dark: The Struggle to Create the American Republic
*Setting the World Ablaze: Washington, Adams, Jefferson,
and the American Revolution*
The First of Men: A Life of George Washington
Adams vs. Jefferson: The Tumultuous Election of 1800
John Adams: A Life
Struggle for a Continent: The Wars of Early America
A Wilderness of Miseries: War and Warriors in Early America
The Loyalist Mind: Joseph Galloway and the American Revolution

INDEPENDENCE

. . .

THE STRUGGLE TO
SET AMERICA FREE

JOHN FERLING

BLOOMSBURY PRESS

NEW YORK   BERLIN   LONDON   SYDNEY

Published by Bloomsbury Press, New York

All papers used by Bloomsbury Press are natural, recyclable products made
from wood grown in well-managed forests. The manufacturing processes
conform to the environmental regulations of the country of origin.

LIBRARY OF CONGRESS CATALOGING-IN-PUBLICATION DATA
Ferling, John E.
Independence : the struggle to set America free / John Ferling. — 1st U.S. ed.
p. cm.
Includes bibliographical references and index.
ISBN: 978-1-60819-008-9 (alk. paper)
1. United States—Politics and government—To 1775.   2. United States—History—
Colonial period, ca. 1600–1775.   3. United States—Politics and government—
1775–1783.   4. United States—Politics and government—Philosophy.
5. Statesmen—United States—History—18th century.   6. Great Britain—Politics
and government—1760–1789. [1. United States—History—
Revolution, 1775–1783—Causes.]   I. Title.
E210.F45 2011
973.3—dc22
2010049366

First U.S. Edition 2011

1 3 5 7 9 10 8 6 4 2

Typeset by Westchester Book Group
Printed in the U.S.A. by Quad/Graphics, Fairfield, Pennsylvania

To Dee Donnelly and Michelle Kuhlman
Who mean more to me than they will ever know

CONTENTS

Preface   *ix*

1. "In the Very Midst of a Revolution":
The Proposal to Declare Independence   1

2. "A Spirit of Riot and Rebellion":
*Lord North, Benjamin Franklin,
and the American Crisis*   8

3. "Defenders of American Liberty":
*Samuel Adams, Joseph Galloway, and
the First Continental Congress*   52

4. "It Is a Bill of War. It Draws the Sword":
Lord Dartmouth, George Washington, Hostilities   88

5. "A Rescript Written in Blood":
John Dickinson and the Appeal of Reconciliation   116

6. "Progress Must Be Slow":
John Adams and the Politics of a Divided Congress   143

7. "The King Will Produce the Grandest Revolution":
George III and the American Rebellion   170

8. "The Folly and Madness of the Ministry":
Charles James Fox, Thomas Paine, and the War   198

9. "We Might Get Ourselves upon Dangerous Ground":
*James Wilson, Robert Morris, Lord Howe,
and the Search for Peace*   224

10. "The Fatal Stab":
*Abigail Adams and the Realities of the
Struggle for Independence*   246

11. "Not Choice, But Necessity That Calls
for Independence": *The Dilemma and
Strategy of Robert Livingston*   278

CONTENTS

12. "The Character of a Fine Writer":
*Thomas Jefferson and the Drafting of the
Declaration of Independence*   294

13. "May Heaven Prosper the New Born Republic":
Setting America Free   318

14. "This Will Cement the Union":
America Is Set Free   336

Epilogue   342

Appendix: The Declaration of Independence   358

Abbreviations   363

Select Bibliography   365

Notes   372

Index   419

PREFACE

Nearly all of us at times fall into the trap of looking back on history's pivotal events as inevitable. Were not the differences between the North and South destined to end in the American Civil War? Surely, Hitler's coming to power was unavoidable. Was not the collapse of the Soviet Union inescapable?

Well, perhaps not. Great events in history, and their outcomes, are seldom bound to happen. They hinge on happenstance, on complex twists and turns, and on choices made or unmade. Make one choice and history goes in one direction. Don't make that choice and events may well veer in another direction.

But once the end of the story is known, there is always a temptation to read history backward. Knowing how things turned out makes it easy to assume that the ending was foreordained.

That may be especially true for many Americans with regard to the declaring of independence in 1776. In recent years popular culture—and not a few writers—has so lionized America's Founding Fathers that many may see them as leaders whose indomitable will set them on an inexorable course toward independence.

History is more complicated. It seems certain that most Americans did not favor independence when what we now know as the War of Independence broke out in April 1775. Even after the war had raged for several months, many Americans—again, probably most—still did not want American independence. At the beginning of 1776 a majority of those who served in the Continental Congress preferred reconciliation with the mother country to American independence. Had the Continental Congress voted on independence in January or February 1776, no more than five of the thirteen colonies would likely have favored a final break with Great Britain.

This is a book about the evolution of the idea of American independence and about the events and decisions that ultimately led Congress, with the backing of most colonists, to set America free of the British Empire. The book's subtitle contains the word "struggle," and in fact those who favored severing all ties with Great Britain faced a long, difficult battle before, at last, they succeeded in declaring independence. Eleven years elapsed between Britain's first attempt to tax the colonists and the Declaration of Independence. What we today call the War of Independence, or the Revolutionary War, had gone on for fifteen months before the Continental Congress declared independence. For more than a year the colonists fought, and died, not for American independence, but to be reunited with Great Britain on America's terms.

A struggle over Great Britain's policy toward the colonies was played out in London as well. Battles were fought in Parliament and within the ministry at every turn, from the passage of the first American tax in 1765 to the decision a decade later to use force rather than to engage in peace negotiations with the Americans. Powerful and articulate members of Parliament always opposed the American policies of their government, fearing that additional provocations would only push the colonists toward independence. Some proposed solutions to the Anglo-American crisis that, if adopted, might have stanched the drift to American independence.

This book is about the struggle in America over how best to resist British actions and secure American interests, and to secure the prevailing interest of individual colonies. It is also about the battles in London over how best to deal with, and respond to, the recalcitrant American colonists. It is a story filled with irony, for in the end the Americans opted for an independence that most of them had wished to avert, while Britain's leaders were confronted with a declaration of American independence that they had sought to prevent, first by peaceful means, later through strident measures.

The choices that were made on both sides were made by individuals, and this book evaluates the key players, important members of the Continental Congress as well as British ministers and their principal adversaries in Parliament. Public officials in that day were not unlike today's officials. Some who held positions of authority were high-minded and sought what they thought was best for the nation. Some were visionaries. Some were inspired by deeply held philosophical convictions. Some were vengeful. Some acted on behalf of narrow provincial interests or sought to protect the entrenched elite. Some were motivated by the hope of enhancing their careers or reputations. Some sought economic gain. Many were driven by a combination of these motives. And no one had a crystal ball. No one could say unequivocally what the long-term results would be if the choice he advocated was adopted.

On the American side, the members of Congress remained deeply divided over the best course to pursue all the way down to July 1776. Some congressmen desperately sought to avoid war and revolution, some held intransigently to the hope of reconciliation, some reluctantly accepted independence, and some surreptitiously yearned for independence years before it was declared. This is the story of able and ambitious politicians—including America's Founders—scrambling to land on their feet; of members of Congress walking a political tightrope between the conflicting interests of New England, the mid-Atlantic colonies, and the South; of men who were daring and men who were timid; of men who were tied to the past and men who dreamed of what might be a glorious future.

Britain's ministers and those in Parliament who opposed them simultaneously groped for the means of saving Great Britain's North American empire. It is a spellbinding tale of a great modern nation blundering into a disaster as its leaders become trapped by their earliest decisions, making them captives in a descent toward tragedy. How the hard and unbending British leaders steered their nation toward an epic disaster provides lessons for politicians in any time period. Britain's rulers coped with the welter of interests in a great modern state. At the same time, they sought to avoid the appearance of weakness. Their story, it seems now, is that of shortsighted leaders on a straightforward path to catastrophe.

Above all, this is a story that could have ended differently. A declaration of American independence, at least in 1776, might never have occurred. There were ways that the imperial crisis might have been resolved, and this book tells the story of the options and alternatives that existed.

But mostly it is a human story. Some forty years after 1776, Thomas Jefferson tried to set the record straight. He was troubled that subsequent generations had come to credit the Founding Fathers with "a wisdom more than human" and to view their achievements with "sanctimonious reverence."[1] With regard to independence, Jefferson knew that the story of what had transpired between the Boston Tea Party in 1773 and the Declaration of Independence in 1776 was far more complex. He knew that the struggle to break America's colonial shackles had been a very human story filled with shards of weakness, opportunism, accidents, deceit, fortuity, enmity, decisions wise and misguided, exemplary leadership, and ultimately heroic boldness.

John Adams would have agreed with Jefferson. He, too, knew how difficult the struggle had been to bring Congress to declare independence, and not long after the battle had been won, he declared: "Posterity! You will never know, how much it cost the [Revolutionary] Generation, to preserve your Freedom."[2]

The leaders on both sides were ordinary mortals who happened to be confronted with extraordinary challenges. This is the story of their response to the uncommon challenges they faced. It is not a story filled with heroes and villains so much as it a history of human beings of assorted virtues, beliefs, motives, and talents who could not see the future with the clarity with which we can see the past.

This is not a history of the American Revolution. While it looks at the Anglo-American crisis from its inception down to the Declaration of Independence, the book largely examines the forty-month period between the Boston Tea Party, in December 1773, and Congress's vote for independence, in July 1776. Its objective is to understand the major players on both sides, what drove them, the choices they faced, their successes and failures, and, above all, why the American Congress moved steadily—seemingly inexorably—toward a final break with Great Britain.

Debts accumulate in the course of writing any book. I am particularly grateful to Matt deLesdernier and James Sefcik for reading the manuscript, pointing out errors, and offering guidance. Four good friends—Edith Gelles, Michael deNie, Keith Pacholl, and Arthur Lefkowitz—answered many questions that I posed. Lorene Flanders graciously found places for me to work in a library that was undergoing a major renovation during much of the time that I was writing the book. Angela Mehaffey and her staff in the Interlibrary Loan Office of the Irvine Sullivan Ingram Library at the University of West Georgia cordially met my rapacious requests for books and articles. Elmira Eidson helped me out of numerous scrapes with my computer and word processing program. Nathaniel Knaebel was an understanding, easy-to-work-with production editor. No author ever had a better copyeditor than Maureen Klier.

Geri Thoma was crucial in the realization of my dream to write the book. Peter Beatty helped in many ways to bring the book to completion, all the while listening to my tales of woe about the Pittsburgh Pirates. This is my sixth book with Peter Ginna, a masterful editor who unfailingly provides encouragement, criticism, and a storehouse of wonderful ideas.

As always, Carol, my wife, encouraged and supported my work, and she joined with me in our annual cookout to celebrate Independence Day on July 2 (yes, July 2—see chapters thirteen and fourteen).

November 12, 2010

CHAPTER I

"In the Very Midst of a Revolution"

The Proposal to Declare Independence

Richard Henry Lee, tall and spare, with a long, pasty face dominated by penetrating eyes and wayward receding hair, left his Philadelphia lodging on the spring-soft morning of June 7, 1776. He set out on the same walk he had taken six days a week for nearly a year. A member of Virginia's delegation to the Continental Congress, Lee was heading for the Pennsylvania State House, the home of Congress.

Philadelphia bustled with forty thousand inhabitants. It was the largest American city, more populous than Bristol, the second-largest city in England, and only slightly smaller than Dublin and Edinburgh, the leading urban centers after London in the British Empire. Philadelphia so impressed a widely traveled British army officer who visited the city in 1765 that he declared it to be "great and noble," "one of the wonders of the world" that "bids fair to rival almost any city in Europe." Colonel Adam Gordon marveled at how this planned city was so "wisely laid out," and he was especially struck by its magnificent public buildings and ethnic and religious diversity.[1]

Philadelphia was something of a melting pot. English, Scots, Welsh, Irish, Germans, and Africans rubbed shoulders, their accents and dialects familiar throughout the city. Lee's stroll on this bright June day was along brick sidewalks, something few American towns yet boasted, and down wide paved thoroughfares alive in midmorning with the rattle and rumble of carts, coaches, and wagons drawn by sweating horses that clattered loudly on the cobbled streets. Lee walked below streetlights that were set aglow only on moonless nights—this was, after all, a frugal Quaker city—under tall elms and lofty Italian poplars, past homes both elegant and modest, all made of brick, and close to the commons, where tethered milk cows grazed. Striding briskly, Lee passed inns, coffeehouses and dram shops, a church and cemetery, an

Pennsylvania State House, a northwest view taken in 1778 and printed in the Columbian
magazine, *July 1787. Home to the Continental Congress in 1775–1776, the structure had
opened about twenty years earlier and served as home to the Pennsylvania legislature
before and after independence. As Congress met here when independence was declared,
it was thereafter popularly called Independence Hall. Illustration from the*
Columbian *magazine from 1787. (Library of Congress)*

outdoor market, the Quaker school, the city jail, and shops of assorted tradesmen, from which the noise of the workplace, and sometimes the sour odors,
flowed through open doors into the streets.[2]

After a few minutes, Lee glimpsed the light red brick State House, known
today as Independence Hall. Located in a square bounded by Chestnut
and Walnut streets on the north and south, and Fifth and Sixth streets on the
east and west, the State House was the city's most imposing structure. Constructed over a quarter century beginning in 1729, it stretched for more
than one hundred feet, was forty-four feet wide, and was crowned by a sixty-
nine-foot-tall masonry bell tower, making it the equivalent of a six-story
building—a veritable skyscraper in an America in which hardly any structure topped two stories. Designed with careful attention to balance and or-
nament, this imposing building was meant to convey dignity and a sense of
orderliness.[3]

There was irony in this, for while Lee's walk took him to the very symbol
of order and authority, his purpose on this day was the essence of revolution.

It was Lee's intention to ask the Continental Congress to declare American independence.

Every day Congress tended to the most vital business. For fifteen months, since April 1775, the thirteen American colonies had been at war with Great Britain, their parent state. Almost everything that Congress had done since the outbreak of hostilities had been related to the war effort. Lee, in fact, knew that the Iroquois and other tribes from the Six Nations Confederation were in town to discuss the war and that General George Washington, the commander of the Continental army, had just departed following several days of consultation with Congress. Lee was mindful, too, that Philadelphia, like a magnet, drew both wealthy merchants and smaller businessmen who were eager to obtain some of the money that Congress was spending to wage war.[4]

The war overshadowed everything. While one congressional committee worked on plans to purchase a warship and looked after getting privateers to sea, another sought to acquire muskets, powder, and flints from abroad. Congressmen wrote home frequently to encourage steps that would help the war effort, urging the fortification of coasts, the construction of river craft to transport artillery, and the recruitment of more men for the army, among other things. On this very morning, John Hancock, the president of Congress, had begun his day by beseeching each colony to gather every scrap of available lead so that it could be recast into cartridges for the army. He also advised the provinces to "remove out of the Way" everything that the British armed forces might possibly utilize "to prosecute their Plans of Violence agt. us."[5]

Lee arrived at the State House a bit before ten A.M., the scheduled time for Congress to begin its daily session, and strode into the congressional chamber on the first floor. It was a spacious room, forty feet by forty feet, with a ceiling that was twenty feet high. Wide, tall windows ran along the north and south sides of the room; substantial fireplaces faced with marble stood on another wall. The walls were paneled and painted a light gray, though when the sun splashed into the room, they took on a bluish hue. One wall was adorned with captured flags and a British drum, seized when a colonial military force had taken Fort Ticonderoga the previous year. Thirteen round tables, one for each colony's delegation, were scattered about the room. Every table was covered with green linen and encircled with hard, uncushioned Windsor chairs.

Knots of delegates were engaged in animated conversations when the bell in the State House tower pealed at ten A.M. That was the signal for Hancock, who was seated on the dais in the president's special cushioned armchair, to gavel the day's session to order. The discussions around the room abruptly ended, and the delegates scurried to their seats. The doorkeeper stepped into the hall and closed the door behind him.[6] The congressional chamber once again was a private reserve, sealed from the outside world.

This day's session began as they all did, with the reading of letters and reports, mostly dispatches from the army's commanders. Lee waited patiently. It was hardly coincidental that he had chosen this grave moment in this desperate war to propose that America break permanently with the mother country. On this very day in Halifax, Nova Scotia, British soldiers were clambering up the gangplanks of troop transports, struggling with their weapons and heavy pieces of field equipment. Part of the greatest armada that Great Britain would assemble in the eighteenth century, these men expected to sail for New York within forty-eight hours. They anticipated a "bloody active campaign" to take Manhattan and seize control of the Hudson River.[7] If they succeeded, the link between the four New England provinces and the nine colonies to the south would be severed and Great Britain almost certainly would win the war.

The members of Congress had received "alarming Intelligence" that Great Britain's army of invasion was coming, not only from Nova Scotia but from England and Europe as well. By midsummer there would be forty thousand British soldiers in North America, several times the number posted in the colonies when the war broke out. "Brittain is Determined to use her utmost endeavors this year to Subdue us," said Congressman Josiah Bartlett of New Hampshire. Like Bartlett, each congressman prayed that his fellow Americans would "play the man for their country & that kind Providence will give us success & victory." There was much to pray for. A British army had landed at Quebec thirty days earlier and already had advanced as far as Three Rivers, on the St. Lawrence River. If that British army plunged farther south and crossed New York's northern frontier, many in Congress feared that it might be unstoppable. America's army was too small to simultaneously defend Manhattan and New York's northern border. Some in Congress thought that Britain's powerful military forces could be defeated only with foreign help. Those same congressmen, including Lee, also believed that only by declaring independence could Congress hope to receive life-sustaining assistance from a European belligerent.[8]

Once the reports were read and discussed, Congress turned to other matters. It voted to give compensation to a merchant whose property, including a vessel, had been seized by the American navy. It spent some time discussing the possibility of raising more men for the army, and it looked into its recent purchase of defective gunpowder from a mill in Frankford, Pennsylvania.[9]

An hour or so into the session, thinking that most of the day's crucial war-related business had been concluded, Lee asked for the floor. When he was recognized, the Virginian indicated that he wished to introduce a resolution.

Lee was a veteran politician. Born in 1732, ten months after George Washington and only five miles below the general's birthplace, Lee had been raised at Stratford Hall, an eighteen-room mansion situated about forty miles above the mouth of the Potomac River. One of six children of Thomas Lee, who held numerous public offices and, for a time, was the acting governor of Virginia, young Richard Henry had been sent to a private academy in England for his formal education. He lived and studied in the mother country for seven years before returning home at age eighteen. During the next six years, while he lived with his parents, Lee read widely and served as a justice of the peace. He married while in his midtwenties, after which he leased five hundred acres three miles downriver from Stratford Hall and built his own oversize mansion, Chantilly, a three-and-a-half story, ten-room frame dwelling that one visitor described as large, though not elegant. It was a working plantation. During most of Lee's life, some fifty to sixty slaves lived and toiled at Chantilly, raising tobacco and grains. Lee lived there for the remainder of his life, fathering twelve children, nine of whom survived to adulthood and two of whom would serve in the Continental Congress.

In 1758, in the midst of the French and Indian War, Lee was first elected to the House of Burgesses, Virginia's assembly. Newcomers customarily rose slowly in the Burgesses, but Lee's ascent was uncharacteristically slow. His progress may have been hampered because he was not a lawyer, though it more likely was due to his transparent ambition, which put off many of his colleagues. Behind his back, some referred to him as "Bob Booty" for his habit of seeking every available lucrative office. Lee's rise may also have been slowed by a yearlong absence from the Burgesses, forced on him while he recuperated from a hunting accident that cost him four fingers on his left hand. Whatever the cause, after eight years Lee still had not achieved a leadership position, ordinarily a telltale sign that a kingpin role was not to be.

However, the colonial protest against Great Britain changed Lee's fortunes. At first, he had been indifferent when Parliament in 1765 passed the Stamp Act, the first time it had ever attempted to levy a direct tax on the American colonists. He had even solicited appointment as a stamp agent—a tax collector. But when he saw Patrick Henry's spectacular leap to prominence as a result of his opposition to the Stamp Act, Lee opportunistically denounced parliamentary taxation as "pernicious to my Country." Lee spoke openly, and often, against the Stamp Act. He unsparingly flayed Virginia's stamp agent, accusing the man who obtained the same post that he had sought of having "endeavored to fasten chains of slavery on this my native country." Lee additionally published a pamphlet condemning Parliament's tax. By 1766 Lee had become not just a legislative leader; he and Henry were also widely seen as Virginia's leading reformers.[10]

If the Stamp Act episode caused Lee to reconsider Anglo-American relations, the recurring frustrations that he experienced as a land speculator after 1765 stoked his burgeoning radicalism. He lost heavily when a land company in which he had invested was beaten out by London insiders in the battle to win legal title to a sprawling domain west of the Appalachians. He lost again in 1769 when the House of Burgesses' appeal to the Crown to permit Virginia to annex a vast western tract—much of what today is western West Virginia and nearly all of Kentucky—ended in failure, with London turning a deaf ear to the Virginians. Beginning in the early 1770s, a series of decisions in London appeared to make it likely that the imperial authorities were bent on stripping Virginia of its land claims north of the Ohio River, a region in which Lee had also invested. Around this time Lee opened correspondence with those who were leading the protest against British imperial policies in Pennsylvania and Massachusetts. Vexed by London's dismaying behavior, and its adverse impact on him and his province, Lee conspicuously displayed his disillusionment with those who ruled England. He hired an artist to paint an eight-foot-tall portrait of Lord Chatham, William Pitt, the leading foe of Britain's ministry and hung the huge portrait in a central hall in Chantilly.[11]

By 1774, when Virginia elected delegates to the First Continental Congress, Lee had become a powerful figure within his province. In fact, he received the second-largest number of votes of the seven delegates that Virginia sent to Congress, outpacing both Washington and Henry.[12] John Adams first met Lee, who was then forty-one years old, at that initial Congress. Adams privately assessed many of his congressional colleagues, describing some as handsome and others as odd-looking, and judging assorted delegates as bookish, talented, plain, unimpressive, lazy, transparently cunning, or "not very promising." Adams was especially impressed by Lee, calling him "a masterly Man" who was earnest, thoughtful, prudent, and the equal of the best orators he had ever heard.[13] Other Virginia deputies told Adams that Patrick Henry was a better public speaker than Lee, so good that his fellow burgesses called him Virginia's "Demosthenes." Lee, they said, was thought of as the colony's "Cicero," for like the ancient who had warned of the decay of the Roman republic, Lee had cautioned of the dangers America faced from the corruption that sullied England. But Virginia's deputies also acknowledged that Lee was an effective and dramatic speaker. (He was known for wearing a black silk glove on the hand that had been disfigured in the hunting accident, a prop that he learned to use to his advantage as he made theatrical gestures while delivering speeches.)[14]

By 1776, Lee was seen by other congressmen as the most influential figure in his colony's delegation. By then, too, he had become a quiet advocate for American independence. The oppressive doubts raised by London's policies in the 1760s had by 1774 led Lee to believe that the colonists' "most desirable connection" with Great Britain should be strictly commercial. When war broke out in 1775, he openly questioned the desirability of reconciliation but did not publicly advocate separation from the mother country. A year later, in the spring of 1776, Lee asserted that Great Britain had severed its ties with the colonies when it boycotted American trade as a war measure. In early June, five days before he took the floor to introduce the resolution calling on Congress to break all ties with the mother country, Lee told acquaintances that American independence was not a matter of choice, but of necessity. Whatever he had felt about independence previously, Lee had come to think that a formal declaration of independence was imperative for gaining victory in what now seemed likely to be a long and profoundly difficult war. America, Lee had concluded, could not win the war without foreign help, and it could not secure adequate foreign assistance unless it offered Britain's foes in Europe some enticement to enter the war. Only American independence, which would drastically weaken Great Britain, might bring European powers into the war on the side of the colonies.[15] Lee and the other members of Virginia's congressional delegation felt that Congress could wait no longer to proclaim American independence. Recognized by Hancock, Lee took the floor on June 7 and read his motion in resounding tones:

> Resolved, That these United Colonies are, and of right ought to be, free and Independent States, that they are absolved from all allegiance to the British Crown, and that all political connection between them and the State of Great Britain is, and ought to be, totally dissolved.[16]

Since the outbreak of hostilities, the colonists' aim in fighting had been reconciliation with Great Britain on terms set by the Continental Congress. Lee was proposing a dramatically new war aim. His resolution urged that henceforth Americans wage this war to set themselves free of Great Britain and to establish a new and independent American nation.

During the past two years Congress had taken many momentous steps, but Lee's motion brought this body face-to-face with the greatest—and most dangerous—decision of all.

CHAPTER 2

"A SPIRIT OF RIOT AND REBELLION"

LORD NORTH, BENJAMIN FRANKLIN, AND THE AMERICAN CRISIS

FREDERICK NORTH, Lord North, was into his fifth year as prime minister during the cool, damp London spring of 1774, a time when war or peace between Great Britain and its American colonies hung in the balance.

In 1770 the king, George III, had turned to Lord North, a political veteran with a background in finance, to form a government. North had entered Parliament in 1755, four years following his graduation from Oxford. After four more years he was brought into the Duke of Newcastle's cabinet as the Lord High Treasurer, a post he held for half a dozen years through several ministries. In 1767 the Duke of Grafton made North the chancellor of the exchequer, the official in charge of financial matters and the ministry's spokesman in the House of Commons, a position for which he was tailor-made, as he had few peers as a parliamentary debater. North still held that post three years later, when the government collapsed and the monarch asked him to head a new ministry. Despite his long service, North was only thirty-five years old when he became the "first minister"—he disliked the title "prime minister"—and moved into the cramped and as yet unnumbered residence on Downing Street that for a generation had been available for the head of the ministry.

North was pleasant, witty, charming, industrious, efficient, and bright. Sophisticated though never pompous, he had a knack for getting on with others, and his performance as chief financial minister had earned nearly universal praise. His appointment to head the ministry was widely applauded. Robert Walpole, the acid-tongued son of the former prime minister, thought North was "more able, more active, more assiduous, more resolute, and more fitted to deal with mankind" than any other possible choice.

Even so, North had readily apparent limitations. He had neither leadership nor executive experience. While good at resolving small, isolated problems, North had difficulty understanding and grappling with larger, more complicated quandaries. When dealing with complexities, moreover, he often turned indecisive and was prone to vacillation. His weaknesses were exacerbated by frequent bouts of poor health and episodic periods of depression—what one member of his cabinet called "his distressing Fits"—that rendered him nearly inert for days on end. North was also utterly lacking in those qualities usually present in great leaders. He possessed not a single ounce of charisma, and lacking gravitas, he was anything but an intimidating figure. He was of average height, obese, awkward, disheveled in dress, and given to slurred speech. Contemporaries limned him as "blubbery" and a "heavy booby-looking" sort. One described him as having a fair complexion, light-colored hair, bushy eyebrows, and lackluster gray eyes. Another observer mentioned that his "large prominent eyes rolled to no purpose (for he was utterly short-sighted)," adding that with his "wide mouth, thick lips, and inflated visage," North "gave the appearance of a blind trumpeter." No one understood his deficiencies better than North himself, and when approached about forming a government, he had sought to persuade the king that he was unsuited for heading the cabinet. George III thought otherwise, and North, who was never able to stand up to the monarch, acquiesced, though on three occasions during his first three years as prime minister he offered his resignation. The king would have none of it.[1]

North had come to power convinced that earlier governments had mishandled the American problem. With better judgment, he said, they "might at first have . . . easily ended" the rebellion when the issue was no more than resistance to taxation. But with time the insurgents had grown bolder and more radical, and better organized, leaving him to face a crisis that was "now grown serious." From the moment he assumed power, North believed the colonies and mother country had reached a deadly impasse. They now were contending "for no less than sovereignty on one side, and independence on the other." He never wavered from that point of view. By the spring of 1774 the issue was "whether we have or have not any authority in that country."[2]

With time and experience North's self-assurance had grown. "I do not find my spirits flag" any longer, he confided to a friend in 1774. One reason for his confidence was that the king remained steadfastly supportive. George III bestowed honors on North and did good turns for his family and friends. The king also often wrote to North following his performance in a debate or an address to Parliament to say, "I thoroughly approve" or "very exactly my way of thinking."[3] But the prime minister was also more poised because he felt that

Frederick Lord North by Nathaniel Dance. A veteran politician, North was asked to form a
government in 1770. He remained the prime minister until near the end of the war. North
privately doubted that Britain could easily crush the insurgency by military means.
Engraving after portrait by Nathaniel Dance, ca. 1773–74.
(National Portrait Gallery, London)

he saw the American problem with clarity, and he believed that there was but
one choice that could be made. "As to America," he remarked in the spring
of 1774,

> *there* is an unhappy necessity, but a great one. We must decide
> whether we will govern America or whether we will bid adieu to it,
> and give it that perfect liberty. ... The dispute is now upon such

ground, unless they see you are willing and able to maintain your authority, they will . . . totally throw it off. There is no man but must be conscious of the necessity to act with authority in that country in order to preserve the country as a subject country to Great Britain.[4]

For North in 1774, the "unhappy necessity" could not have been more apparent. He must take the steps necessary to hold America or it would declare its independence.

The road to American independence was long and twisted, and no one is certain where it began.

For more than a century before 1776, numerous English writers, and occasionally a royal official posted in the colonies, had reflected on the likelihood of the American colonies becoming independent. Some had warned that it was inevitable. Pointing to examples in antiquity when Greek and Roman colonies had thrown off their imperial yokes, many essayists predicted that sooner or later Britain's colonies in America would to do the same. Others were influenced by the cyclical theory of history, quite popular at the time. According to this theory, nations went through the same sequences, or cycles, as humans, beginning as children, growing into young and vigorous adults, passing into a less robust but more enlightened middle age, and finally falling into senescence and decline. The devotees of the cyclical theory cautioned that when the American provinces reached adulthood, the colonists would seek independence. Other writers shunned fancy theories and said simply that the colonists would seek to go on their own when they were convinced that they had become economically self-sufficient.

Still others warned that the descendants of the Puritans, radical Protestants who had migrated to New England in the seventeenth century to escape the Church of England, would not rest until they were entirely free of Great Britain. New England Yankees, it was said, were merely waiting for the right moment to act. Some writers saw the spectacular population growth in the colonies as a threat. They predicted a revolt for American independence when the colonists outnumbered the inhabitants of the parent state.

Not everyone who ruminated on the matter thought independence was probable. Economists and spokesmen for the mercantile sector often ridiculed those who prophesied American independence. They stressed the commercial benefits that the colonists derived from being part of the empire and insisted that proper trade policies would choke off separatist inclinations.

Many English and Europeans crossed the Atlantic to visit North America during the eighteenth century, and several wrote of America's flora and fauna and of the living conditions and cultural practices in the far corners of the colonies. Many could not resist the temptation to ask the colonists whether they believed America would someday break away from the mother country. The colonists invariably answered that independence was inevitable, although all said the break lay in the distant future, a generation or two removed, possibly even a century down the road.

In the first half of the eighteenth century, the Americans—mostly colonial businessmen engaged in transatlantic commerce—who wrote on the question of American independence said it was unlikely. Nearly all, in fact, extolled the mutual benefits of the imperial relationship and argued that the Americans were happy to be part of the British Empire.[5] In the 1750s, Benjamin Franklin, the best-known colonist, took up the matter of the striking growth of America's population. In two thoughtful and widely read essays, Franklin forecast with amazing accuracy that by the mid-nineteenth century America's population would surpass that of the mother country. When that occurred, the imperial capital should be moved from London to Philadelphia, he said, perhaps tongue in cheek. While never predicting that America's swelling population would lead to independence, Franklin did offer pithy counsel to the imperial rulers. A "wise and good Mother," he wrote, would loosen her grip on her maturing offspring, lest tight restraints "distress . . . the children" and "weaken . . . the whole Family."[6]

In the glow of the Treaty of Paris of 1763, which recognized the Anglo-American triumph in the Seven Years' War (sometimes called the French and Indian War), the colonists appeared to think of themselves as blessed to be British subjects. Americans reveled in the glorious peace, which drove the French from North America and Spain from Florida. Great Britain was left in possession of every square foot of territory from the Atlantic coast to the Mississippi River. Many Americans shared their king's pride at "glory[ing] in the name of Britain." They also dreamed of sharing in the coming prosperity they believed would flow from the spoils of victory. Not a few hailed their "indulgent Mother" and praised Great Britain as the freest nation on the planet.[7] Joyous colonists named towns after British heroes. Massachusetts sent a donation to London to help cover the expense of erecting a memorial to a British officer who had fallen in the conflict. When word arrived in 1760 of the sudden death of the king, George II, the colonists mourned. The following year they rejoiced with heartfelt celebrations at the news of the coronation of the new king and queen, George III and Charlotte. As the decade of the 1760s got under way, several royal governors reported that the colonists were loyal and happy. No one captured America's spirit better than Jonathan Mayhew, perhaps the most influential cleric in Boston. He saw colonists and parent state linked in "a mighty empire (I do not mean an independent one) in numbers little inferior to the greatest in Europe, and in felicity to none"[8]

The colonists did not know that sometime around 1740 officials serving in Sir Robert Walpole's ministry had begun to consider steps to expand and tighten Britain's control over its distant colonies. The officials were all too aware that many American merchants engaged in a lucrative illegal trade, ignoring Parliament's century-old commercial regulations and diverting some of their profits into non-British pockets. Rightly or wrongly, Walpole's ministers also believed that America was inexorably drifting toward independence. London was distracted by domestic woes and repeated wars, and its administrative control over the colonies had long been lax. The result, these brooding officials concluded, was that the colonists—three thousand miles away and for generations left to their own devices—had grown steadily more autonomous. Unless checked, the ministers convinced themselves, the colonies would continue to drift apart from the parent state, both politically and culturally, until America could no longer be kept within the empire. To stop this putative slide toward American independence, these ministers wished to tighten London's grip on the colonies as soon as circumstances permitted.[9] However, wars with France and Spain in the 1740s and 1750s, including the Seven Years' War, posed roadblocks to the imposition of more rigorous control of the colonists. But with the Peace of Paris, which finally ended nearly twenty-five years of warfare, there was nothing to prevent London from exerting greater control over its American colonies.

Like their predecessors, Britain's postwar ministers were concerned about America's drifting away from London's control, a worry that took on an additional urgency once France had been removed from the picture in America. Many in London had believed that the French presence, and the threat it had posed, had kept the northern colonies, and especially New England, in line. The Yankees, it was often said, had known that they needed London's protection if they were to be secure. That no longer was the case. In the bright glow of peace, many in the ministry felt that Great Britain not only could act to resolve its potential colonial problem but also that it must act.

Peace ushered in other problems. Great Britain was swamped with debt brought on by years of war. The national debt had doubled during the previous seven years. The debt's interest alone devoured approximately half of the government's annual revenue. Retiring the debt, it was believed, required an increase in taxes, and few in power in London wished to heap the "dreadful" load of taxation entirely on "the gentry and people" of the home islands. Simultaneously, the government hoped in the near future to open to settlement some of the territory it had won in the Peace of Paris. But it was widely believed that only the presence of the British army on America's western frontier would induce the Indians living in trans-Appalachia to relinquish their land to the Crown. Furthermore, as it was widely feared that the Treaty of Paris had ushered in another brief period of peace, many thought troops were needed in America to prevent France and Spain from avenging their recent humiliating defeats.[10] Someone had to pay for keeping the army in America. That too meant new taxes.

Just as peace came, the king named George Grenville to head a new ministry. It was a surprise announcement. Though Grenville was fifty-one years old, had sat in Parliament for twenty-two years, and served in several cabinets, he was generally thought to be in the second tier of leaders. However, his greatest strength was supposed to be his grasp of finance, which at least partially accounted for his appointment. Grenville's cabinet rather quickly made five crucial decisions, though some of them—including the matter of American taxation—had been agreed to in principle by its predecessor, the ministry of John Stuart, 3rd Earl of Bute.[11] The government agreed to heavy new taxes on the citizenry living in the homeland in order to raise revenue for retiring the debt. It opted to leave seven regiments of infantry, or about 8,500 men, in America. It announced the Proclamation of 1763, which forbade migration to and the purchase of land west of the Appalachians until further notice. It enacted the Sugar Act in 1764 both to raise revenue and to tighten the screws on America's merchants. This legislation drastically reduced a prohibitory tariff on the importation of foreign molasses, making it considerably cheaper to import the foreign commodity. But there was a catch. The Sugar Act not only levied a duty on the foreign molasses; it also enhanced the means of enforcing imperial trade laws. Finally, in 1765 the ministry decided to do what it had never previously attempted in the 150 years of the empire's existence. Parliament imposed a direct tax on the colonists. It enacted the Stamp Act, which taxed permits, licenses, and newspapers, among other things. As historian Richard Archer put it, the mother country thought it "time to remind the colonists that they were colonists."[12]

The Sugar Act did not create much of a stir throughout the colonies. It fell largely on the four New England provinces, the principal importers of molasses, which was a key ingredient in their rum production industry. Moreover, while the Sugar Act was certainly a tax, it was neatly camouflaged as a trade regulation measure. Nor were the colonists emotionally or intellectually prepared to protest in 1764. The foes of the Sugar Act in Massachusetts could not even induce the Bay Colony assembly to adopt a petition beseeching the king's assistance.[13]

The Stamp Act was a different matter. It was unmistakably a tax. Ministerial defenders forthrightly declared that Parliament possessed an unqualified right to tax the colonies. Parliament, they said, was the sovereign legislature within the empire and, as such, it "exercises a Power" which the colonial assemblies did not possess, "never claimed, or wished, nor can ever be vested with."[14] The ministry also maintained that it was only fair that the colonies pay for opening the West. After all, the British army had "constantly protected and defended them" from the Indians. Furthermore, without the sacrifice of countless British soldiers, the recent war could not have been won and the vast tracts of frontier lands previously claimed by the French and Spanish could never have been garnered for the benefit of the colonists.[15] More quietly, the ministry moved to stiffen its supervision of American trade. Although no new legislation was enacted, imperial authorities contemplated the more systematic enforcement of century-old parliamentary legislation that restricted colonial trade to the British Empire and subjected foreign trade to imperial duties. Colonial merchants had often ignored the restrictions, seeking out lucrative markets wherever they happened to be. Evading the understaffed Customs Service had not been terribly difficult. All that changed in the mid-1760s, when London implemented the stringent regulations that first had been envisaged by Walpole's government twenty-five years earlier. In addition to drastically increasing the number of customs agents in colonial ports, the British government made it easier to prosecute trade violators by establishing four vice admiralty courts in North America.

Although one or two royal governors, and several colonists who happened to be in London at the time, cautioned that a stamp tax would provoke problems—it "would go down with the people like chopt hay," a Connecticut official advised—the ministry ignored the warnings.[16] It took only a few months in 1765 for the government to realize that it had provoked a tempest. Boycotts were organized against British trade in several port cities in an attempt to force the repeal of the tax. Mobs also spilled into the streets in nearly every large city and a few small towns. In some places the rioters acted with such unrestrained fury that they appeared to be driven by more than anger over a tax. In fact, they often were. The residents of Boston, for instance, had suffered a stunning array of tribulations during the five years before they ever heard of the Stamp Act. One of the worst fires in American history struck Boston in 1760, consuming many businesses and 10 percent of its dwellings. Three years later, hundreds perished when a smallpox epidemic broke out in this port city. Boston had additionally been hit with a severe postwar depression when the French and Indian War concluded, and the economic downturn arrived at a time when its residents groaned under extraordinarily heavy provincial taxes imposed to meet the Bay Colony's staggering war debt.[17] If it was not enough for Bostonians to cope with the steepest tax increase in the British Empire after 1761, one imposed by their own colonial assembly, they now were confronted by the Stamp Act, a levy passed by a legislature three thousand miles away and in which they had no voice.

This new vexation combusted with the Bostonians' pent-up frustrations. The result was a wanton spree of mob violence and destruction in the summer of 1765. In place after place, mobs hanged in effigy high-ranking British political figures, looted and destroyed records of pending customs cases, and laid waste to the property of some stamp collectors and royal officials. That a rampaging throng in Boston tore down the residence of the comptroller of customs in Massachusetts was deplorable, but not especially astounding. Nor was it particularly startling that a frenzied crowd wreaked great damage to the home and well-manicured grounds of Massachusetts's stamp collector. That it demolished the elegant Boston mansion of Thomas Hutchinson, Massachusetts's lieutenant governor, was more surprising. Possibly, the mob turned its sights on Hutchinson, a native-born son of the Bay Colony who had chosen to serve London, because he was thought of as a traitor to his fellow Americans. ("Bone of our Bone, born and educated among us!" John Adams would rant about Hutchinson years later over another matter.)[18]

Virginia was one of the few places that did not experience cruel and frenzied mob violence, but it witnessed decisive protest nonetheless. Twenty-nine-year-old Patrick Henry took the lead in Virginia in rallying opposition to Parliament's tax. One of ten children born to a Scottish immigrant who had married into a prominent Virginia family, young Henry was raised in Hanover County, near the frontier. After four years of formal education, and further tutoring by his father, Henry at age fifteen was put to work as a clerk in a general store. Sometime around his twenty-first birthday, Henry opened his own crossroads store. When it failed, he opened another. When that foundered as well, he went to work as a barkeep in his father's tavern. But Henry wanted more. In 1760, at age twenty-four, he taught himself enough law in a few weeks to open his own practice. Possessed of a fast mind and a silver tongue, Henry flourished as a backcountry attorney. Within five years he was a member of the House of Burgesses. He was sworn in as an assemblyman in May 1765, less than a week before word of the Stamp Act arrived in Williamsburg. When news of Parliament's levy reached the Virginia capital, Henry refused to be silenced by his status as a newcomer. He joined in the debate over how Virginia should respond to the tax. On only his ninth day as a burgess, Henry delivered an electrifying speech, the only one from the debate

Patrick Henry by George Bagby Matthews, after Thomas Sully. Among the early advocates of American resistance, Henry introduced the Virginia Resolves in the House of Burgesses in 1765. Chosen to be part of the Virginian delegation to Congress, he resigned in the spring of 1775. He was never a leader on the national stage as he had been in Virginia.
(U.S. Senate Collection)

that is now remembered. Numerous versions of what Henry said have come down to posterity, but according to popular legend, he defiantly stated: "Tarquin and Caesar had each his Brutus, Charles the First his Cromwell, and George the Third . . ." He got no further before he was interrupted by loud cries of "Treason! Treason!" Henry paused for a moment. But, unflappable as always, he proceeded by observing that the king "may profit by their example! If this be treason, make the most of it."

If Henry's exact words are in question, there is no doubt that following his stirring speech he introduced a series of resolutions, several of which were quickly approved by the House of Burgesses. The Virginia Resolves stated that the earliest settlers "brought with them . . . all the Liberties, Privileges, Franchises, and Immunities . . . held, enjoyed, and possessed, by the People of Great Britain." Their charters, moreover, confirmed that they were entitled to all rights and liberties enjoyed by those "abiding and born within the Realm of *England.*" A "distinguishing characteristick of British Freedom," the Resolves added, was that taxes might only be levied by "the People . . . themselves, or by Persons chosen by themselves to represent them." From the beginning the English colonists had enjoyed these rights, none of which they had ever "forfeited or yielded up."

These resolutions soon were published in nearly every colonial newspaper. Before the spring and summer ended, the Virginia Resolves had been adopted nearly word for word by almost every colonial assembly in America. The point of view embraced by the colonists was believed to be an expression of ideology that traced its heritage to the ancient English constitution, and in fact every official set of American resolutions denounced the Stamp Act as unconstitutional. Parliament, it was asserted, had no legal authority to tax the colonists, for the Americans were not, and could not be, represented in that faraway body. What is more, the colonial assemblies alone could lawfully tax the colonists. Any taxes levied by any other than the colonial assemblies were not just illegal; they were also a violation of the colonists' rights and an irrefutable threat to their liberty. Indeed, the colonists saw a linkage between taxation and liberty. Taxation was a manifestation of government's power, and if that authority was wielded improperly or unconstitutionally, it could destroy all rights and liberty. Americans had embraced a constitutional position from which they would never depart so long as they remained British subjects. In October, seven colonies sent delegates to the Stamp Act Congress, a rare intercolonial assembly that met in New York. It adopted a similar statement concerning the British constitution: Parliament had no authority to levy taxes in America.[19]

Officials in Great Britain did not know, but feared, that the Stamp Act was a transformative event for many Americans. Their fears were well-founded. There were colonial activists, like Patrick Henry, who sensed that their constituents were restive under London's new colonial policies. There were also those, like Richard Henry Lee, who took note when a Johnny-come-lately such as Henry was catapulted overnight to a position of leadership when he denounced those policies. There were lessons to be learned as well from the lot of those who defended parliamentary taxation. Not only was there the destruction of Hutchinson's estate to consider, but there was also the fact that nineteen members of the Massachusetts assembly who had spoken on behalf of the Stamp Act were defeated for reelection in the fall of 1765.[20]

The Stamp Act did far more than reshape the fortunes of a few politicians, however. The Stamp Act, and the protests that followed, was the salient moment when many Americans for the first time contemplated the second-class status of both colonies and colonists within the British Empire. Of course, all had long known that there were limits to how far a colonist could rise. An American might win election to his provincial assembly, but no colonist could hold a seat in Parliament. There was next to no chance that a colonist might become a royal governor or be named to an important imperial board. No colonist had ever held an office in a British ministry, much less become the prime minister. No colonist had ever been appointed as an ambassador to another country. It was difficult for a colonist to secure a commission in the British army or the Royal Navy, and advancement was problematical for anyone who did. An American might become a field officer in his colony's army, but he would be outranked by the lowliest officer in the British army.

Though little had been said of it, the colonists were also all too aware that London alone had always made crucial decisions that impinged on life in the colonies. The British government enacted trade regulations, prohibited certain kinds of manufacturing, negotiated treaties with the Indians, made policy regarding the African slave trade, and sometimes sentenced criminals to exile in America. Without consulting the colonists, London decided when to go to war, dragging their colonial subjects after them and usually ordering them not only to raise their own armies to help with the fight but also to provision and house the British soldiers who were sent to America. London alone negotiated the peace treaties that ended the imperial wars. The colonists were never brought into the peace deliberations. At times, the Americans were convinced that London agreed to treaties that ran counter to the interests of the provincials.

There is little evidence that many colonists were riled by these facts of imperial life before 1765. The Stamp Act changed that. The year 1765 was a "most remarkable Year," thought thirty-year-old John Adams. Reflecting in December on the parliamentary legislation and the colonists' response to it, Adams described the Stamp Act as an "enormous Engine . . . for battering down all the Rights and Liberties of America." It had caused the colonists to reconsider their place in the British Empire, he said. "The People, even to the lowest Ranks, have become more attentive to their Liberties, more inquisitive about them, more determined to defend them."[21] Furthermore, Adams was amazed to learn that it was not just his brethren in Massachusetts who shared his thinking about Parliament's tax and the colonists' inferior status but also colonists who lived far from New England. Half a century later, he would reflect that the American Revolution had its beginnings in the 1765 transformation in the way the colonists saw themselves and their relationship with the far-off imperial government.[22] Though no one in the colonies uttered the word "independence" during the Stamp Act upheaval, the embryo of the idea of American independence was in being by the end of that pivotal year.

Once London realized that the warnings had been correct about the colonists taking exception to parliamentary taxation, those who ruled Great Britain found themselves on the horns of an ugly dilemma. The American uprising against the Stamp Act appeared to confirm the necessity for Great Britain to

*The Stamp Act was greeted by mob violence in several colonies, especially
in New England. Property damage occurred and on occasion tax collectors faced the
threat of violence, including tarring and feathering. This British cartoon is titled
"The Bostonians paying the exciseman, or tarring and feathering."
Published by Sayer and Bennett, London, 1774. (National Archives)*

tighten its control over the colonies. The merest sign of weakness or retreat, many feared, would hasten America's march toward independence. Furthermore, Great Britain continued to need revenue. However, if Parliament stuck to its guns, or responded with punitive measures, colonial resistance might be inflamed into a full-blown revolution for independence. The quandary that the government had brought on itself when it turned to the Stamp Act would bedevil every ministry from 1766 through to 1776.[23]

In 1766 Britain's government readily understood that the Stamp Act was untenable. It covertly decided to repeal the troublesome measure and replace it with an alternative form of taxation. The first step would be to convince the public that a stamp tax had been a mistake. The best way to do this, the ministry concluded, would be to conduct sham hearings in the House of Commons. Its star witness was Benjamin Franklin.

The world has seen few men more ambitious than Franklin, and only a handful who may have worked more assiduously at achieving success. Born in Boston in 1706 to a large working-class family, Franklin was mostly self-educated. As he grew into adolescence, Franklin meditated over how to get ahead. He calculated how to get along with others, worked diligently, lived frugally, and cagily kept his eyes open for every edge that might facilitate his upward mobility, including taking bold risks. Franklin's most daring move came at age seventeen. Leaving home, he traveled alone to Philadelphia, where he did not know a soul. He was drawn to this new, vibrant city on the Delaware River on the assumption that it offered greater opportunities than Boston, which at the time was larger and about twice as old. The following year he sailed for London, gambling that there were even greener pastures in the great metropolis, though he knew no one there either. When things did not pan out in England, he borrowed money for a return voyage to Philadelphia in 1726, and it was there that his amazing arc of ascent really commenced. Franklin started as a clerk in a store. Within two years he and a partner owned a printing press. After two more years he was the sole owner and publisher of a newspaper, the *Pennsylvania Gazette*. Twenty-one years after his return to Philadelphia, Franklin, with income pouring in from a variety of shrewd investments, retired. He was forty-two years old.

But Franklin was hardly the sort to fancy a carefree and indolent retirement. He devoted considerable time to science, winning fame in America and Europe for his electrical experiments and numerous inventions. He loved Philadelphia, and it is likely that never before, or since, has a city benefited so much from the presence of a single resident. Franklin organized a lending library, a fire company, a militia, a philosophical society, an academy, and a hospital for the city's inhabitants. In addition, he taught his neighbors how to make their homes safer and more comfortable, and he worked indefatigably—and successfully—to convince Philadelphians of the wisdom of inoculation against smallpox.

In midlife Franklin turned to politics. Given his penchant for structure and organization, he wasted little time cobbling together one of America's first political parties. It was called the Assembly Party, and it soon dominated the Pennsylvania legislature. To achieve this, Franklin allied with Joseph Galloway, a wealthy twenty-six-year-old who practiced law and moved in silk-stocking circles. There can be no doubt that it was Franklin who took the initiative in forming the partnership. Already the best-known Philadelphian, and perhaps the preeminent American in the mid-1750s, Franklin was old enough to have been young Galloway's father. Franklin brought to the team his notability and skills as a writer and organizer. As a tradesman himself, Franklin also had useful contacts with those in the city who worked with their hands. However, whereas Franklin thought himself a "bad Speaker, never eloquent, subject to much Hesitation in my choice of Words, hardly correct in Language," Galloway was acclaimed as orator.[24] Furthermore, Galloway was well connected in the legal community and with Philadelphia's most affluent merchants.

The Assembly Party stood for reducing the authority of the proprietary Penn family. In 1681 the Crown had given William Penn and his heirs much of the land between New York and Maryland, some forty-seven million acres. The proprietors had been vested with numerous privileges, which in time wore thin with many Pennsylvanians, as did the Penn family's refusal to permit the assembly to tax their lands. Not a few Pennsylvanians were also convinced that the proprietors had chronically mishandled Indian relations. Political activists, moreover, disliked other aspects of proprietary governance. Pennsylvania's governors—the appointed agents of the proprietors—had a vicelike hold on patronage, and judges served at their pleasure, leading many to charge that the judiciary was insufficiently independent. In addition, the governors not only intruded on the assembly's affairs, but they were obligated by their instructions from the proprietors to veto certain types of legislation, making compromise between the executive and legislative branches impossible. In the midst of the French and Indian War, the assembly sent Franklin to London to lobby authorities to "elicit a removal of the grievances we labor under by reason of proprietary instructions."[25] Franklin sailed for London in 1757 and lived there for five years.

Franklin got nowhere on this mission. This prompted the Assembly Party to change its strategy. In 1764 the assembly approved sending Franklin back to London, this time to seek the end of proprietary government. If he succeeded, Pennsylvania, like most other American provinces, would become a royal colony, with a charter granted by the Crown and a chief executive appointed by the king. Rumor had it that if royalization occurred, Franklin stood an excellent chance of becoming the first royal governor of Pennsylvania and Galloway its first chief justice. Franklin, who had been home for only a few months, crossed the Atlantic again in 1764. This time he remained in London for a decade, until the eve of the Revolutionary War.[26]

Franklin had just resumed his residence in London when the ministry first considered a stamp tax for America, and he was one of several colonists consulted about the wisdom of the step. Most of the other Americans had predicted without reservation that parliamentary taxation would lead Britain into a thicket of troubles. Franklin's response was the least in touch with sentiments in America, perhaps because he had spent so little time there of late. While he warned that a stamp tax might arouse opposition because it would be inescapable, Franklin touted alternate forms of taxation. He appears to have been the only colonist in London to have done so. An indirect tax, something like a sales tax, would almost certainly be accepted by the colonists, he said. He also endorsed a requisition system, under which the Crown would determine the amount owed by each colony but the provincial assemblies would decide how to raise the revenue. He specifically espoused a "General Land-Office" plan, a complicated scheme through which the colonies might issue a paper currency at interest, an option that in reality would have been tantamount to a stamp tax on money.[27] Whatever form Parliament chose, Franklin added, the Americans would not be "much alarm'd about your Schemes of raising Money on us. You will take care . . . not to lay greater Burthens on us than we can bear."[28]

None of his recommendations were appealing to the ministry, which, Franklin declared in private, was "besotted" with the desire to impose a direct and visible tax.[29] The ministers, of course, chose the Stamp Act. Though Franklin anticipated some dissatisfaction with the levy, he never imagined that such widespread American protest would occur. Indeed, he nonchalantly secured the post of stamp agent for Philadelphia—the same sort of position that the unwary Richard Henry Lee had sought in Virginia—for a close friend and political ally, John Hughes.

The first notice that Franklin had about how the colonists were responding to the Stamp Act came from Galloway, who wrote that parliamentary taxation had produced "a Spirit of Riot and Rebellion" that threatened to "alienate affections for the Mother Country."[30] Hughes soon wrote with news that his house had nearly been torn down by a mob. He feared for his life, he added.[31] Hughes's letter was followed by one from Franklin's wife, Deborah, who had remained in Philadelphia. The city, she wrote, was bathed in the orange glow of fires set by rioters. The Franklins' brand-new house on Market Street had faced the threat of mob attack. It had been targeted, Deborah said, because the leaders of the mob believed that he had played a key role in having "obtained the Stamp Act" and were also convinced that Franklin and his Assembly Party "were warm Advocates for the carrying it into Execution." She related that friends had come with guns and powder—Franklin was not a gun owner—turning "one room into a Magazin" and proposing to "show a proper resentement" to any hostile crowd that gathered. While a band of friendly artisans that dubbed themselves the White Oaks Company stood guard around the residence, Deborah grabbed a musket and took up a post at an upstairs window.[32] The attack on Franklin's house never materialized, perhaps in part because of the defensive measures taken by Deborah and the White Oaks.[33] But while the house was preserved, Franklin's reputation fared less well.

A friend in Philadelphia advised him that the "People is . . . violent against every One they think" supported the tax. He added that "they have imbibed the Notion, that you had a Hand, in the framing" of a parliamentary tax on America.[34]

The colonial riots and the damage to his stature led to Franklin's transformation, though nearly two years passed before he was truly in step with popular opinion in America. Soon after hearing from his wife, Franklin openly denounced the Stamp Act and defended the colonists as having acted "from a strong sense of liberty" and "a determination to risque every thing rather than submit . . . to what they deem an unconstitutional exertion of power."[35] By then a new ministry was in power. Domestic problems had brought down the Grenville government even before the rioting in Boston. It was succeeded in the summer of 1765 by a cabinet cobbled together by Lord Rockingham, who listened to merchants and manufacturers eager for the repeal of the Stamp Act. Bent on jettisoning the troublesome act, Rockingham scheduled public hearings in the House of Commons for February 1766. Aware that Franklin not only was now critical of the Stamp Act but also was widely esteemed in England, Rockingham thought the Pennsylvanian might be useful. On the third and final day of the Commons' inquiry, the sixty-year-old Franklin was called to testify. Overweight—he called himself "Dr. Fatsides"—with rapidly thinning hair and a heavily lined face, Franklin nevertheless impressed observers as robust and healthy. More than anything, however, he struck nearly everyone as sincere.[36]

On the stand for four long hours, Franklin sought to redeem himself at home while not burning his bridges in London. The result was testimony shot through with ambiguity and contradiction. He told the House of Commons that the Stamp Act was sowing a whirlwind through the colonies. Having by now read the various assembly resolutions denouncing the Stamp Act, he testified that Americans believed that parliamentary taxation was "unconstitutional, and unjust." Where once the colonists had seen the British government as the "best in world," they now had a "very much altered" outlook. Unless the Stamp Act was repealed, the "respect" and "admiration" that Britain had always enjoyed in the colonies would be forfeited and the mother country would henceforth be "detested and rejected." Franklin might have stopped there. Instead, he advised that Americans could live with indirect taxes, which was precisely what Britain's ministers wanted to hear. Franklin defined an indirect tax as "a duty laid on commodities. . . . If the people do not like it at that price, they refuse it; they are not obliged to pay it." The Stamp Act, in contrast, was a tax "forced from the people without their consent."[37]

Nine days later Parliament repealed the Stamp Act. Lest the colonists

A View of the House of Commons *engraved by B. Cole. Benjamin Franklin testified against the Stamp Act in this chamber in 1766. It was the scene of numerous acrimonious debates on policy toward the colonies, including Edmund Burke's major addresses on America. (Private Collection/ The Stapleton Collection/ The Bridgeman Art Library)*

conclude that Parliament was conceding that its authority was limited, it simultaneously passed the Declaratory Act. This measure claimed Parliament's
power to legislate for America "in all cases whatsoever." Parliament had
never previously felt the need for such a declaration, but in the wake of the
colonists' questions about the constitutionality of the Stamp Act, it believed it
had to affirm its sovereignty over the empire.[38] A few months later, Parliament, unburdened by doubt and following the lead of a new ministry headed
by William Pitt, the Earl of Chatham, imposed new taxes on the colonists. It
tried what Franklin had recommended. The Townshend Duties, passed in
1767, taxed commodities, including tea, paper, lead, glass, and paint. Parliament had adopted Franklin's preference for indirect levies.

Little time passed before the ministry and Parliament discovered that Franklin had offered bad advice. Americans were opposed to taxes of any sort levied by Parliament. The colonists were unyielding in their belief that Parliament
did not possess the constitutional authority to lay taxes on them, no matter
what sort of spin was attached to the legislation.

The repeal of the Stamp Act had ended the protests as suddenly as they had
begun. Repeal, said John Adams, "has hushed into silence" the insurgents
and "composed every Wave of Popular Disorder into a smooth and peaceful
Calm."[39] But before the end of 1767 the quiet had been shattered by protests
against the Townshend Duties and, at least in the northern port cities, against
the British government's attempt to enforce the long-neglected trade laws. For
many in those cities, the prospect that the trade laws would be enforced was
no less unsettling than parliamentary taxation. Urban merchants had made
fortunes through illegal trade and the evasion of custom duties. These businessmen provided employment for countless sailors and dockhands, and the
goods they brought into America kept many shopkeepers and craftsmen afloat.
Enforcement threatened the livelihood of families in every economic class. As
if to be certain that every toe imaginable was stepped on, Parliament accompanied the Townshend Duties and the implementation of the trade laws with
a decree that New York's assembly was to be dissolved and not permitted to
meet until the colony complied with the Quartering Act. That law, passed a
few years earlier, mandated that colonies must help meet the expenses incurred by the British army stationed within their borders. New York had
ignored the law and was to be punished for having done so. Only two years
after first learning of Britain's new colonial policies, many colonists were
alarmed at what seemed to be Parliament's reckless intent to exercise its authority.

The colonial protest gained momentum in 1768. This time the popular leaders took pains to establish greater control over unruly mobs. The wild and frightening urban rampages in 1765 had served their purpose. They had alarmed officials in London, helping to convince them to repeal the Stamp Act. However, many American protest leaders feared that the mayhem had also been counterproductive, chasing away some in the colonies who otherwise might have joined in the protest against the tax. In 1768 crowds once more poured into the streets, venting their anger in noisy, assertive demonstrations. But the protests were largely peaceful. While protestors marched and rallied around Liberty Poles in the major cities, the assemblies in nearly every colony once again remonstrated against parliamentary taxation, beginning with Massachusetts, which in February sent a Circular Letter to the other provincial legislatures. It asked every assembly to appeal to the king to protect the colonists from Parliament's illegal taxation. At the same moment, leaders in several colonies organized boycotts of British imports. Not only were more trade embargoes ginned up than had been the case in 1765, but they were also better planned and less porous, their organizers having learned a thing or two from the shortcomings of the previous boycotts.

The American protest was aided by London's clumsy early response to the colonial resistance. Wills Hill, Lord Hillsborough, the American secretary, ordered the dissolution of every assembly that endorsed Massachusetts's Circular Letter. Hillsborough's maladroit overreaction only fueled the American outcry. Pamphlets attacking British policy rolled off the colonial presses in 1768 in record numbers. The most influential was *Letters from a Farmer in Pennsylvania*, written by John Dickinson, in reality a lawyer who lived in Delaware and probably never went near a plow or a pitchfork. Parliament had acted unconstitutionally, Dickinson wrote. It had no authority to levy any sort of tax on Americans—direct or indirect—as the colonists were not, and could never be, represented in a Parliament that met three thousand miles away. Unlike some, however, Dickinson did not suggest that Parliament had no authority over America. Despite the all-too-apparent contradiction in his argument, Dickinson conceded Parliament's power to regulate imperial commerce, something that was "essential . . . and necessary for the common good of all" those living within the empire.[40] Dickinson's more moderate tone appealed to many who longed for accommodation with London.

No one read Dickinson's pamphlet more carefully than Franklin. The two were longtime political enemies, as Dickinson was the leader of the Proprietary Party in Pennsylvania, a faction that had come into being to resist the Franklin-Galloway initiative to royalize the province. Although Franklin did not entirely agree with Dickinson's stance on imperial matters, he thought the conciliatory tone of *Letters from a Farmer* might offer a bridge toward an eventual solution to the Anglo-American quandary. He quietly arranged the publication of Dickinson's tract in London.[41] In fact, Franklin acted so covertly that Galloway was unaware of what his longtime political partner had done.

If any Americans yearned for independence in 1768, Franklin was not among them. When Franklin told an acquaintance late that year that he "wish[ed] all prosperity to both" sides, he meant what he said. He still loved and trusted the king and praised him as "the very best in the world."[42] But there was more than that to his thinking. Having spent most of the past decade in England, Franklin desperately hoped for a settlement that would prevent an imperial clash, enabling him to live out his days in London. In Franklin's time, those who escaped the perils of infancy and childhood had a reasonable chance of surviving into their sixties, though few lived much beyond age sixty-five. Franklin turned sixty-two in 1768.

He loved London, a great cosmopolitan center and a city in which, as he said, he had "made many agreeable connections of friendship."[43] London offered convivial clubs and rich enticements for a man with insatiable social and intellectual appetites. The Continent was nearby, too, and Franklin had already traveled there twice, exploring France and Germany. But London had become his home, and it offered him much more than tiny Philadelphia.

It even offered him at least as much female companionship as he had enjoyed at home. At age twenty-four, Franklin had entered into a common-law marriage with Deborah Read of Philadelphia. She had not been his first choice, but when his other courtships failed, Franklin turned to her. Franklin's marriage—like everything that he did—was a cold, calculated move. Deborah was plain and barely literate, but she brought several virtues to the union. She was prudent, frugal, industrious, and helpful around her husband's shop. She was also willing to raise Franklin's illegitimate son, William, born to another woman. Two years into the marriage, Deborah gave birth to a son, Francis, who died of smallpox when he was four years old. (Though he exhorted others to be inoculated, Franklin had mysteriously failed to take the precaution with little Francis.) As Deborah and Benjamin approached their fortieth birthdays, she bore a second child, Sarah, who was called Sally.

Whatever the nature of their relationship may have been in their early years together, Benjamin and Deborah rarely saw one another once they reached middle age. She refused to accompany her husband on his two Atlantic crossings, possibly from fear of sailing, perhaps from an apprehension that she and the great metropolis would not be a good fit, or, more likely, because Franklin led her to believe that his absences would be brief. Between the time of Franklin's voyage to England in 1757 and Deborah's death near the end of

1774, the two were together for only a few months. They did not see each other at all during the last nine years of Deborah's life. She was disconsolate when they were separated. Her husband, who drifted farther and farther apart from his wife until he appears to have lost interest in her altogether, was quite content with the arrangement.

During the roughly sixteen years that Franklin lived in London after 1757, he lodged in a four-room apartment in Margaret Stevenson's spacious four-story home on Craven Street in the center of the city. Mrs. Stevenson, a widow and the same age as Franklin, provided what he called a "genteel" environment, something other than what he was accustomed to with Deborah. The true nature of the relationship between Franklin and Mrs. Stevenson remains a mystery, but she seems to have fulfilled his needs as Deborah no longer could. Contented as he had not been for some time at his own home in Philadelphia, Franklin preferred the company of Margaret Stevenson to that of his wife and daughter.[44]

While Franklin may have returned to London to facilitate his hopes of becoming the governor of Pennsylvania, his sights might have shifted higher after several years there. By 1768 rumors were swirling that he might be named an undersecretary in the newly created ministerial office of American secretary. The tattle would have caused only sweet sensations for this ambitious man. A subministerial post—the highest public office to which any American could aspire, and which hardly any attained—would be the capstone to Franklin's glorious life. Consequently, the growing imperial strife was a great threat to all of his hopes. If a breach came, Franklin would have to choose between America and England, and he likely already knew that he would choose America. It was his homeland. More important, his property and investments were in America, and they alone could provide security for his last years. But he did not want to have to make the choice between America and the mother country. He wanted to find a solution to the empire's problems so that he might live his final years in London.

Franklin attempted a balancing act. He wished to do nothing that would jeopardize his standing in Pennsylvania or his possible selection to be a subminister. With several irons in the fire, Franklin tried to convince officials in London that the Americans were not as radical as they sometimes appeared to be. He also sought to persuade the Americans to tone down their rhetoric, which he privately labeled "wild ravings."[45]

Increasingly, however, Franklin was coming to believe that it would not be easy to resolve the Anglo-American difficulties. Earlier than most, he saw clearly where the imperial clash appeared to be heading. America, he wrote as early as 1767, "must become a great Country, populous and mighty." It might already be capable of shaking "off any Shackles that may be impos'd on her," and it might even be sufficiently powerful to "place them on the Imposer." Abundant "Respect, Veneration and Affection" for Great Britain yet existed in America, Franklin advised, and if Britain ruled wisely and gently, the colonists "might be easily govern'd [by London] for Ages" to come. Franklin also pointed out that over the long haul, Great Britain would need America more than America would need its mother country. But he warned that if the British were so unwise as to attempt to govern the colonists with a heavy hand, it would drive them to "a Separation," for "the Seeds of Liberty are universally sown" in America and "nothing can eradicate them." The fate of the empire, he predicted, depended on the prudence of those who held power in London. But even at that early moment Franklin did "not see . . . a sufficient quantity of the Wisdom" needed to preserve Britain's ties to America.[46]

Franklin scratched out several anonymous essays for a London newspaper attacking the Townshend Duties. He charged that Parliament was bent on "oppressing and enslaving . . . the last brave Assertors" of freedom. A faction existed in Parliament that "harbors inveterate Malice to the Americans." They had "no true Idea of Liberty, or real Desire to see it flourish and increase," he maintained, even claiming that some in Parliament wished to push things to the brink, giving London the pretext "to hang" every American dissident.[47]

Franklin was not alone in this view. As the colonial protest spread in 1768, calls for Britain to use force to "effectually quell the spirit of sedition" in America grew louder. The ministry, it was said, had placated the colonists by repealing the Stamp Act, but it was clear now that such a course had been unavailing. Appeasement had only "encreased the storm instead of laying it" aside. By that autumn both the undersecretary of state in the American secretary's office and Connecticut's agent in London feared that the ministry was close to a decision to use force.[48] Franklin was sufficiently alarmed that he addressed the matter in a newspaper essay. Five years and an army of more than forty thousand men had been required to reduce one American province—Canada—in the Seven Years' War, he wrote. He added that hostilities with thirteen colonies would likely drag on interminably, bleeding Great Britain of manpower and depleting its treasury, and in the end Britain might lose America.[49]

In the course of this feverish crisis, Franklin's conception of the empire slowly changed. He had earlier come to the conclusion that Parliament had no authority to raise revenue in America, but he equivocated on the matter of Parliament's right to regulate American commerce. Between the middle and the end of the decade, Franklin moved toward the notion of free trade for the colonists. Increasingly, he was coming to believe that Parliament's only imperial role should be to protect all components of the Anglo-American union from foreign competition. Whereas Dickinson saw commercial regulation as in the general interest of America and Britain, Franklin was coming to see it more as a means of advancing the economic interests of powerful sectors within the mother country at the expense of the colonists.[50]

By sometime in 1768 or 1769, Franklin's thinking came into greater focus. With regard to Parliament's power over America, Franklin, unlike Dickinson, saw that there could be "no middle doctrine." Either "Parliament has a power to make *all laws* for us, or . . . it has a power to make *no laws* for us."[51] He had decided that Parliament had no constitutional authority whatsoever over the colonies, a position from which he never wavered. Franklin had already begun to envisage an imperial arrangement in which the colonists owed allegiance only to the king—a union that in the distant future would come to be called the commonwealth theory of empire. It was a concept that within seven or eight years would be embraced by virtually all Americans who opposed British policies. In the late 1760s, however, Franklin, who only three years earlier had found himself so far behind the thinking of most colonists that his popularity had for a time suffered, had come to embrace a more radical position than Dickinson, the most popular American pamphleteer.[52] When asked by officials in London whether there was a solution to the empire's problems, Franklin, in a pensive mood, replied: "*Repeal* the LAWS, *Renounce* the RIGHT [of Parliament to legislate for America], *Recall* the Troops, *Refund* the Money [raised thus far by taxation], and *Return to the old*"—that is, to the easy imperial relationship that had existed prior to the Stamp Act.[53] But should the British government persist in its "unhappy new system of politics"—a system that required "a new kind of loyalty" from America, "a loyalty to P[arliamen]t"—the colonists would be driven "to dissolve those bands of union, and to sever . . . for ever" their ties with Great Britain.[54]

Franklin was not the only American whose outlook was transformed in the late 1760s. For him and many others, the Townshend Duties proved to be more pivotal than the Stamp Act. That was the case with George Washington. Though a member of the Virginia assembly, Washington had been so untroubled by the Stamp Act that he had not been in attendance when the House of Burgesses took a stand against the parliamentary tax. While Patrick Henry was making history in Williamsburg, Washington, according to his diary, "sowed Turneps. . . . Seperated my Ewes & Rams. . . . Finished Sowing

Wheat. . . . Began to Pull the Seed Hemp" at Mount Vernon.[55] But in 1769, Washington, who had been an inconspicuous backbencher during the initial decade that he had sat in the assembly, took the lead in organizing Virginia's embargo of British imports. Reading Dickinson's *Letters from a Farmer,* which he had purchased in Williamsburg, may have contributed to his evolving radicalization. But more than anything, Washington on his own had come to see a menacing pattern in British actions. Like many other Americans, he had looked on the Stamp Act as an aberration. He thought it unconstitutional, but he believed the ministry had stumbled accidentally into the measure. The Townshend Duties convinced him that Parliament was bent on taxing the colonists. Moreover, if Parliament stripped away the Americans' sacred right to be taxed only by their own representatives, other rights and liberties might be imperiled as well. By 1769, Washington was writing of "our lordly Masters in Great Britain," venom dripping from his pen as he contemplated the second-class status of the colonists. That same year, he spoke in private of taking up arms against the mother country, if need be, to defend the rights of the American colonists. Washington, in fact, was one of the first colonists, if not the first, to suggest the possibility of going to war to resist the encroachments of the British government. He was inspired by "an Innate Spirit of Freedom," he claimed, and though he could not "say where the Line between Great Britain and the Colonies should be drawn," he believed that "one ought to be drawn; & our Rights clearly ascertained."[56]

Around the time that Washington grew more militant, growing numbers of New Englanders were also coming to suspect British intentions. In the summer of 1768 royal authorities announced that two British army regiments were being redeployed from the frontier to Boston. It was not an unexpected turn of events. Boston's newspapers had been predicting the soldiers' arrival for three years, always saying that troops would be sent to enforce the imperial laws and usually characterizing their arrival as an "invasion" of the Bay Colony. To many Yankees the presence of the British army smacked of tyranny, and indeed, one newspaper essayist after another pointed out how despots throughout history had utilized armies to become all-powerful. Bolstered by armed might, one screed warned, rulers soon "begin to look upon themselves as the LORDS and not the SERVANTS of the people." In no time, he continued, they "*make laws for themselves,* and enforce them by the *power of the sword!*" "Military power is forever *dangerous* to civil rights," cautioned another writer. Not a few scribblers said the British army was being sent to Boston to enforce both an "unconstitutional" tax and harsh trade laws that would wreck the city's economy. Francis Bernard, the royal governor of Massachusetts who had requested that troops be sent to Boston, was pilloried in the press as a "Great Bashaw," as "freedom's foe," and as a "knave" who longed to run a "tyrant crew."[57]

Some in Boston in 1768 spoke of raising an army of militiamen to resist the landing of the troops, or "lobster backs," as the citizenry habitually referred to Britain's red-clad soldiers. Some later recalled hearing Samuel Adams, the most visible leader of the resistance movement in Massachusetts, call for taking up arms, even for seizing and holding hostage all royal officials in the city. "If you are Men behave like Men . . . and be free," Adams supposedly declared. Other radicals urged the seizure of Castle William, a royal fortress in Boston Harbor, and the use of its artillery to prevent troopships from docking. But cooler heads prevailed, if only because the groundwork had not been laid for uniting with other colonies, a prerequisite for armed resistance. The British army marched ashore peacefully, though all the while a small armada of British war vessels stood in the harbor, their guns trained on the city.[58]

The presence of British soldiers turned Boston, already a city on edge, into a tinderbox. Putting soldiers given to "common insolence" amid civilians who burned with "warm resentment" toward the presence of the army was akin, said Franklin, to "setting up a smith's forge in a magazine of gunpowder."[59] There were repeated violent incidents, though somehow the friction was kept under control for eighteen months. Finally, on March 5, 1770, the long-anticipated explosion occurred.

Some in New England who were given to thinking in terms of intrigue had from the beginning believed that the army had been sent to Boston to provoke a clash. Others—including British officials in Massachusetts and even some residents of the city who sympathized with the American resistance—thought that Boston's popular leaders were no less interested in inciting some sort of confrontation. Rumors of depredations by the soldiers swirled through the city during February and early March 1770, stoking a white-hot atmosphere of suspicion and malevolence.

Around nine fifteen P.M. on March 5, an alarm bell tolled—no one was ever certain who rang it—summoning residents downtown. Some hurried from their homes, others from the grog shops that lined the waterfront, most thinking they were being called to fight a fire. In no time, a crowd of upwards of two hundred men and boys had gathered on snow-covered King Street in front of the Customs House. A squad of eight regulars and one officer stood guard before the building. Little time was required for the mood of the crowd to turn ugly. Men vented their long-standing hostility toward the soldiers, doubtless emboldened by the belief that the disciplined redcoats under an officer's command would not retaliate.

Members of what in an instant had turned into an impassioned, unruly mob jeered and shouted curses at the soldiers. Some pelted the redcoats with snowballs and ice. Others recklessly dared the soldiers to open fire. "Come on you rascals, you bloody-backs, you Lobster Scoundrels; fire if you dare, God damn you, fire and be damned, we know you dare not," hotheads shouted. Heavily outnumbered, the frightened soldiers were edgy. In such a belligerent, tension-packed atmosphere, the worst outcome was predictable.

It took only a few minutes for a catastrophe to occur. No one ever knew exactly what happened, but the best guess was that a soldier, hit with a heavy chunk of ice, was knocked off balance, causing him to accidentally fire his musket. In an instant, other overwrought soldiers fired too. Some soldiers who had not yet discharged their weapons now presumed that, in the bedlam, they had failed to hear their commander's order to open fire. They, too, emptied their muskets into the crowd. There was also the possibility, based on subsequent eyewitness accounts and the number of casualties, that civilians on the second floor of the Customs Building fired into the crowd.

It had taken only an instant for these events to unfold, but in their wake, six in the crowd of agitators were wounded and five lay dead or dying in the bloody, trodden slush. Bostonians immediately called the incident a "massacre." Some, like John Adams, ever after referred to what had occurred as the "slaughter in King Street."[60]

Long before it learned of the Boston Massacre, London was feeling the bite of the colonists' trade embargo. British imports into America were sliced in half in 1769. The boycott in New York City, the second-busiest port in the colonies, shut out 80 percent of the goods normally imported into that colony. Eighteen months after the Townshend Duties became law, the American secretary confessed that the legislation could not be enforced. By early 1770 most members of the ministry had reached a similar conclusion. Though the colonists would not learn of the ministry's action for another six weeks, three days before the Boston Massacre the cabinet voted to repeal the Townshend Duties, save for the tax on tea. Given the Americans' thirst for the beverage, the tea tax was expected to raise twenty thousand pounds annually for the British treasury. Retaining that tax, Franklin reported, also afforded the government the means "for keeping up the claim of Parliamentary sovereignty."[61]

The government that rescinded most of the Townshend Duties had just come to power. The repeal, in fact, was very nearly the first step that it took. It was the government of Lord North. On March 2, six weeks after its formation, North's ministry agreed to repeal the bulk of the Townshend Duties. Parliament rubber-stamped the decision within a few days. There is no evidence that North, who longed for reconciliation with America, ever planned to levy further taxes on the colonists. However, lest he send a signal of weakness, North rapidly purged those in his ministry who had favored the revocation of all American taxes, surrounding himself almost entirely with ministers who had strongly advocated both the Stamp Act and Townshend Duties. Given the composition of his ministry, and the fact that it had sought only a partial repeal of Parliament's taxes, many in America feared that North's government was solidly committed to taxing the colonists. Those concerns were disseminated by Americans in London, including the deputy governor of Maryland, who observed that everything pointed toward North "laying [additional] duties in America on some future occasion."[62]

Whatever North's government stood for, there was no disputing that the American protest had, for the second time in forty months, compelled the British government to back down. In addition, as had happened during the Stamp Act crisis, those in American politics who were coming to be called Tories—because they had either defended British actions or opposed a hardline resistance to London's policies—paid a price. The faction in New York that had championed compliance with the Quartering Act and opposed the commercial boycott was swept from power in the elections of 1769. In Pennsylvania, the Assembly Party suffered staggering losses in the elections in 1770—retribution for its lukewarm support for the boycott and its long campaign for royal government, which few in the colony any longer found attractive. The evidence was overwhelming that there was widespread popular support in America for resisting parliamentary taxation and maintaining whatever slivers of autonomy the colonists had won.[63]

North's ministry largely ignored its American problem during the next three years. North may have been biding his time, waiting for the colonists' boycott of tea to disintegrate, although such an explanation probably gives him more credit for system and savvy than he deserves. He was preoccupied by a crisis with Spain over the Falkland Islands during a portion of this time, a dustup that was successfully resolved, boosting North's self-confidence. Much of his remaining time was consumed by the debt problem, and after a few years on the job, North was able to report that he was making headway toward getting Britain's financial house in order, thanks in large measure to a new lottery he had introduced. Although London was not procuring much tax-based revenue from the colonies—the ongoing embargo had by 1772 reduced imports of tea by some 60 percent throughout the colonies and by nearly 99 percent in both New York City and Philadelphia—the ministry still showed no inclination to rekindle the troublesome matter of colonial taxation.[64]

In the end, North inadvertently stumbled back into the American problem.

By 1773 mismanagement had pushed the mammoth East India Company to the cusp of bankruptcy, a calamity that threatened to plunge Great Britain into a ruinous depression. North's government chose to bail out the beleaguered company, loaning it 1 million pounds. To help the company meet its debt obligation, North's government also secured passage of the Tea Act, a measure that vested the East India Company with a monopoly on tea sales in America and reduced the existing tax on tea. North's thinking was that the cost of the company's tea would be so cheap that no smuggler could compete.[65]

North found what he had done to be distasteful, though only because he loathed the government's intrusion into the affairs of a private enterprise. He appears to have never imagined that an American rebellion could blow up out of the Tea Act, especially because he saw the origins of the legislation as distinct from that which had produced the Stamp Act and the Townshend Duties. But Franklin saw what North could not see. Before the colonists learned of the Tea Act, Franklin published in a London newspaper what may have been his most brilliant satire, a piece he titled "Rules by Which a Great Empire May be Reduced to a Small One." To ensure the ruination of an empire, Franklin wrote, the mother country should send as governors to the colonies men who were "Prodigals who have ruined their Fortunes, broken Gamesters or Stock-Jobbers," and when they have completed their "Mal-administration, Oppression, or Injustice," they should be brought home and "*reward*[ed] . . . with Pensions." That alone would not do, however. The parent state should additionally quarter troops among the Americans so that mobs might be provoked, restrict the colonists' manufacturing and commercial abilities, and "harass them with novel Taxes." Remember, too, he further advised, "to make your arbitrary Tax more grievous . . . by public Declarations importing that your Power of taxing them has *no limit*." Finally, be sure to ignore the colonists' entreaties for redress. Instead, "Suppose all *their* Complaints be invented and promoted by a few factious Demagogues, whom if you could catch and hang" it "shall *work Miracles* in favour" of your getting "rid of the Trouble of governing them . . . for ever."[66]

His biting essay notwithstanding, Franklin remained hopeful. Perhaps he clutched at straws, but it was more likely that he had been impressed with the steady restraint exhibited by North's government during its first forty months in office. Franklin was also cheered by the departure of Lord Hillsborough as American secretary in the summer of 1772. Franklin had initially believed that Hillsborough's "inclinations are rather favourable towards us." He had been wrong. Hillsborough not only had been prone to malicious and ill-advised actions—by "*my Firmness*" the colonists will be "something mended," he had boasted loudly—but also had treated Franklin with a callous snobbishness. Soon enough Franklin realized that both the royalization of Pennsylvania and his elevation to a subministerial post were dead letters so long as Hillsborough held his office. Ultimately, Franklin concluded that the boorish Hillsborough was a man given to "conceit, wrong-headedness, obstinacy, and passion" who was "fond of every one that can stoop to flatter him and inimical to all that dare tell him disagreable Truths." But by the time of the Tea Act, Hillsborough was gone, forced out a year earlier by domestic enemies who believed his land policies in America were injurious to their speculative interests. He had been succeeded in August 1772 by the Earl of Dartmouth, who was quiet and genteel, reputed to be given to calm and rational deliberation, known to have been an advocate of the repeal of the Stamp Act, and, according to Franklin, generally believed to harbor "favourable Dispositions towards the Colonies."[67] If only the Tea Act could be weathered—and Franklin believed it could, provided the colonists responded judiciously—he was hopeful that Anglo-American differences could be resolved.

Ironically, no one did more than Franklin to set the stage for the combustible environment in Boston that greeted the Tea Act. At the very end of 1772—some six months prior to the enactment of the Tea Act—Franklin had made a fateful decision. Someone who has never been identified passed along to him a purloined collection of letters exchanged in the late 1760s between Thomas Hutchinson, by now the royal governor of Massachusetts, and Thomas Whately, a member of Parliament and former undersecretary of the treasury. The missives were filled with volatile passages. Hutchinson had portrayed the popular leaders in Massachusetts as bent on fomenting rebellion, welcomed an unflinching British response to American provocations, and even asked for "an abridgment of what are called English liberties" within the Bay Colony. Given the passionate atmosphere in Boston and the antipathy that residents already felt toward Hutchinson, Franklin knew the letters would have an inflammatory effect.

However, Franklin had convinced himself that the letters would demonstrate that the culprits responsible for imperial troubles were misguided and corrupt lower-level officials, the likes of royal governors and undersecretaries who steered well-intended ministers—such as Lord North—toward bad choices. He was convinced too that the continued presence of Hutchinson, who was widely hated in Boston, only made the already inflamed situation in the Bay Colony even more explosive. Publication of the letters, Franklin reasoned, would lead London to remove Hutchinson. Incredibly, Franklin seemed to believe that by passing along the stolen letters, he was paving the way for the final resolution of Anglo-American differences.[68]

For all his brilliance as a scientist, essayist, businessman, and civic leader,

Franklin the politician not infrequently made monumental mistakes. Dispatching the Hutchinson Letters was his most egregious blunder, both for his own personal fortunes and as a contributory factor to a landmark event in the American Revolution. Seldom has any thoughtful public figure acted on such flawed logic or demonstrated such a shocking lack of political savvy.

Today, it is surprising that a powerful American resistance could be fashioned against a tax that had been in existence for six years and was even being reduced. But by this time many Americans had come to distrust the motives of the mother country. Noxious taxes, occupation by a standing army, and discriminatory commercial regulations had convinced many colonists that the policies pursued by the imperial government "evince[d] a design to reduce them under absolute Despotism," as the Declaration of Independence would eventually assert. Contrary to Franklin's expectations, nothing was more important than the Hutchinson Letters—at least in Massachusetts—in confirming the colonists' suspicions.

Hutchinson's pilfered correspondence was made public in Boston only weeks prior to the arrival of the first news of the Tea Act. The letters hit like a bombshell, causing many Bostonians to imagine a far-flung conspiracy among malevolent authorities—ranging from colonial officials in America to the ministry itself—to victimize the colonists. Many were now assured that the ultimate goal of these conspiratorial officials was tyranny, just as the leaders of the colonial protest had been saying for nearly a decade. Instead of rehabilitating North's reputation, as Franklin had hoped would be the case, the letters convinced many Bostonians that by reducing the levy on tea, the ministry had treacherously schemed to find a way to get the colonists accustomed to paying imperial taxes. Once they acquiesced, the Bostonians thought, Parliament would impose a panoply of taxes on America.[69] It followed, too, that in due time London would strip the colonists of all autonomy and abuse them in the same manner that it had long victimized the Irish.

Coordinated resistance to the Tea Act was possible because an infrastructure of protest had been fashioned since 1765, at least in the principal cities. Operating through organizations such as the Sons of Liberty, which sported networks that reached from harborside barrooms to the richly paneled offices of affluent merchants, the popular leaders listened, managed, taught, manipulated, and planned. With time, they grew more adroit at organizing and provoking. They learned how to turn out crowds and how to control them once they were in the streets, and they found writers with a keen eye for cant who were capable of giving just the right twist to British policies and actions. These polemicists cast everything done by British officials in a bad light. This is not to suggest that those who followed the popular leaders were unthinking automatons. More and more Americans now questioned whether their vital interests could be secured under the current imperial structure. Increasing numbers of colonists wished to have greater control over their destiny, and steadily more of the best educated and the affluent were growing restive with the limitations for advancement that they faced simply because they were colonists. By 1773 many Americans had come to think along the lines of Samuel Adams, who had recently written that it was "the Business of America to take care of itself."[70]

Nor was it solely the residents of the large port cities who had grown disaffected with imperial conditions. Many Chesapeake planters longed to market their tobacco in free markets outside the British Empire. Others, both the wealthy and hordes of land-hungry farmers, some of whom had fought in the French and Indian War to win the trans–Appalachian West for Anglo-America, had grown restive waiting for London to open that lush domain for settlement and speculation. The Tea Act took effect near the tenth anniversary of the Peace of Paris, yet after all that time the lands across the mountains remained nearly as closed to American settlement as they had been when they belonged to France. Nor should it be forgotten that many yeomen in the Carolina and Georgia backcountry, the Scots-Irish in particular, were descendants of immigrants who had fled British victimization, whether economic or religious. To say that they were resentful of London's long reach would be an understatement.[71]

If the nascent American resistance was to succeed, the colonists had to demonstrate a common front against London. Colonists throughout the length and breadth of the land had to realize that opposition to parliamentary taxation, even a growing disenchantment with many imperial policies and practices, was widespread. Early in 1773, just prior to the passage of the Tea Act, Richard Henry Lee in Virginia had taken the lead in inducing the House of Burgesses to open an intercolonial correspondence. The idea, as Thomas Jefferson later recalled, was to foster an "understanding with all the other colonies to consider the British claims as a common cause to all, & to produce an unity of action." Once adopted, Virginia shared information with colonial assemblies throughout America. Within a few months each colony, save Pennsylvania, had its own committee of correspondence and "lovers of liberty in every province"—Lee's characterization—were coming to understand that Americans from New England's rugged coastline to the pine barrens of the Lower South felt threatened by the encroaching policies of Parliament.[72]

The colonists learned of the Tea Act in September, more than two months prior to the arrival of the first ship that brought dutied tea across the Atlantic. From the start, there was a gathering sense in some quarters that this was an epochal showdown. Here, yet again, was another attempt by Parliament to tax them. What is more, the act gave the East India Company monopoly rights in selling the tea, a dangerous precedent that could threaten free trade. Then, too, there was an air of deceit about this law. As the existing tax on tea was lowered, many saw the Tea Act as a sleight of hand to draw the colonists into paying only a light duty. If the maneuver succeeded, the colonists in no time would become accustomed to paying this parliamentary tax; ensnared, they would be ripe for further taxation.

Given months to prepare, those who opposed parliamentary taxation were ready when the tea ships approached the port cities. Confronted by angry mobs, the captains of the *Nancy* and the *Polly*, the tea ships bound for New York and Philadelphia, respectively, turned for home without attempting a landing. The *London* made for Charleston, but when it docked, the local Sons of Liberty seized the cargo, preventing its sale. In Boston, outrage took a different and more destructive form. Late on a frigid, jet-black Saturday night toward the end of November, the *Dartmouth*, carrying 114 chests of tea, slipped into Boston Harbor and tied up at dockside while the city's residents slept. When the Boston resistance leaders learned the next day that the tea ship was in port, it was too late to seize the duty cargo, unless they wished to risk a confrontation with customs officials and possibly British soldiers. Things only got worse for the radical leaders in Boston. A week later a second tea ship, the *Eleanor*, arrived and docked, and after another ten days the brig *Beaver* entered Boston Harbor with still more of the East India Company's tea. (A fourth tea ship, the *William*, ran aground at Provincetown on Cape Cod, but its 58 chests of tea were saved and fell into the hands of the Customs Service.)[73]

Those in Boston who opposed the Tea Act knew that, under a century-old customs regulation, all duties on taxable goods were to be paid within twenty days or customs officials would seize the ship and sell it and its cargo at auction. Whale oil and assorted winter supplies, which were also part of *Dartmouth*'s contents, were rapidly brought ashore, but longshoremen refused to touch the chests of tea. The clock was ticking. Come December 17, time would run out. On that day the tea aboard the *Dartmouth* was certain to fall into the hands of the Customs Service. There could be no doubt that thereafter the tea would be sold by the East India Company to Massachusetts consumers. Should that occur, it was feared, not only would the tax on tea be collected, but the triumphant ministry and Parliament would also impose additional duties on the colonists. To prevent this from occurring, Boston's radical leaders pleaded for three weeks with Governor Hutchinson to send the ships with their cargoes of tea back to England. He turned a deaf ear to their entreaties. Hutchinson had taken an oath to enforce British law. Furthermore, after the publication of his private letters, he was anxious to settle old scores.[74]

Faced with the choice of acting or capitulating, the resistance leaders chose to act. On the bitingly cold, mist-cloaked night of December 16, they took a carefully planned step. Upwards of 200 men, many disguised as Indians, descended on Griffin's Wharf and slipped aboard all three tea ships. While some men held lanterns or stood lookout, others descended into the holds. With block and tackle, the heavy chests of tea—each chest was lead-lined and weighed 80 to 90 pounds when empty and upwards of 450 pounds when filled—were hoisted on deck, where men, sweating despite the raw weather, wielded axes to smash them open. Other "Mohawks," as these men called themselves, shoveled the loose tea into the swirling, sable waters of Boston Harbor. The work was difficult and time-consuming, requiring nearly three hours. Still, considering the amount of goods that had to be moved—90,000 pounds of tea in 340 unwieldy chests—the job was completed relatively rapidly, which suggests that most of the work was undertaken by dockhands accustomed to this sort of labor. Customs officials and the leaders of Britain's armed forces in Boston had known early on that the vessels had been taken over by hostile elements—they could not help but know, as more than two thousand spectators gathered along the waterfront to watch the festivities—but none wished to act without civilian authorization. Governor Hutchinson, who had fled to his country home in Milton, was not present to give the order to stop the plundering. In the crystalline dawn of the following day, December 17, every resident knew of the Boston Tea Party and, in all likelihood, knew it had been a watershed event, what John Adams that morning called "an Epocha in History."[75]

No one recorded Lord North's first response to the news of the Boston Tea Party, but, like Adams, he must have realized straightaway that the incident marked a new level of rebellion. The tea protest had become his American crisis. The prime minister was doubtless angry and shocked, as were some Americans who had thought the Tea Act should be resisted, though by peaceful means. Franklin's initial reaction was that all "considerate Men" must oppose the destruction of private property. Besides, he said, America's dispute was not with the East India Company. On learning what had occurred in Boston Harbor, Franklin appealed to the Massachusetts assembly to indemnify

Some 90,000 pounds of East India Company tea was destroyed in the Boston Tea Party,
on December 16, 1773. This was America's most violent response to the Tea Act,
and led the British government to respond with coercive measures that
the colonists labeled the Intolerable Acts. The Destruction of Tea
at Boston Harbor *lithograph by Sarony*
and Major, 1846. (National Archives)

the company.[76] Washington, likewise, found the destruction of private property indefensible and proposed that Virginia help Massachusetts make repa-
rations to the East India Company.[77]

The outrage expressed by Franklin and Washington paled next to the anger that swept England. More than six months after the passage of the Tea
Act, only 3 percent of the tea the East India Company had shipped to America—
just that salvaged from the shipwrecked *William*—was in the hands of the
Customs Service and ready for sale. Unbridled fury toward the colonists
filled the British newspapers, but the lion's share of indignation was directed
at Boston, the lone site of violence. Bostonians were branded "bigots of the
most dangerous kind" and singled out as the "most turbulent" of all Americans. It was a city, according to a London newspaper, in which "honest Men
and Virgins [were] scarce." One English penman claimed that the American
troubles had originated with "crafty" Boston "smugglers," after which things
were "blown into rebellion by the preachers." Several essayists instantly attributed the Boston Tea Party to the work of the "crafty pettifogger" and
"arch rebel" Samuel Adams, who, it was said, "leads a banditti of hypocrites,"

and the merchant John Hancock, who was widely portrayed in England as the prince of smugglers and the "*Milch-Cow*" of Boston's extremists.[78] Numerous scribblers demanded that Adams and Hancock be arrested and transported to England to stand trial for sedition. One writer suggested that royal authorities in Boston send across the Atlantic "a Cargo of American Scalps, as some Recompense for their Tea," while another proposed that British officials "Hang, draw, and quarter fifty" of Boston's radicals.

One essayist cast a broader net. Britain, he said, confronted a "many headed Monster" in America that threatened the "Peace and Tranquility of the Nation." Others charged that the lingering American problem could be traced to the "Timidity of . . . Tax-repealing" ministries that had capitulated in the face of the Stamp Act protests and largely surrendered again when most of the Townshend Duties were repealed. "Forbearance has long been ineffectual" was the mantra of many who demanded toughness. The time had come, they said, for "an enlarged Fortitude" and "an Exertion of Power." British "supremacy must be maintained and supported. . . . This is no period for . . . temporizing." There were times—and this was one of them, according to one pamphleteer—when "violent remedies must be . . . applied to obstinate diseases." Even the *National Register*, a journal that had opposed American taxation, labeled the Boston Tea Party an "outrage."[79] Franklin, who kept an eye on the British press, notified America of the "great Resentment here" toward the colonists, and he added: "I suppose we never had since we were a People, so few Friends in Britain."[80]

The savage mood in Britain was reflected in the cabinet. The ministers were incensed by the American reaction to the Tea Act, but they were particularly irate at what had occurred in Boston. This was due in part to the Yankees' repeated defiance, but even more so it was because the Bostonians had destroyed the tea. Given the near-sacred status of property in Great Britain—where courts were known to hang paupers who stole a loaf of bread—the ministers looked on the Boston Tea Party as worse than a riot.

From its first meeting, the cabinet resolved to take "effectual steps . . . to secure the dependence of the colonies." But to its credit, North's government did not hastily settle on its response. North was a mild-mannered man. He had come to power free of enmity toward the Americans, and from first to last he hoped that war might be avoided.[81] He presided over calm, unhurried, and thoughtful deliberations concerning the proper response. Over the course of six weeks the ministers met often, sometimes even late into the night, to discuss their options and the likely American response. Each minister understood that if the government stood its ground, refusing any longer to appease the colonists, there was a risk of war. Consequently, at numerous meetings North and his ministers contemplated hostilities. Could Britain win a war? How would it be fought? What was the likelihood of French and Spanish intervention?

From the outset, a majority of ministers believed the colonists would back down if faced with the use of force, a view nourished by General Thomas Gage, the commander of the British army in America, who advised that the Americans would "be lyons whilst we are lambs but if we take the resolute part they will be very meek." It seemed inconceivable to most in the cabinet that colonists who had neither a national army nor a navy of any sort would dare risk war with a nation that could field a professional army and possessed the greatest navy in the world. Virtually every member of North's ministry believed that Britain would prevail, and easily, should the Americans be foolish enough to resort to arms. Some were convinced that only one or two engagements would be sufficient to bring the colonists to heel. Some even thought that the colonists' will to resist could be broken by a naval blockade and that no pitched battles would be necessary. But if fighting did occur, the prospect was not terribly troubling. Given the performance of callow colonial soldiers in the recent war, many were persuaded that the Americans were a "poor species of fighting men." Some questioned that premise, though it was incontrovertible that there was a dearth of officers in the colonies with experience in leading large armies. Most also thought it improbable that colonial militiamen would dare stand up to regular soldiers. Furthermore, the colonists were disunited. During the French and Indian War, Franklin had proposed what came to be known as the Albany Plan of Union, a plea for the colonies to unite in a confederation to more effectively wage the war. Not a single province had endorsed his idea. Given these realities, some in Britain were cocksure, such as the general whom Franklin overheard boasting that "with a Thousand British grenadiers he would undertake to go from one end of America to the other, and geld all the Males, partly by force and partly by a little Coaxing."[82]

Confronted by the colonists' effrontery, not to mention their willful lawlessness, virtually every member of North's ministry believed that retribution of some sort was called for. Differences existed, however. The Earl of Sandwich, First Lord of the Admiralty, and the Earl of Suffolk, secretary of state for the Northern Department (Northern Europe), led those who favored the most punitive measures. Sandwich, a veteran minister who over the years had instituted many useful naval reforms, was the most influential minister, next to North, of course. Walpole thought no other cabinet member was Sandwich's rival when it came to making quick and sound judgments. Suffolk, who was young and good-natured, had been a follower of Grenville and for

*Lord Dartmouth by Sir Joshua Reynolds. Lord North's stepbrother and
the American secretary during the final years of peace, he advocated negotiation to
resolve the crisis. However, Dartmouth signed the order to use force against the American
rebels. (© Coram in the care of the Foundling Museum, London /
The Bridgeman Art Library International)*

ten years an outspoken advocate of American taxation. A second faction also wanted the government to be tough, but less so than demanded by the hard-liners, and these ministers were not entirely certain what steps should be taken. This contingent was led by the Earl of Gower, president of the Privy Council; the Earl of Rochford, secretary of state for the Southern Department and an expert on Spain; and Viscount Weymouth, groom of the stole, who was related to North by marriage. Dartmouth, standing nearly alone, was the most vocal against taking especially vindictive measures. He saw himself as manning the bulwarks "to cover America from the present storm." But Dartmouth was not sanguine. Over the years he had found that Lord North usually gave in to those who were more forceful and acrimonious.[83]

When the cabinet began its deliberations, North set the tone: "Whatever may be the consequences, we must risk something; if we do not, all is over." The king also leaned on his ministers to be resolute. "I do not wish to come to severer measures," he said, "but we must not retreat."[84] The ministry did not have many options. Sandwich and Suffolk strenuously advocated the immediate use of force against Massachusetts. For several days the cabinet also contemplated prosecuting those who were thought to be leaders in Boston's insurgency. The names of Hancock and Samuel Adams, as well as two other readily identifiable activists—Dr. Joseph Warren, a Boston physician and firebrand, and Thomas Cushing, the speaker of the Massachusetts assembly— were frequently mentioned as targets for arrest. The ministry abandoned that avenue only after the solicitor general advised that solid evidence was lacking of their complicity in the Tea Party. For that matter, no corroborative evidence existed for prosecuting a single person for having participated in the destruction of the tea. The cabinet briefly considered merely warning Massachusetts that it would be punished should there be a future incident of property destruction, but the ministers ultimately decided that such a course would "avail nothing," as North subsequently said. The one alternative that was not considered was the repeal of the Tea Act. According to Dartmouth's recollection, anyone who had suggested its repeal would have been thought "mad."[85]

A month after learning of the Tea Party, North's ministry somberly coalesced behind what would be called the Coercive Acts. The government introduced four separate bills in Parliament. The Boston Port Bill would fine Massachusetts for the destroyed tea and close Boston Harbor until the colony paid. The Massachusetts Government Bill would change the charter under which the colony had lived for the past three quarters of a century, blatantly reducing the power of the people while strengthening the hand of royal officials. The bill stipulated that the upper house of the assembly, whose members had always been elected by the lower house, would henceforth be appointed by the royal governor. Town meetings—a New England tradition— were to be prohibited without the chief executive's authorization. Juries, which had always been elected or summoned by local elected officials, were to be placed under the jurisdiction of the governor's appointees. The Administration of Justice Bill would empower the governor to transfer to other colonies, or to England, the trials of indicted government officials. The Quartering Act would authorize the commander of the British army in America to lodge his soldiers wherever necessary, even in private residences.[86]

North's government did not ignore the notion expressed by some newspaper essayists that the disorder in America was widespread. However, the ministry was convinced that Massachusetts was the epicenter of the colonial insurrection. It was additionally guided by an ancient axiom: Sever the head of the serpent and it will die. North's government chose a strategy of divide and conquer, driven by the belief that "the other Colonies would leave them [Massachusetts] to struggle alone," as one minister observed.

North sent the first piece of legislation, the Boston Port Bill, to Parliament on the afternoon of March 7, a sad, gray late-winter's day. In presenting the measure, North charged that the Bostonians had been "the ringleaders of all the riots in America for seven years past."[87] Moreover, if the residents of "Boston . . . can set their faces against" one act of Parliament, he went on, "they might set their faces equally against all" parliamentary legislation until "we have no authority" in Massachusetts. He was taking this step, North added, to secure "the just dependence of the Colonies on the mother country."[88] He acted with the conviction that when confronted with coercion accompanied by the ominous threat of armed force, the radical demagogues in Massachusetts would back down or, more likely, be restrained by what he yet believed was the more prudent majority within the colonies. North did not believe that any colonies to the south of New England would assist their insurrectionary fellow colonists, and he was confident that there would be no war. North prayed that his adamant stand would resolve the American problem, or at least move it to the back burner for a very long time.

The *London Evening Post* reported that when North completed his presentation, "there was a perfect silence for some minutes." If so, it was not because most members of Parliament shrank from punishing Boston. In fact, there was virtually no opposition to the bill, save from a handful of representatives of port cities who feared that closing the port of Boston would be injurious to the pocketbooks of their merchant constituents. Most MPs believed that London had no choice but to take a harsh stand. Even some who had opposed taxation, and were widely known in England as "friends of America," endorsed the bill. For instance, Isaac Barré, who had gained a hero's status in the colonies for his robust denunciation of the Stamp Act, gave his "hearty, and determinate" assent. "I like it, adopt, and embrace it cheerfully," he said on the floor of the House of Commons.[89]

Parliament quickly enacted the Boston Port Bill. The three remaining Coercive Acts faced slightly more opposition, though each passed by a huge majority. At nearly the same time—in June 1774—Parliament enacted the Quebec Act. It was not part of the Coercive Acts, but news of its passage reached America nearly simultaneously with that of the ministry's resort to coercion, and in Virginia it caused as great a stir as the steps taken against Massachusetts. The Quebec Act placed the region northwest of the Ohio River under the jurisdiction of the province of Quebec. Land speculators in Virginia—which included a substantial percentage of politically influential planters—knew in an instant that the Quebec Act severely curtailed their chances of making fortunes in the Ohio Country, a vast, verdant region that Virginia's armies had helped to wrest from the French. No less a figure than Richard Henry Lee would label this legislation "the worst grievance" for Virginians.[90]

During the debates on the Coercive Acts, not a single member of the House of Commons denied that Parliament had the authority to tax the colonists. None questioned the limits of Parliament's authority. Some expressed a sense of betrayal, remarking that they had voted for the Boston Port Bill after having been led to believe that the measures that would follow would be conciliatory. But nearly all who expressed reservations said they believed that Boston's "provocation deserves the fullest arraignment."[91] A small opposition faction around Lord Rockingham, whose ministry had repealed the Stamp Act eight years earlier, argued that there should have been hearings before Parliament acted. Some in this faction said the measures went too far, and it was a Rockinghamite who delivered the lone memorable speech in the course of the debates.

On April 19 Edmund Burke spoke for two hours, addressing not so much the Coercive Acts as the matter of American taxation. His speech drew greater applause than any other in this session and was extolled in the press, with one journal praising him for having "distinguished himself in a masterly manner."[92] Burke was forty-five, portly and jowly, with dark wavy hair. A native of Ireland, he had come to London as a young man to study law and pursue a literary career. He soon abandoned his plans for a legal career, but he enjoyed some success as an essayist and historian. The modest notoriety that he gained as a writer led to his selection as Rockingham's secretary, and that in turn facilitated his election to Parliament in 1765.[93] Though active in the movement to repeal the Stamp Act, Burke had remained surprisingly quiet on the American question until North's government introduced the Coercive Acts. Even then, Burke spoke only once in the debate on the Boston Port Bill, though he had said that the day the legislation was introduced was the day when the world knew that the prime minister "wish[ed] to go to war with all America."[94]

Burke's speech during the debate on the Coercive Acts was the first of three notable speeches he would deliver on the American question in a span of nineteen months. Each address would call for conciliation and, taken together, they won him a reputation in the colonies as America's best friend in London. Burke was convinced that coercion would lead to war and that war almost certainly would result in the loss of the American colonies. To make matters worse, he thought the ongoing crisis with America was entirely avoidable. The Stamp Act protests a decade earlier, he said, had made it folly for subsequent ministries to seek to impose further taxes on the Americans. To do so was akin to setting a torch to dry grass. Besides, the taxes that Parliament had levied would have raised little revenue. They had been imposed primarily to make the point of parliamentary sovereignty. What Parliament achieved was not merely the provocation of "just alarm" among the colonists; London's ill-advised policies had slowly, almost imperceptibly, put the colonists on the road toward union and nationhood.

However, when it came to offering a solution to the American quandary, Burke had few innovative ideas. His views, in fact, were the essence of orthodoxy. He called for the repeal of the Tea Act but did not question the Declaratory Act, which, after all, had been conceived by the Rockingham ministry when it repealed the Stamp Act. Like his fellow Rockinghamites, Burke defended the supremacy of Parliament; he merely wished for its authority to be exercised in ways that the Americans could tolerate. In this speech, Burke asked that Parliament "leave America . . . to tax itself," save for times of dire imperial emergencies. Parliament must instead be "content to bind America by the laws of trade." The trade laws were the "corner stone" of the empire, for they safeguarded and advanced the commerce of all its inhabitants. Should the mercantile laws be the principal imperial regulatory measures, Burke concluded, Anglo-American ties would endure. And if Great Britain spurned coercion in favor of the "old ground," Burke was "persuaded the Americans [would] compromise," and that "subordination and liberty [would] be sufficiently reconciled."[95] But only about 20 percent of those in Parliament sided with him. No mood existed for compromise or conciliation.

In the dark mood of retribution that gripped London, Franklin, once the most venerated colonist, fell from grace. Little compassion for Americans could be found in England in 1774, and when Franklin was identified as the guilty party behind the Hutchinson Letters incident, the decision was made not just to ruin him but also to publicly humiliate him.

Franklin's role in the affair came to light at Christmas 1773, when Thomas Whately's brother challenged to a duel a bureaucrat whom he believed responsible for having put the letters in Samuel Adams's hands. Unwilling to permit the possible death of an innocent man, Franklin confessed to having sent the letters to America. He was widely vilified in the British press as a duplicitous hypocrite and traitor. Franklin's act of passing along the stolen letters of Hutchinson and Whately was worthy of Britain's enmity, but he did not deserve the embarrassing public shaming that followed.

On January 29, nine days after news of the Boston Tea Party reached London, Franklin was summoned to a meeting of the Privy Council for a scheduled hearing on Massachusetts's request that Governor Hutchinson be recalled.

The session was held in the Cockpit, an indoor amphitheater within the government complex known as Whitehall. The hall was packed with officials and spectators who came with a carnival thirst for revenge, taking every seat in the gallery that encircled the lower floor of the chamber. If Franklin arrived expecting to testify on Massachusetts's solicitation, he was greatly mistaken. He was not permitted to speak. Instead, while many in the madly vindictive audience jeered and laughed, Franklin, now sixty-eight years old, was forced to stand for an hour and listen to reproaches against his character made in the most vitriolic manner by Britain's solicitor general, Alexander Wedderburn.

Wearing a coat of spotted Manchester velvet and, as tradition dictated, a white wig, Franklin stood to the left of a large fireplace and faced a table occupied by thirty-five high officials, including Lord North. Wedderburn stood at the table between two privy councillors. From time to time in the course of his harangue, Wedderburn accentuated his points by pounding sharply on the table. Franklin, Wedderburn charged, was "not a gentleman; he was in fact nothing less than a thief." Having stolen the letters for "the most malignant of purposes," Franklin had "forfeited all the respect of societies and of men." From this day forward, the solicitor general added, "Men will watch him with a jealous eye; they will hide their papers from him and lock up their escritoires. He will henceforth esteem it a libel to be called a man of letters." Franklin, he went on in a scornful tone, was "the true incendiary," the "first mover and prime conductor" of the sedition that had bubbled to the surface in Massachusetts. Franklin, Wedderburn charged, had been driven by "secret designs." He had cherished the hope of bringing about American independence and creating "a Great American Republic."[96]

Throughout his ordeal, Franklin, according to one observer, "stood conspicuously erect, without the smallest movement of any part of his body. The muscles of his face had been previously composed, and he did not suffer the slightest alteration of it to appear during the continuance of the speech."[97] Franklin may have concealed his feelings, hoping to cheat the howling crowd from still further merriment at his expense, but he never forgot the debasement he had suffered. From that day forward, retribution against Great Britain's rulers would be a driving force behind the public policies that he pursued, much as it had been for his tormentors on that day in the Cockpit.

Lord North was appalled by the vindictive behavior of his colleagues and subsequently apologized in private to Franklin. But the first minister offered no excuses for the immeasurably harsh Coercive Acts. "Now is the time . . . to proceed with firmness and without fear," he declared.[98]

*   *   *

Franklin was finished in Great Britain and so too, he suspected, were America's ties to the British Empire. In his testimony eight years earlier on behalf of repealing the Stamp Act, Franklin had warned that Britain "will not find a rebellion" in America, but it "may indeed make one."[99] That time had arrived, he now believed. He no longer urged restraint on the colonists. Instead, late in February 1774 he wrote a long piece for the *Boston Gazette* detailing the "Bull-baiting" to which he had been subjected in the Cockpit. He closed with a warning: *"Behold Americans where matters are driving!"*[100]

CHAPTER 3

"DEFENDERS OF AMERICAN LIBERTY"

SAMUEL ADAMS, JOSEPH GALLOWAY, AND THE FIRST CONTINENTAL CONGRESS

WHAT LORD NORTH CALLED the Coercive Acts were referred to by the residents of Massachusetts as the Intolerable Acts. It was a label that resonated with most colonists.

Nearly five months passed before the colonists knew precisely how North's government would respond to the Boston Tea Party. That lengthy period was crucial for the leaders of the Massachusetts resistance movement. It provided them with an opportunity to explain Boston's violent resistance to the Tea Act and to build a common front against London's anticipated reprisals.

On the day after the events on Griffin's Wharf, Boston's popular leaders had called on Paul Revere for help. A muscular thirty-nine-year-old silversmith who had been active in the city's resistance movement since the Stamp Act, Revere may have been among the "Mohawks" who dumped tea in Boston Harbor. The next morning he was asked by the leaders to ride to New York and Philadelphia with dispatches clarifying, and justifying, the Boston Tea Party. Revere sped away on his mission, the first of five long rides that he would make to these two cities. The account of what had occurred in Boston that he carried southward sketched out a narrative showing that Governor Hutchinson and his "Cabal" had turned a deaf ear to the "conciliatory" alternatives proposed by the patriots. It was Hutchinson who had "provoke[d] the people to destroy the Tea," and it was the Royal Governor who was "answerable for the Destruction of the Tea."[1]

Over the next several days the resistance leaders in Boston discovered that the Tea Act had been defied in New York, Philadelphia, and Charleston. To their joy, Boston's radicals learned too that no colony had condemned the violence in Massachusetts and that many newspapers throughout America ecstatically reported the destruction of the tea. The *Pennsylvania Journal*, for instance, presented the story of the Boston Tea Party as a festive "Christmas Box" to its readers. Town after town within New England applauded what had occurred in Boston Harbor, and during the winter the inhabitants of some villages proudly demonstrated that they were made from the same mettle as the Bostonians. When attempts were made in Hull, Massachusetts, and Shrewsbury, Connecticut, to sell East India Company tea—presumably that which had been saved from the fatally damaged *William* in Provincetown—crowds gathered and destroyed the tea chests. When a tavern owner in Weston, Massachusetts, tried to sell the commodity, a mob tore down his inn, though not before its members had helped themselves to all the liquor on the premises.[2]

Throughout the winter and early spring, rumors of how the North ministry would respond spread like wildfire through New England. Some accounts had North caving in and telling the East India Company that it was solely responsible for gaining restitution for its lost tea. Wishful thinking of that sort ended in April, when sobering word arrived of the fury that percolated through the mother country. Some of the news was reported by Franklin, who advised that the "violent destruction of the Tea seems to have united all Parties here" against Massachusetts. Orders for "seizing persons"—that is, for arresting those responsible for the destruction of the tea—could not be ruled out, he added.[3]

On May 10 a vessel from London brought to Boston the jarring texts of the Intolerable Acts. Boston's leaders at last learned that their city and province had been singled out for punishment. They knew at once that Massachusetts could not solely endure Britain's retribution. A united front was essential if London was to be made to back down. Within seventy-two hours of learning the terms of the Intolerable Acts, the Boston Committee of Correspondence, in league with similar committees from eight nearby towns, sent word to their counterparts throughout America. Boston, the message exclaimed, had been "tried and condemned" without a hearing. The Bostonians' bigger concern was that North's ministry and Parliament wished to divide and conquer the colonies. Boston "is now Suffering . . . Vengeance in the Common Cause of America." Be aware, they advised, that next "*you* will be called on to surrender your Rights." Admitting that Boston could not "struggle alone," the Massachusetts committees appealed for "joint Efforts" to resist this "Indignation." They specifically urged "at least" the suspension of all trade with Great Britain by each of the thirteen American colonies and those in the West Indies "till the Act for Blocking up this [Boston] Harbor be repealed." Utilizing dispatch riders and other channels, including the post office, Boston at the same moment appealed to towns and colonies throughout America for food and assorted supplies to sustain its beleaguered citizens while the harbor remained closed. Samuel Adams wrote some of the appeals and edited the remainder, taking pains to score every possible propaganda point. Boston's entreaties were not without success. Within weeks aid poured in from as far away as Nova Scotia and Georgia; New York generously pledged to feed Boston for ten years.[4]

Revere carried Boston's appeal into Rhode Island and Connecticut, after which he made a second ride to New York and Philadelphia. In addition to the pleas for provisions, Revere's saddlebags contained confidential letters from Samuel Adams to leaders elsewhere. Adams once again outlined what he had said in countless newspaper essays. Wealth had corrupted the mother country. The decadence that came from a never-ending chase after "luxury and dissipation, . . . vanity and extravagance," had driven Britain's rulers to try to get their hands on American revenue in order to feed their wastrel habits. To this Adams added what he was not prepared to say publicly: Unless London ceased its exploitive policies and returned to "principles of moderation and equity," its policies would inevitably result in *the entire separation and independence of the colonies.*[5]

Samuel Adams was fifty-two years old in 1774. Though he was sixteen years younger than Franklin, Adams was considerably older than most of those who are thought of as American Founders. Adams was ten years older than Washington, thirteen years older than his cousin John Adams, and nearly twenty years the senior of Thomas Jefferson. At a time when 95 percent of the colonists lived in rural America, Adams was thoroughly urban—so citified, in fact, that he did not know how to ride a horse. Adams may not have traveled much, but his reputation had spread throughout America. After Franklin, he may have been the best-known American by the time of the Intolerable Acts.

Adams's father, Samuel Adams Sr., had been a Boston Puritan who succeeded as a brewer and merchant. The senior Adams had also been a major player in Boston's politics, helping to shape a political faction in the 1730s and 1740s that advocated policies at odds with those pursued by Massachusetts's royal government. Young Samuel, who had been raised in comfortable surroundings, received an excellent education, eventually earning two degrees from Harvard College. But soon after he completed college, his father suffered financial ruin, a calamity brought on when a banking scheme of which he was a part failed in the early 1740s. The financial debacle occurred in part as a result of the opposition of Thomas Hutchinson, who disapproved of

Adams Sr.'s bank, and because Parliament disallowed it. Meanwhile, young Samuel had gone to work for a Boston mercantile firm. Temperamentally un-suited for the world of business, he predictably failed, and he foundered yet again when he took over his late father's brewery toward the end of the 1740s.

Much of Samuel's life in the fifteen years that followed—until he gained prominence in the protest against Britain—is shrouded in mystery. Indeed, the adult life of no other major Revolutionary leader is so obscure for such a long period of time as that of Samuel Adams through the 1750s and early 1760s. It is known that his wife of eight years died in 1757 of complications from pregnancy. He remained a widower for seven years, but in 1764 Adams wed Elizabeth Wells, a twenty-nine-year-old English immigrant who appar-ently had never previously married. Her father, who had emigrated as well, provided Adams with money, as his former father-in-law also continued to do. Without their financial assistance, Adams, his wife, and his two children—both from his first marriage—could not have gotten by as he struggled to earn a living from a series of low-paying municipal jobs, including posts as town scavenger, tax assessor, and tax collector. Contemporaries reported that, even with the beneficence of his fathers-in-law, Adams and his family lived on the margins of poverty, so hard up that kindly neighbors often provided food and clothing.

Adams's economic plight appears to have been brought about by his obses-sion with politics. He had been captivated by politics while still a young boy and had relished listening to his activist father's stories and reflections. Some-times he sat in on political meetings held in his home. John Adams once re-marked that "Mr. Sam. Adams . . . was born a Rebel."[6] More likely, it was the circumstances of his father's financial misfortune that drew Samuel Adams deeper into politics and forged his militancy. From an early age, Samuel was aware that his father's banking scheme, which had been widely popular in Boston, had been laid waste by a handful of officials in a faraway capital and their minions in America.

By the late 1750s Adams belonged to nearly every liberal political club in Boston. Like his father before him, he also was a major player in the Boston Caucus, something akin to a steering committee for the Country Party, the faction that resisted the policies of the royal governor. From the outset of his activism, Adams had been an implacable foe of Hutchinson and others who he believed had helped ruin his father, and the adversary too of a host of royal officials in Massachusetts who had worked tirelessly to seize and sell what remained of his father's estate. It was in the course of his long battle to save the family's property that Samuel learned much about politics, including how to use the press. He published an untold number of essays in Boston's

Samuel Adams by John Singleton Copley. A leader of Boston's protest, Adams served in Congress from 1774 until 1781. Because he frightened many moderates, Adams remained in the background in Congress. He probably favored independence before the outbreak of the Revolutionary War.
(Photograph © 2011 Museum of Fine Arts, Boston)

newspapers excoriating his foes, usually portraying them as inveterate enemies of liberty and property. After years of struggle, he finally won the battle to retain his father's estate.

Given his outlook, and his two decades of political activism, Adams was perfectly prepared to play a crucial role in Boston's resistance to Britain's new colonial policies after 1765. He had few equals as an agitator, a fact subsequently acknowledged by Jefferson, who described Samuel Adams as "truly *the Man of the Revolution*," a master of intrigue, subversion, and propaganda, and the man most responsible for giving birth to the colonial rebellion. John Adams concurred, remarking that Samuel had done more than anyone to shape and guide America's resistance to imperial policies. In the tempest spawned by British taxation and regulation, Samuel Adams rapidly emerged as Boston's premier political figure, drawing on the political skills he had previously honed.

Adams tended to politics with a feverish intensity, entertaining in his home, attending meetings, working with committees, socializing with artisans, drinking with laborers. While not an original thinker, he displayed a deft hand as an organizer. (He even took the lead in forming singing clubs for Boston's artisans, probably as a subtle means of bringing them together, but also as a means of fostering a relationship with them.) In addition, Adams was among the first to understand the use of crowds. There can be little doubt that he was among those who mobilized the feral mobs that rampaged in Boston in 1765 protesting the Stamp Act and tearing down Hutchinson's mansion. Three years later Adams carefully controlled the crowds that poured into the streets to demand the repeal of the Townshend Duties, seeing to it that they remained orderly, though menacing. Adams was a decent orator—one observer said that he spoke with a "nervous eloquence"—though he lacked the flair of Patrick Henry or Richard Henry Lee. His talent as a writer surpassed his ability as a public speaker, at least when it came to composing inflammatory tracts. One of his victims said that Adams's pen "stung like an horned snake." But Adams's greatest strength was his uncanny ability to converse easily with men from every social and economic class, and even with the rustics sent to the Massachusetts assembly by the interior farming communities. Those who respected Samuel Adams and thought of him as a sincere companion ranged from the wealthiest merchants to tradesmen to brawny and uneducated—even illiterate—common laborers.

Stout and of middling height, Samuel Adams was not charismatic. But he was ruggedly handsome and comfortable with male comaraderie. Good politicians are often good actors, and Adams had a chameleonlike skill at self-presentation. His public persona of flinty toughness led to him being described as "staunch and stiff and strict, and rigid," not a man who could be bullied by the powerful and certainly not one who would ever betray his followers. Abigail Adams was struck by Samuel's "obliging, engaging Manners" and thought him a man of "genteel Erudition." Her husband, John, a Harvard graduate, saw Samuel as "polished, refined." Others saw him as an ordinary man who dressed simply, lived modestly, and worshipped regularly, singing in his church choir. Workers must have glimpsed uncontrived down-to-earth qualities in him. On the other hand, Samuel Adams's foremost enemies, including Hutchinson, dismissed him as "a great Demagogue" given to "low art and cunning." No matter how varied and dissimilar, each description captured a side of Samuel Adams.[7]

Virtually alone among America's principal Founders, Samuel Adams seems not to have been driven by personal ambition. An American whose Puritan ancestors had emigrated more than a century before the Stamp Act, Adams may never have been enthralled with Great Britain; and to be sure, whatever affection he ever felt for the mother country vanished after his father's fortunes were ruined by British officials. But private rancor alone did not drive Adams. Eighteenth-century England was in the throes of a great economic transformation, which Adams did not fully understand but which made him uncomfortable, for he feared that what he perceived to be the luxury and dissipation sweeping the mother country threatened New England's old Puritan virtues.

By the 1770s nearly a quarter of England's population was engaged in industry, building, and commerce. What has been called a "commercial revolution" and a "consumer revolution" was afoot with seminal social consequences. Industrial capitalism was reshaping many facets of English life. As historian J. H. Plumb has written, "the hold of the past had been weakened" and "old traditions and old techniques" were tottering. It is easier to comprehend the changes today than it was in Adams's time, but it is clear that he found Great Britain's stupendous growth of wealth, and what he regarded as that wealth's malign influence, to be especially disconcerting. Life in the British homeland seemed to him to be increasingly shaped by an irrepressible urge for ever more riches and by an insatiable lust for sumptuous indulgences. Such things were "*Superfluities*," he said, and likened chasing after them to the "*worshipping of graven images*" worthy of "the *whore of Babylon*." He believed that the inexhaustible covetousness that had seized the ruling class in the mother country was what lay behind their desperate plans for using coercion and force to "enslave the colonists" and render "the greater part of the people in Britain . . . slaves."[8]

While most who would embrace the American Revolution looked to a new world, Samuel Adams was uncomfortable with modernity and sought to preserve an older New England world that lay far from Britain's reach and was as yet untainted by the supposed decay in the homeland. He longed to preserve the old Puritan virtues, what he called "the ancestral Spirit of Liberty" and "the ancient principles" of a moral society. Adams had been careful never to publicly utter the word "independence" before 1774. To do so would have been not just a seditious act; it would have been politically ill-advised. One can only guess when he came to hope for American independence, but, like others, he knew as early as 1765 that a break with Britain was a conceivable outcome of the imperial troubles, and it is not likely that he was troubled by such a possibility.[9]

With Massachusetts singled out for retribution, Samuel Adams's goal in May 1774 was to achieve a united American response. Once he secured the formation of the Solemn League and Covenant, a formal commitment by the towns of Massachusetts to boycott all British imports after September 1, he appealed to the other colonies to adopt a similar embargo. That was all he asked for. Adams knew that some in Massachusetts hoped each colony would send delegates to a continental congress that might hammer out a unified national response, but he was wary. He wanted rapid action and knew that it would take weeks for the colonies to agree to a congress and still more time for them to elect their congressmen and for those delegates to finally assemble. Thereafter, months might elapse before the congress took any action, if it acted at all. Nor could Adams be sure what a national congress would do. The Stamp Act Congress in 1765, given to waffling, had not endorsed an embargo of British trade and had adopted a namby-pamby statement on American rights, even acknowledging that the colonists owed "all due subordination" to Parliament. Even if a continental congress was an improvement and agreed to a trade embargo, additional months would pass before any boycott was finally put in place. The Boston Port Act was to take effect on June 1. Adams wanted a national boycott in place as soon after that date as possible.[10]

While Adams had serious reservations about a congress, others thought such a gathering was essential. By June 1—a day of peaceful protest in numerous colonies, observed by flying flags at half mast, fasting, and the melancholy tolling of muffled bells—momentum was building for a national conclave. Already, several towns and the Rhode Island and Connecticut committees of correspondence had called for a continental congress. Connecticut's committee, in fact, had urged two congresses: a gathering of the northern colonies in July and a national meeting later.[11]

No single motive drove those who desired a national congress. Some wanted a congress in the hope that it would agree to something less provocative than a national boycott. Others, including Philadelphia's merchants, who had lost commerce to nearby Baltimore when Maryland had not joined the embargo against the Townshend Duties, wanted a guarantee that this time the trade stoppage would be observed by every colony. Some believed a display of American unity would be the best means of forcing London to back down. Others prayed that a national congress might be a vehicle for arranging a compromise solution to the imperial crisis. Not a few saw a congress as the best means of restraining the radical firebrands in violence-prone Massachusetts. Still others thought hostilities were unavoidable. For them, a congress was essential for securing American unity prior to the conflict. Others wished to measure sentiment throughout the colonies before they agreed to steps that could lead to war.[12]

By the second week in June the notion of a continental congress had begun to take on an air of inevitability, leaving Samuel Adams with little choice but to endorse the idea. Besides, he glimpsed a promise that something good could come from a congress. Colony after colony had condemned the Intolerable Acts. The Boston Port Act had been widely denounced as a measure that would make the innocent suffer along with the guilty. A number of colonies had seen the Administration of Justice Act as confirmation that Britain aimed to negate all aspects of American autonomy. But it was the Massachusetts Government Act that aroused the most concern and scorn, for in that legislation

Parliament had arbitrarily altered the Bay Colony's charter. Issued by the Crown at the time each province came into being, the charters were viewed by most colonists as sacrosanct written constitutions that structured the provincial governments and guaranteed the colonists the "rights of Englishmen." As was true of the residents of Massachusetts, whose charter had been in place for nearly a century, few Americans could remember a time when their colony's charter had not existed. But if London could arbitrarily obliterate Massachusetts's charter, it could do the same with any colony's. And if London could unilaterally change a charter, what would it change next? Would suffrage rights be curtailed? Would the number of elected officials be decreased? Would the Anglican Church be made the established church in each colony? Would the Quakers in Pennsylvania and other minority sects still be able to worship freely?[13]

By early August every colony, with the exception of Georgia, a new and remote province, had chosen to participate in a national congress and had appointed its delegates. As governors dissolved or prorogued the assemblies in the hope of preventing them from meeting, the assemblymen in many colonies simply acted through illegal bodies. In Virginia, for instance, the members of the House of Burgesses learned on May 24 that the royal governor, John Murray, the Earl of Dunmore, had dissolved the legislature. The next day, most of the burgesses gathered at the nearby Raleigh Tavern in Williamsburg, reconstituted themselves as an "association," and urged a boycott of East India Company tea. Some seventy-five days later, after two other southern colonies, Maryland and South Carolina, had voted in extralegal assemblies to send delegates to a continental congress, the former members of the House of Burgesses convened again in Williamsburg as the Virginia Convention. This time they endorsed a continental congress and chose seven delegates to attend.[14]

Formidable opposition to a congress existed only in New York and Pennsylvania. Soon after word of the Coercive Acts arrived in May, a meeting of three hundred Manhattan merchants created the Committee of Fifty-One. In this hub of commerce, the merchant-dominated committee controlled New York City politics throughout that summer. The committee was deeply divided from the outset. Many businessmen had no stomach for another ruinous trade embargo and no particular empathy for Massachusetts. Some not only resisted the push for a national congress but also urged that the committee adopt a statement applauding the change in Massachusetts's charter. Committee meetings were so heated that fistfights were common, and on one occasion Isaac Sears, who was sometimes thought of as the "Samuel Adams of Manhattan," was subjected to a "good drubbing," according to a colleague. The committee wrangled for nearly ten weeks before it sanctioned the province's participation in the congress, and then it selected a slate of Manhattan-only delegates that did not include Sears. When elected, the delegates announced that "at present" they favored an embargo. New York was backing a continental congress, but reluctantly, and largely as its merchants believed that such a meeting offered the last best hope for reaching an accommodation with the mother country and avoiding rebellion and social upheaval.[15]

Pennsylvania's merchants were no more enthralled with the prospect of a congress and the loss of trade than their counterparts in Manhattan, and they resisted both steps through the Assembly Party, the political party that Franklin and Joseph Galloway had created two decades earlier, The Assembly Party had been formed prior to the imperial crisis, and the cornerstone of its existence had been to make Pennsylvania a royal province. For a very long time after Franklin went to London in 1764 to campaign for a royal charter, Galloway continued to believe that such a change was likely. Galloway's optimism arose in no small part because of Franklin's buoyant reports. To say that Franklin was not always candid with Galloway would be an understatement. By 1768 at the latest, Franklin correctly concluded that all hope was lost that the British government would royalize Pennsylvania. With Galloway, however, Franklin put on a sanguine face. It was true that the current ministry would never consent to royalization, Franklin reported in 1768, but he inexplicably predicted that better days lay ahead. A "Party is now growing in our Favour," Franklin said. Five months later he told Galloway that "our Friends are . . . increasing." In 1770 he intimated that as Lord North held Pennsylvania in high regard, his ministry might recommend royalization, but only if the colony remained quiet and caused no problems for the British government. Franklin's ongoing cheeriness about royalization was a stretch at best, a calculated falsehood at worst. Not infrequently, Franklin exhibited a penchant for duplicity, and in this instance, whether from his burning hatred of the proprietors or his all-consuming ambition, he strung Galloway along. Franklin enticed his friend to oppose the foes of Parliament's taxes. Meanwhile, quietly and covertly, Franklin opened channels with John Dickinson and other Proprietary Party leaders, who were managing Pennsylvania's resistance to parliamentary taxation. For a long time—a fatally long time—Galloway believed what Franklin was telling him. After all, they had been friends and allies for years, and Franklin was on the scene in London. By the time Galloway understood Franklin's guile, he had painted himself into a corner from which escape was nearly impossible.[16]

Forty-four years old in 1774, Galloway was considerably younger than Franklin. He had been born into a comfortable and upwardly mobile Quaker family in Anne Arundel County, Maryland, though while he was still a child, his parents moved to Kent, Delaware. Galloway had not attended college, but after years of private tutoring and an apprenticeship to a lawyer, he moved to Philadelphia and opened his own law practice at age eighteen. As his practice flourished, Galloway rose rapidly in Philadelphia society. He joined elite clubs and fraternities, gained entrée to intellectual and scientific circles (he served for a time as the vice president of the American Philosophical Society), and in 1753 married Grace Growden, the daughter of a wealthy Philadelphia merchant who simultaneously sat as a judge on Pennsylvania's highest court and served as the speaker of the house in the Pennsylvania assembly. Long before Galloway reached his thirtieth birthday, he owned a large town house on Market Street in Philadelphia and five country estates, the greatest of which, Trevose, stood majestically in Bucks County, north of the city.

With expressive eyes and soft features, Galloway's countenance was appealing, but he was not an expansive or approachable person. To all but his closest friends, Galloway came across as stiff, austere, and unreachable, though his manner was not entirely a liability in the sometimes stuffy, premodern world of colonial politics. His unflagging industry was crucial to his political ascendancy, as was his unquenchable ambition. Galloway's drive could make him hard and ruthless in the assembly's political brawls. His tart manner once led him and his acrid rival John Dickinson to engage in fisticuffs. One of Galloway's greatest assets was his unmatched skill as an orator, a talent he had honed before innumerable juries and which was so exceptional that his fellow assemblymen called him the "Demosthenes of Pennsylvania." Galloway's wife thought him an honest man, though naive in his personal and political relationships. Possibly thinking of her husband's relationship with Franklin, she subsequently remarked that he had often been undermined by those whom he regarded as his friends. Galloway's only child, a daughter who was entering adolescence in 1774, knew him as a doting father. While his political enemies acknowledged that Galloway was "sensible and learned," they also impugned him as pushy, haughty, and egotistical. He habitually chased after "eternal Fame," they charged, and daily sought to make his social inferiors aware of his overarching supremacy and their lowly subservience. After meeting the Pennsylvanian once or twice, John Adams wrote that Galloway comported himself with an "Air of Reserve, Design and Cunning."[17]

Without Franklin, Galloway might not have risen so far or so fast. On the other hand, without Franklin he may not have fallen so far and so hard. Franklin and Galloway probably met in the early 1750s. It is possible that they were first brought together by Franklin's son, William, who was a close friend

Joseph Galloway by Max Rosenthal. This depiction shows an older and harder Galloway, as he may have appeared in 1774. He refused to serve in Congress after hostilities broke out and he died in exile in England. (Print Collection, Miriam and Ira D. Wallach Division of Art, Prints and Photographs, New York Public Library)

of Galloway and a fellow lawyer. However, in a city the size of Philadelphia—it had about twenty thousand inhabitants in the 1750s—it is hardly surprising that the paths of two such active and ambitious men would cross. Franklin was the first of the two to enter politics, but once Galloway was elected to the assembly, each must have rapidly glimpsed potential advantages through collaboration. Franklin made Galloway his legislative assistant in 1756. By the next year they were full-fledged partners, jointly running the Assembly Party, which controlled the Pennsylvania assembly for most of the next two decades. With Franklin abroad much of that time, the party itself was controlled by Galloway, who year in and year out served as the speaker of the house.[18]

The Assembly Party managed Pennsylvania's war efforts during the French and Indian War, and as hostilities died down after 1759, it turned its attention to making the province a royal colony. It is difficult to escape the conclusion that the principal impetus for the party's campaign was Franklin's hope of becoming the royal governor of Pennsylvania and Galloway's longing to climb the political ladder, perhaps starting as a Crown-appointed magistrate and ending who-knew-where. For Galloway, his single-minded focus on royalization, together with his personal and political shortcomings, would in the long run prove to be a toxic mix.[19]

By the time word of the Stamp Act reached Philadelphia in 1765, Galloway, cheerily optimistic as always, was convinced that Pennsylvania soon would be a royal province and that Franklin's appointment as governor was imminent. To assure success, he believed that he had to keep Pennsylvania in "every way moderate." He could not prevent Philadelphia's fiery protests against the Stamp Act, but with Dickinson's Proprietary Party leading the opposition to parliamentary taxation, Galloway unwisely made the Assembly Party into a cheerleader for Britain's new policies. Spokesmen for the party aspired "to state the Conduct of the Mother Country in a true Light" and to demonstrate the "reasonableness of being Taxed." Galloway himself portrayed the foes of the Stamp Act as "wretches" and "Villains," and he publicly defended Britain's "Good Disposition towards America." At the very moment that Franklin was testifying before the House of Commons on behalf of repealing the Stamp Act, Galloway wrote to him boasting that the Assembly Party had been "the only Loyal Part of the People." It alone had "oppose[d] the Torrent" and sought to "discredit" those who denounced the law.[20]

With Franklin dropping hints from London that Hillsborough and others in the ministry were favorably disposed toward Pennsylvania's royalization, Galloway and the Assembly Party stood foursquare behind the Townshend Duties in 1769 and 1770. Even as the colony embraced a trade embargo and Franklin surreptitiously attacked the new taxes in London newspapers, Galloway told his political partner that he was working to assure Pennsylvania's "Dutiful Behaviour during these Times of American Confusion." Galloway's actions were tantamount to political suicide. By October 1770, when the annual assembly election was held, the Assembly Party was anathema in Philadelphia. Galloway, who had been elected to one of the city's eight seats in the assembly for fifteen years, had to run in rural Bucks County to win reelection.[21]

Despite its collapse in Philadelphia, the Assembly Party remained in control of the assembly until 1774. It survived because it remained the overwhelmingly dominant faction in rural eastern Pennsylvania, a region with 50 percent of the colony's population but nearly three quarters of the allotted seats in the assembly, and Galloway continued in his post of speaker. Though hardly powerless, his loss of popularity in Philadelphia weighed on Galloway, and for a time in the early 1770s he contemplated abandoning politics.[22] During the same period, perhaps concluding that his troubles had mounted because of his naive trust in Franklin, Galloway drifted away from his old partner. While Franklin wrote to him several times each year, Galloway answered with only three letters in the forty-eight months after January 1771.

Galloway remained politically active, but he changed course after 1771. Among other things, he abandoned his open defense of parliamentary taxation, emphasizing instead the benefits that the colonists derived from their connection with Great Britain. Galloway and others among the most conservative Americans increasingly stressed that the colonies were an extension of British civilization, nourished and protected by the mother country. They asserted that the British and the Americans not only were the freest people on the planet both politically and religiously but that the colonies also prospered from imperial trade. Pointing to the vast quantities of British manufactured goods that were consumed annually by Americans, they portrayed the Anglo-American union as "a commercial Kingdom." However, it was not only material plenty that made the empire desirable. The existence of a strong, central imperial government assured stability and the rule of law in America. The many benefits of empire had made the colonists "the happiest People . . . under the Sun." But, conservatives warned, all was threatened by the colonial dissidents.[23] If the American radicals pushed the imperial crisis to the point of American independence, social revolution would be the result. Even conservatives who resisted parliamentary taxation and the extension of British hegemony shared this view. For instance, New York's Gouverneur Morris— who would support the Revolution and ultimately sit in the Constitutional Convention in 1787—warned in the early 1770s that "the mobility [the upwardly mobile patriots] grow dangerous to the gentry." It was in the interest of the most affluent Americans, Morris added, "to seek for reunion with the parent State."[24]

After 1770, Galloway's mission was to save the Anglo-American union, but even he understood that it could not endure in a relationship in which Parliament claimed the right to legislate for the colonists in all cases whatsoever. Accordingly, Galloway denounced Britain's dissolution of the New York assembly and asserted that only the colonial assemblies could tax the colonists. There can be no "Union either of Affection or Interest between G. Britain and America until . . . there is a full Restoration of its [America's] Liberties," he proclaimed. Inching toward some sort of compromise solution to the imperial woes, he also excoriated the colonists' growing distrust of Great Britain as "mad."[25]

In 1773, Galloway neither defended the Tea Act nor made an effort to have the cargo aboard the *Polly,* the tea ship bound for Philadelphia, unloaded and sold. When London answered the Boston Tea Party with the Intolerable Acts, Galloway immediately understood that American resistance meant war. However, his response was not politically adroit. Once Paul Revere's sweaty mount galloped into Philadelphia in May 1774 carrying Boston's appeal for a national boycott of British trade, Galloway led the fight against another trade embargo. He did so as much from the fear that an embargo would lead to war as from the hope of saving Philadelphia's merchants from additional grievous losses. Galloway was swiftly outmaneuvered. The city's radicals organized a mass rally that called for both a boycott and a continental congress. Galloway at first opposed both steps and refused to convene the assembly, which ultimately would have to decide Pennsylvania's response to Boston's entreaty. In mid-June the radicals struck with yet another outdoor meeting attended by thousands in downtown Philadelphia. The gathering endorsed the idea of summoning an extralegal assembly into session, seemingly the only means by which Pennsylvania might be represented in a continental congress. Faced with the prospect of a revolutionary body—one that would surely give proper representation to the western counties that long had been underrepresented in the Pennsylvania assembly, and which would supplant the colony's legitimate legislature—Galloway caved in.[26]

He called the assembly into a special session. By the time it met, Galloway knew not only that a continental congress was inevitable but also that New York's conservatives had agreed to such a meeting in the hope of restraining New England's firebrands. Galloway suddenly saw an opportunity to act in concert with other delegates from the mid-Atlantic region, and perhaps elsewhere. Thus, when the Pennsylvania assembly met, it agreed, under the guidance of Galloway, to a continental congress and proposed that it be held in centrally located Philadelphia early in September. The assembly also elected seven delegates to the congress, all conservatives and moderates. Galloway was included in the delegation, and he saw to it that his old rival Dickinson, next to Franklin the most popular Pennsylvanian, was not chosen. The assembly instructed its delegates to "establish a political union between the two countries," Great Britain and its American colonies.[27] A day or two later, one of Pennsylvania's delegates, Thomas Mifflin, a Philadelphia merchant, informed Samuel Adams that his colony would vote to boycott British trade only if "some previous Step" was taken by the congress to peacefully resolve the crisis.[28]

Neither Samuel Adams nor Joseph Galloway had initially desired a continental congress, but in the end both accepted it. For Adams, a national congress offered the only hope of obtaining a national boycott of British trade and, perhaps, of preparing for war. For Galloway, if it acted with what he called "Temper and Moderation," a national congress that spoke for America would subsume "the illegal conventions, committees, town meetings, and . . . subservient mobs" that Adams and his ilk had controlled.[29] Moreover, as the heat-blistered summer of 1774 set in, Galloway had come to believe that an intercolonial congress offered the best hope, if not the only hope, of preventing war.

From the southern low-country to northern New England, the delegates to what became known as the First Continental Congress—fifty-five men in all—descended on Philadelphia in August and early September. Most traveled by carriage and in the company of other delegates. The four congressmen from Massachusetts, together with their four servants, met on August 10 at Thomas Cushing's residence in Boston and set out from there. Three weeks later Patrick Henry and Edmund Pendleton stopped at Mount Vernon to pick up George Washington. Accompanied by slaves, they started the long, dusty journey to Pennsylvania on a day that Washington described as "Exceeding hot."[30]

The Virginians completed the trip in five days, but the delegates from Massachusetts were on the road for three weeks. The congressmen from South Carolina and Rhode Island were the first to reach Philadelphia. Those from North Carolina arrived last, not entering the city until nearly the last week in September, some twenty days after Congress had begun.[31]

The journey of the Massachusetts congressmen was time-consuming in part because the delegates refused to travel on the Sabbath. But they also paused in nearly every town along the way to meet with noteworthy locals, hoping to demonstrate that they were not militant incendiaries. Furthermore, as most had never been outside Massachusetts, they spent considerable time sightseeing. They inspected gardens, toured the campuses of Yale and the College of New Jersey (now Princeton), and once in New York—where they lingered for a week—the deputies gawked at public buildings, fortifications, statues, the prison and hospital, churches, cemeteries, King's College (now Columbia), and climbed into a tall church steeple for a panoramic view of the city.[32]

As the Massachusetts delegates neared Philadelphia in the muted light of sunset on August 29, they were greeted by several congressmen from Pennsylvania and Delaware, who in turn were accompanied by a dozen or so leading citizens of the city. Forming a small caravan, the Yankees were escorted into Philadelphia and welcomed along the way by a scrum of well-wishers

City Tavern of Philadelphia as depicted in an early twentieth-century color lithograph.
Many congressmen resided at the City Tavern. Congress held its initial meeting here in
September 1775 to decide on a site for its sessions. (Library of Congress)

who waved happily. Though "dirty, dusty, and fatigued"—they had been on the road for more than eight hours that day alone—the rumpled Massachusetts congressmen were taken to the City Tavern on second street above Walnut for drinks and dinner, a long, festive session that extended past eleven P.M.[33]

Most congressmen found lodgings in private homes. The entire Massachusetts delegation rented rooms in the home of Jane Port on Arch Street. Washington and Richard Henry Lee lived at the home of Dr. William Shippen, Philadelphia's most esteemed physician and Lee's brother-in-law. Others were scattered here and there, including in taverns, the hotels of the day.[34]

Probably many of the delegates were apprehensive that they might not measure up to the most talented congressmen from other colonies. John Adams imagined that Congress would be "an assembly of the wisest Men upon the Continent," a gathering that would be a far cry from the caliber of the "sordid, venal Herd" ordinarily sitting in the Massachusetts legislature. He was not particularly confident that he would be adequate to the challenge. He knew law but fretted whether he was "fit for the Times," that is, up to the great challenge that he would face. "I feel unutterable Anxiety," he confided to his diary, adding, "God grant us Wisdom, and Fortitude" so that this congress would not in the end submit to British tyranny. "God forbid! Death in any Form is less terrible," he declared.[35]

As Congress was not scheduled to meet until Monday, September 5, the delegates who arrived early whiled away the time looking over the city. Several climbed the steep, narrow ladder into Christ Church's tall steeple for what one deputy said was a "full View of the Whole City and of [the] Delaware River." Most delegates were intrigued by Philadelphia. Many were unaccustomed to a large city, while those from Boston, New York, and Charleston were eager to see how the Pennsylvania metropolis compared with their own. A New Englander was amazed to find that "Wheat Fields crowd into the very Squares of the City," by which he apparently meant that farms abutted the edge of Philadelphia. John Adams was struck by the "Regularity and Elegance of this City," for unlike Boston, Philadelphia was a planned city that had been laid out in an uncomplicated gridiron pattern. The streets "are all equally wide, straight and parallel to each other," Adams marveled. If in that respect Philadelphia differed from its counterparts, it was a typical walking city, quite similar to every American city of that day. More than six thousand houses and close to forty thousand inhabitants were squeezed inside a space that was only twelve blocks wide and some twenty-five blocks long. In an age before automobiles and mass transit, cities had to be compact so that the residents could daily get from their dwelling to their place of work, and back home again, by foot. Philadelphia was also typical of other cities—and quite unlike today's American cities—in that neighborhoods were hardly segregated along social and economic lines. The small houses and shops of artisans frequently stood next to the fashionable homes of the affluent.[36]

Not even Philadelphia's "Exceeding hot, Sultry" weather, which the New Englanders found nearly unbearable, kept the delegates from sightseeing. Several toured the hospital and listened to a lecture on human anatomy by Dr. Shippen. Some went for an excursion to the "Cells of the Lunaticks," where they found the incarcerated to be "furious, some merry, some Melancholly." To his astonishment, John Adams discovered in what passed for the insane asylum an inmate whom he had once represented. "I once saved [him] . . . from being whipped . . . for Horse stealing," Adams recalled. Others visited the shipyards and the poorhouse, which could accommodate five hundred residents. Many were taken with the four-hundred-yard-long city market, though a Yankee deputy opined that while the meat was excellent, the fruit and vegetables were inferior to those in New England. Nearly all toured the College of Philadelphia (now the University of Pennsylvania). On Sundays, many worshipped in churches not to be found at home. Washington and John Adams, for instance, attended the local Roman Catholic

Church, a first for the New Englander and probably for the Virginian as well.[37]

Nearly every evening, socially prominent Philadelphians invited a delegate or two from several colonies to a sumptuous dinner party. At one affair, said a congressman, the table groaned with "Curds and Creams, Jellies, Sweet meats of various sorts, 20 sorts of Tarts, fools, Trifles, floating Islands, whipped Sillabubs &c &c—Parmesan Cheese, Punch, Wine, Porter, Beer &c &c." On another occasion the guests had a dessert of "Melons, fine beyond description, and Pears and Peaches as excellent." In between what John Adams referred to as the "incessant Feasts," clusters of congressmen gathered over steaming pots of tea and cold tankards of beer to chat, and to size up one another. On September 1 the twenty-five delegates already in town spent a long evening dining together in a private room at the City Tavern. "My time is totally filled from the Moment I get out of Bed, until I return to it," one congressman exclaimed, adding that much of each day was given over to "feast[ing] upon ten thousand Delicacies" and consuming spirits for hours on end. At times, some of the congressman drank too much. Adams said that at one party he "drank Madeira at a great rate." He remained sober, or so he said, but he noted that Richard Henry Lee and Benjamin Harrison from Virginia got "very high."[38]

These festive occasions enabled the congressmen to become better acquainted. Each delegate knew the other members of his own delegation, but those from other colonies were for the most part total strangers. For a century and a half the colonists had looked across the sea toward the mother country, largely ignoring their neighboring provinces in America. Surprisingly little trade occurred between the colonies, and it, of course, was conducted by businessmen, not politicians. But businessmen often traveled and sometimes they became active in politics. For instance, Pennsylvania delegate Thomas Mifflin had met John and Samuel Adams a year earlier while on a business trip to Boston. Furthermore, some delegates had become acquainted with their soon-to-be colleagues through the committees of correspondence network. For a year or more, Samuel Adams had been exchanging numerous letters with leading political figures in several colonies, some of whom would serve in Congress.[39] Thus, it was largely but not entirely true, as one congressman remarked, that this conclave brought together "Strangers" who were unacquainted "with Each others Language, Ideas, Views, Designs" and who were also "jealous . . . fearfull, timid, skittish" in the company of one another.[40]

Sometimes, too, the delegates struggled to overcome their own biased first impressions of those from other parts of America. The Yankee John Adams, for instance, immediately concluded that every New Yorker was rude and ungentlemanly. With some irritation he declared that they "talk very loud, very fast, and alltogether. If they ask you a Question, before you can utter 3 Words of your Answer, they will break out upon you, again—and talk away."[41]

Above all, the delegates were eager to discover the political outlook of their fellow deputies. Every word uttered, every toast offered, every sign conveyed by body language could divulge something of a colleague's sentiments. John Adams had been in town less than twenty-four hours before he uncovered "a Tribe of People here" who were identical to those in orbit around Governor Hutchinson back in Massachusetts. One was Galloway, whom Adams instantly marked as identical in his thinking to those in Boston who had defended the Stamp Act back in 1765. On the other hand, Adams was delighted with Richard Henry Lee, who confided—presumably while he was sober—that he favored the repeal of all British taxes and the Intolerable Acts, the removal of the British army from American soil, and sweeping reforms in the mother country's regulation of colonial commerce. Adams got the impression that most in the Virginia delegation shared Lee's convictions, leading him to pronounce that those Southerners were filled with "Sense and Fire [and] Spirit."[42]

No one was at a greater disadvantage than Galloway, as Congress was meeting in his province. Legions of enemies that he had made in the course of twenty years in Pennsylvania politics appear to have spoken ill of him while meeting with deputies from other colonies. On the afternoon that the Massachusetts delegation had neared Philadelphia, Dr. Benjamin Rush, a leading physician in the city, had been among those who had ridden out to greet the New Englanders. He boarded the Yankees' carriage, said John Adams, and immediately "undertook to caution us" about Galloway. Thomas Mifflin and Joseph Reed, a Philadelphia lawyer, showed the Massachusetts delegates about town and, while at it, enlightened them about Galloway's past record, portraying him as a "Tory" who could be counted on to defend British policy. John Dickinson, whom Galloway had kept off Pennsylvania's congressional delegation, frequently came to town to converse with the congressmen, and he entertained several at Fairhill, his nearby country estate. It hardly stretches credulity to imagine that Dickinson spoke with disfavor about Galloway in the course of these conversations.[43] Even before Congress formally met, Galloway was a marked man, at least among the more radical delegates.

Politicians all, the congressmen were struggling to discover what actions the Continental Congress might take, and what they might have to do to steer the assembly in what they thought was the proper direction. The congressmen knew that each colony was opposed to parliamentary taxation of Americans, but where most provinces stood on the issue of the limits of Parliament's authority was far from clear. As eight of the colonies had instructed their delegates to vote for a trade embargo, that step seemed a certainty, though no one knew whether Congress would lean toward a total or partial boycott. Nor did anyone know what Congress would decide about how the boycott was to be enforced.[44] No one knew whether a majority would favor condemning all, or only some, of the Intolerable Acts. None knew how Congress would define the rights of Americans, or if Congress might be willing to relinquish some rights that colonial assemblies had previously claimed. To be sure, none knew whether Congress would consent to take steps to prepare for the possibility of war.

On September 5, almost four months to the day since word of the Intolerable Acts had reached Boston, the delegates to the First Continental Congress assembled at the City Tavern in Philadelphia. Their first order of business was to select a permanent meeting site. As politicians are wont to do, they made that seemingly uncomplicated matter into a test vote. Galloway offered the Pennsylvania State House. His rivals rallied behind Carpenters' Hall. (A week earlier John Adams had noted in his diary that while touring the city, he had "visited . . . the Carpenters Hall, *where the Congress is to Sit*," an intriguing remark that suggests delegates from several colonies must have colluded days before to thwart Galloway on this issue.)[45] As the State House was more spacious, it is likely that nearly everyone thought it the more desirable site, but the vote was seen as an assessment of Galloway's strength. Congress chose to meet at the recently constructed Carpenters' Hall, a Georgian brick building that served as a guildhall for tradesmen. The bottom floor included a spacious room, large enough for Congress's sessions, while a library dominated the second story. The building was set back from Chestnut Street, offering privacy and quiet, and a colorful garden—suitable for exercise and conversing—was merely a step outside its rear door.[46]

After walking three blocks to Carpenters' Hall in a heavy gray mist that clung to the city, the delegates rapidly got down to business. They chose Virginia's Peyton Randolph to be the president of Congress and appointed Charles Thomson, a nonmember but a Philadelphia activist and longtime foe of Galloway, as secretary. Thomas Cushing proposed that this urgent assembly commence with a prayer. When Congress assented, Samuel Adams took the floor and asked that Jacob Duche, an Anglican priest in Philadelphia, be permitted to deliver the invocation. The pious Adams may have genuinely wished to appeal for divine guidance, but, as was usually true with everything he did, there was a political component to his entreaty. He hoped to show that the New England Puritans not only were "no bigot[s]" but also were

Carpenters' Hall. The First Continental Congress met here in September and October 1774. Congress moved to the larger Pennsylvania State House in 1775. An 1896 lithograph from Harper's *magazine. (http://www.harpers.org/archive)*

more moderate than many suspected. Adams's gesture was a "Masterly Stroke," gushed a Delaware congressman, as it led some in his delegation, and some Pennsylvanians as well, to grow "more favourable" toward Massachusetts. Duche prayed with "fervour," one delegate declared.[47]

One additional hurdle had to be cleared before Congress could proceed. What would be the voting procedure in this assembly? The smaller provinces, wanting an equal voice, naturally pushed for giving each colony one vote. If these proceedings led to war, Samuel Ward of tiny Rhode Island candidly asserted, the smallest colony "would suffer as much as the greatest."[48] The larger colonies argued for basing voting strength on population. Patrick Henry of Virginia, the most populous American colony, was the chief spokesman for their cause. As he had so often done before Virginia juries and in the House of Burgesses, Henry resorted to histrionics, leading one observer to compare him to "a Presbyterian clergyman, used to haranguing the people."[49] Henry contended that the colonies had ceased to exist and that all Americans were "in a State of Nature." Though he would steadfastly defend Virginia's interests during the next several weeks, on this day, and in this cause, Henry declaimed: "I am not a Virginian, but an American." He added that Congress must be structured in what he called a "democratical" manner. A majority of those present and voting should decide every question.[50]

It was a magnificent, though futile, speech. In truth, the larger colonies never had a chance. The smaller colonies had no intention of being led where they did not wish to go, and Massachusetts, one of the larger colonies, needed all the help it could get in resisting the Coercive Acts. In short order, Congress decided that each colony would have one vote, a procedure that remained in effect through the next fifteen years.[51]

This critical choice would color the proceedings of Congress on every substantive issue. Throughout the American Revolution the members of Congress represented colonies or states, not people. Down to its final day, the members of the Continental Congress were never popularly elected. They were always chosen by the provincial assemblies, which almost everywhere were malapportioned. The conservative eastern counties were nearly always overrepresented at the expense of the usually more radical western counties. Sentiment in Congress often lagged behind popular opinion. That, and the pressing need for unity and the ever-present necessity of securing the approval of at least seven provinces in order to pass any measure, would not only pose roadblocks to the independence movement but also make the American Revolution more conservative than most modern revolutions.

Congress immediately agreed to meet in secret, a practice from which it also never varied. Its members wished to speak as they pleased, free from intimidation by noisy spectators. More important, they realized that there would be times when it was imprudent for London or the American people to be privy to matters under consideration. They also wished to hide from North's government all evidence of differences within Congress. In keeping with this, the delegates opted to publish a journal of their proceedings, but one that often contained only the scantiest record of what had transpired.

After only three sessions, the Massachusetts delegates knew for certain that next to no one in Congress was willing to bow to the demands of North's ministry. "A Tory here is the most despicable Animal in the Creation. Spiders, Toads, Snakes, are their only proper Emblems," John Adams concluded, and with some exaggeration he wrote to his wife that Massachusetts was seen by most congressmen as the "Saviours and Defenders of American Liberty."[52]

While the Massachusetts delegates had reason to be hopeful, they, like other perceptive congressmen, rapidly discerned two distinct factions within

Congress. It was hardly unexpected that there would be divisions. Some degree of discord had existed in every colony since the onset of the imperial crisis. While most Americans were indignant at parliamentary taxation, they had never seen eye to eye on how—and how far and how hard—to push back against those policies. There was always uneasiness over how Great Britain might respond to their protests. Moreover, breaches had developed in the colonists' attitudes toward the mother country. Some had grown suspicious of the motives of Crown and Parliament, and wary of a mother country they believed to be in the thrall of decadence.

But alongside those reservations, a deep and abiding love, even adoration, of Great Britain remained strong. Americans felt an ingrained allegiance to Britain, and many were unable to shake the age-old belief that, like it or not, dependence on the parent state remained unavoidable and essential. Britain not only safeguarded the colonists from Europe's predatory powers, but the most timorous and conservative colonists felt safer knowing that as a last resort, London could also be depended on to maintain social and political order in America. By the second half of the eighteenth century, moreover, America was flooded with English consumer goods, changing the colonists' consumption patterns in ways that only increased their appreciation of the British Empire. Finally, the political culture in the colonies had fostered a profound devotion to the British monarchy. Each year numerous scheduled celebrations of British kings and their families were held, including remembrances of their deeds and linkage to the founding of the various provinces, as well as frequent reminders of the triumph of these Protestant monarchs over their Catholic rivals.[53]

The question facing this congress was how to respond to the Tea Act and Coercive Acts. But behind that question lay myriad emotions, ambitions, certitudes, unknowns, and apprehensions.

One faction in Congress consisted of what might be called the hard-liners, those whom Galloway privately referred to as the "violent party."[54] They were united by a belief that Parliament possessed no authority over the colonies and that the monarch alone had jurisdiction throughout the empire. For some delegates of this persuasion, constitutionalism was the heart of the matter. A quest for personal advancement, or the dream of pecuniary gain for themselves or their province, drove others. Some were incensed by the colonists' unshakable second-class status within the British Empire. At a minimum, they desired greater American autonomy. The belief that the colonies had matured and were able to stand alone inspired others, a conviction abetted by the defeat and removal of France from North America, lessening the need for British protection. Many felt betrayed. After sacrificing to help the mother country win the Seven Years' War, the colonists' recompense had been taxes, standing armies, and coercion.

Most members of this hard-line faction were bent on making London not only repeal the Tea Act and Coercive Acts but also retreat from the new colonial policies it had sought to impose since 1763. They did not come to Philadelphia seeking a compromise with the mother country. Although notoriously tight-lipped, the members of this faction had almost certainly concluded that America could not have its way short of war, and some, including Samuel Adams, probably already believed that only independence could solve America's problems with London. Delegates from three New England colonies—Massachusetts, New Hampshire, and Connecticut—banded with a majority of Virginia's congressmen to make up the heart of this contingent.

The other, more moderate, faction consisted chiefly of delegates from the four mid-Atlantic colonies—Pennsylvania, New York, New Jersey, and Delaware. Dominated by mercantile interests with deep economic ties to the empire, these colonies longed for reconciliation and the survival of the Anglo-American union. Their economies were thriving. Businessmen in New York and Philadelphia profited handsomely through extensions of credit from London's bankers, and their ships and cargoes were secured by marine insurance acquired in England and protected by the Royal Navy. They had no financial reasons for protesting. Indeed, as one Philadelphia merchant remarked, protest was "unnatural, and will assuredly prove unprofitable." But, in addition, these colonies featured heterogeneous populations of English, Scotch-Irish, and German immigrants, topped off by large numbers of African slaves. Of all the colonies, those in the mid-Atlantic region were thought to be the most likely to experience internal unrest during a revolutionary upheaval.[55]

Almost to a man, the deputies from the mid-Atlantic colonies hoped for a restoration of the placid relationship between the colonies and mother country that had existed before 1763. Nevertheless, the moderates also felt that London's recent colonial policies posed dangers to American rights and had to be resisted, and nearly every one of them came to Philadelphia prepared to support a trade embargo. But they favored a more tempered defiance than their counterparts, and some were convinced that both the colonies and the mother country had to give ground if war was to be averted. Above all, most members of this faction still believed that Britain's leaders were wise and prudent. If Congress responded with a mixture of firmness and moderation, most of these deputies confidently believed that Great Britain would back down short of war.

Some congressmen were not hard-and-fast members of either faction. This was especially true of some deputies from Maryland and the Carolinas, who now and then sided with one faction and from time to time with the other. Rhode Island's voting pattern was the most unique of all. Its two delegates often took contrary stands. Samuel Ward usually sided with other New England hard-liners, while Stephen Hopkins was drawn to more conciliatory proposals. With its two congressmen often deadlocked, Rhode Island had a voice, but not a vote, on many matters.

Whether hard-liners or moderates, or somewhere in between, most delegates were prepared to ride the whirlwind to destinations unknown. On the eve of this historic gathering, John Adams doubtless captured the feeling of most: "the die was now cast; I had passed the Rubicon; swim or sink, live or die, survive or perish with my country, was my unalterable determination."[56]

Samuel Adams walked a tightrope. He favored a hard-line approach, but he knew that Massachusetts could ill afford to frighten away the moderates. It was crucial that America respond with a unified voice. Adams also knew that while each colony had a single vote, each delegation consisted of numerous congressmen, ranging from a high of nine (New York) to a low of two (New Hampshire and Rhode Island). Often, the members of these delegations differed in outlook. By winning over one swing voter here and another there—or by losing one here and there—a colony's final vote could be altered.

Adams arrived in Congress with a reputation as a violence-soaked incendiary, and, by dint of coming from Massachusetts, the three other members of that delegation were similarly, if unfairly, tainted. Led by Samuel Adams, the delegation set out to palliate the fears of the other congressmen, adopting what John Adams called a strategy of "great Delicacy and Caution." He and his Bay Colony colleagues, John Adams remarked, had "been obliged to keep [them]selves ought of Sight, and to feel Pulses, and Sound the Depths—to insinuate our Sentiments, Designs and Desires by means of other Persons, Sometimes of one Province and Sometimes of another." Keeping a low profile, the Massachusetts delegates permitted every procedural resolution offered at the outset of Congress to be made by delegates from southern colonies, mostly by Virginians. Those steps almost surely came after private consultation with Samuel Adams, but they were not associated with the Massachusetts delegation. Furthermore, the three other congressmen from Massachusetts—Cushing, John Adams, and Robert Treat Paine—seldom spoke in the congressional debates, and Samuel Adams appears to have been virtually stricken mute. The Massachusetts delegates turned instead to their newfound comrades from Virginia, and especially to Richard Henry Lee and Patrick Henry, to walk the point for them on the floor of Congress. But Samuel Adams was active behind the scenes, planning and scheming and orchestrating the machinations of radical activists from Massachusetts. He and his comrades back in Boston kept Paul Revere on horseback so often to bring in news designed to sway Congress that the poor dispatch rider must have developed saddle sores.

Massachusetts's strategy was effective. Joseph Reed, the savvy Philadelphia lawyer, was fooled into believing that the Bostonians were "mere Milksops." A Maryland congressman concluded that the Massachusetts delegates were the "most moderate" in Congress. South Carolina's Thomas Lynch thought the Massachusetts men were "truly heroic." Not only were they acting "Without rashness," but theirs had been "a steady, manly, cool and regular conduct" as well. Three weeks into the Congress, Samuel Adams privately gloated that whereas his colony had once been thought of as "intemperate and rash," it now was "applauded as cool and judicious."[57] But not everyone was hoodwinked. Recognizing that the Bostonians wished to be seen as "modest" in their hopes, Galloway glimpsed through the "Straws and Feathers" they "throw out . . . which Point of the Compass the Wind comes." He rapidly deduced too that Samuel Adams was a master of "popular intrigue, and the management of a faction." Galloway added that Adams, "though by no means remarkable" intellectually, was nearly unequalled in his skills as a politician. "He eats little, drinks little, sleeps little, thinks much, and is most decisive and indefatigable in the pursuit of his objects." Adams's manner, Galloway continued, was "secret and hypocritical, and . . . [leaves] no art, no falsehood, no fraud unessayed to conceal [his] intentions . . . to incite the ignorant and vulgar to arms, and with those arms to establish American independence." Others may have been more favorably disposed toward Adams, but, like Galloway, many understood that the Bostonians and Virginians had joined together to move Congress in a more immoderate direction.[58]

Galloway and his confederates played a somewhat similar game to achieve their ends. Though hardly a shrinking violet, Galloway maintained a low profile during the first three weeks of Congress. While he disagreed with some of Congress's early steps—especially the selection of his bitter provincial rival Charles Thomson as secretary—Galloway went along quietly. He joined in only one floor debate, taking such a strong stand on behalf of American rights on that occasion that he acknowledged "my Arguments tend to an Independency of the Colonies." His rhetoric was a subtle ploy to rehabilitate his reputation. In fact, Galloway hoped that Congress would petition for redress while avoiding "every measure which tended to sedition, or acts of violent opposition." In quiet conversations out of doors with numerous delegates, he also floated the idea that Congress send commissioners to London to negotiate an accommodation. These agents could also provide "solid Information" about the position of the North ministry, so that we "shall be no longer misled by ... private Letters," he added, almost surely with Franklin in mind.[59]

Once Congress got the procedural hurdles out of the way, but before it could do anything else, an express from Boston brought word that the city had been bombarded for an entire night by British armed forces. The report was false, but the response of Philadelphia—muffled bells rang throughout the city and its residents displayed what one Yankee called "unfeigned marks of sorrow" for the Bostonians—heartened the New Englanders. The news also provoked Congress's first full-fledged debate on substantive issues. By the time it was learned that the news of the British attack had been inaccurate, Samuel Adams and fellow hard-liners knew that a majority of congressmen had exhibited "firmness, sensibility, Spirit" in the face of presumed hostilities. They were foursquare for the "Interests of America," said one New Englander.[60]

Once Congress was certain that Boston had not been subjected to British shelling, it created the Committee on Rights, or Grand Committee, as some called it. Consisting of two delegates from each colony, it was charged with stating "the Rights of the Colonies & the several Instances in which they have been violated ... & the means most proper to obtain Redress." Expecting the committee to report within two or three days, Congress suspended its daily sessions. However, in this deeply divided Congress, the committee's deliberations spun on endlessly in bitter wrangling on crucial issues as well as in hairsplitting over the language in the report. Days passed. Those congressmen who were not on the Grand Committee spent their time doing still more sightseeing. For those on the committee, the novel experience of hammering out what might be a historic document was initially pleasing. After its second meeting, John Adams wrote that the daylong committee debate had been "ingenious, entertaining." After a few more blather-filled sessions, he changed his tune. The meetings were nothing but "nibbling and quibbling," he grumbled, adding that there was "no greater Mortification than to sit with half a dozen Witts" who saw themselves as "refined Genius's" and were "fond of shewing" their supposed intellect. Things had gotten "very tedius," he declared.[61]

After ten days of congressional inertia, Revere again galloped into town, this time with a declaration recently adopted by Suffolk County, Massachusetts, which included Boston. The timing of Revere's arrival suggests that Samuel Adams and his lieutenants at home had preplanned such actions to steer Congress along the path they desired. The Suffolk County Resolves denounced the Intolerable Acts as a violation of the British constitution and American rights, urged that Massachusetts boycott "all commercial intercourse with

Great Britain, Ireland, and the West-Indies, and abstain from the consumption of British merchandise and manufactures." It additionally appealed to the residents of every town in the Bay Colony to "use their utmost diligence to acquaint themselves with the art of war as soon as possible"—in other words, for local militia units to begin training. Congress rapidly came back into session to discuss these impassioned declarations and, after a daylong debate, unanimously endorsed the Suffolk Resolves and ordered their publication. Not every congressman was happy with his vote, nor was every American contented with what was published. John Adams saw "Tears gush into the Eyes" of some Philadelphia Quakers, though he proclaimed the occasion "one of the happiest days of my Life."[62]

Congress then fell back into its inactive mode for nearly another week while the Grand Committee plugged along with its interminable discussions. Finally, on September 24—nineteen days into this Congress—the committee at last announced that it was ready to report a draft statement on American rights and grievances. Congress was summoned back into session that same day and commenced a debate that rapidly built into a pitched battle over the acceptable limits of resistance and accommodation. Fearing that taking an unyielding and intractable stance would mean war, the more conservative and moderate congressmen urged deference. The hard-liners feared that showing the least sign of meekness would not only be mocked in London, but would sow further divisions among the colonists. The members of this faction argued for congressional pugnacity. Some zealots insisted that the statement on the rights of the colonists must be accompanied both by an appeal to each colony to raise and train its militiamen and by the raising of a national army of twenty thousand men. Tempers flared to the breaking point, leaving some to wonder whether Congress could survive the tempest.[63]

At this moment, hoping to get something concrete from Congress before it possibly self-destructed, Virginia acted. On September 26, Richard Henry Lee moved for the adoption of a boycott of British imports that would take effect on December 1. There was never the slightest doubt that non-importation would be approved, and it was agreed to by Congress on that same day.

But soon there was trouble. Immediately after the vote to embargo British imports was taken, a Massachusetts delegate—probably Cushing—urged a boycott on all American exports to Great Britain. New England sold virtually nothing to England, but the southern colonies exported tobacco, rice, indigo, sea-island cotton, and naval stores (including tar, pitch, resin, and turpentine) to the British Isles. Nearly every Southern congressman opposed non-exportation. Southern indebtedness would soar, Maryland's Samuel Chase declared, and he added that in a very short time bankruptcy would follow.

Other congressmen from the Chesapeake region cried that a prohibition of exports would be especially unfair to them, as their tobacco had been planted before the Boston Tea Party and would not be ready to ship for another sixty days or more. With no opportunity to prepare for non-exportation, such a measure would leave tobacco producers in Maryland, North Carolina, and Virginia without an income for an entire year. This furious two-day dispute was the first North-versus-South battle in American politics, and it was nasty. As the delegates walked to Carpenters' Hall on September 28, many feared the continuation of this combustible struggle. Instead, Galloway cleverly chose this moment to act.[64]

His strategy, which he had decided on during the summer, was to seek a resolution of the imperial dilemma through compromise. By choosing to present it at this volatile juncture, Galloway hoped to appear to be the very voice of reason and moderation. His great objective was to save the Anglo-American union and prevent a disastrous war. If Congress adopted a temperate declaration of American rights accompanied by a compromise proposal, Galloway believed the worst possible scenario could be avoided. On that point, he may have been correct, for in retrospect, when Congress debated and voted on his plan, it made its choice for peace or war.[65]

September 28 was a pivotal day for America. The day began with a fog-wreathed dawn, but by ten A.M., when Congress started its session, it was clear and uncommonly warm for early autumn. Galloway soon took the floor and offered his plan in a lengthy prepared address that must have consumed two hours or more, and was probably the longest speech made in the First Continental Congress. It was a dramatic presentation, offered with all the oratorical talents that had facilitated his ascent in provincial politics. Galloway divided his speech into three parts, beginning with an elaboration of how the colonists had benefited from the British Empire. "[N]ourished and sheltered" under the mother country's "wings and protected by its wealth and power," American agriculture had flourished and the "liberal arts and sciences . . . ripened to a degree of perfection, astonishing to mankind." Furthermore, "liberty, peace and order" had always been the American hallmark. Not only did free speech and a free press exist to a degree unknown in most corners of the world, but Americans were also safe from "all manner of unjust violence." Nowhere were so many people so prosperous. Even greater good fortune awaited future generations of colonists, for given its dynamism and prowess, the Anglo-American union would rapidly expand westward to the Pacific Ocean and southward into Central and South America. Untold riches would flow into the colonies, creating limitless opportunities.

In the second portion, Galloway warned that America's rosy future could be dashed should Congress choose the wrong response in this crisis. Britain would never back down again, he said. If Congress defied the mother country, war was inevitable, and it would be a conflict that the Americans probably could not win. America had no army or navy, he reminded his colleagues, and it lacked the means of fighting a protracted war. The colonists, he added, had survived the French and Indian War only through Britain's help. America's lone hope of victory in a war with Britain would be through the assistance of France or Spain, and to accept the assistance of either would be to run the risk of becoming the dependent of an autocratic Catholic power. Was it not better, he asked, for Americans to be free and prosperous colonists of Britain than to be vassals of despots in Madrid and Versailles?

Galloway completed his address by stressing that while vassalage to a faraway tyrant was frightening enough, a war was likely to be accompanied by a movement for radical domestic change throughout America. An American revolution was brewing, stoked by the fiery, demagogic rhetoric of agitators, he cautioned. Once change was unleashed, it might be impossible to stop or undo. If war came, and if by some miracle the Americans won the war, Galloway predicted that calamities such as class warfare and democratization would surely be the result. Democracy had long been the great apprehension of most political theorists, and it was especially feared by society's elite in Europe and America. Galloway did not have to catalog the horrors of democracy for the audience he addressed in Carpenters' Hall. Popular licentiousness was the least of it. Stay laws to prevent the recovery of debts, the seizure of property, the heavy taxation of the wealthy, and even the redistribution of wealth were thought to be the inevitable accompaniments of popular tyranny brought on by democracy.

There was a way to prevent these dire misfortunes, Galloway insisted. Both the colonies and the mother country were partially correct in the constitutional positions they had taken. American rights were violated by a Parliament in which they were not represented. London, on the other hand, was correct in its assertion that there must be a sovereign head of every government, an entity that could not only oversee but also protect and defend the national interest. Galloway proposed constitutional revision. He urged Congress to adopt what he called his "Plan of Union." He proposed the creation of a third house of Parliament. In addition to the House of Lords and House of Commons, an American Branch, as he called it, must be created. It would consist of an American Congress, not unlike the Continental Congress, and a president general appointed by the Crown. No act of Parliament that impinged on America could become law without the consent of the American Branch.[66]

Nothing that occurred in this Congress threw a greater scare into the hard-line delegates than Galloway's proposal. In fact, John Adams later said it was "the most alarming" obstacle "in the way of effective and united action" prior to independence. Galloway's motion was seconded by John Jay of New York. It won the endorsement of some congressmen from New England and South Carolina—Edward Rutledge of Charleston called it "almost a perfect Plan"—and it was defended by nearly every delegate from the mid-Atlantic colonies. In fact, it may actually have been favored by a majority of those in attendance—twenty-four of the fifty-five congressmen came from the four mid-Atlantic colonies, some southern and even New England delegates joined with them in support of Galloway's plan—but what counted was the vote of the twelve colonies. A motion to table Galloway's plan until another day was carried by one vote—six colonies against five—while Rhode Island's two congressmen divided and did not cast a vote.[67]

No one reason can account for the opposition to Galloway's plan. Most delegates wanted relief for Boston as rapidly as possible. A constitutional debate in Congress, and possibly in London as well, would have interminably dragged out a resolution of the crisis. In addition, years earlier the hard-liners had come to believe that Parliament had no authority over America. They had no wish to revisit that issue. Some congressmen wanted more autonomy for America than would have existed under Galloway's plan. Others longed for their colony to be nearly self-governing and were loath to surrender authority to a national congress. Given the multiplicity of reservations, Galloway faced an uphill climb from the outset, an ascent made even steeper by his soiled reputation. That the vote to table Galloway's plan was so close was due in part to his political skills, which included his supposedly radical speech early in Congress and his superb timing in offering his compromise solution. But mostly the narrowness of his defeat stemmed from the fear on the part of many delegates that an undiluted American response would make war inevitable.

With Galloway's proposal shelved, the pace of Congress quickened. During the next three weeks, the delegates rapidly moved through a breathtaking series of substantive decisions. Furthermore, while there were heated moments, the earlier rancor subsided considerably. Indeed, the realization that Galloway's plan had been tabled, not voted down, and that it would eventually come up for a final vote, may have made the hard-liners more amenable to joining hands with their moderate colleagues.

Another reality also haunted the more radical New Englanders. It was readily apparent, as John Adams noted, not only that "absolute Independency" was an idea "which Startles People here" but also that the feeling was so widespread that should Massachusetts provoke "a Rupture with the [British] Troops all is lost." In other words, if Yankee hotheads were thought to have started a war, American unity would be shattered. Every mid-Atlantic colony, and perhaps others as well, would abandon New England. Similarly, should Massachusetts push for steps that many congressmen believed were certain to lead to war, that too would likely destroy American unity. Most members of Congress were "fixed against Hostilities" unless the British fired the first shot, Adams continued. Even then, many anguished that should war come, it "would light up . . . the whole Continent" with flames "which might rage for twenty year, and End, in the Subduction of America, as likely as in her Liberation."[68]

In the more conciliatory—even genial—mood that prevailed by early October, Congress voted to prohibit all exports to Great Britain, Ireland, and the British West Indies, though it agreed that non-exportation must be delayed for one year, until September 1, 1775. Congress also agreed to non-consumption, under which British goods already ordered or acquired by American merchants could be sold for five more months, until March 1. A few days later Congress created the Continental Association, the mechanism for enforcing the trade embargo. Under its provisions, every city, town, and county in the colonies was to create a committee to assure adherence to the boycott. The committees were to be elected by "those who are qualified to vote for representatives" in the provincial assembly. Congress also vowed to boycott trade with any colony that refused to adhere to the Association.[69]

While the bargaining over the boycott played out, Congress dealt with the Declaration of Colonial Rights and Grievances brought in by the Grand Committee a few days prior to Galloway's presentation. Congress tinkered with the document, adding here, subtracting there. It finally agreed on a statement in mid-October. Much of the document repeated, sometimes verbatim, the declarations adopted by various colonies going back to the Virginia Resolves nine years earlier. It denied that Parliament could legislate for America "in all cases of taxation and internal polity," and it specifically denounced Admiralty Courts, the Intolerable Acts, the deployment of the British army in America in peacetime, and the Quebec Act, which it disingenuously assailed not as an economic grievance but as having established "the Roman Catholic religion in . . . Quebec." But while it denied much of Parliament's power over America, the Declaration was leavened with the statement that the colonists from "necessity . . . and a regard to the mutual interests of both countries . . . cheerfully consent" to Parliament's "regulation of our external commerce."[70]

The question of whether Parliament could regulate American trade was the stumbling block that had tied up the Grand Committee for three long weeks. The mid-Atlantic colonies insisted on Parliament's regulatory power—as Dickinson had asserted years before—because they had enjoyed nearly uninterrupted profits through imperial commerce, deriving credit from London's lending houses, protection on the high seas from the Royal Navy, reduced overhead costs through marine insurance available in the metropolis, and invaluable assistance provided in foreign ports by British diplomats. New England had not wanted to recognize any powers of Parliament, but it relented yet again, and John Adams, who took his marching orders from Samuel Adams at the First Congress, wrote the section on commerce that made possible the passage of the Declaration of Rights.[71]

If the hard-liners had once again bowed to the moderates, one further matter came before Congress on which most from New England and Virginia were unwilling to yield. Both Massachusetts and Virginia wanted Congress to order military preparations, and Lee brought it up early in October. In as much as a huge British army was in America, Lee said, the colonies must be ready to defend themselves. Therefore, each colony should raise a militia, and Congress should furnish arms and ammunition to these citizen soldiers. Lee's motion touched off the last angry debate in this Congress. South Carolina's John Rutledge denounced the motion as both beyond the scope of why Congress had been called to meet and a "Declaration of Warr." Lee's colleague from Virginia, Benjamin Harrison, spoke against it as well, contending that it would inflame passions, whereas "Our Business is to reconcile." After several delegates from the middle colonies had taken a similar stance, Patrick Henry, a hot mass of feelings, jumped in with the most candid remarks offered during the roiling debate: If the trade boycott failed to secure redress, a resort to arms would be the only course left to America. In fact, there was a strong likelihood that the British army might attack even before the embargo had an opportunity to work. Given the gloomy road ahead, Henry emphasized that military preparedness was essential. "Arms are Necessary, & . . . Necessary Now."[72] (Half a century later, John Adams remarked that of all the delegates to the First Continental Congress, Henry best understood "the Precipice or rather the Pinnacle on which he stood, and had candour and courage enough to acknowledge it.")[73]

As military preparedness hung in the balance, Paul Revere arrived in Philadelphia after yet another long ride. This time he brought word that General Gage had ordered the construction of military fortifications in Boston. Revere reported that many feared that Gage was taking this step in preparation for unleashing his army, while others worried that the ramparts built by the soldiers would sever all communication and trade between Boston and the hinterland. This crisis brought Samuel Adams from the shadows. Speaking at last, Adams proposed that Congress inform Gage that it considered his action to be a provocation that threatened "all America [with] the Horrors of a civil War" that would open a "Wound which would never be heald." Both Lee's call for arming the provincial militias and Adams's advocacy of a harsh response to Gage were too drastic for Congress. Instead, with Lee raging privately that the timorous "majority had not the spirit" to prepare for war, Congress adopted a temperate response to Gage. Claiming that it was pursuing "every dutiful and peaceful measure to procure . . . reconciliation," Congress appealed to Gage to do nothing that would take on "so hostile an appearance" that it might "irritate & force a free people . . . into hostilities." Congress further temporized by merely requesting the colonies to ready their militia; it took no steps to provision the militiamen. Before adjourning, however, Congress—without spelling out the details of what it had in mind—resolved to support Massachusetts militarily in the event that it was attacked.[74]

In the waning days of Congress, a move was made to bring Galloway's compromise scheme up for a vote. But Congress wanted no more of it. Galloway's plan was not just left on the table; all record of its existence was expunged from Congress's published journal.[75]

The congressmen had been away from home—and in about a third of the cases, away from their legal practices—for upwards of two months. They were eager to wrap things up, especially as they knew that the substantive business of this Congress was now complete. When the committees charged with preparing an address to the king and separate addresses to the people of Britain, Quebec, and America reported in October, the delegates approved the drafts rapidly and with few meaningful changes, though the congressional editing was not devoid of niggling.

The address to the king was couched in humble tones. "[Y]our majesty's faithful subjects . . . beg leave to lay our grievances before the throne," it began. After reciting the grievances, it prayed that "Your royal indignation . . . will rather fall on those designing and dangerous men" responsible for attempting to sunder the liberties that the colonists had always enjoyed "under the auspices of your royal ancestors." It concluded with the statement, "We ask but for peace, liberty, and safety. We wish not [to] . . . solicit any new right." And it implored the monarch to use his "royal authority and interposition . . . for our relief." It was signed by each member of Congress.[76]

What in the long run was most memorable about the address to the monarch was that it had been drafted by John Dickinson. As was its custom, Pennsylvania conducted its annual elections early in October. The results were striking. In district after district, the Assembly Party went down to defeat. Once the assembly met, it deposed Joseph Galloway as speaker and elected Dickinson to Congress. Dickinson took his seat on October 17, nine days before Congress adjourned and just in time to be given this one important assignment. The meaning of what had occurred in Pennsylvania was lost on no one. The election outcome was "a most compleat and decisive Victory in favour of the American Cause," declared John Adams. He added that it would "change the Balance" in the next Congress, which the delegates voted to open on May 10, 1775, unless the imperial crisis had been resolved in the interim.[77]

"This day the Congress dissolved," a delegate noted in his diary on October 26. Fifty-two days after its initial session, the First Continental Congress was at an end. Defeated in his bid for a compromise settlement, Galloway went home to nearby Trevose. Suffused with despair, he bristled that those of "Violent Temper" had won out, the "Spirit of American Independency breathing throughout all of them." He was certain that their victory made war unavoidable. Samuel Adams must have been buoyant as he returned home from Philadelphia. Nearly all that he had dared to hope for from a continental congress had been realized. But whereas Galloway presumed that war would result because he had failed, Adams appears to have believed that hostilities would occur because he had succeeded. Already, Samuel Adams was writing that the colonists must "provide themselves without Delay with Arms & Ammunition [and] get well instructed in the military Art" so that "they may be ready in Case they are called to defend themselves against the violent Attacks of Despotism."[78]

CHAPTER 4

"It Is a Bill of War. It Draws the Sword"

Lord Dartmouth, George Washington, Hostilities

Some delegates left Philadelphia early, but Colonel Washington and Richard Henry Lee stayed to the end, finally setting off for home on a dismally foggy morning on the day following adjournment. Every inch of Washington's carriage was packed. An inveterate consumer, he had spent more than one hundred pounds—roughly what a skilled tradesman would earn in four years—on shopping sprees during his eight weeks in the city. He had purchased silk stockings and ribbed hose, a toothbrush, a razor strop, shoes, shoe polish, gloves, pamphlets, bed linen, and a nutcracker, and for Martha he had bought gloves, a pocketbook, a nightgown, and snuff. For his house, Washington acquired a bell, twenty yards of fabric, and twenty-six yards of ribbon. He was taking home wool and cotton to be spun by his female slaves. He had also bought shoes and boots for his body servant, Billy Lee. The extra weight on the carriage did not slow the travelers. They reached Mount Vernon toward the end of their fourth day on the road.[1]

Neither Washington nor Richard Henry Lee believed that war was imminent. Lee thought the ship that crossed the Atlantic with the news of the boycott would return with word that North's government had backed down. Based on what he heard from correspondents in England during the fall and winter, Washington felt that "the Ministry would willingly change their ground" rather than risk using force that would "be inadequate to the end designed." He certainly acted as if there would be no war. Soon after returning to Mount Vernon, he purchased land and indentured servants and sent a team of hired hands, servants, and slaves to develop property that he owned in what now is West Virginia. He even skipped the autumn meeting of the Virginia legislature in order to tend to his business affairs. Yet while he hoped for peace, Washington provided money and time to help get the nascent Fairfax Independent Company, a contingent of fifty-six aspiring soldiers, onto the drill field. He rode to Alexandria on several occasions to observe their musters and act as something of a consultant to its inexperienced young officers, who were attired in buff and blue uniforms that he had designed for the unit. What is more, Washington did his part to get the Continental Association up and running in Fairfax County.[2]

Life, with all its anxieties and uncertainties, its hopes and sorrows, went on that fall and winter for all the congressmen. Confident that Congress's unyielding stand would "save us . . . an effusion of blood," John Dickinson made improvements to Fairhill, his country estate, six miles outside Philadelphia. If he was wrong and war came, Dickinson confidently expected that history would exonerate the colonists. Future generations, he said, would understand that the blame for "wrecking the whole Empire" was due to the misguided policies of North's government. Not every congressman was so sure of that. North Carolina's William Hooper thought the great imperial crisis had in part been brought on by the "intemperate folly of . . . Deluded Men" from Boston. James Duane said that he and his fellow New Yorkers were in a "Pitch of Anxiety" over whether "our Friends in Boston [would] precipitate an Attack on the King's Troops." Patrick Henry spent the winter grieving. His wife, Sarah, who was mentally ill, died shortly after he returned from Philadelphia, possibly a suicide. Samuel Adams negotiated with Iroquois representatives over the winter, hoping to persuade the Native Americans to remain neutral in the event of war. Every colonist was apprehensive over how North's ministry would respond to what Congress had done. The "Times . . . are . . . as bad as they can be," John Adams lamented. "I doubt whether War, Carnage and Havock would make us more unhappy than this cruel state of Suspense we suffer."[3]

Nor was it only the congressmen who waited expectantly through that long winter, wondering whether war would follow the latest American defiance of the mother country. Several provinces prepared for war. Like the men in Alexandria who were trained by Colonel Washington, militiamen and volunteers in nearly half the American colonies were drilling on lonely, muddy fields, trying to learn quickly how to be soldiers. Even while the Continental Congress was meeting, the rebel government in Massachusetts directed each town to organize its militia—which in many instances had been dormant since fighting ended in the French and Indian War, fifteen years earlier—and train the men at least three times each week. If some men had no musket, local officials were ordered to "take effectual care, without delay, to provide the same." The Lexington, Massachusetts, militia company drilled only two days each week, but for four hours each time, and when winter's cold was unbearable, the men were put through their paces inside a barn. Before the end of February the British army's intelligence network informed General Gage that thousands of Yankees were under arms and would rally "to oppose the troops" should the commander order his regulars to "attempt to penetrate into the Country."[4]

The first person in London to learn what Congress had done was the Earl of Dartmouth, the American secretary. Born in 1730 as William Legge, Dartmouth had entered the cabinet three years earlier, and because he was responsible for the North American colonies, he found himself at the center of the storm. Dartmouth had joined the government with relatively little experience in public office, but he had the closest possible ties to Lord North. When Dartmouth was only six years old, his widowed mother had married North's father. Dartmouth was two years older than his new half-brother, and the youngsters grew close. Raised together, they were side by side at Oxford and later shared a thirty-month grand tour of Europe. Dartmouth was twenty-four when he returned home. He married soon thereafter, became a patron of the arts, was devoted to Evangelicalism, and acquired a deserved reputation for philanthropy. Among other things, he contributed to the endowment of the Indian Charity School in Hanover, New Hampshire, an institution that slowly evolved into today's Dartmouth College.

Dartmouth took his family's seat in the House of Lords in 1754, the same year that North was first elected to the House of Commons. North's ascent in politics was more rapid. He entered a ministry five years after becoming an MP; Dartmouth sat in Parliament for eleven years before he was named to the Board of Trade by the Marquis of Rockingham. Dartmouth immediately played a pivotal role in the repeal of the Stamp Act, a step that won him a reputation as a friend of America, including a unanimous vote of gratitude by the Massachusetts assembly for his "noble" efforts on behalf of the colonists.

After the Rockingham ministry collapsed in 1766, Dartmouth held no political office for six years, though he was an active player among the Rockinghamites who worried over both what they saw as the monarchy's attempt to increase its power and the disaster that would befall Britain's merchants should war with America occur. Though they never devised a coherent American policy, Rockingham's faction steadfastly opposed the government's colonial policies from 1766 onward, even sharing with many Americans the belief that all English were threatened by the possibility of monarchical tyranny.[5]

In 1772, when Hillsborough was forced out, North turned to his stepbrother, offering Dartmouth the post of American secretary. The prime minister hoped that Dartmouth's appointment would be seen in America as a signal of a new ministerial course. Dartmouth, who was forty-two years old at the time, was gray and balding, with soft features and kind eyes that bespoke the warmhearted temperament for which he was noted. Although he knew that he would be out of step with most members of the cabinet, Dartmouth accepted North's tender, delighted by his half-brother's "friendship and good will." He took office confident that he could "heal the Breach" between the colonies and the parent state, differences that he told himself were "rather in the head than in the heart." Dartmouth's appointment won the applause of wary colonists, including Franklin, who remarked that the ascension of the new American secretary "gives me room to hope . . . to obtain more in favour of the Colonies . . . than I could for some time past."[6]

Like North, Dartmouth played for time, hoping that, in the long run, reason would prevail and the American problem would go away. He sometimes acted in an unorthodox manner to smooth out differences. A year after taking office, Dartmouth made the unprecedented step of writing directly to Speaker Cushing in Massachusetts, bypassing the royal governor. Telling Cushing that he believed Parliament was sovereign, Dartmouth astoundingly confided that he also thought that its "right [of sovereignty] . . . should be suspended and lie dormant" until some imperial emergency—another war, perhaps—rendered its "exercise . . . obvious."[7]

Given enough time, Dartmouth might have had some success, although even in a ministry headed by his close kin, he stood virtually alone. When the East India Company's troubles surfaced in 1773, Dartmouth foresaw the dangers posed by the Tea Act and fought a lonely battle against it. "He is a truly good Man," Franklin said of Dartmouth at the time, but he "does not seem to have Strength equal to his Wishes." Franklin also believed, probably accurately, that to survive politically, Dartmouth was compelled on many occasions to display a *"Firmness"* toward the colonies that he secretly abhorred.[8]

Some Americans had seen Dartmouth as their only hope when the ministry debated its response to the Boston Tea Party. It was widely believed that he would press the cabinet to demand nothing more than compensation for the East India Company. Some hoped that he would push the notion that the "Idea of Taxation might be waived" as the best hope for assuring that the "Dispute might Subside."[9] But few thought Dartmouth could succeed. Some suspected his limitations, seeing him as weak-kneed, with "no will or judgment of his own" and a proclivity to shrink from battle. Others thought more highly of him, but doubted that he could "singly . . . stem the torrent." Many hoped that if Dartmouth saw that he could not prevail, he would resign rather than "dip his hands in blood." It would be a courageous gesture that might inspire the foes of coercion and possibly stay the hand of those who were crying that the colonists must be severely punished.[10]

In the early-1774 cabinet battle over how to respond to the Boston Tea Party, North provided Dartmouth with every opportunity to present his case for leniency. The American secretary, in turn, seized the chance to defend the colonists from what he called the "madness of the people" for revenge. Dartmouth first fought to limit Boston's punishment to the arrest and prosecution of those responsible for the destruction of the tea. When such a mild response was greeted with scorn, Dartmouth urged that coercion be accompanied by a repeal of the Tea Act, but even North refused to back his kin in rescinding the tax on tea. In the end, Dartmouth stood alone. The best he had been able to do was to secure the cabinet's authorization for the royal governor in Massachusetts to act with leniency toward colonial offenders. Dartmouth did not resign when the ministry embraced the Coercive Acts.[11]

Dartmouth had been most troubled by the Massachusetts Government Act, sensing that the government had gone too far when it changed the colony's charter. As the summer of 1774 approached, Dartmouth's only hope had been that the other colonies would not unite behind the Bay Colony. However, in midsummer he had learned of the colonists' plans for a continental congress, and thereafter he feared the worst. Others had as well. With war beginning to look ever more likely, Lord North had advised the monarch to dissolve Parliament and call elections. George III complied and, as expected, the autumn elections returned a huge majority for the government. Not only did the Rockinghamites lose a dozen seats, but also North reported to the king in November that three of every five members of the House of Commons would unwaveringly support his government and many more would fall in line behind most of his measures. If war came, the government would enter it backed by a huge majority.[12]

Although Congress had met in secret, some of what it was doing reached Dartmouth during the fall. Galloway disclosed to friends the details of his Plan of Union, and one of them, probably Benjamin Franklin's son, William, passed along the information to Dartmouth; Joseph Reed, the Philadelphia lawyer, knew from other sources some things that were happening behind closed doors at the State House, and he was secretly corresponding with the American secretary. However, while Dartmouth gathered scraps of information, news from Philadelphia had always been sketchy, and rumors were plentiful in London. One bit of tattle had Congress looking to Benjamin Franklin, who was still in London, for guidance. According to other hearsay, Congress would do nothing more than petition the king's help.[13] The first definitive word had reached London in October. It was Congress's published approval of the Suffolk County Resolves. With that, Dartmouth knew that all was lost. "They have declared war on us," he moaned.[14]

In early December, Dartmouth, through his informants, had learned that Galloway's constitutional reform plan had been narrowly rejected by Congress. Around the same time, he also received official word of what else Congress had done. The American secretary had reacted positively toward Galloway's proposal, but as it had been discussed in secret by Congress, he could hardly respond to it, at least in any official manner. However, it should have been clear to any perceptive politician—and it seems to have been to Dartmouth—that serious divisions had existed within Congress. While Congress had adopted a trade stoppage, it had not only appealed to the king in a deferential fashion but also urged a return to colonial policies that, until a decade earlier, had been in place for 150 years. Furthermore, Galloway's compromise proposal had been defeated by a narrow vote. Clearly, many in Congress yearned for reconciliation. It appeared to Dartmouth that the way was open to defuse the crisis, or at the very least to avert an immediate showdown, by opening negotiations with the colonists based on Congress's address to the king. Dartmouth suggested to North that a commission be sent to America to begin discussions.

North took the American secretary's recommendation to the king, though there was no reason to expect the monarch to acquiesce to Dartmouth's request. Thirty-six years old in early 1775, George III had come to the throne in 1760. He was agreeable and good-humored, conscientious, and so diligent that he agonized over wasted time. He took pains to present a public persona as a venerable, responsible, modest, and seemly individual. The king had never crossed the Atlantic to visit his colonies. Had he done so, the experience might have recast some of his views. As it was, he had no qualms with the colonial policies that commenced in the aftermath of the Seven Years' War. He had joined in the push for the Stamp Act and looked askance at making concessions when the colonists protested. At the time, he predicted that the American dilemma would be the greatest problem his generation would face, and he was not at all sure that there was sufficient "candour and temper" in Parliament to prudently cope with it. The king did not question Parliament's passage of the Townshend Duties, and when those levies met with protest, he made no attempt to prevent the deployment of troops in Boston. Nevertheless, until the Boston Tea Party, George III appears to have been disposed toward leniency and was open-minded with regard to searching for a means of settling differences.[15]

But once he learned of the Boston Tea Party, the king was tough and inflexible, telling Lord North that the colonies were "in a State of Rebellion." Later, he said that "blows must decide whether they are to be subject to this Country or independent. . . . [W]e must either master them or totally leave them to themselves, and treat them as Aliens." On another occasion, the king had advised his first minister that further appeasement would mean the loss of the colonies. The "dye is now cast," he had said famously, adding that "the Colonies must submit or triumph. . . . [W]e must not retreat." When General Gage had privately proposed the suspension of the Coercive Acts, the king not only refused to consider such a step; he also made clear to the cabinet that the general must be replaced by a commander with greater backbone.

Now, on learning what steps the Continental Congress had taken, the monarch predictably remained firm and unbending. He spurned the notion of dispatching a commission to America, fearing it would brand London as weak-kneed and embolden the radical leaders in America. Should negotiations be attempted and fail, he added, it would only further unite the colonists. However, the monarch opposed negotiations primarily because he did not wish to yield on any of the major points in dispute. There would be no negotiations. He made that clear to North: "I do not want to drive them to despair but to Submission."

But given a couple of weeks to reflect on the matter, the king appeared to waver, if only slightly. He received Congress's address to him "very graciously" and promised Dartmouth that he would present the entreaty to Parliament. The king even insisted that "reason not passion must point out the proper measures" to be taken. With the holidays on them and Parliament not due to meet until deep into January, George III asked North's ministry to defer its decision for up to a month so that whatever was decided would be well "digested."[16]

When the ministers scattered in December, nothing had been decided. But in the course of three meetings in January the cabinet reached its decision. The contours of its final determination were shaped by several factors. The alarming reports submitted by General Gage were especially influential. He told the cabinet that "popular Fury was never greater" throughout New England. The people in the backcountry "openly threaten Resistance by Arms." They were stockpiling weapons and ammunition and "threaten to attack any Troops who dare to oppose them." Gage insisted that "Conciliating, Moderation, Reasoning is over. Nothing can be done but by forceable Means." He also said that the rebellion was not confined to Massachusetts. Even Pennsylvanians "talk . . . of taking [up] Arms with an Indifference, as if it were a Matter of little Importance," the general wrote. Nevertheless, Gage stressed that New England, and especially Massachusetts, was the cockpit of the American rebellion. If the Yankees could be brought to submission, he counseled, the American rebellion would be over. However, Gage cautioned that the pacification of New England might not be easy. It would require an army of at least 20,000 men, and he reminded London that he had only 4,521 under his command. Gage additionally advised that striking the first crumpling blow would be crucial to his success. A successful "first stroke" by his redcoats would "decide a great deal," he said in one letter. In another, he predicted that a surprise strike "wou'd be fatal" to the rebels.[17]

Many ministers had previously questioned Gage's appraisals as unduly pessimistic, but this time his judgment appeared to be confirmed by the daunting assessments by several Crown officials from outside New England. John Penn, Pennsylvania's proprietary governor, told his superiors in London that winter that the "general temper of the people . . . here as in other parts of America is very warm." Similar tidings arrived from every royal governor in the southern colonies. Governor Dunmore reported on "the turbulence and prejudice which prevails" in Virginia. From New Bern, North Carolina, Governor Josiah Martin cleaved to the notion that his subjects were in the thrall of diabolical rebel demagogues. He claimed that the people were moved "to the will of those . . . [who] practice on their ignorance and credulity" in the same fashion as the "magical wires to the figures in a puppet-show" were pulled by the all-controlling puppeteer. Notification came from Governor William Bull in Charleston that the "spirit of opposition to taxation . . . is so violent" that "it will not be soon or easily oppressed." Sir James Wright, the governor of Georgia, had already informed the ministry that most colonists in his province favored independence. The "licentious spirit . . . has now gone to so great a length and is at such a height" that there was nothing he could do to "settle matters." Only a pugnacious stand by London, he declared, could favorably resolve the imperial crisis.[18]

While royal officials in America appeared to say that only force could bring the Americans to heel, there were those in the mother country who urged conciliation. Merchants from thirteen major urban centers flooded the ministry, Parliament, and the Crown with petitions—collectively containing thousands of signatures—asking that the colonists be placated. Some petitions and addresses specifically defended the colonists' rights against the claims of the government. Some urged the repeal of the Coercive Acts. During the winter of 1775, tradesmen also staged a sizable march through London, observed by large and friendly crowds. The demonstrators advocated the withdrawal of all British troops from the colonies.[19] Several pamphleteers rushed into print a variety of reconciliation schemes that winter. One anonymous writer, who insisted that the colonists were due greater rights and liberties as a result of the price they had paid in settling the hostile American wilderness, urged commercial concessions. The right of Americans to trade more freely would add to the colonists' prosperity, and that in turn would add to Britain's revenues, he reasoned. "Natural means" will save the empire, the writer said, but "violent measures" will destroy the Anglo-American union. Another pamphleteer proposed an end to parliamentary taxation and the creation of a "Supreme Council" composed of elected representatives from each North American and West Indian colony. This colonial council would be sovereign throughout America, but its decisions would be subject to royal veto. To replace the revenue that might have been realized through colonial taxation, the author advocated that churches in England be taxed.[20]

But most of the press defended North's government and urged firmness. Many essayists spun out legalistic arguments demonstrating that there must be a sovereign head to every government. There could be no middle ground, they insisted. Either the colonies must recognize Parliament's supremacy in all matters, or they must be independent, and the latter choice was intolerable.[21] Most editors and writers defended the government's "judicious" policies and denounced the "wicked and treasonable" colonists. No American, not even Samuel Adams, came in for as much vitriol in the press as Benjamin Franklin. Labeled "old Doubleface," "Judas," the "grand incendiary," and the "living emblem of iniquity," he was portrayed as the cause of "much of the present troubles in America." With war likely, one editor predicted that Franklin would soon return to the colonies to see "whether he cannot do more mischief with the Sword than with the Pen."[22]

Lord Dartmouth, however, hoped to use Franklin's pen, and his wits, to prevent swords from being drawn. Once he discovered the lengths of Congress's defiance, and possibly the minute that he learned of Galloway's Plan of Union, the American secretary set in motion a covert approach to Franklin. It was Dartmouth's last-ditch attempt to prevent catastrophe. Aware that Franklin was Galloway's old friend and political partner, and knowing that the king had not made a final decision regarding sending commissioners to America to negotiate a peaceful settlement, Dartmouth hoped that Franklin could be persuaded to suggest viable terms for reconciliation. If Franklin cooperated, Dartmouth thought there was a chance that the monarch might agree to open negotiations in America. Dartmouth must also have hoped to use Franklin to drive a wedge between the various factions in America, shattering colonial unity and compelling the Americans to abandon all thoughts of armed resistance.

Dartmouth selected David Barclay and John Fothergill to serve as intermediaries. Both were Quakers with ties to Pennsylvania, and each knew

Franklin. Barclay, who had invented a home fire protection plan, had become acquainted with Franklin through scientific circles. Fothergill was a physician to both Franklin and Dartmouth. Franklin met with the two during the first week of December and, at their behest, drafted a set of "Hints . . . of Terms that might probably produce a durable Union between Britain and the Colonies." Among his proposals: the East India Company was to be compensated by Massachusetts or the Continental Congress for its destroyed tea; Parliament was to repeal the Tea Act and Coercive Acts; Britain was to agree to end its monopolization of American trade; Parliament was to agree not to tax the colonists in peacetime; in wartime, the colonists would pay a land tax equivalent to one quarter of the land tax levy in England; and "all powers of Internal Legislation in the Colonies [were] to be disclaim'd by Parliament."[23]

Dartmouth saw at a glance that Franklin's proposals would go nowhere. They would have required an abject British surrender. But the American secretary did not give up. He arranged a meeting between Franklin and Admiral Richard Howe. Dartmouth probably chose the flag officer because he was seen as a moderate on colonial issues. Furthermore, London was buzzing with rumors that if a peace commission was sent to America, Howe would be one of the commissioners. Given his stature, Howe might persuade Franklin to moderate his demands, which in turn might convince the king to reconsider sending a peace commission across the sea.

Fothergill and Barclay brought about the meeting between Franklin and Howe in a roundabout manner. First, they persuaded the admiral's sister, Catherine Howe, to invite Franklin to her fashionable Grafton Street residence for an evening of chess shortly before Christmas. Things went well, and she asked him to return for another night of chess on December 28. Whatever Franklin might have expected, Admiral Howe was present when he arrived on that cold winter evening.

Howe was an impressive figure. Tall and swarthy—he was popularly known as "Black Dick" Howe—the admiral was somber and dignified, and in the course of his thirty-five-year naval career he had won a reputation for courage and boldness. After warmly greeting Franklin, Howe lamented his contemptible treatment in the Cockpit a year earlier. With that out of the way, Howe got down to business, telling Franklin that "there was no likelihood of the admission" of his "Hints." He asked the American to tender a new, more temperate set of proposals. In a blatant attempt at bribery, Howe also promised Franklin that if he cooperated, he could "with reason expect any reward in the power of government to bestow."

Howe's naked promise of preferment made Franklin aware of what he had probably suspected all along: He was being used by Dartmouth. Franklin

Richard Lord Howe by John Singleton Copley. A British admiral who also sat in Parliament, Howe hoped for a negotiated settlement that would prevent war. He sought to find acceptable terms through talks with Benjamin Franklin in 1774–1775, and was sent to America as a "peace commissioner" in 1776. (Wikimedia Commons)

wanted no part of it. He had decided to leave England a year earlier, following his humiliation by Wedderburn, though he had stayed on after learning of the Boston Tea Party "to see if my Presence may . . . be of use," he said. Franklin had doubtless hoped to rehabilitate his reputation in England by playing a role in settling Anglo-American differences, perhaps enabling him to live out his life in London. But he would not betray America, and that was what Howe and Dartmouth were asking. On the final day of 1774, Franklin provided Howe with his second list of proposals. Aware by this time of what the delegates in Philadelphia had demanded, Franklin's second list of terms essentially recommended that the ministry comply with the demands of the Continental Congress.[24] A despondent Dartmouth knew immediately that Franklin had failed to help him and that all hope of peaceful reconciliation was lost.

Franklin knew too that he was finished in London, and a few weeks later he sailed for home, ending a stay that had begun in late 1764. Just before he embarked, Franklin wrote Galloway a letter making clear that he already favored American independence. It was one of many things that Franklin divulged to his longtime political partner for the first time. Franklin declared his conviction that should the colonists remain in the British Empire, the mother country would "drag us after them in all the plundering wars which their desperate circumstances, injustice, and rapacity may prompt them to undertake." He also expanded on the "extreme corruption . . . in this old rotten state," adding that if the colonists remained tied to Great Britain, it "will only . . . corrupt and poison us." Franklin, who twice in the past had urged Galloway to propose a compromise solution that might resolve the crisis and enable the colonists to remain happily within the British Empire, closed by saying that he had chosen to side with "our rising country," America.[25]

North's cabinet finally met on January 13 to decide how to respond to its refractory colonists. In that meeting and two others, which followed in a span of eight days, the ministers recapitulated the pros and cons of going to war that they had considered the previous January. From the outset it was clear that the great majority thought there was no choice but to use force, though the ministers wished to employ a carrot-and-stick policy. At the January 21 session, held at the home of the Earl of Sandwich, the cabinet agreed to what it considered the carrot: Should the colonies in peacetime furnish the amount of revenue desired by London, and in time of "war contribute extraordinary supplies, in a reasonable proportion to what is raised by Great Britain," Parliament would "desist from the exercise of the power of taxation, except for commercial purposes only."[26]

The stick came next. Dartmouth sought to forestall the clash by pushing for sending commissioners to America to open discussions with the colonists, but the ministers were adamant. Not only had the king already rejected negotiations, but also nothing fruitful had come from the clandestine talks with Franklin. The cabinet took a hard line in its remaining steps. In reprisal for Congress's boycott of British trade, it agreed to deny the four Yankee colonies access to the fisheries off Newfoundland, a vital economic resource for New Englanders. The ministers also voted to reinforce the Royal Navy and the British army in Boston. The navy was to be augmented by 2,000 men. The cabinet initially agreed to send an additional three regiments to the army, but after further deliberation it decided to send four regiments and 400 marines as well as to bring Gage's existing regiments up to strength. The ministry anticipated that by early summer Gage's force would be nearly doubled, to 7,500 men. Though that would be only a third the number that he had requested, the ministers thought the army would have the manpower to suppress the rebellion in New England, which in turn, they were convinced, would bring to an end the American insurgency. Finally, North's government agreed to two steps that were guaranteed to provoke hostilities: Gage was to be ordered to use force and to seize the leaders of the rebel government in Massachusetts.[27]

It was cruelly ironic that it fell to Dartmouth, who for three years had been the ministry's most strenuous advocate for moderation and a peaceful resolution of the imperial crisis, to issue the order to go to war. He might have resigned rather than carry out such an unpalatable task, but he stayed on and did as the ministry wished, perhaps out of loyalty to his stepbrother. On January 27, 1775, Dartmouth ordered Gage to apply "a vigorous Exertion of . . . Force," adding that if the colonists resisted, "Force should be repelled by Force." Whereas Gage until now had "act[ed] upon the Defensive," Dartmouth told the general that henceforth he was "to take a more active & determined" course, including "sending out Detachments of your Troops" into the interior of Massachusetts to smash the rebellion.

As so often had been the case in North's ministry, an air of unreality permeated Dartmouth's order. To the very end, the ministers had willfully ignored evidence that the situation in America was much more challenging than they acknowledged. Both Dartmouth and his fellow ministers, who insisted on reading and approving the order before it was dispatched, still held to the belief that a small "tumultuous Rabble" in New England was causing the American problem. They confidently believed that the use of force in Massachusetts would bring the other provinces to their senses. Dartmouth, like his colleagues, expected little in the way of a military challenge from the Americans. He broke the news to Gage that he would not be getting the twenty thousand men he wanted. However, as if in dreamland, Dartmouth nonsensically advised Gage that, as "a rude Rabble without plan, without concert, & without conduct" formed the core of the American rebellion, a small British army "would be able to encounter them with greater probability of Success than might be expected from a greater Army." When Dartmouth issued the order that would launch the war, he and his colleagues appeared to believe that only "a single Action"—one that might "perhaps be accomplished without bloodshed"—would break the back of the American rebels. Even should the American insurgents choose war, Dartmouth added in closing, their resistance "cannot be very formidable."[28]

Parliament faced two strikingly different alternatives with regard to America when it reconvened following the holidays. Five days after Dartmouth wrote the secret order to go to war, William Pitt, the Earl of Chatham, the most esteemed public figure in Great Britain, introduced a plan of American conciliation in the House of Lords. The architect of victory in the Seven Years' War, Chatham was the Winston Churchill of eighteenth-century Britain and a revered figure in America, where his portrait hung in many homes, including Richard Henry Lee's Chantilly. Convinced that the ministry was guided by a flawed strategic vision for the empire, and equally certain that he could find the means of preserving the Anglo-American union, Chatham came forward in this crisis. Old and suffering from numerous physical debilities as well as melancholia, Chatham nevertheless summoned the energy to meet four times with Franklin in the course of preparing his plan for imperial salvation. Once he even was driven into London and called on the Pennsylvanian at his Craven

Street residence, leading to a two-hour conversation in which Franklin informed Chatham of the details of Galloway's Plan of Union.[29]

Chatham was famous for his spellbinding oratory, and with all expecting that this would be his last great speech (which, in fact, it was), and with London awash with rumors that war was imminent, the peers must have listened with rapt attention as Chatham struggled to complete his address. He called his scheme a plan "for settling the Troubles in America." Much of what he proposed was hardly distinguishable from that offered by Burke in the spring. Chatham not only left the limits of Parliament's authority unquestioned; he also stressed that it must continue to regulate imperial trade. However, he insisted that prudence dictated that Parliament no longer exercise its powers in matters where the colonists were competent to govern themselves. After indicating his opposition to American independence, Chatham got to his specific proposals. The army must be removed from Boston. Convinced that the Americans must bear some of the costs of empire, Chatham additionally proposed that the Continental Congress—which North's government regarded as illegal—make a "free grant . . . of a certain perpetual revenue," which Parliament might use as it saw fit. Finally, Chatham urged the suspension of all parliamentary acts to which the Continental Congress had objected.

Chatham cautioned against going to war. The Americans will not back down, he warned. Possessed of the virtues of the English people, the Americans were motivated by a sense of honor and a belief in their natural rights and their rights as Englishmen. They "will not be slaves." This "sleeping and confounded ministry" could not understand that, he declared. North's government seemed capable only of offering "plan[s] of mis-administration." It was taking Great Britain into a war that could not be won by an army of forty thousand regulars. Rather than go to war, Great Britain must do something "that can restore America to our bosom: you must repeal her fears and her resentments; and you may then hope for her love and gratitude." Parliament must understand that "taxation is theirs, commercial regulation is ours." Parliament "must recognize . . . the Americans . . . supreme unalienable right in their property."[30]

North spoke the following day for two hours. He largely ignored what Chatham had said. Instead, he unveiled a portion of the government's planned response to events in America. Asserting that Britons paid a tax burden fifty times greater than that borne by the American colonists, the prime minister pronounced it absurd for Massachusetts to rebel against meager taxes levied by Parliament. He declared that the law must be enforced, and he proclaimed that it would be. North revealed that military reinforcements were being sent to America, but he disclosed neither that Gage would be getting far fewer troops than he wanted nor that the general had been ordered to use force to crush the rebels. In the vaguest terms, North said that his government would attempt to redress American grievances once order had been restored. He closed by presenting the question that divided America and the mother country as lying "within a very narrow compass." At issue, he said, was "whether we have or have not any authority in that country." The nation, he added, must decide whether it wishes to abandon the claims of parliamentary sovereignty over America and "give up every advantage arising from . . . the sovereignty," or whether Britain should "ensure" its hegemony over the colonies.

The issue was never in doubt. By large majorities in both houses, Chatham's plan was rejected, and over the next few days North's hard line was approved. The bills denying the New England colonies access to the fisheries and increasing the size of the navy in North America passed easily.[31]

Even so, it was widely appreciated that a large portion of the population was unhappy with the government's American policy. Lord Camden told North that he did not have "half of the nation on your side." The prime minister did not disagree. In fact, he told the king that "the cause of Great Britain is not yet sufficiently popular."[32]

With that in mind, North on February 20 made his final major address on the American crisis prior to hostilities. He presented the American taxation scheme that the cabinet had approved the previous month. Having earlier pushed for coercive measures, North in this speech made a show of offering the olive branch. Characterizing his remarks as "Propositions for conciliating the Differences with America," the prime minister unveiled what came to be popularly known as the "North Peace Plan" or "North's Conciliatory Proposal." In reality, North confided privately to George III his hope that his plan would cause "great utility . . . to arise to the publick" on "this side of the water." In other words, his peace plan did not seek to avert war but to solidify public opinion in Great Britain behind the coming war. In private, he had already told the monarch that his plan "gives up no right" to the colonists.[33]

North told Parliament that his purpose was to uphold "the doctrine that every part of the empire was bound to bear its share of service and burthen in the common defense." Revenue must be raised, and never more so than now, as the annual interest alone on the national debt totaled 1.8 million pounds. If the Americans persisted in denying the authority of Parliament, he went on, "we can enter into no negociation, we can meet no compromise." But if the colonists through their assemblies should agree to contribute "their proportion to the common defense (such proportion to be raised [by each] . . . assembly . . . and disposable by parliament)," the government of Great Britain would "forbear . . . to levy any duty, tax, or assessment" on that colony. Furthermore, the colonial assemblies could raise the revenue by "any mode"—direct or indirect taxes, lotteries, land sales, whatever—they chose.[34]

North made clear that it was his intention to deal with each province separately. He never mentioned the Continental Congress. In fact, he categorically declared, "I am not treating with rebels."[35] He was advancing the doctrine that Crown and Parliament remained sovereign in every respect. The ministry and Parliament would make the key decisions. They would determine what constituted the common defense, how much revenue was to be raised annually, what percentage of the revenue would come from America, and how much was to be raised by each colony. Each colonial assembly would possess the authority only to decide how to raise the revenue that London had assigned as its quota. Parliamentary sovereignty remained at the heart of North's proposal. Furthermore, as one of Dartmouth's subministers remarked privately, under North's plan the Americans would have "no security" for London's lasting adherence to North's plan "but our own good faith."[36]

North's so-called peace plan stirred remarkably little debate, though two MPs delivered especially striking speeches in opposition to the course the prime minister had outlined. Charles Pratt, 1st Baron Camden, spoke compellingly in the House of Lords. The sixty-two-year-old Camden had sat in two previous ministries. Though at times he had expressed his exasperation with the colonists, Camden never wavered in his opposition to the Declaratory Act. Over the past decade, he had opposed the stamp tax, Townshend Duties, Tea Act, and Coercive Acts. On March 16, with an air of doom dangling on every phrase, yet with greater clarity than was expressed by any other MP, Camden took the floor to warn against following the government's belligerent course. The "true character" of what North had proposed, he began, was "violent and hostile. . . . [I]t is a Bill of war; it draws the sword" and will plunge the empire into "the calamities of civil war." Before resorting to hostilities, he continued, "wise and good men" must ask "whether the war in which they are going to engage be just, practicable and necessary." War with the colonists would be unjust, he declared. The colonists' grievances were the outgrowth of the "oppressions you have accumulated on America." Furthermore, North was taking Great Britain into a war that it might not be able to win. Indeed, Camden spoke of the "impracticability of conquering America." The army, he said, could never "conquer a great continent of 1800 miles, containing three millions of people, all indissolubly united on the great Whig bottom of liberty and justice." It was possible, though by no means certain, that a naval blockade could quash the American rebellion. Britain would go to war filled with "discontent and division," whereas the Americans were "prepared to meet these severities [of war] and to surmount them" through "a union as renders her invincible. . . . They are allied in the common defence of every thing dear to them. They are struggling . . . in support of their liberties and properties, and the most sacred rights of mankind."[37]

Camden was answered principally by Sandwich. Fifty-seven years old in 1775, the first lord of the Admiralty had been part of every ministry over the past eight years. In each, he had been a tenacious advocate for taking a harsh stance toward the colonial protestors. In 1775 Sandwich expected to lead the navy in the war that was about to begin, and it was a challenge that he relished. He anticipated no problems whatsoever from armed Americans. With an imperturbable air, Sandwich predicted that the "American heroes" would show themselves to be "egregious cowards," much as their forebearers had done in the French and Indian War. The "very sound of a cannon" will "carry them off" in flight. "They are raw, undisciplined, cowardly men," he proclaimed.[38]

Edmund Burke once again was North's principal adversary in the House of Commons. His long speech—it lasted nearly three hours—instantly gained a wider circulation than the address by Camden. "The proposition is peace," Burke began. "Not peace through the medium of war; not peace to be hunted through the labyrinth of intricate and endless negotiations. . . . It is simple peace." Peace, he went on, implies reconciliation, and reconciliation requires concessions by one side or the other. He urged that the concessions be made by Great Britain, for the "fierce spirit of liberty" that was characteristic of Americans would not permit them to surrender "what they think [is] the only advantage worth living for." If North's government refused to yield ground, Great Britain would lose its colonies. That would be disastrous for the mother country. One third of Britain's overseas trade was with America, Burke observed, an amount equivalent to all of Britain's trade only seventy-five years earlier. But if the government succeeded in reconciling with America, Burke went on, the colonists "will cling and grapple to you, and no force under heaven will be of power to tear them from their allegiance."

Camden had not offered an unambiguous solution to the imperial crisis. Burke was more specific, though barely so. He urged the repeal of the Coercive Acts and all taxes, contending that sufficient revenue would come from America through the regulation of its trade. Taxation, he said, was the heart of the matter. Reconciliation could not occur unless the Americans were satisfied on this score. But what Burke offered was less than the Continental Congress had demanded. Burke knew that Congress had disavowed the Declaratory Act, but he refused to deny Parliament's supremacy over the colonies. On the other hand, he knew of Galloway's plan and he spoke of Irish and Welsh representation in Parliament, leaving the impression that he was suggesting that the colonists be represented, perhaps in an American branch. Great Britain must, he said, "yield as a matter of right, or grant as [a] matter of favour," the admission of "*the people of our colonies into an interest in the Constitution.*" But he did not define the constitutional rights of the colonists. Once again, Burke left the impression that he was suggesting a federal system for the empire. The empire, he said, should consist of "the aggregate of many states under one common head," with "the subordinate parts [having] many local privileges and immunities."

Burke had spoken in a statesmanlike manner. From the outset, he knew that his speech was futile. He and the others who responded to North, he said privately, "spoke in opposition . . . more for the acquittal of their own honour, and discharge of their own consciences . . . than from any sort of hope" of success. But while Burke provided a breath of fresh air, he in fact proposed nothing more concrete than a return to pre-1763 practices. Typically, however, he closed with a flow of splendid rhetoric:

> All this, I know well enough, will sound wild and chimerical to the profane herd of those vulgar and mechanical politicians, who have no place among us . . . and who . . . [are] far from being qualified to be directors of the great movement of empire. . . . Magnanimity in politics is not seldom the truest wisdom; and a great empire and little minds go ill together. . . . We ought to elevate our minds with the greatness of that trust to which the order of Providence has called us. By adverting to the dignity of this high calling, our ancestors have turned a savage wilderness into a glorious empire, and have made the most extensive, and the only honourable conquests, not by destroying, but by promoting the wealth, the number, the happiness of the human race. Let us get an American revenue as we have got an American Empire. English privileges have made it all that it is; English privileges will make it all it can be.

Burke's warning that Great Britain must offer conciliatory terms or risk the loss of its American colonies fell on deaf ears. The House of Commons rejected his proposal by nearly a four-to-one vote.[39]

Thereafter, both houses went along placidly, overwhelmingly endorsing North's program. Once they had acted, David Hartley, who had been Dartmouth's intermediary to Franklin before Christmas, literally had the final word in Parliament's debate on conciliation. Parliament had chosen war, he said. Had it "pursued a plan of equity and justice," peace and the British Empire might have been maintained.[40]

No one listened, and not solely because of Hartley's reputation as an uninspiring and verbose orator. (Behind his back, colleagues called him the "dinner bell." When he spoke, many MPs left the chamber for a repast.)[41] In this instance, Hartley's effort went unheard because, in truth, North's government, and its commanding majority in Parliament, had decided on war a full year earlier unless the Americans accepted absolute parliamentary supremacy. Once word of the Continental Congress's action reached London, Britain's recourse to the use of force was never in question. Despite what most knew to be the possibility—even the likelihood—of military difficulties, ministry and Parliament marched into hostilities persuaded that humbling the colonists would not be a formidable task. Not for the last time would a government underestimate its enemy as it took its people into the costly, bloody wasteland of war.

During the six months that separated the First and Second Congress, including the three months spent by North's government arriving at its American policy, the colonies put in place the Continental Association, the mechanism for enforcing the stoppage of trade with the mother country. Here and there, bitter battles were fought over adherence to the boycott that Congress had adopted, though in the end only Georgia failed to immediately create a provincial Association committee. In New England and Virginia the boycotts adopted in the spring and summer never ceased operation, while elsewhere most of the Association committees were up and running sometime during the winter. In its first month of operation, before the bugs were ironed out, the New York City committee seized and sold imports that brought only 350 pounds in auctions. A few months later a royal official in the colony lamented that the boycott was ironclad and "ever rigidly maintained in this place."[42]

Occasionally, a congressman served on an Association committee. John Adams, for instance, was already a member of the Board of Selectmen in Braintree, Massachusetts, which was given responsibility for enforcing the boycott in the village. Adams's committee superintended the embargo and regulated prices brought on by the scarcities caused by the boycott. In addition, it published the names of violators so that "all such foes to the rights of British America may be publickly known and universally Contemned as the enemies of American liberty and thence forth We respectively will break off all dealings with him or her."[43]

Some Association committees instituted loyalty oaths. Those who signed the oath pledged their willingness to abide by the boycott. Those who refused to take the oath were designated as Tories. This was the first instance in the colonial protest that an entire segment of the population was readily identifiable as Loyalists or Tories, and the first time too that those who were seen as hostile to the popular cause were placed under surveillance. In some locales Tories were disarmed. In rare instances they were incarcerated. Nearly everywhere Tories were forced to resign from public office. In some villages throughout Massachusetts, the local Association committee denied Loyalists admittance to worship services, though the Boston Committee of Correspondence inveighed against that practice. Many committees compelled Tories to make public apologies for their transgressions. Shots were fired into the home of one outspoken Tory in Taunton, Massachusetts, though no one was injured.[44] When General Gage sought to recruit Loyalists into a newly formed Tory "Corps of Infantry," Massachusetts militiamen in Bristol County, about forty miles south of Boston, turned out on April 10 and rounded up those who volunteered. They were stripped of their weapons, and eleven men who had signed on to soldier for the king were imprisoned in an abandoned salt mine.[45]

As in England, the colonies witnessed an explosion of pamphleteering during the winter of 1775. Pamphlets defending and attacking British policies had appeared in America since Parliament's initial attempt to tax the colonists, but never had so many tracts been issued by both sides in such a brief period. With war hanging in the balance, most of these publications assumed a strident, urgent tone rarely seen before. A wave of pamphlets attacking the First Continental Congress appeared first. Most of the authors were Anglican clerics and one, Jonathan Boucher, the priest of Saint Barnabas Church in Prince George's County, Maryland, was an acquaintance of Colonel Washington and the former tutor of his stepson. Several who condemned Congress's actions were lawyers, including Jonathan Sewall and Daniel Leonard in Massachusetts and Galloway in Pennsylvania.

Few of the Tory publications shed new light on the American crisis. Rehashing what the defenders of parliamentary taxation had been writing throughout the past decade, most attributed the empire's woes to American troublemakers who supposedly had a hidden agenda: independence and democratization. The Tories attacked Congress for having failed to seek a settlement with the mother country. One after another wrote that there could be only one sovereign government and, if the empire was to survive, that government must be the Crown and Parliament. Some played on class prejudices, warning that the rebellion would elevate tradesmen and maybe even those without property to high office, and that they would confiscate the wealth of their social superiors. Joseph Galloway produced the shrillest pamphlet. He predicted that "companies of armed, but undisciplined men, headed by men unprincipled" would enter "your homes—your castles—and sacred repositories of safety for all you hold dear and valuable—seizing your property and carrying havock and devastation wherever they head—ravishing your wives and daughters, and afterwards, plunging the dagger into their tender bosoms." Other writers warned that when unchecked turbulence prevailed, the natural order of things would be turned on its head. "When the pot boils, the scum will rise" was a favorite Tory epigram. By it, they meant that war and revolution inevitably resulted in the triumph of those whom they called the "lower sort."[46]

The one newsworthy Tory publication was Galloway's *Candid Examination of the Mutual Claims of Great Britain and the Colonies*. What set it apart from the others was that he not only revealed, and fleshed out, the compromise plan he had introduced in Congress, but he also notified the colonists and residents of the mother country alike of the deep divisions that had cleaved Congress. He described a Congress under the control of ambition-mad "demagogues" who had chosen a course certain to lead to hostilities, for war offered their only hope of attaining their secret "scheme of independence." He had waited patiently through the first three weeks of Congress for another delegate to introduce a plan for reconciliation, Galloway claimed. When none stepped forward, he introduced his plan of union in the hope of preventing a catastrophic war. But by the narrowest margin his formula for "*harmony* and *liberty*" was defeated, and for reasons that he was willing to "let America determine," the radicals who had dominated Congress chose a path of "industriously concealing it from the world."[47]

The Tory pamphleteers were answered in numerous essays by patriots, or "Whigs," as they were usually called. Though obscure at the time, two who countered the detractors of Congress would become among the best-known members of the Revolutionary generation. John Adams hurriedly dashed off thirteen newspaper essays to rebut Leonard. Nineteen-year-old Alexander Hamilton responded to Samuel Seabury, the Anglican rector of the town of Westchester, New York.

Adams was a marvelous letter writer, invariably composing his missives with clarity and often with spice and humor. When he wrote for publication, however, his literary style regularly turned cloudy and ponderous, and his articles were nearly unreadable. Writing as "Novanglus" in 1775, Adams poured out an overly lengthy and legalistic opus that could not have been read and understood by many colonists. Even Adams appeared to recognize the hopelessness of reaching an audience with what he had written, as near the end of his slog he characterized his work as a "fatigueing ramble." Through a haze of

Latin and legalese—"*Nos itaque* . . . says King Ed I"; "This statutum Walliae . . . is well worthy of the attention and study of Americans"; "Another incontestable proof of this, is the *ordinatio pro statu Hiberniae*"—Adams set out to prove that the colonies were not subject to the Parliament's jurisdiction. He conceded, as had Congress, that the Americans would submit to Parliament's regulation of imperial commerce, but to be subject to parliamentary taxation would be to accept the yoke of slavery.[48]

Though only an undergraduate at King's College, Alexander Hamilton was the better polemicist of the two. Late in 1774 he answered Seabury with two lively rejoinders. Hamilton, who would later grow famous for his lacerating pen, waged a slash-and-burn offensive against his Tory adversary, denigrating the cleric's writing abilities and thought processes. Most of what Hamilton had to say with regard to constitutional issues had been said before many times over. What was new in Hamilton's pamphlets was his contemplation of hostilities with the mother country, a topic that had been largely off-limits before the worrisome winter of 1775. Of course, Hamilton was responding to a Tory pamphleteer who had asserted that the colonists could not win a war against Great Britain. Hamilton proved to be the superior prophet. He not only took for granted that war was inevitable; he also said that it could be won by the Americans. The colonists could arm more men than Britain could send to subdue the rebellion, he said, and he added that it was inevitable that France and Spain—and, less directly, the Dutch—would aid the Americans. Hamilton granted that the British would have field trained, professional soldiers while the Americans were amateurs, but he forecast that the colonists could win the war by employing Fabian tactics. He explained: "The circumstances of our country put it in our power to evade a pitched battle. It will be better policy to harass and exhaust the [British] soldiery by frequent skirmishes and incursions [than] to take the open field with them."[49]

The tract that appears to have reached the largest audience between Congress's adjournment and the outbreak of hostilities was written by neither Adams nor Hamilton, but by Lieutenant Colonel Charles Lee, a native of Great Britain who had been a redcoat officer for nearly twenty years. He had fought in America in the French and Indian War, suffering wounds in an engagement at Fort Ticonderoga. Shortly after that war, he resigned his commission and moved to Virginia. An acid-tongued eccentric, Lee, who was well educated and capable of wielding a corrosive pen with panache, answered one of the Loyalist pamphleteers. With a writing style that was seldom equaled in rhythm and cadence, Lee defended Congress and devoted some space to the argument that the best way to prevent a war was to prepare for one. But the heart of his piece addressed the question of whether the Americans could win a war against Great Britain. Lee left no doubt that the colonists would be victorious. The British soldiers were overrated and often led by incapable officers who owed their positions more to wealth and politics than to talent. The Americans were inexperienced, he acknowledged, but the art of soldiering was not a mystery. Americans could learn combat skills in short order. Besides, the Americans had a psychological asset. They were fighting for something tangible and invaluable: their liberty. The colonists seemed to welcome Lee's pamphlet as evenhanded and illuminating. For many, it demystified war; while for others, it tore down the mystique of invincibility that shrouded the British army.[50]

The colonists' world changed forever on April 19, 1775, the day that General Gage acted on Dartmouth's order to use force to smash the American rebellion.

Three months elapsed between the dispatch of the American secretary's order and its implementation, a delay occasioned because the ship carrying Dartmouth's order to America was forced by storms to return to England. On its second attempt, the vessel succeeded in making the long, slow Atlantic crossing, docking in Boston during the second week in April. Gage had already drawn up plans for an operation to destroy an arms depot that the rebels had constructed in Concord, about twenty miles west of Boston. It was hardly the only rebel arsenal, but it was the one closest to Boston, and attacking it offered the best hope of completing a lightning strike before the American militiamen in the surrounding countryside could respond. Dartmouth had also ordered Gage to seize the ringleaders of the Massachusetts insurrection. Gage's intelligence had correctly reported that John Hancock and Samuel Adams were residing in Lexington, a tiny village about seven miles east of Concord, near where the rebel provincial assembly was meeting. Like a good soldier, Gage acted rapidly to carry out his orders. He spent a few days ironing out the final details of the march on Lexington and Concord. All the while, he took precautions to keep his plans secret. No one knew better than Gage that surprise was vital to the success of his operation.

Gage's efforts at stealth came to grief. The rebels had their own surveillance network. Through spies, abundant clues, and loose-lipped British officers (and possibly their wives), American intelligence gleaned a day or two in advance that Gage was preparing a march. By about ten P.M. on April 18 the rebels knew that Concord was the target. An hour later Paul Revere set off on his most famous ride, and at about the same time William Dawes, a Boston tanner, also set off to carry the alarm to Lexington, though he rode a different route. Revere had been given Brown Beauty, the fastest horse available. Speed was crucial for Revere. He was to race westward from Charlestown and alert Hancock and Adams to flee before the regulars arrived. While in Lexington, Revere was also to awaken the residents and let them know that Gage's soldiers were coming. Next, he was to spur his mount to Concord and spread the alarm. It is likely that Revere and Dawes were only two of several riders who set off from near Boston on that clear, mild night. Others likely rode different routes to towns scattered through the hinterland. Their mission was to awaken militiamen—and especially the so-called minutemen, some one third of the men in each Massachusetts militia company who were to be ready to march "on a minute's notice"—so that they could descend on the Concord Road and intercept the redcoats' formidable striking force of more than nine hundred men. Furthermore, once a town was alerted, it almost always sent one of its own to neighboring towns to sound the alarm.

Thinking the lobsterbacks were only a step behind, Revere pushed Brown Beauty to her limit. He had more time than he realized. At midnight, the regulars marched to Boston's Back Bay, but the navy bollixed the plans for rapidly transporting the soldiers across the Charles River. It was past two A.M. before the redcoats actually stepped off along Concord Road. The first streaks of sunrise were visible in the eastern sky by the time they finally reached Lexington. Nearly five hours had elapsed since Revere, whose ride was four miles shorter than Dawes's, had reached the town, sounded the alert, and persuaded Hancock and Adams to flee. Long before the regulars arrived, some sixty Lexington militiamen under Captain John Parker, a forty-six-year-old farmer and mechanic who was deep in the fatal clutches of tuberculosis, had assembled on the village green to await them.

When the regulars entered Lexington, Lieutenant Colonel Francis Smith, whom Gage had put in charge of the day's operation, detached six companies—about 240 men—under Major John Pitcairn to disband and disarm the rebel militiamen under Captain Parker. Pitcairn marched his regulars toward the village green. The immaculate, red-clad regulars advanced smartly on the ragged, white-faced Americans. As the early-morning light glinted off the bayonets of his soldiers, Pitcairn wasted no time on pleasantries. Visibly contemptuous of the armed yeomen and tradesmen before him, Pitcairn loudly and curtly commanded, "Lay down your arms, you damned rebels!" One of the villagers heard another British officer cry out, "Ye villains, ye rebels, disperse, damn you, disperse!" Seeing that he was outnumbered by as much as four to one, and hardly wishing to be arrested and charged with treason, Parker rapidly ordered his men to hold their fire and disperse. But he did not command them to surrender their arms. As the men disbanded, someone fired a shot. It might have been a horribly ill-timed accidental discharge of a weapon. Or, just as likely, a nervous or trigger-happy soldier on either side may have squeezed off the shot. Many thought it was fired by someone hiding behind a nearby stone wall, someone who was not a soldier. Whoever it was that discharged his weapon, he had fired the first shot in what was to be an eight-year war.

The musket's loud blast set off a chain reaction among the edgy redcoats. Several fired into ranks of the militiamen. To Revere, who was still in Lexington, the volley sounded like a "continual roar of musketry." A handful of militiamen answered with fire of their own, though most of the citizen-soldiers broke and fled for safety. British officers screamed the order to cease firing, but they had difficulty controlling their men, who were now flooded with adrenaline. With a febrile intensity, scores of redcoats charged after the bolting Americans. By the time order was restored, a pall of white smoke and the odor of burnt powder hung heavy over Lexington Green. Bodies littered the commons—some the victims of gunfire, some of bayonets. From start to finish, the incident in Lexington had lasted no more than a couple of minutes, but the carnage was incredible. Seventeen Americans were casualties, many suffering horrid wounds. Eight colonists were dead. One regular had been hit, though his wound was not life-threatening.

Colonel Smith did not linger in Lexington. His objective was Concord, nearly seven miles away. Revere and Dawes, who had rendezvoused in the village, had long since departed to warn the residents of Concord and those who lived along the way. Neither Revere nor Dawes succeeded in reaching their destination. Near Lincoln, about halfway to Concord, Revere was taken captive by a patrol of British regulars, but he was released after a brief detention. He returned to Lexington and witnessed the shooting. Dawes barely escaped the same patrol, after which he too came back to Lexington. But Concord was warned during the still, dark night by Dr. Samuel Prescott, a local physician who was courting his girlfriend in Lexington when he heard the alarm carried by Revere. He galloped home to spread the word.

Thus, by nine A.M., when the redcoats at last marched into Concord under a bright sun high in a blue sky, the residents had known for several hours that they were coming. Nevertheless, the regulars marched into the village unopposed. Colonel James Barrett, the Middlesex regimental commander who was the officer in charge of the five trainband companies that were present in Concord—probably a bit fewer than two hundred men—found himself, like Captain Parker, badly outnumbered and unwilling to order his men to resist the king's troops.

The regulars set right to work destroying the arsenal. During their first hours in town, few of the hardworking, sweaty soldiers saw the Concord militia, which remained passively on its muster field across the Concord River, nearly a mile away. As the morning progressed, Concord's militiamen were joined by minutemen who arrived from neighboring towns. Slowly, steadily, the American force grew. By midmorning nearly five hundred militiamen were present. Wired and eager for a fight, some pleaded with Colonel Barrett, a sixty-year-old miller who had taken the field this day wearing his soiled leather work apron, to do something. Still outnumbered, Barrett refused to budge. But around eleven A.M. the militiamen spotted black smoke curling above the bare trees in Concord. Though the regulars had torched only ordnance in the arsenal, word spread like wildfire that the British army was burning the town. Barrett could wait no longer. He ordered his men to load their pieces and march to the North Bridge that spanned the river. The Americans found 115 redcoats guarding the bridge on the other side. Men on both sides were jittery and armed, a dangerous combination. The lead element among the militiamen crowded onto the bridge and moved forward. As the rebels advanced, a shot rang out. This time there was no mistaking its source. A British soldier had fired his musket. As had happened at Lexington, the sharp, jolting sound of the shot caused men on both sides to open fire. The exchange was brief but deadly. Six Americans were wounded, two fatally. One who died was Captain Isaac Davis, an Acton farmer who had built a firing range behind his house to hone his skills as a marksman; he was shot through the heart in the first nanosecond of his combat experience. Twelve regulars were cut down by the return fire of the rebels. Three suffered mortal wounds, the first of the king's soldiers to perish at the hands of colonists.

The regulars at the bridge fled after one volley, joining their comrades in town. Colonel Smith had long since known that the hoped-for secrecy of his mission had been lost. With the arsenal nearly destroyed, and faced with a march to Boston that would require hours, he immediately abandoned further work in Concord and set his force on its return home. Throughout that golden afternoon, a seemingly endless stream of American militiamen arrived and took up positions along bucolic Concord Road. Before the sun set, men from at least twenty-three Massachusetts villages were present and fighting, and their numbers had swelled to almost three thousand, providing the colonists with a considerable numerical superiority. Firefights raged up and down the road. Militiamen, concealed behind stone walls, trees, barns, and haystacks, laid down a triangulated fire on the retreating regulars. It was a bloodbath, and only the arrival of redcoat reinforcements summoned after the skirmish in Lexington prevented the killing or capture of the entirety of Smith's original force.

War brings out the best and the worst in people. Catherine Louisa Smith,

Abigail Adams's sister-in-law, who lived about halfway between Concord and Lexington, helped a badly wounded grenadier into her house and tried to nurse him; the soldier died and was buried on the Yankee farm.[51] Heroism was displayed by the fighting men on both sides, but wanton cruelty was in evidence as well. Victimized by snipers who fired from inside houses, contingents of regulars at times stormed dwellings in search of partisans. When the soldiers invaded a home, they often gave no quarter. Those who entered the houses following the battle sometimes found bodies strewn about, and one witness exclaimed that the butchery in one residence was so immense that "Blud was half over [my] Shoes." Others reported finding civilians who had been stabbed, bludgeoned, and shot, and one told of discovering the inhabitants' "brains out on the floor and walls." Not infrequently, the king's soldiers plundered and burned houses and killed livestock.[52]

As darkness spread over the blood-soaked landscape, the regulars at last reached Boston, and safety. By then, 94 colonists were dead or wounded. The British army had suffered 272 casualties. Dartmouth had said in his order to use force that Gage should not expect much opposition. Sixty-five of Gage's men lay dead at day's end on April 19.[53]

As that cold, gray spring of 1775 little by little crept toward disaster, George Washington, who was more than a thousand miles removed from Lexington and Concord, frequently hunted, passionately landscaped Mount Vernon, and oversaw the preparation of his fields for the season's crop of wheat.[54] He had returned home from Congress doubting that war was likely, but the imperial crisis was never far from his thoughts.

Washington had attended the Continental Congress persuaded that North's ministry was advancing "a premeditated Design and System . . . to introduce an arbitrary Government into his Majesty's American Dominions." He had thought of the Tea Act and Coercive Acts as "despotick Measures" that were part of a "regular, systematic plan" to "fix the Shackles of Slavery upon us." No less important, Washington had come to understand that Britain had "a separate, and . . . opposite Interest" from that of the colonies. He had openly stated that the colonies must be "treated upon an equal Footing with our fellow subjects" in England under a "just, lenient, permanent, and constitutional" framework.[55] He was fed up with "Petitions & Remonstrances" even before Congress met. Truth be told, he probably already favored American independence. What seems abundantly clear is that long before the march on Lexington and Concord, Washington had been prepared to go to war unless the British government backed down.[56]

The events in Lexington and Concord made it apparent that London would not back down. Washington was convinced that the colonists must not give in. A "Brother's Sword has been sheathed in a Brother's breast," he immediately declared when word of the carnage in Massachusetts reached Mount Vernon late in April. He added that the "once happy and peaceful plains of America are either to be drenched with blood, or Inhabited by Slaves." His choice was never in doubt. Indeed, he emphasized that no "virtuous Man" could "hesitate in his choice."[57]

Washington departed Mount Vernon for Philadelphia and the Second Continental Congress on May 4, 1775, taking with him his military uniform. He was going to war. Unlike Dartmouth and North, Washington harbored no illusions that this would be an easy war. "[M]ore blood will be spilt" in the coming conflict, he predicted, "than history has ever yet furnished instances of in the annals of North America."[58]

CHAPTER 5

"A RESCRIPT
WRITTEN IN BLOOD"

JOHN DICKINSON AND THE
APPEAL OF RECONCILIATION

IT TURNED COLD AND RAINY overnight in Boston, but all through the jet-black evening that followed the battle-scarred day in Lexington and Concord, armed men from throughout New England had descended on the city. Some had abandoned workbenches and farms on a moment's notice to take up arms. Israel Putnam, for instance, a fifty-seven-year-old yeoman who had endured a lifetime of adventure while soldiering in the French and Indian War, literally dropped his plow in his field in Pomfret, Connecticut, picked up his sword and musket, and headed for the scene of action, ready to serve yet again. One company of exhausted minutemen from Nottingham, New Hampshire, arrived outside Boston at daybreak on April 20, having made an incredible fifty-five-mile march in twenty hours.[1]

By morning's gray dawn on April 20, thousands of armed men had congregated on Boston's doorstep. They came as four separate armies, one from each of the New England colonies. But as they were on Massachusetts soil, the highest-ranking officer in the Bay Colony, General Artemas Ward, a forty-seven-year-old Shrewsbury farmer, businessman, and judge with two degrees from Harvard College, was in overall command. His army swelled rapidly. Men arrived all through April 20 and the days that followed, until, after a week, some sixteen thousand Yankee soldiers were present. While the rage for soldiering prevailed, Ward wisely had the men take an oath to serve for the remainder of the year. Impassioned and eager for heroics—and confronted with incredible peer pressure—most of the men signed on. A few thought better of it and went home, in many instances fearing that their farms and families would suffer during their prolonged absence. Some, however, may have suspected that the chaos all about them was an augury of miseries ahead. After all, the newborn army lacked tents, hygienic conditions were

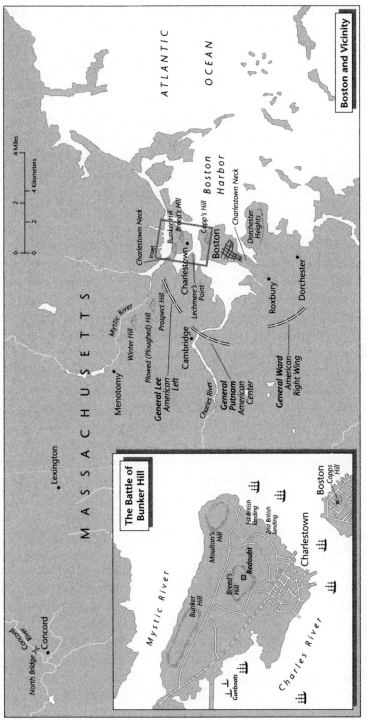

Boston and Vicity

ATLANTIC

OCEAN

M A S S A C H U S E T T S

Lexington

North Bridge
Concord
Concord River

Menotomy

Mystic River

Winter Hill

Plowed (Ploughed) Hill

Prospect Hill

General Lee
American
Left

Cambridge

Charles River

General Putnam
American
Center

General Ward
American
Right Wing

Roxbury

Dorchester

Charlestown Neck
Inlet
Bunker Hill
Breed's Hill
Copp's Hill

Charlestown

Lechmere's
Point

Boston

Charlestown Neck

Dorchester
Heights

Boston Harbor

0   2   4 Miles
0   2   4 Kilometers

The Battle of Bunker Hill

Mystic River

Bunker
Hill

Moulton's
Hill

Breed's
Hill

Redoubt

1st British
landing

2nd British
landing

Charlestown

Boston

Copps Hill

Gunboats

Charles River

(Gary J. Antonetti, Ortelius Design)

deplorable, and a thousand and one logistical details were yet to be worked out.

Nevertheless, after a few days Ward knew that he had an army of roughly twelve thousand men, more than double the number that Gage was thought to possess. Yet Ward never considered attacking the British. At least until the Continental Congress reconvened as scheduled on May 10, nearly three weeks in the future, Ward saw his army's mission as one of containing the British army within Boston. New England newspapers quickly dubbed the siege army the "Grand American Army," and General Ward just as rapidly deployed his men all along the periphery of Boston in a twelve-mile arc that stretched from east of the Mystic River to the north to Roxbury and Dorchester to the south of the city.[2]

Those who had been chosen to sit in the Second Congress were preparing to leave for Philadelphia, and their responses to the outbreak of hostilities differed wildly. Galloway, though reelected, had decided to resign his seat and quit the Pennsylvania assembly as well. He did not wish to be part of any government that was at war with the mother country. Galloway also feared for his safety. It was bad enough to be regarded as an "apostate" by the other congressmen, but he was badly unnerved when someone sent a box to his home containing a noose and a note asking that he kill himself and "rid the World of a Damned Scoundrel."[3] New York's Robert R. Livingston, who was every bit as conservative as Galloway, was elected to Congress on the day before word of the Lexington and Concord battles reached Manhattan. Friends urged him not to attend the Congress, but he refused to listen. "My property is here [and] I cannot remove it," he told them. "I am resolved to stand or fall with my country."[4] John Dickinson, who charged London with having started an "impious War of Tyranny against Innocence," was eager to be part of this congress.[5] So too was Richard Henry Lee, who raged that General Gage had launched "a wanton and cruel Attack on unarmed people . . . brutally [killing] Old Men, Women, & Children."[6]

John Adams declared that Britain's use of force had "changed the Instruments of Warfare from the Penn to the Sword." He laid aside his quill, mercifully bringing to an end his Novanglus essays, and hurried to Lexington, wishing to speak with witnesses to the incident on Lexington Green, as well as to residents along what was now and ever after called Battle Road. He found that his fellow colonists were ready for war. The "Die was cast, the Rubicon passed," they told him, adding that they had fought on April 19 because "if We did not defend ourselves they would kill Us." He saw abundant evidence of the recent engagement. Adams rode down Battle Road, still littered with the rotting corpses of horses and other residue of the bloody clash, and he spoke with civilians and militiamen, some with ghastly wounds. It was a profoundly disturbing experience. Aside from any haunting questions that might have troubled him regarding his accountability for having brought on hostilities, Adams was anxious for the well-being of his wife and four children, who lived even closer to Boston than did the inhabitants of Lexington and Concord. Would they, too, face similar horrors? Overwrought by his day at the scene of suffering, Adams fell ill that evening "with alarming Symptoms."[7]

War created a new set of political problems for Samuel Adams. For one thing, he feared that some Americans, including the most conservative congressmen, might be swayed by Lord Chatham's February peace proposal. Chatham, after all, was lionized in America, and his plan for saving the empire could be distilled to a simple and possibly attractive means of avoiding war: The colonies would recognize parliamentary sovereignty in return for Parliament's renunciation of American taxation. Adams went on the offensive, writing some of his congressional colleagues to implore them to "take Care lest America in Lieu of a Thorn in the Foot should have a Dagger in her heart."[8]

Notwithstanding what his cousin John had written in excitement, Samuel Adams, and the coterie of radical leaders who surrounded him, realized that the pen, as well as the sword, was an essential weapon in this war. They rapidly set out to convince colonists throughout America that the British regulars, acting on orders from London, had been responsible for firing the first shot. They also wished to persuade both colonists and residents in the mother country that the American militiamen had bravely stood up to the British regulars and, in fact, had defeated them.

On the day after the fighting, Revere saddled up again. This time he rode at the behest of the Massachusetts Committee of Safety, which from the Hastings House in Cambridge directed day-to-day activities for the defiant rebel government in Massachusetts. Revere spent seventeen days on the road disseminating the committee's account of what had occurred on Lexington Green and the North Bridge in Concord. One Boston firebrand called the story that Revere broadcast an "authentick account of this inhuman proceeding." In fact, the purpose of the Committee of Safety was to wage what historian David Hackett Fischer has called "the second battle of Lexington and Concord": the battle for public opinion. It moved quickly to tell its version of the events of that historic day, dispatching numerous riders to committees of correspondence inside Massachusetts and beyond. The Committee of Safety also published a broadside—a single-page handbill—with a description of the attack on Captain Parker's militiamen under the screaming headline BARBAROUS MURDERS. It additionally subsidized the *Massachusetts Spy*, whose editor had wisely removed his printing press from Boston to the safety of Worcester just three days before the fighting. In the days following, that newspaper ran repeated hyperbolic accounts of the engagements. Its motto was "Americans! Liberty or Death: Join or Die!"[9]

As the Massachusetts Committee of Safety hoped would be the case, newspapers across America promptly ran accounts of the events of April 19, virtually all of them utilizing materials distributed through the committees of correspondence. Within seventy-two hours the story was in print in every New England colony, and in less than a week residents of New York and Philadelphia could read a narrative of what had transpired. The newspaper accounts played on a few simple themes: "his *Brittanick* Majesty commenced Hostilities upon the People" of America; the tragedy was the result of the "sanguinary Measures of a wicked Ministry"; the citizens of Lexington and Concord, and the residents along Battle Road, had suffered cruelties no "less brutal than what our venerable Ancestors received from the vilest Savages of the Wilderness"; and by day's end the British regulars had been "decisively defeated."[10] Some newspapers ran their stories inside black borders. One ran the headline: BLOODY NEWS. A New England broadside depicted a row of coffins beneath the headline BLOODY BUTCHERY BY THE BRITISH TROOPS. The *New-York Journal* told its readers that "our good mother [country is] . . . at last revealed to all the world . . . a vile imposter—an old abandoned prostitute—crimsoned oe'r with every abominable crime, shocking to humanity."[11]

These lurid though vague accounts of what had occurred were augmented by the publication of depositions taken from more than one hundred civilians and militiamen—and even captured British regulars—who had been in Lexington or Concord or somewhere along Battle Road on April 19. Within four days of the fighting, representatives of the Massachusetts Committee of Safety began taking sworn statements, which were rushed into print. Needless to say, these accounts stated that the regulars had fired the first shots in both Lexington and Concord. There were slight differences in the various accounts of the historic instant when the first shot was fired on Lexington Green, but all fixed the blame on the redcoats:

> A British officer shouted "damn them, we will have them," and immediately the regulars "shouted aloud, run, and fired on the *Lexington* Company, which did not fire a gun before."

> The regulars' commander "flourishing his sword and with a loud voice giving the word fire; which was instantly followed by a discharge of arms by said Regular Troops."

The regulars' commander ordered his men, saying "Fire, by *God*, Fire; at which moment we received a very heavy and close fire from them."

"[W]hilst our backs were turned on the Troops we were fired on by them . . . Not a Gun was fired by any person in our Company."

"[S]ome of our Company were coming to the parade with their backs towards the Troops, and others on the parade began to disperse, when the Regulars fired . . . before a gun was fired by any our Company on them."

The commander of the regulars shouted "'Fire! Fire, damn you, fire!' and immediately they fired before any of Captain Parker's Company fired."[12]

The Massachusetts Committee of Safety additionally published several letters that it claimed had been written by captured or killed British soldiers. On encountering the "peasants" in Lexington, wrote one redcoat, his commander "ordered us to rush them with our bayonets fixed . . . and the engagement began." Another divulged that "We . . . burnt some of their houses." Several mentioned the suffering of Boston's residents. As there "is no market in *Boston*, the inhabitants [are] all starving," one reported, while a comrade wrote that the "people in Boston are in great trouble, for General Gage will not let the Town's people go out" to gather provisions.[13]

On April 25 the Committee of Safety learned that General Gage's report of the battle was to be conveyed to London that same day by the *Sukey*, a two-hundred-ton brig loaded with cargo and owned by a Boston merchant. Knowing the importance of first impressions, the committee moved hurriedly to present its version to London before the *Sukey* crossed the Atlantic. It chose as its courier Captain John Derby of Salem, owner of the *Quero*, a lean and speedy sixty-ton vessel with a schooner's rigging. He departed from Salem four days after the *Sukey* weighed anchor in Boston. To hasten his voyage, Derby sailed without cargo. He did not even carry any correspondence, save for that provided by the committee: copies of the hastily transcribed eyewitness depositions; two issues of the *Salem Gazette*, each of which carried accounts of the April 19 engagements; and a letter from the committee addressed "To the Inhabitants of Great Britain." Written by Dr. Joseph Warren, the letter declared that the regulars had started hostilities by firing on the Lexington and Concord militiamen, acts that he characterized as a premeditated mark of "ministerial vengeance against this Colony." Warren vowed that Americans "will not tamely submit . . . we determine to die or be free."[14]

Derby won the race. In a day when Atlantic crossings often took six weeks or more, the *Quero* sped across the white-capped ocean in thirty days. Despite his rival's head start, Derby outpaced the *Sukey* by nearly two weeks. Within forty-eight hours of the docking of the *Quero*, Arthur Lee, Richard Henry Lee's brother, who lived in the English metropolis, put a note in a London newspaper revealing that the depositions were available for public perusal at the office of the lord mayor of London. Edward Gibbon, a member of Parliament who later achieved greater renown as a historian, was one of many who read Lee's squib and hurried to the mayor's Mansion House to read what Derby had brought. Gibbon's reaction was not untypical. "This looks serious," he exclaimed, but Gibbon was less startled by the bloodshed on April 19 than by the news that the "next day the Country rose" to besiege Boston.

During the next few days it was apparent that the Massachusetts Committee of Safety had won at least the initial battle of public opinion in London. Several newspapers printed accounts of atrocities supposedly committed by Gage's soldiers, and one cried out against the "cruel and inhuman proceedings of our army there," adding that the conduct of the redcoats had "as never before disgraced the character of British soldiery." A week after the *Quero* arrived, a despondent friend of the administration wrote in a London newspaper that the Yankees had persuaded many in England of American blamelessness. "The Bostonians are now the favourites of all the people of good hearts and weak heads in the kingdom," he said, adding that the New Englanders "saint-like account of the skirmish at Concord, has been read with avidity . . . [and] believed."[15]

Within two weeks of the fighting, delegates from throughout America began their trek to Philadelphia for the Second Continental Congress. They found a country in the grip of war fever. Great Britain's unsparing callousness, said one congressman, had "roused a universal Military spirit." Companies of soldiers greeted the congressmen on the edge of many towns and, with flags waving and often a small martial band playing spirited tunes, escorted them into the village. Sometimes the delegates reviewed the troops—the volunteers "go thro their Exercises extremely Clever," gushed one deputy—and in the larger cities they were often part of a substantial parade, riding through downtown flanked by proudly marching soldiers and gaudily clad cavalrymen astride sleek mounts. (As the Massachusetts delegates rode through New York City, the sounds of the martial band spooked the horse pulling John Adams's carriage, causing the vehicle to overturn and be dragged for several yards; its driver was badly banged up in the accident, but only moments before, Adams had fortunately shifted to another carriage.) The grandest reception was the one that Philadelphia threw for the Massachusetts, Connecticut, and New York delegations, which approached the city together. The congressmen were escorted into Philadelphia by nearly three hundred city officials and soldiers, many bearing fearsome-looking swords. As they entered the city, the congressmen found the "Bells all ringing, and the air rent with Shouts and huzza's" from the large crowds that lined the streets.[16]

John Adams, who had anguished after discovering that a majority at the First Congress abhorred the thought of war, exulted at the militant spirit that he encountered en route to Philadelphia. He was especially happy to see the pugnacity on exhibit in Manhattan, whose delegates the previous autumn had been Galloway's greatest supporters. "The Tories are put to Flight here," Adams rejoiced as he passed through New York City. By the time he reached Philadelphia, Adams was confident that every colony would join the war effort, and he was hopeful that the colonies could replace their lost British trade with commerce from Europe, for he was certain that America's "cause . . . interests the whole Globe."[17]

Before it had adjourned in October, the First Congress had set Wednesday, May 10, as the day for reconvening. However, given the woeful state of America's roads, which were made worse by heavy spring rains, not every delegate reached Philadelphia on time. Congress began anyway. As the Massachusetts delegates circulated among their colleagues, recounting treacheries allegedly committed by the British soldiers and spreading the falsehood that Captain Parker's men had not returned the regulars' fire on that fateful morning, Congress spent a couple of days tending to housekeeping.[18] The delegates presented their credentials, reelected Peyton Randolph as president of Congress and Charles Thomson as secretary, agreed once again to meet in secret, and—with Galloway not in attendance—voted to meet in the capacious Pennsylvania State House rather than Carpenters' Hall. With sixty-five members expected, ten more than had attended in the fall, the delegates needed a larger space. "We have a very full Congress," Washington noted, and when the Pennsylvania assembly once again offered to surrender its downstairs chamber and move upstairs, he and his fellow delegates readily accepted.[19]

Though larger than its predecessor, this Congress had a familiar look. Fifty of the delegates who had sat in the First Congress returned. They were joined by a delegate from Georgia, the only colony that had not been represented at the earlier meeting, and by congressmen from four colonies that had expanded their delegations. Two of the newcomers were already widely known: John Hancock had been added to the Massachusetts contingent and Benjamin Franklin, safely home from London, was elected to Pennsylvania's delegation shortly after he disembarked at the Philadelphia docks.

Within a week of landing, but before Congress assembled, Franklin used a carriage provided by Galloway to ride to Trevose, north of the city, to see his old political partner for the first time in more than a decade. Franklin's purpose was to persuade Galloway not to retire from public affairs. "[Y]our Abilities are so much wanted," Franklin told him in a note that he sent a day or two prior to his visit. Franklin remained at Galloway's estate overnight, and the two men discussed the Anglo-American crisis into the wee hours of the morning. Franklin tried to convince Galloway that reconciliation with the mother country was impossible, save on London's terms, and as proof he read to his younger associate from the journal he had kept during his discussions in December and January with the surrogates of Lord Dartmouth. Galloway was unmoved. His health had been ruined by his public service, he said, and indeed he was gaunt and looked considerably older than age forty-five. Galloway had other, better, reasons for remaining detached from public life. While he wanted no part of a war against the mother country, he also realized that his public attacks on Congress and his published revelations of what had occurred in the First Congress's secret sessions had burned his bridges. He could never again be a power in the Continental Congress. Sullied with the taint of Toryism, he knew all too well that he was "despised and Contemned by all," as a New England congressman in fact remarked in private that very week. Two days after Congress was gaveled into session, Galloway formally submitted his resignation. Franklin did not give up easily. On two other occasions during the ensuing months, he met with Galloway and pleaded with him to rejoin Congress. He also urged Galloway to support the war. Galloway was not swayed. He would remain neutral, loyal neither to Congress nor to Great Britain, he said.[20]

By the time Congress reconvened, the delegates were aware that Parliament had spurned Chatham's early-winter peace proposal. Every member believed that North's government wished the total subjugation of the colonies. General Gage's dispatch of his regulars on April 19 only confirmed in their minds that the ministry was unwilling to back down. Every delegate to the Second Congress was committed to waging war.

Even so, there were divisions among these delegates. The first difference to surface would be the greatest of all. In the initial days of this congress, South Carolina's John Rutledge asked his colleagues what America was fighting for: "do We aim at independency? or do We only ask for a Restoration of Rights & putting of Us on Our old footing?"[21] A wide-ranging debate followed, in the course of which it was evident that the overwhelming majority remained committed to reconciliation. But it was just as plain that the delegates were divided over what steps to take, if any, beyond the use of force and the ongoing boycott to restore harmony with London.

The previous congress had been splintered, and the question of how to seek reconciliation with the mother country likewise split this congress into two factions. The more moderate faction was led by John Dickinson.

Dickinson, who was forty-three in 1775, was tall and slender and "pale as ashes," so sickly looking that some of his fellow delegates at first thought "he could not live a Month." The cause of his chronic health problems is unknown, though by this time his physical woes were exacerbated by gout, perhaps the reason that his gait was noticeably stiff and awkward. Dickinson's backswept hair had already turned gray, and his heavily lined face was dominated by an aquiline nose and warm eyes that shone with earnest sincerity. Although he was reserved, new acquaintances invariably thought him modest, friendly, restlessly intelligent, eloquent, and persuasive.[22]

Dickinson was born into an affluent Quaker family in Talbot County, Maryland. His father was a lawyer, magistrate, tobacco planter, and land baron who own owned more than sixteen thousand acres. When tobacco prices collapsed in the 1740s, the Dickinsons moved to Kent, Delaware, and shifted to grain production. Most of John's youth was spent at Poplar Hill, a handsome three thousand-acre estate not far from Philadelphia. At age eighteen, after years of study with a tutor, he moved to the city to read law with a practicing attorney, the conventional means of becoming a lawyer in the colonies. But ambitious and well-to-do, Dickinson after three years sailed for London, where in 1754 he enrolled in the Middle Temple, the only law school in the empire. If Samuel Adams was a rarity among colonists in that he earned two degrees, Dickinson was one of only a handful of eighteenth-century Americans who was awarded a formal law degree.

Dickinson was also one of the few native-born colonists who had experienced life in the mother country. He crossed the Atlantic alive with excitement at the prospect of living in the imperial capital. At first, he admitted his "awe & reverence" at nearly every thing he encountered, but soon Dickinson grew jaded. Early in his three-year stay, he exclaimed that the English "nobility in general are the most ordinary men I ever faced." Their prominence, he concluded, was attributable more "to fortune than to their worth." In due time he came to believe that England was in the throes of decadence. Traditional religion was on the wane. The gentility "despised" their social inferiors. The successful colonist was "nothing" in their eyes. He came to equate English

*John Dickinson by Charles Wilson Peale, 1770. Dickinson led the faction in Congress
that sought reconciliation with Great Britain. He supported the war but refused to vote for
independence. (Independence National Historical Park Collection, Philadelphia)*

political practices with those in Rome in its last, debased days. He noted that
bribery was "so common" it was a mainstay in parliamentary elections; he
estimated that more than a million pounds was spent buying votes each election. "It is grown a vice here to be virtuous," he remarked. It took Dickinson
less than six months to reach the same conclusion that took the reluctant
Franklin more than a decade. The "corruption of the age" had eddied into
nearly every corner of English life, Dickinson thought, but the political structure in particular had become a cesspool of degeneracy. It made him yearn
for his homeland. "America is, to be sure, a wilderness, & yet that wilderness
to me is more pleasing" and pristine than England.[23] More than anything,
he hoped to keep British officials out of America, lest the venality that
spawned them spread to the New World.

Dickinson was disillusioned with the mother country when he returned
home in 1758, but he was not a revolutionary. He plunged into his legal practice in Philadelphia, which flourished immediately. Rapidly rising to the top
of his profession, he surpassed other prominent lawyers, among them Galloway, who had been practicing law for the better part of a decade before Dickinson embarked on his legal career. Like Galloway, Dickinson became a
member of several prestigious Philadelphia clubs and quickly entered politics. He served first in the Delaware assembly before being elected to Pennsylvania's legislature in 1762. He entered it together with Franklin, who had just

returned from his initial long stay in London seeking to alter proprietary practices.

During his first year in the assembly, Dickinson sided with Franklin and Galloway on most issues. In fact, Dickinson's background was so remarkably similar to Galloway's that the two initially got along well enough. Only two years separated them, and both hailed from Quaker families that had moved in the same year from the same part of Maryland to Kent, Delaware. However, in 1764, when Galloway was thirty-four and Dickinson was thirty-two, politics turned them into bitter enemies. The break came when the Assembly Party petitioned the king to strip the proprietors of all authority and transform Pennsylvania into a royal colony.

Dickinson was appalled by the thought of royalization. He was close to the Penns, so close that while he was in England, Thomas Penn, the proprietor of Pennsylvania, had taken him to St. James's Palace for George II's birthday reception. Even more, after witnessing what he thought was the dissolution throughout English society and politics, Dickinson had no wish to see the reach of the mother country extended any deeper into the affairs of the colonies. He particularly feared that the Pennsylvania assembly, which he saw as the "guardian of the public liberties" enjoyed by Pennsylvanians, would be fatally weakened should the proprietary governor be replaced by a Crown-appointed chief executive.[24] During 1764, Dickinson joined what came to be known as the Proprietary Party, or New Ticket, a faction that was strongest in the western counties, whose inhabitants felt exploited by the dominant eastern counties in matters of taxation and services.

Eloquent, sophisticated, and probably the best-educated public official in the province, Dickinson almost immediately assumed the lead in the fight against Franklin and Galloway. In hot and intemperate assembly debates, Dickinson's conservative stance presaged the position he would often take later in Congress. To Dickinson, change—almost any change—was inadvisable. He seldom wished to run the risk that accompanied making even the slightest transformation. As to royalization, Dickinson cautioned that the gamble was too great. The change might lead to the loss of those bountiful guarantees of religious freedom that Pennsylvanians had enjoyed since William Penn established the colony seventy-five years before. Freedom had been lost in ancient Rome and, more recently, in Denmark by a "neglect of . . . prudence," which had resulted in the surrender of "liberties to their king," he warned. Wariness must be the watchword of Pennsylvanians. "Power is like the *ocean*, not easily admitting limits to be fixed in it," he asserted. In the torrid daily debates that ensued, Dickinson came close to charging that the

Assembly Party's campaign for royalization was a thinly disguised endeavor to fulfill Galloway's and Franklin's insatiable ambition to hold loftier offices and gain ever more power.[25]

Galloway responded that the Crown "shews its Limits; they are known and confined." Only rarely, he added gingerly, has any monarch made "any Attempts ... to extend them." But an air of fatalism permeated Galloway's retort. The Crown and Parliament were sovereign over the colonies and could do as they wished. All Americans, he said, were at the mercy of what "Our Superiors think ... convenient."[26]

As Franklin's and Galloway's Assembly Party was in the majority, the legislature adopted the petition to the king in May. Thereafter, both Galloway and Dickinson published the speeches they had delivered in the legislative battle. Both carefully excised the ill-tempered remarks they had made in the floor debate.[27] As was so often the case, however, Franklin stirred the pot. In a preface to Galloway's tract, Franklin sarcastically attacked "Mr. Dickenson"— likely deliberately misspelling his name—whom he portrayed as a parvenu who passed himself off as "a *Sage* in the Law, and an *Oracle* in Matters relating to our Constitution."[28] Dickinson responded with a second pamphlet. Though he shrank from rebuking the more popular Franklin, he went after Galloway, and in a petty and vituperative manner. He assailed Galloway's want of "humanity and *decency*," his "cruel" rhetoric, lack of understanding of history, faulty reasoning, "falsehoods," and penchant for "calumnies and *conspiracies*." Dickinson even alluded to Galloway's allegedly "continual breaches of the rules of grammar; his utter ignorance of the English language; the *pompous obscurity* and *sputtering prolixity* reigning through every part of his piece; and his innumerable and feeble tautologies."[29] Dickinson had declared war on Galloway.

Galloway gave as good as he got, at one point portraying Dickinson as driven by a "restless thirst after promotion."[30] The acrimonious charges and countercharges brought things to the breaking point. The two squared off in a fistfight in the yard outside the Pennsylvania State House. Galloway appears to have gotten the best of it. Toward the end of the battle, he was flaying Dickinson with his cane when bystanders intervened to halt the brawl. Dickinson immediately challenged his foe to a duel, though cooler heads prevailed and further violence was averted.[31] Each man thereafter refrained from further publications that defamed the other. But a combustible environment had been created, and party members on both sides joined the fray during the fall election campaign. Some who were bolder than Dickinson lashed out at Franklin, calling him a libertine devoid of moral principles, even breaking the news to the world that young William Franklin was his father's illegitimate child. Astoundingly, when the balloting was completed in October 1764, Dickinson was reelected and both Galloway and Franklin were defeated, although their Assembly Party retained control of the legislature.[32] The losers complained of election fraud, though Franklin candidly acknowledged that he and his partner had been injured among German-American voters by anti-German comments he had made. Primarily, however, Franklin and Galloway had gone down to defeat because many voters shared Dickinson's apprehension about converting Pennsylvania into a royal colony.[33]

It was in this white-hot atmosphere of partisanship that word of the Stamp Act reached Philadelphia. Dickinson and the Proprietary Party waged a battle against it, as much from opposition to parliamentary taxation as from the hope of destroying Galloway and Franklin and wrecking their cherished scheme of royalization. Though lacking a majority in the assembly, the Proprietary Party succeeded in having the legislature send a delegation to the Stamp Act Congress in New York that autumn. Chosen to be part of the delegation, Dickinson played a key role in that conclave and had a hand in writing the Declaration of Rights. When he returned to Philadelphia, Dickinson published a broadside proclaiming that the "critical time is now come" for Pennsylvanians to decide whether they "shall be Freemen or Slaves." He followed that with *The Late Regulations Respecting the British Colonies*, his first pamphlet aimed at reaching a national audience. It was published in London as well and reached such a large readership that it went through two printings.[34]

Continuing to speak out, Dickinson in 1766 authored a pamphlet that aimed at arousing opposition to parliamentary taxation in Great Britain's Caribbean colonies.[35] But it was what he penned the following year that made Dickinson not only the most renowned American political figure but also the most widely respected public official in all the colonies.

Dickinson had been stirred in 1766 by Parliament's suspension of the New York assembly for its defiance of the Quartering Act. The Townshend Duties came hard on the heels of that step. Beginning in November 1767, Dickinson answered both actions of Parliament with a series of a dozen essays—he called them "letters"—which first appeared in the *Pennsylvania Chronicle*. In the habit of the time, Dickinson wrote anonymously, signing his pieces "A Farmer." (Galloway immediately suspected that Dickinson was the "Farmer," though he believed his rival had collaborated with others of the "damned republican breed" to produce what he huffed was "damned ridiculous! mere fluff!, fustian! altogether stupid and inconsistent.")[36]

From the outset, Dickinson's essays created a sensation. Other Philadelphia newspapers rapidly reprinted his letters, and eventually nineteen of the twenty-three American newspapers printed his dozen essays. In March 1768, after the final letter in the series appeared, all twelve compositions were compiled and published as a pamphlet titled *Letters from a Farmer in Pennsylvania to the Inhabitants of the British Colonies*.[37]

Letters from a Farmer was an overnight sensation. Some sixty pamphlets on the imperial crisis had previously been published in America,[38] but none had equaled its sales. In fact, sales of Dickinson's tract likely exceeded the combined sales of all previous pamphlets on Anglo-American troubles. Multiple printing runs were required to meet the public demand. A few years earlier, Dickinson—who, like most public figures, was terribly ambitious—had told a friend that someday he would "enjoy making a bustle in this world." With *Letters from a Farmer*, he had achieved his goal in spades. By 1770 engravings of his image were published in almanacs and some editions of the pamphlet, his figure had been added to a waxworks museum in Boston, and a newly launched ship had been named for him, with his likeness adorning the figurehead on the vessel's bow. In 1769 he was awarded an honorary degree by what is today Princeton University (and so too was Galloway that same year). "To the Farmer" became the most popular toast from Maine to Savannah. Numerous town meetings endorsed his publication. Several members of Parliament who were regarded as friendly to America lauded the pamphlet, as did Voltaire in France, where a French-language edition was soon published. Lord Dartmouth clipped items pertaining to Dickinson from London newspapers, though he made no public comments. Franklin in 1768 paid for the publication of *Letters from a Farmer* in England and, cognizant of the shifting attitudes in America and the growing popularity of critics of ministerial policy, contributed a brief preface. Whereas he had earlier directed acerbic jabs at Dickinson, calling him an upstart, Franklin now praised his "able learned Pen" and called him "a Gentleman of Repute" who was widely extolled in the colonies for his "Knowledge of . . . Affairs." So popular was Dickinson that when his younger brother, Philemon, stood in for him at a Sons of Liberty rally in Boston in 1769, a record crowd of several hundred turned out.[39]

No one factor explains the brilliant success of *Letters from a Farmer*. Dickinson wrote in a coherent and elegant manner, though he was not given to catchy, head-turning phrases, and no single sentence in the lengthy tract was widely quoted by contemporaries. The disenchantment with England and disillusionment with its leaders, which Dickinson had come to feel during his residence in London, spilled over in his writing and resonated with a colonial populace whose eyes were just opening to the threat posed by Parliament. Yet, Dickinson's tone was not that of a fire-breathing radical, which was crucial, as most Americans were not ready for militancy. Dickinson not only specifically denounced independence but he also, with considerable optimism, promised his readers that redress would come if only the colonists united in a peaceful protest. Dickinson benefited too, in that he was among the first colonists to take up his pen against the Townshend Duties, leading sympathetic newspapers to embrace his work.

Dickinson was also his own publicist, and he possessed a sure instinct for self-promotion. Knowing that Galloway and his followers would do all they could to limit his appeal in Pennsylvania, he reached out to activists in Boston, sending them copies of his newspaper essays with the hint that their publication would help "Kindle the Sacred Flame" of liberty throughout New England. Boston's popular leaders found Yankee publishers for *Letters from a Farmer* and helped make famous "A Song for American Freedom" that Dickinson wrote early in 1768 and sent along to them as well.[40] Using the melody of a popular English song of the day, Dickinson's "Liberty Song," as it was often called, urged for boldness and sacrifice. It began

Come join hand in hand brave Americans all,
And rouse your bold hearts at fair Liberty's call.
No tyrannous acts shall suppress your just claim,
Or, stain with dishonour America's name.
In Freedom we're born and in Freedom we'll live,
Our purses are ready,
Steady, Friends, Steady.
Not as Slaves, but as Freemen our money we'll give.[41]

In *Letters from a Farmer*, Dickinson started with the presumption that Parliament's attempts to tax the colonists were "unconstitutional" and "destructive to the liberty of these colonies." He continued: "No free people ever existed, or can ever exist, without keeping . . . 'the purse strings' in their own hands." He reiterated what many colonial assemblies had said during the Stamp Act crisis. A tax was a tax, whether it was an internal or an external tax. From this, it followed that Americans must "answer with a total denial of the power of parliament to lay upon these colonies any 'tax' whatever." However, Parliament must have the authority to regulate imperial commerce, and it was the "*duty* and *prudence*" of Americans "to maintain and defend" the power of Parliament to do so. In an oblique slam at Galloway and Franklin and other leaders who appeared unwilling to stand up to the British threat, he warned that a "*people* is travelling fast to destruction, when *individuals* consider *their* interests as distinct from *those of the public*." He emphasized that he was not writing as an advocate of independence. The "happiness of these provinces indubitably consists in their connection with Great Britain," he contended. Although he had cautioned about a "decay of virtue" in the mother country, he believed that peaceful protest from throughout the colonies would secure the repeal of the objectionable taxes. "Our *vigilance* and our *union* are [our] *success* and safety," he said, for Americans understood that they "*cannot be* HAPPY, *without being* FREE," and "we cannot be free, *without being secure in our property.*" He fervently believed, he said near the end, that "several of his Majesty's present ministers are good men, and friends to our country," and when they understood the "*truths*" that Americans held dear, they would hasten to abandon parliamentary taxation.[42]

Dickinson's newfound celebrity was only one change in his life. In the summer of 1770, at age thirty-eight, he married into the powerful Norris family. Mary, his thirty-year-old bride, was the daughter of the speaker of the house of the Pennsylvania assembly, as Grace Growdon had been seventeen years earlier, when she married Joseph Galloway. Like Grace Growdon Galloway's father, Mary Norris Dickinson's father was one of the wealthiest men in the colony. Rumor had it that Mary brought a dowry of eighty thousand pounds to the union. Dickinson also acquired Fairhill, the Norris property just outside Philadelphia. The sprawling estate—appraised by the tax office at a value of twenty thousand pounds—exceeded five hundred acres and included a luxurious two-story house and two separate dependencies, one of which Dickinson planned to use as a library. Even so, Dickinson wanted to put his stamp on the mansion. He immediately plunged into a major remodeling job, enlarging and recasting it in a classical Georgian manner. He additionally expanded the already grand gardens and paved a five-hundred-yard driveway. In 1773, Josiah Quincy, a Bostonian who toured several middle and southern colonies, visited Fairhill and called it the most magnificent residence that he saw south of New England. With money to burn, Dickinson additionally acquired a lot on Chestnut Street in Philadelphia, just across from the Pennsylvania State House, and in 1771, at a cost of eight thousand pounds, began construction of a magnificent two-story town house. But in 1775, when the Second Continental Congress met, the dwelling was still not completed, and in fact, Dickinson would never live in the house. (During the war, it was used first as a hospital and then, after 1778, leased to the French minister to the United States.) Dickinson also started a family in these years. When he was forty, Mary gave birth to a daughter. A second daughter, the couple's last child, was born shortly before the outbreak of the war.[43]

Distracted by the many changes in his personal life, and attached to the minority party in the Pennsylvania legislature, Dickinson kept a low profile in the early 1770s. He was reelected annually to the assembly, usually by a near-unanimous vote. He reemerged on the bigger stage only when the *Polly*, the tea ship bound for Philadelphia, neared the American coast in the fall of 1773. Writing his first major essay in five years, Dickinson penned a piece for the *Pennsylvania Journal* that denounced the Tea Act. Calling the legislation insolent, oppressive, and "Madness," he urged that "no Man . . . receive the Tea . . . nor suffer the Vessel, that brings it, to moor at his Wharf, and that if any Person assists in unloading, landing or storing it, he shall ever after be deemed an Enemy to his Country."[44]

The following year, when word of the Intolerable Acts reached the colonies, Dickinson attacked the repressive measures in several published letters. He took the line that London had long wished to carry out repressive actions against Massachusetts and was merely using the Boston Tea Party as a pretext. Perhaps because events were moving so rapidly that summer, these essays failed to attract the notoriety of *Letters from a Farmer*. In fact, by the time he wrote the final letter in the series, Pennsylvania was afire with the battle over sending a delegation to the Continental Congress. Dickinson's target in his final epistle was Galloway, who was preventing the assembly from supporting a congress. The foes of British coercion, Dickinson said, were "now strenuously endeavouring, IN A PEACEFUL MANNER . . . to preserve our freedom." But if Galloway thwarted the planned congress and British tyranny prevailed, he would be "justly chargeable with all the dreadful consequences to the Colonies." Dickinson asserted that if only a congress of all the colonies could meet and institute a national boycott, North's government would have to back down, as Great Britain is "So dependent . . . on us for supplies."[45]

During the spring and summer of 1774, Dickinson played an active role in the public rallies that were designed to force Galloway's hand. He spoke to an overflow gathering of some three hundred in the City Tavern in June and the following month presided over an outdoor meeting that drew more than eight thousand Philadelphians. Galloway, of course, yielded in the end, but he kept Dickinson out of the First Continental Congress. However, the fall elections brought about the decisive swing in power within the Pennsylvania assembly that enabled Dickinson to enter Congress just prior to its adjournment.

Given the tectonic shift in Pennsylvania politics and Dickinson's national renown, it was hardly surprising that he would be a major player in the Second Continental Congress. To this point, Dickinson had been seen as a radical—an archfoe of encroaching royal authority, an opponent of the Stamp Act, a critic of the Townshend Duties, and a sworn enemy of the Tea Act and Intolerable Acts. But anyone who perused his writings over the past decade would have found that Dickinson had steadfastly espoused the merits of

America's ties to the British Empire. Furthermore, he had always insisted that Great Britain's leaders would back down when faced with peaceful protests by the united colonists.

Until 1775, he had been correct. Then came Lexington and Concord. Dickinson had been confident that the measures taken by the First Congress would lead London to assuage the colonists in some way or other. He had been certain that peaceful reconciliation was on the horizon. Instead, war had come. In shock, he declared that London had responded to Congress with a "Rescript . . . written in Blood."[46] War with the mother country, he thought, was "unnatural & astonishing," but like every other delegate to this Congress, he supported America's armed resistance. He believed that Great Britain had launched an "impious War of Tyranny against Innocence," a "cruel War" brought on by a "mad or villainous . . . Ministry" dominated "by a few worthless persons," men whom he referred to as "Fools or Knaves." America's cause was "a righteous Cause," he said, adding, "I hope every Man of Sense & Virtue will draw his Sword."[47]

Yet, Dickinson remained attached to reconciliation. Most of those who would be his colleagues when Congress reconvened in May shared his hope that harmony with the mother country could be restored. The great divide between Dickinson and many of his fellow deputies would not come over whether to reconcile with London but over how best to restore the Anglo-American union. Jolted by the outbreak of hostilities, Dickinson appears to have spent the next few weeks in restless contemplation. Few congressmen understood the reality of the imperial troubles, or of the war that lay ahead, with such clarity as did Dickinson.

Before Lexington and Concord, Dickinson had optimistically believed that a unified, tenacious, and peaceful resistance by Congress would be sufficient to topple North's government and bring on a new ministry committed to peace. The outbreak of war caused the scales to fall from his eyes. Within days of learning of the bloody combat along Battle Road, he concluded that North's "Ministry will stand." It enjoyed large majorities in both houses of Parliament and would not face another election for up to seven years. He conceded too that North had been an "artful" leader in the run-up to war, succeeding even in persuading the most influential residents in the homeland that "Great Britain is contesting for her very Existence in this Dispute with America." It was a bitter truth, he thought, that the actions taken by North's government were popular with the British people. America had friends in Great Britain, but not enough. There were merchants for whom the war would be economically disastrous, but they had little political influence. Wise men, the likes of

Chatham, Camden, and Burke, sat in Parliament and spoke for a "small Band of independent virtuous Spirits" who loathed North's policies, but they were "personally odious to the King."

Dickinson was no less sensible—prescient, in fact—about the war. He foresaw a long, difficult conflict, and he worried that wars were unpredictable. He had no doubt that before this conflict ended, Americans would "taste . . . deeply of that bitter Cup" of adversity. Battles would be lost. Diseases would sweep through the army's camps. To supply armies spread over a continent as vast as North America would be a demanding, perhaps impossible, assignment. The northern colonies should expect invasions by forces of Canadians and Indians. Slave insurrections in the southern colonies were an all-too-real likelihood. America would face a "forbidding" adversary in the Royal Navy. In the face of such daunting peril, it would be difficult to sustain morale. Dickinson knew that as tribulations increased, and persisted, there would be those who "in a tumultuary Passion or rather Phrenzy for Peace" would "cast away in one Day of Haste & Weakness" all that had been gained "by Years of Blood." That made it imperative that America engage in a sincere effort to achieve reconciliation before the war became long and bloody and war weariness set in.

The solution that Dickinson hit on was not for Congress to abandon armed resistance, but for it to accompany its war effort with an appeal to the king. The monarch, unlike Lord North and the members of Parliament who represented local districts, was responsible for the security and best interest of the entire British Empire. Dickinson was convinced that the time was right to approach the Crown. Britain "has lost a Battle—& all America is more united & more determined" than those in the mother country could ever have imagined would be the case. Persuading himself that the monarch had not had a hand in the decision to resort to force—he and many other reconciliationists clung to the notion that the war had been brought on solely by a conniving set of ministers—Dickinson believed that the king would want to act to prevent a civil war once he saw that the American people were "vigorously *preparing*" for armed resistance. Furthermore, a petition would demonstrate to the king that the colonists were acting in self-defense and harbored no secret agendas. Even if an appeal to the monarch failed, to have tried for reconciliation would be useful. Should this indeed become a long war, an unsuccessful appeal to the king would unite the colonists, for no one could subsequently say that Congress had "omitted proper applications for obtaining Peace."

Dickinson was driven by his belief that American prosperity and security stemmed from its ties to the empire, but much like Galloway, he was haunted by a conservative's fear of the forces for change that so often were unleashed by war. As the leader of the faction that for a decade had represented the disenchanted inhabitants of western Pennsylvania, Dickinson knew full well that many Americans longed for substantive change. He had in fact ridden those cravings as the means of forcing Galloway to permit Pennsylvania to participate in the First Congress. But Dickinson understood that it was easier to start making reforms than to stop making them. Once a reform movement commenced, it built a momentum for further change. "[A] people does not reform with moderation" was how he had put it in one of the *Letters from a Farmer.* He knew, too, that a people driven by the passions of war to hate everything that was British might be especially unrestrained.[48]

Like Galloway, Dickinson was convinced that shattering political, social, and economic changes could best be prevented by remaining tied to Great Britain. In the absence of a rapid settlement of Anglo-American differences, Dickinson feared the war could have only two possible outcomes. Hostilities might end in a terrible defeat followed by brutal oppression and reprisals. Or, the exigencies of a desperate war would drive Congress to declare independence. If America won the war and achieved independence, Dickinson was certain that such an outcome would bring immeasurably greater tribulations than those threatened by the recent string of British ministries. An independent America would be a strife-filled land of democracy that bore little resemblance to its British past. Moreover, the fragile new American nation would be thrust onto the world stage before it was capable of defending itself against the "rapacious & ambitious Nations" of Europe.

To prevent the horrors that he envisaged, Dickinson believed that Congress must emphasize to the king the colonists' "Readiness & Willingness at all Times" to commit "our Lives and Fortunes to support, maintain & defend the Interests of his Majesty & and our Mother Country." He hoped that Congress's appeal to the Crown would be carried to London by agents of Congress who were empowered to negotiate a peace treaty leading to a constitutional settlement. A "treaty can do Us no Harm" and it "may do Us Good," he believed.[49]

Dickinson did not wait long before he opened the fight to appeal for the king's intercession. Congress had started slowly, leisurely tending to organizational matters as it awaited the arrival of more delegates. Finally, after a "Number of Members arrived" on Monday, May 15, nearly a week behind schedule, Congress went into a committee of the whole to consider "the state of America." Richard Henry Lee, as was often the case, was the first on the floor. He proposed the creation of a national army to replace the Grand American Army, which was composed entirely of soldiers from the four New England colonies. But this was too fast for some delegates. It was at this point, in fact, that John Rutledge raised the all-important question about the aim of the war: Was this a war for reconciliation or independence?[50]

John Adams was still suffering from whatever had caused his collapse on the day of his journey to Lexington, but not too ill to enter the debate. He discoursed in what one delegate thought, no doubt correctly, was an "Argumentative" manner. Adams spoke at length, though the essence of what he said was simple. America was not fighting for independence. Nor was it fighting for what the First Congress had sought. In the Declaration of Rights and Grievances adopted the previous October, Congress had recognized Parliament's power to regulate American trade. That no longer was acceptable. Parliament's decision to make war on America had changed everything. The colonists could no longer recognize Parliament's authority in any way, shape, or form. America's aim was reconciliation with the mother country, but the only British authority the colonists could recognize was that of the king.

The minute Adams concluded, Dickinson was on his feet. If Adams had been contentious, Dickinson likely answered in the combative manner that had long been his custom in floor debates in the Pennsylvania assembly. What is certain is that he aired at least some of his views on patching up differences with the mother country. Like Adams, Dickinson saw reconciliation as the object of the war, but he wished to restore the Anglo-American relationship that had existed prior to 1763, before there were parliamentary taxes and a British army in America in peacetime—a time when the colonists happily acquiesced in Parliament's regulation of American trade.

With the conflict less than a month old, Congress was divided over what it was fighting for. Some were also put off by what they saw as Yankee extremism in Adams's remarks. Some from New England, on the other hand, found that Dickinson's stance "gives . . . disgust."[51] This spelled trouble, and at the very moment that word was reaching Congress of urgent military issues that needed tending. Congress postponed further debate on America's war aims for a week, hoping that passions might cool in the interim.

But Congress did not put off the debate strictly from fear of divisions. These were experienced politicians. None expected unanimity on every issue. Nor did they anticipate debates that were free of rancor. They were simply overwhelmed with the number of things they had to deal with. "Such a vast Multitude of Objects, civil, political, commercial and military, press and crowd Us so fast, that We know not what to do first," John Adams remarked without exaggeration.[52]

Congress knew that it first must deal with a series of military issues that simply could not be ignored or postponed. It was common knowledge that London was sending reinforcements across the Atlantic, and many believed the destination of some troops would be New York. On May 15 Congress received an inquiry from resistance leaders in New York City asking how the colony should respond if threatened with a landing by the British army. Congress put together a committee—which included George Washington—to consider the matter, and within a few days New York was directed not to resist the redcoats. They were to use force only if the soldiers attacked or invaded homes or businesses.[53]

Hard on the heels of the New York issue came word of military actions taken by Massachusetts and Connecticut. Fearing a British invasion from Canada, those two colonies, each acting without knowledge of what the other was doing, had raised military forces to seize the British-held installation of Fort Ticonderoga on Lake Champlain in New York. Colonel Benedict Arnold commanded the Massachusetts force. Ethan Allen was in charge of the army raised by Connecticut, a band of rowdy frontiersmen who called themselves the Green Mountain Boys. The two small armies set off at about the same time and ran into each other in western Massachusetts. Thereafter, they more or less cooperated in a joint campaign to take the fort. On May 10, the day that Congress reconvened, Allen and Arnold led their men on the last leg of the expedition, a half-mile march along a narrow path that hugged Lake Champlain. They moved with stealth through the early morning darkness, bringing their force to the south side of the British installation. When the men were ready, Allen gave the order to attack. The Yankees charged out of the black night and into the fort, screaming at the top of their lungs. They encountered next to no resistance. The British had posted only two sentries, and both were thoroughly surprised by Allen, who roared that the colonial force was taking Fort Ticonderoga "in the name of the great Jehovah, and the Continental Congress." The remaining redcoats, forty-two in all, were sound asleep. They were awakened and taken captive, along with twenty-four women and children, and all were herded into the stockade. The entire operation lasted less than ten minutes. Flushed with success, the Americans also took Crown Point, another British fort twelve miles farther north. By the time Congress learned about these actions, it also discovered that Arnold was talking wildly of going after the British post at St. Johns on the Richelieu River, not far from Montreal.[54]

Fort Ticonderoga may have been seized in the name of the Continental Congress, but the action had not been taken with Congress's authorization. In fact, the members of Congress were surprised to learn of the campaign. The authorities in New York were even more astonished, as they had never been consulted by Massachusetts and Connecticut about an operation on their soil. The whole affair raised several troubling questions. As both Massachusetts

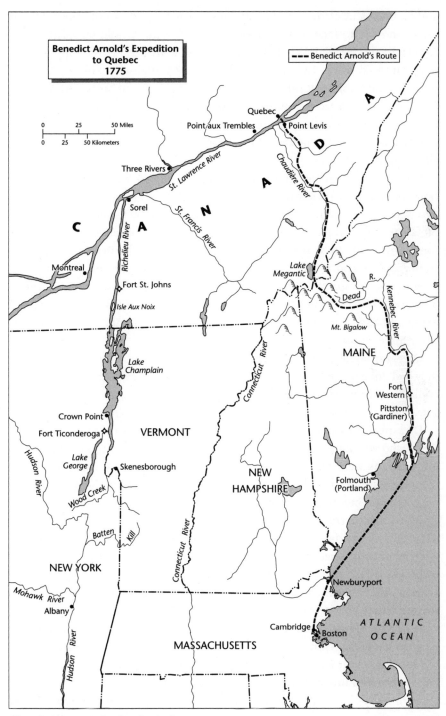

(Gary J. Antonetti, Ortelius Design)

and Connecticut claimed to lack the resources for garrisoning the captured forts, who was to take on that commitment? Should Arnold be permitted to campaign in Canada? What should be done with the British supplies that were captured in the two installations? Were individual colonies to be permitted to take military initiatives without congressional authorization? But two larger questions loomed over and beyond these matters. One was the question of who was responsible for running this war. An infinitely more thorny question concerned America's relationship with London while the war was being waged.

Congress first tackled the questions that required an immediate resolution, though in a preview of how slow this deliberative body could be, nearly two weeks were required for it to reach its decisions. By the end of May, Congress had directed Arnold to take no further action, ordered the removal of some provisions from the recently seized forts—lest the British army come from Canada and retake them—and asked Connecticut and New York to provide the troops for garrisoning Forts Ticonderoga and Crown Point.[55] (Congress was presented with some of the trophies, including a captured drum and flags, which soon adorned one wall of its chamber in the Pennsylvania State House.)

On Saturday, May 20, the congressmen dined together at the City Tavern, as they had done the previous Saturday evening. When they resumed their deliberations on Monday, they took up Dickinson's proposal, labeled by one delegate, "shall we treat."[56] In other words, should Congress petition the king?

Dickinson was among the first to speak. He began with a stark warning. If those who wished to raise a national army and undertake attendant military preparations were to get what they wanted, they must first agree to pursue reconciliation by appealing to the Crown. "We must know the one Measure will be taken before we assent to the other. If We [the more moderate delegates] will go on with Measures of War, They [the more radical congressmen] must go on with [a] Measure of Peace." After he threw down the gauntlet, Dickinson took issue with John Adams's view that the colonists no longer owed any allegiance to Parliament. Dickinson insisted that Congress must acknowledge Parliament's right to regulate imperial commerce. In fact, he seemed to say, Congress should only deny Parliament's right to tax the colonists, for on all other matters "They have the Power, We cant take it away." Next he called on Congress to compensate the East India Company for the tea destroyed in the Boston Tea Party. Toward the end of a speech that must have consumed hours, Dickinson introduced three motions. He asked Congress to adopt a "humble & dutiful Petition to his Majesty, praying Relief from . . . the System of Colonial Administration adopted since [1763]"; to send agents to London to negotiate "an Accommodation"; and to inform General Gage of its petition to the monarch and request that he "forbear further Hostilities . . . untill an Answer can be received to our Answer & proposals."[57]

Dickinson privately said in advance that his remarks would doubtless "inflame" many of his colleagues. He could not have been more accurate. His speech on May 23 touched off the second raging debate within a week, both triggered by speeches that he had given. Most of the furor swirled about the issue of petitioning the king. America was "between Hawk and Buzzard," John Adams muttered. It should not be wasting its time with a petition. It should be resolutely preparing for war, creating the national army that Lee had urged a week earlier and establishing a navy as well. Moreover, Adams and many others who hoped to receive aid from Britain's enemies feared that an appeal to the monarch would send the wrong signal. It would make America appear weak in the eyes of the world. Furthermore, he feared that a petition would provide Lord North the "Opportunity . . . to sow divisions among the States and the People." If all that was not enough, Adams and others were convinced that it was "fruitless" to beseech the king to end the war.[58]

Nor was petitioning the king all that bothered some congressmen. Many thought that time had passed Dickinson by, that he spoke the language of yesteryear, a time before the colonists' constitutional viewpoint had crystallized. To many, his views on the Anglo-American relationship must have seemed nearly identical to those of Galloway. Expressing shock at Dickinson's stance, some of his longtime allies within the Pennsylvania delegation broke with him. Others were openly critical. Lee denounced any thought of yielding any American rights. Patrick Henry warned that natural rights "must never be receded from." John Rutledge spoke of Dickinson's proposal "with the utmost Contempt," said one listener, and insisted that Congress never consider "any Concession" to the "Ultimatum" issued by the British ministry.[59]

Dickinson had indeed inflamed delegates from every corner of America, and few supported his recommendation to consider modifying the rights that Americans were certain they possessed. But a majority in Congress was willing to make an entreaty to the king and, if the monarch was disposed to talk, to negotiate with him. Some, like Dickinson, anticipated success. Others thought it prudent, for even if the attempt failed, having made the effort would in the long run unify the colonists behind the war effort. No delegates were more viscerally opposed to approaching the king or to negotiation than those from New England, but they were painted into a corner. The Yankees knew that their jerry-built siege army might not last much longer. They also knew that they might not get a national army unless they conceded to Dickinson and his numerous allies.

After two days of savage debate, Congress agreed to four resolutions. Three passed by unanimous votes. Congress blamed hostilities on Lord North's ministry, which it said was seeking to "carry into execution, by force of arms, several unconstitutional and oppressive acts . . . for laying taxes in America . . . and for altering and changing the constitutional and internal police of . . . these colonies." As the British army was responsible for having fired the first shot of the war, Congress resolved to immediately put "these colonies . . . into a state of defense." It agreed to petition the king. Lastly, though many congressmen voted against the measure, it consented to "opening a Negotiation in order to accommodate the unhappy disputes."[60] Dickinson had won round one.

CHAPTER 6

"PROGRESS MUST BE SLOW"

JOHN ADAMS AND THE POLITICS OF A DIVIDED CONGRESS

IT HAD BEEN NEARLY inevitable that John Dickinson would take charge among the delegates to the Second Congress who wished to follow a moderate course, but there was no such obvious leader for those who favored a harder line. Patrick Henry and Samuel Adams were the best-known among the congressmen who thought it wrongheaded to petition the king, but both lacked the attributes—and possibly the trust—needed to be an effective manager in a deliberative body. Henry's great gift was his oratorical skills, while Adams was unsurpassed as an organizer and propagandist, but the members of Congress were not the sort to be swept up by a flamboyant speaker or an accomplished agitator.

Perhaps because he understood early on that he could never hold sway at this level, Henry left Philadelphia for home only a few weeks after Congress reconvened, never again to be a major force in the national government. Samuel Adams remained in Congress until 1781 and never ceased to be an important figure, though he mostly stayed in the background, possibly somewhat by choice. He was aware that his reputation as a radical revolutionary led some to see as pernicious anything that he advocated. Besides, though not without ambition, Adams appears to have been less driven to win national accolades than most who played on that stage. From start to finish, Adams's focus was on Massachusetts. He longed for autonomy for his province and battled for the preservation of the way of life that had long prevailed within the Bay Colony, free from the dictates of a strong central government, whether in London or Philadelphia. Loosening the shackles that North's ministry envisaged for the colonies was paramount for Adams, and in the first fifteen months of this Congress he worked quietly to achieve his goal, leaving to others a more public role.

Benjamin Franklin sat in the Second Congress, but standing front and center in an assembly had never been his style. Even when his Assembly Party dominated the Pennsylvania legislature in the 1750s and 1760s, Franklin had turned to Galloway to lead and manage the party's business. Franklin was both a poor public speaker and never comfortable joining in the rancorous and fast-moving floor debates that were part of the day-to-day activity in an assembly. Franklin's behavior as a congressman astonished some of his colleagues, who, aware of his widespread fame, expected a more flamboyant and outgoing personality. John Adams, for instance, was surprised to discover that Franklin was "composed and grave and . . . very reserved. He has not . . . affected to take the lead; but has seemed to choose that the Congress should pursue their own Principles and sentiments and adopt their own Plans."[1]

Franklin's reserve in 1775 also stemmed from his protracted absence from America. Nearly every member of Congress was a stranger to him. He knew most in Pennsylvania's delegation, but several of them had been political enemies when he had last been active in his province's politics. He must have wished to remain in the background, at least for a time, to gain the lay of the land. Something else weighed on Franklin when he took his seat in Congress: Many of his fellow congressmen distrusted him. After all, he had been a resident of London for the past decade, where he had once publicly endorsed parliamentary taxation of America. Furthermore, Franklin had once advocated the royalization of Pennsylvania; the despised Galloway was his longtime political partner; and his son, William, was now the royal governor of New Jersey. Both Richard Henry Lee and Samuel Adams thought Franklin "a suspicious doubtful character." Adams's doubts increased when he learned of Franklin's overnight visit with Galloway at Trevose. One deputy confided that some in Congress "entertain a great Suspicion that Dr. Franklin" had returned to America "rather as a spy than as a friend." Some even thought he hoped "to discover our weak side & make his peace with [Lord North] by discovering it to him."[2] Seldom have fears been so badly misplaced.

When Franklin sailed from London in March, he no longer thought Anglo-American reconciliation was likely or desirable. Still fuming over his despicable treatment in the Cockpit, Franklin acknowledged his lust for revenge, a sentiment for which he was "ashamed," he said. But he was not especially dismayed to learn upon landing in America that hostilities had erupted during his Atlantic crossing. He was pleased by Massachusetts's response to Gage's attack. Even more, he rejoiced that Britain's decision to begin the "cutting of throats" had only "more firmly united" the American people. Franklin delighted in regaling America's friends in England with accounts of the action along Battle Road, writing sardonically that the regulars had made such a "vigorous Retreat" that "the feeble Americans . . . could scarce keep up with them."[3]

Franklin alternated between sorrow for what need not have occurred—the British Empire was being wrecked "by the mangling hands of a few blundering ministers," he said—and a sense that historical inevitability was being played out. As he saw it, "a new virtuous People, who have publick Spirit," were coming of age and severing their ties with "an old corrupt" nation. Franklin saw no hope for the Olive Branch Petition, as Dickinson's proposed appeal to the king was being called. It would "afford Britain one chance more of recovering our Affections and retaining the Connection," Franklin remarked, but he was certain that Britain's leaders had "neither Temper nor Wisdom enough to seize the Golden Opportunity." He never doubted that American independence was on the horizon. "A separation will of course be inevitable," Franklin said shortly after he entered Congress.[4]

Nor could there be any doubt that he was pleased with what he saw as America's inexorable march toward independence. Despite how much he loved London and hoped to live out his life there, once it became clear that Parliament and North's ministry had "doomed my Country to Destruction"—to "murder our People," was how he put it—he had cast his lot with America.[5] In letter after letter written to acquaintances in England in the first weeks after he entered Congress, Franklin alluded to "your Ministry," "your Ministers," "your Nation," "your Ships of War." When he referred to America he spoke of "our Seaport Towns," "our Sea Coast," "our Liberties."[6]

Franklin's first task after entering Congress was to convince his colleagues that his support for America's war was genuine. It took a few weeks, but by midsummer John Adams had aptly sized up his fellow congressman. Franklin supported "our boldest Measures," Adams had concluded. In fact, he believed that Franklin "rather seems to think us too irresolute, and backward." At present, Adams continued, Franklin believed America was "neither dependent nor independent. But he thinks that We shall soon assume a Character more decisive. He thinks, that even if We should be driven to . . . a total Independency . . . We could maintain it." To which Adams added: Franklin "is . . . a great and good Man."[7]

Though not a commanding figure in Congress, Franklin was hardly inactive. Esmond Wright, a biographer, fittingly described Franklin as "the organizer of revolution" during that crucial summer of 1775. He had a hand in preparing Philadelphia's defenses, planning a continental currency, securing munitions, and creating an American post office.[8]

Franklin's most daring act that summer was to call for organizing a national government under a constitution. Two decades earlier, while Pennsylvania's representative at an intercolonial conference that met in Albany to prepare for the French and Indian War, Franklin had offered a plan of union for the thirteen colonies. London had not been happy with the idea of an American confederation, nor had any colony embraced the scheme. No American province had been willing to surrender even a smidgen of authority to a central government.[9] But in July, Franklin tweaked his twenty-year-old plan and presented it to Congress.

Franklin's proposed constitution would have come close to creating an independent United States. Under his plan, Congress would have possessed the authority to levy taxes, create new colonies, conduct diplomacy, form alliances with foreign powers, and make war and peace. A plan of this sort never stood a chance of passage. Those who clung to the hope of reconciliation were horrified by it, and some who were ready for independence distanced themselves, fearing that deliberations would sow bitter, perhaps fatal divisions at a moment when unity was imperative. Franklin rapidly withdrew his scheme, claiming that he had merely wished to provide his colleagues with ideas to ponder. But, as was almost always true of Franklin, there was a hidden motive. His proposal was part of his campaign to convince skeptics that he was an ardent supporter of America's war.[10]

Vacuums do not last long in politics, and in June and July 1775 it was John Adams who stepped up to take the lead of those who were restive with the moderate course advocated by Dickinson.

Adams was anxious to redirect the delegates' attention to Richard Henry Lee's May 16 resolution calling for a national army, a proposition that had gathered dust for three weeks. The New England army camped outside Boston—the so-called Grand American Army—was not so grand. There were men aplenty, but the four provincial armies that made up the force were incapable of conducting a lengthy siege operation. Not only were there appalling shortages of arms, artillery, and ammunition, but New England also lacked the means of indefinitely paying the soldiery. Besides, the Yankees did not think that they alone should have to foot the bill for an army that was resisting British tyranny. British actions were an American problem, not a New England problem. It was clear, too, that some of the higher-ranking officers in the army were unfit. They owed their selection to politics, not merit. Furthermore, hardly any of the middle- and lower-grade officers were experienced soldiers. This army needed to be rebuilt, or "new modeled," in the parlance of the day.[11] It would require the resources of all the American colonies and a leadership

The Yankee Doodle Intrenchments near Boston. A British lampoon of the American siege of Boston and the amateur colonial soldiers. The siege began on the day after Lexington and Concord and continued until the British abandoned the city a year later. (Archive of Early American Images, John Corter Brown Library, Brown University)

that shied away neither from initiating drastic changes nor from imposing the discipline necessary to mold the army into a decent fighting force.

As May slipped by without congressional action, Massachusetts activists wrote to their delegates in Philadelphia in what appears to have been an orchestrated campaign to secure change. The soldiers were defying orders, cried one correspondent. If something was not done soon, the army might turn into an armed mob and plunder civilians. What was needed, said another, was "a regular general to assist us in disciplining the army." A writer cautioned, "Every days delay . . . will make the task more arduous." One urged the appointments of Colonel Washington and Charles Lee "at the head" of the army. Even some officers in the army reported "the impossibility of keeping the army together, without the Assistance of Congress." At the very moment that the Massachusetts congressmen were sharing these thoughts with their colleagues from outside New England, Massachusetts's rebel assembly asked Congress to assume "the regulation and general direction" of the Grand American Army so that its "operations may more effectually answer the purposes designed." It sent its request by express, which not coincidentally arrived as Congress was spinning its wheels over the wording of the petition to the king.[12]

But Congress moved at a glacial pace. Before acting decisively, it discussed how to finance a national army, looked into securing gunpowder and other supplies, and solicited the thoughts of the authorities at home regarding who they preferred as officers in a national army.[13] John Adams was irritated by the delay. This "continent is a vast, unwieldy Machine," he sighed. A good army has to be fashioned and quickly, he thought, for it alone offered "the most efficacious, Sure" means of securing "our Liberty and Felicity." Samuel Adams was no less impatient, though he told his friends at home that something would soon be done. "Business must go on slower than one could wish," he said. "It is difficult to possess upwards of Sixty Gentlemen, at once with the Same Feelings upon Questions of Importance."[14]

In mid-June, four days after Samuel Adams wrote his letter, John Adams brought matters to a head. He knew that "many of our staunchest" friends in New England thought the best means of obtaining a truly national army was through the appointment of someone from outside the region to command it. He knew too that many Southerners heartily agreed. Adams said privately that a "Southern Party" in Congress was not only suggesting that Southerners might refuse to serve in an army under Yankee leadership but was also backing Colonel Washington for the post of commander in chief. But some New Englanders were opposed to removing General Ward. They worried that New Englanders, who were certain to make up the lion's share of the soldiery at least through the end of 1775, might only follow a commander who hailed from New England. Some also feared a harmful political backlash if Ward was dumped. The matter was further complicated by John Hancock's longing to be chosen to head the army. The Massachusetts delegation was badly divided, and some—including Samuel Adams—were "irresolute," as John put it.

Before Congress convened on June 14, John consulted Samuel Adams in the yard outside the Pennsylvania State House. They walked and talked at length on that warm summer morning, as John sought to persuade his more influential colleague of the wisdom of creating a national army headed by Washington. Aside from getting the job done so that the army could be improved and Congress could get on to other things, Adams wished to act because he was persuaded that Washington was the right man for the job. John subsequently recollected that Samuel did not agree, but neither did he disagree, and during that day's session John, like Lee a month earlier almost to the day, moved that Congress "Adopt the Army" that was besieging Boston. Congress was ready to take this step, and it acted swiftly to take over the Grand American Army, transforming it into what the official congressional journal called the "American Continental Army," or what almost immediately—and lastingly—would be known simply as the Continental army. Once that step was taken, John Adams was on his feet again, this time to address the issue of who was to be the army's commander. There was a member of Congress, he said, "whose independent fortune, great Talents and excellent universal Character, would command the Approbation of all America, and unite the cordial Exertions of all the Colonies better than any other Person in the Union." Thinking that Adams was speaking of him, Hancock listened with "visible pleasure," Adams later recalled. But when Adams recommended Colonel Washington to command the new national army, Hancock's expression changed suddenly to "Mortification and resentment." The moment that Adams concluded his remarks, Thomas Johnson of Maryland formally nominated Washington to be the commander in chief of the Continental army.[15]

Washington immediately left the chamber so that Congress could freely deliberate the motion. The delegates discussed the matter for the remainder of that day and half of the next, but their decision was never in doubt. As no record of Congress's deliberation has survived, no one knows what was said. Years later Adams recalled that some objected to Washington's appointment. That likely was true. The delegates must have spent some of the time discussing the ramifications of removing General Ward, but most of the discussion likely focused on learning as much as possible about Washington's character from his fellow Virginians. It was already known that Washington was the right age—at forty-three he was young and strong enough to have a good chance of enduring a long war—and he had ample experience, having commanded Virginia's army in the French and Indian War for nearly five years. What the congressmen really wanted to know, however, was whether Washington could be trusted with an army. The members of Congress knew that throughout history many generals had used their armies to make themselves dictators.

Virginia's congressmen must have assured their colleagues that Washington was trustworthy, a conviction that many in Congress already shared, for they had been his associate at both congresses, observing him and even questioning him about his feelings regarding the subordination of the military to civilian authority. Washington passed every test. The congressmen saw him as "Sober, steady, and Calm," no "harum Starum ranting Swearing fellow," as one said. They thought him "sensible . . . virtuous, modest, & brave," very formal and reserved, tough as nails, and possessed of an indomitable will. He commanded respect. One observer remarked that Washington "has so much martial dignity in his deportment that you would distinguish him to be a general and a soldier from among ten thousand people. There is not a king in Europe that would not look like a valet de chambre by his side." The capstone perhaps was that Washington was hardly a social revolutionary. His selection "removes all [sectional] jealousies" and solidly "Cements" the new American union, one congressman proclaimed. It was of no little importance that Washington was seen as sturdy enough to reconstruct the army and that he possessed the mettle to make citizens into good soldiers. He was appointed on June 15.[16]

Until he nominated Washington, John Adams had not played a key role in Congress. But when Adams took charge of the creation of the army and the selection of its commander, it signaled that change was in the air. Convinced of his abilities and probably concerned that Samuel Adams's point of view was too parochial for the epic challenges that lay ahead, John Adams had begun his ascendancy in Congress. During the next twelve months, he would lead those who opposed John Dickinson and his adherents.

John Adams's background could hardly have been more different from Dickinson's. Adams had been raised on a small farm in Braintree, just south of Boston. His father, Deacon John Adams, probably never owned more than fifty acres and never produced much for market from his rocky fields. In fact, during the long, cold Massachusetts winters, Deacon Adams worked as a shoemaker to supplement the family's meager income. Through frugality and industry, Deacon Adams and his wife accumulated the resources to provide a formal education for one son—the eldest child—including four years at nearby Harvard College. John was the firstborn.

Young John acquired a no-nonsense work ethic from his father and a passion for reading from his mother, but he had little idea what he wanted to do with his life when he entered Harvard in 1751. He knew only what he did not want to do. His father hoped he would become a Congregational pastor. John was not enticed. He was put off by hairsplitting theological disputes and, given his gruff and acerbic manner, he understood better than anyone that he was thoroughly ill-suited for providing solace to the troubled. His mother wanted him to become a physician, but in a day when medicine was more art than science, he found the calling unappealing. No one suggested that he pursue a mercantile career and he never gave it a thought. That left the law.[17]

John was captivated by the prospect of matching wits with other attorneys. He knew too that successful lawyers were held in high esteem throughout Massachusetts, and particularly in Boston. Nor did it escape his attention that by the 1750s increasing numbers of political leaders in the Bay Colony came from a legal background. Alive with ambition, Adams yearned even as an adolescent to gain a "Reputation" and escape the fate of "the common

Herd of Mankind, who are to be born and eat and sleep and die, and be forgotten." Longing for "a Prospect of an Immortality in the Memories of all the Worthy," he fixed on the law as the surest path toward becoming "a great Man."

After graduating from Harvard, Adams taught for two years in a Latin school in Worcester to earn the money to pay for his legal apprenticeship, which he completed under that town's only attorney in 1758. Unlike Dickinson and Galloway, Adams neither started at the top of the legal profession nor soared to its pinnacle. Practicing in terribly competitive Boston, he made excruciatingly slow progress and survived by living at home with his parents for several years. He had only two clients during the first year and did not win a case before a jury until the end of his second. Years passed before his earnings were sufficient to marry Abigail Smith, whom he was courting. In 1764 the twenty-nine-year-old Adams and his patient fiancée, the daughter of a Congregational minister, finally wed.[18]

Adams owed his success, in part, to his work ethic. After consulting with several leading lawyers in Boston, he mapped out an exacting regimen of postapprentice study. At a time when many attorneys entered practice scant months after beginning their studies, and presumably read little law thereafter, Adams willed himself to learn the law in great breadth and depth. "I will master it. . . . I will . . . break thro . . . all obstructions," he vowed as he burned the midnight oil. His work paid off. In 1765 a Boston town meeting chose him, together with Jeremiah Gridley and James Otis—the city's most esteemed lawyers—to speak for it before the royal governor during the Stamp Act crisis. Five years later Adams represented some seven hundred clients, which he thought—probably correctly—made his the largest legal practice in Massachusetts.[19]

When choosing a career, Adams had been lured to the law partly because it offered access to political office. Yet before 1770—when he turned thirty-five—he shied away from politics, fearing that what he did in politics might harm his law practice and his growing family, which at the time consisted of a daughter and two sons. During the Stamp Act crisis he had represented the Boston town meeting, but in a legal capacity, and he had written Braintree's protest against the tax, though he had done so anonymously. Adams had penned several essays for Boston newspapers, including some that lashed out at London's plan to "enslave all America" and accused royal officials of having "trifled with, browbeaten, and trampled on" the colonists. But these too had been unattributed, as he used pseudonyms such as "Clarendon" and "Humphrey Ploughjogger."[20]

After 1767, however, with his reputation as a lawyer growing and the imperial crisis in full glow, Adams was increasingly pressured to play an active role in politics. Both sides wanted him. Through an intermediary, Thomas Hutchinson offered him the post of solicitor general of Massachusetts. Adams spurned the offer "in an instant," he subsequently recalled. By then, Otis, Dr. Warren, and Samuel Adams, his cousin, were working on him to join with them in open opposition to the mother country's new colonial policies. They wanted him to address Boston town meetings, but he rebuffed their entreaties, remarking privately that the radicals only wished him to "deceive the People," to "conceal from them . . . essential truth[s]." Not easily put off, some of the militants told Adams that "many" of their collaborators believed he "was not hearty in the Cause," and some even supposedly conjectured that he might be a Tory. Adams was so badly shaken that in 1769 he attended a public Sons of Liberty rally. But he would do no more. Although he shared the radicals' fears of ministerial intent, Adams suspected that Boston's firebrands had a hidden agenda. He believed that Samuel Adams and his compatriots were plotting American independence. Fearing revolution and war, Adams said privately of his cousin's designs: "That way madness lies."[21]

But Adams was haunted by the whispers of his alleged Toryism, and in 1770, as never before, he contemplated an active role in politics. It was a difficult decision. If he held office, he would make enemies. Yet, if he remained uncommitted, he would fall under a cloak of suspicion that could be even more detrimental.[22] The Boston Massacre in March 1770 appears to have been the decisive event in resolving his personal struggle. After several British soldiers were arrested and charged with the killings, Dr. Warren and Samuel Adams pleaded with John to defend the redcoats. The radicals did not want the soldiers to go unpunished and could not imagine that any jury in Boston would exonerate them, but they did not wish the trial to be a sham. They wanted an eminent Boston lawyer to serve as the defense attorney for the soldiers.

Adams always insisted that he agreed to take the case because he believed that every man deserved a fair trial. That doubtless was a factor in his decision, but so too was his intuitive understanding that this would be a historic case that might win him lasting fame. Nevertheless, there was a downside to taking on the assignment. Adams worried that he was "hazarding a Popularity very general and very hardly earned" by "incurring . . . prejudices" among those who hated the British soldiers. But that concern was mitigated by a bargain that he appears to have struck with Samuel Adams: In return for defending the hated redcoats, Samuel would to see to John's election as one of Boston's four representatives in the Massachusetts assembly. From that perspective, taking the case was a win-win deal for John. By defending the king's soldiers he would gain the approval of the most conservative citizens; as an assemblyman who supported the radical faction in its resistance to the Town-shend Duties, still being debated that spring, all suspicions of his Toryism would vanish.[23]

Adams conceived a masterful defense for the soldiers, winning the acquit-tal of seven of the nine. Two were convicted of manslaughter, not homicide, and they were set free through a legal artifice. Adams's reputation as a lawyer soared, and true to his word, Samuel Adams delivered an assembly seat to his cousin. John Adams had hardly assumed his place in the assembly, however, before he realized that he had made a dreadful mistake. Given a behind-the-scenes view of Samuel's intrigue, John's suspicions of the sinister motives of the radicals were confirmed. Samuel Adams and other militants engaged in what John soon saw as "a laboured controversy"—a contrived campaign, in other words—to turn public opinion against the Crown officials. Fearing the disapproval of the resistance leaders if he did not participate in "all the dis-putes" that were part of his cousin's "disagreeable Causes," John reluctantly joined in what he saw as their dishonest endeavors. He anguished that the role he was playing would bring his "family to ruin" and that he "was throw-ing away as bright prospects [as] any Man ever held before him." It was too much. Already weighed down with anxiety from the recent Boston Massacre trials, and grieving over the recent death of his fifteen-month-old daughter, Susanna, Adams collapsed under the strain. He was too ill to complete his term and did not seek reelection in 1771. John Adams's political career, which had lasted only a few weeks, appeared to be over.[24]

Adams later said that he was transformed into a revolutionary partly as a result of having immersed himself in European and English radical thought. He was drawn to the literature of European Enlightenment rationalism, espe-cially the works of Voltaire and Montesquieu. Even more important were the late-seventeenth- and early-eighteenth-century essays of John Locke and other Englishmen, writings that historian Caroline Robbins characterized as a veritable "textbook of revolution" for Americans. These tracts not only de-scribed an England in which liberties were imperiled by internal corruption, but also warned of a ministerial conspiracy to eradicate the rights of Ameri-cans. While influenced by what he read, Adams believed that it was the 1773 publication of Thomas Hutchinson's purloined letters that pulled together his disparate thoughts and converted him into a dissident. He called those letters his "grand discovery." The scales fell from his eyes and he at last understood that London's policies threatened to render Bostonians "more unhappy than the basest Negro in Town." He now believed that Great Britain's leaders were "cool, thinking, deliberate Villain[s], malicious, and vindictive, as well as ambitious and avaricious." Unless stopped, they will "ruin the Country," he added. What is more, Adams also believed that Hutchinson's letters confirmed what Samuel Adams and his collaborators had been saying all along: A "profoundly secret, dark, and deep" plot indeed existed among royal officials to quash the rights of the colonists.[25]

Adams's retrospective account might have exaggerated the immediate impact of Hutchinson's letters, but there can be little doubt that the three years that followed his illness, or breakdown, in 1771 was a crucial time for him. Adams turned thirty-seven in October 1772, and he noted on his birthday that he had reached a point when most men's lives were half over.[26] Taking stock, Adams concluded that he had achieved everything that he had dreamed of accomplishing as a lawyer, and more. Yet, the world had changed. Now it was not lawyers that attained fame, but political activists, the likes of Samuel Adams and John Dickinson. By 1773 and 1774 he yearned to resume the political career he abandoned in 1771. As he wrestled again with becoming politically active, the Hutchinson Letters helped allay the misgivings he had earlier exhibited at participating in the radicals' orchestrated campaigns to arouse popular resistance to royal authority.

Samuel Adams and other popular leaders aided John in overcoming the last hurdles, calling on him frequently and placating his fears. They utilized every artifice in their bag of tricks to persuade him of their temperate outlook. Wanting to believe in their cause, John was easily swayed. Soon he was writing that Samuel Adams was driven by the purest motives of "public Service."[27] A couple of years earlier he would have denounced an act such as the Boston Tea Party, but when Adams heard of the destruction of the East India Company's tea, he effusively remarked that the action "charms me." If it led to a war that cost the lives of thousands, the carnage would be "very profitably Spent," he declared.[28] John Adams had become a radical.

When the colonies responded to the Coercive Acts by calling the First Continental Congress, the Massachusetts assembly chose John Adams as one of its delegates. In memoirs that he wrote a quarter century later, Adams matter-of-factly described his election as if it had been inevitable.[29] In fact, Adams owed his selection to Samuel Adams, who never explained why he added to the delegation an individual who was not only politically inexperienced but also only a recent convert to the colonial protest. Samuel's likely motives are not difficult to fathom. As it was imperative that the Massachusetts congressmen appear to be the antithesis of fire-breathing militancy, it was a savvy move to include in the delegation a member who was untainted by extremism as well as a leading lawyer who had defended the British soldiers charged with the Boston Massacre. Samuel no doubt also thought it a plus that John was a political innocent who would look to his older cousin for guidance.

John had not expected to play a major role in the First Congress, and indeed, like his three colleagues from Massachusetts, he remained in the background, saying little and taking pains to be circumspect on the rare occasions when he spoke. Furthermore, John had come to Philadelphia in September 1774 very much aware that he was a political novice. He had expected to be overshadowed—overawed, in fact—by the bevy of "wise Statesmen" in attendance.[30] Adams was additionally convinced that he had not been graced with the qualities exhibited by most political standouts. Leaders, he thought, were almost always tall and graceful men who readily filled every room with their commanding presence. But he stood only five feet seven, the average height of American-born males in the late eighteenth century, leading him to sadly acknowledge that "By my Physical Constitution I am but an ordinary man." In addition, Adams was awkward, portly, balding, and, by his own admission, a rather careless dresser. Nor was he especially warm and engaging. He admitted that he did not possess a knack for telling jokes. When it came to what he thought were men's three favorites subjects—women, horses, and dogs—Adams could barely join in a conversation. Instead, he was a cantankerous sort given to arguing. That led others, including Jefferson, to describe him as "irritable." Adams characterized himself as "irascible."[31]

Adams had sat on the First Congress's Grand Committee, and it had turned to him to draft the section on Parliament's authority over colonial commerce, the great roadblock to completing its statement on American rights. Otherwise, he had watched and listened, and what he had seen and heard boosted his self-confidence. By the time Congress adjourned, Adams had come to see himself as intellectually superior to nearly all of his colleagues and the equal of most as a public speaker. He eagerly looked forward to playing a greater role in the Second Congress.

But Adams, who had collapsed following his tension-laced visit to Lexington soon after the war's first battle, was still ill when he reached Philadelphia two weeks later. In letter after letter to Abigail that spring, he complained that he was "completely miserable," "not well," "quite infirm," "wasted and exhausted," and "weak in health." "I am always unwell," he despaired in the early weeks of Congress. He suffered with "smarting Eyes" and dim vision. He was afflicted with a skin disorder, night sweats, insomnia, weakness, fatigue, tremors, arrhythmia, depression, and acute anxiety.[32] These were the same symptoms he had experienced during his illness four years earlier, and they would haunt him again in 1781. Each of Adams's illnesses occurred in times when he endured great stress. Today, stress is thought to be one possible trigger

of hyperthyroidism, and the cluster of symptoms Adams displayed is symp-
tomatic of an overactive thyroid, or thyrotoxicosis. Physicians in Adams's
time were unaware of the thyroid, much less its maladies, but medical records
from the next century—prior to the discovery of modern therapies—
demonstrate that while the disease was usually fatal, some patients lived for
years, because in some instances hyperthyroidism lapsed into remission and,
on occasion, never reappeared.[33]

The cause of Adams's poor health is uncertain, but the source of the tension that gripped him is not difficult to find. At the height of his illness,
Adams remarked that "a vast Variety of great objects were crowding upon my
Mind," including worries over the safety of his family in a colony that was
"suffering all the Calamities of *Famine, Pestilence, Fire,* and *Sword* at once."[34]
Furthermore, Adams knew that he was part of a body in rebellion against
king and Parliament. If the war was lost, every congressman would be liable
to arrest and prosecution for the capital crime of treason, a grim fact that allegedly led Franklin to quip that the members of Congress must hang together or they would hang separately. Adams was not a coward, and from the
start he believed the war was necessary and just. He also believed America
would win the war. However, he was profoundly troubled by the knowledge
that he had helped bring on a war in which others would be compelled to face
hazards on the battlefield that he had never confronted. He was uneasy over
the fact that he was the first male in the Adams family who had never served
in the military. His burden of guilt only grew when one of his brothers, Elihu,
died that summer of a camp disease while soldiering in the siege of Boston.
When not writing home about the alarming symptoms of his illness, Adams
filled his letters with remorseful pledges to fight for his country. "Oh that I was
a Soldier!—I will be," he exclaimed. "We must all be soldiers," he said, adding:
"Every body must and will and shall be a soldier." But deep down he knew that
he would never bear arms or come under fire, and it gnawed at him, feeding
his anxieties and perhaps fueling his illness.[35]

In May 1775 Adams was too ill to mount a strenuous opposition to Dickinson's campaign to petition the king. Even had he been well, he may not have
fought too hard. Massachusetts's fundamental priority at that stage was to
preserve unity, at least until Congress created a national army that would
displace the sectional Grand American Army.

By mid-June Adams felt better. He told Abigail that his eyes were improving and some of his other ills had abated. His health seemed to get better—
and his spirits soared—on learning of America's "astonishing" military spirit
and Congress's unanimous support of the war.[36] The action that he had taken
to break the logjam in Congress by urging the creation of a national army,

and Washington's subsequent appointment as its commander, were signals that Adams was ready to play a greater role. As the summer heat and humidity settled over Philadelphia, one observer remarked that Adams had emerged as "the first man in the House," the leader of those who favored taking a firmer line toward Great Britain than did Dickinson's faction.[37] Adams's ascent was breathtaking. Virtually devoid of political experience prior to the First Continental Congress, he had come to be a leader in the Second Congress after only a few weeks.

The legendary determination and industry that led Adams to flourish as a lawyer served him again in Congress. Pursuing what his colleagues might have thought was a sleepless pace, Adams tended to congressional business from early morning until well past dark, six days a week. He sat through the daily sessions of Congress and served on at least thirty-five committees during the year that began in June 1775. The committees often met before Congress convened or following its late-afternoon adjournment, and many required long hours of intense work in order to meet the pressing deadlines set by Congress.[38] Characteristically, Adams also sought to become the best-informed congressman on a wide variety of subjects. He brought to Philadelphia several books from his considerable library and from time to time asked Abigail to send down others. He rose early and stayed up late reading and studying, straining to see the pages by the dim light of a flickering candle. His hard work paid dividends. In time, his colleagues came to see him as Congress's foremost expert on political theory, diplomacy, and even military ordnance.

Nor was his diligence all that he had going for him. Adams's years in the courtroom had made him both a talented debater and an able orator. He lacked Henry's flair for the dramatic, but his speeches were eloquent and rational, prompting one congressman to remark that Adams was unequaled in his ability to grasp "the whole of a subject at a single glance." Jefferson described Adams as "profound in his views . . . and accurate in his judgment." Finally, while Adams's penchant for argumentation was irritating, once the other congressmen got to know him, most grew to like him. Adams had "a heart formed for friendship," as one of his fellow Boston lawyers remarked, and he so badly wanted to succeed that he overcame his naturally reserved habits.[39] Adams never conquered his prickly manner, but he grew to be more outgoing and a good conversationalist. He had the ability to talk about numerous subjects, and he was blessed with the rare virtue of being a good listener. It may not be an exaggeration to say that John Adams made more lasting friendships with deputies from throughout America than any other member of Congress. Curiously, too, while John was no less radical than

Samuel Adams by the summer of 1775, he was from first to last seen by most of his colleagues as something of a moderate, at least as far as Yankees went. Their perception only gave greater credibility to the tough and unsentimental line that he advocated.

By fits and starts that summer, Adams saw hopeful evidence that things were falling in place for those of his persuasion. He remained vexed that many in Congress, probably most, believed that North's ministry and Parliament would come to their senses when they learned of what happened at Lexington and Concord. Adams predicted with certainty that Britain's government would give America nothing "but Deceit and Hostility." He was displeased too that the selection of the general officers who were to serve beneath Washington had been shot through with politics, leading to the appointment of some men who he feared were strikingly incompetent. Nothing that Congress had ever done gave "me more Torment," he raged, although he knew that some good men had been chosen and was delighted that the top two officers were General Washington and Major General Lee, just as Massachusetts had wished. He may even have shared Samuel Adams's belief that Washington and Lee jointly exhibited so many wonderful qualities that they would "make good all Deficiencies" of the other general officers. Adams was additionally thrilled that Congress had voted to raise soldiers from several colonies south of New England, a step that would make the Continental army a truly national force while giving the siege army at least a two-to-one superiority over Gage's regulars. Among those raised were ten companies of riflemen from Pennsylvania, Maryland, and Virginia. Adams exclaimed that these men, armed with rifles rather than the notoriously inaccurate muskets that most eighteenth-century soldiers carried, could "kill with great Exactness at 200 yards Distance." He was unruffled by their vow to hone in on the officers in the British army. Indeed, he hoped "they perform their oath."[40]

Adams's confidence grew as Congress redoubled its efforts that summer to find powder and weapons and to create an American currency. What truly made him happy, however, was evidence that the country was firmly behind the war. In some instances the people appeared to be out in front of their congressmen. Pennsylvanians were a case in point. Whereas Adams believed that many of that colony's leaders were "timid" and only "lukewarm" in their support of the necessary military preparations, Pennsylvanians were rallying to arms. Philadelphia had rapidly raised three battalions—nearly two thousand men—"all in Uniforms, and very expert" in their "Wheelings and Firings." There were riflemen in backcountry garb, gaudily clad cavalry, Highlanders in kilts, and "German Hussars," who sported "a deaths Head" emblem on their waistbands. The latter, said Adams, were the "most formidable" men he had ever seen. As General Washington prepared to leave Philadelphia for the front in Boston, Adams rejoiced that the "Spirit of the People is such as you would wish" and that every colony had embraced the "Cause of America."[41]

After his selection as commander, Washington remained in Philadelphia for a week to wrap up his personal affairs—among other things, he had a will drawn—and also probably to listen to Congress's discussion surrounding the general officers, virtually all of whom were strangers to him. In addition, he served as a consultant on the drafting of the Articles of War, the judicial code governing army conduct. Washington also awaited his orders from Congress, much of which limited, or at least restrained, his authority. Though given "full power" to repel "hostile invasion[s]" and defend American liberties, he was directed to seek the advice of his general officers in councils of war before making substantive decisions. He was made responsible for the appointment of lower-grade field officers but was forbidden to name general officers. Fearful of wayward and disorderly soldiers, Congress told its new commander that it expected him to keep "strict discipline" in the Continental army.[42]

At sunrise on Friday, June 23, every member of Congress gathered outside the Pennsylvania State House to bid farewell to General Washington, who at last was ready to ride north to take command of the army. In the gathering dawn, while scores of spectators watched, Washington bowed gravely, said good-bye, and easily sprang aboard his great white charger. The congressmen who would escort him to the edge of the city climbed into carriages. The city's militia units and a spirited martial band took their places at the head of the column. When all were in line, the procession set off, clattering over Philadelphia's cobblestone streets. It had been the simplest of ceremonies. But it was an epochal moment. America's commander in chief, tasked with compelling Great Britain to reconcile with the colonies on Congress's terms, was on his way to a most uncertain future.[43]

Snippets of news about a second great battle had reached Philadelphia shortly before Washington's departure. An express rider from the Bay Colony galloped into town at eleven o'clock on Wednesday night and headed directly for the boardinghouse where the Massachusetts delegation stayed. Despite the late hour, word spread quickly that something big must have occurred. In no time, more than a hundred men had gathered in the street, each straining to hear what was said. But the facts were "very Confused," according to one man in the crowd. There had been a battle at Bunker Hill, just north of Boston.

Losses were heavy on both sides. That was about all that was known for certain. Several New England congressmen rushed to their lodging to write home for more information. The sketchy account of the battle had provoked the "most uneasy of all Situations," said one, while another wrote that the news "leaves us in suspence" and "the greatest possable anxiety." "We wait to hear more particulars," a congressman told a source near Boston, adding: "Our Hopes and Our Fears are alternately very strong."[44] The Battle of Bunker Hill would be profoundly important to both sides in this war, and it would have an impact on congressional decisions during the next couple of weeks.

Unaware of the steps being taken by Congress to create a national army and name its commander, General Ward had acted on his own to cope with military exigencies facing his siege army. Receiving intelligence that the British planned to occupy Charlestown Heights, hilly terrain across the Charles River from Boston, Ward moved swiftly to beat his adversary to the punch. On the night of June 16, the day after Washington's appointment in faraway Philadelphia, Ward dispatched a sizable force to Bunker Hill with orders to fortify the site. Ward's plan was simple. American artillery deployed on these heights could command Boston Harbor, the British army's lifeline to the outside world. General Gage would face a choice of emerging to fight the entrenched rebels or of quitting Boston.

Just before dawn, Gage learned of Ward's action. The British commander rapidly decided to fight. In fact, unable to imagine that America's callow soldiers would stand up to his regulars, Gage scorned suggestions that the Royal Navy be utilized to simply seal off the rebels' only escape route, giving the British a bloodless victory. Gage ordered a frontal assault. He hoped to humiliate the rebels, who he thought would flee when they saw the king's soldiers advancing on their positions. Gage also hoped to kill as many colonial soldiers as possible. That would dampen the ardor of other colonists who were eager to take up arms. Gage was cocksure not just of victory but also of inflicting a disaster of such proportions on the Grand American Army that the colonists' will to continue the rebellion would be broken.

Gage gave General William Howe, a veteran with a deserved reputation for bravery, responsibility for the attack. Howe never considered any option other than having his men fight as they were trained to fight on European battlefields. The regulars would march slowly and methodically up the open hillside toward their enemy. In Europe, opposing armies clashed on open battlefields. Howe knew things would be different here. His men would face an entrenched foe. But like Gage, Howe did not believe the Americans would stick around for the fight.

Howe was given 2,300 infantry. In addition, the navy was ordered to shell the nearby village of Charlestown, hoping to flush out any rebel units or snipers

The Battle of Bunker Hill occurred on June 17, 1775. The British armed forces succeeded in retaking the hill from the Grand American Army, but suffered heavy losses, which convinced many colonists that the untrained Americans could stand up to British regulars. (Archive of Early American Images, John Corter Brown Library, Brown University)

in that sector. Slightly more than 2,000 American soldiers were atop the hill, under the command of Colonel William Prescott. A lithe and trim six-footer, the forty-nine-year-old Prescott had soldiered in the past two intercolonial wars. He had so impressed his regular commanders during the French and Indian War that they had offered him a commission in the British army. He declined, and at war's end returned to his farm in Pepperell, Massachusetts. Now he was soldiering again, and at Bunker Hill his men were armed with muskets and ten artillery pieces. The Yankee soldiers had precious little ammunition, but many were ensconced inside a hastily constructed four-sided, square redoubt. Others were hunched behind earthworks and stone walls.

One aspect of Gage's strategy unfolded as planned. The navy laid down a shuddering bombardment, setting Charlestown ablaze. The "merciless Dogs" reduced the little village to "a heap of Ruin with nothing standing but a heap of Chimneys," one enraged Yankee reported.[45] Otherwise, nothing went as Gage and Howe had imagined it would. Foremost among their disappointments was that the American soldiers did not immediately flee in panic. Ordered to husband their powder and not to fire "until you can see the whites of their eyes," the Americans stood their ground, watching as the regulars marched unhurriedly, and unwaveringly, up the hillside. An eerie silence fell over the scene, broken only by the clatter of equipment as the redcoats struggled at times to climb over the fences and walls that dotted the landscape. With determination the regulars moved closer, steadily closer, in what many Americans later marveled was a "very slow march."

When the regulars closed to within twenty-five yards, the Americans at last opened fire. It was akin to "a continual sheet of lightning" and sounded like "an uninterrupted peal of thunder," one of Howe's men thought. They "picked us all off," he added.[46] Men clad in red fell all across the battlefield. One who went down with a mortal wound was Major John Pitcairn, who two months earlier had commanded the regulars on Lexington Green. (He was allegedly struck only a second after shouting "The day is ours!")[47] That blood-drenched moment when scores of British regulars were gunned down produced *"a Moment that I never felt before,"* Howe acknowledged afterward.[48] The British fell back, and "with a quicker step than they came up," a Yankee noted with satisfaction.[49]

But the British came on again. The Americans continued to stand their ground. For a second time the regulars were repulsed. Howe summoned reinforcements from Boston. When the additional units were in place, he ordered his men forward a third time. This time the regulars succeeded, but only because the Americans finally ran out of ammunition. Without the means of fighting, the rebels at last broke and ran. The regulars, atop the heights, poured a merciless fire on the fleeing Yankees, killing many, including Dr. Warren, the rebel firebrand who unwisely had come to the battlefield to watch the fighting.

The carnage was nearly indescribable, and it was mostly suffered by the regulars. Fifty percent of the British soldiers who saw action were killed or wounded. Of the British officer corps stationed in Boston, 40 percent were casualties. Altogether, Gage and Howe lost 226 killed and 928 wounded, nearly a quarter of the British army in Boston. The Americans took heavy losses too. Some 330 rebels were killed or wounded.[50]

Four British generals had been present, and each was shocked and dismayed by what had taken place. After the battle, Howe walked among his wounded on the slopes of Bunker Hill, listening to their mournful cries, his white leggings laced with streaks of red by the tall, blood-drenched grass. On this "unhappy day," he remarked, "success [was] too dearly bought." Sir Henry Clinton called it a "dear bought victory," and added that "another such would have ruined us." General John Burgoyne, who had watched the engagement from Beacon Hill in Boston, described the battle as "a picture . . . of horrour." Though a veteran of the fighting in Europe in Britain's previous war with France, Burgoyne thought Bunker Hill had featured "the greatest scenes of war" he had ever witnessed.[51]

It fell to Gage to file the official report with Lord Dartmouth. The general minced no words. British losses were "greater than our force can afford to lose." Gage's view of his adversary had been transformed. The "rebels are not the despicable rabble too many have supposed them to be." They fight with "zeal and enthusiasm," evincing "a military spirit" never displayed when they soldiered alongside the British in the French and Indian War. Gage closed with a warning: The "conquest of this Country is not easy, and can be affected only by time and perseverance, and strong armies attacking it in various quarters and dividing their forces."[52]

By the end of June, Congress knew what had occurred and its members were exultant. Samuel Adams "greatly rejoiced at the tryed Valor" of the New England soldiers. A South Carolinian dared to believe that the British army might fear "to face the provincials again" after suffering "so severe a drubbing." Jefferson said that "every one rejoices" at the news of Pitcairn's death. When writing to friends in England, Franklin emphasized the "two severe Repulses" suffered by the British army. But with a wink and a nod he skipped over the rebels' shortage of powder, claiming instead that the redcoats finally succeeded only because the Americans had lacked the time to complete their entrenchments.[53]

Word of Bunker Hill almost immediately influenced a matter before Congress. In May, Congress had stopped Colonel Benedict Arnold in his tracks when he was poised to advance from Crown Point into Canada. But in early June, after Arnold reported that the British authorities in Canada were inciting the Indians to attack along New York's northern frontier, the question of an American invasion of Canada had resurfaced. New York and New England supported such an action, but the other colonies were uncertain. Congress waffled for days before agreeing to postpone a decision until it learned whether the inhabitants of Canada, for the most part people of French descent, were likely to assist an American invasion force. Congress was still waiting for an answer when the news of Bunker Hill arrived. One day later Congress decided on "making an Impression into Canada," as Hancock curiously worded his missive that broke the news to General Washington. Given the Americans' performance along Battle Road and on Bunker Hill, Congress thought that Canada, which was weakly defended by the British, would fall whether or not the Canadian population provided assistance.[54]

Canada was not the only item on Congress's agenda when word of Bunker Hill arrived. Late in May, Congress had referred to a committee the North

Peace Plan, the prime minister's wishful pitch for reconciliation based on the fatuous notion of permitting each colonial assembly to raise whatever amount of revenue was stipulated by Parliament. Calling it an "example of the moderation of Parliament," and praying that it would bring an end to the colonists' "trivial and groundless complaints," Dartmouth had sent the plan to each governor, directing them to submit it to their assemblies for approval. Dartmouth ignored the Continental Congress.[55]

Ten days before the Second Congress met, the Pennsylvania assembly had been the first to take up North's plan. Still meeting in the room that Congress would soon take for its own, the Pennsylvania legislature—in a carefully worded message written by Dickinson—told the governor that it would be "a dishonorable desertion of sister colonies . . . for a Single Colony to adopt a measure so extensive in consequences." It forwarded North's plan to Congress, as did every colonial assembly that considered the scheme, though some spoke out harshly on the so-called peace plan. Virginia's House of Burgesses adopted one of the stronger statements, a resolution penned by Thomas Jefferson. North's ploy of levying quotas was "a stile of asking gifts not reconcilable to our freedom," Jefferson had written. He added that "the British Parliament has no right to intermeddle with . . . civil government in the Colonies."[56]

By the time Congress finally got around to North's plan, Jefferson had been added to the Virginia delegation in Philadelphia. When Congress turned to him in July to draft its resolution on North's proposal, it was clear that every member held the prime minister's scheme in contempt. Maryland's Thomas Johnson doubtless spoke for all his colleagues when he remarked that "Lord North's proposition" was "insidiously devised to wear the face of peace," although in reality it was a "villainous" move designed to "Embarrass us in the Choice of evils." Jefferson's draft rejecting North's plan was even more hostile than the document he had written for Virginia. This time Jefferson labeled North's plan "uncandid[,] unreasonable[,] unequal[,] and insidious." Congress toned down his rhetoric a mite. It styled North's plan merely "unreasonable and insidious."[57]

Three days before Congress learned of Bunker Hill, it received the committee's draft of the Olive Branch Petition. In May, when Congress had approved Dickinson's proposal to petition the king, it created a committee to draft the entreaty. That panel was packed with moderates—Dickinson, John Jay of New York, John Rutledge, and Johnson of Maryland. Franklin was the lone member who was inclined to a harder line. Not a single New Englander was placed on the committee, one of the few times in the long history of the Continental Congress that a section was denied a role in a substantive undertaking. Dickinson, the principal author of the committee's draft, churned out the "humble and dutiful petition" he had advocated, but his hope that Congress would send peace commissioners to London to open negotiations with the Crown was stymied, doubtless because of Franklin's opposition. Franklin knew all too well the games that officials in London could play when it came to negotiations. Furthermore, he had no wish to see Congress backed into a corner with an option of accepting or rejecting a bad accord sent home by negotiators in London. As a result, the petition's final draft threw the ball into the king's court. If there were to be negotiations, it was left to George III to "direct some mode" for beginning discussions.[58]

Congress received the committee's draft on June 19, but it delayed considering it for fifteen days. By the time it took up the document, on July 4, it knew of Bunker Hill, the second time in as many engagements in this war in which colonial soldiers had inflicted great damage on the British army.

As all of Congress's sessions were secret, it is not known for certain what occurred on July 4 and 5 when the delegates discussed the Olive Branch Petition. But as deliberations spun out over two days, tempestuous debates almost certainly ensued. It is likely that the more hard-line congressmen sought to recast the unctuous tone of Dickinson's draft. It is also probable that the moderates waged a last-ditch fight to send peace commissioners to London.

The only record of what transpired was left by John Adams in memoirs penned a quarter century later. Adams's memory sometimes betrayed him, and in his account of this battle he listed as a participant a congressman who had left Congress two weeks earlier. Nevertheless, Adams probably recaptured the essence of what had occurred. He recalled that the debate commenced with lengthy speeches by several moderates from Dickinson's faction. They were answered by delegates from the other side, some of whom addressed Congress with "Wit, Reasoning and fluency." Adams portrayed himself as the leader of the opposition to Dickinson, speaking with passion against what he privately depicted as a petition filled with "Prettynesses [and] Juvenilities, much less Puerilities" that were unbecoming "a great Assembly" in the midst of war.[59] It was in this battle with Dickinson that Adams almost surely assumed the leadership of the faction opposed to the moderates' conciliatory course.

Dickinson, Adams recalled, grew "terrified" that his petition would be emasculated, if not rejected altogether, by a Congress emboldened by Bunker Hill. In the course of the stormy session, Adams was called away into the yard outside the State House to meet with someone on some sort of business. Adams later recollected that he grabbed his

Hat and went out of the Door of Congress Hall: Mr. Dickinson observed me and Darted out after me. He broke out upon me in a most abrupt and extraordinary manner. In as violent a passion as he was capable of feeling, and with an Air, Countenance and Gestures as rough and haughty as if I had been a School Boy and he the Master, he vociferated out, "What is the Reason Mr. Adams, that you New Englandmen oppose our Measures of Reconciliation. . . . Look Ye! If you don't concur with Us, in our pacific System, I, and a Number of Us, will break off, from you in New England, and We will carry on the Opposition by ourselves in our own Way." I own I was shocked by this Magisterial Salutation. . . . These were the last Words which ever passed between Mr. Dickinson and me in private. We continued to debate in Congress . . . But the Friendship and Acquaintance was lost forever . . . [through] Mr. Dickinsons rude Lecture.[60]

A short time later, Adams, still seething at Dickinson's tone and his threat to abandon New England, wrote a friend at home that a "certain great Fortune and piddling Genius whose Fame has been trumpeted so loudly, has given a silly Cast to our whole Doings."[61] Unfortunately for Adams, the bearer of his missive was taken into custody by the British as he crossed Narragansett Bay. Finding Adams's letter, the British gleefully turned it over to a Tory editor in occupied Boston, who happily published it in the *Massachusetts Gazette*. It also appeared in two London newspapers in September, leading some readers to speculate that the "piddling Genius" was John Hancock. But Dickinson knew whom Adams had referred to, giving him further grounds for enmity. From this point forward these two congressmen never again spoke to one another. When passing in the State House hallway or on Philadelphia's busy sidewalks, each in glowering silence looked straight ahead, never acknowledging the other.

After Adams's caustic letter appeared in public, he was shunned for a time by Quaker merchants and others in Philadelphia who saw him as an obstacle to reconciliation. According to one observer, he was also viewed with "nearly universal detestation" by the moderates in Congress, much as Galloway had been reviled by the radicals at the First Congress. But the incident did not cause lasting damage to Adams, and in fact, it appears to have immediately made him more popular among the foes of Dickinson. Adams continued to participate in Congress without missing a beat, and his colleagues continued to choose him for important committee assignments.[62]

After the second day of debate, Congress approved the committee's draft of the Olive Branch Petition. Back in May, when he had first raised the matter of a congressional appeal to the Crown, Dickinson had couched the issues of petitioning the king and creating the Continental army as trade-offs. The moderates would agree to the military preparations sought by the hard-liners; the hard-liners, in return, would consent to the Olive Branch Petition.[63] Dickinson must have reminded the petition's foes of the quid pro quid agreed to six weeks earlier. In fact, that is what he must have pointed out to Adams in the State House garden, to which he almost certainly added that the hard-liners could not now break their word without shattering unity within Congress. Dickinson had his way. Congress adopted the Olive Branch Petition as it was reported out of committee. At some point, perhaps on the day of the dustup with his rival or on the day that Congress approved the petition, Adams wrote to a friend at home: "I dread like Death" petitioning the king, but "We cant avoid it. Discord and total Disunion would be the certain Effect of a resolute Refusal to petition." Adams's only hope was that the monarch and his ministers "will be afraid of Negotiations as well as We [the congressional hard-liners], and therefore refuse it."[64]

But if Congress had agreed to seek the monarch's intervention, it had not agreed to send envoys to London with the Olive Branch Petition. Instead, it asked Richard Penn, the son of Pennsylvania's proprietor, to carry the petition across the sea. Penn lived in Philadelphia, had entertained several congressmen in his home, and was trusted by most deputies. Even so, Penn was instructed to deliver to Arthur Lee and other colonial agents in the metropolis the secret document that he carried with its seal unbroken.[65]

Penn sailed three days later. As he departed, John Adams almost audibly sighed that Congress "is a great, unwieldy Body. Its Progress must be slow. It is like a large Fleet sailing under Convoy. The fleetest Sailors must wait for the dullest and slowest. Like a Coach and six—the swiftest Horses must be slackened and the slowest quickened, that all may keep an even Pace."[66] Now and again Adams was driven to despair, but he never lost hope that in time a majority in Congress would come around to see that reconciliation with Great Britain was unlikely, perhaps even undesirable. From the onset of hostilities he sensed that the war would alienate the colonists from the mother country. Inevitably, it would call forth decisions that would widen the breach between America and Great Britain. In short, the war would radicalize his countrymen. He was certain, too, that British officials would take steps that would be seen as "Cruelties more abominable than those which are practiced by the Savage Indians." With each "fresh Evidence" of "Deceit and Hostility, Fire, Famine, Pestilence and Sword," more and more Americans would "be driven to the sad Necessity of breaking our Connection with G.B." With each British act of "War and Revenge," the American people would better understand the immeasurable "Corruption to the System" of politics in the mother country, until most at last understood that the "Cancer is too deeply rooted, and too far spread to be cured by any thing short of cutting it out entire."[67]

Dickinson scored another victory—what would be his final major triumph—the very next day. On June 23, the day General Washington departed for the front, Congress had created a committee to draft what was tantamount to a declaration of war. Hoping to have Washington publish the statement when he arrived in Massachusetts, Congress must have directed the committee to work with haste, for the following day the panel submitted a draft penned by John Rutledge. However, Congress found Rutledge's work unacceptable—the document has vanished, and its contents are unknown—and directed the committee to try again. It also added Dickinson and Jefferson to the committee. Dickinson no doubt wanted the assignment. The "famous Mr. Jefferson," as one congressman referred to him, was chosen because others in the Virginia delegation had spread the word that he had a "reputation for literature." In fact, the committee asked Jefferson to pen the new draft.[68]

Jefferson agreed and within a few days shared his draft with his colleagues on the committee. Dickinson strenuously objected to some of its contents and over the next couple of days, using the Virginian's handiwork as an outline, wrote his own statement. Adams would have thought it intolerable to have his work repudiated. Jefferson, who was both a newcomer to Congress and a less-confrontational individual, neither quarreled with Dickinson nor bore enmity toward him. Years later Jefferson said simply that he had acquiesced to Dickinson's "scruples" as he "was so honest a man, and so able a one."[69]

At the time, New Jersey's William Livingston, who sat on the committee, criticized what Jefferson had written as containing "faults common to our Southern gentlemen." Southerners believe, he went on, that "a reiteration of [British] tyranny, despotism, [and] bloody" actions was all that was necessary when asking the citizenry's support of the war.[70] Livingston implied that the declaration must also stress that Great Britain had violated the imperial constitution. But in fact Jefferson had not ignored constitutional issues. Livingston—and Dickinson, the real power on the committee—in reality wished to have Congress embrace a declaration that espoused the moderates' view of the limits of parliamentary authority.

Jefferson, like John Adams, believed the king was the sole "link of union between the several parts of the empire." Dickinson was critical of Parliament: It had evinced, he said, "an inordinate Passion for [unlimited] Power" over the colonies, including the hope "to extort from us, at the point of the Bayonet . . . unknown sums." But while he blamed it for the imperial crisis and the war, he did not wish to proclaim that it possessed no authority over America. In a lengthy section Dickinson explained to the monarch that the American people had taken up arms solely to defend their liberties. Furthermore, he underscored that Congress did not seek independence: "We have not raised Armies with ambitious Designs of separating from Great-Britain, and establishing Independent States."

But a declaration stating the reasons for war had to resonate with a people who were being asked to sacrifice, and possibly die, in that war. It also had to assure the people that the war could be won. Near its close, Dickinson retained a passage that Jefferson had written: "Our cause is just. Our union is perfect. Our internal Resources are great, and, if necessary, foreign Assistance is undoubtedly attainable." Americans, it added, have "resolved to die Freemen rather than to live Slaves." On July 6, Congress saw only the version of the Declaration on the Causes and Necessity for Taking Up Arms that Dickinson had prepared. With some minor editing, but little debate, Congress adopted it.[71]

In two bruising months the Second Congress had rejected the North Peace Plan, created an army, named its commander, declared war, and petitioned the king. Its one substantive link to the prewar First Continental Congress was that the dominant faction repudiated independence, insisting that America yearned to be reconciled with Great Britain, but on its own terms—the restoration of the imperial relationship as it had been before anyone had dreamed of the Stamp Act or other taxes and encroachments. Still, so sweeping, so revolutionary, had been Congress's actions since Lexington and Concord that John Adams wrote on the day the declaration of war was adopted that he expected "Lord North [would] compliment every Mothers Son of us with a Bill of Attainder"—a decree of outlawry for having committed treason.[72]

CHAPTER 7

"THE KING WILL PRODUCE THE GRANDEST REVOLUTION"

GEORGE III AND THE AMERICAN REBELLION

WHEN THE PACKETS BROUGHT to London by the *Quero* were opened on May 28 and news of the losses suffered by the British force sent to Lexington and Concord spread across the city, members of the government reacted with skepticism. Most thought the reports must be American propaganda. Given a couple of days for reflection, the king privately allowed that General Gage might have dispatched an inadequate force to Concord. Possibly, there had been some trouble, but George III would not budge from his belief that the accounts in the Salem newspapers on display at the lord mayor's office were exaggerated. Even so, while it awaited Gage's official report, the government used friendly newspapers to counter the rebel allegations that the king's soldiers had committed atrocities. The *General Evening Post* cautioned readers, "Impartiality cannot be expected from Men when they are giving an Account of their own rebellious Proceedings." It added that the version spread by the "rebel Vermin" was "stuffed with many Falsities."[1] The *London Gazette* and *London Magazine* also ran unfounded stories claiming that the Americans had not only committed atrocities—they had both scalped wounded redcoats and cut off their ears, it was alleged—but also fired the first shot on April 19.[2]

Two weeks later Gage's own report on the bloody first day of war arrived in London. Lord North learned that the accounts carried across the sea by Captain Derby had not been overstated. Although Gage emphasized that the force sent to Concord had accomplished its mission of destroying the arsenal—after the colonists fired the first shot, he said—the general revealed that on the return to Boston his soldiers had been "a good deal pressed" as they took "Fire from . . . every Hill, Fence, House, Barn, &c." The "whole country was

Assembled in Arms" against the British army, he confided. Disconcertingly, Gage did not divulge his losses, but aside from the matter of the source of the first shot, his report more or less confirmed the colonists' accounts of the action. North summoned his cabinet, which had not met in weeks, to his office on Downing Street.[3] Having expected that a show of force would resolve the crisis, North instead had a war on his hands. He and his ministers now had to prepare for hostilities they had not foreseen.

The mood was glum when the cabinet gathered on June 15—the very day that the American Congress, three thousand miles away, appointed General Washington to command the Continental army. Some were upset at learning just how erroneous had been the repeated bluster that the Americans would back down when confronted. Others were disturbed at discovering on the very eve of their meeting that New York, which they had been led to believe was safe from rebel control, was acting in "association with other colonies to resist Acts of Parliament."[4]

The ministers may have been in low spirits, but as far back as January 1774, when the cabinet considered the Coercive Acts as a response to the Boston Tea Party, they had known that a heavy-handed approach could lead to war. They had never wavered from the belief that if war came, Great Britain would be victorious. That attitude yet prevailed, and according to one account, Dartmouth alone, at that initial cabinet meeting after Lexington-Concord, urged an alternative to a military response.

The American secretary got nowhere with his pleas for peace. His colleagues were certain that it would be disastrous for Great Britain to show a hint of weakness. Besides, they were convinced that American firebrands were to blame for the bloodshed. That view was confirmed by General Gage, who told them that this was "a preconcerted Scheme of Rebellion, hatched years ago in Massachusetts Bay." The ministers knew, too, that going to war was popular in the British home islands. Driven by outrage that the colonists had killed British soldiers, the "nation . . . is in a manner unanimous against America," Sandwich told friends. Edward Gibbon, the MP, described the mood as a "national clamour" to employ "the most vigorous and coercive measures."[5] At that June 15 meeting, and three others later in the summer, North's government took steps to escalate the conflict.

During the first meeting, the ministers agreed to reinforce Gage's army by shifting troops from England and Ireland, recruiting one thousand Highlanders in Scotland, and directing Guy Carleton, a general and the governor of Quebec, to raise a force of two thousand citizen-soldiers—if the solicitor general deemed it legal to recruit Catholics—and to persuade his Indian allies to attack along the northern frontier of New York. The cabinet also discussed hiring upwards of three thousand foreign mercenaries, though it came to no decision. Finally, the ministry agreed to send four frigates to America.

By the ministry's second meeting, a week later, Wedderburn had ruled that Catholics could be recruited. North's government then directed Carleton to raise six thousand Canadians—triple the number first contemplated—and assigned them the objective of retaking Fort Ticonderoga, the loss of which London had just learned. The ministers additionally voted to transfer three regiments from Gibraltar and Minorca to America, replacing them with soldiers hired in the German province of Hanover. The cabinet also contemplated how to utilize the Royal Navy in suppressing the American rebellion. The navy was directed to blockade not only the New England coast but also the ports of New York and Charleston and the entrances to Delaware Bay and Chesapeake Bay. At this stage, Britain's blockade was designed to obstruct commerce between the thirteen colonies. The colonies were allowed to trade with both the mother country and the British West Indies, though naval commanders were instructed to stop American vessels and search for arms and munitions, and for illegal foreign goods. The cabinet took two more steps at this busy meeting. It agreed to ship arms to the royal governors in the southern colonies. It also commanded Dartmouth to ask the northern Indian superintendent in New York to "lose no time in taking such steps as may induce" the Six Nations Confederation of Iroquois "to take up the hatchet against His Majesty's rebellious subjects."[6]

The decision to raise Native American warriors was taken after Gage reported that Indians were part of the siege army at Boston. "You may be tender of using Indians," the general had advised, "but the Rebels have shewn us the Example, and brought all [the Indians] they could down upon us." Gage's communiqué was accurate. The Stockbridge Indians, a tribe that had allied with the New England settlers during their eighteenth-century wars with the French, had cast their lot with the Yankees once again. As the Grand American Army took shape in May, some fifty Stockbridge braves formed a light infantry company within the siege army. Prior to Washington's arrival, the Indians were active in ambushing British outposts and surprising sentries. During April and May at least six redcoats died at the hands of the Indians and several others had been wounded (and plundered, according to British reports). Washington continued to utilize his Indian allies—his secretary, Joseph Reed, referred to them as "our Stockbridge Indians"—even though congressional policy after late June was to secure the "strict neutrality" of the Indians.[7]

In the course of its two meetings the ministry had agreed to send some five thousand more regulars to Gage. North's government had deployed two thousand troops to New England at the beginning of the year, when it directed Gage to use force. With the reinforcement agreed to in June, there would be an army of some thirteen thousand men in Boston by late autumn, nearly a 150 percent increase over the number posted in the city only a year earlier.[8] The huge force raised in Canada was expected to bring the number of British under arms in America to nearly twenty thousand, more than double the number in service on the continent when the war broke out.

When the weeklong second cabinet meeting concluded, North was confident that his ministry had done all that was necessary to cope with the American problem. He hurriedly departed London for Wroxton, his 150-year-old country house in Oxfordshire. As Parliament was not in session between May and October, North had spent the spring at his country estate and expected to remain there until autumn. His hopes were quickly frustrated. Late in July, London was jolted by tidings of the Battle of Bunker Hill. The prime minister once again called the cabinet to an emergency meeting and sped to Downing Street.

When the ministers gathered on July 26 for their third meeting on the American war, the atmosphere was even more somber. Their frame of mind was captured perfectly by William Eden, an undersecretary of state: "We certainly are victorious . . . but if we have eight more such victories there will be nobody left to bring news of them."[9] North, at last, grasped that his government faced a more formidable challenge than he had realized. The "war is now grown to such a height, that it must be treated as a foreign war," he told the monarch, adding that "every expedient which would be used" in a contest with a major European adversary "should be applied" to hostilities in America. Privately, North confided to a neighbor and friend that he doubted victory could be won. Not only had the stout performances of the American soldiers awakened him to the realities of this war, but also North was not confident that the nation possessed the financial means of carrying on a widespread, protracted war. But he did not take his reservations to the king.[10]

While North remained silent, others expressed their misgivings. Viscount Barrington, the secretary at war, told the prime minister that the Americans might be brought to their knees through a naval blockade, but they could not be defeated in a land war. Dartmouth pushed harder than ever for a negotiated settlement. London, he argued, must make sufficient concessions so that the leaders in the mother country and the colonies could "shake hands at last." The Duke of Grafton, Lord Privy Seal and a veteran of many past ministries, urged North to "go to great lengths to bring about . . . a reconciliation."[11]

But most ministers remained intransigent, sure of victory, though they implicitly acknowledged that this would be a tougher war than they had formerly imagined. No one any longer presumed the war could be won in 1775.

Every minister understood that victory required more troops than had been thought necessary only thirty days before, and all presumably understood that, at the moment, the British army did not have sufficient men to do what it was to be asked to do. On paper, the British army in 1775 consisted of 48,647 men, but the ministry knew that no more than 36,000 regulars were under arms.[12] Somehow, somewhere, men had to be found. In the wake of Bunker Hill, five regiments in Ireland, six more battalions in Gibraltar and Minorca, and four artillery companies in the home islands were ordered to sail for America at once. In addition, 6,000 men were to be recruited to bring the regiments already in America up to strength—that is, up to 811 men per regiment, not counting officers and noncommissioned officers. North's government had gone to war thinking the job could be done with as few as 7,000 regulars. Word of Lexington-Concord and Bunker Hill caused the ministry to increase its estimates of how many men were needed to suppress the colonial rebellion. By the time the late-July cabinet meeting adjourned, North was committed to deploying more than 30,000 redcoats in North America. Between January and July, the ministry had taken steps to nearly quintuple its army in America. Some of the reinforcements were expected to reach the colonies by early autumn, but it would be the spring or summer of 1776 before the last British soldier crossed the sea.[13]

Three days after the third emergency cabinet meeting, North learned from Carleton that none of the 6,000 Canadians, and none of the Indians, that the ministry had anticipated would be available to augment the British army. When asked to take up arms, both had "showed . . . backwardness," the governor exclaimed. An incursion into New York to reclaim the lost forts was out of the question, at least in 1775. In fact, Carleton was not even sanguine about securing Canada. He needed money and reinforcements, he said, to defend his province against a possible rebel invasion.[14]

More bad news cascaded on North in the weeks that followed. First, recruiting went badly in August and September. Next, the secretary at war convinced the monarch that sending to America all the reinforcements agreed to would leave merely 4,500 regulars in all of England and Scotland, too few to defend the homeland in a worse-case scenario. By early autumn North feared that the British army in America would have insufficient manpower to conduct a broad campaign in 1776. He took the only step left to him. North sought to hire foreign soldiers, turning first to Russia's czarina, Catherine the Great.[15]

With England facing a bigger, more dangerous war than had been foreseen, changes in high places seemed imperative. Sometimes the king demanded the changes, but North also realized that new faces were needed. General Gage was the first to go.

The king had turned against Gage a year earlier, convinced after reading the general's reports that he was a defeatist. Gage had bluntly told North's government that all America, not merely the Yankees, would fight if London did not back down. He suggested suspending the Coercive Acts, though only in order to buy time for making the necessary preparations for war. Winning a war against the Americans would not be easy, he had advised. He would need a huge army, and he wanted it at his disposal on the first day of war. He would be fighting a formidable foe and would have to pacify not merely the coastal areas but the interior of the colonies as well, no easy undertaking. "If you think ten Thousand Men significant, send Twenty, if one Million is thought enough, give two." In another missive, he added, "send me a sufficient Force to command the Country, by marching into it, and sending off large Detachments to secure obedience thro' every part of it."[16]

Although Gage's reading of the situation had been uncannily prescient, word of the disasters on the day of Lexington and Concord, and on Bunker Hill, convinced North that Gage was not the man for the job. As usual, it fell to Dartmouth to do the dirty work. "From the Tenor of your Letters," he wrote to Gage on August 2, "the King is led to conclude that you have little Expectation of effecting any thing further this Campaign, and has therefore commanded . . . that you . . . return to England." He was to be succeeded as commander of the British forces in America, Dartmouth went on, by General Howe, who had led the assault on Bunker Hill.[17] Gage, a good soldier with an excellent sense of the situation throughout the colonies, was gone, replaced by a commander who would prove to be his inferior in every respect.

Dartmouth was the next to go. Out of step with this hard-line ministry for the past eighteen months, he had survived as long as he did largely because of his familial ties to North. But with a tough war ahead, the first minister understood that Dartmouth could not be kept on. North tried to make Dartmouth's ouster as painless as possible by offering him another, less important, cabinet position. But that meant someone else had to be removed from his seat to make room. Weeks were consumed in delicate negotiations, during which one insider claimed that North sweetened the pot by promising Dartmouth that America would be offered new terms for reconciliation. At long last Dartmouth resigned as American secretary in November and was named Lord Privy Seal. In the words of North's biographer, Dartmouth "retired into honorable unimportance in the cabinet."[18]

Lord George Germain succeeded Dartmouth as the American secretary.

He would in time become a veritable secretary of war and, Lord North aside, the most powerful man in the ministry. A noted war hawk, there was no question that Germain would be more forceful than his predecessor. Yet, his appointment was somewhat surprising. He was considerably older than most leaders on both sides in this war—he was sixteen years older than both Lord North and General Washington—and he was "a man with a past," as historian Piers Mackesy described him.[19] Born to great wealth in Kent, Germain chose to soldier after several indifferent years as a student. It seemed an excellent choice, as he rose to the rank of major general within only fifteen years.

When the Seven Years' War broke out, Germain was named second-in-command of the British army in the European theater. But three years into that conflict, he was accused of disobeying orders and behaving cravenly during the Battle of Minden. Though cleared of the charge of cowardice, he was dismissed from the service and endured years of ridicule and incivility, sometimes at the hands of those who had once been close friends. Nevertheless, some believed him unfairly wronged and stood by him, even seeing to his agonizingly slow rehabilitation. First, they helped Germain get appointed to a series of minor offices. Eventually, he took a seat in Parliament, where he supported the Declaratory Act and the taxes levied on the colonists. In 1774 Germain demanded that the Yankees be punished for the Boston Tea Party. As North's government contemplated its response to the destruction of the tea, Germain spoke on the floor of the House of Commons in favor of "a manly and steady perseverance" to end the "state of anarchy and confusion" in America and to restore "peace, quietude, and a due obedience to the laws of this country." He caught North's eye with that assertive speech.[20]

Germain continued to speak in Parliament on the American problem, earning a reputation in some circles as an authority on the matter. From beginning to end he characterized New England's radicals as "a tumultuous and riotous rabble" that harbored "dark designs," including American independence. He belittled compromise, scorning the abdication of any parliamentary authority. "Support your supremacy," he exhorted. He contended that the colonists would have been brought to heel a decade earlier "if the Stamp Act had not been unfortunately repealed."[21]

Germain's unvarnished optimism and skill in debate impressed the first minister, who increasingly thought him the ideal candidate to present and defend the government's American policies. Germain, meanwhile, won the support of several hard-liners inside the government, among them Wedderburn, undersecretary of state William Eden—a close friend to whom North often turned for advice—and the Earl of Suffolk, the secretary of state for the Southern Department. They brought Germain's recommendations for dealing

*Lord George Germain by George Romney. A former soldier, Germain entered
the ministry as American secretary soon after hostilities commenced.
He steadfastly urged a hard line and was opposed to negotiations with the colonists.
(William L. Clement Library, University of Michigan)*

with the recalcitrant colonists to the prime minister's attention: Raise Loyalist
regiments to augment the army; unleash Canadian troops on New York's
northern frontier; and retake New York. "We are equal to the contest; our internal resources are great," he insisted. "I shall be for exerting the utmost force
of this Kingdom to finish the rebellion in one campaign." In the wake of Bunker Hill, North thought Germain "the fittest man in the Kingdom" for directing the American war and was eager to move him into Dartmouth's slot.[22]

Many opposed bringing Germain into the government. Some could never
forgive him for his behavior at Minden. Others feared that his obsession with
personal redemption would color his judgment in making military decisions.
Those who believed that only negotiations could lead to reconciliation with
America knew that Germain thought in terms of the total subjugation of the
colonists. Not a few were put off by what they saw as his cold, unapproachable
manner. North's brother, the bishop of Worcester, was among those who cautioned against Germain's appointment, warning that he was "not a popular
Man, & is reckoned impracticable and ambitious." But North chose Germain.
Even at sixty years of age, Germain remained an impressive figure, tall and
muscular. He radiated a dignity that commanded respect and fear among many,
scorn among some. North was swept up by Germain's confidence and arsenal
of ideas, not to mention his sharp tongue, which would be useful in managing

MPs. Above all, the prime minister believed that the inflexibly tough Germain was the man who could "bring the colonists to their knees."[23]

One item remained. In the first hours after learning of Bunker Hill, the ministers considered having the king officially proclaim that the colonies were in a state of rebellion. They turned to Wedderburn to draft the document. During the several days that were required for Britain's chief legal officer to complete his task, word arrived that Richard Penn had sailed from Philadelphia during the previous month, bringing with him some sort of petition adopted by the Continental Congress. Though North's government had never recognized Congress, some officials wished to delay any royal pronouncement until the details of Congress's appeal were learned. North was one who hoped to forestall any action until Penn arrived, and he dawdled more than usual in revising the solicitor general's handiwork. But few in the ministry saw any reason for waiting, and fewer still were disposed to receive any product of the Continental Congress.

Nor was the king prepared to accept any communiqué from the Continental Congress. Nine months earlier, George III had concluded that force alone could resolve the American problem. He had seen no reason then, and he saw none in the summer of 1775, for believing that the colonists would peacefully agree to terms of reconciliation that were consistent with what he believed to be in Great Britain's national interest. On learning of Lexington and Concord, the king told North that "any other conduct but compelling obedience would be ruinous." When he received word of Bunker Hill, the king wrote North: "we must persist and not be dismayed by any difficulties that may arise on the other side of the Atlantick; I know I am doing my Duty."[24]

North had no stomach for confrontation with the monarch. At no time in the fourteen years that he headed the ministry did North possess the mettle to stand up to the king. Had Great Britain been led by a more adroit prime minister—a Disraeli rather than a North—perhaps the monarch could have been brought around to a less intransigent strategy. War might have been avoided or, in the aftermath of the early military catastrophes, Great Britain might have been set on a course leading to concessions and peace.

As it was, North did not even make an attempt to bring the cabinet around to his way of thinking. He simply went along with those who believed that war, and war alone, could resolve the Anglo-American dispute. During the third week in August, the prime minister sent the reworked version of the royal proclamation to Windsor Castle. On August 23—one day before Penn and Arthur Lee presented the Olive Branch Petition to the American secretary—George III issued the Proclamation for Suppressing Rebellion and Sedition.[25]

The monarch proclaimed that many Americans, "misled by dangerous and ill-designing men, and forgetting" their allegiance to the mother country, had "proceeded to open and avowed rebellion" that included "traitorously preparing, ordering, and levying war against us." The king also pledged "condign punishment [for] the authors, perpetrators and abettors of such traitorous designs."[26] Great Britain had declared war on America. London's response to the American moderates' attempt at reconciliation was much as Franklin had expected, and as John Adams had prayed it would be.

North's government had worked tirelessly during the two months since it learned of the outbreak of war, and in September and October the prime minister continued his exertions to furnish General Howe with adequate troops. Early in September the prime minister also authorized his new commander in chief in America to abandon Boston and transfer operations to New York, a step earlier recommended by Gage and advocated by Germain. Britain's army could be more easily supplied in New York, and possession of the Hudson, Germain said, would be "the decisive blow" of the war.[27]

The mood on Downing Street remained grim, all the more so when in late summer London newspapers carried the story of the arrival in Plymouth of the *Charming Nancy*, a three-master whose passengers included nearly two hundred soldiers wounded on Bunker Hill, "some without legs, and others without arms; and their cloaths hanging on them like a loose morning gown." Scores of widows and children of the slain redcoats disembarked as well. It was "a most shocking spectacle," one newspaper reported.[28] Thereafter, North mostly marked time, awaiting the annual autumn opening of Parliament. That day finally arrived on October 26, and as had long been customary, Parliament was welcomed into session by the king.

The bright and sunny day was a holiday of sorts, and sixty thousand Londoners—twice the number of residents of America's largest city—turned out to watch the parade of royal grandeur. The pomp was in marked contrast to the simple ceremonies that had attended the gathering of the American Congress or General Washington's departure for the front. Mounted grenadiers, with swords drawn, led the long procession of majestic carriages filled with noblemen and noblewomen. Horse guards and footmen in red and gold livery surrounded the king's splendid coach, a massive vehicle weighing four tons and drawn by eight cream-colored horses.

At about three o'clock the thunderous roar of artillery announced that George III had completed his journey from St. James's Palace to Westminster. The monarch alighted to the cheers of the spectators and, moments later, was escorted by peers wearing red robes to the throne in the forefront of the House of Lords. The Lords sat. Members of the House of Commons, lacking chairs, stood in the rear of the chamber. The king was not introduced. He simply began his address, the entirety of which concerned America.[29]

He added little to the proclamation he had issued sixty-four days before. Demagogues have "successfully laboured to inflame my people in America." The deluded colonists "now openly avow their revolt, hostility, and rebellion. They have raised troops . . . and assumed to themselves legislative, executive, and judicial powers." Parliament had offered "conciliatory propositions" during the winter, but they were spurned by the "authors and promoters of this desperate conspiracy." The end they sought was the establishment of "an independent empire." He had augmented Britain's army and navy in America in order to "give a further extent and activity to our military operations." He also said that he had "received the most friendly offers of foreign assistance," the first official hint that foreign mercenaries might be sent to assist the redcoats in quelling the colonial rebellion. The king vowed "to put a speedy end to these disorders by the most decisive exertions" of force. He pledged "pardons and indemnities" to the "deluded multitude" when they "shall become sensible of their error." He did not promise mercy for the leaders of the "conspiracy."

For a second time the king had proclaimed that America was in rebellion. For a second time he had pledged to crush the insurgency by armed might.

George III by Johann Zoffany. Britain's monarch after 1762, George III took a hard line toward the colonists, refusing to negotiate or to receive Congress's petitions. He ultimately advocated the use of force to suppress the American rebellion. (Royal Collection. All rights reserved © 2010 Her Majesty Queen Elizabeth II)

He offered no concessions and said nothing about negotiations. However, there was one intriguing line in the address. The king had spoken enigmatically of giving "authority to certain persons upon the spot" who would be "so commissioned" to "restore [to the empire] such provinces or colony so returning to its allegiance."[30] The meaning of that sentence was unclear, and during the months that followed, it spawned rampant speculation. Rumors floated, but all in all the king's answer to the events in America seemed unmistakable. He was going to wage war on America.

The First Continental Congress had met for eight weeks before adjourning. The Second Congress adjourned on August 2 after only twelve weeks, its members crying that they had "Set much longer than . . . expected" and "We are all exhausted." As war was raging and soldiers and civilians alike were being asked to make enormous sacrifices, it may seem odd that the congressmen laid aside their responsibilities at this juncture, especially as the only reasons they gave for returning home were fatigue and a desire to escape Philadelphia's "Very Close & Hot" summer.[31] Actually, this was a good time for a break. Until the delegates learned of the king's response to the Olive Branch Petition—which was not expected until deep into the fall—many thought Congress was at a standstill. Besides, they had done what could be done to prepare for America's defense, and with the beleaguered British army apparently incapable of emerging from Boston until reinforcements arrived, there was little likelihood of another major battle in Massachusetts any time soon. There was another reason for suspending activities at this point. Many congressmen thought it prudent that they be at home to assist the local authorities in implementing the war measures that Congress had taken since May.[32]

John Adams, for instance, spent the break serving on the Massachusetts Council, which acted as the rebel government's executive authority within the province. A member of a congressional munitions committee charged with finding lead, Adams also took the initiative in pushing his colony to obtain and refine the metal. En route home, Jefferson swung by Richmond, where the Virginia Convention was meeting, and assisted with the expansion of Virginia's militia and the selection of Patrick Henry as its commander in chief. Franklin, Silas Deane of Connecticut, Samuel Chase of Maryland, and James Duane of New York spent a portion of their recess procuring powder for the army of the Northern Department, which was preparing to invade Canada. Franklin also oversaw the manufacture of arms in Pennsylvania. Samuel Ward was engaged in the erection of shore batteries in Providence.[33]

After their working vacations, the congressmen reassembled on September

13, a week later than scheduled because of the want of a quorum. The entire New Hampshire and North Carolina delegations arrived a week late, and numerous other delegates were tardy. One notable event occurred during the Massachusetts delegation's trek back to Philadelphia: After much tutoring by John Adams, Samuel Adams learned to mount and ride a horse. Though plagued with saddle sores, he stayed with it for three hundred miles, and by the time the party reached its destination, he made what one colleague called "an easy, genteel Figure upon the Horse." Samuel Adams's aide could not resist baiting the other Massachusetts delegates by proclaiming in Philadelphia that his boss now rode "fifty per Cent better" than any of them.[34]

Some congressmen returned to Philadelphia expecting Congress to mark time, and in fact much of September and October was consumed with the wearisome yet crucial task of managing the war. Contracts were let for the acquisition of flints, powder, muskets, and field artillery. Innumerable army officers were commissioned. On occasion Congress interviewed a candidate who aspired to become a general officer. Atop all this, Congress directed the completion of defensive works, looked after recruiting, found winter clothing for the soldiers, took care to keep inflation in check, and audited the books to determine what it had spent since convening in May. After the angry clashes and momentous decisions made early on by the Second Congress, these sessions were tame and tedious, moving one delegate to sigh: "Much precious Time is indiscreetly expended" on "Points of little Consequence" by "long winded and roundabout" oratory.[35]

At times there were bitter wrangles, but on the whole the congressmen got on remarkably well. Several reserved a table at the City Tavern and dined together each evening. Moreover, the practice begun by the First Congress of all the delegates joining for a Saturday repast was continued through 1775. Relations between the delegates were so good that after a few weeks a Southerner even exclaimed that the "Character of the New Yorkers is no longer suspicious." The glaring exception to what one described as the prevailing "perfect harmony" was the relationship of Dickinson and John Adams.[36] Four days after Congress resumed in September—by which time Adams's intercepted letter about Dickinson had been published in a Tory newspaper—the two congressmen encountered one another while walking along Chestnut Street. "We met, and passed near enough to touch Elbows," Adams said, but Dickinson "passed without moving his Hat, or Head or Hand. I bowed and pulled off my Hat. He passed hautily by. . . . I shall for the future pass him, in the same manner," Adams vowed.[37]

Of course, from time to time other feathers were ruffled. The intercepted packet containing Adams's letter about Dickinson also included a missive from Virginia's Benjamin Harrison to Washington in which he commiserated with the general for having to deal with New Englanders. Harrison knew how exasperating that could be, he said, based on "the Sample [of Yankees] we have here." The Loyalist newspaper editor gleefully published that letter as well.[38] Most of the problems that arose sprang up between delegates from different sections of the country, but at times congressmen from the same delegation did not get along. Some had been foes in provincial politics long before the Anglo-American conflict, but in some instances divisions over congressional policies produced enmity. For instance, John Adams's relations were strained with both Thomas Cushing and Robert Treat Paine. The Adams-Paine clash may have been nourished by their long rivalry as lawyers in pre-Revolutionary Massachusetts. At times, it was said, Adams and Paine barely exhibited "Decency and Civility" toward one another. As the fall session wore on and the delegates faced an escalating number of difficult issues, the strains between the congressmen increased. "[W]e grow tired, . . . Captious, Jealous and want a recess," one congressman sighed at the beginning of December.[39]

Part of the problem was that the congressmen faced long days—and evenings—of hard work six days a week. With the exception of Tuesday, October 24, when Congress adjourned for the funeral of Peyton Randolph—the president of Congress since its inception who died suddenly of a stroke two days earlier—Congress never missed a session that fall. It met for about six hours each day, and nearly every day one or more committees met prior to the day's session or following its adjournment. The daily schedule that faced Silas Deane was typical. "I rise at Six, write [letters] untill Seven dress & breakfast by Eight go to the Committee of Claims untill Ten, then in Congress untill half past Three or perhaps four—Dine by five, & then go [to additional committee meetings] until Nine, then Sup & go to Bed by Eleven." His routine, he lamented, "leaves little Room for Diversion, or any thing else." Several delegates complained of a "Want of Exercise as we are obliged to Set" for hours on end.[40]

Many congressmen were voluminous letter writers, devoting hours to keeping in touch with family, friends, and political allies at home. Franklin, who was at home, spent some of his time writing influential acquaintances in England whom he knew to be foes of the war. Doubtless hoping that David Hartley would continue to speak in the House of Commons against hostilities, Franklin told him that the colonists looked on the people of England as friends, but "Our respect for them will proportionately diminish" the longer hostilities continued. "[S]end us over hither fair Proposals of Peace," Franklin advised a friend in London, and he would use his influence in Congress "to promote their Acceptation." To others he wrote that in 1775 the entire British army in America had lost 1,500 men while it killed only 150 colonists—which came to a cost of "£20,000 a head," he calculated—and during "the same time 60,000 children have been born in America." At that rate, he asked, how much will it cost and "how long will it take for England to conquer America?"[41]

The delegates worried that their businesses—mostly farms and legal practices—would suffer irreparable harm during their absence, but nothing was as painful as being separated from one's family. Some sent instructions to their wives about managing affairs while they were away, and a few utilized what might best be described as insider information as they urged them to hold or sell the produce of their farms. Others were content not to intrude on their wives' management of family matters. Elizabeth Adams, Samuel's wife, moved from one house to another without consulting her husband. When he learned what had occurred, Samuel responded that he was "exceedingly pleasd with it."[42] Several delegates felt guilt pangs at their lengthy separation from their young children. Samuel Ward wanted his children to understand that he did not enjoy being away from them. He exhorted his wife to make the children aware that their "most indulgent Father" was serving his country "at the Risque of Life" and at the "Expence of many of the Amusements & Pleasures of this World." John Adams said that he felt "like a Savage" because of his protracted absence from his family, but he justified his months—and eventually years—of separation by saying that he believed his patriotic sacrifices would result in the establishment of greater opportunities for his children.[43]

As the delegations were large and each colony had but one vote, many delegates slipped away every three months or so on brief trips home. Sometimes that was not possible. At one point in the fall of 1775, for instance, with some delegates already on leave, some out with illness, and 10 percent of the congressional membership away on committee assignments in Cambridge and Fort Ticonderoga, Congress refused to give John Jay a leave of absence to return home. When he was finally permitted to go home, Jay told his wife that "nothing but actual Imprisonment" could now keep him in Philadelphia.[44]

A spate of humdrum days, and even weeks, was not uncommon for the congressmen, but trouble was never long in resurfacing. The dull and wearisome late-summer sessions were soon enough interrupted by the first wartime crisis. It unfolded in stages and involved the new Continental army. Late in

September, Congress was jolted by a disturbing letter from General Washington. The period of enlistment for the several thousand soldiers who had entered the Grand American Army under General Ward back in April and May
was due to expire at year's end. Happily, Washington advised that he believed
most men would reenlist. However, he told Congress that he feared the officers would leave the army if changes were not forthcoming. The problem,
said Washington, was that the pay of the subalterns—the ensigns, lieutenants, and captains—was "inadequate to their Rank." If their remuneration
was not increased for 1776, the commander in chief thought it likely that most
would resign their commissions at the end of the year. Washington urged
that their pay be increased. He did not request a pay raise for the enlisted
men. In fact, he asked that they be paid by the calendar month rather than
the lunar month—a New England militia tradition that had been continued
in the Grand American Army and carried over by Congress into the Continental army—a step that would result in an 8 percent annual pay cut for the
men.[45]

It was readily apparent that if most of the junior officers quit, the army
would face a potential calamity. But something subtler lay behind Washington's letter and Congress's ultimate response. General Washington was attempting to reshape the very nature of the Continental army. New England,
the most egalitarian section within the American colonies, had historically
fielded militia characterized by relative equality between the ranks. The pay
of a Massachusetts lieutenant, for instance, was only twice that of a private,
and the pay of the highest-ranking officer—a colonel—was just six times
greater than that of the lowest-ranking soldier. In the southern colonies, the
least egalitarian American provinces, militia lieutenants were paid about five
times as much as privates and colonels about twenty times as much. When
Congress established the Continental army in June, it more or less adopted
the New England pay schedule, save for the general officers, which were
newly created ranks. Thus, a Continental lieutenant's stipend was twice that
of a private, and a Continental colonel's pay was just seven and one-half times
that of a private. But general officers were paid twenty to twenty-five times what
privates were. Washington's remuneration as commander in chief was
seventy-five times greater than that of his lowest-ranking soldier.[46]

When General Washington urged Congress to increase the pay of officers,
he had a hidden motive. He sought an officer corps gathered from the elite
within American society. Washington's hope may have been to eradicate the
"Familiarity between the Officers & Men" that he had found when he reached
Cambridge, and that he believed was "incompatible with [the] Subordination

& Discipline" required to build an effective army.[47] Whatever Washington's motivation, some congressmen welcomed his letter, as they had come to fear an egalitarian citizen-army as a potential agent for social change. These congressmen believed that a rigidly disciplined army whose leadership was drawn from the socially superior was unlikely to be a force in favor of innovative social reform. Those who saw the rebellion as both a protest against British policy and an opportunity for meaningful social and political change understood what was implicitly at stake. But they were as reluctant to engage in this battle as John Adams had been to fight Dickinson over petitioning the monarch, and for the same reason. Unity remained their priority. The more radical congressmen understood that Congress was fully behind the war—"there is a serious Spirit here—Such a Spirit as I have not known before," John Adams exclaimed on October 1—and they wished to avoid actions that might jeopardize the national mood that had crystallized behind waging war against the mother country. Besides, the war had to be won before any lasting social changes could be put in place.[48]

Congress responded to Washington's letter by creating a three-member Camp Committee to hurry to Cambridge and meet with the commander in chief. As two of the three committee members were Southerners, it was a foregone conclusion that Congress would oblige Washington. Those congressmen who disliked what was unfolding did not exert themselves, one dissatisfied deputy remarked.[49] As a result, Congress in November endorsed the Camp Committee's recommendation of pay raises for all subalterns. The pay of a lieutenant jumped from two to three times that of a private, while a captain's pay rose from three to four times that of a private. This, it turned out, was merely the first step. While the pay of enlisted men fell, that of all subalterns was further increased in the fall of 1776—by then lieutenants' pay was four times and captains' six times that of privates—and the pay of those holding the rank of majors, lieutenant colonels, and colonels (untouched in 1775) jumped by about one third.[50] The fear of an army that would be used to bring on radical change—a concern best articulated by Galloway in 1774 but felt by every conservative congressman—was largely laid to rest. The ordinary citizens who comprised the lower ranks of enlisted men would be held in check by an officer corps drawn almost entirely from America's social and economic elite.

By mid-autumn Washington had gotten what he sought, but his victory was accompanied by a more serious crisis.[51] As the gray, scudding clouds that heralded the approach of winter gathered over Cambridge, the enlisted men—those whom Washington had thought would remain in the army—left for home in droves the moment their enlistments expired. In a matter of days the size of the army declined by almost 80 percent, prompting the commander to rage at the men's "dearth of Public Spirit" and their "dirty, mercenary" character. Pay was a factor in soldiers' decision to go home. The enlisted men found the salary "Alterations disgusting," one congressman remarked. But other factors prompted their return to civilian life. The men felt that they had done their duty. Now it was someone else's turn to sacrifice. Many were yeomen who feared their farms would go to rack and ruin if they stayed away for a second consecutive year. Many were simply fed up with soldiering, having discovered that it often was a hard and lonely life filled with discomfort and danger and a disconcerting lack of freedom.[52]

Washington and Congress had to scramble to meet the unanticipated emergency. The commander held out the promise of furloughs and additional blankets to induce men to reenlist, and he persuaded the four New England governors to send sufficient numbers of militiamen to Boston until another army could be raised. Congress refused to provide bounties as a recruiting tool, but with some success it persuaded the colonies to be generous. A few provinces gave those who enlisted, or reenlisted, a cash bonus—usually an additional month's pay—as well as a blanket, a shirt, and "1 pr. Shoes, 1 pr. yarn stocking & a felt hat." By February 1776 the army had grown to 12,510, ending the manpower crisis and also thwarting Washington's next request. Telling Congress that the army had been saved only by "the finger of Providence," Washington asked Congress to terminate the practice of enlisting men for one year. He wanted a standing army composed of men who signed on to serve for the duration of the war.

That was too much for most congressmen. Like Samuel Adams, most deputies believed that standing armies were "always dangerous to the liberties of the people." Many probably also agreed with John Adams, who said that a standing army would consist of "the meanest, idlest, most intemperate and worthless" men in society. Having an officer corps drawn from the elite was one thing, but John and Samuel Adams, and most other members of Congress, wanted a soldiery that was broadly representative of the population and, as much as possible, they wanted men to volunteer to serve because they believed in the cause.[53]

Before the year was out, wartime pressures led Congress down other paths that few could have anticipated. For instance, the First Congress had embargoed British imports and, beginning in September 1775, American exports to the mother country. Long before autumn it was becoming apparent that the commercial prohibitions were causing problems. New York's Robert R. Livingston pointed out in October that "we suffer" from stoppage of trade.

Money had dried up. Weapons and ammunition would remain in short supply "unless We open our Ports" to other nations. What is more, Livingston
cautioned, the boycotts had put ten thousand sailors and dockhands out of
work. The unemployed not only posed a potential threat to the domestic tranquility, but from desperation they also might be driven "into the Hands of
our Enemies." Thomas Willing of Pennsylvania added that salt was in dan-
gerously short supply. Richard Henry Lee responded by proposing that Congress throw open American ports to all nations that wished to trade with the
colonies. "We shall get necessary Manufactures and Money and Powder" if
such a step was taken, he said, for the Royal Navy would not dare attack the
vessels of Europe's neutral nations that sailed into American harbors. Lee
thought it especially likely that France, which he fancifully claimed was "in
Distress" for American commodities, would leap at the chance to trade with
the colonies.[54]

Many moderate delegates were horrified. Opening trade with all of Europe
was nearly tantamount to declaring independence. The reconciliationists first
wanted to hear the king's response to the Olive Branch Petition. Even if that
proved to be disappointing, some held out hope that in time—perhaps following American victories in Canada—London would make concessions.
Sounding as if he was clutching at straws, South Carolina's Christopher Gadsden, a planter-merchant, warned that the colonies would not share equally in
the foreign trade. The mid-Atlantic and Chesapeake colonies—the former
America's breadbasket, the latter the producer of both grains and tobacco—
would do almost all the business. Those colonies that were left out would be
resentful. Throwing open the ports "will divide us. One colony will envy another, and be jealous."[55]

Like Gadsden, Georgia's John Joachim Zubly looked askance at opening
trade with Europe, but he also acknowledged, "We cant do without Trade.
We must have Trade." Zubly, a Presbyterian minister who had emigrated from
Switzerland to Savannah, where he delivered his sermons in English, French,
and German, spoke broken English, but his colleagues had no difficulty understanding the point he made: "I came here with 2 views. One was to secure
the Rights of America. 2. A Reconciliation with G. Britain." Congress, he
continued, "must regulate our Trade so that a Reconciliation be obtained,"
but also so that "We [are] enable[d] to carry on the War." Thomas Johnson of
Maryland was not so sure. "I see less and less Prospect of a Reconciliation
every day. But I would not render it impossible." The rub, Zubly responded,
was that "We must trade. We must trade with Somebody" to obtain the weapons of war. Great Britain, he reminded his colleagues, was not going to furnish the colonists with military supplies.[56]

Once again, the more radical colonists shrank from pushing too hard, lest Congress's solidarity behind the war be shattered. Besides, as Zubly's comments demonstrated, many moderates recognized that the war required that some change be made to America's trade policies. On October 26 the congressmen compromised. The Association was altered to permit trade with foreign ports in the Caribbean. It was done, said one moderate, "for the purpose of purchasing ammunition &c." Zubly rejoiced that it would additionally procure "supplies to keep soul and Body together."[57]

While the radicals did not get everything they wanted concerning trade, opening commerce in the West Indies made possible the attainment of something they had sought for the past six months. Since the creation of the Continental army, New England's delegates had pushed to establish a Continental navy, and in August Rhode Island formally proposed "building and equipping . . . an American fleet." Aside from the Yankees, few in Congress thought such a step was a wise idea. Some objected to the cost. It would "mortgage the whole Continent," said one congressman, who thought it better to spend the money on fortifying the Hudson. Zubly added that nothing was needed for waging war but "Powder and Shot" for the army. Maryland's Samuel Chase, a tall man (he stood over six feet) with a ruddy complexion—behind his back, some colleagues referred to him as "Bacon Face"—called the creation of a navy "the maddest Idea in the World," as the costly American fleet would be tiny and in no time would be swept from the sea by the giant Royal Navy. Angered, Silas Deane of Connecticut retorted, "I dont think it romantic, at all." Gadsden agreed that Congress should consider "some Plan of Defence by Sea." His colleague from South Carolina, John Rutledge, was willing to consider a navy, but he was not prepared to commit to it until he learned its size and cost. What was the point of having a navy, some asked? A New Englander answered that "a Fleet . . . might make prey enough of the Trade of our Enemies to make it worth while." Thomas Willing from Pennsylvanian was horrified. Any step that was seen as waging offensive warfare would only make reconciliation infinitely more difficult. The proponents of a navy answered that the creation of a fleet would be "a defensive Measure."[58]

Until October, there appeared to be no likelihood that Congress would agree to a navy. Wartime realities changed that, much as they had compelled a change in the trade policy. On October 5 Congress learned that in mid-August two brigs filled with military supplies had sailed without convoy from London, bound for Quebec. Congress wasted no time creating a committee to consider a response. The committee's composition was highly unusual. All three members were New Englanders, a sign that Congress wanted action, and quickly. Only one hour after its creation, the committee recommended that the New England colonies be authorized to raise a squadron to intercept the brigs. Congress agreed and sent expresses northward that same day to notify the New England authorities. The next morning, the committee made another recommendation. It urged Congress to commission two armed vessels to cruise for ninety days in search of British shipping. This led to more debate. Zubly declared, "We must have a Navy," which he argued would protect the coastal trade between the colonies and gather needed intelligence.

Deane jumped in with a proposal to create a navy of at least ten vessels, a squadron equal to the number of warships that Great Britain was expected to send to American waters in 1776. Act now, Deane declared, and "if We get early to Sea [in 1776], these Shipps" can "surprise, & intercept" the troop transports carrying additional redcoats across the Atlantic. That was going too far for many delegates. As the British blockade was concentrated off the New England coast, several delegates wanted only to try to "protect & secure the Trade of New England," which could be done by a handful of vessels. Congress tabled the proposal to create a navy and authorized only the committee's proposal to dispatch two armed vessels for a three-month cruise. It was a small victory for those who wanted a naval arm, but it was a victory, and John Adams rejoiced: "We begin to feel a little of the Seafaring Inclination here."[59]

A few weeks later, Congress recognized that vessels engaged in the new trade with foreign ports in the West Indies required protection. It created the Naval Committee to look into the matter. Its recommendations triggered the last great debate at this juncture over the creation of a navy. George Wythe of Virginia, who had been in Congress for only a month, made a long, impassioned speech on behalf of a navy, and to some degree he spoke as if America were already independent.

> Why should not America have a Navy? No maritime Power, near the Sea Coast, can be safe without it. It is no Chimera. The Romans suddenly built one in their Chartheginian War. Why may We not lay a Foundation for it. We abound with Furs [fir trees], Iron ore, Tar, Pitch, Turpentine. We have all the materials for construction of a Navy.

With a navy, Wythe added, "We shall distress our Enemies." Moreover, he said, if defended by an American fleet, the "British Navy will never be able to effect our Destruction." Richard Henry Lee concurred. Until America received help from France—and at the moment, that was no more than "a Glimmering Hope"—America had to supply itself, and for that a navy was required.[60]

Chase, who had earlier opposed a navy, once again spoke against building a fleet. It was a long speech and, as was his custom, he delivered it in a derisive manner, his irritation and fervor palpable. (John Adams thought Chase was "very sarcastic, and thinks himself very sensible.") He returned to Willing's earlier point that the creation of a fleet would jeopardize reconciliation and lead America to break with the mother country, a step that he said would "end in the total destruction of American Liberty." He again insisted that it was folly to believe that America could ever build a fleet that could compete with the Royal Navy. "G.B. with 20 ships can distroy all our Trade, and ravage our sea Coast—can block up all your Harbours." The trade embargo remained the "best Instrument [for waging war that] We have." In time, the loss of its trade with America would bankrupt Great Britain. He reasoned: Southern tobacco alone financed Great Britain's annual debt; Ireland needed American flax; Britain's sugar islands were dependent on American grain, fish, and lumber; without American participation, Britain's African slave trade faced ruin. His conclusion: "Britain can never support a War with Us at the Loss of such a valuable Trade."[61]

It was a bitter fight. In the end it was resolved not through hot-tempered rhetoric but, as was rapidly coming to be commonplace, by jolting military news. On October 23—two days after Wythe and Chase clashed—word reached Philadelphia that in mid-October a royal squadron had carried out a devastating raid on Falmouth, Massachusetts (now Portland, Maine). Early in the month, the British had dispatched four ships from Boston to "chastize" Falmouth for having fired, albeit without success, on a royal vessel. On October 17 the village was presented with an ultimatum: Surrender all munitions and its leading rebels within twenty-four hours or face destruction. When the town's leaders refused, the four British vessels subjected the town to a merciless bombardment lasting eight hours. They fired balls, bombs, incendiary shells, and antipersonnel devices into the town, and when civilians were spotted trying to extinguish the flames, the British put ashore a landing party to prevent firefighting activities. By sunset a thick pall of smoke hung like a shroud over what once had been a town. Falmouth's houses and buildings, its wharves, and the eleven vessels in its harbor had been reduced to ashes.[62] With winter rapidly approaching, Falmouth's entire population had been stripped of shelter. The residents of every coastal city and village expected that they might be the Royal Navy's next target. (Benjamin Franklin, away on congressional business, wrote home to suggest that his daughter might want to remove her children from Philadelphia, and he added, "remember to secure my Account Books and Writings . . . in my Library.")[63]

Congress was livid. Washington told Congress that Britain's act was "an Outrage exceeding in Barbarity & Cruelty every hostile Act practised among civilized Nations." Samuel Adams denounced the "Barbarity of our Enemies," and for once, every congressman agreed with him. During the next several days, Congress created the Continental navy and voted to raise two battalions of marines. It appropriated $100,000 for the purchase of four existing vessels and their conversion to warships, and it voted to spend $866,000 for the construction of thirteen frigates—about $66,000 per ship.[64]

Inexorably, each month of war made reconciliation less likely. Hard on the heels of Falmouth, more bad news arrived for those who clung desperately to the hope of the permanence of the Anglo-American union. By midsummer 1775 the royal governors in Virginia, North Carolina, and South Carolina had fled to the safety of British warships or fortifications. Only Georgia's chief executive remained in the governor's official residence, but he told North's ministry that "the powers of government are wrested out of my hands." He added that he had been reduced to "a mere nominal governor" with "scarce any power left." All four southern governors spoke wistfully of large loyal populations and predicted that if London would only send help, the British flag would fly once again over their provinces.[65] Only Governor Dunmore of Virginia acted unilaterally to crush the rebellion with force.

A forty-three-year-old Scotsman with dark eyes and long black hair, Dunmore had failed to advance either as a soldier or as a member of Parliament. In 1770 he tried a different route to prominence and greater power. He agreed to become the governor of New York. A year later he moved to Williamsburg as Virginia's royal governor. From the days of the Coercive Acts onward, Dunmore watched helplessly as the defiant rebels took power from him. And when hostilities erupted, he felt personally threatened—with justification. In July, while at Porto Bello, his farm six miles from the capital, he was fired on by a party of rebels. He barely escaped capture or harm. Even before this alarming incident, Dunmore had vowed to resist the "open violences" of the rebels, much of which he laid at the feet of Patrick Henry. By autumn, in possession of two royal vessels—a sloop and a schooner—and three armed merchantmen, and in command of a few score Tories and sixty regulars deployed from Florida, Dunmore commenced open warfare. In October he conducted a series of successful raids against small bands of Virginia militia. The next month he scored a victory in a pitched battle at Great Bridge, below Norfolk. Emboldened by his triumph, Dunmore on November 7 issued a proclamation promising freedom to all rebel-owned slaves who were "able and willing to bear Arms" and joined "his Majesty's Troops" to help with "the speedy reducing" of Virginia's rebels to "a proper Sense of their Duty, to His MAJESTY'S

Crown and Dignity." A few weeks later he ordered his small fleet to shell Norfolk, destroying two thirds of the town.[66]

Word of Dunmore's proclamation shocked white Southerners. Virginia's countryside was swept by apprehension that planters would lose their labor force and that bloody slave insurrections would follow. Fearing that Virginia planters who had hitherto supported the rebellion would defect in order to safeguard their property, General Washington told Congress that Dunmore must be stopped. If successful in causing Virginians to defect to Toryism, Washington warned, Dunmore "will become the most formidable Enemy America has—his strength will Increase as a Snow ball by Rolling." Southern congressmen required no warning from the commander in chief. One member of Virginia's delegation called Dunmore a "monster" and another railed at his "Diabolical scheme." North Carolina's delegates were no less alarmed than their Virginia colleagues. They feared that Dunmore would take his growing army into their province and set free their slaves. To Southern rebels, what Dunmore had done was precisely the sort of abomination by British officials that John Adams had forecast. In December, Edward Rutledge of South Carolina predicted that Dunmore's act had done "more effectually to work an eternal separation between Great Britain and the Colonies, than any other expedient, which could possibly have been thought of."[67]

The mood of the delegates had begun to shift in the ten weeks or so since Congress returned in September from its late-summer recess. For some, the fervent longing to remain part of the British Empire waned. As it did, the dominance of the reconciliationists grew weaker. Worse was to come for those still determined to reconcile with the mother country. Word of the king's August proclamation asserting that America was in rebellion reached Philadelphia early in November.

"We are all declared Rebels," a Yankee said, adding with exaltation that most of "those who hoped for Redress . . . now give . . . up & heartily join with us in carrying on the War vigorously." Samuel Ward wrote home that one reconciliationist—sadly, he did not identify him—who had been in the habit of calling his counterparts "Brother Rebel," declared that he had now received "a sufficient Answer" from the Crown. The congressman, Ward continued, had abandoned his hope for reconciliation and pronounced that he was at last "ready to declare Ourselves independent." No one was more jubilant than Samuel Adams. The "Councils and Administration" of Lord North, as well as the policies of "our most gracious King," he crowed, "will necessarily produce the grandest Revolutions the World has ever yet seen." Adams knew that the choices made by Great Britain's leaders and the pressures of the war were immeasurably sweeping America headlong toward independence. Not even the "most industrious and able Politicians" could hurry the colonies more rapidly to a final break with the mother country, he said.[68]

It was in this atmosphere that Congress tackled one final crucial issue before autumn turned to winter in 1775. Since the bloody day of Lexington and Concord, pressure had been building in some provinces to cast aside the old colonial governments under Crown-issued charters and create new ones. After all, few Americans any longer recognized the authority of the royal governors, and most of the king's courts had long since been closed. In addition, some rebels were growing anxious that, in the unsettled conditions spawned by the absence of legitimate government, unsavory changes might be in the offing. The leaders in some eastern counties were keeping a wary eye on the western counties, where most residents took the Whig rhetoric of self-government and equal representation seriously. Just as Galloway had prophesied a year earlier, the rebellion was churning up the potential for drastic political and social change. Talk of equal representation for westerners in the provincial assembly, fairer taxes for those living on the frontier, and democratic political practices filled the air. Not every rebel wanted to see those changes come about. Even those who were sympathetic worried that substantive domestic change would prove to be so divisive that it would jeopardize the march toward independence.

The issue of creating new provincial governments had come up previously. In June, even before the Continental army had been created, Massachusetts told Congress that its "system of colony administration" was "vigorously opposed by the collected wisdom" of its citizens. The Massachusetts Provincial Congress asked the Continental Congress for its "most explicit advice" concerning what to do regarding its government. The Bay Colony had brought up the matter at the moment when John Adams was emerging as the leader of the more radical faction in Congress, and he was the one who managed this explosive issue. Adams realized at once that authorizing the colonies to create whatever government they desired would be seen by many as a virtual declaration of independence. He also knew that the most conservative colonists would be horrified should any colony institute truly radical political changes. Either occurrence could be fatal to the war effort.

Back in June, Adams had led his colleagues toward a solution that preserved as much as possible of the Bay Colony's old colonial government. Massachusetts was instructed to revert to its government under the charter of 1691, which had been taken away by the Coercive Acts. It was to restore the bicameral assembly under which it had lived for three quarters of a century.

If the royal governor refused to recognize the legislature—which was a fore-gone conclusion—the council, or upper house, was to assume executive authority. The most radical members of the Massachusetts Provincial Congress had hoped to go further. They had wished to elect their own chief executive and to redistrict the assembly. But they complied. "At this Congress," Adams explained to them, "We do as well as we can. . . . Your Government was the best We could obtain for you." He told a friend, "The colonies are not yet ripe to assume the whole government."[69] Adams's explanation was true enough, though he had left unsaid his fear of provoking a congressional breach that could prove to be harmful to conducting the war.

The question of governments for the colonies resurfaced in mid-October. This time it was raised by New Hampshire at the behest of its congressional delegation, which sensed the shifting sentiments in Philadelphia. Once again, John Adams was at the forefront of the congressional debate, though this time he approached the issue differently. He strongly endorsed permitting New Hampshire to create its own government. Such a step, he said, would attract the attention of both America's friends in England and those in foreign nations who wished to provide assistance. Both would "believe us United and in earnest, [and would] exert themselves very strenuously in our favour." Adams was immediately gratified by the reaction to his bold stand. Many delegates, he thought, "began to hear me with more Patience, and some began to ask me civil questions." After a warm debate, Congress created a committee, packing it with delegates certain to recommend giving New Hampshire the go-ahead. Four of the five members of the committee, including Adams and Richard Henry Lee, had steadfastly pushed for a harder line toward Great Britain.[70]

The committee was slow in reporting, probably intending to withhold its recommendations until the question of creating an American navy had been resolved. But once Congress learned of the king's proclamation of an American rebellion, the committee rapidly reported. Congress wasted no time approving what the committee proposed. New Hampshire was instructed to "form . . . Such a government as shall be most Agreable to the Province" as determined through a "full and free representation of the people." Unlike its directions to Massachusetts in June, Congress specified nothing regarding the nature of the government. New Hampshire was given a free hand. The only restriction was that whatever government was created was to exist only so long as hostilities continued, and that stipulation, a delegate reported home, was made solely "to ease the minds of some few persons, who were fearful of Independence." The next day, November 4, John Rutledge obtained Congress's consent for South Carolina to form whatever government it pleased, prompting Samuel Adams to predict in private that the "Time is near" when nearly every province would scuttle its charter government.[71]

John Dickinson had been missing in action since the late-summer recess. In September he moved upstairs in the Pennsylvania State House to the chamber where the Pennsylvania assembly met and remained engrossed in its transactions until November. Pennsylvania's legislature wrestled with crucial questions ranging from defense issues to the civil and religious rights of Quakers in wartime, and Dickinson may have believed—with some justification—that Congress would do nothing drastic before it learned of the king's response to the Olive Branch Petition. He withdrew from some of his congressional committees, and there is no record that he was an active participant in any of Congress's debates that fall. However, when Congress authorized New Hampshire to create its own government, Dickinson became a player once again.[72]

He helped to write new instructions from the Pennsylvania assembly in which he sat to the colony's congressional delegation, on which he also served. The congressmen were "strictly enjoin[ed]" to "dissent from and utterly reject any propositions . . . that may cause or lead to a Separation from our Mother Country." The task of Pennsylvania's representatives in Congress, the message continued, was to obtain "Redress of American Grievances" and restore "Union & Harmony" with Great Britain. Maryland, Delaware, and New Jersey quickly adopted similar instructions to their congressmen. But when New Jersey considered sending its own olive branch petition to the Crown, Dickinson, accompanied by two other congressmen—John Jay and George Wythe—hurried to Burlington and addressed the assembly. Dickinson took the position that a petition from an individual colony would only further persuade North's ministry that the colonists were hopelessly divided, leading it to fight harder and spurn reconciliation. The New Jersey legislators backed down.[73]

The year was speeding to a close. Great events and important changes had occurred since the eruption of hostilities seven months earlier, but the future remained clouded. Some delegates from the mid-Atlantic provinces continued to believe that most Americans yearned to remain tied to the mother country. The "people call out for reconciliation," said Robert Morris, a newcomer to the Pennsylvania delegation. A New York delegate, John Alsop, concurred: The "people . . . are intirely against . . . independency but ardently wish [for] a reconciliation free from Taxation." Franklin might have agreed that a considerable number of his fellow Pennsylvanians longed to be reconciled with London, but he accurately predicted that Great Britain would continue fighting until it aroused the "enmity, hatred, and detestation" of nearly every American for all things British. Thomas Jefferson shared Franklin's assessment. Unless George III offered meaningful concessions, Jefferson prophesied, the monarch would "undo his empire." Americans would never again "crouch under his hand and kiss the rod with which he deigns to scourge us." Jefferson added that after taking up arms "there is but one step more" left to the colonists—to declare independence. He closed with his own prediction: The coming year, 1776, "will probably decide everlastingly our future."[74]

CHAPTER 8

"The Folly and Madness of the Ministry"

Charles James Fox, Thomas Paine, and the War

GEORGE III READ HIS ADDRESS to Parliament on October 26 and in a matter of minutes was on his way back to St. James's Palace. Even as the monarch's carriage clattered through London's streets, the two houses of Parliament met separately and debated their response to what he had said. There was never a chance that the opposition could repudiate the king's bellicose stand. Most members of Parliament believed the war would be short, not lasting beyond the campaign of 1776, and they were confident that victory was assured. Nevertheless, the debates were spirited and lasted for two days. As word of Lexington and Concord had arrived just hours after Parliament's session ended in May, this was the first opportunity to discuss the American crisis since the outbreak of hostilities. Several opposition MPs wished to reopen the issue of the use of force and to consider alternatives to the government's approach to the crisis.

As the king had declared war, it was more difficult than ever for the opposition to raise objections to the government's American policies. But if ever there was a moment for those who disliked the resort to force to unite behind a different approach, the moment had arrived. Two factions opposed to the majority in power had long existed in Parliament: those who coalesced around the Marquis of Rockingham and those who were satellites of the Earl of Chatham. But the two contingents were divided over domestic policies. Moreover, rancorous personal feuds and jealousies got in the way of their unification. Even with regard to Anglo-American differences, the two were at odds over the exercise of parliamentary supremacy. In the end, the two opposition groups failed to present a united front against the king and his prime minister. But even had they combined, their union likely would have been ineffectual. Like North and his followers, not even the best and brightest

among the government's critics appeared capable of the unorthodox thinking that might have led to a peaceful solution to the imperial crisis.[1]

Foes of the war were vocal and passionate. Some blasted North's government for taking the country into an unnecessary conflict. The prime minister's plan for dealing with America was "butchery" plain and simple, said
Henry Conway. John Wilkes savaged the cabinet for having pursued policies
that had dragged "the nation into an unjust, ruinous, felonious, and murder-
ous war." Other critics forecast that hostilities would end badly for Great
Britian. It would result in "ruinous consequences," said one, in "ruin and
destruction, . . . grief and horror," said another. Many in the opposition predicted that Great Britain could not achieve "unconditional submission of a
country infinitely more extended than our own." Colonel Isaac Barré forecast
that if the war continued, "the whole American continent was lost for ever."
The solution to the American woes that was most frequently recommended
by the ministry's adversaries was the immediate repeal of all American legislation passed by Parliament since 1763.[2]

Three speeches were notable. The Duke of Grafton created a sensation by
breaking with the government. Rail-thin and with a long, hooked nose, Grafton was a former prime minister—his government had enacted the Townshend Duties—who had accepted the position of Lord Privy Seal in North's
cabinet in 1771. He took on the assignment because he believed his experience
would prove useful in leading North to a solution of the American problem.
But by the fall of 1775 Grafton not only was disappointed with North; he also
probably divined that he was about to be forced from the ministry so that his
post could be given to Dartmouth. Grafton opened his speech by claiming to
have been deceived by North's policies. He had thought North meant to pursue conciliation, when in fact the prime minister had adopted one war measure after another throughout the recent summer, a course that would send
government and country "headlong on their own ruin." If Grafton presumed
his remarks might be his swan song, he was correct. The king soon thereafter
ordered his removal from the ministry.[3]

Lord Shelburne gained notice by raising a new and crucial point. Shelburne wondered why the king had not addressed the Olive Branch Petition.
The American Congress had not threatened independence, he pointed out. In
fact, it had almost pleaded with London to open negotiations leading to peace.
Congress's entreaty, he said, offered the best "opportunity . . . of extricating
this country from the ruinous situation in which the folly of [North's] administration has involved us."[4]

A speech by Charles James Fox criticizing North's government garnered
the greatest attention, partly because he was unsurpassed as an orator, but

also because to this point he had never defended the American dissidents. In fact, Fox had been almost entirely silent on the American question before the fall of 1775.

Brilliant and rakish, Fox had entered Parliament when he was only nineteen years old. By then, he had attended Eton and Oxford, lived on the continent for more than two years, and become fluent in French and Italian. Born to wealth and influence—his father had served as a secretary at war—Fox had inherited one hundred thousand pounds, a prodigious fortune, which over the years he supplemented with sinecures worth thousands annually. At times, he appeared bent on spending his fortune in record time. A bachelor when he came to London to take his seat in the House of Commons—he did not marry until he was forty-five years old, and wed only after a ten-year courtship—Fox soon earned a reputation as an "egregious coxcomb" and a "prodigious dandy." He wore tight-fitting and outlandishly cut clothing, a style that Londoners called the "Macaroni." Fox's standing as a boulevardier was not derived from good looks. He was heavyset with a swarthy complexion, long black hair, a perpetually heavy beard, and massive, unbroken sable brows that gained him the nickname "the Eyebrow."

His status as a carefree ladies' man paled next to his repute for gambling. The Earl of Carlisle, a friend, noted that Fox "was incapable . . . of any restraint when the gratification of his appetites were concerned," and that was especially true of his compulsion to test his luck. Many nights he sat down to play whist, piquet, or baccarat and remained at the gaming table until past sunset the following evening. (Told once in these years that his son might marry, Fox's father allegedly quipped that nuptials meant there was at last a possibility of Charles's going to bed for one night.) Fox, like many gamblers, wore a mask to hide his emotions while wagering and a broad-brimmed straw hat embellished with ribbons and flowers. He played for high stakes. The wager on some hands was as much as ten thousand pounds. On one occasion, he and his brother lost thirty-two thousand pounds in three nights. One friend in the House of Commons estimated that on occasion Fox lost five hundred pounds an hour when he gambled. Nor was he drawn solely to the gaming table. Fox visited the track on a regular basis and eventually invested in a string of racehorses.[5]

But Fox's standing as a political figure soon overshadowed the tattle about his personal habits. As a student, Fox had been thought the most gifted speaker in his class, and during his first five years in the Commons he spoke 254 times. Only eight of his colleagues spoke more frequently. His speeches were seldom prepared in advance, and many were delivered following a night with little or no sleep. But this precocious young man took on the giants of

Edmund Burke and Charles James Fox by Thomas Hickey. Members of the House of Commons, Burke and Fox were the foremost critics of the government's policy of coercion and force. They insisted that ministerial policy would drive the colonists to declare independence. (National Gallery of Ireland)

his time and held his own, a talent that astounded veteran politicians. While Fox was an adroit speechmaker, he was nearly unequaled in the give and take of a debate. A contemporary exclaimed that many spectators who watched as he debated "all off-hand" found his performances "a most extraordinary thing." One of his biographers wrote that Fox "in unprepared arguments . . . transcended any speaker in the history of Parliament." Edmund Burke concurred, noting that Fox "rose by slow degrees to be the most brilliant and accomplished debater that the world ever saw."[6]

Fox launched his career as a Tory. He served North well in his initial years and was rewarded with seats on the Admiralty and Treasury boards. Some thought he might have been brought into the ministry had it not been for his youth. (Fox did not reach his majority until four days after North became the prime minister.) But in 1772 Fox broke with the government over a series of domestic issues and resigned from the Admiralty Board. "Charles Fox is turned patriot and is already attempting to pronounce the words 'country,' 'liberty,' 'corruption,' with what success time will discover," Edward Gibbon noted happily as his young colleague commenced his transition to Whiggism. If the Whigs were delighted by Fox's apostasy, George III was outraged. The king told the prime minister that "the Young Man has so thoroughly cast off every principle of common honor and honesty that he must become as contemptible as he is odious." Ever obliging to his monarch, North saw to Fox's removal from his remaining government post. In dismissing Fox from the Treasury Board, North informed him of the decision in a scornful note: "his Majesty has thought proper to order a new commission of the Treasury to be made out, in which I do not perceive your name." Fox at first thought he was the victim of a practical joker. When he learned the truth, he was furious, and he concluded that it was unlikely that he would ever be asked to be part of a ministry so long as George III sat on the throne. Furthermore, Fox was estranged from both North's government and the opposition.[7]

It was in the midst of this predicament that Fox discovered the American problem. Until 1775 he had been silent when the American debates stirred the Commons. He had not taken a stand during the heated battles over the Coercive Acts. He had merely responded to a fellow MP who had framed the issue as a "dilemma of conquering or abandoning America" with the remark, "if we are reduced to that, I am for abandoning America." Fox remained in the background during the debate on the supposedly conciliatory terms that North offered the colonists in February 1775, only prophesying that "the Americans will reject them with disdain." Though his criticism of the North Peace Plan was muted, the prime minister publicly responded that Fox was backing the

American rebels because of his resentment at having been ousted from the Treasury Board. Fox denied the charge—had his conduct been driven by rancor, he said, he would long ago have revealed instances of North's "unexampled treachery and falsehood"—but on the floor of the Commons, he pledged to join henceforth with Burke to compel the prime minister "to answer [for] the mischiefs occasioned by his negligence, his inconsistency, and his incapacity." He also shared with all who would listen his newfound conviction that having followed Lord North was "the greatest folly of his life."[8]

Fox made good on his pledge to ally with Burke. As a boy, he had known the Irishman, who was twenty years his senior; and when the two became colleagues in the House of Commons, they drew close, forming a warm friendship that seemed to grow from their mutual appreciation of literature and art, not to mention their deep respect for each other as penetrating thinkers and effective politicians. Burke looked on the gifted young man as a pupil and protégé, and he described Fox as "one of the pleasantest men in the world, as well as the greatest Genius that perhaps this country has ever produced."

Burke's critique of North's policies in 1774 helped shape Fox's thinking about American issues. But whereas Burke took up the cause of America because he understood that North's policies would result in the loss of the colonies and the diminution of British power and prestige, Fox was drawn to the colonists' plight in some measure because of the political opportunities that such a stance might yield.[9] In the fall of 1775, in the wake of the king's address, Burke and Fox began to work hand in hand against what they saw as the mad and misguided direction that their country was being taken. They drew on each other's talents. Burke was a spectacular orator. Fox was equally dazzling as a debater. Burke was informed and reasonable. Fox was eloquent, passionate, and biting, and as if wielding "the wand of the magician"—according to one observer—he was able to hold an audience in the palm of his hand.[10] From October 1775 through July 1776, and beyond, Burke and Fox emerged as the strongest voices for the much-outnumbered factions fighting in Parliament against the government's policies toward America.

Fox's speech in the debate on the king's address was his first on the American war. He said little that had not been said on numerous occasions by others. He characterized North as "the blundering pilot" who had conveyed the nation to this crisis. He agreed that "the Americans had gone too far," but he took issue with the monarch's contention that the colonists sought independence. And like Grafton, Fox said that he had been deceived by the ministry. He had voted to send more troops to America in 1774 because North's government had said that doing so would "ensure peace" without bloodshed.

The ministers had been wrong. Fox pronounced that he could no longer "consent to the bloody consequences of so silly a contest about so silly an object, conducted in the silliest manner that history . . . had ever furnished . . . and from which we were likely to derive nothing, but poverty, misery, disgrace, defeat, and ruin."[1]

North largely left the government's defense to Sandwich, who despite the bloodbaths suffered along Battle Road and on Bunker Hill, ludicrously raised the familiar canard about American "cowardice and want of spirit."[2] The implication of his remarks was that victory would be easily attained. To no one's surprise, when the debate concluded, both houses brushed back the opposition to the king's position. By huge margins each house announced its "entire concurrence" with the monarch's wish to "suppress this rebellion" with "the most decisive exertions."[3]

Ending the debate did not close the matter. Too many MPs wanted to discuss waging war. Some questioned the ministry's authority to hire the foreign troops that were sent to the Mediterranean, and others raised doubts about the government's estimates of the cost of expanding the naval and land forces in North America. In addition, the discussion kept coming back to the Olive Branch Petition. Congress's entreaty to the king was read in the House of Lords early in the month, and on November 10 Richard Penn, who had carried the supplication across the Atlantic and was still in London, was summoned to testify. Among other things, he told the legislators that the sentiments of Congress reflected public opinion in the colonies and stressed that the Americans had gone to war "in defence of their liberties," not to secure independence.[4]

Many opposition MPs seized on Congress's petition to assert that "the colonists were disposed to an amicable adjustment of differences." Peace was possible, several observed. Others questioned the wisdom of pursuing a conquest that would be difficult, perhaps impossible, to achieve. One said that time would tell whether or not the colonists were cowardly, but there could be no question that they possessed arms and knew how to use them. More than one observed that the Americans also knew their country intimately and would use its rivers and other "natural barriers" to their advantage. Shelburne, who had been the first to ask why the king refused to receive Congress's solicitation, spoke at length for a second time on the opportunity presented by the Olive Branch Petition for peacefully resolving the American question. Shelburne raised another matter that was on the minds of many. If the war lasted beyond 1776, he warned, the danger would grow that France would enter the fray. French belligerency, he said, would increase the likelihood that Congress would declare American independence and that America would win the war and make good on its break from the empire. Sandwich responded for the government. To concede to the demands of the rebels, he said, would "render up the rights of this country into the hands of the colonists." To back down, he continued, would bring "disgrace" and lessen Great Britain's standing "in the eyes of all Europe," perhaps with fatal consequences.[15]

A few days later, on November 16, Burke delivered the last of his three major speeches on the American crisis before independence. In the spring of 1774, and again during the following winter, he had made long, impassioned addresses attacking Britain's taxation of the colonists, his second effort coming when war hung in the balance. Burke's final oration was also incredibly lengthy—it consumed nearly four hours—and while his critics thought it "tedious" and not his best effort, many believed it was superior to Chatham's antiwar speech during the previous winter.[16]

Burke maintained that three approaches existed to the American problem. First, Great Britain could seek to crush the rebellion solely by the use of force. He doubted that victory could be achieved and was certain that it could not be accomplished by the number of troops that North had proposed sending to North America. Second, Great Britain could mix war and negotiation. Once the Continental army had suffered a sharp blow at the hands of the redcoats, terms could be offered to the colonial assemblies. Burke thought such a plan was fanciful. Rather than humbling the colonists, Britain's use of force would render the Americans less willing to reunite with the mother country. The third, and surest, way to "restore immediate peace," according to Burke, was to offer genuine peace terms without delay. The terms must not—could not—include the repeal of the Declaratory Act or of all American legislation enacted since 1763. To rescind the Declaratory Act would strip Parliament of all authority over America. To invalidate all recent acts might destroy Anglo-American commercial ties. Instead, Burke proposed offering the Continental Congress terms that included the renunciation of Parliament's authority to tax the colonists; recognition of the Continental Congress's authority to legislate for the colonies; repeal of the Townshend Duties and Coercive Acts; revocation of decades-old legislation that prohibited certain forms of manufacturing in the provinces; and pardons for all who had borne arms against Great Britain in this war.

Burke closed with an assessment of political realities in the colonies. A majority in Congress, he said, wished to reconcile with the mother country, and he believed that the terms he proposed were consistent with the conditions stipulated by the First Continental Congress. Shrewdly, Burke told the House of Commons that an offer of generous terms "would be the true means of dividing America" and crippling its solidarity behind the war, thus compelling

Congress to accept peace.[17] Burke had hit upon the great fear of the likes of John Adams. Because Galloway had exposed what had occurred in the First Congress, and because of the correspondence of Adams and Harrison that had gone awry, London knew that deep divisions existed among the rebels. Burke held forth the option of exploiting those breaches as the best means of finding a peaceable solution to the crisis.

Fox had said in private that Burke's speech "will be the fairest test in the world to try who is really for war and who is for peace."[18] The first to answer Burke was Lord Germain, who during November's American debate had finally succeeded Dartmouth as the American secretary. This was Germain's maiden speech as a minister. It was midnight when he obtained the floor. Germain struck one observer as "much flustered," and the new minister in fact confided to a friend that he "felt very awkward."[19] He began by saying that he would never surrender the right of taxation. If that meant war, he did not shrink from it. Great Britain had great resources and was "equal to the contest." The government, he went on, was sending the reinforcements asked for by the "officers serving on the spot." They believed the increased numbers of regulars would be sufficient "to restore, maintain, and establish the power of this country in America," and so did he. Germain pointed out that Congress had spurned the North Peace Plan. Indeed, it had not responded to the peace proposals made by Camden, Chatham, Burke, and Hartley during the previous winter. He declared that what Burke had proposed would not win over the Americans. The Americans, he argued, would see the terms proposed by Burke only "as gratuitous preliminaries" and would demand still more concessions, which "would put us on worse ground."[20]

North had been silent throughout the debates, but he rose when Germain took his seat. The first minister concurred with his new American secretary. Offering little that was new, North even repeated word for word some points made by Germain. At four A.M., immediately after North concluded his speech, the House of Commons rejected Burke's conciliatory terms by a two-to-one margin.[21]

Parliament had been in session for nearly a month, and North had divulged only his plans for increasing Britain's armed forces in North America. Nothing had been said about palliative measures, though rumors were swirling that the government planned to send a peace commission across the sea. The talk had largely been inspired by the cryptic passage in the king's address alluding to "persons . . . so commissioned" to restore the colonies to their proper allegiance. Germain had also fueled expectations of peace commissioners. In his rejoinder to Burke, Germain alluded to "the plan of sending commissioners," adding that he hoped they would "inquire into grievances."[22]

Four days after Burke's long speech, North spoke at length and finally informed Parliament of the government's plan. He revealed that commissioners would be sent to America to grant pardons and "enquire into . . . any . . . real grievance that would be remedied." He offered no new conciliatory proposals. He merely reiterated the plan that Parliament had approved in February: that the colonies tax their inhabitants to raise an amount of revenue stipulated by the imperial government, in return for which Parliament would no longer levy taxes on America. North clung to the slender hope that his supposed peace offering, counterbalanced by the full might of the British army and navy, offered the best chance of avoiding total war. Coercion and the threat of subjugation alone could sunder American unity and bring at least some of the colonies to their senses.

Given his pugnacious outlook, North introduced one new policy. Hoping to ratchet up the pressure on the colonists, the prime minister introduced the American Prohibitory Bill, soon to be labeled the "Capture Bill" by its foes. North's proposed legislation called for a naval blockade of each colony, the seizure of American goods discovered at sea, and the impressment into the Royal Navy of captured American seamen. North was confident that the measure would bring a rapid end to the colonists' "treasonable commotions." Not only would it frustrate the insurgents' every hope of obtaining foreign assistance, North thought, but also the threat of austerity posed by a blockade would result in an American capitulation before June or July, when the military campaign of 1776 was likely to begin in earnest. Should that not be the case, North continued, it was the government's intent to deal with the American rebels by coupling maximum force with severe economic coercion. When the colonists had been brought to their knees by defeat on the battlefield and privation sown by the prohibition of their trade, the so-called peace commissioners would accept the American surrender and grant pardons to at least some of the colonists.[23]

Burke and Fox never for a moment believed that the Americans would yield to North's strong-arm tactics. They believed, in fact, that further duress would only fuel the colonists' resolve to stand up against their mother country. Burke, answering North in his rich Irish brogue, retorted that the administration's "plan of this year is to enforce the conciliatory motion of last year by military execution." Working in tandem, Fox followed and spoke longer than his newfound ally. The Americans would see through North's deception and understand that the ministry had no intention of negotiating. They would understand that North's real purpose was "a declaration of perpetual war." The American Prohibitory Bill, Fox raged, lays bare "the want of policy, the folly and madness, of the present set of ministers."

The history of this crisis, Fox asserted, was that first Parliament imposed on the colonists "cruel and tyrannical laws." When the Americans objected, they were answered with "another [law] more rigorous than the former." When the colonists complained further, government sent "fleets and armies against them." The American Prohibitory Bill would be the final step. Whereas Burke had offered a peace plan built around genuine conciliation, North offered a "wretched policy" tantamount to total war. It would not divide the Americans; it would unite them against the mother country. It would push America to declare independence. Burke concurred with Fox, and in very nearly the final word in the debate, predicted that the day would come when the "damnable doctrines of this Bill would fall heavy on this country." Burke's oration fell once more on stony ground. The House of Commons passed the bill by more than a four-to-one margin.[24]

When Congress adopted the Olive Branch Petition, John Adams had prayed that the British government would be afraid to pursue negotiations, for he feared that serious talks would bring about a peace that left the Americans with less than they could achieve by continuing the war. Franklin had never for a moment thought that North's government would act on Congress's petition. "It now requires great Wisdom" on the part of Britain's leaders "to prevent a total Separation" of the colonies from the mother country, he had said back in the summer. "We shall give you one Opportunity more of recovering our Affections and retaining the Connections," he had remarked when Penn departed to carry the petition across the sea, but Franklin had not been sanguine.[25] Adams's prayers had been answered, and Franklin's suspicions had been borne out. Great Britain's last chance of preventing American independence by peaceful means had come and gone, spurned by a king and ministry that saw negotiation as weakness and gambled that the Americans were too feeble, divided, and craven to effectively resist the use of force.

Very near the time in December that the American Prohibitory Bill was passed by Parliament, a young Frenchman disembarked from a vessel in the harbor of Philadelphia. Achard de Bonvouloir was a French army officer, but he was dressed as a civilian and posed as a merchant from Antwerp. He had been in Philadelphia once before, in the fall of 1774 while on a tour of American cities, and he had quietly met with some delegates to the First Congress. He may have been sent to America in 1774 as a secret agent of the French government. There was no question that he returned just before Christmas 1775 as the representative of the French foreign minister, Charles Gravier, comte de Vergennes.

Following his initial visit, Bonvouloir had hurried to London, where he met with comte de Guines, France's ambassador to Great Britain, and reported on the rebellion that was simmering in the American colonies. While he thought hostilities were likely, Bonvouloir did not know whether the colonists possessed the resources to adequately wage war. After listening intently, Guines wrote to Vergennes to urge that the young soldier be sent back to Philadelphia to take "a good look at them [the colonists] politically and militarily."[26]

Vergennes had been France's foreign minister for only a few months, but like his predecessors, he had kept a watchful eye on Anglo-American relations. Since the Stamp Act troubles, France had sent a string of secret agents to America, and all had reported hearing talk of independence by many colonists. Prudently, France opted not to try to foment a rebellion, but just the same, it had devoted its energies to rebuilding its navy—which Great Britain had decimated in the Seven Years' War—and to solidifying its alliance with Spain, both necessary precursors to any conflict with Britain. In the meantime, it watched and waited.

Vergennes, who was fifty-five in 1775, was large, handsome, polished, and charming but suitably grave, thoughtful, and renowned for his industry. The foreign minister knew that an Anglo-American war would present France with both opportunities and dangers. It could produce a realignment of the European balance of power in France's interest. It might additionally open to the French a lucrative transatlantic trade that otherwise would remain closed so long as the American colonies remained part of the British Empire. On the other hand, a misstep could be ruinous for France. The most obvious miscalculation would be to openly support the American rebellion, only to learn that the colonists lacked either the means to fight capably or the will to persevere in the face of adversity. Above all else, Vergennes wished to avoid a situation in which France would find itself alone at war with Great Britain. That, almost certainly, would result in a worse defeat than France had suffered in the Seven Years' War. So it was also vitally important for Vergennes to learn whether the Americans would really wage war for independence, as a reconciliation with their mother country offered no benefits to France.[27]

By late summer 1775, Vergennes had discovered much through his careful observation of Anglo-American relations. He knew that the colonists had fought valiantly and effectively along Battle Road and atop Bunker Hill, Congress had authorized an invasion of Canada, and George III on August 23 had declared the colonists to be in rebellion. News of the king's action convinced Vergennes that reconciliation between the Americans and British was unlikely. But he needed more information before acting decisively. He wanted to know whether the Continental army could stand up to British regulars. He also wished to learn what France could do to assist America's war effort. For six months Vergennes had sat on Guines' recommendation that Bonvouloir be sent back to Philadelphia. Late in August the foreign minister made his decision. Bonvouloir was to return to America to report on the military situation. He was also to assure Congress that France had no aspirations to repossess Canada, to divulge that France admired the American quest for liberty, and to intimate that American merchant vessels would be welcome in French ports.[28] Vergennes had decided to do what he could to move the Continental Congress toward a declaration of independence.

Bonvouloir sailed from London late in the summer and reached Philadelphia about a week before Christmas. Through the contacts he had made a year earlier, Bonvouloir likely was routed to John Hancock, the president of Congress, who in turn must have arranged a meeting between the French agent and the members of the Committee of Secret Correspondence. The committee was new, having been created three weeks earlier, when Congress sanctioned trade in the Caribbean with foreign nations. At that time, Samuel Chase had proposed sending an agent to France to discuss trade possibilities, a motion seconded by John Adams. Most saw such a move as too radical, or at least premature, and opted instead for the creation of the Committee of Secret Correspondence, a five-member panel that was charged with establishing communication with America's friends in both the mother country and Europe. Though most members of the committee were confirmed reconciliationists, every member hoped to open commerce with foreign nations. Trade was essential for waging a war. In addition, for Dickinson, Jay, and Thomas Johnson, foreign trade might be the ploy that would force North's ministry to the negotiating table. For Franklin and Benjamin Harrison, trade with France was a crucial precursor to an alliance.[29]

In the first days of its life, the committee wrote to Arthur Lee in London and to Charles-Guillaume-Frédéric Dumas at The Hague. Lee, the thirty-five-year-old brother of Richard Henry Lee, had lived in London since 1768 and not only was deeply enmeshed in English politics but also had close ties with many opposition figures. Dumas, a man of letters who had long corresponded with Franklin, knew nearly every envoy at The Hague, a hub of European diplomacy. The committee directed Lee to act with "great Circumspection and impenetrable Secrecy" in forging links with America's friends in the mother country. It set Dumas on a different course. Franklin, in a letter signed by Dickinson and Jay, confided that during 1776 America expected to be "threatened from England with a very powerful force." Consequently, Congress found "it necessary to ask aid of some foreign power. . . . [W]e wish to know whether any . . . from principles of humanity, is disposed magnanimously to step in for the relief of an oppressed people." Or, the letter continued, if the Americans "declare ourselves an independent people," would any European nation "be willing to enter into an alliance with us for the benefit of our commerce." At this same moment Franklin also wrote privately to the heir apparent to the Spanish throne, thanking him for the gift of a book. Franklin went on to make it sound as if independence was inevitable and that the United States and Spain would share mutual concerns. America, Franklin wrote, was "a rising state" destined "soon to act a part of some Importance on the stage of human affairs." It will be "a powerful Dominion . . . whose interest it will be to form a close and firm alliance with Spain" against the predatory nations of Europe who will look covetously on North and South America and the Caribbean.[30]

Serendipitously, Bonvouloir arrived in Philadelphia just days, perhaps only hours, after these letters were written. He met with the committee three times. Each session was held at night in Carpenters' Hall. The Committee of Secret Correspondence wanted no one outside Congress to know that talks were under way with a French agent. It is also likely that the committee did not want every member of Congress to know of the discussions. Bonvouloir drank in what the committee told him. His report to Guines, which eventually reached Vergennes in March 1776, was exceedingly optimistic. "Everyone here is a soldier," he exclaimed. At least fifty thousand men had volunteered to serve without pay. Those who were in the Continental army were "well clothed, well paid, and well commanded." The Canadian invasion was proceeding smoothly, and Quebec was expected to fall shortly. The Americans needed arms, munitions, and military engineers but nothing else.[31]

Seemingly by coincidence, while Bonvouloir conversed with the Committee of Secret Correspondence, two other Frenchmen arrived in Philadelphia and met with another congressional committee. Around the time that Bonvouloir had come down the gangplank in Philadelphia, Pierre Penet and Emmanuel Pliarne, who were representatives of a private firm in Nantes— but in good standing with the French government, which almost certainly had sanctioned their venture—arrived in Providence, Rhode Island, hoping to do business with the colonists. In return for whale oil and tobacco, they offered to supply "the Continent with Arms & Ammunition." Merchants in Providence immediately escorted their French counterparts to Washington's headquarters in Cambridge, Massachusetts, The American commander in chief just as rapidly sent them to Philadelphia. Washington was so eager for them to meet with Congress that he even picked up the tab for the expenses they incurred on their journey southward from New England.[32]

Penet and Pliarne reached Philadelphia on December 29 and within

forty-eight hours were meeting with Congress's Committee of Correspondence, a nine-member panel created in September and entrusted with con-
tracting for arms from abroad. But when the committee members realized
that the Frenchmen were not agents of the French government, they reacted
warily. Discussions had continued for three fruitless weeks when, on January
17, Congress's session was interrupted by the arrival of a courier bearing "disagreeable Accotts [accounts] from Canada."[33] No news that reached Philadelphia after the outbreak of the war had a greater impact on Congress than
the dire tidings from Canada.

The Canadian campaign had originated with Congress late in June. Expectations of success had abounded, as all signs indicated that Canada was lightly
defended. Major General Philip Schuyler, a member of New York's delegation
to Congress prior to being named one of the original general officers in the
Continental army—and the commander of the Northern Department—was
vested with discretionary authority to advance only if he found that the
Canadians welcomed the invasion and the Indians appeared likely to remain
neutral. Congress was also confident that Schuyler would have sufficient men.
Nearly three thousand troops were scattered throughout New York, many New
Englanders were thought likely to join in, and Ethan Allen and his Green
Mountain Boys were available.[34]

With the formidable Canadian winter on everyone's mind, the original
plan was for Schuyler to lead his invasion force down Lake Champlain in July.
In the best-case scenario, Schuyler was to take the British installation at St.
Johns, advance on Montreal, and reach Quebec City long before the first snow-
fall. Taking Quebec was the great plum, for its conquest would be tantamount
to laying hold of Canada.

Trouble surfaced immediately. Recruiting and logistical difficulties caused
delays, as did Schuyler's health. Throughout the late summer he complained of
a stunning array of physical ailments that beset him with "Inflexible Severity."
First there was "a bilious Fever," next a "Barbarous Complication of Disorders,"
after which "violent rheumatic Pains" set in, followed by "a violent flux." These
myriad afflictions led him to speak of "the shattered Condition of my Constitution." July passed, then most of August. The invasion force was still at Fort
Ticonderoga. It had not taken a single step northward. As the weeks of inactiv-
ity passed, some officers grew to believe that Schuyler's maladies were psycho-
somatic. Some thought him indecisive and lacking the "strong nerves"
necessary for high command, and they may have been correct. Schuyler was a
political appointee whose military background was in the supply service. Commanding an operation of this magnitude may have been beyond his abilities.[35]

With his own doubts about Schuyler increasing, General Washington intervened to get the campaign under way. On his own initiative, Washington on August 20 proposed sending a secondary force of some one thousand men through Maine to Quebec. His idea was that if the British regulars in Quebec City came after Schuyler, the men coming up from Maine could easily take the city. If the redcoats debouched to take on the Maine expedition, the way would be open for Schuyler. If the British remained at Quebec, the two American forces would unite and attack the city. With overwhelming numerical superiority, a rebel victory seemed assured.

Schuyler consented to Washington's plan. Nearly two months to the day after Congress authorized the invasion, the army of the Northern Department at last moved northward, though Schuyler, still pleading illness, was not with his men. He remained at Fort Ticonderoga, leaving his second-in-command, Brigadier General Richard Montgomery, a sixteen-year veteran of the British army who had resigned his commission and emigrated to New York in 1771, to lead the army. Every inch the soldier, Montgomery provided excellent leadership, though by the time he and his men set out, the nights were already cold and the British had been given three months to prepare for the invasion. A couple of weeks after Montgomery's army started north, the second force, under Colonel Benedict Arnold, whom Washington had selected to be its commander, sailed from Massachusetts for the Kennebec River in Maine. It was to advance on Quebec in newly constructed bateau and by portaging between Maine's wild rivers.[36]

Every imaginable problem, and some that would have been difficult to conceive, plagued the American forces that autumn. Montgomery never had more than 1,700 men, too small a number for such a difficult undertaking. There had been little time to train them, the supply system was an inefficient work in progress, and the army launched its campaign with a piteously inadequate train of artillery—merely five field pieces and three mortars. Moreover, whereas Congress had imagined that the army might reach Quebec in September, it was November before Montgomery successfully completed a siege operation at St. Johns, and Montreal still had to be taken. Montgomery and his men finally reached Quebec during the first week in December. The city was already in the depths of winter.

Montgomery's problems paled next to those that confronted the secondary force. Arnold's men, many of whom lacked experience in roughing it on the frontier, faced a tortuous seven-week advance through more than two hundred miles of wilderness. Almost from the first day, bateau loaded with the expedition's supplies overturned, dumping their precious contents to the bottom of Maine's swirling, frigid rivers. Only a couple of weeks into the campaign the hungry soldiers were eating tree bark and candle wax, not to mention pet dogs that some of the men had unwarily brought along for companionship. There were too few blankets, especially after many wound up underwater. Habitually wet shoes disintegrated, leaving many men to proceed barefoot. Their plight was exacerbated by rain and snow, and incredibly by what appears to have been a hurricane that struck a month into the march. By mid-October some men had died and many others suffered from diarrhea, rheumatism, and arthritis. On October 25 an entire battalion of some 200 men deserted, taking with them about 150 others who were too ill to continue. Nor were they the only deserters. Upwards of 50 additional men appear to have deserted singly or in small parties. On November 9, about the time Montgomery was launching operations to take Montreal nearly 150 miles downriver, Arnold and his survivors reached Quebec City. Intelligence reported that a British force of 800 men were inside Quebec's walls. Arnold had some 650 men, a bit more than half the force that he had started with fifty-one days earlier. He decided to await the arrival of Montgomery.

The two rebel forces united on December 2 at Pointe-aux-Trembles, twenty miles down the St. Lawrence from Quebec City. Attrition in Montgomery's force had exceeded even that in Arnold's. Montgomery had only 300 men when he linked up with Arnold. Some of Montgomery's men had been lost in action; many more had died of disease; desertion had been heavy; more than 300 had to be left behind to garrison St. Johns and Montreal; and not a few soldiers had left for home when their enlistments expired in November. In command of a paltry army of about 950 men—one third of the number that had set out from New York and New England—Montgomery on December 3 ordered his troops to march through the swirling snow to the Plains of Abraham, just outside Quebec's formidable walls. Over the next few days the American army was augmented by the arrival of about 175 Massachusetts troops as well as some 200 men who formed a Canadian regiment that had been raised after the fall of Montreal, the grand total of *habitants* who had stepped forward to fight with the rebels. By the second week in December the American army stood at some 1,300 men.[37]

The numerical superiority that Congress had anticipated did not exist. The defenders of Quebec City were now known to number nearly 1,800 men, as the original garrison had been augmented by the survivors of the fighting at St. Johns and Montreal. Furthermore, Quebec City's topography offered natural defensive features. The city stood on a tall, nearly unassailable promontory above the St. Lawrence and St. Charles rivers. It was further protected by formidable man-made defenses, including a thirty-foot-tall wall buttressed by a stone foundation on the more exposed western side of the city. Lacking the manpower and artillery to conduct a siege, Montgomery tried to lure the British out of their citadel to fight on the Plains of Abraham. When that failed, the American commander had only one choice: to attack. Unable to persuade those soldiers to reenlist whose tour of duty ended on December 31, Montgomery knew that he had to attack before the end of the month.

Montgomery had to realize that the odds were heavy against success, though there was some reason for hope. The British might possess numerical superiority, but many of their men were militiamen. The British garrison also had to defend an enormous area with relatively few troops. If the Americans surprised their adversary and massed their firepower, they might succeed. Waiting patiently for stormy conditions, Montgomery plotted torching the town, hoping for a raging, wind-driven conflagration that would sow confusion among the defenders and burn at least a portion of the palisade.

Montgomery waited until the last possible moment, December 31. His plan was to open the engagement by launching feints designed to fool the defenders. While Montgomery's deceptive actions unfolded, Arnold, with half the army, was to break through a sturdy barricade defended by redcoats on the northeast side of the city. Montgomery, with the other half of the army, was to fight his way through a similar barricade on the southwest side. When both divisions were through, they would link up and charge into the lower city, setting it afire.

Things began propitiously. A heavy snowstorm struck that day, leading the Americans to hope that the unsuspecting British would be caught by surprise. But the British were not taken unaware. And the diversionary attacks that Montgomery ordered fooled no one. That set the tone for what lay ahead. The Americans failed to achieve any of their objectives. Neither barricade was taken. Montgomery died at the very outset of his assault, nearly decapitated by a burst of fire by the British defenders. After heavy fighting, Arnold was felled with a disabling wound to his Achilles tendon.

By seven A.M. it was over. The American attack had been repulsed with staggering losses. Nearly five hundred of the rebel soldiers had been killed, wounded, or captured. In three hours more than one third of the American army in Canada had been destroyed. The British lost only eighteen men.[38]

More than two weeks passed before news of the disaster reached Philadelphia. It struck Congress with the force of a body blow, and the residents of Philadelphia, at least according to one delegate, reacted as if "universally struck with grief."[39] All knew that the "events of war are always uncertain," as Franklin had written to Dumas a month earlier, but a failure of this

The Death of Montgomery *by John Trumbull. General Richard Montgomery,*
commander of the American army that attacked Quebec on December 31, 1775,
was killed in the engagement. One third of Montgomery's army was lost, nearly
five hundred men. (Yale University Art Gallery/Art Resource, NY)

magnitude was shocking. The dire news hit all the harder because this was the
first real defeat sustained by the rebels. The drubbing inevitably raised troubling questions about the colonists' ability to successfully conduct the war.

There were those, like New York's Robert R. Livingston, who wished to
pull out of Canada immediately. The place would bleed the colonies to death
both in human and economic terms, he argued, adding that it was "most evident that the Canadians are not to be relied on" to bear arms. He thought it
wiser to withdraw and prepare defenses along the Canadian border. There
were also some congressmen who saw the debacle as a "needfull" demonstra-
tion of "our Dependence" on foreign assistance, especially as the notion was
growing that this might be a protracted war, one in which America's staying
power hinged on acquiring a wide variety of military supplies from abroad.

But the viewpoint around which a majority of congressmen coalesced in
January was to send another army into Canada "with the utmost Dispatch."
The delegates reasoned that Quebec City might still be taken before British
reinforcements arrived, which would not occur until the St. Lawrence thawed
in the late spring. Some believed there was no choice but to continue to fight
for Quebec. Should the British regain their citadel, they warned, the royal

authorities would mobilize the Canadians and the Indians against the colonists, and they would strike the northern provinces with "a force . . . more
formidable than that of all the British Troops they can import into America."

Some saw another urgent reason for continuing to campaign for Quebec.
Word had reached Philadelphia of both the king's address and Germain's remarks hinting that peace commissioners might be sent across the sea. Some
believed that if Canada could be taken before the envoys arrived, it would be
an important bargaining chip in the negotiations with the commissioners.
Within seventy-two hours of learning of the defeat at Quebec, Congress not
only ordered seven regiments to be raised and sent to Canada but also, for the
first time, authorized the payment of bounties to raise recruits for the Canadian army. Quietly, too, news of the setback at the gates of Quebec stirred the
Committee of Correspondence to let contracts with Pliarne and Penet, the
two Nantes merchants who had languished impatiently for weeks in Philadelphia. With the sanction of Congress, trade was opened with France in order
to secure arms and munitions.[40]

Just days before word of the Canadian calamity reached Congress, an express
arrived with the first tidings of George III's October address to Parliament.
"It is decisive," a New Englander instantly responded. No greater proof was
needed that Britain's monarch "meant to make himself an absolute despotic
Tyrant." Samuel Ward added that "Every Man must now be convinced that . . .
our Safety depends wholly upon a brave, wise and determined Resistance."
Samuel Adams told others that this proved the king was the driving force behind British policy. War guilt "must lie at his Door," he added. A Virginian,
Francis Lightfoot Lee, concurred. The king's speech laid bare his and North's
"bloody intentions" and demonstrated beyond doubt that it was folly to any
longer continue "gaping after a reconciliation."[41]

Thirty-six hours after the express brought the king's speech to town,
Thomas Paine's *Common Sense*, the most important pamphlet published in
the American Revolution—indeed, the most influential pamphlet published
in seventeenth- and eighteenth-century America—hit Philadelphia's streets.
Its central argument was cogent and timely: Reconciliation was not in the
best interests of the colonists.

The thirty-seven-year-old Paine was an Englishman who, like Patrick
Henry and Samuel Adams, had failed at numerous endeavors. Unemployed,
divorced, and at loose ends, he had left his homeland in 1774 to begin a new
life in America. He claimed that he came to the colonies planning to start a
school for girls, but if that was his intention, he never got around to it. In his last
years in England, with time heavy on his hands, Paine had taken to writing

essays. He discovered that he had a facility for writing. Furthermore, he could earn a modest living as an author, enabling him to avoid toiling for sixty hours a week, as his other jobs had required. Paine had hardly landed in Philadelphia before he took up his pen. He published a newspaper or magazine article roughly every two weeks during his initial ten months in the city. He wrote about the war, calling it wicked and "unworthy [of] a British soldier," attacked slavery, and reflected on science, mathematics, dogs, dueling, women ("at all times and in all places" women have been "adored and oppressed"), love, ancient history, and unhappy marriages.[42]

Within a few months, it was apparent to Paine's growing number of readers that he was no ordinary writer. His essays, typified by a seldom-equaled clarity, also brandished an unmatched passion and verve. Sometime in the autumn of 1775—most likely when Dickinson persuaded the Pennsylvania assembly to instruct its delegates to Congress to seek redress and reconciliation—some congressmen and private citizens in Philadelphia appealed to Paine to pen a tract urging American independence. Dr. Benjamin Rush, one of Philadelphia's leading physicians, somewhat artlessly though accurately told Paine that he had nothing to lose by writing such a radical essay. What, Rush asked, could happen to someone who was already unemployed and nearly penniless?

The thought had already crossed Paine's mind. Though he had previously intended to write a series of short newspaper pieces on American independence, the entreaties of influential men set him to thinking in terms of writing a longer essay suitable for a pamphlet, and in November he commenced work. Paine made writing look easy, though in reality it was hard, slow work for him. He lashed himself to his desk for a few hours daily and over the course of a month crafted an essay of some eighteen thousand words. Not much of his argument was original. He had heard the ideas bandied about in coffeehouses and taverns, and some of his polemic—especially those portions dealing with governance in England—was the staple of eighteenth-century English radicalism. It was Paine's genius to marshal the disparate arguments in a cohesive and straightforward manner. Above all, Paine presented his arguments to readers in an inviting literary style. *Common Sense* was free of nearly indecipherable jargon and minus the recurrent Latin phraseology so popular with the lawyers who wrote most of the pamphlets. It was crucial for Paine to write in an accessible manner, as he was seeking to do what few other pamphleteers had ever tried. Most pamphleteers wrote for the best educated in society. Paine consciously sought a wider audience. His object was to convince the mass of colonists that it was desirable and feasible for America to sever its ties with Great Britain, and he especially wished to bring on a

Thomas Paine by John Wesley Jarvis, ca. 1806–1807. Paine's Common Sense,
issued in January 1776, was the first pamphlet to openly advocate independence.
He wrote that independence would be the birthday of a new world,
and that it would lead to peace and prosperity for the American people.
(National Gallery of Art, Washington D.C.)

transformation in how American independence was viewed by the inhabitants of the most recalcitrant colonies, including Pennsylvania.

The first few pages of *Common Sense*, which are no longer well remembered, were not unimportant. Paine explained that government was much simpler than the common people had been led to believe by the best educated and socially elite, who, of course, wished to continue monopolizing power. As government's purpose was to secure the safety and well-being of the citizenry, Paine wrote, it was only "common sense" that the citizenry should share in the governing process. In sketchy terms, he outlined republican governance. All that America needed for its government was a unicameral assembly (which it had in Congress) that was broadly representative of the people (which was not particularly true of Congress, though Paine did not point this out). In such a system, Paine continued, the elected representatives would have "the same concerns at stake [as] those who have appointed them" and would share "a common interest with every part of the community."

Great Britain's system was the very antithesis of what he had described, Paine told his readers. Dominated by a monarch—who came to the throne through hereditary succession—and a titled nobility who inherited seats in one house of Parliament, Britain's rulers seldom displayed "fidelity to the public" and "contribute[d] nothing towards the freedom of the State." The Crown—the monarchy—was the "overbearing part in the English constitution," the engine that drove the entire system, Paine added. As *Common Sense* appeared at the same moment that word of the king's October speech to Parliament arrived in the colonies, what Paine said appeared to be dead on target.

"The evil of monarchy," Paine asserted, was that it had left England groaning under kings who all too often were "foolish . . . wicked, and . . . improper," sometimes too young, over and again too old, on many occasions "ignorant and unfit," their "minds . . . early poisoned" by the belief that they were "born to reign, and others to obey." Not least among the iniquities of monarchy was that royal families were sequestered from their subjects to the point that they were unfamiliar with the wants and needs of the people. Kings, Paine went on, had little to do but create titles and make wars, and the wars they had started had "laid . . . the world in blood and ashes." The staggering result of war after war, not to mention the cost of creating sinecures for favorites and sycophants, was that the citizenry had been shackled with oppressive taxes to pay for it all.

But above all else, if monarchy contributed little of benefit to the people of England, it was actively baneful to colonists who lived three thousand miles away and whose outlook and interests were usually strikingly different from those of the English Crown and nobility.

However, by remaining tied to Great Britain, Americans were victimized by far more than monarchs and aristocrats. The American people and the British nation had dissimilar interests, but imperial governments sought almost solely to advance the interests of the latter. As a result, the connection to royal Britain left Americans to suffer "injuries and disadvantages."

This moved Paine to challenge Congress's very reason for fighting the war: to reconcile with Great Britain. To remain tied to the mother country would not only inhibit American commerce; it would also subject the American people to a "second hand government" on the other side of the Atlantic Ocean. "America is only a secondary object" to that British government, he contended. "England consults the good of this country no further than it answers to her own purpose." It will drag America into European wars that are of no concern to the colonists. It would fight those wars as long as it wishes. It would make whatever peace on whatever terms it pleases without consultation with the provincial authorities.

There were those who said that "America has flourished under her ... connection with Great Britain [and] the same connection is necessary towards her future happiness," Paine wrote. This was a "fallacious" assertion, he responded. "We may as well assert that because a child has thrived upon milk, that it is never to have meat." Others said that Britain has protected America. True, Paine wrote, but London safeguarded the colonies in order to exploit their wealth and trade. Dependence was no longer necessary. America was capable of standing on its feet.

Paine took a swipe at "all those who espouse the doctrine of reconciliation," including those in Congress and none more clearly than Dickinson. He charged that they were "Interested men, who are not to be trusted; weak men, who *cannot* see; prejudiced men, who *will not* see; and a certain set of moderate men, who think better of the European world than it deserves; and this last class, by an ill-judged deliberation, will be the cause of more calamities to this continent, than all the other three."

He then threw down the gauntlet: "I challenge the warmest advocate for reconciliation to show a single advantage that this continent can reap by being connected with Great Britain." None existed, Paine insisted. Once independent of Great Britain, Americans could govern themselves and secure the true interests of America. Peace and prosperity would ensue. "Our plan is commerce, and that, well attended to, will secure us the peace and friendship of all Europe; because it is the interest of all Europe to have America a free port." The time had come to declare American independence. "'TIS TIME TO PART."

Once it was independent, republican America would be an example to the world. American independence would strike "a new era for politics"—it would be nothing less than the 'birthday of a new world." Sounding very much like the revolutionary that he was, Paine proclaimed, "We have it in our power to begin the world over again."

In the final section of *Common Sense*, Paine maintained that victory in a prolonged war for independence could be won. America was unified and debt-free, and it had the resources and manpower for creating powerful armies and a sturdy navy. (America needed a fleet only one-twentieth the size of the Royal Navy to be "an over-match for her," he claimed.) Paine implied—he was careful not to make this a categorical argument—that help from Great Britain's traditional European enemies, France and Spain, could be had and that it would be useful. What he did say unreservedly was that it was "unreasonable" to expect French and Spanish assistance so long as reconciliation—"strengthening the connection between Britain and America"—was the object of the war. When Congress declared independence, he implied, Versailles and Madrid would find that intervention on America's behalf was desirable; for if London lost its colonies, Great Britain would be seriously weakened. Aside from Paine's assaults on monarchy and reconciliation, it was this cogent passage—merely one long sentence—that made *Common Sense* so timely. The pamphlet had no more than appeared before word arrived of the disaster at Quebec. Where once many would have taken umbrage at the thought of a foreign alliance, the horrific failure in Canada led many to see that close ties with France were perhaps America's only hope of saving itself.[43]

Four days after *Common Sense* hit the streets, a New Hampshire delegate reported that it had been "greedily bought up and read by all ranks of people" in Philadelphia. Another congressman related that it "has had a great Sale." John Hancock said that the pamphlet "makes much talk here." Franklin informed a correspondent that it "has made a great Impression here." Samuel Adams, one of the first to purchase the tract, immediately sent copies to friends in Massachusetts, informing them that it had "fretted some folks here." Other delegates eagerly wished to learn what the authorities back home thought of "the general spirit of it," and some explicitly asked provincial leaders if they had been converted by *Common Sense* to "relish independency."[44]

Common Sense hit like a bombshell. Some 250 pamphlets on the Anglo-American crisis had been published in America during the previous decade, and none had come close to equaling the sales of Paine's tract. Dickinson's *Letters from a Farmer in Pennsylvania* had outsold all rivals before 1776, but within a few months, nearly one hundred times more copies of *Common Sense* may have been sold than Dickinson's immensely popular leaflet had realized during its eight-year life span. Timing was obviously crucial for Paine's success, as was his crisp and lucid writing style. But so too was his palpable rage at Great Britain. Unbridled fury seemed to leap from the pages of the pamphlet. Paine's wrath struck a responsive chord with Americans who were beside themselves with anger at a mother country that made war on its colonies and willfully destroyed port cities, incited Indian attacks, and fomented slave insurrections.

Paine's euphoria at an American Revolution—a term that had not yet come into common usage—also transported readers. He provided a transcendent meaning for the events that were churning up the lives of the inhabitants of the colonies. Not only did the fate of contemporaries hang in the balance, Paine said; unborn generations of Americans and Europeans also depended on the creation of an independent America. "'Tis not the concern of a day, a year, or an age; posterity are virtually involved in the contest, and will be more or less affected even to the end of time, by the proceedings now," Paine wrote. He proclaimed that "a new era" had begun on April 19, 1775—the day the war began—an epoch that would be ushered in by cleansing changes, none more important than the republicanism that would supplant rule by monarchy and privileged nobility, preserving "the RIGHTS OF MANKIND." "The *time hath found us*," he declared, and it had brought forth the "seed-time of continental union, faith, and honor," and above all of American nationhood and American independence. No one had said such things in print previously, but across the broad landscape countless Americans took to heart what Paine had written, and their ready acceptance of his radical message quickened the pace toward American independence.[45]

CHAPTER 9

"We Might Get Ourselves upon Dangerous Ground"

James Wilson, Robert Morris, Lord Howe, and the Search for Peace

One "Event has brot another on," Samuel Adams remarked early in 1776.[1] He understood that the war was driving nearly every step that Congress took. The dynamic of hostilities was reshaping attitudes and shredding the already tattered remnants of the colonists' devotion to the mother country. The hard and bitter feelings that had swept over Great Britain in the wake of Lexington and Concord were now matched in an America that had learned of Falmouth and Lord Dunmore's proclamation. But nothing to this point in the war had shaken the reconciliationists as badly as the simultaneous blows of the king's fierce and unbending stance and Thomas Paine's assault on the very idea of maintaining ties with the mother country.

With the tide running against those who favored reconciliation, and with their options increasingly limited, Dickinson and his followers launched a final initiative at the outset of 1776. In August, and again in October, the king had justified the use of force on the premise that Congress was committed to American independence. On January 9, the day after the text of the monarch's address to Parliament reached Philadelphia, James Wilson, a Pennsylvania delegate who looked on Dickinson as his mentor, moved that Congress "declare to their Constituents and the World their present Intentions respecting an Independency." A New Jersey congressman noted in his diary that Wilson was "strongly supported," and it is a safe bet that at a minimum all four delegations from the mid-Atlantic colonies backed his motion.[2] Wilson and his adherents had two objectives. They wished to show America's friends in England that the king was wrong to insist that the American rebels secretly planned to declare independence when the time was right. In addition, by disavowing independence, Wilson hoped to lay the groundwork for talks with the envoys that George III in October had so tantalizingly suggested were to be sent to America. On the day after Wilson spoke, *Common Sense* appeared. That provided the reconciliationists with an additional—and especially urgent—reason for acting. They prayed that a congressional repudiation of independence would derail whatever groundswell might be aroused by Paine's persuasiveness.

The thirty-four-year-old Wilson, who served as the point man for this latest sally to halt America's drift out of the empire, had grown up in a farming family in Caskardy in the Scottish Lowlands. Provided with a formal education that was to prepare him for the clergy, Wilson instead fell under the influence of the Enlightenment during his years at the University of St. Andrews. He endured one listless year of theological study following graduation, after which he dropped out of school and worked briefly as a tutor and bookkeeper. Unhappy and adrift, he sailed for America in 1765, hoping, like numerous other immigrants, to find some purpose to his life. Wilson landed in New York, though he quickly moved to Philadelphia, the larger of the two cities. Not long after his arrival, the *Letters from a Farmer* appeared and Dickinson bolted to fame. Ambitious and drawn to politics himself, Wilson in 1767, at age twenty-five, applied to study law with Dickinson. Completing his apprenticeship in less than a year, Wilson moved to Reading, a town of a few hundred inhabitants northwest of Philadelphia, and opened a legal practice. With little competition, he rapidly succeeded. Filled with confidence, Wilson after two years moved to Carlisle, a larger frontier town teeming with immigrants, including many from Scotland. He prospered there as well. Within two years he had the largest caseload of any attorney in town, and in 1771, merely six years after crossing the Atlantic, he married a wealthy heiress, the stepdaughter of an influential ironmaster.

Like John Adams, Wilson largely remained aloof from politics until the Tea Act and Intolerable Acts crises, when he served on local committees that opposed parliamentary taxation. Later, he was part of the movement that pressured Galloway to have the assembly sanction the Continental Congress. Also like Adams, Wilson published a pamphlet in 1774 that attacked Parliament's claims of unlimited power over the colonies. In most respects, Wilson shared Dickinson's outlook, especially with regard to American independence. The one significant difference in their outlook was that, by the eve of the war, Wilson denied that Parliament could exercise any authority over the colonies.

Dickinson and his former student remained close. When Galloway resigned

James Wilson. A staunch reconciliationist and follower of John Dickinson, Wilson opposed independence until the last minute, when he voted to break with Great Britain. He had a long career as an American public official following independence. (Private Collection/ The Bridgeman Art Library)

from the Pennsylvania delegation to the Second Continental Congress, Dickinson had a hand in securing Wilson's appointment to the vacant seat in May 1775. Wilson remained a backbencher throughout his first year in Congress, in part perhaps because his somewhat standoffish manner and forbiddingly cold exterior prevented close relationships with delegates from other colonies. In addition, like Adams at the First Congress in 1774, Wilson, somewhat unsure of himself, likely was overawed for a time by his more experienced colleagues. Yet while Wilson seldom entered debates, he served on numerous committees, where he established a reputation as a bright, thoughtful, and dependable colleague. In the summer of 1775 John Adams pronounced that Wilson's "Fortitude, Rectitude, and Abilities too, greatly outshine" those of Dickinson.[3]

When Wilson took the floor in January 1776, he may have felt that the time had arrived for him to play a more prominent role. He may also have been driven by desperation, given the increasing plight of the reconciliationists.

The possibility exists, too, that those who shared his outlook selected him to take the lead in this fight not only because he was a fresh face but also because his outlook on Parliament's supremacy was slightly more progressive than Dickinson's. Or, Wilson may have acted when he did because of the role he was playing at the time in a largely forgotten episode—negotiations with a self-appointed emissary of Lord North.

Through contacts with talkative New York and New Jersey delegates who had attended the First Congress, Thomas Lundin, Lord Drummond, had learned in December 1774 of the narrow defeat of Galloway's compromise proposal. Drummond, a Scotsman who had crossed to America and settled in New Jersey three years after Wilson's emigration, also appears to have gleaned that the initial Congress had been deeply divided and that many moderate congressmen distrusted their more radical colleagues from New England. Armed with this inside information, Drummond hurried to London shortly after the First Continental Congress adjourned. During the winter of 1775, hard on the heels of Dartmouth's failure to lure Franklin into meaningful negotiations, Drummond was given an audience with Lord North and the American secretary. The Scotsman presented a peace proposal that he had drafted, a plan that bore a striking similarity to the so-called North Peace Plan recently presented to Parliament. Both North and Dartmouth thought Drummond might be useful, but the prime minister made no decision about using him as an emissary for another six months.

In the wake of Lexington-Concord and Bunker Hill, with the ministry scrambling to find additional troops to send to America, and with North at least privately despairing of ever suppressing the American rebellion by force, the prime minister decided to put Drummond to use as an unofficial envoy. North asked him to return to Philadelphia. Drummond was to use his contacts to determine what Congress would accept, and what London would have to relinquish, to settle Anglo-American differences. No doubt, too, Lord North was searching for a means of sowing fatal divisions among the congressmen. It seems clear that Drummond was instructed not to drag his feet. North wanted to know whether any chance existed for fruitful negotiations before substantive military operations began in the spring or summer of 1776. The thirty-three-year-old Scottish nobleman sailed from London in September and reached Philadelphia late in December, arriving in the city around the same time as Bonvouloir, Penet, and Pliarne. Within days, possibly hours, Drummond had quietly opened discussions with delegates from at least four colonies: New York, New Jersey, South Carolina, and Pennsylvania. One of the delegates with whom he met was James Wilson.

Not every member of Congress welcomed Drummond's presence or wanted his colleagues to meet with the Scotsman. Samuel Adams hurriedly demanded that Drummond be arrested, as did the Pennsylvania Committee of Safety, which feared that the Scotsman might share with the British military what he learned of Philadelphia's defenses. However, several congressmen from the middle and southern colonies objected with "grt Warmth" to Adams's proposal and by an eight-to-three vote—if Drummond is to be believed—Congress sanctioned the unofficial talks.[4]

Drummond told the congressmen with whom he met that North's ministry was "heartily tired of the controversy" with America and "astonished at the Union and Strength of the Colonies." The prime minister, he added, was confident that the differences between the colonies and mother country "might be easily settled." Drummond advised that under North's conciliation plan the amount of revenue each colony would be asked to provide would be "a very small sum Annually so as to save appearances." If Congress would consent, Drummond went on, North would ask Parliament to repeal the Tea Act and the Coercive Acts.

The discussions between Drummond and several delegates spun out for nearly two weeks until, in mid-January, North's envoy was convinced that seven congressional delegations were willing to accept what North had offered. Drummond may have been so eager to succeed as a peacemaker that he imagined greater support for North's offer than actually existed, but at that point he was certain that a majority of congressional delegations were prepared to accept the Declaratory Act if, in turn, Parliament renounced the right to tax America, agreed to remove some restraints on colonial trade, and relaxed the restrictions on American manufacturing. Drummond also believed that the seven delegations with which he had supposedly reached an accord would ask Congress not only to approve the terms that had been hammered out but also to send a three-member delegation—consisting of John Jay of New York, Thomas Lynch of South Carolina, and Andrew Allen of Pennsylvania—to London to conduct formal negotiations.[5] Reading between the lines of Drummond's sketchy notes, it seems likely that the seven provinces with which the Scotsman believed he had come to an agreement were New York, New Jersey, Pennsylvania, Delaware, South Carolina, North Carolina, and Georgia. It is a safe bet that James Wilson was ready to make peace with the mother country on these terms. Wilson also doubtless saw his motion to have Congress declare where it stood on the issue of American independence as inextricably linked with the Drummond negotiations.

Tall, ruddy, and solidly built, Wilson, as was his custom, wore thick glasses and a white wig when he addressed Congress on January 9. Like many lawyers, he had polished his speaking talents before countless juries, but Wilson surpassed most rivals, winning a reputation in Pennsylvania as a consummate orator blessed with "the powers of a Demosthenes and a Cicero."[6] Wilson had been in Congress long enough to know that his oratory was unlikely to win any converts, but there can be little doubt that what he said that day in his thick Scottish accent was well organized and carefully crafted.

Wilson hoped that a congressional repudiation of independence would lead to successful negotiations with Drummond. An agreement with Drummond, he thought, would make it easier for both North and the king to accept the terms desired by a majority of the congressional delegations. Eighteen months after Galloway had failed to persuade the First Congress to adopt a compromise scheme, another Pennsylvanian—and an archfoe of Galloway at that—was deeply involved in yet another attempt to preserve the Anglo-American union through negotiation and compromise.

Congress deferred consideration of Wilson's proposal for three days, which was not uncommon, then delayed action for twelve additional days. The second postponement likely occurred in part because talks with Lord Drummond were still in progress. In addition, Samuel Adams may have had a hand in putting off consideration of Wilson's surprise proposal. Adams wanted time to better organize the opposition. It was rare for Adams to emerge from the shadows to play an open and leading role in a floor battle, but he did so in this instance because John Adams, like several congressmen, had returned home in December for a visit with his family. It quickly was apparent that Samuel Adams's method of coping with the reconciliationists was considerably different from that of his cousin. Patience and negotiation had been John's watchwords, as he had steadfastly believed that if Congress's unity behind the war could be maintained, events would in time transform most of his foes into advocates for independence. Samuel was more confrontational. He countered first by pulling strings with his allies at home to have Thomas Cushing recalled as a member of the Massachusetts delegation. Cushing was replaced by Elbridge Gerry, who was thought to be favorably disposed to American independence. Before January ended, all of Congress knew of the change among Massachusetts's representatives, and all knew what it meant. Previously, three of the Bay Colony's five congressmen—Cushing, Hancock, and Robert Treat Paine—had been either staunch reconciliationists or willing to consider concessions in order to restore ties with the mother country. Those three Yankees found a peaceful Anglo-American reunion on acceptable terms preferable to declaring independence and waging a long, costly, and uncertain war. But a change of one individual in Massachusetts's delegation altered everything. Gerry and the two Adamses barely hid their yearning for independence.[7] But this was not Samuel Adams's only way of fighting back. He also resurrected Franklin's proposal to write an American constitution, a step that had been tabled six months earlier, as it was seen as tantamount to a declaration of independence.

The actions of Wilson and Samuel Adams brought Congress to the brink of a potentially great crisis. About half the delegations in Congress appear to have been willing to renounce independence and dispatch emissaries to London to conduct peace talks. But with American independence seemingly so close that they could taste it, the other half were desperate to prevent their congressional foes from ruining their dream of setting America free of Great Britain. This was not the first time that Congress had been deeply divided, though not since the First Congress had a clash of such diametrically opposite choices confronted the delegates. The war was raging, and all knew that it would broaden and deepen as the military campaign of 1776 unfolded. Thomas Paine had brought talk of independence into the open. The war and all that went with it had hardened the attitudes of many in Congress. But just as surely, hostilities had increased the apprehensions of other deputies, quickening their desire to bring the war to a suitable conclusion. For at least some among the latter, the belief was palpable that Drummond's mission presented them with a great opportunity—perhaps their last—to snatch back reconciliation from the seeming maw of independence.

Congress set January 24 as the day for taking up Wilson's motion. All knew the stakes were high. George Read of Delaware, who had returned home to nearby New Castle to tend to urgent personal matters, hurried back to Philadelphia when he learned from reconciliationist friends in the North Carolina and Pennsylvania delegations that Wilson needed support for his "business of the last importance." Read rounded up Caesar Rodney, his Delaware colleague who was also at home, and both were back in their seats when Congress assembled. Samuel Adams was ready for a fight as well. Wilson's move had to be defeated, lest "we might get our selves upon dangerous Ground," he said. Adams confided to one of New England's general officers in the Continental army that rather than renouncing independence, the time had come for Congress to throw off Great Britain's "Chains & Slavery" and "assume that Character" of independence that the "great Law of Nature points out" for America.[8]

When Wilson's motion came to the floor for discussion on that cold January morning, John Dickinson was the first congressman on his feet. Dickinson's attendance in Congress had been spotty during the past several months, as he divided his time between the Pennsylvania assembly and his service as a colonel of one of the four militia battalions raised by Philadelphia. He took soldiering seriously. Even John Adams admitted that Dickinson "setts a fine

Example [and] is much talk'd of and applauded" by the members of Congress for the time he devoted to drilling his men, procuring and inspecting weaponry and powder, and planning the city's defenses.[9]

But Dickinson knew the crucial nature of this debate. He returned to be heard and to lead the fight. He opened the discussion with a lengthy, impassioned, and legalistic speech that aimed at demonstrating the colonists' "Constitutional Connection" with the Crown at every step from the founding of the British Empire down to 1776. However, the heart of Dickinson's presentation was his call for Congress to renounce independence and dispatch diplomats to London to seek to open negotiations leading to peace. He moved that Congress in a "humble and dutiful" manner petition the king once again—it would be Congress's third address to the monarch in fifteen months—informing him that America was not "contending for Empire & Independence," but that it sought a "mutually beneficial Accommodation" with the mother country.

Dickinson proposed that two or more members of Congress carry the petition to London, and if the monarch was willing, conduct talks with his representatives. Congress's envoys were to tailor their demands to what they found in England. For example, if they discovered that the armed forces being sent for the campaign of 1776 were so great that the colonies seemed certain to be "in Danger of suffering any great Calamity . . . likely to have a Decisive Influence on the Event of the War," Congress's representatives were to scale back their demands. If that was not the case, America's diplomats were to demand an immediate armistice and exchange of prisoners of war, followed by negotiations aimed at securing a renunciation of Parliament's power to tax the colonies, a guarantee that the colonial charters were inviolate, greater freedom for colonial manufacturing and trade outside the empire, the right of the colonies to issue their own currency and pay the salaries of their civil officials, and the "Redress of Grievances." The principal American concession envisaged by Dickinson was to consent to the prime minister's February 1775 peace plan proposal that each province agree to furnish a stipulated amount of revenue to the imperial government in London. Dickinson concluded by asking Congress to inform the American people that it was committed to reconciliation, not independence.[10]

Dickinson had not mentioned the negotiations with Drummond, but the terms of his proposal were strikingly similar to those that some congressmen appear to have reached with North's envoy.

Dickinson's stance in January 1776 revealed that changes had occurred in his outlook over the years. He now demanded greater trading rights for Americans. Even so, he appeared willing to consent to more British control of

American affairs than Galloway would have yielded in his compromise scheme back in the autumn of 1774.

"Most of the day was spent" in deliberating what Dickinson had said, one delegate noted in his diary.[11] The discussion focused on whether to make a statement espousing reconciliation and disowning independence, not on the matter of negotiations. It was Dickinson's misfortune that so much had occurred—that radicalizing events just kept happening, to paraphrase Samuel Adams—in the two weeks since Wilson's speech and in the several days following the culmination of the talks with Lord Drummond. Many southern congressmen, including some who had been ready to concede much in negotiations leading to reconciliation, were outraged at learning on January 16—scant hours after the discussions with Drummond concluded—that Governor Dunmore had bombarded Norfolk. William Hooper of North Carolina knew all too well "the defenceless State" of his colony and feared that its hamlets would also experience "total destruction" unless outside assistance was provided. That help, Hooper had to know, might depend on keeping the Yankees in Congress happy. The following day, January 17, word reached Philadelphia of the failed invasion of Canada, America's first real setback in the war. The news "restrain[ed] the Expectations"—to use Dickinson's words—of America's chances of securing favorable terms in negotiations with the Crown. Not only that, but even some who had been in on the talks with Drummond now spoke of "making alliances" in order to successfully wage the war, a step that they acknowledged required "a total seperation with Britain." Finally, by the time of Dickinson's speech, every congressman had been startled by the "Surprizing run" of Paine's *Common Sense* and by the popularity of his call for cutting all ties with the mother country.[12]

As the long shadows of late afternoon fell over the State House, Congress voted against petitioning the king or sending envoys to London. It also declined to take action on Samuel Adams's move to consider Franklin's plan for a national government. But with the thought of solidifying the bond between the colonies, it appointed a committee, which included both Dickinson and Wilson, to draft an address to the American people on the reasons for waging the war. Congress hoped that the address would persuade the colonists that neither British armed forces nor Lord North's machinations could break up the American union.[13] Dickinson and Wilson agreed with that, but both intended to produce an address that renounced American independence. Their foes, expecting as much, anticipated a savage floor fight to resolve the issue.

Had the committee completed its work rapidly, it might have won a more favorable response from Congress. But a week slipped by, then a second week, and ultimately a third week passed while Wilson and Dickinson dithered over what to include in the document, and even over the choice of words. The committee selected Wilson, who had first asked Congress to declare where it stood on independence, to write the initial draft. Dickinson, objecting to much that Wilson included, rewrote entire passages, liberally adding and deleting sections. Wilson, in turn, struck out much that Dickinson had penned and crafted the document as he saw fit. In the end, they produced an incredibly lengthy document. It ran some six thousand words, one third as long as *Common Sense* and five or six times longer than most newspaper essays. Wilson was a political novice, and Dickinson was mulish and accustomed to having his way, and in this instance neither was the least bit savvy.

While Wilson and Dickinson wrangled, things continued to happen that hardened attitudes within Congress. Five days after the committee was formed, a packet of London newspapers from November reached Philadelphia. They contained two crucial bits of news. For the first time the congressmen learned what they had suspected all along: North's government was sending large numbers of reinforcements to America for the military campaign of 1776. The papers reported that not only were twenty-five thousand additional redcoats crossing the Atlantic but also that there were indications some troops were to be deployed in the southern colonies. The congressmen also gleaned from the accounts of the autumn session of Parliament that North was sending what he called "peace commissioners" across the sea.[14]

John Adams, who returned to Congress in mid-February, noted that "a deep Anxiety, a kind of thoughtfull Melancholy" pervaded the southern delegations. The southern congressmen found themselves in the same disquieting situation that Bostonians had faced on the eve of hostilities nine months earlier. But it was not solely Southerners who were anxious. Every deputy knew that a "very critical time is approaching," as one remarked, a time of the harshest tests on the battlefield, of talks with Lord North's envoys, and possibly of further urgent discussions with the French.[15] In this uneasy environment few members of Congress wished to risk making an unnecessary public pronouncement that might be attended with unforeseen, and possibly pernicious, consequences. What might seem innocuous in the winter could in the spring or summer prove to be injurious to wartime morale or unity, or it could undercut the most crucial negotiations that Congress would ever be called on to undertake, whether with London or Versailles.

Wilson's proposed Address to the Inhabitants of America was dead on arrival when at last it was presented to Congress on February 13. It had defended using force to resist the "Calamities" that would result from Great Britain's unconstitutional acts, and it denied that Congress had ever intended to establish "an Independent Empire." "We disavow the Intention," it stipulated.

Instead, the address stated: "We declare that what we aim at . . . *is the Defense and Re-establishment of the constitutional Rights of the Colonies.*" It concluded with a rhetorical flourish: "That the Colonies may continue connected, as they have been, with Britain, is our second Wish: Our first is—THAT AMERICA MAY BE FREE."[16]

Wilson's proposal was "very long, badly written & full against Independency," thought a New Jersey delegate, who added that "the Majority did not relish his Address & Doctrine." That much was sufficiently clear after a brief discussion. Wilson never asked Congress to vote on his Address.[17]

Thirty days had elapsed between the moment when Lord Drummond believed that a majority of congressional delegations were prepared to make peace on the basis of North's Peace Plan and the day that Wilson presented his draft document renouncing independence. During that month, sentiment for making peace and reconciling with the mother country—if Lord Drummond's sense of congressional attitudes was correct—crested and began to recede.

The Drummond episode also underscores that, from 1774 onward, Lord North and the Crown missed one opportunity after another to resolve the quarrel with the colonies and, with only minimal concessions, to save the empire. Had peace commissioners been sent to America before the war began, as Dartmouth had wished, there might never have been a war. Had North and his ministers stood up to the king and softened, or prevented altogether, his strident proclamation in August 1775 and his speech to Parliament in October, reconciliation might have been possible even after hostilities had begun. Had North named and dispatched peace commissioners in November—when he told Parliament that he planned to do so—and had those envoys been entrusted with the authority to engage in authentic diplomacy, a majority in Congress might have consented to the terms that they were ostensibly willing to commit to with Drummond. Above all, the Drummond episode laid bare the desperation of many congressional delegates who favored reconciliation, raising the possibility that an artful government in London might have gained its ends by fatally dividing Congress, the very strategy that Burke had shrewdly urged North to pursue the previous fall.

But from the moment in January 1774 that they had learned of the Boston Tea Party through the end of 1775, and beyond, the king and an overwhelming majority of his ministers held inflexibly to the premise that all was lost if they conceded to the colonists even the slightest authority that London exercised over America. Beginning with its discussions over how to respond to the destruction of the tea in Boston Harbor, North's government preferred coercion to making concessions. By 1776 North's government was committed solely to the use of armed force to resolve its American problem. If it proved to be unavailing, Great Britain would lose its American colonies. Moreover, many believed that Great Britain had to succeed in 1776. If the Continental army survived 1776, it would thereafter be a seasoned and more formidable foe, and it might be joined by French or Spanish forces.

Though it is more apparent in hindsight than it was to contemporaries, Congress's response to Wilson's address on February 13, 1776, was a pivotal moment. The reconciliationists were finished. They had dominated Congress and constrained its actions from the beginning. No more. The war now controlled Congress, and a majority of delegates were prepared to do whatever had to be done to gain victory. With one event bringing on another, as Samuel Adams had remarked, the likelihood was considerable that wartime exigencies—as Wilson and Dickinson surely must have known—were moving Congress steadily, and rapidly, toward an irrevocable breach.

Forty-eight hours after Congress rebuffed Wilson and Dickinson, Robert Morris, a member of the Pennsylvania delegation who had been an unbending advocate for reconciliation, wrote a friend that it was inevitable that Congress would declare American independence, most likely sometime during 1776. In jumbled syntax, he allowed that war had "prepared Men's minds for an Independency, that were shock'd at the idea a few weeks ago." He also predicted that if Great Britain failed to crush the rebellion in 1776, it "may bid adieu to the American Colonies."[18] Morris was adapting like a chameleon. He was a congressman cut from different cloth, a man from a mercantile background who in large measure viewed the war and America's break with the mother country from the perspective of its impact on countinghouse ledger books. That was not necessarily good news for those who favored reconciliation.

The forty-four-year-old Morris sported a middle-age spread, a thick mane of graying hair, and dark, furtive eyes. He was pallid, as might be expected of a man who spent his days indoors at a desk. His demeanor was that of a man obsessed with profits and losses. He tended toward briskness and formality. He was not unfriendly, but he was neither warm nor outgoing. He had few close friends, and no one who worked with him in business or public affairs ever characterized him as engaging or recalled any spark of humor or kindness on his part.

Born in Liverpool in 1735, Morris had emigrated to America with his father just as he entered adolescence. They settled in Maryland, where his father worked as a tobacco agent, but after only a year in the colonies young Morris was orphaned following his father's death. The youngster's guardian

sent him to Philadelphia to begin an apprenticeship in the mercantile firm of
Charles Willing. Morris and Willing's son, Thomas, separated in age by less
than two years, developed a close relationship and in 1757—following the elder Willing's demise in a yellow fever epidemic—established their own firm,
Willing, Morris and Company.

As was true of the Franklin and Galloway political partnership, Willing
and Morris brought dissimilar but essential talents to their business partnership. Willing had ties to powerful Philadelphia families. His mother was a
Shippen, a family that had long produced professional and civic leaders, including Philadelphia's first mayor; his father was one of the city's more influential merchants and had also held the post of Philadelphia's mayor. Young
Willing was well educated, having attended preparatory schools in the mother
country and read law at the Inns of Court in London. He was amiable, cosmopolitan, well connected, and quite affluent, if not wealthy. He was also
politically active and deeply involved in the life of the city. Willing dabbled in

*Robert Morris by Charles Willson Peale. A Philadelphia merchant, Morris entered
Congress in 1775. He favored reconciliation and refused to vote for independence,
but in August 1776 Morris signed the Declaration of Independence.
(Pennsylvania Academy of Fine Art/ The Bridgeman Art Library)*

Indian diplomacy, sat in the assembly between 1764 and 1767, and, like his father, served as mayor of Philadelphia. He was additionally a trustee for a charitable school, director of the College of Philadelphia, and judge of the Orphans' Court.[19]

Yet it was Morris who set his and Willing's company apart from its rivals. Fortuity had brought him into a field of endeavor for which he was perfectly suited. Meticulous, industrious, and persevering, Morris seemed to have the Midas touch when it came to commerce. He landed government contracts for the nascent firm during the French and Indian War, turning that conflict into a bonanza for Willing, Morris and Company. The company continued to flourish during the dozen years before the Revolutionary War broke out, in part because Willing and Morris had an easy collaborative relationship. Early on Willing told his partner that "my house shall be your home and myself your friend." After two decades in business together, Willing told Morris of his "esteem and friendship" for him, adding that his partner remained "the Man in the World I love most, and for whom I have every feeling of affection and regard."[20] By 1775 Willing, Morris and Company sent out some twenty ships annually, exporting grain from the Pennsylvania heartland (and from the Chesapeake and even Quebec) and importing wine, salt, and lemons from Portugal and Spain. But the heart of the company's trade was with Great Britain and the West Indies. The company shipped corn, wheat, and flaxseed to Ireland and lumber, flour, and fish to the Caribbean, and its vessels returned home laden with manufactured goods, luxury items, and casks of rum. In the last years before the war, the company branched into land speculation schemes, investing in what the proprietors thought would be a citrus-producing tract near the Mississippi River. Before he turned thirty-five, Morris, with his wife (the daughter of a prominent lawyer) and two sons, lived in a stone mansion on an eighty-acre estate that sprawled along the Schuylkill River only three miles from downtown Philadelphia.[21]

Both Willing and Morris supported the nonimportation boycotts against the Stamp Act and Townshend Duties, and each shared the outlook of Dickinson with regard to opposing London's policies. Willing was the more politically active of the two—he was a member of the provincial convention in 1774 that compelled Galloway to have the assembly consent to the First Continental Congress—and he was elected to the Second Congress in May 1775. Morris remained largely aloof from politics until war broke out, but in the first election thereafter he ran successfully for the assembly. He had hardly taken his seat before the legislature added him to the colony's delegation in Congress in November 1775. Both Willing and Morris were unswerving advocates of reconciliation, but the two were businessmen who never lost sight of what their public service could do for Willing, Morris and Company's earnings. They knew that war could be both good and bad for business. "[W]e judge that Business must be very valuable, so long as the other Colonies are shut up" by the Royal Navy, they said. Obtaining a sizable chunk of that business often appeared to be their guiding light.[22]

In September 1775 Willing was among the initial batch of delegates chosen to serve on the Secret Committee, Congress's panel for making sub rosa arms purchases. However, hard on the heels of Morris's election to Congress six weeks later, Willing resigned from the committee, and Morris—who not only had a proven track record in landing government contracts but also had been privately trading for munitions in the West Indies since the outbreak of the war—took his place. In no time, Willing, Morris and Company obtained several contracts from Congress for trafficking in gunpowder, gunlocks, arms, artillery, and bayonets. It also had a share of the nearly three hundred thousand dollars that Congress appropriated for opening trade in Europe and a guarantee of 5 percent of the profits turned by that commerce. Morris developed cozy ties with the army's paymaster in Virginia, who channeled business to Willing, Morris and Company in return for government contracts that the congressman secured for him. Morris saw no ethical conflicts in his actions. "[I]t seems to me," he said in 1776, that "the present opportunity of Improving our Fortunes ought not to be lost especially as the very means of doing it will Contribute to the Service of our Country at the same time." By mid-February 1776, when Morris came to think that a congressional declaration of independence was a certainty, he was working hard to land a contract to export tobacco from the Chesapeake colonies to France, commerce that long had been illegal under Great Britain's trade laws. Morris badly wanted a share of that trade.[23]

Morris appeared to be playing every angle. Early in 1776, he let business contacts in England know that he believed "the Power of Great Britain [was] insurmountable" and that he favored reconciliation. But what Morris really believed was that the war would not go on long before nearly every nation in Europe would "be glad to treat and trade with us on our own terms." He wanted a role in that traffic, for as commerce with Great Britain dried up in the course of the war, the European trade would be his company's salvation. Morris had another reason for wanting to get involved in trade with Europe. He thought the most likely outcome of the war would be a stalemate. Great Britain would be unable to crush the rebellion; the colonists would lack the ability to gain victory; a stalemated war would end in a negotiated peace. Morris appeared to believe that after all was said and done, the America colonies would remain part of the British Empire, but London would have to grant greater autonomy to the colonies, including more liberal trading rights outside the empire.[24] Morris presumed that the European trade connections he forged during the war would serve him well following hostilities.

Robert Morris and Thomas Willing were still part of the anti-independence bloc in Congress. Each had lived in England, loved England, and was loyal to old country ties. Willing, Morris and Company had innumerable commercial contacts throughout the British Empire and had prospered within the Anglo-American union. As Morris observed just before Christmas 1775: "I abhor the Name & Idea of a Rebel. I neither want or wish a Change of King or Constitution."[25] But both men—Morris especially—were opportunists, and Morris in particular knew that a declaration of American independence was on the horizon. The colonists, he said, "have been drove into it step by step with a reluctance on their part that has been manifested in all their proceedings."[26] He also believed that American independence might serve his interests. If Willing and Morris were typical of the powerful Philadelphia merchants, and of merchants throughout America's cities, they were a weak reed for Dickinson to depend on in his continued fight against American independence.

"Where the plague are these [peace] Commissioners," Morris exclaimed as spring dawned in Philadelphia. Nearly one hundred days had passed since the colonists learned of the king's address, with its vague reference to commissioners, and not a single envoy had been seen. Morris, who had been willing to make peace on the terms worked out with Lord Drummond, prayed for the arrival of a commission empowered to offer "terms fit for Freeman." If and when the commissioners arrived, he added, they must be willing to negotiate with Congress. Should that not be the case, he said, "they may as well stay where they are."[27]

When Morris offered his thoughts in April, the peace commissioners alluded to by the king in October had not been formally appointed. The long delay in dispatching the commissioners was not due to the novelty of the idea. The notion of sending an envoy to America to negotiate a settlement went back at least to early 1774, when Dartmouth, in the course of the debate over how to respond to the Boston Tea Party, had proposed that the ministry send an emissary to the colonies. A year later, during the cabinet's final peacetime discussions on using force, Dartmouth had again pressed for sending a representative across the sea armed with authority to conduct talks with the colonists. A mission of the sort had been politically untenable for North prior to the outbreak of hostilities, and the prime minister—and, above all, the monarch—also thought it ill-conceived. North had remained convinced that when confronted with the prospect of British force, the colonists would come to their senses, throw out the firebrands and demagogues who had come into power since the Stamp Act crisis, and accept London's terms leading to reconciliation.

But as news of the bloody disasters suffered by the British army along Battle Road and on Bunker Hill poured into London in the summer of 1775, North quietly grew to think that a negotiated settlement offered Great Britain the best possible way out of its American dilemma. While North was unbending on the issue of parliamentary sovereignty, he privately considered almost everything else to be fair game for negotiations, though he was too adept politically to say so openly.

North's first challenge was to secure authorization for a peace commissioner. As was customary, the prime minister had a hand in writing the king's address that opened Parliament in October 1775, and it was North who inserted in the rough draft the puzzling sentence about "persons . . . so commissioned" to restore the rebellious colonies to the empire. For North, the passage meant that a commissioner would be sent to America to negotiate with the rebels. It is not clear what George III believed he was consenting to, but once the king agreed to the insertion of the passage, North set about naming a commissioner. Dartmouth, in one of his final acts as American secretary, offered Lord Howe the post of peace commissioner. He did so, of course, with North's approval.[28]

The prime minister knew that many within his ministry, as well as in Parliament, looked unkindly on any negotiations with the American rebels, at least until the provincials announced their compliance with the Declaratory Act and the North Peace Plan unveiled in February 1775. North additionally believed that the commissioner would need as much leverage as possible to bring the colonists to acquiesce in parliamentary sovereignty. Since July, North had dramatically augmented the power of Britain's armed forces in America and secured passage of the American Prohibitory Bill, the measure that was to shut down all colonial commerce. He saw both steps as necessary precursors for securing Parliament's approval of a peace commission and for making the Americans accede to Parliament's sovereignty. North got what he wanted. Just before Christmas Parliament consented to sending a peace commissioner who was to "confer with proper persons" and accept the Americans' recognition of parliamentary authority. North believed that the American capitulation—for that is what acquiescence to parliamentary authority amounted to—would be followed by the removal of all restrictions on colonial commerce, the repeal of the Tea Act and Coercive Acts, and by real and fruitful negotiations aimed at resolving other provincial grievances.

With a bit of luck, Lord Howe, the peace commissioner, might have alighted in America before the end of January 1776, announcing his readiness to parley and capitalizing on the spadework done by Drummond. But nothing was ever simple in British politics. Five months elapsed before Howe sailed for America.

Howe not only was an admiral; he also had sat in Parliament for nearly fifteen years. Never firmly aligned with any faction, he usually voted with those in orbit around Earl Chatham. He favored a conciliatory policy toward America, though he never advocated the surrender of parliamentary sovereignty. Like Burke, Fox, and Dartmouth, among others, Howe wished to avoid compelling the colonists to profess their utter capitulation to Parliament. To do so, he feared, would only drive the Americans to armed rebellion. Howe never doubted that the Americans could be crushed by force. But he knew that war would engender an American bitterness toward the mother country that would not vanish until generations had passed. However, Howe was a warrior and did not shrink from his responsibilities. When hostilities commenced, he accepted appointment as the commander of Great Britain's North American squadron. Crushing the rebellion on land, if it came to that, would be the responsibility of his brother, General William Howe. A month after he was commissioned to command the navy in American waters, and thirty days before Parliament agreed to a peace commission, Admiral Howe was asked by Dartmouth to go to America as the government's envoy to negotiate peace. Howe readily accepted. He appears to have believed that North favored negotiations and that he would have the latitude to conduct peace talks more or less on the terms demanded by the First Congress.[29]

Howe had wished to sail for America before the end of 1775, but wrangles within the ministry over his selection, and friction over his instructions, led to interminable delays. Sandwich, the head of the Admiralty, did not relish having his naval commander serve as a peace commissioner. This view was shared by Germain, who entered the cabinet a few days after Howe's appointment. Germain feared that Howe was too soft on American issues to handle the responsibility. Howe responded to their caviling by threatening to resign as naval commander, a step that North desperately wished to prevent, fearing a political firestorm. The squabble dragged on from November until February 1776. It was resolved when the king intervened. Howe agreed to stay on after he was promoted to the rank of vice admiral. Sandwich and Germain were mollified by the appointment of General Howe to serve with his brother as a peace commissioner.

Skirmishing over the instructions for the Howe brothers was no less time-consuming. North left to Germain the responsibility for drafting the commissioner's instructions. Since before taking office, Germain had been adamant that there was to be no negotiation with the American rebels. In his maiden speech as American secretary, he had told the House of Commons that the colonists must lay down their arms and accept parliamentary sovereignty. Their refusal to do was to be met by British force until all "rebellious resistance" was suppressed.[30] If anything, Germain's position grew more rigid once he was in power. Never wavering, he asserted in one cabinet meeting after another that the Howe brothers must not be authorized to conduct negotiations until the Americans agreed to the authority of Parliament "in all cases whatsoever." It struck William Knox, who as an undersecretary in the American Department had worked with Germain on a daily basis, that the new American secretary—a man who had once suffered the grossest humiliation for his purported failure as a soldier—was eager to resolve the Anglo-American quandary by military means. Germain, Knox implied, "having now collected a vast Force and having a fair prospect of subduing the colonies," could not resist the allure of smashing the insurgents with armed force.[31]

Howe, in contrast, wished to have the latitude to conduct serious negotiations when he thought it opportune to do so. Some opposition MPs saw the prudence of Howe's position. Offering the Americans both the carrot and the stick held the greatest hope of peace. Furthermore, Howe and his brother would be in America—"upon the spot," as the king himself had said—where they could see clearly, and immediately, whether negotiations might be productive. It seemed to some to be injudicious, if not reckless, to refuse to negotiate. Thomas Walpole, for instance, chastised Germain for failing to "know of human nature." It was unthinkable, Walpole said, that colonists who were willing to die "in the defense of their supposed rights" would abjectly surrender with no "adequate or just provision . . . for obtaining" those rights having been agreed to by British representatives through formal negotiations.[32] Others in Parliament made one last stab at forcing the government to negotiate. Grafton introduced a resolution in the House of Lords calling on the king to issue a proclamation announcing an armistice to be followed by genuine negotiations with the colonists. This would forestall what he called Germain's "new doctrine of unconditional submission," a quite different policy, he believed, than Parliament had consented to when it approved the North Peace Plan a year earlier. Camden supported the motion, saying that negotiations alone could "lay the foundation for a treaty, which can be the only safe road to conciliation." Grafton's motion was voted down by a three-to-one margin.[33]

In the House of Commons, Fox tried to avert further hostilities by calling for an inquiry into "the disgraces the British arms [army] had suffered." In a lengthy speech he left no doubt that he believed the two costly defeats in

Massachusetts had arisen from "folly in the cabinet." Some, like Isaac Barré, endorsed the proposal and charged North's government "with the loss of America." Barré directly confronted Germain: "Give us back our colonies! You have lost America! It is your ignorance, blunders, cowardice, which have lost America." Some, he said, were calling Germain "the [William] Pitt of the day," which Barré thought was balderdash. "Pitt [was] a great man," Barré said, but Germain was taking Great Britain down the road to ruination. "America would never submit to be taxed," he declared. Germain and his fellow "architects" were leading Great Britain deeper into a needless and tragic war that would result in the nation being "buried in its ruins." Fox's call for an investigation was defeated by a two-to-one vote.[34]

While the battle raged in the cabinet and Parliament, North and Dartmouth threatened to resign, hoping their ploy would prompt ministers and MPs alike to grant the Howe brothers the freedom to conduct negotiations. As had been the case when Howe threatened to resign, this tempest was resolved by the intervention of the king. After persuading North to stay on, the monarch directed his prime minister to obtain, and follow, the advice of William Murray, Lord Mansfield, the lord chief justice. Mansfield agreed with Germain, who clearly had a majority of Parliament on his side. It was not what North had hoped for, but he and Dartmouth complied. Howe did not. He threatened for a second time to resign. Adding that his brother would probably refuse to serve as well, Lord Howe said that he was "disqualified" from serving in a capacity in which he was to offer the Americans the choice of surrender or the continuation of British military operations. Lord Howe proposed instead that he and his brother be authorized to declare an armistice should the Americans consent "to offer a contribution in lieu of taxation, lay down their arms, [and] restore the civil government" that had existed in each colony before the imperial troubles began. Howe envisaged this as only a first step. He also asked for the authority to open talks on the colonists' additional grievances once the armistice took effect.

Germain vociferously objected. He demanded that the Americans formally assent to Parliament's sovereignty before any further steps be taken. Once again, Lord Mansfield was called on to resolve the dispute. After a joint visit by North and Germain, the lord chief justice proposed the slightest compromise: The commissioners were not to demand the colonists' acquiescence in the Declaratory Act but were to wait to see what concessions the Americans offered. Only if the colonists voluntarily accepted the unlimited authority of Parliament, said Mansfield, should the envoys proceed. Having won again, Germain promptly consented. Howe, probably hoping to save face, did not accept Mansfield's terms, and during a span of six weeks he and Germain haggled, mostly over negligible points. Ultimately, Howe accepted instructions that in substance hardly differed from those that Germain had first drafted four months earlier.[35] At last, on May 3—some 125 days after Wilson and Dickinson sought to lay the foundation for talks with the commissioners— the king formally named the Howe brothers as his peace commissioners and vested them with their instructions. The commissioners were forbidden to negotiate with Congress or any colony still under a rebel government. Once the legitimate colonial assemblies agreed to adhere to the laws of Parliament and consented to make restitution to the Loyalists for the property losses they had suffered, and after all American armed forces had laid down their arms and all fortifications had been dismantled or surrendered, the Howe brothers were authorized to issue pardons, suspend the Coercive Acts and the American Prohibitory Act, and listen to the colonists' additional grievances.[36]

Lord Howe and his brother were so-called peace commissioners, raising in the public mind in England, and among some wishful-thinking reconciliationists in Congress, the presumption that they were being sent to America to engage in sincere diplomacy to resolve the colonists' grievances. North would have liked for them to do that, but the vast majority in his cabinet and in Parliament never had the slightest intention of sending envoys for such purposes. From start to finish, the whole point of dispatching the commissioners was to secure the colonists' servility to the imperial government, an outcome that nearly all in the British government believed could be achieved through economic coercion and the triumph of British arms on American battlefields.

No one in the mother country understood better than Edmund Burke what was occurring, and why, and what almost certainly would be its outcome. He appeared to think that the Tory mentality—that is, the cast of mind of the most politically conservative of his countrymen—habitually fixated on resolving matters through the use of force. People of such persuasion "always flourish in the decay, and perhaps by the decay of the Glory of their Country," he lamented. As Howe sailed away on his mission of futility, Burke added, "we are a people who have just lost an Empire."[37]

As early as mid-March the members of Congress knew from London press reports that one or more peace commissioners were to be sent. Only the most gullible, or desperate, believed this step would satisfactorily resolve Anglo-American differences. Grasping at straws, North Carolina's William Hooper chose to think that the commissioners would be empowered to present Congress with "proffers [that] will be liberal." Drawing on the most optimistic puffery in English newspapers, he took as gospel that the "haughty monarch" had accorded his envoys the authority to negotiate "without limi-

tations," and even "to part with us" rather "than hold us upon . . . an igno-
minious condition."[38]

Few in Congress were so sanguine. As the months piled up following the
king's mention of peace commissioners, some delegates even suspected the
monarch's emissaries would never come. Oliver Wolcott of Connecticut
called them the "Phanptom . . . Commissioners." If they did materialize, he
added, it was an "idle Whim" to imagine that they would do more than offer
pardons.[39] John Adams thought only the deluded could expect substantive
negotiations, and he predicted that a commissioner empowered to truly con-
ciliate was "a Messiah that will never come."[40] Samuel Adams was certain
that George III would concede nothing to his American subjects. He is "more
unrelenting and malignant than was [the] Pharaoh towards the Israelites in
Egypt." But something good might come of it, Adams believed. Once and for
all, "the doubting and . . . timid" colonists would see that London had nothing to offer America but the sword, and when at last they understood that
truth, all their hopes "of reconciliation must vanish."[41]

CHAPTER 10

"The Fatal Stab"

Abigail Adams and the Realities of the Struggle for Independence

For fear of shattering wartime unity, the word "independence" had seldom been uttered in Congress in 1775. Times had changed by the spring of 1776. The delegates were daily "disputing . . . about independency," one congressman remarked. Some deputies were certain that the severance of all ties with Great Britain was not far away. Elbridge Gerry had been in Philadelphia barely a month before he pronounced that the day when America will "give Law to herself . . . will soon take place." John Adams and others believed that wartime exigencies dictated that independence must be declared before long. As colonists, "We have hitherto conducted half a War," Adams said, but independence would enable Americans to trade with foreign nations, and that was essential for waging war more forcefully. Others thought the combination of British policies and hostilities had rapidly eroded the mood for reconciliation. The war, according to Richard Henry Lee, had made Americans aware of the "British crimes" of killing its colonists and seeking the "barbarous spoliation" of its colonies. Lee added that all but Tories and the most intransigent reconciliationists realized that one might as well "expect to wash an Ethiopian white, as to remove the taint of despotism from the British court."[1]

When John Adams returned to Philadelphia on February 8 from his winter furlough at home, he arrived with a list of measures that he planned to advocate at the appropriate times. They included issuance of an American currency; a ban on the exportation of gold and silver; a national tax to finance the war; congressional subsidies for flax, hemp, cotton, and wool; commercial treaties with France, Spain, Holland, and Denmark; a *Declaration of Independency*"; a constitution for the new American nation; and alliances with France and Spain.[2]

As the winter of 1776 faded, Congress appeared to be swept by the sense that it was treading water, awaiting events that would push it to do what by then almost certainly a majority of delegates were ready to do: set America free of Great Britain. Those who favored independence did not have long to wait. In a span of roughly seventy-five days beginning in late February, a series of occurrences and circumstances pushed Congress to the brink of declaring independence.

The first pivotal moment came on the next-to-last day of February. Freshly arrived newspapers from London brought word of the American Prohibitory Act. Listening as some of the newspaper accounts were read on the floor of Congress, the delegates learned that since New Year's Day American ships sailing off the coasts of England, Scotland, and Ireland had been subject to capture. As of March 1, less than forty-eight hours away, all colonial vessels bound for or departing from American ports were "to be seized & confiscated" by the Royal Navy.[3] New England had been under a blockade since the outset of the war, but henceforth the commerce of every colony was to be interdicted. "Firmness in the strongest terms" was London's intractable answer to Congress's petition for conciliation, said one delegate, who also believed that Parliament's latest step "shew[s] that the Colonies are of but very little consequence to Britain."[4]

It may seem odd that word of London's having resorted to all-out war—economic as well as military—could so inflame the colonists. After all, a state of hostilities had existed for ten months, and the colonists had long since boycotted all trade with the mother country. Yet the news of the American Prohibitory Act was a savage blow to most Americans. In some measure this was because of their long and ardent affection for Great Britain. Throughout the eighteenth century the belief had been deep-seated in America that the mother country was the most benevolent, nurturing, and enlightened of all nations. But now, atop the realization that London was sending a huge army and a large fleet to crush the rebellion, the colonists had received the disquieting tidings that the British government was prepared to deprive colonial civilians of essential goods. For some, this confirmed the newfound wisdom that the English in reality "know so little of our feelings or character." For others, it heightened the malevolent image of the parent state that had taken root during the past two years. Wishing to leave nothing to chance, Congress had its president, John Hancock, notify the colonies of the "Strain of Rapine and Violence" that drove the British government.[5]

The timing of the American Prohibitory Act was important as well. For one thing, news of the legislation arrived at the same moment that word spread through the colonies of recently intercepted letters from Germain to Governor Eden of Maryland. The letters revealed not only that Maryland's chief executive had been transmitting sensitive military information to London but also that the ministry envisaged an invasion that year of the Carolinas and possibly Virginia. The purloined letters were sent to General Charles Lee, commander of the Continental army in the Southern Department, who passed them on to Richard Henry Lee in Congress. Like their northern brethren, southern colonists now knew that their trade was to be blocked and that their provinces faced an imminent assault by British military forces.[6] News of the blockage of trade also hit many colonists with singular intensity because they had expected the arrival of peace commissioners, not an escalation of punitive measures. Conjoined with what one congressman called Lord North's "declaration of war" came word—happily divulged by Franklin, who had gotten the information from friends in London—that Parliament had adjourned at Christmas 1775 without having confirmed any peace commissioners. Moreover, Parliament had no plans to reconvene until late January. London seemed to be in no hurry to parley with the colonists.[7]

Every member of Congress understood that Britain's all-encompassing war on the colonists' trade meant that America must establish commercial ties outside the British Empire. To protect its economy, America would have to act as if it was independent, whether or not it had formally proclaimed itself a sovereign nation. Once again, the harsh realities of war were moving Congress a step closer to actually declaring independence. "It cannot surely after all this be imagind that we consider ourselves or mean to be considered by others in any State but that of Independence," said Samuel Adams. Other delegates saw things in a similar light. The American Prohibitory Act "will cause a final separation," New Hampshire's William Whipple predicted. Joseph Hewes, a delegate from North Carolina who had yearned to be reunited with the mother country, saw that there no longer was any "prospect of a reconciliation." Despairing, Hewes said that "nothing is left now but to fight it out." Some delegates, he reported home, already "urge strongly for Independency and eternal separation." Others, he said, wished "to wait a little longer" until the voice of the people was heard or conversations with the peace commissioners took place, though not a few were so outraged that they hoped Congress would refuse to receive the peace commissioners if and when they arrived.[8]

No one was happier than John Adams to learn of the American Prohibitory Act. He thought the legislation might more aptly be titled the "Act of Independency." The "King, Lords and Commons have united in Sundering this Country, and I think forever. It is a compleat Dismemberment of the

British Empire," he rejoiced. He lamented that Congress was hamstrung awaiting the peace commissioners. "The Tories, and Timids . . . expect great Things from them," though the majority anticipated only "Insults and Affronts." But for the sake of unity the majority had to wait for the minority's inescapable disillusionment. Even so, Adams was not despondent. Less than three weeks after learning that Britain hoped to strangle the colonists' trade, Congress threw open every American port to trade from all nations. Parliament's age-old restrictions on American trade—to which the First Congress had been willing to adhere—had been repudiated. This prompted Adams to ask: If "This is not Independency . . . What is?"[9]

The wrathful atmosphere created by word of the American Prohibitory Act also enabled John Adams and his faction to enact a measure they had unsuccessfully sought for months. Within days of learning of Parliament's sanction of a total American blockade, Congress legalized privateering, acting on a motion by Samuel Chase, who only a couple of months earlier had opposed the creation of a navy. Privateering was common in the warfare of the day and had long been an American practice during Great Britain's wars with France and Spain. Entrepreneurs invested in armed vessels and seamen signed on, all hoping to strike it rich. The prizes that were taken—that is, the enemy ships that were captured intact—were brought to port and the vessel and cargo were sold. The booty was then divided between the financiers and the armed ship's officers and crew. Since America lacked a navy, merchants and rebel leaders in New England had sought to have Congress make privateering lawful almost the minute that the war began. Their hope, of course, was that hundreds, perhaps thousands, of American privateers would sail, intercepting shipments from Great Britain to its army. But many in congress were opposed, largely from fear that North's government would retaliate by attempting to halt the commerce of all the colonies. Now that North's government had done just that, congressional inhibitions instantly collapsed.[10]

The American Prohibitory Act, especially as it followed hard on the heels of the debacle in Canada, drove Congress to take another step. Three days after learning of Parliament's legislation, Congress agreed to send Silas Deane to Paris to explore the depth of France's friendship for the American cause. Deane, a lawyer-merchant who had served in the Connecticut delegation from the beginning until January 1776, was chosen because he knew the mind of Congress and, as a former colleague observed, he had been "really Very Usefull here & much esteemed in Congress."[11] This first-ever American envoy was to meet with private citizens whose names were supplied by Benjamin Franklin. Congress hoped that through these intermediaries Deane would be given access to Foreign Minister Vergennes. In his talks with the French, Deane was to attempt to establish commercial ties, but his first priority was to secure clothing and "Quantities of Arms & Ammunition," including one hundred pieces of field artillery, for an army of twenty-five thousand men. Revealingly too Deane's instructions—written by Franklin and four reconciliationist congressmen, including Dickinson and Morris—also stipulated that he was to determine "whether, if the Colonies should form themselves into an Independent State, France would . . . acknowledge them as such" and enter into an alliance "for Commerce, or defence, or both."[12]

After word of the disaster in Canada, Congress yearned for good news from the military front. It got it before winter ended. When General Washington took command of the Continental army, he inherited the siege of Boston, which had begun on the day after Lexington and Concord. It had been successfully conducted for some seventy-five days before Washington arrived, and he maintained it for the next eight months. The operation succeeded in part because, save for the brief recruiting crisis late in 1775, the Americans were always numerically superior. The Continentals usually outnumbered General Howe's redcoats by nearly two to one, and if Yankee militiamen were to be summoned in an emergency, the British army would be confronted by an adversary that was several times its size. Even so, the British had total naval superiority, and Howe might have attempted to break the siege had he thought it worth the trouble. But he saw no sense in running the risk. From the moment he assumed command, Howe planned to withdraw from Boston and launch a campaign to take New York and the Hudson River. Unbeknownst to Washington, Howe remained in Boston through the fall and winter only because the troop transports that would take his army from the besieged city had not arrived.[13]

All the while, Washington was eager for action. Vigorous and enterprising, the American commander was temperamentally ill-suited to passive behavior. Besides, he knew that some in Congress and many in New England wanted him to do something, and he also may have chafed under the realization that Artemas Ward—whom he had supplanted—had scored what was seen by all as a daring and magnificent victory at Bunker Hill. Washington also wished to act before British reinforcements arrived. In a September council of war he had raised the possibility of attacking Boston, but his officers nearly unanimously rejected such a course. They thought it too likely to result in an American defeat as great as the one the enemy had suffered at Bunker Hill.[14]

Washington was frustrated—he privately complained of the "backwardness" of his officers—but he did not abandon his thoughts of an attack. When the first of autumn's inclement weather arrived in November, making a British attack highly unlikely, Washington sent Henry Knox, the twenty-five-year-old commander of the Continental army's artillery regiment, to Fort Ticonderoga to fetch the British ordnance that Benedict Arnold and Ethan Allen had captured in May. Knox performed brilliantly. Early in February 1776 he and his party reached Boston after an epic trek through the steep, ice-cloaked Berkshire Mountains. Knox presented to Washington thirty-nine field pieces—about four times the number previously available to the siege army—as well as two howitzers and fourteen mortars.[15]

Washington wasted no time summoning his generals to another council of war. He presented them with three options: send the army across the frozen Charles River to attack Boston; attack the British on Bunker Hill and reclaim that site overlooking Boston Harbor; or occupy Dorchester Heights, which overlooked the harbor from south of the city. Taking either Bunker Hill or Dorchester Heights, said Washington, would compel Howe either to attack or to abandon Boston, for with adequate artillery the Continentals would be in a position to close Boston Harbor, the British army's lifeline to the home islands. Washington implied that he leaned toward an assault on the besieged British army in Boston. A "Stroke well aim'd . . . might put a final end to the War," he said. His officers wanted no part of the first two options, thinking that offensive operations were too risky for an untrained army. However, they approved of taking Dorchester Heights by stealth and inviting Howe to attack the entrenched Continentals.[16]

Washington worked out the final plan for the operation in frequent meetings with his officers. It called for a steady bombardment of Boston during the nights of March 2 through March 4. On the last evening, while the redcoats were distracted by still another thunderous artillery barrage, two thousand Continentals were to steal up Dorchester Heights and under cover of darkness prepare the army's defensive installations. Just before dawn, they were to be replaced by three thousand fresh troops under General Ward. These men were to await Howe's expected assault.[17]

The operation could hardly have gone more smoothly. A low-lying fog blanketed Boston on the evening of March 4, hiding the heights in Dorchester from the British army. But the crest of the ridgeline in Dorchester was above the fog, and the Yankee soldiers worked under a brilliant moon and starry sky. The men were mostly heavily muscled farmers accustomed to physical labor. They did their work briskly, despite having to excavate earth that was frozen to a depth of eighteen inches. Dragging the artillery to the peak of the heights was the most difficult task. Most of the night was needed to complete that mission, and long before the job was done, great, muddy ruts defaced what only hours earlier had been the grassy, sloping hillside. Well before dawn, Dorchester Heights bristled with a breastwork constructed of felled trees, fascines (bundles of long stakes), chandeliers (wooden shells tightly packed with dirt-stuffed baskets called "gabions"), and thick, wide bales of nearly impenetrable hay.

As the dense fog burned off under the day's sun, the British discovered that an American force was entrenched on Dorchester Heights with its artillery trained on Boston Harbor. What most amazed the British was how quickly the Americans had carried out the undertaking. Howe allegedly exclaimed, "[T]hese fellows have done more work in one night than I could make my Army do in three months." Later, he supposedly said that Washington must have employed ten thousand workers. The chief engineer in the British army estimated that twenty thousand Continentals had been put to work.[18]

Howe, who had been leisurely biding his time until he could leave Boston, suddenly faced a difficult decision. Some troop transports had arrived, and he knew that others would soon reach Boston, affording him the option of abandoning Boston within a few days if he chose to do so and his adversary would permit him to leave. Howe knew full well that there were compelling reasons for departing without a fight. Considering the Continentals' new-found firepower, to storm Dorchester Heights would almost certainly bring on a battle more bloody than Bunker Hill. In addition, as one of his officers had long before remarked, the British army was "so small that we cannot afford a victory, if attended with any loss of men."[19] Howe may also have thought that it made no sense to ask men to die for the sake of holding a city that was slated to be relinquished. Besides, it would be best to preserve his soldiers for the looming battle in New York, a contest that would probably determine the fate of the American rebellion.

On the other hand, to quit Boston without a fight would be seen by many as a sign of weakness. Some of Howe's officers urged him to fight. The red-coats should kill every rebel they could find, after which they must put Boston to the torch and leave behind the smoldering ashes, advised General James Grant. If the army sowed terror, Grant reasoned, "the American Bubble must soon burst."[20] He may have been on to something. The razing of Boston would have had a profound impact on opinion in Philadelphia, New York, Charleston, and other colonial cities, and it might have halted Congress's steady progress toward declaring independence. But Howe spurned such a ghastly course. He and his brother were peace commissioners, and he continued to believe that they might succeed in negotiating a happy reconciliation between the mother country and its colonies. Howe feared that should his army engage in a deliberate policy of annihilation, the colonists would be lost forever.

On March 7, forty-eight hours after he had learned that the rebels had occupied Dorchester Heights, Howe offered Washington a deal. If the rebels
permitted the redcoats to board their troop transports unmolested, the British army would depart, leaving Boston intact. Now it was Washington who
faced a painful decision. He could attempt to capture or destroy Howe's army,
virtually the entire British army then in America. If Washington succeeded,
not only would London's plans for the campaign of 1776 be dealt a severe
blow, but also yet another staggering military loss might bring down North's
ministry and shatter Britain's implacable hostility toward reconciliation on
America's terms. On the other hand, if Washington failed, the utter destruction of Boston would follow, and that might stanch the momentum for declaring independence. It might even destroy the will to continue the war in
some colonies.

Washington appears to have longed for American independence since
1774, if not much earlier, and he knew that public opinion and perhaps a majority of congressmen were inching toward a final break with Great Britain.
Better than any American, Washington also knew that declaring independence was crucial for waging a long war. He accepted Howe's offer. On March
17 the British army sailed away for Nova Scotia, to await reinforcements for
the invasion of New York. As the last British soldier left, an American regiment, with Generals Ward and Putnam riding before it, marched in to reclaim possession of Boston.[21]

Ecstasy swept Congress. For some, this was fresh proof that the British
army was hardly "invincible." For others, it seemed likely that Britain's latest
"Disgrace" would encourage France and Spain to offer the colonists trade and
military assistance, if only America declared independence. America's victory was widely celebrated, and in Boston people poured into the streets. It
was said that the British army had "disgracefully quitted" the city and "took
refuge on board their ships." One newspaper declared that it hoped the Bostonians never again had to breathe "air . . . contaminated by the stinking
breath of toryism." Harvard College awarded Washington an honorary degree, and Congress ordered a gold medallion struck for its triumphant commander. Lady Liberty and an image of the departing British fleet—"all their
Sterns toward the Town"—adorned the medal.[22]

When asked in the spring by a constituent whether a declaration of independence was imminent, a Virginian responded that "it is probable" Congress
"will wait till the people brings it before them."[23] By April the delegates knew
that a sea change in popular opinion was occurring.

In the first months of war a colonist who had dared to publicly urge independence could have found himself in a world of trouble with American authorities. In the autumn of 1775, for instance, Thomas Anderson of Hanover County, Virginia, was forced by the local committee of safety to publicly recant his statement "declaring that this Country was in a state of rebellion, and aimed at a state of independence, more than opposition to parliamentary taxation." Nearly simultaneously the Chester County, Pennsylvania, Committee of Safety—chaired by Anthony Wayne, who shortly was to become a general officer in the Continental army—was appalled when the local militia battalion trumpeted that its men had taken up arms "to overturn the Constitution, by declaring an independency." The committee condemned "an idea so pernicious in its nature" and compelled the officers to recant and publicly swear that they and their men soldiered to secure "a happy and speedy reconciliation" with Great Britain.[24]

Wars often reshape thinking, and this one was part of a rebellion that had been refashioning thought since 1765. By early 1776 the Anglo-American conflict, little more than nine months old, was causing the colonists to see both their mother country and themselves in a different light. Dunmore's proclamation, the razing of Falmouth, and battlefields steeped in blood had hardened feelings toward the mother country. Even the most conservative congressmen found their loyalty to Great Britain shaken to the core by knowledge that "the sword of ministerial vengeance . . . has been drawn," causing "innocent blood [to have] been shed," as New York's James Duane exclaimed.[25] Whatever love had once existed for the parent state vanished entirely when a son, father, or brother died fighting against British soldiers. A New Hampshire farmer who lost a son in the Canadian campaign wrote in his diary that his child had died "defending the just Rights of America" against the "wicked Tyranical Brute (nea worse than Brute) of Great Britain."[26] Some towns experienced a staggering death toll during 1775. On the first day of the war, four men from Lynn, five from Needham, six from Cambridge, seven from Danvers, ten from Lexington, and a dozen from Menotomy (now Arlington) had perished.[27] That was only the beginning. Others from those villages, and dozens of additional towns, fell in action or from camp diseases in the ensuing months. Enmity toward Great Britain rose in step with the increasing casualty rate, until by the spring of 1776 Franklin spoke of "a rooted Hatred" for England throughout America.[28]

Concurrently, the idea gathered force that the inhabitants of America were Americans, not British. Many colonists were third- or fourth-generation Americans. In addition, Americanism was nourished by the training received by thousands of soldiers who had to be readied for fighting British regulars. General Washington, for instance, frequently sent messages to his troops telling them that this was not a war to resolve the problems of Massachusetts or New England. All Americans, he said, were confronted by "a diabolical Ministry" bent on "Inslav[ing] this great Continent." The "great Cause we are engaged in" is one of protecting "Life, Liberty, & Property" from the ravages of "a brutal, savage enemy," a foe that threatened "every thing we hold dear," that had laid "our towns . . . in ashes" and driven "innocent Women & Children . . . from their peaceful habitations."[29]

In the three years since the tea ships had set sail for colonial ports during the warm summer of 1773, America had become a far different place. The offices of the king's chief executives, solicitors, and customs officials had been shuttered and the officials who had once occupied them were only a dim memory from a rapidly receding past. In nearly every colony, sovereign authority was wielded by a revolutionary assembly, often called the "provincial congress" or "provincial convention." Many who sat in these bodies were new to such lofty power, having been thrust by the rebellion, and especially the war, into their elevated position. A notch lower, in the counties and towns, committees of safety—sometimes called the committee of inspection or observation—enforced the boycott of trade with the mother country instituted by the First Congress, managed the war effort, and maintained security on the home front. Many, perhaps most, who sat on these committees had never before occupied a civil office. Nor would they have much hope of ever wielding power again if royal authority was reestablished.[30]

While the overwhelming majority of colonists supported the war, those whose behavior violated the laws of Congress or was judged harmful to the conduct of the war faced the possibility of harsh treatment from the committees of safety. Men who refused to sign an oath to abide by the Continental Association, and especially those caught violating the non-importation, non-exportation, and non-consumption laws, might be placed under surveillance or have their names published as "enemies of the country," a clarion call for patriots to cruelly ostracize them.[31] Incidents of open infidelity were relatively uncommon, although in January 1776 some four hundred inhabitants of Queens County, New York, were made to publicly apologize for having failed to establish a committee to enforce the Association.[32] Those caught selling goods to the British army suffered harsher punishments. Some were briefly jailed, after which they were compelled to pay the costs incurred in their confinement.[33] One Edward Parry was exiled from his coastal Massachusetts village and ordered to "be immediately sent to some inland Town, which shall be more than seventy miles distant from the seaports in this Colony."[34] Maryland's rebel assembly removed from local office a violator of the Association.[35] When the local committees could not get their hands on

Tory authors of newspaper essays or pamphlets, they did the next best thing: They publicly burned the offending tract. Freehold, New Jersey's committee even condemned one pamphlet to "a suit of tar and turkey-buzzard's feathers."[36]

Many men also got into trouble because of things they said. Citizens were jailed or fined for disloyal pronouncements. Some were made to recant utterances such as "the English would be an overmatch for the *Americans*" or "damn . . . the honourable Continental Congress." Men were punished for having publicly defended "British taxation," "scandalously aspersed the characters" of American leaders, engaged as "a retailer of falsehoods," denounced the "rascally Rebels," spoke "injuriously of the distressed people of . . . Boston," and maintained they would rather "be under a tyrannical King as a tyrannical Commonwealth." Action was taken against those who through their "wicked and mischievous striving [had attempted] to bring destruction and ruin on . . . [this] bleeding country."[37] Those who recanted often had to pledge to henceforth "conduct myself as a true friend to *America*," acknowledge "being too backward . . . with regard to the liberties of my country," vow to hereafter "sacrifice my interest and venture my life in the defence of my Country," or "beg forgiveness of God, and all friends to *American* liberty."[38] During the first months of 1776 there were fewer and fewer openly unpatriotic acts that cried out for punishment. What is more, punitive actions against those who openly called for American independence appear to have ceased altogether.

The lucid wording of the statements published by the committees of safety early in 1776 made clear that a new frame of mind was taking shape in America. Increasing numbers of colonists saw themselves as Americans, saw America as their country, and believed that America should be governed solely by Americans. In astonishingly short order, the belief had taken hold that Great Britain was a foreign land that groaned under a "wicked system" that drove those who held office to seek "the destruction of *American* liberty."[39] On America's farms and at its workbenches, in villages along the coastal plain and throughout the rolling, wooded backcountry, people were discovering that their interests all too often differed from the interests of those who governed the British Empire. Moreover, they were coming to find that they could get along fine, perhaps better, when they were removed from British jurisdiction. Age-old loyalties to the mother country were vanishing—in many places had already disappeared—like snow under a warm sun. With the new way of thinking came a growing tolerance, even fervor, for the idea of American independence. The gathering transformation in the thinking of Americans appears to have outpaced that of many who sat in Congress.

Public opinion polls were not taken in those days, but it is difficult not to believe that a considerably smaller percentage of reconciliationists lived in America by the spring of 1776 than sat in the Continental Congress.

Nothing in the Americans' worldview changed more drastically, or rapidly, than their opinion of the monarchy. Even into the 1770s, George III's coronation and his birthdays were celebrated throughout America with balls, games, "Gun-firing," and repeated toasts at elaborate dinners. The monarch was lauded in sermons, pamphlets, almanacs, and widely sold biographies. The royal likeness and the king's arms adorned mass-produced china, ceramics, and glassware, and George III's portrait hung in government buildings and many shops. Throughout the eighteenth century, Great Britain's kings had been not just revered but also loved by Americans, who thought of them as benevolent figures who presided over the relationship between the colonies and the mother country. Benjamin Rush, a Philadelphian who later signed the Declaration of Independence, said that, as a youngster, he had believed that kings were "as essential to political order as the Sun is to the order of our Solar System."[40]

This veneration of monarchy eroded badly after the enactment of the Intolerable Acts. In their wake, some southern Anglican clergy who prayed for the king were forced from their pulpits and fled into exile, and here and there throughout the colonies mobs set on those who openly defended the king or accepted a royal appointment. When Timothy Ruggles, who nine years earlier had been the president of the Stamp Act Congress, was named by royal authorities to the Massachusetts council under the provisions of the Intolerable Acts, a mob descended on his Worcester County estate, damaging his home, disfiguring his horse, and killing his livestock.[41] The onset of hostilities and the king's repeated refusal to hear Congress's petitions further dampened emotional support for the monarch, and Thomas Paine's visceral and nearly unanswerable assault on royal rule in *Common Sense* drove a stake through the heart of homage to monarchy. It "put the torch to combustibles," said Edmund Randolph, a Virginia activist, who clearly thought that Paine had voiced sentiments that already existed.[42]

The colonists had long been accustomed to political and social systems modeled on those of England, but there had always been significant differences. North of the Potomac, America was devoid of aristocratic hierarchies, and it was less deferential and more egalitarian. Furthermore, colonists everywhere had for years believed that the real authority in their province was—or at least should be—the assembly, a body chosen in elections in which some two thirds or more of all adult white males were qualified to vote. And from Patrick Henry's Virginia Resolves until the First Continental Congress, it was the assemblies that had largely led the protest against British policies. Invisibly but inexorably, the sense coagulated in the colonies that America's resistance to the ministry's supposed conspiracy against liberty was nothing less than that of a struggle by a republican people through its elected representatives against a corrupt mother country dominated by an ossified aristocracy and mostly dissolute commoners. Republican America, untainted by England's luxury, extravagance, and servility, gradually came to be seen as the embodiment of virtue and purity. Such thinking added a deeply moral dimension to the American protest. For some, that meant that independence was imperative to ensure that America would not be poisoned by Britain's corruption. For others who shared Paine's conviction about starting the world anew—those who, perhaps, were the most idealistic, ideological, ambitious, and opportunistic—it meant that the belief in American independence and a republican revolution were inextricably linked. For these colonists, American independence was merely the beginning of the American Revolution. Independence was to be followed by an expunging of privileges for the few and by the institutionalization of equal opportunities.[43]

Vivid testimony to the alterations in the colonists' outlook welled up across the land in the spring of 1776. With breathtaking suddenness, numerous localities adopted their own declarations in favor of severing ties with Great Britain. Often following a step behind public opinion, the revolutionary governments in several colonies rewrote their instructions to their congressional delegations authorizing them, if they saw fit, to declare American independence.

Stunningly, South Carolina, whose delegates had largely and intransigently remained part of the reconciliation faction in Congress, was the first colony to act. The previous fall Congress had freed New Hampshire and South Carolina to scrap their governments under royal charters and, if necessary, to create new ones. The Yankees acted quickly, but South Carolina's provincial congress did not finally act until mid-February 1776. Its decision to write its own constitution triggered a firestorm. Powerful elements in the colony resisted, claiming with considerable justification that doing so was tantamount to declaring independence. But others, notably Christopher Gadsden, who had sat in Congress since its inception, not only urged a new constitution but also demanded that it specify that South Carolina was free of all British ties. Inspired by *Common Sense*, Gadsden, who had just returned to Charleston from Philadelphia, spoke publicly in favor of "the absolute independence of America." His assertion startled and alarmed many in the same fashion as would an unexpected "explosion of thunder," according to a fellow rebel in South Carolina's capital.[44]

Gadsden's remarkable stance was thought by most to be untimely, not to mention shockingly audacious, and it went unheeded. The foes of a new constitution prevailed until the third week of March, when news of the American Prohibitory Act finally reached Charleston. It hit with the impact of a bombshell. Within two days of learning that London was bent on sweeping South Carolina's trade from the high seas, the provincial congress instructed its congressional delegation to act with the majority to secure the "defence, security, interest, or welfare" of both South Carolina and "America in general." The word "independence" did not appear in the instructions, but a sixth sense was not required to know that the colony's congressmen were being told that, if need be, they should vote to sever all ties with Great Britain. Three days after taking this step, the provincial congress adopted a new constitution. The word "independence" was not in its text either. Like its predecessor in New Hampshire, South Carolina's new fundamental charter was to exist until the Anglo-American differences were resolved, whether by reconciliation or independence.[45]

What did this mean? Was South Carolina still part of the British Empire? On April 23, after living with the ambiguity for a month, William Henry Drayton, the chief justice of the province, handed down a ruling that provided clarification. Calling the upheaval against Great Britain "the late revolution"—as if the American Revolution was already complete—Justice Drayton wrote that South Carolina was "independent of Royal authority." He grounded his judgment on the precedent set by Parliament when it forced James II from the throne during the Glorious Revolution nearly a century earlier. Parliament had acted because the king had broken his contract with his subjects by having failed to protect "their lives, liberties, and properties." George III, Drayton reasoned, had similarly "broke the original contract" between ruler and ruled "by not affording due protection to his [American] subjects."[46] In a stupendous act of judicial activism, Justice Drayton had ruled that South Carolina was independent.

The news that South Carolina had adopted a new constitution led John Adams to exclaim that this was convincing evidence that America was "advancing by slow but sure steps to [a] mighty Revolution." If what South Carolina had done spawned similar acts in the three other southern colonies, he went on, their "Example . . . will Spread through all the rest of the Colonies like Electric Fire."[47]

Unbeknownst to Adams, that fire was already spreading. North Carolina's provincial congress had just instructed its congressional delegation "to concur with the delegates of the other Colonies in declaring Independency, and forming foreign alliances." It was the first time that a provincial body had authorized a break with the mother country by actually using the word "independence."[48] Before the end of April every member of Congress knew what North Carolina had done, and it led Samuel Adams to rejoice that the "Ideas of Independence spread far and wide." It would not be long, he thought, before Congress acted. Members of the Virginia delegation had already told him that the provincial authorities in Williamsburg would shortly dispense with the old instructions that had "tied the Hands of their Delegates" on the matter of declaring independence. Adams was confident that similar moves would be made in the coming weeks in nearly every colony. Only New York and Pennsylvania troubled him, but he did not believe that Congress could do anything, or needed to do anything, to spur them toward independence. It was "Events which excite" people to take bold and surprising steps, he said, and at every twist and turn since the Tea Act, events had "produce[d] wonderful Effects." Samuel Adams was confident that the next pivotal event would be either the return of British armed forces or a great battle. Thereafter, all—or nearly all—of the provinces would be ready for "a Declaration of Independency."[49]

Samuel Adams had expected that Virginia would be the next to act, but Rhode Island moved more quickly. On May 4 its assembly decreed that officials in the province should no longer take an oath of allegiance to the king. Like Justice Drayton, the Yankees reasoned that George III had broken his compact by "departing from the . . . character of a good king." Rather than having defended his subjects, he was "endeavoring to destroy the good people" of Rhode Island. That same day, the assembly instructed its two delegates in Congress to act in concert with the other colonies. It did not mention independence by name, but like South Carolina, Rhode Island was telling its congressmen to vote for the final break with Great Britain if that was what the majority in Congress thought was in the best interests of the American people.[50]

On May 15, eleven days after Rhode Island took that step, the Virginia Convention finally acted. Some had wanted the colony to declare independence, but after wrangling for more than a week, it settled on instructing its delegates in Philadelphia to recommend that Congress declare independence. The instructions previously adopted in South Carolina, North Carolina, and Rhode Island had been passive in that they emphasized concurrence with the majority opinion in Congress. Virginia's congressional delegation in contrast was instructed "to propose" that Congress "declare the United Colonies free and independent States, absolved from all allegiance to, or dependence upon the Crown or Parliament of Great Britain." That same day, moreover, the Virginia Convention resolved to prepare a Declaration of Rights and a constitution for the citizenry of what it expected would soon be the independent state of Virginia.[51]

In the wake of South Carolina's move toward independence, three grand juries in that colony adopted statements in favor of a final break with the mother country. But localities did not always wait on action by the provincial assembly. Four Virginia counties had adopted ringing declarations of independence prior to the action taken by the Convention, and each appropriated ideas laid out by Paine, especially his critiques of monarchical rule.[52] The local committees of safety were swept by the fervor that gripped Americans everywhere in early 1776, but they may additionally have been nudged a bit by Virginia's congressmen, some of whom wrote home during the spring advising that support on the home front was imperative. For instance, Francis Lightfoot Lee—Richard Henry's brother, who had entered Congress the previous autumn—informed a powerful local figure in the Old Dominion that France and Spain had refused to supply badly needed military equipment until the colonies declared independence. America was being driven by "hard necessity . . . to extremity," he expounded. Either it would have to choose "absolute submission [to Great Britain] or foreign assistance." If Congress opted for the latter, it would have to declare independence. Lee asked his correspondent: "Which will be your choice?" In a second letter Lee said that America's alternatives were "slavery or separation." Would it not be prudent, he continued, to prepare Virginians for Congress's "inevitable" decision? Lee wrote a third time, and in that missive he was even more direct. Congress would not declare independence, he explained, until it knew that its constituents wanted America to be set free of Great Britain.[53]

Lee must have been happy with the declaration on independence adopted on April 23 by the sixteen members of the Charlotte County, Virginia, Committee of Safety. It began with the assertion that the government of Great Britain had pursued a "despotick plan . . . these twelve years past, to enslave *America*." The king, Lord North, and Parliament, it continued, "have turned a deaf ear to the repeated petitions and remonstrances of this and our sister Colonies." Instead, those rulers had sought "to enforce their arbitrary mandates by fire and sword," including "encouraging . . . our savage neighbours [Indians], and our more savage domesticks [slaves], to spill the blood of our wives and children." It concluded: As "nothing is intended for us but the most abject slavery" and as "all hopes of a reconciliation . . . [are] now at an end," it wished the Continental Congress to "immediately cast off the *British* yoke, and to enter into a commercial alliance with any nation or nations friendly to our cause."[54]

* * *

Congressmen may have been pleading for direction from home, but through the winter and spring of 1776 they were aware that calls for independence—formerly a taboo topic—filled newspapers across the land. Once *Common Sense* was greeted with unbridled exuberance, pleas for independence were commonplace. Most of the scribblers in the press argued that wartime realities made a declaration of independence essential. Between their bravado-filled lines, many proponents of independence acknowledged that America would need considerable assistance from France and Spain if it was to win a protracted war, and foreign aid would require that Congress sever all ties with Great Britain. Several writers hinted, though few said it explicitly, that it was essential for Congress to declare independence in the near future. Some wanted it done before the peace commissioners arrived, anxious that Lord North's game of divide and conquer might succeed. Others, believing that Versailles was favorably disposed, wanted to act while French help was still possible. Still others, concerned about damage to morale that might accompany military setbacks, urged that independence be declared prior to the onset of the campaign in the summer of 1776. An anonymous New York writer touched all bases in April when he posed the following question to Congress: "Should the American Colonies neglect the present critical moment of asserting and securing their freedom, is it not probable that a few months will put it out of their power of doing it forever?"[55]

Some essayists sought to convince their readers that reconciliation on favorable terms was no longer possible. One, who called himself a "strenuous advocate for independency," maintained that "Blood once shed puts a final period to all other accommodations." Thomas Paine, writing as "The Forester," took a similar position. Reconciliation, he wrote, was a "false light." All hope of being reunited with Great Britain "'Tis gone! 'tis past! The grave hath parted us, and death, in the persons of the slain, hath cut the thread between *Britain* and *America*." American submission was the only condition on which the colonies could be reunited with the mother country, said many writers. One observed that "If we reject . . . Submission and Dependence, we must of consequence be Independent."[56]

Many writers attempted to demonstrate the positive aspects of independence, and especially to equate independence with liberty. "The day in which the Colonies declare their independence, will be a jubilee" to all "heroes who have offered themselves as sacrifices upon the altar of liberty," Paine declared. Another essayist tried to show that "dependency is slavery," whereas independence would enable Americans to secure their "safety, honour, and . . . interest" on their own terms. Some argued, as had Paine in *Common Sense*, that an independent America wresting liberty from the grasp of tyrants would be a beacon to others around the world. "The lovers of liberty abroad have their eyes turned toward us," one New Yorker wrote, while another asserted that like "the waves of the sea," the example of American independence would have a breathtakingly wide impact.[57]

Some saw a glorious future for an independent America. With independence would come "peace, plenty, and liberty," said a Maryland polemicist. In March the author of "Plain Hints" equated colonial America to a tree that was surrounded by impediments and could not grow to its full potential. Free the tree, he said, and it "might soon become the largest tree in the forest." That same month "An American" insisted that an independent America would be on the road to "eminence and glory."[58]

The foes of a break with the mother country busily turned out essays and pamphlets of their own, though they were forced by *Common Sense* to shift gears. Previously, they had mostly proffered solutions to the crisis or urged that the king be petitioned for redress, but on the defensive after Paine's tract, they focused largely on the dangers that would accompany independence. A total break, said some advocates of reconciliation, would cost the colonists its friends in Parliament, powerful figures who could be of help to America. Furthermore, they warned, London would fight tenaciously to prevent independence: A declaration of independence "will unite the whole force of *Great Britain* and *Ireland* against us—a force that has hitherto been much divided, from an opinion that we only seek peace, liberty, and safety, in a constitutional connection with *Great Britain*." Prolonged wars, these writers added, were filled with uncertainties and dangers. Americans might lose their freedom while attempting to gain it. The colonists might fall victim to a standing army or an American tyrant; more likely, they would become the prey of a European ally who turned on them once the war ended. But the most probable outcome was that hostilities would end in a stalemate leading to a negotiated settlement. Stalemated wars in Europe usually ended in the partition of the territories that had been fought over. Should that happen in this Anglo-American war, the anti-independence writers cautioned, Great Britain, France, and Spain would divide the spoils, transferring some star-crossed parts of colonial America to the jurisdiction of foreign and Roman Catholic nations ruled by autocratic monarchs.[59]

"Independence will not produce happiness," said those who were opposed to breaking ties with Great Britain. Above all, it would be a "leap in the dark," a gamble that might very well result in untold miseries. Some woes were predictable, they asserted. Only America's ties to the empire had held together peoples who embraced a rich diversity of religions, languages, ethnicity, and interests. That unity would "burst asunder" with independence, and in its place "the entrails, the heart, the very life of the Colonies" would be rent. When that occurred, America would resemble Europe. A multitude of sovereign governments would dot the North American landscape. Each would be hostile toward the others. War after war, the plague of Europe, would ensue. These writers charged, too, that the proponents of independence were visionaries and "ambitious innovators," but mostly they were "adventurers who have nothing to lose," men who had been "exalted by the present confusions into lucrative offices" and who had a vested interest in keeping alive "the publick calamities" that offered their only hope of retaining power. Such men were committed to republicanism, a word these writers employed with a shudder. It was a mantra of many who opposed independence that the whole history of republicanism was a sorry chronicle of anarchy and chaos, of "domestick violence and rapine, war and bloodshed." Independence, they warned, would usher in republican "instability and unwieldiness," bringing to an end the order and comity that had happily existed in British America.[60]

The advocates of independence fought back. "I see no terror in [independence]," said one, "but in an unconditional dependence . . . I see a thousand."[61] "We must separate, or become the labouring slaves of Britain," said a North Carolinian, who added that independence would set America free from "a cruel, blood-thirsty people, the cause of all our woes."[62] As for America's friends in Parliament, they "may be sincere and zealous in our cause, but they have not been able to do us any good," said one writer. "If they are generous friends, they will . . . still exert themselves in our favour; but if they should forsake us, we shall lose nothing."[63]

After *Common Sense* there was a sameness to the pro-independence essays, a redundant elaboration on the themes of monarchical tyranny, British corruption, and London's habitual warfare. The one exception—and the most important piece pertaining to independence after *Common Sense*—came from the pen of John Adams. What made Adams's effort notable was that he answered those who were predicting mayhem in an independent and republican America. Adams laid out a plan of government that was to be an antidote to disorder.

Adams had been writing about political theory since he was a young lawyer in Boston. As a congressman, he had spoken out on governance when the issue of replacing colonial charters first came up, earning a reputation among his colleagues as the best-informed member of Congress on the subject. In 1776 Adams again spoke out often on governance in America. The impetus for his frequent homilies was not the warnings advanced by reconciliationists and Tories, but the prescription for government outlined by Paine in *Common Sense*. Adams had applauded Paine's cogent arguments on behalf of independence. He had also acknowledged Paine's unmatched talent as a writer, even admitting to his wife that he "could not have written any Thing in so manly and striking a style." However, Adams was appalled by Paine's formula for government. Paine "has a better Hand at pulling down than building," Adams fumed. Paine's views on governance, he went on, were not just "inadequate"; they were "despicable" and "ignorant." If the form of government that Paine had recommended was instituted, Adams added, it "will do more Mischief . . . than all the Tory writings together." Though Adams did not say so, he had to be worried that Paine was reaching a huge audience. In addition to the thousands who read *Common Sense*, countless others listened as Continental army officers or town criers read it to them.[64]

Paine had suggested that each state be governed by a popularly elected unicameral assembly that was more broadly representative of the people than had been the case in the colonies. Each state in turn would popularly elect at least thirty representatives to a unicameral national congress. Its membership would be around four hundred, in contrast to the fifty or so delegates in the Continental Congress. A 60 percent majority would be necessary for enacting legislation. Paine, of course, did not want an American monarch. Instead, he thought an official akin to the British prime minister would suffice, and he proposed that this official be chosen annually by his fellow congressmen.

Several aspects of Paine's formula for government troubled Adams. The size of Paine's national congress would make it unwieldy. Adams was all too aware of how hard it was to get anything done in a body as small as the Continental Congress. Adams additionally abhorred the absence of checks and balances in Paine's plan. Nor would Paine's chief executive be a truly national figure with a capability of overriding the provincial interests of the members of Congress.

Adams spoke out on these matters in Congress, and he may have intended to write an essay addressing his concerns. In any case, before he could act on his own, he was asked by William Hooper and John Penn—North Carolina congressmen who were about to return home to participate in writing a constitution for their province—to commit to paper his ideas on government. Adams consented. "Borrow[ing] a little Time from . . . sleep," as he put it, Adams "wrote with his own Hand, a Sketch" on proper governance that ran six or seven pages in length. Subsequently Richard Henry Lee and George Wythe also asked for copies, and Adams obliged. With Adams's authorization, Lee paid to have the piece published, and it appeared during the fourth week of April under the title *Thoughts on Government*.[65]

Adams began by insisting that the purpose of government was to promote "the happiness of society." Republican governments, he maintained, were the best instruments for achieving this end. These were governments in which power was given by "the many, to a few of the most wise and good." Adams proposed that the structure of government consist of a bicameral assembly that was to be balanced by executive and judicial branches. Like Paine, Adams understood that the legislature would be the focal point of the system. It was therefore essential that the assembly "be in miniature, an exact portrait of the people at large. . . . Great care should be taken" to see that the representatives of the people "feel, reason, and act like them." Adams maintained that a two-house assembly was superior to a unicameral legislature, as bicameralism reduced the likelihood that legislation would be enacted in a fit of passion. Adams urged that the representatives in a small lower house be popularly elected by the qualified voters in each state, in elections conducted according to the "established modes to which the people have been familiarised by habit." The lower house, in turn, would elect the members of the upper chamber, whose size should not exceed thirty members. The executive, who should be elected annually by both houses of the assembly, was to possess veto powers over bills passed by the legislature. Judges, he argued, should be appointed by the executive with the consent of the upper house of the assembly. They should hold office for life. Adams maintained that his formula would result in the "dignity and stability of government." Moreover, because this structure was strong, sturdy, and popular, "THESE Colonies, under such forms of government, and in such a union, would be unconquerable by all the Monarchies of Europe."[66]

Nothing else that Adams ever wrote rivaled the impact of *Thoughts on Government*. Many of his previous publications had been overly long and dense. This one was crafted with a lovely clarity. Perhaps the literary quality was improved because Adams did not realize that what he wrote would be published. Or he may have been inspired to try to match Paine's felicitous style. Neither he nor anyone else was Paine's equal as a writer, yet Adams reached a large audience of articulate citizens and succeeded in easing many fears about America's ability to govern itself. Some concerns remained. An independent America would be a huge nation—the settled portions of the thirteen provinces were several times larger than most European nations— and it was certain to be frayed by wildly dissimilar interests. But Adams's essay was pivotal because it offered a rational formula for constructing a government that would be insulated from those "ambitious innovators" that so worried the most conservative colonists. Adams succeeded in convincing many Americans that they could live in an independent nation and still preserve what they chose to keep from their treasured colonial past.

*   *   *

On May 5, ten days before the Virginia Convention called on Congress to declare independence, a vessel docked in Philadelphia loaded with thirteen tons of gunpowder and other war-related materials that had been taken aboard in Port l'Orient, France. The cargo was welcome, but the ship also brought a two-month-old issue of a Dublin newspaper that was filled with unwanted news. The North ministry, it disclosed, was dispatching forty-five thousand troops to America, among them German mercenaries.[67]

Congress had known for months that the mother country might utilize mercenaries. The king had cryptically alluded to offers of foreign assistance in his October address to Parliament. Even before that, Americans had learned from accounts in the British press, including debates in Parliament, that North's government was attempting to negotiate a treaty with Catherine the Great to obtain Russian soldiers. Rumors buzzed in Philadelphia just after Christmas that "a great Number of Foreign Troops are coming over." One report claimed that thirty thousand Russians were already crossing the Atlantic. As Great Britain had frequently employed mercenaries to augment its own army during its wars with France and Spain, few were surprised that London would once again turn to this expedient. The ministers "must Certainly have recourse to Foreigners as they cannot meet success in" raising adequate numbers within Great Britain, Robert Morris responded rather matter-of-factly.[68]

Americans learned in midwinter 1776 that North's Russian diplomacy had failed. The csarina had declined to sell her soldiers to the British. No one in Congress thought that was the end of the story. Most believed the Crown would next try to hire German soldiers. That was precisely what it did. In February the British government concluded treaties with the rulers of four German principalities to lease twenty thousand soldiers. The opposition in Parliament had fought hiring foreign troops, calling such a step "disgraceful and dangerous." When the government submitted the treaties for ratification in February, Isaac Barré charged that this was fresh proof that North and Germain were "not fit to conduct the affairs of a great nation." David Hartley called it a "fatal measure," for "when foreign powers are once introduced in this dispute, all possibility of reconciliation is totally cut off." The treaties passed in the Commons by a three-to-one margin.[69]

Congress may not have been surprised to learn in May that thousands of German troops had been hired, but nothing since word of the American Prohibitory Act so riled the delegates. For some, the news that the king planned to use foreigners to kill his American subjects was the final confirmation of the corruption and despotism that stalked the mother country. The "Tyrant of Britain and his Parliament," said John Hancock, "have proceeded to the last Extremity." Several congressmen described the use of mercenaries as "infamous," but to hire German soldiers, who had a reputation as cruel and barbarous warriors, was unthinkable. Great Britain has "added near half of Germany" to its army, a North Carolina delegate raged, while a Yankee said that it meant London intended "to push the war with the utmost fury." James Duane of New York, who had steadfastly been aligned with the reconciliationists, worried that the Germans would not leave even if they subdued the rebellion. "[L]ike all other Barbarians," he fumed, they would remain to "set up their own Empire on the Ruins of Americans." His compatriot from Pennsylvania, Robert Morris, was no longer so blasé. The "Dogs of Warr are now fairly set loose upon us," he said, adding that the Germans "are coming to Slaughter us." No one better captured the temper in Congress than New Hampshire's Josiah Bartlett. George III, he charged, planned to use "Britons, Hessians, Hanoverians, Indians, negroes and every other butcher [he] can hire against us."[70]

Intermingled with these thoughts was one other idea. Most colonists had always believed that they could "safely venture our strength . . . against that of Great Britain only." But on learning of the hiring of the Germans, many an American quickly concluded that "we are . . . unequal to a Contest with her and her Allies without any assistance from without." And substantial assistance from without—from France, in other words—might be had only if America declared independence.[71]

By early May Congress had been in session without a break since September 13. During that time some delegates had relinquished their seats and others had been recalled and replaced, as when Gerry took Cushing's place in the Massachusetts delegation. Among those who stayed on in Congress, most had managed to squeeze in a trip home, and some who did not live far from Philadelphia had visited their families two or three times. For those confronted with a long journey, to New England or the lower South for instance, a trip home inevitably meant a lengthy absence from Congress. John Adams was away from Philadelphia from December 8 until February 8, spending almost half that time on the road. Some congressmen never went home. Connecticut's Oliver Wolcott told his wife, Laura, that he could not leave while Congress was considering matters that would "decide the Fate of this Country" for generations to come. Samuel Adams wrote to Elizabeth that he badly wanted to be with her, but "I thought my self indispensably obligd . . . to deny my self." He added soothingly: "Whenever I shall have the pleasure of seeing you, to me it will be inexpressible."[72]

Long before May 1776 most congressmen were exhausted, "worn down with long and uninterrupted Labour," as one put it, or "almost wore down . . .

owing to the multiplicity of business," according to another. Lawyers, business-men, or planters, for the most part, many congressmen wrung their hands over the personal cost of public service. "My private affairs . . . are hurrying fast into Ruin [and] really require some Attention," one despaired. It was worrisome enough that his business affairs at home were left to the "discre-tion of [inadequately superintended] workmen," said one congressman, but the cost of living in Philadelphia was an additional burden. The city was at least six times more expensive to live in than a small New England town, one Yankee congressman despaired. But nothing worried the congressmen more than their health, and with good reason. During the first weeks of 1776 one member of Congress, Thomas Lynch of South Carolina, suffered a stroke. Though he was "better than he has been" within two weeks, his congressional service was at an end. Rhode Island's Samuel Ward, who said in January that he was "not like to get time to be Inoculated" against smallpox, was stricken with the disease in March. He perished after a brief illness. Ward was the second congressman to die since the opening of Congress eighteen months earlier; Virginia's Peyton Randolph had died suddenly the previous autumn. Delegates wrote home complaining of frequent headaches, coughs, fevers, ir-ritated eyes, and gout. Many thought their maladies attributable to "being So long Confined [indoors] without any Bodily Exercise." Given their daily regi-men of up to six hours at a desk while Congress was in session, and often still more time in committee meetings, some delegates sought to compensate with long early-morning walks or horseback rides. At least one congressman at-tempted greater "discipline in living." He curtailed his diet from three meals to two each day and ate "a pretty light Breakfast of Sweetened Water and Milk with some Toast."[73]

Harmony prevailed in many delegations, but in others, bitter differences separated the deputies, sometimes causing open ruptures between old friends and adding to the strains attendant to congressional service. The Massachu-setts delegation was one of the most deeply divided. Hancock and Robert Treat Paine opposed much that John and Samuel Adams supported, and in the end their wrangles led to resentments and downright hostility. Paine es-pecially complained of "the cold, haughty, disrespectful behaviour of the two Adams towards me," and he found John Adams's perceived superciliousness to be especially galling. "I flatter my self I deserve [such treatment] from no body," Paine raged, adding that "I am sure I dont from him." Paine's indigna-tion in part rose from jealousy of his colleague's rising stature. Paine was mortified that Adams, who had been his junior as a lawyer in Massachusetts, had been "ranked above" him by the Massachusetts Provincial Congress and was convinced that a conspiracy among "a Junto of 2, 3, or 4 men"—doubtless

Samuel Adams and some of his Virginia friends, including Richard Henry Lee—had raised John Adams to great prominence in Congress. John Adams was aware of Paine's enmity, but shrugged it off. "[W]hat cant be cured must be endured," he remarked.[74]

No strain equaled that of the anxiety caused by separation from wives, children, and loved ones. "I have been waiting impatiently for a Letter from you. . . . [Y]ou cannot do me a greater Pleasure than by writing to me often," one delegate told his spouse, a sentiment echoed by most of his colleagues. One congressman, a widower, was courting a woman at home—you should have seen them "*Cheese* together," said a colleague who had observed them during a trip home at Christmas—and missed her company. Sometimes the tidings from home were gloomy and unwelcome. New York's Robert R. Livingston lost both parents while he attended this lengthy session of Congress. John Adams learned of his brother's death while on military duty. One of Samuel Ward's sons was captured during the attack on Quebec and was confined in a smallpox-riddled prison. Even when the news from home was not bad, many congressmen agonized over the "unhappy situation" of family and friends who lived close to the British army or in an area likely to see fighting during the campaign of 1776. Brooding over their family's fate at the hands of British or Hessian regulars occasioned more "gloomy Ideas in my mind" than all the wrangles on the floor of Congress, said one delegate. Many grieved at not being home to "be an Instrument in forming the Minds & Manners of my dear Children," and not a few purchased toys and clothing to send to them.[75]

Those left at home were no less anxious for their spouses. They were also eager to know what was occurring in Congress. "Pray write me every opportunity every thing that transpires," Abigail Adams begged her husband, and she told him that she prayed that whatever he did in Congress "may be directed into the wisest and best measures for our Safety."[76]

The Adamses were accustomed to prolonged separations. While practicing law, John had been apart from Abigail for up to a third of each year since 1764 as he rode the legal circuit throughout Massachusetts and what today is Maine. But aware of her husband's fragile health, Abigail was beside herself with worry when John departed for Philadelphia a few days after Lexington and Concord. When almost three weeks passed without hearing from him, she grew frantic. When his first letter finally arrived and she learned that he had gotten there safely, Abigail admonished him to be as careful in his work habits "as you can consistent with the Duty you owe your Country."[77]

Concern for her husband's well-being was merely one of Abigail's worries. With Boston Harbor shut and the city besieged, she and her neighbors were afflicted with scarcities and soaring prices. From time to time she sent her husband a shopping list in the hope that he could find certain items in Phila-delphia, including pins, black pepper, fabrics, rhubarb, nutmeg, cloves, cinna-mon, and handkerchiefs. She was frustrated too by her lack of free time. As managing the farm had been added to her customary responsibilities with the children, Abigail said that her life was akin to that of "a nun in a cloister."[78]

Those aggravations paled in comparison to the fear triggered by the out-break of dysentery that swept the region in the summer and fall of 1775, a scourge that in some measure was spread to civilians by the two armies in and around Boston. In some towns more women and children died that year from the unfurling camp disease than did the males from the village who were away soldiering.[79] This "Distemper," this "pestilence," this "general putrefac-tion," this "voilent Dysentery," as Abigail variously called the affliction, soon enough struck her household. Two servants, a child—Thomas Boylston—and Abigail herself fell ill "in a violent manner. . . . Our House is an hospital in every part," she told John. Patty, one of the servants, perished, as did others in town, including Abigail's mother, who succumbed to the stubborn malady on October 1. "Woe follows Woe and one affliction treads upon the heel of an other," Abigail grieved, every bit as much a victim of war as a soldier who faced dangers on the front lines. "I sit down with a heavy Heart to write to you," she told her husband in one letter. "Have pitty upon me, have pitty upon me o! thou my beloved," she continued. Inconsolable, Abigail ranted at Brit-ain's leaders for the devastation they had unleashed. "O [Lord] North! may the Groans and cryes . . . Harrow up thy Soul," she lashed out. By November she favored independence. Great Britain was no longer America's parent state, she said. It was America's "tyrant State. . . . Let us separate, they are unworthy to be our Breathren."[80]

Though John was writing home about twice each week, his letters miscar-ried at this critical juncture, leaving Abigail to worry yet again about his fate while she was ensconced in her sorrow. "[T]is only in my Night visions that I know any thing about you," she lamented. His letters finally arrived—five in one day—and she drew sustenance from them, exclaiming that they "admin-ister comfort to my wounded Heart."[81]

John and his fellow congressmen were hundreds of miles from the front lines, but Abigail lived only a stone's throw from the British army in occupied Boston. Every conceivable sort of rumor about impending British or Conti-nental actions swirled through her neighborhood. Some were not that fanci-ful. Hearsay had it that the Royal Navy might sail into Quincy Bay and shell Braintree, laying waste to it as it had destroyed Falmouth. The story circu-lated too that Howe might land an invasion force near Braintree in an at-tempt to outflank Washington's Continentals. In that event, Abigail knew

Abigail Adams by Benjamin Blyth. The wife of John Adams, she remained at home near Boston and was close to early fighting during the war. She was a proponent of independence and encouraged her husband to seek greater rights for American women following the break with the mother country. (Massachusetts Historical Society)

that the battlefield would be very "near my dwelling." During the first days of the siege of Boston, she had lived "in continual Expectation of Hostilities." She moved her husband's library to his brother's house, which she thought might be in a safer location in the event of an attack, and she tried to be brave. "Danger they say makes people valiant," she remarked. As it turned out, the closest thing to a battle in her locality was brought on by Washington's Dorchester Heights operation. The army was but a short distance from Braintree, and the heavy Continental bombardment shook her house. "No sleep for me to Night. . . . [M]y Heart Beat pace with [the cannonade] all night," she wrote John. She said she had hurried up nearby Penn's Hill, "whence I could see every shell which was thrown. . . .'Tis now an incessant Roar. . . . My Hand and heart . . . tremble, at this domestick fury."[82]

Though absorbed with the challenge of daily sessions of Congress, John responded with concern and sensitivity to Abigail's travails. "I long to know, how you fare, and whether you are often discomposed" by the war's dangers and disruptions, he said. He tried to be reassuring: "I think you are in no Danger—dont let the . . . fruitful Imaginations of others affect you." He gently reminded her from time to time that American liberty was at stake and the struggle required sacrifice, to which he added his praise of how she was bearing up: "It gives . . . Pleasure . . . that you sustain with so much Fortitude, the Shocks and Terrors of the Times. You are really brave, my dear, you are an Heroine." But John's letters were devoid of romantic sentiments, and it irritated his wife. After he had been absent for months, Abigail bluntly told him: "I want some sentimental Effusions of the Heart. I am sure you are not destitute of them." The letters she received in return must have been disappointing. Perhaps fearing that his correspondence would be intercepted once again and published by some delighted Tory editor, John scrupulously avoided all evidence of amorous feelings.[83]

In the first days of the siege of Boston, Abigail notified John that she had permitted soldiers to lodge or take a meal at their home, and she had even taken in refugees from the city—total strangers—for up to a week at a time. John praised her "generous Solicitude." He also asked her to try to extract information from those who had fled Boston about how the beleaguered British soldiers were faring. However, if she learned anything, John advised, she should discreetly pass it along to the local revolutionary government rather than send it through the mail to him. When the dysentery epidemic spread to Braintree, John was beside himself with anxiety and considered rushing home. "I tremble for you" and the children, he wrote, and pledged to come home for good or to transport his family to Philadelphia should he receive "more disagreable" news from her. He fell back on his religious beliefs for solace, counseling Abigail that God's "designs are often inscrutable," though "always wise and just and good." When he learned of the death of Abigail's mother, John wrote his wife a long, compassionate letter in which he extolled his late mother-in-law's "Purity . . . Piety and Virtue" and reflected on the heartaches of life. He also reminded her that the afflictions besetting so many colonists were the consequence of what he often called "the glorious struggle" to resist British tyranny.[84]

In the wake of the epidemic, John not only began to write his children but also poured out to Abigail his sorrow over his absence from his sons and daughter during their formative years. He advised her on how they should be raised: All must be properly educated and the boys must learn the meaning of courage, industry, and ambition. They must be taught "to scorn Injustice, Cowardice, and Falshood. Let them revere nothing but Religion, Morality and Liberty." John may have borne a heavy burden of guilt over being away, but he never said that his public service was unmerited. In fact, he proclaimed that in the long run, his children would be the beneficiaries of his sacrifices, for his service in Congress was designed "to procure a free Constitution for them to solace themselves under."[85]

Before Adams returned home in December for a brief vacation, he told Abigail that he would not serve again in Congress until others from Massachusetts took their turn. He also vowed never to return to Philadelphia unless accompanied by Abigail.[86] But in February he resumed his seat in Congress and returned to Philadelphia alone. What privately transpired between John and Abigail in December and January cannot be known for certain. They probably agreed that he would continue to serve in Congress until independence was declared. Until then, Abigail must remain at home to care for the children and the farm. During the previous October, John had told Abigail that since the Stamp Act crisis, he had foreseen that the Anglo-American "Controversy was of such a Nature that it would never be settled" short of war and that ultimately "Things would be wrought up to their present Crisis" over "breaking our Connection" with Great Britain. At this decisive moment in American history, he had continued, "I dare not consent" to leave Congress.[87]

Having met with General Washington while at home, John gleaned that the siege of Boston was probably headed toward an impending showdown. He departed Braintree for Philadelphia late in January 1776 filled with "many Pains, on your Account," he told Abigail. But in mid-March, when word of Washington's occupation of Dorchester Heights reached Congress, Adams also learned that the British were quitting Boston. With the liberation of the city and the unmistakable approach of independence, the tone of both John's and Abigail's letters changed. "I feel very differently . . . to what I did a month ago," Abigail wrote early in April. With the British gone from Boston, she continued, all those in the vicinity of the city may "sit under our own vine and eat the good of the land." But she wanted more: "I long to hear that you declared an independency." John responded that America was all but independent. "[B]e patient," he advised in April, for the formal declaration of independence could not be far away. Abigail's response was audacious: "Remember the Ladies" when independence was declared and the laws for the new nation were enacted. Protect the rights of women, she pleaded, and she additionally urged that Congress take steps to end slavery. "[Y]ou are so saucy," John replied noncommittally, sounding very much like the pragmatic politician that he had become.[88]

The idea of declaring independence was coming to fruition in the spring of 1776, brought steadily closer by the groundswell of public opinion. As May approached, those congressmen who favored independence were confident that every New England delegation and all four from below the Potomac were ready "to declare off from Great Britain," as one quaintly put it. There were signs as well that Maryland and New Jersey were coming around. "Every Post and every Day" brought fresh word of the fervor for independence, John Adams said, adding that the good news "rolls in upon Us . . . like a Torrent." Independence was "unavoidable," a Connecticut delegate remarked in April, but he and his fellow advocates for independence desperately wanted Congress's most significant decision to be by a unanimous vote.[89]

New York, Delaware, and Pennsylvania were seen as the greatest obstacles to unanimity, though most thought "there is but very little doubt of N. York" ultimately siding with those who favored independence. Everyone also thought that Delaware would do whatever Pennsylvania chose to do. As had been true since the First Congress, it was Pennsylvania above all that marched to a different drummer, but those in Congress who longed for independence radiated confidence in April that it too was "coming over with great Rapidity" to their position. In the very near future, Richard Henry Lee happily predicted, Pennsylvania would cease to "obstruct and perplex the American machine."[90]

"It requires time to bring the Colonies all of one mind, but time will do," John Adams said. ("It requires Time to convince the doubting and inspire the timid," Samuel Adams had similarly remarked the previous day.) "I do not att all wonder, that so much Reluctance has been shewn to the Measures of Independency," John Adams added. "All great Changes are irksome . . . especially those which are attended with great Dangers." Be that as it may, as April drew to a close, Adams was confident that they were "hastening rapidly to great Events."[91]

One reason for optimism was that May 1 was election day in Pennsylvania. Adams and others expected the pro-independence candidates to win control of the assembly and "repeal their deadly Instructions to their Delegates in Congress," directions that—according to Adams—had made Pennsylvania "So exceedingly obnoxious to America in General."[92] But the outcome of the election was disappointing. Although the pro-independence candidates captured thirteen of seventeen contested seats, those who favored reconciliation retained a majority of the assembly seats. In Philadelphia, Thomas Willing, the reconciliationist congressman, was defeated, but a majority of those elected were foes of independence, who garnered a narrow 50.5 percent of the vote in the city. Thomas Paine, perhaps correctly, thought the outcome due to the fact that numerous pro-independence citizens were away in the Continental army and could not vote.[93]

Thwarted at the ballot box, the leaders of the pro-independence faction in Pennsylvania turned for help to John Adams, leader of the pro-independence faction in Congress. He was more than willing to do something. The "dullest and slowest" sailors, as he had once characterized the congressional faction that favored reconciliation, had too long inhibited the push for independence. First, Adams sought to have Congress pass a resolution discouraging all colonies from instructing their delegates. Congress rejected that idea as the antithesis of representative government. Next, on May 10, a day when Dickinson was absent—he had returned to his farm near Dover, Delaware—Adams introduced a resolution urging the colonies to create new governments if their old colonial charters were unable to meet "the exigencies of their affairs."[94] Adams's act was a thinly veiled maneuver to terminate Pennsylvania's government under its seventeenth-century charter. His objective was the creation of an assembly in which the western counties—home to roughly half of the colony's population, and the region that was the most supportive of American independence—were afforded equal representation. Such a government was virtually certain to be dominated by Pennsylvania's radicals, who would rewrite the instructions to Pennsylvania's congressmen.

Congress adopted the measure, but deferred its publication until a preamble could be written and adopted. Adams handled that as well, and his preamble gave a new meaning to the resolution passed five days earlier. The preamble stated that given the king's refusal to receive Congress's petitions and his willingness to make war on America in concert with German mercenaries, it was "absolutely irreconcilable to reason and good conscience" for Americans to any longer adhere to any government whose authority was derived from Crown-issued charters.

The debate, conducted while Dickinson remained absent, produced "much

heat," one delegate observed. But its foes no longer openly demanded reconciliation. (Later, Dickinson claimed that after the Olive Branch Petition had
been rejected, not one deputy in Congress ever urged reconciliation.)[95] Instead, the preamble's opponents urged that Congress go slowly. "Why all this
Haste? Why . . . this driving?" James Duane asked. Samuel Adams played a
major role in defending the preamble. Wartime realities demanded that the
provincial governments be altered and modernized, and quickly, he said. It
was miraculous, he added, that the people, bound by Crown charters, "have
conducted so well as they have" against the king's "Fleets and Armies." But
now they are about to be confronted with his "Mirmidons from abroad." Indeed, that morning the *Pennsylvania Gazette* had reprinted a story from a
London newspaper that reported an armada of fifty-seven warships loaded
with thirty-five thousand men—including German mercenaries—was crossing the Atlantic. The debate raged for three days before Congress adopted the
preamble on May 15.[96]

That night, writing to a friend at home, John Adams rejoiced that Congress
had at that day's session "passed the most important Resolution, that ever was
taken in America." Two days later he wrote to Abigail that Congress's act was
tantamount to a "compleat Seperation" from Great Britain, "a total absolute Independence" of America.[97] Adams was not alone in seeing things this way.
Maryland's Thomas Stone exclaimed: "The Dye is cast. The fatal Stab is given to
any future Connection between this Country & Britain."[98] Congress had taken
a step that would have been unthinkable only a few weeks earlier. It had all but
declared American independence.

CHAPTER 11

"NOT CHOICE, BUT NECESSITY THAT CALLS FOR INDEPENDENCE"

THE DILEMMA AND STRATEGY OF ROBERT LIVINGSTON

BEFORE MAY ENDED, Richard Henry Lee and his colleagues in the Virginia delegation learned that the provincial convention in Williamsburg had in midmonth agreed to ask Congress to declare independence. Lee quietly shared the tidings with John and Samuel Adams, who, he said, responded with "Joy and exultation." Things were moving their way. Every day seemed to bring another scrap of news indicating that "a Seperation will take place," and in the near future.[1]

The Maryland Convention, while not calling for independence, had just prohibited the taking of oaths to Great Britain. Given Maryland's steadfast commitment to reconciliation since the First Congress, the pro-independence faction saw this as a positive sign. Indications of change were also apparent in Pennsylvania, Delaware, and New Jersey, leading Francis Lightfoot Lee to conclude that they too were "going fast into Independency."[2]

Several things appeared to be behind the gathering momentum. "Great Britain may thank herself for this," one delegate observed. In the space of seven days in late May and early June, Congress first learned that Lord Dartmouth, still thought by some to be a friend of America, had asserted during a March debate in Parliament that the peace commissioners would not suspend hostilities "till the Colonies own our legislative sovereignty." One gleeful congressman remarked that Dartmouth's comment would at long last "shut the mouths of all Gapers after [peace] Commissioners." Hard on the heels of that news came word that when London's mayor and aldermen had petitioned George III in March to seek peace, the king's response had been that the use of force was the only "proper and effectual means" of dealing with rebels.[3]

But military realities overshadowed everything else in pushing the colonists to declare independence. More bad news from Canada provided the impetus for the final drive to break with Great Britain.

Following the Continental army's defeat at Quebec on the last day of 1775, only a few hundred soldiers had remained outside the walls of the city. Montgomery was dead, Arnold was incapacitated by his wound, and some five hundred rebel soldiers had been killed or captured in the desperate attack. Its ranks depleted and nearly devoid of artillery, the tiny American army could do little but await reinforcements and try to sustain itself in the face of the brutal Canadian winter.

Even before it was aware of the debacle in Canada, Congress had voted to raise a regiment to replace the men whose enlistments were due to expire at the end of 1775. Within hours of learning of the repulse of Montgomery's attack, Congress agreed to raise still more men. For the first time it also authorized cash bounties to entice men to enlist. As it searched for supplies—clothing, blankets, arms, wagons, tents, axes, tomahawks, and above all, specie that would enable the army to purchase goods in Canada—Congress redeployed some existing Continental units to Canada. The first of those men were marching northward within five days of Congress's receiving word of Montgomery's disastrous assault.[4]

Congress also replaced General David Wooster, who had become the acting commander in Canada following Montgomery's death. Now sixty-five years old, Wooster had been the second-oldest of the original general officers appointed by Congress. He was an experienced soldier, having served for several years during the French and Indian War—in which he tasted combat—but by 1775 few any longer thought him equal to the task. One observer caustically remarked that Wooster might function best as "general . . . of a hayfield."[5] Nonetheless, Wooster was part of the army that invaded Canada, and when Montgomery died, he became the highest-ranking officer in that force. He took charge of the siege operation at Quebec and maintained it for months through the harsh Canadian winter. He won praise from some in Congress, including John Adams, who thought that "Wooster has done that in Canada which Schuyler could not have done. He has kept up an Army there through the Winter."[6]

But many congressmen thought Wooster too old for the challenge. Some habitually referred to him as "old Wooster." Several deputies also wanted to change commanders in Canada because they believed a better man was available. John Thomas had shined during the long siege of Boston. A fifty-two-year-old physician who had served for six years as a surgeon's mate in Massachusetts's army during the last war, Thomas had practiced medicine and served in local offices in Kingston, Massachusetts, in the interim between the

French and Indian War and the Revolutionary War. When the Continental army was created, Thomas had been appointed one of the brigadier generals. Washington, a shrewd judge of men, gave Thomas command of the key Roxbury sector during the siege of Boston and also put him in charge of the operation to occupy and fortify Dorchester Heights. Impressed by what it had seen, Congress in March promoted Thomas and named him the commander of all forces in Canada. Congress told Thomas that it wanted a leader in Canada "whose Skill, Courage and Capacity will probably insure Success. In Major General Thomas they flatter themselves they will not be disappointed."[7]

Initially, Congress remained incredibly optimistic. John Hancock predicted that the "speedy arrival of troops in Canada will . . . in all probability put us in possession of Quebec" sometime during the winter or spring. His sanguine mood sprang from the belief that the besieged British within Quebec would run out of food and be compelled to surrender before the St. Lawrence thawed in April or May, enabling the Royal Navy to bring up supplies and reinforcements. "This is a Critical period," stressed Caesar Rodney, the Delaware congressman, and he added: "We are determined (God willing) to have Quebec before the frost Break's up." Robert Morris summed up congressional opinion: The "possession of Canada [is] essential to the welfare of the United Colonies," for taking Quebec might induce London to negotiate an Anglo-American settlement. At the very least, seizing Canada would shut the door to a British invasion through upper New York.[8]

Congress may have expected that Quebec would be taken, but mindful of all that had gone wrong in the fall, it sent a team of commissioners northward along with the fresh soldiers. The commission included two congressmen, Benjamin Franklin and Samuel Chase of Maryland, as well as two prominent Roman Catholics who were not members of Congress, Charles Carroll (a Maryland planter who had written eloquent tracts attacking parliamentary taxation) and his second cousin John Carroll, "a popish Priest," as a New Jersey delegate crudely referred to the Maryland clergyman. The commissioners were to seek support from Canada's inhabitants, who had remained perplexingly uncommitted since the beginning of the campaign. Among other things, they were to try to persuade the *habitants* to form a rebel government. That province might then join the American union and enjoy "a friendly intercourse with these colonies." To facilitate that end, the commissioners were to begin their mission by conveying Congress's pledge that it respected the Canadians' right to a "free and undisturbed exercise of their religion."[9]

Little time passed before Congress was awash with gloomy tidings from Canada. It was nearly May before General Thomas and the commissioners reached Montreal, their arduous journeys having been slowed by ice-bound lakes and rivers, and roads that had long since turned into muddy quagmires. (Three weeks into the trek Franklin, now seventy years old, so feared that he could not survive the grueling mission that he sat "down to write to a few Friends by way of Farewell.")[10] Thomas rapidly discovered that none of his regiments were at full strength. He estimated that he would have some 20 percent fewer men than promised. He realized too that the artillery and powder Congress had ordered northward had not arrived and that the Continentals' food supply would be exhausted within two weeks. Thomas additionally reasoned that if he had gotten through from Albany to Canada, it could not be long before British reinforcements—the ones that Lord North had worked so hard to find during the previous summer—reached Quebec. Should they land before the Continentals took the city, "some disagreeable consequence must ensue," Thomas told Congress in a classic understatement. The only repercussion that he spelled out was that it would mean "we cannot expect . . . any assistance from the inhabitants." The commissioners were even more pessimistic. The inhabitants of Canada, they said in their initial report on May 1, would provide no assistance. Whatever the *habitants* may once have thought about backing the American cause, they were unwilling to cast their lot with a Continental army, which they believed was certain to "be driven out of the Province as soon as the King's troops can arrive." With "few friends . . . here," the commissioners added, Congress must send lots of money—at least twenty thousand pounds—for the purchase of supplies. It should additionally send more men, "sufficient . . . to secure the possession of the country."[11]

Thomas kept Wooster in charge of the siege at Quebec, but he had already begun to formulate a strategy for what should be done when the British reinforcements arrived. With the concurrence of his officers, Thomas planned to retreat to Three Rivers, about halfway between Quebec and Montreal, and attempt to prevent the redcoats from advancing beyond that point. Once again, the commissioners were less optimistic than the Continental officers, or perhaps they felt less constrained about airing their real feelings. Unless Congress deployed massive numbers of men northward, they told Philadelphia, it would be "better immediately to withdraw" the army from Canada.[12]

Unbeknownst to the commissioners, the long-anticipated flotilla bringing British reinforcements had arrived at Quebec early in May 1776, two days before they passed on their recommendation to Congress. More than five thousand redcoats were on board, but General Carleton, who had been confined within the walled citadel at Quebec for six months, could not be restrained. He was spoiling for a fight. At the first sight of the British sails, Carleton and several hundred of the ragged defenders of Quebec poured out of their lair and came after General Wooster's Continentals. What followed was not pretty. The mere sight of Carleton's advancing soldiers created a "panic so violent" that the rebels dropped whatever they were doing and fled for safety. They left behind five hundred muskets, all of their artillery, and massive amounts of powder. So great was their terror that the rebels even abandoned nearly two hundred sick comrades who were too ill "to come off," as one soldier put it. Some officers had been the first to flee, deserting their men. The commissioners reported that the army's "flight was made with the utmost precipitation and confusion." Seeing what was occurring, several British vessels sailed farther upriver and landed parties of marines here and there in the hope of cutting off the frightened and disorganized rebels. Over the next two days, before Thomas at last brought things under control, the Americans rushed along the muddy river road with "loaded carts driving full speed," in the words of one British observer. The fleeing Continentals had "dwindled into a mobb," said an American witness, that was so driven by hysteria that for a second time some disgracefully forsook their comrades, deserting men in poor health who had made it that far but could not keep up.[13]

General Thomas rushed forward and stanched the retreat. He even refashioned the panicked men into something approaching soldiers. As he did so, he rethought his strategy. Jettisoning his plan to make a stand at Three Rivers, Thomas now envisaged withdrawing to the confluence of the Richelieu and St. Lawrence rivers, near Montreal, where his army would dig in and await the advancing British. But given the number of redcoats known to be disembarking at Quebec, it was the height of optimism to think that the American army could long remain on Canadian soil. In fact, the commissioners advised Thomas that his best bet was to fall back to Isle-aux-Noix, an island in the Richelieu River above Lake Champlain. Thomas was still pondering his options when the commissioners concluded that they could "render our Country no further Services in this Colony." Franklin and Father Carroll started for home on May 11. Before Charles Carroll and Chase departed a few days later, they beseeched Schuyler, the commander of the Northern Department, to make available every conceivable vessel so that the army could escape Canada.[14]

By now, the commissioners had concluded that the American army in Canada was rotten to the core: Numerous officers were "unfit," the men were untrained and undisciplined, "confusion . . . prevails thro' every department," the soldiers had not been paid, and the army had been "reduced to . . . the scanty & precarious Supplies of a few half Starved cattle & trifling quantities of flour." If one man was to blame for this gathering disaster, the commissioners appeared to say, it was General Schuyler, who had permitted thousands of men to enter Canada without having "taken care to have Magazines formed for their Subsistence." But the commissioners also seemed to say that a failure of this magnitude was not the fault of only one man. During their journey to Canada the four commissioners had stopped at Fort Constitution, the only installation on the Hudson River that guarded the highlands above Manhattan. Although the war was a year old, the commissioners found that no artillerymen were garrisoned at the fort, half the soldiers had not been furnished with muskets, two thirds of those with arms lacked bayonets, and the pantry was bare of vegetables. In their own way, the commissioners seemed to be telling Congress that while Schuyler bore responsibility for some of the failures under his command, America faced a bigger problem. The Continental army needed foreign help in waging this war.[15]

With so many things going badly, the commissioners thought that conditions could not worsen. But the situation soon deteriorated further. General Thomas died of smallpox during the third week in May. Once again, Wooster was in charge. Chase and Charles Carroll, who were still in Canada, had no confidence in him. Wooster's very presence in Canada is "prejudicial to our Affairs," they reported on May 27, and they urged Congress to recall him.[16]

Many in Congress shared the commissioners' feelings about Wooster, especially after he had lost control of the army at Quebec. That "old woman suffered himself to be surprised" when Carleton and his half-starved army had emerged from behind the walls of Quebec, one delegate raged.[17] A sufficient number agreed. Before the end of May, Congress recalled Wooster and named Brigadier General John Sullivan to command the army in Canada. One can only wonder whether many congressmen thought Sullivan would be much of an improvement. He was half Wooster's age, but before the war he had been a Portsmouth, New Hampshire, lawyer with little military experience. He became a militia officer only in 1773, and before the siege of Boston, the only action he had seen had been in marching his men around the parade ground. Sullivan served in the First and Second Congress and appeared to owe his inclusion in the initial batch of general officers solely to politics. When Chase learned of Congress's decision, he despaired, remarking that Sullivan was unfit to command the army.[18]

Chase was prescient. Sullivan hurried to Canada thirsting for action and glory. "I now think only of a glorious Death or a Victory," he announced. Even though he acknowledged that it was "a serious truth" that the army was "extremely weak," Sullivan ordered an advance to Three Rivers, where, with about one third of his Continentals, he attacked a British force that was three times larger. Predictably, his men were not only mauled; they were also cut off from the remainder of their comrades. They escaped only because the British failed to follow up their advantage. The rebels' good fortune sprang from Carleton's adherence to antiquated orders from London directing that he merely clear the St. Lawrence of the rebel invaders. Sullivan, who had already begun to think of how to explain his blunder to Congress—"Ill Success never happen'd by my Rashness Imprudence or Cowardice," was his ultimate and unpersuasive defense—finally decided toward the end of May to do what the congressional commissioners had recommended thirty days earlier: He retreated to Isle-aux-Noix. But even there calamity dogged this miserable army. Smallpox, dysentery, and malaria struck the men encamped on the swampy, mosquito-infested island. A dozen or more men died daily; some three hundred perished within two weeks. "Death reigns triumphant," an army physician announced, and Sullivan remarked that his soldiers were "Dropping off Like the Israelites before the Destroying Angel."[19]

About two weeks before Sullivan's misguided attack on Three Rivers, Richard Henry Lee had learned that Virginia wished its delegation to ask Congress to declare independence. At that juncture, Lee remained optimistic that something could be salvaged from the Canadian adventure. Though the commissioners "seem to be on the fright," Lee had said, he still believed that the American army might make a valiant defensive stand that would prevent the enemy from reaching the "Upper Country," by which he meant New York's northern border. If the Continentals could pull that off, Lee reasoned, the Indians would remain neutral and the long and bitter Canadian campaign would "answer every good purpose."[20]

Lee was one of the few in Congress who still harbored hope for success in Canada. Thomas Stone of Maryland, who read the same dispatches, thought the American army would retreat out of Canada and that "a most bloody & distructive war" was in the offing on the New York and New England frontier. Another delegate foresaw "hard rubs" in the Northern Department. By early June, Lee had changed his tune. News arrived that another five thousand reinforcements from London were crossing the Atlantic, headed for Quebec. This ended all hope for success in Canada. "[O]ur Affairs in that Quarter wear a melancholy Aspect," the president of Congress notified each colony.[21]

Many in Congress were beginning to fear that the disasters in Canada might only be a small foretaste of wartime woes to come. Howe was expected to strike around New York City during the summer and it now appeared certain that another British army would simultaneously invade upper New York. All knew that Washington's army would face a "violent struggle" when the redcoats and their German allies landed near Manhattan with what one congressman called a "dreadfull Armament." Not a few feared that Sullivan's army, which was "in a very bad way," would be unable to hold the line on the frontier. Worry spread that the British might in time seize control of the Hudson River.[22]

As the first week of June sped past, the feeling gathered impetus that America might not be able to stand alone in the coming military trials. The realities of the war were forcing a stark choice. Either Congress must accept London's untrammeled sovereignty or it must break with Great Britain completely. Proclaiming American independence offered the only hope of securing foreign assistance. Foreign aid alone would enable America to wage what now seemed certain to be a long struggle against Great Britain's formidable military. To wage war unilaterally would lead to ruin, as the recurring debacles in Canada demonstrated. A majority in Congress was now convinced that the colonists were "certainly unequal to a Contest with [Great Britain] and her Allies." For most congressmen, submission to London's arbitrary rule was unthinkable, which made declaring independence unavoidable. "It is not choice then, but necessity that calls for Independence," wrote Richard Henry Lee on June 2. One day later, John Adams wrote to Patrick Henry in Williamsburg: "The Importance of an immediate Application to the French Court is clear." It was equally clear that Adams believed independence was a foregone conclusion and that he had begun to think of life in the independent United States. "The Decree is gone forth, and it cannot be recalled," he told Henry, that "a more equal Liberty, than has prevail'd in other Parts of the Earth, must be established in America."[23]

With a vote on independence almost certainly near at hand, more than one reconciliationist in Congress must have wrestled with a decision that he had hoped never to have to make: to support or to resist the final break with the mother country. No delegate had been a more resolute advocate of reconciliation than Robert Robert Livingston of New York. He hailed from a family of New York bluebloods that had been a dominant force in the colony's politics for nearly a century. The first New York Livingston—also named Robert—had emigrated from Scotland in 1673 and accumulated a fortune from land and the fur trade. Thereafter, Dutchess County sent one or more members of each generation of the Livingston family to the New York assembly. Over the years, assorted Livingstons held a wide array of important offices. Congressman Livingston's father (named Robert Robert Livingston to distinguish him from numerous other Robert Livingstons in the extended family) was the grandson of the clan's founder. Like many others in the dynasty, he too held lofty offices, serving as an admiralty court judge as well as a justice on the

New York Supreme Court. Not surprisingly, the Robert Robert Livingston who sat in the Continental Congress, was destined for a political career.

Born in 1746, Robert R. Livingston graduated from King's College in 1765, married the daughter of a land baron, and inherited from Judge Livingston thousands of acres, more than 350 tenants, and mills, stores, and iron forges. Clermont, his mansion, was so palatial that it dwarfed the homes of most other rich Americans; measuring 104 feet by 91 feet, it had roughly as much square footage as the Pennsylvania State House. Young Livingston was admitted to the bar in 1770 and soon formed a legal partnership with John Jay, a friend from college days. Livingston held one Crown office, recorder of the city of New York, a position that London took from him in 1775 because of his activism in the colonial protest. Five days after the war began, Livingston, who had no legislative experience, was added to New York's congressional delegation. Only twenty-nine years old at the time, he was one of the youngest men to serve in Congress during the American Revolution.

Livingston came to Philadelphia in 1775 with a view of the imperial crisis that was similar to Dickinson's, as well as his father's. Judge Livingston had exhorted his son to oppose London's colonial policies but had also counseled that New York should "not desire . . . [to] be wholly independent of the mother country" because of the "benefits we receive of protection." The elder Livingston had attended the Stamp Act Congress in 1765 and supported America's opposition to that parliamentary tax. After Lexington and Concord, Judge Livingston advised his son to use the Continental Congress as a vehicle for "lay[ing] hold of Lord North's overtures, to open a negotiation" leading to reconciliation. Congressman Livingston did just that. He steadfastly supported policies that he believed might resolve the "unnatural Quarrel" between the mother country and her colonies. Thus, he had no objection to America's armed resistance, for, like Dickinson, he thought it would compel North to make a settlement "on the solid Basis of mutual Justice and constitutional Liberty."[24]

John Adams once speculated that extraordinarily wealthy men such as Livingston were unswerving reconciliationists because deep down they feared that the British military would confiscate their property.[25] Livingston's own remarks suggest that, like Galloway, he was more apprehensive of radical American revolutionaries. Livingston feared that a break with Great Britain would be accompanied by sweeping political changes and social unrest. In the aftermath of independence, American society would lack that "influence that is derived from respect to old families wealth age etc."[26]

Livingston's concerns notwithstanding, he was often out of step with Dickinson. From the outset, Livingston knew that he would support independence if that was what a majority in Congress desired. Within a week of the beginning of hostilities, he declared: "I am resolved to stand or fall with my country. My property is here[.] I cannot remove it & I will not hold [it] at the will of others." When Bonvouloir was in Philadelphia, Livingston was warm for pursuing commercial ties with France. During the tempestuous debates on trade in the fall of 1775, Livingston openly broke with Dickinson. He advocated the exportation of tobacco to Europe and urged that shipments of assorted northern commodities to the British West Indies be permitted. Such commerce, he argued, would raise revenue for the purchase of arms and munitions. He also claimed that the northern colonies' trade in the Caribbean was essential in order to alleviate the plight of farmers and laborers. The income of farmers had declined by two thirds, he contended, while some three hundred thousand workers had been idled in the year since the Association was first adopted. Unless the northern provinces could conduct this trade, Livingston asserted, there was a danger that morale would collapse and northern men, who made up the lion's share of the Continental army's soldiery, would no longer volunteer. But while he called for trade in northern produce, Livingston opposed the exportation of some southern staples. Planters could get by because they lived on self-sufficient plantations, he said, adding tactlessly, though forthrightly, that their "Blacks go naked till 14" anyway.[27]

Livingston was never a leader in Congress, and he was almost certainly less influential within New York's delegation than either Jay or James Duane. But he was respected by his colleagues in each major faction and frequently was chosen for important committee assignments. Among other things, Congress had put him on one panel charged with writing a letter to the people of London, another that was to draft an address to the inhabitants of Great Britain, and on the committee that met with General Washington when he came to Philadelphia in May 1776. Livingston's most important assignment came in November 1775, when he served with Robert Treat Paine and New Hampshire's John Langdon on what Congress called the Committee to the Northward. With Montgomery and Arnold advancing on Quebec, the three congressmen were to travel to Fort Ticonderoga to meet with General Schuyler and, if need be, to proceed into Canada and rendezvous with General Montgomery, Livingston's brother-in-law.

The congressmen faced a grueling two-week journey. It began with an overland ride to New York City. Thereafter, the men sailed up the Hudson River to Albany, after which they spent days on horseback first negotiating "very rutted" roads, then coping with primitive thoroughfares that had turned to a fetid ooze following heavy autumn rains, and finally making a long ride across "hard frozen" terrain laden with "considerable snow & Ice." None of the three were accustomed to roughing it. What is more, although they were traveling to the far north in November and December, Livingston and his comrades shortsightedly had "brought but one blanket with us." Sleeping several nights on "hemlock beds," they built roaring fires and somehow managed to survive temperatures that plummeted well below freezing. In the course of their mission the congressmen examined Fort Constitution and recommended improvements—which clearly had not been made when Franklin and his companions dropped in five months later—recommended repairs to Fort Ticonderoga, and took steps to secure additional troops and supplies for Montgomery. They eschewed a journey into Canada, in part because none of the three spoke French. On the final leg of the trek, the congressmen stopped in Albany to confer with one hundred Iroquois sachems and warriors and beseech them to remain neutral.[28]

Livingston was not eager to return to Congress. He missed his family and believed that his health had suffered from his heavy workload and sluggish lifestyle as a congressman. He had long before moaned that he was "sick of politicks," and now he said that he dreaded returning to that "hot room" in Philadelphia. He reached home around Christmas and tarried there for nearly seventy-five days, not rejoining his fellow New York delegates in Congress until mid-March.[29]

Much had occurred during Livingston's long absence from Philadelphia, including the publication of *Common Sense* and word of the American Prohibitory Act. When Livingston returned to Congress, he knew the day was not far off when he would probably have to make a decision on independence. While he continued to support the "Glorious struggle [to be] emancipated from the tyranny of an inhuman prince," Livingston still opposed independence. His actions during the spring of 1776 were those of a man who sought to delay the decision on independence in the hope that it would never have to be made. Indeed, Livingston spoke in private of pursuing a strategy of "well-timed delays." That, in fact, was the strategy not only of Livingston but also of the entire New York delegation and a string of provincial congresses back home. The plan of action, or inaction, was grounded on twin convictions. Livingston and his New York comrades not only believed that a large number of MPs opposed Lord North's American policies and were "prepared to give up the right of [Parliament's] taxation" of America, but they also were convinced that the opposition faction in Parliament would swell if the British suffered setbacks during the coming campaign of 1776. Therefore, if the decision on independence could be staved off, military realities by late in 1776 might make both sides more willing to consent to terms of reconciliation. In

February, Livingston summed up his outlook: "I wish to join hands with a nation which I have been accustomed to respect."[30]

The best of all worlds for Livingston was to prevent independence from ever occurring. The second-best alternative for Livingston was to delay independence until New York's traditional colonial leaders could write and adopt a constitution for the independent state of New York, a charter that would preserve as much as possible of the old order.[31]

In late winter, just after word of Montgomery's failed campaign reached Philadelphia, Livingston appears to have believed that independence could be forestalled for months, and perhaps forever. By mid-May he knew that his earlier assessment had been wrong. A decision on independence could not be averted much longer, though he remained willing to fight against it in every congressional floor debate. Nevertheless, all along Livingston knew that if, or when, the question of independence came to a vote, he would vote for the final break. He understood, as he put it, "the propriety of swimming with a Stream which it is impossible to stem" and conceding "to the Torrent" in order to "direct its course."[32] First and foremost, Livingston's goal was to continue to hold power, for only then could he hope to prevent or minimize social and political change in the new United States. If independence was unavoidable, he wished to assure that the American Revolution would be guided from the top down rather than from the bottom up.

Richard Henry Lee did not act immediately on the Virginia Convention's directive to ask Congress to declare independence. He waited nearly two weeks to make his move, in part because Generals Washington and Gates were in town for talks and it would have been awkward to raise the issue of declaring independence.[33] Lee's timing may also have been influenced by the Canadian debacle. He may have waited for that ongoing misadventure to play out, as each day bad news arrived and the ill tidings played into the hands of those who insisted that foreign assistance was essential for winning the war.[34]

Lee himself appears to have believed that the British could not do much more damage on New York's northern frontier during 1776. After conferring with Washington, Lee may also have concluded that the British might take New York City and all of Manhattan Island in 1776, but the campaign would be long and hard, and—as General Washington put it—the "place shall not be carried without some loss" to the redcoats, losses proportionally far in excess of those they had suffered on Bunker Hill. At the beginning of June 1776, Lee was convinced that the Americans could survive that year's campaign, but he appears to have believed that without foreign assistance he and his countrymen would be in a world of trouble during the campaign of 1777.[35]

During the first week of June, Lee and his fellow Virginia delegates must have conferred and decided that the time had come to act. When Lee walked from his lodging to the Pennsylvania State House on that bright morning of June 7, he knew that he would offer a resolution that very day calling for American independence. If he had any reservations over whether the timing was appropriate, they vanished during the initial moments of the session. The final reports sent from Montreal by Chase and Charles Carroll were read. The news was so "truly alarming" that Congress directed its president to inform Washington that the army of the Northern Department was "almost ruined" and barely maintained a toehold above Ticonderoga.[36]

Sometime shortly after the customary daily business was completed, Lee took the floor. He slowly read his resolution. It contained three parts. Lee urged Congress to declare that the thirteen American colonies were "free and independent States . . . absolved from all allegiance to the British Crown." The resolution also called on Congress to undertake "the most effectual measures for forming foreign Alliances" and to prepare a "plan of confederation"—a constitution for the American union of states—that was to be transmitted to the states for ratification.[37]

Some delegates objected to beginning debate on Lee's resolution on that day. There was another pressing matter to tend to: how to cope with the circulation of counterfeit congressional bills of credit. Some delegates said that issue was too important to wait. In all likelihood, they wanted time to organize their response to what Lee had proposed. Congress voted to defer consideration of Lee's resolution until the next day.

In an unusual plea, Hancock "ordered" the congressmen to "attend punctually at ten o'clock" the next morning, a Saturday session that the president of Congress must have expected to be lengthy. Presumably, most delegates obliged, and once the customary business was out of the way, Congress formed itself into a committee of the whole. Lee's motion was reread, and for the first time an entire session was devoted exclusively to the question of declaring independence. According to a New Englander, the issue was "cooly discussed" in a very long debate. The session stretched until seven in the evening, three hours or more beyond the normal quitting time, and on Monday the discussion resumed.[38]

The case against an immediate declaration of independence was made by Dickinson, Wilson, Livingston, and Edward Rutledge. Little had been seen of Dickinson since early in the year, when he had tried without success to send delegates to London to seek to open negotiations with the Crown. But on June 8 Dickinson notified his colleagues in the Pennsylvania assembly that Congress's business "in a very particular Manner demand[ed] his Attendance this Morning." He hurried down to the first floor to join the fight against separating from the mother country.[39]

Dickinson was often the first to speak when reconciliation was threatened. While it is not certain that he was the first to obtain the floor on this day, he likely spoke longer than anyone else. Dickinson's prepared, though sketchy, notes ran several pages, indicating a speech that probably would have required more than an hour to deliver.

Dickinson's speech against declaring independence was organized around three arguments. He pointed out that several colonies had not authorized their representatives to vote for independence. Most delegations had been charged with defending the colonists against British actions, nothing more. Besides, to "change a Government" required "a full & free Consent of the People plainly exprest." Secondly, he denied that military necessity demanded independence. Never mentioning Canada, he pointed to Bunker Hill and Dorchester Heights as evidence that the colonists could adequately resist Britain's armed forces. He knew that Congress was avid for French assistance, he said, but warned that "We must pay some price for it." No one knew what that price would be. He raised the specter of falling under France's thumb. That would only be the beginning of problems for an independent America, he continued. An independent America would be a republican America, and the history of republicanism was one long dismal record of "Convulsion" that invariably ended in despotical rule, the only means of restoring order.

Finally, Dickinson fell back on his hard-wearing theme that reconciliation with Great Britain was in America's best interest. The commercial advantages offered by the British Empire were too great to be relinquished. Was it not preferable, he asked, to be allied with the British people, whose "Religion, Blood, Manners, Customs" were similar to those of the American people, rather than to join hands with the French, who were different in every way from Anglo-Americans? He begged Congress to do nothing before the peace commissioners arrived. Americans were united behind the war, but the British were deeply divided, he said. Congress could play on those divisions in the negotiations with the commissioners. Furthermore, following the heavy losses that the British army would almost certainly suffer in the fighting for New York, the colonists could win a just settlement that permitted them to enjoy the fruits of the empire while being "render[ed] . . . independent" within it.[40]

The other foes of independence mostly offered variations on the themes presented by Dickinson, but some of what they said was novel. Wilson and Livingston said they thought reconciliation an "impossibility," but they opposed a formal break "at this time." They observed that during the month since Congress had voted "for suppressing the exercise of all powers derived from the crown," not a single mid-Atlantic province had authorized its delegates to vote for independence. This demonstrated that the inhabitants of these four colonies "had not yet accommodated their minds to a separation from the mother country." Should Congress declare independence, there was a danger that those colonies—Pennsylvania, Delaware, New York, and New Jersey—"might secede from the Union." If even one or two colonies seceded, it was inconceivable that France or Spain would remain interested in providing assistance to the rebels. One of these speakers—it is not clear who—even declared that France and Spain would never aid the American rebels. It was "more likely," he asserted, that they "should form a connection with the British court" to suppress the American rebellion and secure "a partition of our territories." To keep its European rivals neutral, London would return Canada to France and Florida to Spain. Rutledge contended that it was ludicrous—in private he said that "a Man must have the Impudence of a New Englander" to consider such a thing—to declare independence and claim to be a sovereign state without first having written and ratified a national constitution.[41]

These presentations, by delegates from what Rutledge in private called the "Sensible part of the House," were answered by Lee and Wythe from Virginia; several Yankees, including John Adams; and one of Georgia's two delegates in attendance, either Button Gwinnett or Lyman Hall. Their arguments, in the opinion of Elbridge Gerry, reflected the views of "the vigorous" delegates and were directed at "the slow people" who for too long had "retarded" the Congress.[42] Adams asserted that a declaration of independence would merely confirm what already existed. The colonists, he and others maintained, had "alwais been independent" of Parliament and they had ceased to be bound by allegiance to the king once he consented to "levying war on us." Some who spoke contended that the overwhelming majority of Americans favored independence. Others took the position that most Americans "wait for us [Congress] to lead the way." They stressed that it "would be vain to wait either weeks or months for perfect unanimity," as that was unlikely to ever be realized. But the heart of their argument centered on military necessity. France was willing to provide help now, but it might not be so inclined should America "be unsuccessful" on the battlefield in 1776. They warned, too, that time would be required to negotiate an alliance, making it imperative that talks begin soon in order to ensure assistance before the campaign of 1777. Finally, some of these speakers asserted that had independence been declared months earlier, not only might foreign assistance have prevented the disasters in Canada, but also a French alliance probably would have deterred the German principalities from furnishing soldiers to Great Britain.[43]

Sometime after the conclusion of Saturday's session, Rutledge decided to move on Monday that the issue be postponed for up to four weeks. In the meantime, Congress could consider a constitution and the terms it would and would not accept in a treaty of alliance with France. Others were thinking along the same line. Not a few also hoped that within the ensuing twenty-five or thirty days, each holdout colony would authorize its representatives in Congress to vote to fall "from the parent stem," as one delegate put it.[44] There was one other matter to consider. Since its inception, Congress had accompanied every major step with a formal pronouncement. If it declared independence, it would probably wish to accompany its vote with a declaration explaining its action. Delaying the discussion on Lee's resolution would provide time for the declaration to be drafted.

When Congress gathered again on Monday, the debate began again. This time it was short-lived. After a bit of discussion, someone—almost certainly Rutledge—introduced a motion "to postpone the final decision to July 1." The motion carried, terminating debate on independence for the time being.

Congress then voted to create a committee "to prepare a declaration of independence," though it did not flesh out the committee until the following day. Overnight, possibly as a result of discussions among key delegates from each of the three geographical sections in Congress, an agreement was reached on the composition of the committee. On Tuesday, June 11, Congress named Franklin, Jefferson, Livingston, Roger Sherman of Connecticut, and John Adams to sit on the committee. In the next day or two Congress created separate committees to cope with the two other components of Lee's motion. One committee, composed of Dickinson, Franklin, Morris, Harrison, and John Adams, was "to prepare a plan of treaties to be proposed to foreign powers." The other, composed of one delegate from each colony—Livingston was chosen to represent New York, Samuel Adams for Massachusetts, and Dickinson for Pennsylvania—was to draft "a plan of confederation."[45]

With the creation of the five-member committee charged with drafting a declaration of independence, it seemed assured that the "Grand Question of Independence" would be answered on July 1, or a day or two thereafter. Virtually every congressman now took for granted that "Every Thing is leading to the lasting Independancy of these Colonies." On June 15 Connecticut's Oliver Wolcott proclaimed that the American people "seem at present to be in the Midst of a great Revolution," a sentiment that echoed the view John Adams expressed on June 9: "We are in the very midst of a Revolution, the most compleat, unexpected, and remarkable of any in the History of Nations."[46]

CHAPTER 12

"The Character of a Fine Writer"

Thomas Jefferson and the Drafting of the Declaration of Independence

THE COMMITTEE CHARGED WITH drafting a declaration of independence had to act rapidly. Formed on Tuesday, June 11, the Committee of Five, as many delegates referred to it, faced a deadline of Monday, July 1. During that time, a draft had to be written and a majority of the committee had to agree to its wording, and it all had to be done while those on the panel were busy with the daily sessions of Congress and committee assignments. Given the time constraints it faced, the Committee of Five probably met for the first time either late on the day it was established or before the next morning's session of Congress.

The five committee members were hardly strangers. Adams and Sherman had known each other since the First Congress. Livingston and Franklin had entered Congress in May 1775, Jefferson a month later. Only the appointments of Franklin and Adams to this committee had more or less been a foregone conclusion. Franklin was Congress's most renowned member and its most prolific writer. For the past year, Adams had led the faction that leaned toward independence. Livingston's choice was curious. It may have stemmed in part from his competent service on other committees that had prepared documents for publication, but he was probably selected mostly because the proponents of independence thought his inclusion would sway votes among those delegates who still clung to the hope of reconciliation.

Jefferson enjoyed a deserved reputation as a writer, and that alone accounted for his selection to the Committee of Five. Most delegates were unknown outside their province when they entered Congress, but Jefferson was renowned for his flair with the pen when he arrived in Philadelphia in 1775. An essay that Jefferson had written a year earlier had gained notice in three London periodicals and sparked rumors—which were untrue—that his name had been added to a bill of attainder passed by the House of Lords.[1] So great was Jefferson's reputation as a wordsmith that he had barely unpacked his luggage before Congress assigned him to the committee that was to prepare the Declaration of the Causes and Necessity for Taking Up Arms. His colleagues on that committee, in turn, asked Jefferson to draft the document. Pleased with his work, Congress a few days later asked him to write its response to the North Peace Plan.

Jefferson's reputation as an essayist notwithstanding, happenstance played a crucial role in his inclusion on the Committee of Five. For one thing, Jefferson had written to the authorities in Williamsburg in mid-May requesting that he be recalled so that he might join in the writing of the state's first constitution. The Virginia Convention had ignored his plea.[2] Furthermore, had Richard Henry Lee wished to write the Declaration of Independence, or at least to have a hand in its composition, he almost certainly would have been chosen for the committee instead of Jefferson. The leader of Virginia's delegation, Lee not only had introduced the motion on independence; he also had served in Congress considerably longer than Jefferson. But like Jefferson, Lee was anxious to return home and play a role in provincial affairs. Lee's fervor to do so was quickened by his understanding that late in June the Virginia Convention would take up the proposed sale of lands in the Ohio Country, a region in which he had invested heavily. Lee simply announced that on June 13 he would be leaving Philadelphia for Williamsburg. His impending departure opened the way for Jefferson's selection to the Committee of Five.[3]

If it seems odd today that Jefferson and Lee preferred to tend to state business rather than to seize the opportunity to gain immortality by writing the Declaration of Independence, it should be recalled that no one in Congress anticipated that the Declaration would long be remembered. Every delegate knew that declaring independence would be Congress's most important act, but nothing that Congress had adopted and published in the two previous years had caught the public's fancy. There was little reason to think its declaration on independence would be any different.

As two delegates on the Committee of Five had been chosen from mid-Atlantic colonies, the last member almost had to be either a Southerner from outside Virginia or a New Englander from one of the three provinces other than Massachusetts. Six delegates from the seven eligible colonies had served since the First Congress. Matthew Tilghman and Joseph Hewes were backbenchers who neither had risen to a leadership role nor were considered when crucial assignments were doled out. Maryland's Samuel Chase did not return to Congress from his trying Canadian mission until the day the Committee of Five was named. Rhode Island's Stephen Hopkins had begun his congressional career by supporting Joseph Galloway in 1774 and shrank from endorsing independence until May 1776. Twenty-six-year-old Edward Rutledge had taken a back seat in South Carolina's delegation until his older brother, John, left Congress in the autumn of 1775. When he came into his own, Edward had steadfastly opposed independence.[4] Congress, of course, was not committed to packing the Committee of Five only with those who had served since 1774, as the selection of Livingston, Franklin, and Jefferson demonstrated. But none among those who had become delegates since May 1775 especially stood out, and none overshadowed Connecticut's Roger Sherman, who had been in Congress from its first day.

Fifty-five years old in 1776, Sherman was a native of Massachusetts who had moved to Connecticut when he came of age, eventually settling in New Haven. Sherman, who had grown up in a comfortable farm family, had only a "slender" formal education, as one of his congressional colleagues put it, but he was enterprising and a quick learner. By the time he was thirty, Sherman had farmed and worked as a cobbler, spent a few years as a self-taught surveyor, speculated in frontier lands, and published an almanac. Before he turned forty, Sherman had become a lawyer, launched a potash business on the side, continued as an absentee farmer, and ultimately opened several retail shops that sold books, cloth, tea, coffee, indigo, and assorted imported goods from England. By then too he had entered public life, serving first as a selectman— or town councilman, as it would be called today in most communities—then as a member of the Connecticut assembly.

Busy as he was, Sherman found time for family life. He married at the relatively late age of twenty-nine. His first marriage lasted eleven years. Following his wife's death, he remained a widower for three years before marrying a second time. He fathered fifteen children in his two marriages.

A conservative in Connecticut's internal politics, Sherman actively resisted parliamentary taxation from the outset. He joined the protest against the Stamp Act in 1765 and never wavered in his opposition to London's policies. In 1772 he declared that it was "a fundamental principle in the British Constitution . . . that no laws bind the people but such as they consent to be governed by." By then, at least in the view of his biographer, Sherman already favored American independence. He told John Adams that his constitutional views had been shaped by the writings of James Otis, Adams's friend and legal mentor, and from the First Congress onward there was little difference in the outlook of Sherman and Adams with regard to the proper response to British policies. (That may explain why, from the day they met, Adams characterized Sherman as "a solid sensible Man.") Once the war broke out, Sherman openly embraced a hard-line position. When he learned a few weeks after

Bunker Hill that Lord North was sending massive military reinforcements to North America, Sherman declared that every colony ought to "take Government fully into their own hands."[5]

Sherman was one of three Connecticut delegates who attended the First Congress. He was the last to be chosen, picked after four others declined to serve. In some respects, Sherman was an impressive figure. At six feet tall, he towered over most of his colleagues. Despite a slender build, he was surprisingly muscular and powerful. His eyes were a sparkling bright blue-gray. Even in his fifties, he still had a full head of hair, which had not yet turned from its youthful brown to gray. Sherman wore it close-cropped, and he shunned a wig, which some of his fellow congressmen insisted on wearing.[6]

Sherman's striking attributes were counterbalanced by what many saw as shortcomings. He was conspicuously ungainly, prompting John Adams to remark that Sherman's "Air is the Reverse of Grace. There cannot be a more striking Contrast to beautiful Action." His movements," Adams added, were "Stiffness, and Awkwardness itself." He is as "Rigid as Starched Linen." A colleague from Georgia found Sherman so inelegant in his gestures and gait that he thought there was something "unaccountably strange in his manner." What is more, Sherman was unpolished as a public speaker and awkward as a conversationalist. One of his fellow deputies from Connecticut was embarrassed that Sherman was part of the delegation. He "is as badly calculated to appear in such a company [as the Continental Congress] as a chestnut bur is for an eye stone," that congressman thought. Adams noted that Sherman spoke "often and long, but very heavily and clumsily." If a fellow Yankee was put off by Sherman's manner of speaking, it is hardly surprising that others from outside New England were repelled by it. Delegates from the middle and southern colonies were annoyed by Sherman's "countrified cadence" and "strange New England cant." One congressman disdained Sherman's "vulgarisms"—his less-than-sterling grammar—which made everything that he said sound "grotesque and laughable." While Sherman's speech habits tried the patience of many, others were vexed by his pious Puritanism. He would not listen to off-color jokes, and once, when Congress was so busy that it contemplated an unheard-of Sunday session, Sherman headed off the proposed violation of the Sabbath out of "a regard for the commands of his Maker."[7]

But Sherman's failings were outweighed by his striking intelligence and consummate common sense. Adams thought that Sherman possessed "a clear Head and sound Judgment" and proclaimed that he was "one of the most sensible men in the world." A southern delegate thought that "in his train of thinking there is something regular, deep and comprehensive." Jefferson allegedly told an acquaintance that Sherman "never said a foolish thing in his life."[8]

Trumbull's Declaration of Independence. *The Committee of Five is shown presenting the draft of the Declaration of Independence to Congress. (Architect of the Capitol)*

Sherman was never a leader in Congress, but his fellow deputies respected his diligence, industry, and pragmatism. Sherman was not absent from Congress for "So much as ten Minutes" between September 1774 and September 1775. He did not take a leave of absence until November 1775, and then he remained at home only half as long as did John Adams during his year-end sabbatical. Sherman's only other absence before June 1776 came in the spring, when Congress asked him to deliver money to the authorities in Connecticut. His fellow congressmen may have looked on Sherman as inelegant and uncultivated, but they thought him dependable and assigned him to one committee after another. Before June 1776 he had served on panels created to deal with Indian affairs, raise shoes and clothing for the army, prepare instructions for the commissioners sent to Canada, and draft a statement on Lord North's hiring of foreign mercenaries. About the same time that he was chosen for the Committee of Five, Sherman was selected for the Board of War and Ordnance, a committee for overseeing affairs in the Continental army, a panel that Congress thought was as important as any it ever created.[9]

The Committee of Five did two things during its initial meetings. John Adams subsequently recalled that it first discussed the "Articles of which the

Detail from Trumbull's Declaration of Independence. *John Adams, the shortest of
the five, stands on the left. Richard Sherman is next to him. Robert R. Livingston
is in the middle. Thomas Jefferson, the tallest individual, is to Livingston's left.
Benjamin Franklin is at the far right. (Architect of the Capitol.)*

Declaration was to consist." That is, the committee pondered the general
shape and content of the document. Adams remembered that "several meetings" were required before a decision was made.[10] His memory may have
betrayed him, though it is not inconceivable that two or three sessions were
necessary to reach a consensus on, among other things, the length of the
document, the audience—or audiences—to which it was to be directed,
whether it was to be framed like a lawyer's brief, whether it should chronicle
the history of the Anglo-American dispute, how it was to legitimate revolution, and what, if anything, it should say about the future of an independent
America.

Once the committee came to an accord on the outline of the Declaration
of Independence, it agreed on who should draft the document. In his memoirs, written in 1805, and in a letter to Timothy Pickering in 1822, Adams said
not only that the committee asked him and Jefferson to form a subcommittee
and jointly write the draft but also that Jefferson appealed to him to retire to
"make the Draught." According to his two accounts, Adams said that he declined both the committee's and Jefferson's invitations on three grounds: It
would be better to have someone other than a New Englander write the
document; his "obnoxious . . . and constant Zeal" on behalf of independence
had made him many enemies, which might increase the difficulty of securing
approval of any document that he authored; and he thought Jefferson was the

superior writer. When Jefferson was an octogenarian, he learned of Adams's version of events. He provided his own account of what had transpired, telling James Madison in 1823 that the committee "pressed on myself alone to make the draught," and he consented.[11]

Memory is often weak bedrock for a historian, and particularly so when trying to decide who had the best recollection of something that had occurred nearly fifty years earlier. Some scholars have given the nod to Jefferson's recollection because Adams noted in his diary only three years after the event that "We appointed Jefferson . . . to draw it up." That might at first blush seem conclusive, except that in the same passage Adams muddied the waters by demonstrating even then that his memory of the events of June 1776 was hardly infallible. He evidently had forgotten that Sherman and Livingston had served on the committee, for in his 1779 diary entry Adams recollected that Virginia's Benjamin Harrison and a mysterious "Mr. R."—in all likelihood Edward Rutledge—were among the committee's five members.[12]

That Adams's memory was untrustworthy when it came to the Declaration of Independence imparts some weight to Jefferson's recollection. However, circumstantial evidence also lends support to Jefferson's version of events. During the previous two years, Congress had put together innumerable committees for the purpose of writing addresses, resolutions, petitions, and declarations, and the committees nearly always made a habit of selecting one member, and only one, to prepare a draft. The Committee of Five probably acted in a similar manner.

Neither Adams nor Jefferson recalled that the committee ever considered any of the three other members as a possible draftsman. It is improbable that Livingston or Sherman would have been thought of for the task. Ordinarily, Franklin would have been a candidate for authoring the document, as he had few equals as a writer. But he had only recently returned from his grueling Canadian mission and was exhausted and in poor health. When he reached Philadelphia, about ten days prior to the committee's creation, he was suffering from boils, edema, and possibly psoriasis. A few days later he fell ill with "a severe Fit of the Gout." Franklin appears to have attended the June 3 and 4 sessions of Congress, but none thereafter until July, and he may not even have attended any meetings of the Committee of Five.[13]

Assigned the task of drafting the document, Jefferson returned to his apartment at the corner of Market and Seventh streets, west of the State House, and set to work. No one could have doubted that declaring independence would be the most momentous step that Congress had ever taken, and no one presumed that the Declaration of Independence would be inconsequential.

But there is no reason to believe that Jefferson could have imagined the impact his composition would have on his contemporaries, much less how it would inspire generations in decades to come. Nor could any of Jefferson's colleagues have foreseen what would spring from his pen. While he was acknowledged to be a talented writer, nothing that Jefferson had previously authored was regarded as an unforgettable achievement.[14]

Born in 1743 at Shadwell, a plantation surrounded by the lush green hills of frontier Albemarle County, Virginia, Jefferson was the third child and first son of Peter and Jane Randolph Jefferson. Peter Jefferson was a self-made man. Obsessed with wealth and status, he had learned to survey, a trade that facilitated his slow, steady accumulation of land and slaves. In time, Peter had sufficient amounts of both to elevate him to a planter's rank, joining what passed as the aristocracy in colonial Virginia. A third-generation American, Peter had surpassed his colonial predecessors. He owned six times as much land as, and scores more slaves than, his grandfather, and he ultimately became the first in his family to sit in Virginia's House of Burgesses. But when Thomas Jefferson was only fourteen years old, Peter succumbed to one of the perilous fevers that stalked the southern landscape.

Brave, adventurous, and driven, Peter had lived long enough to acquaint his son with a masculine world that exalted ingenuity and fortitude. He taught Thomas to survey and, probably mostly by example, how to manage a plantation and its labor force. He made Thomas a good horseman and saw to it that the young man was comfortable with the outdoors, including the dense forests surrounding Shadwell. Thomas inherited his father's ambition, all-consuming materialism, and love of books and learning, but in many ways the youngster appears to have been cut from a different cloth. Thomas seems to have been more a dreamer and thinker than a doer, more at home indoors reading poetry, singing, playing the violin, and contemplating architecture.

The differences in father and son were not surprising. Whereas Peter had been self-taught, Thomas had received a formal education, and a good one. It began around age five, when he was sent to Tuckahoe, his mother's ancestral home, a sprawling estate on the James River. Thomas studied there under a tutor, after which he spent nine years in Latin schools, one on the James and another a few miles from Shadwell. He subsequently described his schooling as the happiest phase of his youth. James Maury, one of his teachers, was an Anglican minister who lavished love and attention on him, perhaps more than young Jefferson had ever received at home. Maury additionally introduced his pupil to the best scientific and literary works of the blossoming age of Enlightenment, opening to Thomas a new world of ideas and questions that challenged traditional assumptions. It was like a beacon of light that shone into his dark and dreary adolescent years.

Late in life Jefferson looked back on his youth as an unhappy time that he would not wish to repeat, a time so painful that he equated it with "colonial subservience." Thomas was proud of his father's achievements and saw him as a larger-than-life figure. He said little about his mother, though his tone hints at a relationship that he found lacking in love and affirmation. If Thomas esteemed his father, he loved Reverend Maury, who had acquainted him with the means through which he could set himself free from the real or imagined fetters of his youth.[15]

At age seventeen, Thomas had already received more schooling than most planters and was due to receive five thousand acres and more than two score slaves when he reached his majority. But he never considered terminating his education. He wanted to attend college, both because of his love of learning and because he thought a college degree was essential for his ascent in public life. In the fall of 1760 Jefferson enrolled at William and Mary College in Williamsburg, a small school that consisted of two buildings on a leafy campus. The college may not have been physically impressive, but in the quarter century between 1750 and the Revolutionary War, it graduated two United States congressmen, a chief justice of the U.S. Supreme Court, a renowned political theorist, an Anglican bishop, numerous Virginia assemblymen, and Thomas Jefferson. Once in college, Jefferson traveled further down the road that Maury had opened to him. He described himself as a "hard student" who was enjoying "the passion of my life." His classmates thought him obsessive, as he studied several hours each day and, unlike them, could rarely be tugged from his books to the gaming table or other diversions. At least some of the seven faculty members appear to have regarded him as one of the best students they encountered. The school's most distinguished professor, William Small, took Jefferson under his wing and introduced him to the governor and lieutenant governor of Virginia, as well as to George Wythe, a local attorney who some thought possessed the best legal mind in the colony.[16]

Jefferson graduated after two years, half the time it had taken Samuel and John Adams to complete their studies at Harvard, and immediately began a legal apprenticeship under Wythe. He planned to enter public life and saw the law as essential if he was to have a chance to become a notable public official. Living with Wythe in Williamsburg some of the time, otherwise studying on his own at Shadwell, Jefferson obtained his license to practice law in three years. He came to love Wythe, calling him his "beloved mentor and . . . most affectionate friend" and saying that no one else had a more "salutary influence on the course of my life." But Jefferson never demon-

strated a fondness for practicing law. Though he rapidly established a successful practice—it had taken John Adams several years to garner as many clients
as Jefferson had in his first year—Jefferson was uncomfortable addressing
judges and juries, did not find the law to be intellectually stimulating, and
grew contemptuous of most lawyers. He described lawyers as a "disagreeable
crowd" that, like parasites, subsisted off the greed and malice of others. He
practiced law for seven years, largely because his earnings facilitated his avid
consumerism.[17]

Jefferson's dissatisfaction with practicing law came about in some measure because he had never aspired to a lifelong legal career. He had always
looked on the law as a means to other ends: to further his political ambitions or perhaps to facilitate his expensive tastes. In addition, his legal career coincided with another dark, melancholy phase of his life, a period
about which he could find nothing good to say in the brief memoirs that he
penned much later. Twenty-four years old when he opened his legal practice,
Jefferson was single and living a solitary existence in remote Albemarle
County. Most of his classmates had married when they graduated from college
several years earlier, and Jefferson was openly envious of them. Profoundly shy
and socially awkward, he had failed in his one attempt at courtship while in
college.

Bewitched by sixteen-year-old Rebecca Burwell, who lived at her uncle's
estate near Williamsburg, the nineteen-year-old Jefferson apparently wished
to ask her to marry him. He attempted to propose on two separate occasions,
but floundered badly each time. On his first attempt, he said, he was overcome by a "strange confusion" that rendered him able only to stammer "a few
broken sentences . . . interrupted with pauses of uncommon length." On his
second try, Jefferson told Rebecca that he wanted to marry but that matrimony would have to wait until he returned from England in perhaps eighteen
months or two years. Curiously, there is no indication that Jefferson planned
a trip to England. That he was in love is beyond dispute; he evidently wanted
to postpone marriage until he had completed his legal studies and had an active practice. But Jefferson could not bring himself to admit that to Rebecca,
possibly fearing she would spurn his proposal if confronted with what might
be a long and indeterminate wait. As it turned out, Rebecca refused his fum-
bling proposal and within a short time was engaged to another man, whom
she married in 1764.[18]

After losing Rebecca, Jefferson made no attempt at courtship for eight years.
Immersed in his studies, distracted by the launching of his legal practice, and
perhaps fearing both rejection and commitment, Jefferson remained with-
drawn and reclusive during long stretches between 1762 and 1770. Embittered

by Rebecca's rebuff, which he acknowledged had shattered his dreams, a growing misogyny appeared to take hold of him for a time.[19] Nevertheless, he continued to crave the warmth and happiness that a family could bring, the very comforts that he had found lacking in his youth.

As painful as these years were, Jefferson was never dysfunctional. He completed his legal training, established a flourishing legal practice, undertook the construction of Monticello—his own mansion, which he planned for a hilltop within sight of Shadwell—and in 1768 was elected to fill the seat his father had once occupied in the House of Burgesses. Jefferson's life was coming together. Some fifteen months after he entered the assembly, he was "touched by heaven," as he put it.[20] He met and began to court Martha Skelton, a twenty-one-year-old widow who lived with her wealthy planter father at the Forest, a plantation near Williamsburg. Like many shy men, Jefferson may have fallen in love with the first woman who took notice of him, but it is just as likely that, with his personal affairs at last in order, he felt at liberty for the first time to fall in love. Family members, and some who worked at Monticello, described Martha as "pretty," a slight, graceful, shapely woman of medium height with auburn hair and large, vivid eyes. As was true of her suitor, Martha was musically inclined, intelligent, and well read. She exhibited a pleasant demeanor and struck everyone as a good conversationalist. Her appeal was enhanced by her experience in managing a plantation and by her wealth.[21] Thomas and Martha were married on New Year's Day 1772. Jefferson was twenty-eight, rather old for matrimony by eighteenth-century standards, but not unusually so for an ambitious man who had set his sights on going places. Washington, Samuel Adams, and John Adams had each married at nearly the same age.

Jefferson had completed two terms of the Burgesses by the time he married and had shown promise that one day he would play a leading role in the assembly. His education and remarkable intellect were obvious attributes, and he literally stood out physically. At six feet two inches in height, he towered six inches or more above most assemblymen. Slender, with sinewy arms and legs, Jefferson had sandy-red hair and struck others as pleasant-looking, if not exactly handsome. But what many observers first noticed, aside from his height and exceptional intellect, was his poor posture and somewhat awkward manner. One onlooker commented on his lack of "external grace," and another said that Jefferson reminded him "of a tall, large-boned farmer."

Jefferson's greatest obstacle to success as a legislator stemmed from his reserved demeanor. Some of his more gregarious colleagues thought him cold and unfriendly, though Jefferson worked hard to be "considerate to all persons." In time, most of his fellow assemblymen appear to have come to see him as kind, gentle, and affectionate. When Jefferson grew comfortable with an acquaintance, he relaxed and was more open, so that in time his associates found him to be a provocative and humorous conversationalist. But Jefferson could never overcome his innate shyness. He shrank from the backslapping and bonhomie that was second nature to the most successful legislators. Aware of his defects as a public speaker, he rarely joined in the floor debates in the legislature. He may have been self-conscious of his voice, described by a female observer as "femininely soft and gentle" and by numerous others as weak and barely audible. Whatever held him back, no one remembered Jefferson being a frequent participant in the give-and-take among the assembly-men. Nor did anyone recall ever hearing him deliver a rousing speech.[22]

Jefferson appears to have remained a secondary figure in the Burgesses until the eve of the American Revolution. His shortcomings as a legislator had something to do with this, but the distractions in his private life were more responsible. He and Martha had two children prior to the outbreak of the Revolutionary War, though only one, Patsy, lived beyond infancy. Jefferson was a doting father and loving husband, a man who found marriage to be as blissful as he had imagined it would be. He abandoned his legal career, hoping to spend more time at home with his family. Jefferson was so content that, had the Anglo-American crisis somehow been peacefully resolved, he might have been content to play only an insubstantial role as a legislator. Living at Monticello, raising his family, reading books, playing music, and from time to time writing an essay for publication might have been sufficient for his happiness.

But Jefferson entered public life during a troubled time, taking his seat in the Burgesses during the Townshend Duties crisis. In 1772, his fifth year as a legislator, he joined with Patrick Henry and Richard Henry Lee in a campaign to link the colonies with committees of correspondence. It was the first sign that he aspired to play a greater role as a legislator. By the next year he chaired one of the six major committees in the assembly, an essential step on the road to becoming a leading assemblyman.[23]

By then his views on Anglo-American relations had taken shape. Jefferson's surviving papers from the early 1770s, though spare to be sure, suggest that above all he was concerned that the autonomy of the colonists was being "circumscribed within narrow limits" and that London was bent on compelling Americans "to direct all labors in subservience to her [Great Britain's] interests."[24] He was doubtless thinking of the dangers threatened by parliamentary taxation, but as a large land holder, tobacco grower and exporter, and slave owner—his "family," as he was wont to say, included some 175 slaves by 1774—Jefferson's economic interests sometimes suffered in the face of imperial policies.

Like Washington, Jefferson was distressed by London's failure to open the lands west of the mountains that had been wrested from France in the Treaty of Paris. In addition, as was true of all tobacco planters, he was compelled by Parliament's trade laws to export his crop solely to British markets. Tobacco prices suffered after 1750 and many planters attributed their woes to the lack of free markets. Virginia's planters were convinced that, had they been able to trade in Europe and elsewhere, the value of their tobacco crops, and their earnings, would have increased. Jefferson did not address that issue directly, but he spoke heatedly of forces beyond the control of Virginia's planters. He also alluded to royal officials who "might sweep away the whole of my little fortune."[25]

Faced with distressed markets, many planters additionally found themselves in possession of an oversupply of bondsmen. In 1772 the House of Burgesses voted unanimously to petition the Crown to disallow the Atlantic slave trade, a move aimed at producing shortages of slaves in Georgia and South Carolina, where rice—and slavery—flourished. If the imperial authorities consented, Virginia would be able to sell its excess slaves to the low-country South. But George III refused to play along. The Crown not only turned a deaf ear to Virginia's petition; it also vetoed acts passed in 1767 and 1769 by the House of Burgesses that would have stopped slave imports into the Old Dominion. The king's actions prompted one planter to exclaim that never before had Virginians felt such a "galling yoke of dependence." Jefferson sensed that and something else as well. The king's conduct, he thought, demonstrated with crystal clarity that the Crown preferred England's slave merchants "to the lasting interests of the American states."[26]

Jefferson's sense of how the policies of a faraway British government damaged his personal interests was filtered through his understanding of Enlightenment liberalism, the law, and the history of English government. From reading John Locke and English Whigs who had produced a remarkable abundance of radical tracts two or three generations earlier, Jefferson came to think of England as a decaying and corrupt land drifting toward tyranny. Already persuaded that England had been defiled for centuries by a feudal monarchical system, Jefferson by 1774 was convinced that not only did the mother country threaten to contaminate America but also that London schemed to reduce "a free and happy People to a Wretched & miserable state of slavery."[27] On the eve of the First Continental Congress, Jefferson said that he hoped the colonies could "establish union" with Great Britain "on a generous plan," a remark that suggests that he already believed the traditional terms of the Anglo-American union to be obsolete.[28]

Jefferson played an important role in Virginia's radical activities in 1774.

When Governor Dunmore prorogued the House of Burgesses in the spring, in retaliation for its resolutions denouncing the Coercive Acts, the legislators met defiantly in the Apollo Tavern—a few steps down dusty Duke of Glouces-ter Street from the capitol—and urged a national congress. It also agreed to meet again in August to select the delegates to the conclave, if the other colo-nies had by then consented to such a body. Jefferson might have been in-cluded in Virginia's delegation to the First Congress, but while en route to the August assembly session, he fell ill with either a migraine or a cluster head-ache, which sent him to bed for several days. (Jefferson had suffered his first such agonizing headache eleven years earlier, when he learned of Rebecca Burwell's engagement. Over the years the affliction recurred in moments of great tension and anxiety until his retirement from public life in 1809, after which he never again endured another debilitating headache.)[29]

Earlier in the torrid summer of 1774, Jefferson had written a lengthy set of instructions—in reality, a learned essay—for the guidance of Virginia's dele-gates. In all likelihood, he hoped that his composition would lead to his inclu-sion in Virginia's delegation to Congress. The Virginia Convention spurned his ideas as too radical, but friends published what he had written as a pam-phlet titled *A Summary View of the Rights of British America*.

Much that Jefferson wrote had been said by others. But he went further than most pamphleteers in elaborating how the colonists had founded, main-tained, and expanded their provinces without British help. Jefferson also ad-vanced the unique argument that the Americans had chosen to be part of Great Britain through their voluntary consent. Nor had they ever relinquished their rights as freeborn Englishmen. He wrote in a graceful, flowing manner, reminiscent of Dickinson's in *Letters from a Farmer*, and with a refreshing brevity that few could equal. Although Jefferson missed the First Congress, his *Summary View* was widely read before war broke out, establishing his reputa-tion as a literary craftsman. John Adams, for instance, called it "a very hand-some public Paper" that gave Jefferson "the Character of a fine Writer."[30]

Virginia sent the same delegation back to Philadelphia for the Second Congress in May 1775, but Peyton Randolph returned home after only two weeks, preferring to preside over the provincial assembly rather than to serve as the president of Congress. Chosen by his fellow legislators as Randolph's replacement, Jefferson hurried northward in June 1775 to take his seat. In mid-June he arrived in Philadelphia in an expensive carriage drawn by two horses and attended by two slaves.[31]

Jefferson was no different as a congressman than he had been as a Virginia assemblyman. He rarely entered the floor debates—Adams later said that he never heard Jefferson "utter three Sentences together" in Congress—but he was less inhibited as a member of small committees, where his associates found him to be "frank, explicit, and decisive."[32] Nonetheless, his colleagues did not see much of him. Jefferson had been in Congress only six weeks when it recessed at the beginning of August 1775. After a month in Virginia, he returned to Philadelphia and served from early October until late December, when, like numerous other delegates, he asked for a leave to return home. He planned on remaining with Martha for about ninety days, more than twice the time spent at home that winter by most congressmen, but Jefferson's absence was considerably longer than he had anticipated. Late in March he fell ill with another excruciating headache, brought on perhaps by his mother's death on March 31 or by anxiety over his imminent departure. He did not leave Monticello for five more weeks, finally taking up his seat in Congress again in mid-May. On this occasion, he made the long trip from Albemarle County on horseback attended only by fourteen-year-old Robert Hemings, his personal servant, or body slave.[33] Within three weeks of his return to Philadelphia, Jefferson sat down to compose the Declaration of Independence.[34]

Jefferson had moved to a new residence when he returned to Philadelphia. Previously, he had lived on the east side of downtown, but he was bothered by the city's "excessive heats" in the summer, finding Philadelphia far hotter and stickier than his remote hilltop in Virginia. He was now lodged on the second floor of the three-story, red brick home owned by Jacob Graff, a successful mason. The apartment was not only cooler but also, with a bedroom and parlor, larger.[35]

Jefferson's residence in Philadelphia when he wrote the Declaration of Independence. Owned by Jacob Graff, and situated at Seventh and Market, Jefferson lodged here between May and August 1776. He drafted the Declaration of Independence in his two-room parlor on the second story. (Drawing from John T. Scharf and Thompson Westcott's History of Philadelphia, *1884.)*

Jefferson likely began writing the draft of the Declaration on Wednesday or Thursday, June 12 or 13. Accustomed to rising early, he probably worked in the relative coolness of early morning. He may also have taken up his pen again in the evening, when the traffic beneath his windows faded and an occasional night breeze stirred. It is conceivable too that he skipped some sessions of Congress and worked through the day. Lee, with Wythe in tow, had left for home, but four other members of Virginia's delegation were present, affording Jefferson the luxury of staying away if he chose to do so.

Only two things are known for certain about Jefferson's work on the draft: He wrote it while seated in a revolving Windsor chair with a small, folding writing desk placed across his lap, both of which had been custom-made for him by a Philadelphia cabinetmaker.[36] And he delivered the draft quickly. Adams later recalled that only "a day or two" was required for Jefferson to complete the task.[37] While Adams may not have meant for his comment to be taken literally, Jefferson was ordinarily a rapid writer.

On a "Friday morn" Jefferson sent a copy of the draft to Franklin—he addressed it to "Doctr. Franklyn"—and asked that he "suggest such alterations as his more enlarged view of the subject will dictate." By then, Jefferson had already shown Adams what he had written.[38] Thus, in all probability Jefferson completed his draft within three to five days and gave it to Adams sometime between Monday, June 17, and Wednesday, June 19. Jefferson probably transmitted the draft document to Franklin on Friday, June 21.

Years later Adams, consumed with jealousy at the laurels Jefferson had reaped as the author of the Declaration of Independence, carped that the document was "a juvenile declamation" that merely rehashed what others had said. There was "not an idea in it, but what had been hackneyed in Congress for two years before." But Adams had forgotten that neither he nor his colleagues on the committee or in Congress wanted Jefferson to write something novel. It would have been ludicrous to have done so. Jefferson correctly understood, as he put it years later, that his task was to avoid "aiming at originality of principle or sentiment." He was to prepare a draft that captured the "tone and spirit" of "the American mind" toward the mother country's imperial policies and the king's decision to make war on them. Along these same lines the document had to make clear why Congress, which had repeatedly insisted that it was not bent on independence, was indeed declaring independence. Within these parameters, Jefferson subsequently said, he merely sought to avoid copying "from any particular and previous writing."[39]

As the draft sprang from Jefferson's pen, it became clear that the Declaration of Independence was to be more than simply a justification of revolution. It need not have been. The English Declaration of Rights, with which Jefferson and every educated colonist was familiar, began with "Whereas" and proceeded to list the charges against the king, James II. When Adams, a month earlier, had written the resolution directing the colonies to abandon their charters and create new, independent governments, he had begun: "Whereas his Britannic Majesty, in conjunction with the Lords and Commons of Great-Britain, has . . . ," followed by a compilation of the wrongdoings by Britain's leaders during the past decade. That Jefferson's draft did not follow those models may have been his unique contribution to the eventual Declaration of Independence. Or, it may have been the result of the instructions provided by the Committee of Five. For instance, in his private correspondence near the time the committee first met, Adams had fervently declared that an independent America must embrace "a more equal Liberty, than has prevail'd in other Parts of the Earth" and must repudiate hereditary rule by the "Dons, the Bashaws, the Grandees, the Patricians, the Sachems, the Nabobs, call them by what Name you please," but in short, the "insolent Domination, in a few, a very few opulent, monopolizing Families."[40] He and others on the committee may have instructed Jefferson to go beyond merely amassing charges of British despotism and to delineate the meaning of the American Revolution.

Jefferson's draft included two segments that consciously sought to do more than merely justify the break with Great Britain. Jefferson penned a draft that enunciated in the broadest terms the principles upon which the new nation would stand and around which its citizenry could rally. After all, until recently, the colonists had considered themselves to be British, but those feelings had evaporated. Furthermore, the colonists identified first and foremost with their province and hardly, if at all, with the Continental Congress or the concept of an American Union. But the "united colonies" were about to become the "United States." Jefferson's draft, therefore, was meant not only to bring to a close America's days as colonies of another nation, but to also announce the creation of the American nation.

This was also meant to be a war document. The meaning it gave to the American Revolution should foster a willingness to fight for the new nation and the resplendent ideals for which it stood, while at the same time sustain morale on the home front throughout a lengthy war. However, this document was not to be directed solely at the American citizenry. Its audience included "mankind" in a "candid world," and none more so than America's friends in Great Britain who might someday play a useful role in the termination of hostilities and recognition of the United States. The draft referred to "our British brethren" who had long been remarkable for their "native justice & magnanimity," and especially those among them who had been "our common kindred" in opposing the measures of Lord North's ministry. As declaring independence at this juncture was due in large measure to the need for foreign assistance, the document was of course directed toward those nations in Europe that might trade or ally with America. (The minute that the Declaration was adopted and printed, the Committee of Secret Correspondence sent a copy to Silas Deane in Paris with instructions that he not only see to its publication in French newspapers but also "communicate the piece to the Court of France, and send copies of it to the other Courts of Europe." Congress additionally ordered that the Declaration "be proclaimed . . . at the head of the army.")[41]

Very little in Jefferson's draft was changed before the document was submitted to Congress. Adams appears to have made two alterations and Franklin five, all dealing with phraseology. For example, "his present majesty" was changed to "the present king of Great Britain." Jefferson subsequently remarked that no changes were made by the Committee of Five, but it seems unlikely that Sherman and Livingston would not have suggested at least one or two alterations. Altogether, sixteen slight modifications were made to the original draft during the roughly ten days between Jefferson's completion of his task and the document's presentation to Congress.[42] Some of the changes may have been made by Jefferson himself. Like any good author who is never satisfied with what he has written, Jefferson may have been unable to resist the temptation to tinker with his handiwork. Or, he may have been responding to oral suggestions that were made at the one or more committee meetings that were held, and some of these recommendations may have been made by Livingston or Sherman. But what is abundantly clear is that the document submitted to Congress was almost exclusively the work of Jefferson.

Jefferson had drawn on several sources, including the English Whig polemicists he had read in his youth. He was familiar with the sentiments of his fellow congressmen, even having taken copious notes on what they said in the debates on independence on June 8 and 10. He was familiar with the Declaration of Rights enacted by the First Congress, a statement that both enumerated the rights enjoyed by all freeborn Englishmen and laid out America's prewar complaints. Since the commencement of hostilities, Congress had adopted two statements that explained in detail the colonists' grievances. Jefferson had been one of the authors of the Declaration on the Causes and Necessity of Taking Up Arms, and he was intimately familiar with Adams's May 10 resolution on jettisoning charter governments.[43] Jefferson was additionally conversant with some of the pamphlet literature produced by

American protestors since the Stamp Act, and he was acquainted with at least some of the declarations on independence promulgated since March by several provincial congresses and local committees of safety.

However, nothing influenced Jefferson more than the draft of Virginia's Declaration of Rights. It had been submitted to the Virginia Convention in May and was published in a Philadelphia newspaper on the day after the Committee of Five was created. The language of a portion of the Virginia document foreshadowed what Jefferson wrote. It stated, among other things, that "all men are born equally free and independent, and have certain inherent natural rights . . . among which are the enjoyment of life and liberty, with the means of acquiring and possessing property, and pursuing and obtaining happiness and safety." It additionally stated that "all power is vested in, and . . . derived from the people," and that the purpose of government was to secure the people's "greatest degree of happiness and safety." But if the government "shall be found inadequate or contrary to these purposes . . . a majority of the community hath an indubitable, unalienable and indefeasible right to reform, alter, or abolish it."[44]

Jefferson's draft included four sections. The preface consisted of a seldom-remembered though important introductory paragraph. It hinted that America's dependent status had been temporary. The time had arrived "to dissolve the political bands" that had tied the colonists to Great Britain and "to assume among the powers of the earth the separate and equal station to which the laws of nature and nature's god entitle them."[45]

Beginning with a melodic encapsulation of the natural rights of humankind, Jefferson proceeded with a lyrical but forceful affirmation of the right of revolution:

> We hold these truths to be self-evident; that all men are created equal; that they are endowed by their Creator with inherent and inalienable rights; that among these are life, liberty, and the pursuit of happiness; that to secure these rights, governments are instituted among men, deriving their just powers from the consent of the governed; that whenever any form of government becomes destructive of these ends, it is the right of the people to alter or to abolish it, and to institute new government, laying it's foundation on such principles, and organising it's powers in such form as to them shall seem most likely to effect their safety and happiness. prudence indeed will dictate that governments long established should not be changed for light & transient causes, and accordingly all experience hath shewn that mankind are more disposed to suffer, while evils are sufferable, than

to right themselves by abolishing the forms to which they are accustomed. but when a long train of abuses and usurpations, begun at a distinguished period, & pursuing invariably the same object, evinces a design to reduce them under absolute despotism, it is their right, it is their duty, to throw off such government, & to provide new guards for their future security.

Jefferson was clearly using the draft of Virginia's Declaration of Rights as a template, though he improved it stylistically. With one exception, he adhered to it faithfully. Virginia's statement enumerated the natural rights of humankind as including life, liberty, and property. Jefferson did not mention property. It has been conjectured that Jefferson may have sought to simplify the long and cumbersome phraseology of his Virginia friends.[46] But as this was a war document, Jefferson must have understood that in a protracted conflict—which by June 1776 looked increasingly likely—the military service of nonproperty owners would be an unavoidable necessity. Jefferson probably deliberately sought to say that this was a revolution in which all free Americans, not just those who owned property, had a stake.[47]

Jefferson's lengthiest section was a bill of indictment cataloging the despotic design of Britain's rulers. He levied twenty-one accusations of illegal and tyrannical behavior against George III, shameful actions that unmasked the "character" of this man and revealed him as "unfit to be the ruler of a people." Although Parliament was never mentioned by name—Jefferson alluded to it as "their legislature," differentiating it from America's legislatures—he charged it with nine additional despotic acts. Somewhat vaguely, Jefferson grouped the charges: He commenced with allegations that the king had refused to govern or to permit the colonists to govern themselves properly; next, he stressed how the rulers in London had violated the rights of the colonists; and finally, he charged the Crown with violence and cruelty toward the colonists.[48]

He began with a vague accusation. The monarch, he wrote, had "refused his assent to laws the most wholesome and necessary for the public good." That was probably a reference to the Privy Council's disallowance of some 5 percent of laws passed by colonial assemblies during the 150 years of colonial subservience, but Jefferson must also have had in mind the Crown's rejection of the three Virginia laws passed since the 1760s that would have forbidden the further importation of African slaves. So that no one misunderstood, he later specifically arraigned the king for having waged "cruel war against human nature itself" by having refused to stop the Atlantic slave trade. Jefferson did not mention the most famous complaint of the colonists—"imposing taxes on us without our consent"—until he had arraigned king or Parliament on sixteen other charges. Parliament's claim to have the authority to "legislate for us in all cases whatsoever" was twenty-second on his list.

Despite all the heated debates in Congress over Parliament's power to regulate American commerce, Jefferson was silent on that score. However, he wrote that London had "sent hither swarms of officers to harass our people," an illusion in part to the increase in customs officials after 1765. The Coercive Acts were condemned in several separate items in the list, as was the Quartering Act, American Prohibitory Act, Quebec Act, and the Crown's efforts during the past several years to eliminate an independent judiciary in the colonies. The king was also charged with keeping a standing army in America in peacetime, making war on the colonists, burning its towns, inciting Indians to go on the warpath, and hiring foreign mercenaries. For having fomented slave insurrections, Jefferson in effect branded George III a war criminal, writing that he had enticed "those very people to rise in arms among us, and to purchase that liberty of which he has deprived them, by murdering" their masters and other colonists.[49] Jefferson additionally took aim at the monarch for having "endeavored to prevent the population of these states," a reference to parliamentary legislation in 1773, which restricted emigration to the colonies.[50]

No charge brought by Jefferson was composed in a more impassioned manner than his arraignment of the king for his complicity in the African slave trade and for his allegedly having imposed slavery on the colonists. Jefferson wrote that the king had enslaved "a distant people, who never offended him, captivating and carrying them into slavery in another hemisphere, or to incur miserable death in their transportation thither." By engaging in "this piratical warfare," Britain's monarch had acted as an "*infidel*" ruler, not as "the *Christian* king of Great Britain." Furthermore, he had disallowed "every legislative attempt to prohibit or to restrain this execrable commerce." If this "assemblage of horrors" was not sufficient, the king was "now . . . exciting those very people to rise in arms among us, and to purchase that liberty of which he has deprived them, by murdering" the American colonists.

Every colonist who supported the rebellion, and every member of Congress, would have applauded the final charge on Jefferson's list: "In every stage of these oppressions, we have petitioned for redress in the most humble terms; our repeated petitions have been answered only by repeated injury."

The final section contained Lee's resolution on independence, although to it Jefferson added a flourish of rhetoric: "these states, reject and renounce all allegiance and subjection to the kings of Great Britain, & . . . we utterly dissolve all political connection between us and . . . Great Britain. . . . [W]e do assert and declare these colonies to be free & independent states" that now "have full power . . . to do all [the] acts and things which independent states may of right do."[51]

Jefferson and the Committee of Five faced a precise and pressing deadline. The document they were to write was to be submitted by July 1, only twenty days after the committee's creation. As some time was spent discussing the nature of the document and selecting a draftsman, and as there were three Sabbath days between them and their target date, the document's author and his colleagues had only some fourteen to sixteen working days in which to complete the task. They succeeded. Once the draft was "approved by them [the committee]," Jefferson noted in an offhand manner in the terse log of proceedings that he kept, "I reported it to the house on Friday the 28th of June when it was read and ordered to lie on the table"—that is, not to be considered by Congress—until the following Monday, July 1.[52]

At the time the Declaration of Independence was submitted, the floodgates for independence had fully opened. By then, two thirds of the towns in Massachusetts had urged a final break with Great Britain, usually by a unanimous vote.[53] Connecticut, New Hampshire, and Delaware had authorized their congressmen to vote for independence, though the latter—like North Carolina two months earlier—had not actually mentioned the word. It simply authorized its delegates to act with others to secure American "liberty, safety, and interests." During the third week in June, New Jersey instructed its delegates to make "the United Colonies independent of *Great Britain*," prompting a member of its assembly to remark that "We are passing the Rubicon and our Delegates in Congress . . . will vote plump"—that is, one and all would vote for independence. New Jersey even elected five new congressmen, replacing the delegation that in mid-May had voted against Congress's resolution excoriating royal government in the colonies. The new congressmen were "all independent souls," remarked a member of the New Jersey Provincial Congress. Maryland likewise freed its congressmen to vote for independence, taking that step on the very day that the Committee of Five submitted the draft Declaration to Congress.[54]

The proponents of independence had always regarded Pennsylvania as the major stumbling block to congressional unanimity in the battle for American independence. But it too came around in June, though an internal political revolution unlike that in any other province was needed. As intended, Congress's May 15 recommendation that the colonies adopt governments equal to the exigencies of the times lit the fuse for the final explosion in Pennsylvania. Within twenty-four hours of Congress's action, radicals in Philadelphia summoned a mass meeting on May 20. Taking "the sense of the people," this meeting of some four thousand Philadelphians, who gathered in the rain on the State House lawn, not only called for a constitutional convention; it loudly, and "with great Unanimity," condemned the Pennsylvania assembly's instructions forbidding its congressmen from voting for independence. Fighting to escape extinction, the assembly at last caved in, withdrawing the instructions that Dickinson had crafted for the congressional delegation six months earlier. On June 8, by a three-to-one margin, the Pennsylvania assembly authorized its congressmen to vote for whatever they believed was essential for securing American liberty and safety. Two weeks later an extralegal Conference of Committees, meeting at Carpenters' Hall to plan for the election of the constitutional convention, voted its "willingness to concur in a vote of the congress, declaring the united colonies free and independent states." By late June, therefore, Pennsylvania's congressmen had two sets of instructions. Each sanctioned a vote for independence.[55]

On the day before Congress was scheduled to take up the question of independence, Francis Lightfoot Lee wrote to his brother Richard Henry in Williamsburg that "Our affairs in Canada are . . . brot to a conclusion." All American troops had "retire[d] out of the Country," leaving the colonies to "contend with all the bad consequences" that must flow from Britain's possession of Canada, including what he thought was the likelihood of imminent assaults on Crown Point and Ticonderoga. To his "dismal Acct," Lee added that word had just reached Philadelphia that Howe's invasion flotilla had been spotted off the coast of New York. It was a massive fleet, the largest expeditionary force that Great Britain had ever assembled, or would muster again until World Wars I and II. One New Yorker described what he saw as "a forest of masts," some 130 vessels bearing a portion of the huge force that Lord North had gathered after learning of the colonists' armed resistance at Concord and along Battle Road.[56]

There was no sign of panic in Congress. The American forces had been routed in Canada, but most believed the poor showing had been uncharacteristic. The Canadian campaign had been "thrown away . . . in a most Scandalous Manner," one remarked, probably thinking of the poor leadership exhibited by Wooster, Sullivan, and Schuyler, and also probably speaking for most of his congressional colleagues. Congress devoted more attention to the looming battle for New York. Most were optimistic, confident of Washington's abilities and also buoyed by the realization that the British forces would not have the numerical superiority they had enjoyed in Canada in May and

June. Many also believed, as did John Adams, that the war was "in all . . .
Probability . . . in its Infancy." America would have many advantages in a
protracted war, especially if France provided assistance.[57]

Independence first had to be declared, of course, and the "grand question,"
as one congressman referred to it, was scheduled for debate on July 1. The
proponents of independence were confident. On the day that Jefferson submitted his draft, North Carolina's Joseph Hewes predicted that Congress
would declare independence "by a great Majority." John Adams felt that most
understood that the realities of war demanded that "we . . . must be independent states," though he knew that "Still Objections are made to a Declaration
of it." In fact, at that same moment, Edward Rutledge remained confident
that he and his fellow foes of independence might prevail. It "will depend in a
great Measure," he thought, "upon the Exertions of the Honest and sensible
part of the Members" of Congress.[58]

CHAPTER 13

"MAY HEAVEN PROSPER THE NEW BORN REPUBLIC"

SETTING AMERICA FREE

JOHN ADAMS HAD WAITED for this day for a very long time, at least since April 1775, when the war began, and probably since the summer of 1773, when he read Thomas Hutchinson's purloined letters sent to Boston by Franklin. It was Monday, July 1, 1776, the day Congress had designated for a resumption of the debate on independence.

Adams rose early, as was his custom. Before leaving for the State House, he wrote to Archibald Bulloch, a Georgian who had been in Congress in the fall of 1775 but who had returned to Savannah to become chief executive of the provincial convention (his title was "President of Georgia"). "This morning is assigned for the greatest Debate of all," Adams told his former colleague. Congress was to consider a "Declaration that these Colonies are free and independent States, and this day or Tomorrow is to determine its Fate," said Adams, who could barely hide his exhilaration. He expected Congress to decide in favor of independence. In fact, Adams wrote to Bulloch as if Congress had already made its decision: "May Heaven prosper, the new born Republic,—and make it more glorious than any former Republic has been."[1]

During the past few weeks Adams had rejoiced at his "ride in the Whirlwind," as he put it. From the moment in February that Congress learned of the American Prohibitory Act, he had sensed a dramatic shift in the mood of many of his fellow deputies. "We are not in a very submissive Mood," Adams said at the time, adding that he believed "We are hastening rapidly to great Events." Throughout the spring he had seen abundant signs that the residents of Philadelphia shared the outlook of most members of Congress. Local military units paraded and drilled almost daily in the city's streets, and the St. George's Day Festival, an English holiday that had been celebrated every April 23 for as long as anyone could remember, had been canceled in 1776. Adams's barber, John Byrne, was the source of much of his information about the sentiments of ordinary Philadelphians. A "little dapper fellow" with an "active and lively, Tongue as fluent and voluble as you please," Byrne frequented the city's grog shops every evening and the next morning, while shaving Adams, related what he had heard. Before April ended he was telling Adams that nearly every Philadelphian was "zealous on the side of America."[2]

Adams believed that Congress's mid-May vote to scrap all provincial governments that derived their authority from the Crown had been "the last Step" before a formal declaration of independence. It indicated that thirteen "mighty Revolutions"—one in each colony—were under way, upheavals that had "sett many violent Passions at Work. Hope, Fear, Joy, Sorrow, Love, Hatred, Malice, Envy, Revenge, Jealousy, Ambition, Avarice, Resentment, Gratitude, and every other Passion, Feeling, Sentiment, Principle and Imagination."[3] All those emotions, and more, Adams appeared to be saying, were driving Americans toward the final break with their mother country.

Jefferson also wrote a letter early on the morning of July 1, to an old college chum, William Fleming, a judge in Virginia. Unlike Adams, Jefferson dwelled almost exclusively on the worrisome military situation. He was troubled by the debacle in Canada and Howe's imminent landing in New York, and he urged Fleming to play an active role "to keep up the spirits of the people" in Virginia in the face of news of further adversity, which he thought likely.[4] Before leaving his apartment for the State House, Jefferson devoted some time to another committee assignment. He took notes on an interview with a Montreal merchant who had passed on word that most inhabitants of Canada hoped that the thirteen colonies achieved their goals in the war with Great Britain.[5]

Other congressmen were writing home too. The war made New Hampshire's Josiah Bartlett anxious. The setback in Canada and the imminent campaign in New York made Bartlett, long a supporter of independence, believe more than ever that the break with Great Britain could not be delayed. The moment had come to push the reconciliationists aside, close ranks behind the establishment of the United States, and seek foreign assistance. He thought, "we are now Come to the time that requires harmony, together with all the wisdom, prudence, Courage, & resolution we are masters of to ward off the Evils intended by our implacable Enemies." It was time to save the "Grand American Cause." North Carolina's John Penn could not have agreed more. July 1, he told a friend at home, would go down in history as a "remarkable" day, as "Independence will be ajitated" and declared. He added that he prayed that "things may answer our expectations after we are Independent."[6] John Dickinson was also up early on the morning of July 1. He was about to make his last stand in the Continental Congress.

* * *

The temperature on Jefferson's thermometer had already climbed into the mid-eighties by nine A.M. It was going to be oppressively hot and humid, the sort of sticky summer day in Philadelphia that congressional veterans had come to dread. As usual, some delegates were at work well before Congress was gaveled to order. In the creeping light of early morning, John Adams left Sarah Yard's stone boardinghouse at Walnut and Second, where he and all the other Massachusetts delegates had resided for the past year, and in all likelihood crossed the street to the City Tavern for breakfast with a handful of his colleagues. From there, he walked three blocks west to the State House, where sometime after eight he met with the Board of War. But at ten A.M. Adams and some forty-five fellow deputies were in the congressional chamber when John Hancock climbed the dais to start that day's session.[7]

Despite the air of anticipation that must have permeated the room, Congress first tended to its daily business. Numerous letters and papers from Generals Washington, Schuyler, Ward, Arnold, Sullivan, and Andrew Lewis—an old Indian fighter from Virginia who in March had been named a brigadier general—were read. Dispatches from two colonels who were with the army that had retreated from Canada were introduced, as was a report by the army's paymaster in the Southern Department. Communications from the New Hampshire and New Jersey assemblies came next, followed by a reading of Maryland's resolution—adopted the previous Friday—that freed its delegation to "concur with . . . a majority" of the other delegations "in declaring the United Colonies free and independent States." Congress then voted to permit brigadier generals to have aides-de-camp. It was just about to proceed to the question of independence when another letter from Washington, written on Saturday, arrived and was read. The commander broke the news that the militia was slow to come in, adding that he hoped their tardiness would not cause "disagreeable circumstances" during his defense of New York.[8]

Finally, the order of the day—the business that Congress had put on its schedule—was read: "Resolved, That this Congress will resolve itself into a Committee of the Whole, to take into consideration the Resolution respecting Independency." After the resolution was adopted, the delegates, as they had done on many occasions when forming into a committee of the whole, chose Virginia's Benjamin Harrison, highly thought of as a parliamentarian, to chair the session. Harrison, who was obese and six feet four inches tall—a Yankee described him as "uncommonly large"—shuffled to the dais to supplant Hancock. Once in his chair, Harrison turned to Charles Thomson, Congress's secretary since the first day of the First Congress at Carpenters' Hall, to reread Richard Henry Lee's motion calling for independence. With that, the floor was open.[9] It was no surprise that, at this critical juncture, Dickinson was the first delegate on his feet.

Leaving nothing to chance, Dickinson had prepared his speech in advance, something he almost always did when he planned to deliver a major address. Dickinson knew that this would not only be an important speech but also his final oration in the Continental Congress. If independence was declared, he planned to resign his seat before Pennsylvania's new legislature, under its new constitution, removed him from the state's delegation, which it very likely would do.

Dickinson had known for weeks that he had lost his fight against American independence. And he had lost much more. Once he had controlled the Pennsylvania assembly, having wrested the leadership from Galloway, but that body, a casualty of the American Revolution, had not met since June 14—and it would never meet again. Once, too, he had been the most revered public figure in his province, exalted above even Franklin. But Dickinson was now reviled by many. In June an editorial in Philadelphia's most influential newspaper, the *Pennsylvania Gazette*, denounced his "ruinous . . . reconciliation" policies, charging that since the war began, Dickinson had held "no fixed object in view than [advancing] HIMSELF." Old provincial political allies had abandoned him and some friends had forsaken him. When the soldiers in three of Philadelphia's four militia battalions voted nearly unanimously in June for independence, other general officers had wondered aloud how Dickinson could lead these men in battle. Some had bluntly told him that he had "lost the confidence and affections of the people." Some urged him to resign his commission. As spring gave way to summer, acquaintances from other colonies implored Dickinson to support independence, which, they said, offered the best hope for a short war. Charles Thomson, related to Dickinson by marriage, tried in the last days of June to persuade his old friend and in-law to join the majority in Congress "for a declaration of independence." Thomson reminded Dickinson that he had once pledged to support independence should Great Britain "employ foreign mercenaries to cut out throats."[10]

But Dickinson could not be swayed. He had waged desperate, courageous fights throughout his public career, and he had always been vindicated. He had contested Galloway and Franklin when they sought the royalization of Pennsylvania, and in time nearly every American had applauded the stance he had taken. At great risk he had led his colony in resisting Britain's imperial policies, and in the process, he had helped his countrymen from New England to Georgia to see the dangers posed by Parliament. There had always been a stubborn streak in Dickinson. It was perhaps stronger than ever in

1776, as he must have felt that he had already burned his bridges. In all probability, he realized that he would never attain the lofty status in an independent America that he had enjoyed in colonial days. He may also have been driven by an obsessive and gnawing unwillingness to take a back seat to the likes of John Adams, a steadfast antagonist whom he despised. No one, and no line of reasoning, could persuade Dickinson to abandon reconciliation and support independence.

It must have been close to noon when Dickinson began to speak. The sun was approaching its zenith, and outdoors the temperature had risen above ninety degrees. Congress's chamber, with its windows shut to preserve privacy and some two score delegates crammed into the room, was a sweatbox. That did not deter Dickinson, who launched into the lengthy speech he had crafted.

He began by mentioning the "Burthen assigned me," possibly a hint that those in Congress who opposed independence had selected him to speak first. He could count heads, too, and he as much as conceded in the first minute or two that he was speaking on behalf of a lost cause. In a sense, he said, he "rejoice[d]" that his fight was nearly over and that he would shortly "be relieved from its Weight." What he said this day would win no friends, he admitted. Instead, it would "give the finishing Blow to my once too great, and [now] . . . too dimish'd Popularity." But he felt compelled to say his piece. "Silence would be guilt. . . . I must speak, tho I should lose my Life, tho I should lose the Affections of my C[ountrymen]." There was at least one consolation: "Drawing Resentment [is] one proof of Virtue."

Dickinson opened his litany against independence with the assertion that Congress and the American people were "warm'd by Passion." Their bitterness was fueled by a "Resentment" born of "injuries offered to their Country." He did not deny that America had been wronged or that Americans were right to resist British tyranny. Nothing was more laudable than to die rather than to submit to a tyrant. Yet, reason screamed that independence was not in America's long-term best interests. America would be better served by reconciliation with Great Britain on the fair and just terms that Congress had long since laid out.

Dickinson next proceeded to enumerate the reasons for not declaring independence:

> a war for independence would last longer than a war for reconciliation; Britain would resist independence "with more severity;" far from increasing American morale, independence would diminish it; it was risky to declare independence before adopting a constitution; a long

war would plunge America deeply into debt; the American union was unlikely to survive long after independence; an independent America might become a vassal of France; and a stalemated war might end in Europe's partition of America.

Dickinson had added nothing new. There was nothing new to be said. In a letter written ten days earlier John Adams had accurately inventoried the objections to independence that the reconciliationists could be expected to make. Still later, once this session was complete, Adams remarked that the day's debate had been "an idle Mispence of Time for nothing was Said, but what had been repeated and hackneyed in that Room before an hundred Times for Six Months past." (Another proponent of independence grumbled that all the arguments on both sides were "as well known at the Coffee House of the City as in Congress.")[11]

The speech had gone on and on, probably lasting past two o'clock. The congressional chamber had grown even more intolerably hot as Dickinson's oration wound to a climax with a warning that the "Book of Fate" portended a "dreadful" future for an independent America.[12]

Dickinson had hardly taken his seat before Adams was on his feet. He had not prepared a speech or even scribbled notes for his talk. They were not needed; he had made these same arguments many times. Adams may not have been Dickinson's equal as an orator, for Dickinson was nearly as good as they came. But there was a studied expertise to Adams's talents as a public speaker, honed before countless juries and in innumerable presentations in Congress. Jefferson once remembered that a typical Adams speech was composed of "deep conceptions, nervous style, and undaunted firmness."[13] On this day, in this speech, Adams summoned all his powers of oratory and delivered a superb address.

No record of Adams's speech has survived, but he must have answered each objection to independence that Dickinson had raised. If the speech resembled his correspondence of recent months—not to mention the compendium of London's abominable behavior contained in Jefferson's draft declaration—Adams probably described in detail the British policies and actions that had driven America to independence. There can be no question that Adams argued that the harsh realities of war left America no choice but to declare independence. Nor is it likely that he minimized the "Calamities" that America would confront during the long "bloody Conflict We are destined to endure," as he remarked in a missive written just after that day's session concluded.

Whereas Dickinson had emphasized the potential dangers that independence might bring on, Adams almost certainly accentuated the benefits that would accrue from breaking with the mother country. Nothing had ever been more important to Adams than the opportunities for ambitious individuals. Above all, he believed that by escaping Great Britain's fetters, talented Americans would have the chance to attain the highest reaches of political power. He knew, too, that independence would better provide the means by which Americans—individuals and powerful economic interests alike—might control their destiny. He may even have sounded somewhat like Thomas Paine, who had asserted that independence offered the promise of better things than could ever be hoped for by Anglo-Americans within the British Empire. "Freedom is a Counterballance for Poverty, Discord, and War, and more," Adams wrote that night, and he likely expanded on that deep-seated conviction in his speech.[14]

Adams's speech was probably as long as, or longer than, Dickinson's. As the afternoon wore on, the puffy white clouds of morning gave way to low, gray scudding clouds, then to angry black thunderheads. In time the thunder, at first distant and muted, grew steadily louder. An hour or so into Adams's speech, Philadelphia grew very dark, as if night was approaching. Candles were lit. Soon, lightning was on top of the city and the thunder was as deafening as a nearby artillery barrage. For a minute or two, large drops of rain splattered loudly on the tall windows. Then, sheets of rain lashed the city.

Adams and his listeners were not distracted. Adams paused only once, when the door to Congress's chamber opened and four of the five newly chosen New Jersey delegates—all freshly authorized to vote for independence—entered. One of them, Richard Stockton, asked Adams to summarize what he had previously said. Adams obliged. Then he pushed forward. Finally, near Congress's customary four P.M. adjournment time, Adams brought his speech to a conclusion. Perhaps no one could have answered Dickinson with a finer speech. Jefferson later said that Adams was the "pillar" in support of independence, "its ablest advocate and defender." Stockton was enthralled with the "force of his reasoning" and subsequently called Adams "the Atlas of American independence." A Southerner exclaimed that he "fancied an angel was let down from heaven to illumine Congress."[15]

Congress might as well have voted on independence when Adams sat down. Little could be added to what he and Dickinson had already said. But each delegate sensed that he was face-to-face with the pivotal moment of his public life. Nearly every member of Congress wanted to speak, to have the satisfaction of having said something on this historic occasion. Each must have hoped that what he said would be memorable. The thunderstorm had cooled the air. The room was now more bearable. One delegate after another took the floor.

Jefferson later recalled that the entire debate had lasted for nine hours. Hour after hour "without a pause," he said, the delegates spoke, many with such passion that they summoned all the "powers of the soul" in their calls for independence or their entreaties not to break with the mother country. Night was gathering over the city when the last speaker uttered the last word to an utterly spent and famished audience.[16]

The time had come to vote on independence. Two votes were necessary. A vote was needed to favorably recommend the question from the committee of the whole. If that vote carried, Congress would then cast the decisive vote.

Everyone expected the measure for independence to carry, but no one knew for certain by what margin. New York's delegation, having not been instructed by the provincial authorities, would abstain. Most doubted that Delaware would cast a ballot. As Caesar Rodney was at home in Kent County, only two of the province's three deputies were present and they differed in outlook. Thomas McKean was a clear-cut supporter of independence. George Read, a cautious forty-two-year-old lawyer, was not. Some of Read's congressional colleagues had been whispering that he was "better fitted for the district of St. James's [in England] than the [Delaware] region of America."[17] McKean and Read were expected to negate each other's vote, so that Delaware would not cast a ballot on this crucial question.

Most thought that Pennsylvania would vote against sending the question of independence to Congress for a vote. Among its seven delegates, only Franklin and John Morton, the speaker of the late provincial assembly, had never wavered on breaking with Great Britain. James Wilson was a question mark, but the four remaining congressmen—Willing, Morris, Dickinson, and Charles Humphreys, an archconservative who had been a follower of Galloway in the assembly after 1763—were seen as foes of independence. Most delegates also regarded South Carolina as a doubtful supporter of independence. Thomas Heyward—he pronounced his name "Haywood"—a thirty-year-old Charleston lawyer who had steadfastly supported cutting all ties with the mother country, was the sole member of South Carolina's delegation who could be counted on by the proponents of independence. ("On him We could always depend for sound Measures, though he seldom spoke in public," John Adams wrote many years later.)[18] Rutledge, Arthur Middleton, and Thomas Lynch Jr. were not so much opposed to independence as to declaring it at this juncture. The best bet was that the measure would be voted out of committee by a margin of 10–1 or 9–2. Either margin would be short of the unanimous vote that most congressmen believed desirable for a step of such magnitude.

It was nearly dark when the committee of the whole at last voted. The measure carried by a 9–2 vote. New York abstained. Delaware was deadlocked.

Pennsylvania and South Carolina voted against the motion to send the question of independence from the committee of the whole to Congress for the historic vote.

The balloting had gone more or less as most delegates expected. Once the vote was taken, a parliamentary practice was carried out. Harrison stepped down from the dais, and Hancock returned to the president's chair. Harrison reported the outcome of the committee's vote, whereupon Hancock asked whether Congress was ready for the formal vote on independence. Before anything could be done, Rutledge took the floor. He asked that the vote be postponed until the following morning. He told Congress that though "they disapproved of the resolution," he believed at least two members of South Carolina's delegation would join Heyward "for the sake of unanimity."[19] The weary and hungry congressmen happily agreed to Rutledge's proposal and adjourned.

American independence would be declared on July 2, that much was certain. John Adams thought the vote would be "by a great Majority," probably by a margin of "almost Unanimity," a remark that suggests he expected Pennsylvania to cast a negative vote. Despite Rutledge's assurances, Adams could not be sure how the South Carolina delegation would vote. There was another matter to worry over. The vote had been close in a couple of delegations, close enough to cause Adams to fret that arms might be twisted overnight, or deals struck, that could lead "one or two Gentlemen" to make a turnabout and "vote point blank against the known and declared Sense of their Constituents."[20]

It was still raining in Philadelphia, though more softly, when the delegates awakened on Tuesday morning. They hurried to the State House, splashing through the puddles on the city sidewalks. All delegates were in place when the session was called to order. Congress first listened to and discussed letters from Washington, the Massachusetts assembly, the governor of Connecticut, and the army's paymaster.[21] Though politicians tend to be talkative, it is not likely that the discussion occasioned by these dispatches consumed much time. Most congressmen were probably anxious to resume consideration of independence and, finally, to cast their vote on what must have seemed to them to have been the climax of a trajectory begun long ago.

It was going on eleven A.M. when Congress returned to the recommendation of the committee of the whole that independence be declared. Lee's resolution, which by now must have been committed to memory by many deputies, was read yet again. It is unlikely that any speeches were made. Congress was ready to vote.

Secretary Thomson prepared to call the roll of the colonies. It would be the last time the provinces would be called "colonies." The moment this vote was completed, the provinces would be transformed from British colonies into American states.

All knew the measure would carry. Even so, an air of suspense, perhaps apprehension, swathed the chamber. Some worried that this most crucial of decisions would carry by a margin that was disappointingly short of unanimity. Even more, each delegate understood that if America lost the war, the members of a Congress that had declared American independence—a rogue assembly from the start, in Parliament's eyes—would be marked men.

Secretary Thomson may have called the roll in alphabetical order, beginning with Connecticut. Wolcott had gone home, but his two colleagues, Sherman and Samuel Huntington, voted for independence. There had never been any doubt about Huntington's support for cutting ties with the mother country. A forty-five-year-old lawyer from Norwich who had entered Congress in January, he and William Ellery of Rhode Island were the only delegates who had been active members of a Sons of Liberty chapter.

Delaware may have been next. To the astonishment of some delegates, Delaware's delegation had swelled to three members. Caesar Rodney, who had not attended a session of Congress for nearly four weeks, had joined his colleagues Read and McKean. Delaware would not be deadlocked on this day. It would cast a vote.

Few matters in the history of the Continental Congress were the subject of as many legends as those that surrounded Rodney's activities in the weeks prior to July 2. Some yarns had him confined at home in Delaware by sickness—in the popular 1960s musical *1776*, Rodney was depicted as suffering a stroke on the floor of Congress early in June—and others placed him at the bedside of his seriously ill wife, an especially fanciful story as Rodney was a lifelong bachelor.[22] The one thing that the tales agreed on was that in order to be present and cast his historic ballot, Rodney had made a stupendous horseback ride through the dark, rainy night, his mount galloping sixty miles— eighty in some versions—in about twelve hours, which brought him to the Pennsylvania State House just in the nick of time.

Rodney was a forty-eight-year-old veteran politician who had supported the American protest since its inception. John Adams thought him a man of "Sense and Fire, Spirit, Wit and Humour," though he was "the oddest looking Man in the World. He is tall—thin and Slender as a Reed—pale—his Face is not bigger than a large Apple." Adams did not mention that Rodney suffered from advanced skin cancer, which had ravaged his nose and spread to one cheek, leading him at times to wear a silk covering to hide the disfiguration.

*Statue of Caesar Rodney by James Kelley in Rodney Square in Wilmington, Delaware.
Rodney's vote on July 2, 1776, broke a tie in Delaware's delegation, enabling the state
to vote for independence. At home leading the militia against armed Loyalists,
Rodney returned to Congress only an hour or two prior to the historic vote.
(Historical Society of Delaware)*

Rodney embraced independence in the spring of 1776, declaring that it was absurd to "Swear Allegiance to the power that is Cutting our throats."[23] Soon thereafter, he left Philadelphia for New Castle to campaign to have the provincial assembly authorize its congressional delegation to vote for independence. As he was a high-ranking militia officer, Rodney stayed on in Delaware to help suppress a Loyalist uprising.[24]

His colleague Thomas McKean subsequently recalled that after he and Read deadlocked in their vote on July 1, he sent a messenger to fetch Rodney back to Philadelphia by ten the following morning. McKean's memory must have been faulty. It stretches credulity to imagine that within fourteen hours a courier could have ridden sixty or more miles, searched for and found Rodney, after which Rodney could have made his own ride to Philadelphia.

It is more likely that McKean, knowing that Congress was scheduled to vote on independence on July 1 and that he and Read would cancel each other's vote, sent an express rider sometime in late June to retrieve Rodney. Detained by his military activities, Rodney may not have started his ride until June 30, or possibly sometime on July 1, but that he arrived at the State House well before Congress voted seems certain. McKean recalled that on the morning of July 2 he met Rodney "at the State-house door in his boots and spurs, as the members were assembling."[25] Thus, Rodney was present when Thomson called on Delaware for its vote, and to no one's surprise he joined with McKean. Delaware, like Connecticut, cast its vote for independence.

Georgia was probably next in the roll call. Only three of Georgia's five delegates were in Philadelphia. One, Lyman Hall, was a native of Connecticut who had moved to Georgia in 1758 after being ousted from the clergy for immoral conduct. Once in Georgia, he became a physician. Hall was disliked by many of fellow Georgia congressmen because he always seemed to vote the way a majority of the Connecticut delegation voted.[26] On July 2 all three Georgians—Hall; Button Gwinnett, a planter-businessman who lived on St. Catherine's, a ten-mile-long island that he owned off the Georgia coast; and George Walton, a Savannah lawyer who hated both of his colleagues—voted for independence.

Maryland may have followed. Maryland's three deputies who were in Philadelphia had learned only twenty-four hours earlier that they could vote for independence. One, John Rogers, declined to cast such a vote. His colleagues, William Paca and Thomas Stone, both Annapolis lawyers, had supported the American protest and the war from the beginning, but with considerable reluctance. Each preferred reconciliation, but at the last minute—in some measure because no peace commissioners had arrived from London—each voted for independence.[27]

There was never any question how Massachusetts would vote. Each of its five congressmen—John and Samuel Adams, Hancock, Gerry, and Paine—voted for independence.

The New Hampshire delegation, which was likely polled next, consisted of two members. Josiah Bartlett, a Kingston physician who had married his cousin, had been a congressman for ten months. His colleague, William Whipple, a Portsmouth merchant who on occasion went to sea, had come to Philadelphia in February. It was hardly a surprise that men whom John Adams regarded as "excellent . . . in Principle and Disposition, as well as Understanding," voted for independence.[28]

New Jersey probably followed. Four of New Jersey's delegates had arrived the day before, during Adams's long speech, joining Francis Hopkinson, who had entered Congress the preceding Friday and for two days had been the colony's lone representative. All five voted for independence. For the four newest of the newcomers—Abraham Clark, John Hart, Richard Stockton, and John Witherspoon—their votes on independence (in the committee of the whole and on July 2) were probably the very first votes they cast as members of Congress.

When New York was polled, one of its seven, possibly eight, members—no record exists of who it was—rose and spoke on behalf of the province. He told the members of Congress that "the delegates for New York . . . were for it [independence] themselves, & were assured their constituents were for it, but that their instructions having been drawn near a twelvemonth before [on April 22, 1775], when reconciliation was still the general object, they were enjoined . . . to do nothing which should impede that object. they therefore thought themselves not justifiable in voting on either side."[29] With that explanation, New York abstained, as everyone knew it would.

Two of North Carolina's three congressmen were in Philadelphia on July 2. Joseph Hewes, a forty-six-year-old businessman, had been a delegate since about a week after the First Congress convened. He never questioned the war, but until the spring of 1776 he had favored reconciliation. Jefferson once characterized him as "sometimes firm, sometimes feeble, according as the day was clear or cloudy." Another delegate recalled that when word arrived in Philadelphia that a majority of North Carolinians favored independence, Hewes "started suddenly upright, and lifting up both his Hands to Heaven as if he had been in a trance, cry'd out 'It is done! and I will abide by it.'"[30] His colleague John Penn, a thirty-six-year-old lawyer, had come to Congress the previous October and shared Hewes's outlook. Both North Carolinians voted for independence.

Most deputies came to the State House on July 2 expecting Pennsylvania to vote against independence. But Pennsylvania sprang two surprises. Startlingly, Dickinson and Robert Morris withdrew "behind the bar," as one congressman put it, which is to say that overnight they had decided to vote neither for nor against independence, but to abstain.[31] It was a breathtaking moment, perhaps the least-expected happening to this point in the history of the Continental Congress.

Three weeks later Morris explained his action to a friend. He had never wavered, he said, in his conviction that a restoration of the Anglo-American union was in the best "interest of our Country and the Good of Mankind." But there were those in Congress who thought reconciliation was "high Treason against the States." Such men, he bristled, hated the reconciliationists. They "wou'd sooner punish a Man for this Crime than for bearing arms against us." He could not bring himself to vote for independence, he continued, but he thought it best not to vote against it. Rather, he would bide his time, awaiting the arrival of the Howe brothers, Lord North's peace commissioners. If they offered good terms, he would continue to support reconciliation. On the other hand, if "no good can possibly arise" from talking with them, Morris promised to declare in favor of independence.[32]

Dickinson never offered an explanation for his abstention. Many delegates emphasized the need for American unanimity and the responsibility of congressmen to reflect the wishes of their constituents, and either or both may have provoked his decision. A cynic might argue that Dickinson, who remained politically ambitious and enjoyed the taste of power, was merely seeking to avoid the total ruin of his political career.

With great suddenness, everyone in the chamber realized that Pennsylvania's swing vote was in the hands of James Wilson. Willing and Humphreys would vote against independence. Franklin, though still weak from his June bout with the gout, had returned to Congress the previous day. There was no question how he would vote. Nor was there any doubt that his colleague, John Morton, would join with him in voting for independence. Morton, a fifty-two-year-old surveyor, former sheriff, and judge—though devoid of legal training—had little formal education and spoke, as did most Quakers, in sentences sprinkled with "thee" and "thou." He had sat in Congress from day one in 1774, though he was quiet and never a leader. Once he became convinced early in 1776 that independence was inevitable, Morton never wavered in his support of breaking with Great Britain. With the Pennsylvania delegation divided two against two, the deciding vote would be left to Wilson. Little in his record as a congressman pointed toward an affirmative vote, but Wilson was clearly aware which way the political wind was blowing.

In January, Wilson had led the fight to have Congress renounce American independence. In the spring, when Congress first debated independence in earnest, he had been an unwavering foe of breaking with the mother country. At the time, Wilson told his colleagues that he wished to hold in abeyance his decision on independence until he learned the outcome of Pennsylvania's May 1 elections. Some colleagues thought him canny and dishonest, a judgment that increased in May and June. Although the electoral results left little doubt that most Pennsylvanians favored independence, Wilson fought against the May 15 resolution of Congress that aimed at securing new instructions for Pennsylvania's delegates. His argument struck many as disingenuous. Perhaps he could support independence, he said, but not until the Pennsylvania assembly authorized such a vote; on the other hand, he was opposed to Congress's attempt to force the assembly to authorize independence. Three weeks later, in the debates on June 8 and 10, he spoke against Lee's resolution calling on Congress to declare independence.

In June, Wilson's steadfast opposition to independence aroused "violent spirits" against him within Pennsylvania, as a friend put it. Wilson was openly vilified by pro-independence forces, including in his home county, which had fallen under the control of radical militiamen and democrats. Wilson's domestic enemies campaigned to force him to alter his stance. Some would have been happier to see him removed from Congress. Foes published records revealing Wilson's record of duplicity: In public, he had postured as open-minded on the question of independence; in Congress's secret sessions, he had done everything possible to prevent a final break with Great Britain. One report alleged that an unidentified congressman had confided to the revolutionary authorities in Carlisle that after dealing with Wilson, he would "never trust a Scotchman again. They Cannot be honest when liberty is in question."[33]

With his political career in jeopardy, Wilson in early June had taken the extraordinary step of asking his colleagues in Congress to "testifie" about his "behavior during the Debate on Independence" and "clear his Character" with the citizens of Pennsylvania. Congress had never done anything of the sort, and it initially refused to help Wilson. But on June 20, leading figures in the pro-independence faction in Congress came to his rescue. In a statement signed by all but two of the twelve congressmen from Virginia and Massachusetts, and six others who would vote for independence, Wilson was portrayed as having been an "un-restrained" advocate of independence who merely wished to postpone a vote until unanimity could be assured. John and Samuel Adams, Jefferson, and Francis Lightfoot Lee knew that the statement they were signing was balderdash. Theirs was a purely political move. They were throwing the embattled Wilson a lifeline to help him in Pennsylvania's domestic political brawling; he, in turn, would vote for independence when the issue came to the floor within the next couple of weeks.[34]

On July 2, the time had come for Wilson to cast his vote. Whatever he thought about breaking with Britain, Wilson had made his decision in mid-June when he solicited the aid of his pro-independence colleagues. The ambitious Wilson feared that unless he voted for independence, he had no future in politics. When the roll was called, he cast his vote with that of Franklin and Morton. By a three-to-two margin, Pennsylvania voted for independence.

Rhode Island's vote was never in question. Stephen Hopkins—at sixty-nine, one of the oldest congressmen—had long championed reconciliation, even voting for Galloway's plan at the First Congress. Something of a professional politician, he changed colors once it was clear that Rhode Islanders favored independence. Hopkins was liked by all, including John Adams, who thought him a man of "Wit, Sense, Knowledge, and good humour" and marveled at Hopkins's habit of drinking rum and water until midnight nearly every evening with any and all colleagues who would join him for a conversation on history, science, poetry, or politics.[35] William Ellery, a forty-eight-year-old Newport lawyer and Harvard graduate, had been in Congress only six weeks. Thought by some to be slow and lazy, he seldom spoke in Congress, but when he did, there was no question that he favored independence. Hopkins and Ellery put Rhode Island in the pro-independence column.

South Carolina was the last question mark with regard to unanimity. Its ballot the night before indicated an opposition to independence, but Rutledge had hinted that the delegation's vote might change overnight. An air of mystery pervades the delegates' behavior. Why would the South Carolina delegates who opposed independence on July 1 reverse themselves on July 2? Most likely, they wanted a deal. Jefferson's draft declaration had been available since Friday, and South Carolina's delegates were not happy with the anti-slavery tone of one of the indictments against the king. After casting a negative vote on the evening of July 1, the South Carolinians must have sought, and received, assurances that what they found offensive in the Declaration of Independence would be toned down or dropped altogether.

When Secretary Thomson polled South Carolina, the three holdout delegates joined Heyward in voting for independence. Of the three, Rutledge had been the most outspoken foe of independence. Arthur Middleton, a thirty-four-year-old rice planter who owned more than two hundred slaves, had taken his seat in Congress on the same day as Ellery. Whereas Ellery seldom spoke, Middleton joined in every debate, though Adams thought him ill-informed on nearly every question, not to mention rude and sarcastic in his manner of speaking. But Middleton never questioned the need to break with Britain, which led Adams to see him as "honest and generous . . . with all his Zeal in this cause." Thomas Lynch Jr. had entered Congress with Middleton. Only twenty-seven, a year older than Rutledge, Lynch was among the best-educated congressmen, having studied at Eton, Cambridge, and the Middle Temple. When he returned to South Carolina from England, Lynch discovered that he had no interest in practicing law. Instead, he was managing the family's estate when his father, who had sat in Congress since its beginning, suffered a debilitating stroke in February 1776. Provincial authorities hastily chose Lynch to succeed his father. Politically inexperienced and with little apparent interest in politics, Lynch seemed to think—as did those who held power at home—that his job was to do as his father probably would have done. The elder Lynch had emerged as a staunch reconciliationist in the Second Congress and had even led that faction when Dickinson was distracted by events in Pennsylvania. During the six weeks that he had been in Philadelphia before the question of independence was debated, young Lynch followed

*The Vote on the Motion to Declare Independence. The motion to
declare independence was first introduced by Richard Henry Lee on
June 7, 1776, and again in the final debates on July 1 and 2.
This document contains the handwritten motion and notes:
"resolution for independency agreed to July 2."
It also indicates the approval of twelve states. (National Archives)*

Rutledge, the clear leader of the delegation. When Rutledge voted for independence, Lynch did so as well, and their votes guaranteed congressional
unanimity on the issue.

How Virginia would vote was never a mystery. Neither Jefferson nor Francis Lightfoot Lee had ever hidden their sentiments on independence. Virginia's three other deputies, each of whom was also a planter aristocrat, had
supported their colony's opposition to British policies since the Stamp Tax.
Thomas Nelson—described by John Adams as corpulent but "alert and lively,
for his Weight"—had lived and studied in England for seven years. Joining
Congress during 1775, he had gone home in February 1776 but returned in
June, about three weeks before the final debate on independence. Many New
England proponents of independence disliked Benjamin Harrison, but they
always knew that they could count on him on the question of breaking with
Great Britain. Carter Braxton was another matter. He was as conservative as
Galloway on social and political issues. During some congressional discussions he argued that America should not declare independence until it had
secured an alliance with France. In other debates he argued that an American constitution should be adopted prior to declaring independence. Though
he did not broadcast his fears, Braxton doubted that the northern and south-

ern colonies, which were strikingly different in many ways, could long maintain their union; he was not even sure that they could remain united until victory was gained in the Revolutionary War. But Braxton's greatest concern was that independence would open the floodgates for sweeping political and social change. He believed that the Yankees, whom he hated, would try to spread "their darling Democracy" throughout the southern states. Braxton was filled with fears about independence, but like his four colleagues he voted for it.[36]

Congress declared independence by a vote of 12–0. The poll of the colonies had not taken long, perhaps only a couple of minutes, but every member of Congress understood the magnitude of what had just taken place. None captured what most must have felt better than Abraham Clark, the fifty-year-old surveyor, father of ten, and veteran politician who had entered Congress as part of New Jersey's delegation only the day before. "We are now . . . embarked on a most Tempestuous Sea. Life very uncertain. Seeming dangers Scattered thick Around us. . . . Let us prepare for the worst, we can Die here but once. May all our Business, all our purposes & pursuits tend to fit us for that important event."[37]

CHAPTER 14

"THIS WILL
CEMENT THE UNION"

AMERICA IS SET FREE

BEFORE DAYBREAK the next morning, July 3, John Adams sat at his desk in his small room at Mrs. Yard's boardinghouse and in the light of a flickering candle wrote to Abigail. He wished to let her know that the "greatest Question was decided." It had been the most crucial decision ever made in America, he said, perhaps the most fateful that ever "was or will be decided" in the history of the world.

"The Second Day of July," he predicted, "will be celebrated, by succeeding Generations, as the great anniversary Festival. It ought to be commemorated ... with Pomp and Parade, with Shews, Games, Sports, Guns, Bells, Bonfires and Illuminations from one End of this Continent to the other from this Time forward forever more."[1]

But when Congress voted to break with Great Britain, it had not completed its work on declaring independence. Congress wished to issue a "declaration on independence," as its *Journal* put it.[2] With regard to that declaration, the delegates had four choices: They could adopt the draft submitted by the Committee of Five; revise the committee's draft; send the draft back to the committee for rewriting (which is what Congress had done a year earlier with the draft of the Declaration of the Causes and Necessity of Taking Up Arms); or it could reject the draft, appoint a new committee, and start from scratch. The two latter options were never considered. Not only had Jefferson captured the thinking of Congress and the provincial assemblies, but also the deputies believed they had to act quickly. They wanted to promulgate the Declaration of Independence before the fighting for New York began, and with British soldiers about to land near Manhattan, a clash of arms was thought to be only days away. Yet while Congress was in a hurry, it also wished to carefully consider Jefferson's draft. With some four dozen delegates perusing each sentence, some changes were inevitable.

It was probably shortly before noon on July 2 when Congress declared American independence. As two thirds of Congress's normal working day remained, it formed itself into a committee of the whole and took up the draft. After presumably spending the remainder of the day editing the document—neither the *Journal* nor any other existing document makes clear precisely what transpired as Congress labored over Jefferson's draft—the delegates must have realized that the process was going to take longer than they had imagined. Before adjourning on July 2, the members agreed to begin the next day's session at nine A.M., an hour earlier than customary. It is known that Congress continued its deliberations for two more days, though on each day it allotted some time to pressing war-related issues.

On July 3 and 4, for instance, Congress asked Pennsylvania, Delaware, and Maryland to send troops to the front for the looming battle of New York; sought supplies for the army; appropriated money to hire workers to build a fleet for the defense of Lake Champlain in the face of the anticipated British invasion of northern New York; focused on efforts to keep the Indians neutral; created one committee to superintend defensive preparations in Philadelphia and another to prepare a "Seal for the United States of America."[3] The delegates also took up a letter from General Washington. The commander requested that Congress "repeat and press home" on the foot-dragging provinces that they must "furnish their Quota's [of militia] with all possible dispatch."[4] It was this letter that prompted Congress to lean on the three states to rush its militiamen to General Washington.

The bulk of the sessions on July 2, 3, and 4—probably ten hours or more altogether—were devoted to scrutiny of Jefferson's draft. It is likely that Congress had ordered the draft document to be printed. If so, the delegates were able to read in advance what the Committee of Five had submitted and could follow the dissection of the draft line by line as the editing proceeded.[5]

That Congress devoted so much time to editing and revising the Declaration of Independence is an indication of just how important it understood this document to be. Fancifully, some congressmen thought the Declaration would somehow motivate America's friends in Great Britain to bring down the war ministry and make peace. Others, no less optimistic, believed that a document that rang with the passionate rhetoric of freedom might inspire the most-enlightened Europeans, perhaps quickening support for America's cause. But every member of Congress knew that the Declaration's primary audience resided in America. Its task was to proclaim for Americans the credo of the new nation, stating what the yet-to-be created government stood for and against. Inescapably, too, Congress hoped that the Declaration would sustain Americans through what was certain to be the fiery trial of war that lay ahead. They wanted a ringing statement that would with crystal clarity lay bare for every American the reasons why the war was being fought.

The congressmen who pored over Jefferson's draft were keen, unsparing editors. They altered nearly half of the introductory paragraph, though the changes were only stylistic, and they made a handful of similar modifications to the second and best-remembered paragraph. For instance, "We hold these truths to be sacred & undeniable" became "We hold these truths to be self-evident." These congressmen-editors wished both to find just the right phrases and to strike out all unnecessary words. Two thirds of Jefferson's allegations against the king and Parliament came through unscathed; in four indictments Congress altered only one word. But here and there Jefferson's colleagues made substantive changes to his accusations.

Congress added more bite to some allegations. The accusation that the monarch was pursuing policies of "cruelty & perfidy unworthy the head of a civilized nation" instead became "cruelty & perfidy scarcely paralleled in the most barbarian ages and totally unworthy the head of a civilized nation." Congress altered some passages in order to be more accurate. Jefferson had stated in one indictment that the king had closed all colonial courts, though in fact only the superior courts had been shuttered.[6] The wording became "he has obstructed the administration of justice." Congress deleted two charges against the king. Jefferson's rant on the origin and perpetuation of African slavery was cut at the instigation of South Carolina and Georgia, which had never envisaged the American rebellion as an abolitionist crusade, and probably of Rhode Island, a province filled with influential men who were making money hand over fist from the slave trade.[7] Uncomfortable with the charge that George III had incited "treasonous insurrections of our fellow citizens," Congress revised it to read that the king had "excited domestic insurrections." That blanket statement served as a condemnation both of Dunmore's proclamation and of the monarch's having at least implicitly roused America's Tories to take up arms.

Toward the end of his draft, Jefferson had charged that the king had not answered Congress's petitions for redress. However, one portion of this lengthy section alleged that Great Britain had done nothing to help the earliest colonists survive in the wilds of America, while another part rebuked the British people for having turned a deaf ear to America's repeated entreaties to their "native justice and magnanimity." What Jefferson had written about Congress's petitions to the king survived intact, but the congressmen-editors were merciless with the remainder of that section. Congress blue-lined more than half of it as incorrect, imprudent, or simply redundant. Aside from the long passage on slavery, more than 90 percent of what was struck from Jefferson's draft came out of this section. Congress also modified the final paragraph—the actual declaration of American independence—by largely substituting for Jefferson's embroidered rhetoric the simple resolution on independence that Richard Henry Lee had offered and Congress had adopted on July 2.[8]

Jefferson's draft was improved by Congress's attention. Congress made the Declaration of Independence a leaner document, one that was more forceful and, in its brevity, more likely to be read. Altogether, Congress pruned the draft by nearly a third.[9] Even with the additions made by Congress, the Declaration of Independence runs just over 1,400 words, not much longer than an op-ed piece in a modern daily newspaper. Only one congressman was anguished by what Congress did to Jefferson's draft, and that was Jefferson himself. Like any writer, he suffered silently in acute distress as his colleagues critiqued his composition, adding words, tinkering with a phrase here and there, and expunging entire sentences. Seeing his colleague's anguish, Franklin tried to comfort Jefferson by explaining—as has many an editor to many a despairing author—that brevity can be more compelling. In his customary manner, Franklin sought to persuade Jefferson through a parable:

> When I was a journeyman printer, [Franklin began,] one of my companions, an apprentice hatter, having served out his time, was about to open shop for himself. His first concern was to have a handsome sign board, with proper inscription. He composed it in these words, "John Thompson, Hatter, makes and sells hats for ready money," with a figure of a hat subjoined. But he thought he would submit it to his friends for their amendments. The first he showed it to thought the word "Hatter" tautologous, because followed by the words "makes hats," which showed he was a hatter. It was struck out. The next observed that the word "makes" might as well be omitted, because his customers would not care who made the hats. If good and to their mind, they would buy them, by whomsoever made. He struck it out. A third said he thought the words "for ready money" were useless, as it was not the custom of the place to sell on credit. Every one who purchased expected to pay. They were parted with, and the inscription now stood, "John Thompson, sells hats." "Sells hats!" says the next friend. "Why, nobody will expect you to give them away. Why then is the use of that word?" It was stricken out, and "hats" followed

it, the rather as there was one painted on the board. So the inscription was reduced ultimately to "John Thompson," with the figure of a hat subjoined.[10]

Franklin's attempt at mollification was, at best, only partially successful. In the notes he took as the editorial work proceeded, Jefferson raged at the "pusillanimous" character of his colleagues for having softened the charges he had brought against the king. He also took the trouble to make a hand-written copy of his draft and to send it to Richard Henry Lee so that he might "judge whether it [the Declaration of Independence] is the better or worse for the Critics." In an effort to placate his simmering friend, Lee responded that Congress had "mangled" Jefferson's draft, to which he added a measure of treacle: "However the *Thing* is in its nature so good, that no Cookery can spoil the Dish."[11] Nearly half a century later John Adams told an acquaintance that Congress had "obliterated some of the best" in Jefferson's draft, though it had "left all that was exceptional." (To which he added, in typical Adams fashion, "if any thing in it was" exceptional.)[12]

Sometime on July 4—Jefferson's notes say "in the evening," though the journal kept by Charles Thomson, Congress's secretary, points toward late morning—Congress completed its editorial work.[13] Adhering to proper parliamentary procedure, the committee of the whole made its recommendation that the document be approved. The Declaration of Independence was read in its entirety and adopted by Congress, after which it was ordered to be printed and distributed, including in handbill editions that were to be "Sent to the Armies, Cities, Countys, Towns, &c."[14]

The members of Congress responded to what they had done in various ways. No reaction was more laconic than that of Robert Treat Paine, whose diary entry for July 4 was simply: "The Independence of the States voted & declared." He was not so nonchalant in the letters he wrote to friends at home. Paine warned that the new nation could not be "saved by good words" alone. "Our hearts are full, our hands are full; may God . . . support us," he added. William Ellery was of like mind. It "is one Thing for Colonies to declare themselves independent and another to establish themselves in Independency," he cautioned. Elbridge Gerry was relieved that independence, "long sought for, solicited and necessary," had at last been declared. John Adams thought the step "compleats a Revolution." Samuel Adams fretted that much "has been lost by delaying to take this decisive Step." Had independence been declared the previous autumn, he carped, the United States not only would now possess Canada; it also would be better prepared to defend against the impending blows of the British military. John Adams thought Samuel was correct with regard to the military situation, yet he believed it was for the best that the decision on independence had been delayed. By July 1776, he said, all "Hopes of Reconciliation" had been "totally extinguished." By then, too, the question of independence had been thoroughly debated in newspapers and pamphlets, in town meetings, county committees, and provincial assemblies. The great majority of Americans, he was assured, were solidly in favor of independence. Rather than injuring the cause, John Adams said he was convinced that the delay in declaring independence "will cement the Union."[15]

Forty-two months, almost to the day, had passed since Lord North had learned of the Boston Tea Party and summoned his cabinet to decide how to deal with the American colonists. The road from London in January 1774 to Philadelphia in July 1776 had been long. Leaders on both sides had many opportunities to choose an alternative course. But North and his ministers, and their king, had spurned every American proposal for change, accommodation, and negotiation, instead holding inflexibly to the position the colonists must submit to British sovereignty in all matters whatsoever. Americans had answered Britain's rulers in stages. In the fall of 1774 Congress had embraced the rule of the king and Parliament's regulation of trade. In 1775 the American people had mobilized for war and Congress repudiated Parliament's authority over the colonies. In July 1776 Congress gave its final answer to a mother country that was bent on war, not concession. It voted unanimously for American independence.

EPILOGUE

THE BROADSIDE CONTAINING the Declaration of Independence, which Congress ordered on July 4, hit the streets of Philadelphia the next day. The only congressman whose name appeared on the Declaration was Hancock. (Congress did not publish a copy of the document containing the names of all the signatories until year's end, when the Continental army scored its first victory following independence.)[1] On July 6 the Declaration appeared in a newspaper, the *Philadelphia Evening Post*.

Congress set Monday, July 8, for the official celebration of independence in Philadelphia. The festivities, attended by "a great Crowd of People" in the State House yard, kicked off at eleven A.M., when nine Pennsylvania soldiers ripped the royal crest from above the entrance to the State House and committed it to a roaring bonfire. Next, a member of Pennsylvania's Committee of Safety read the Declaration of Independence. One resident noted in his diary that the Declaration was "received with general applause and heart-felt satisfaction," including three loud cheers of "God bless the Free States of North America!" When the reading was complete, Philadelphia's militia battalions, one of which was commanded by Colonel John Dickinson, paraded smartly and, according to John Adams, who could hardly have missed the irony of the occasion, "gave us the Feu de Joy, notwithstanding the Scarcity of Powder." Throughout that day and into the night, bells at the State House and in every church steeple across the city rang out joyously. As night descended, bonfires were set and many Philadelphians celebrated by putting a lighted candle in every window in their homes.[2]

By the day of Philadelphia's celebration, printed copies of the Declaration of Independence had already reached towns as far as seventy-five miles from the city. Thereafter, slowly but inexorably, the text appeared in handbills and newspapers in great towns and small. More than a month after July 4, word of the Declaration of Independence at last reached Savannah and its environs, among the last places in America where the citizenry learned that they were living in a new nation free of all links to Great Britain. The Declaration of

George Washington, in a print by Jenn-Baptiste Le Paon, ca. 1781, shown holding the
Declaration of Independence. Washington served in the First and Second
Continental Congress, but left to command the Continental army in June 1775.
He ordered that the Declaration of Independence be read to his
assembled soldiers in July 1776. (Brown University Library)

Independence was printed in London newspapers at almost the same moment that Georgians first read the document, though in England it was reported to have provoked laughter.[3]

Soldiers posted here and there were assembled to listen as the Declaration
of Independence was read. Sometimes the military commander made the
reading part of a worship service. That was not the case with the principal
contingent of the Continental army in and around New York City. On July 9
those soldiers marched to hear the document read "with an audible voice," or
so General Washington had ordered. When the reading was complete, the
Declaration "was received by three Huzzas from the Troops," according to
one officer. Washington thought his men had given "their most hearty assent" both to American independence and the Declaration of Independence,
an assessment confirmed by one of his colonels, who thought the document
was "highly approved by the Army."[4]

Public ceremonies were held in many villages and cities, always at a central location—the commons, the courthouse, a city square, or around the Liberty Pole. Abigail Adams heard it read from the balcony of the Massachusetts statehouse. As soon as the reading was completed, vessels in Boston Harbor fired salutes to American independence.[5] In most places church bells pealed during the festivities, militia companies paraded, occasionally a few rounds of artillery were fired, clergy prayed and sometimes sermonized, dignitaries spoke, and a man of strong voice—in rural areas it was frequently the sheriff— read the Declaration of Independence. Listeners sometimes discovered a magical quality to the Declaration that was not always readily apparent to readers. Jefferson, who was a talented musician, possessed a genius for the cadence of composition, for what one scholar described as the "rhythmical pauses . . . comparable to musical bars."[6] Public readings were also in a sense theatrical events, and the audiences, as if attending a play, sometimes felt the pain, disappointment, reproach, and anger that had captivatingly flowed from Jefferson's pen.[7]

In some locales effigies of the king or other royal officials were hung. In one town on Long Island the monarch's effigy featured a black face to remind onlookers of Dunmore's proclamation. Savannah staged a mock funeral for George III. Massachusetts directed all clergymen to read the Declaration of Independence to their congregations following the next worship service. One of the stranger ceremonies occurred in Watertown, Massachusetts, where the Declaration of Independence was interpreted to assembled Indian sachems. The translation went as follows: "You and we . . . have now nothing to do with Great Britain; we are wholly separated from her."[8]

In some places the popular enmity toward Great Britain turned destructive. The king's picture was often burned, crowds tore symbols of royal authority from the walls of public buildings and Anglican churches, and signs were ripped down at taverns, inns, and coffeehouses whose names were tainted with royal trappings. After the proprietor of the Kings' Arms tavern in Worcester, Massachusetts, was made to remove his sign, the crowd helped itself to his liquor and drank twenty-four toasts, the last being: "May the Freedom and Independency of America endure until the Sun grows dim with age, and this Earth returns to Chaos." A great statue of George III—one witness called it "the IMAGE of the BEAST"—was pulled down in New York City, after which it was sent to Litchfield, Connecticut, where it was recast into 42,088 cartridges for muskets. (One rebel was moved to write to Horatio Gates, a Continental army general, that the redcoats would have "melted Majesty fired at them.")[9]

Independence was well received everywhere. New Jersey's authorities reported that whereas the citizenry had been confused about fighting the king's army while professing loyalty to the Crown, the break with Great Britain had given a "great turn to the minds of our people. . . . Heart and hand shall [now] move together." General Washington expressed similar sentiments, adding that he thought it might make his soldiers act with greater "Fidelity and Courage," as they knew that henceforth they would be fighting for their own country. Congress learned from state authorities in New Hampshire that the Declaration of Independence had transformed the thinking of many who only months before had been "greatly averse to anything that looked like independence." A soldier at Fort Ticonderoga said that independence had been "well relished in this part of the world." Abigail Adams noted that "every face appeard joyfull" in the crowd that heard the document read in Boston.[10]

Perhaps the most important approval for independence came from the New York Provincial Convention, which was meeting in White Plains. On July 9, the same day that Washington's army heard the Declaration read, the Provincial Convention unanimously resolved that Congress's action was "cogent and conclusive," and it published the document, though it "lament[ed] the cruel necessity which has rendered that measure unavoidable." On hearing of New York's affirmation, one of the Yankee delegates in Congress exalted that "the Declaration of Independency . . . now has the sanction of the thirteen United States."[11]

Once it learned that every state was in line, Congress on July 19 ordered "that the Declaration passed on July 4 be fairly engrossed on parchment" and "when engrossed, be signed by every member of Congress."[12] The printing was completed on August 2, and on that day the delegates who were present signed the Declaration of Independence. John Hancock probably led off. With a bold flourish, he signed in large, easily distinguishable letters, as if to shout his approval of the break with the mother country. Thereafter, he must have summoned each delegation to the dais one at a time. It was a solemn and anxious moment, captured by Benjamin Rush, a new delegate from Pennsylvania, who later remembered "the pensive and awful silence, which pervaded the house when we were called up, one after another, to the table of the President of Congress to subscribe what was believed by many at that time to be our own death warrants."[13]

Those who were absent that day subsequently affixed their signatures. Elbridge Gerry, for instance, "worn out of Health, by the Fatigues of this station," had left Philadelphia in mid-July for rest and recuperation at home. He so badly wanted his name on the Declaration of Independence that he proposed it be added by proxy. That was not necessary. Congress wanted everyone who had voted for independence to sign the Declaration, and it even gave leave to sign to those who had been delegates during the spring debates on independence but had not been present for any of the votes between July 1 and July 4. It even permitted those who had voted against independence but subsequently changed their minds to sign. It also welcomed the signatures of those who entered Congress between July 5 and mid-autumn.[14]

Every congressman who voted for independence on July 2 ultimately signed the Declaration of Independence, including Gerry, who scribbled his signature sometime after he returned to Philadelphia on September 2. Several who signed the document had not voted for independence. North Carolina's William Hooper signed, though he had been absent from late March until mid-July. Richard Henry Lee, Samuel Chase, George Wythe, and Oliver Wolcott had gone home on the eve of the vote on independence and had come back to Philadelphia at varying times—it was October before Wolcott returned—and each signed shortly after resuming his seat.[15] Congress permitted Connecticut's William Williams, who had been elected in October 1775 but had not come to Philadelphia until four weeks after independence was declared, to sign the Declaration. Maryland's Charles Carroll of Carrollton signed, though he did not become a member of Congress until July 17. Given the political upheaval in Pennsylvania, five new faces were added to that state's delegation and took their seats between July 22 and September 6; each—Rush, George Clymer, George Ross, George Taylor, and James Smith— signed the Declaration. Four New York delegates, who were not authorized to vote for independence until July 9, eventually signed the document. That contingent did not include Robert R. Livingston, who left Congress on July 5 and never returned. New Hampshire's Matthew Thornton was probably the last man to sign the Declaration of Independence. Elected in September, he could not have signed it until after he took his seat on November 4.[16]

Two congressmen who had voted against independence on July 2 ultimately signed: George Read and Robert Morris.

Before all the signatures were affixed to the Declaration of Independence, one final stab at reconciliation had to be played out. The Howe brothers, the long-awaited peace commissioners, had arrived in New York in July. At the time they had sailed, both William and Richard Howe still thought it possible that war might be avoided by a last-minute peace accord. However, just as each soldier-commissioner disembarked on Staten Island, American independence had been declared and was being celebrated with gusto. The Howe brothers immediately sent Germain a copy of the Declaration of Independence, to which they appended their belief that there was "no prospect of a disposition in those who now hold the supreme authority over the colonies to make any advances towards a reconciliation."[17]

Even so, the Howes launched their mission by contacting both General Washington and Benjamin Franklin, hoping that the former might agree to talks and that the latter would serve as a conduit for opening discussions with Congress. They got nowhere with either man. Washington accepted their invitation to meet with one of General William Howe's officers, but it was an unproductive get-together. The American commander was willing to discuss the release of the American prisoners of war held in Canada, but when he made clear that he had no authority to engage in peace negotiations, the talks abruptly ended.[18] With the authorization of Congress, Franklin answered Lord Richard Howe's missive on July 20. His response was not heartening. As it appeared that the peace commissioners were to be unable to do more than extend "Offers of Pardon upon Submission," Franklin wrote curtly, "Reconciliation . . . [is] impossible on any Terms given you to propose."[19]

That stopped the peace commissioners in their tracks until the first battle in the campaign for New York was fought. The British army began landing on Long Island in August. Their blow fell on August 27, just two weeks after the last grand American celebration of independence had occurred in Savannah. The Continentals were routed in a brief engagement that culminated with thousands of American soldiers breaking and running in a panic for the safety of redoubts in Brooklyn Heights. American losses were heavy—nearly 1,500 killed, wounded, or captured, including two rebel generals, John Sullivan, who had fared poorly in Canada, and William Alexander, who called himself Lord Stirling.

Given this American debacle—pretty much what many in North's ministry and Parliament had predicted would occur on American battlefields—the Howes made one final stab at a meeting with the representatives of Congress. Lord Howe dined with Sullivan. The admiral advised his captive that he was empowered to make a just peace, adding unofficially that he could make real concessions to the colonists. Would Sullivan carry his message to Congress? Sullivan consented, and early in September he passed on to the deputies the substance of Howe's remarks.[20]

Hardly a congressman believed the Howes' were prepared to engage in serious discussions. Instead, they suspected that the real objective of the Howes was to sow deep, harmful divisions inside and outside Congress. John Adams raged that it was the Howes' intent "to seduce us into a renunciation of our independence" by crippling American morale. Their offer to talk was "an Ambuscade, a mere insidious Manoeuvre, calculated only to decoy and deceive."[21] But Adams and his fellow deputies also feared that if Congress refused to talk, the public would blame it for "the Odium of continuing this War." Boxed in, Congress wrangled for four days over whether to send negotiators to meet with the Howe brothers before finally deciding that it had no choice but to parley.[22]

Congress dispatched three of its own to meet with North's peace commissioners: John Adams, Franklin, and Rutledge. On September 11 they met with Lord Howe—General Howe, who was about to invade Manhattan Island, was busy—in what Adams thought was a shabby house on Staten Island. Adams subsequently described how he and his colleagues "walked up to the House between Lines of Guards of Grenadiers, looking as fierce as ten furies." Howe greeted the American envoys cordially and treated them to a dinner of ham, mutton, tongues, bread, and claret.[23]

Once Howe got down to business, it was readily apparent that these discussions would not be fruitful. The admiral began by saying that he had no authority to recognize American independence. It was too bad, he went on, that they could not have talked just after Congress sent the Olive Branch Petition, as it could have resulted in "an Accommodation to the Satisfaction of both Countries." Nevertheless, it was "His Majesty's most earnest desire to make his American Subjects happy, to cause a reform" leading to the "Redress of any real Grievances." Taxing the colonists was of little importance to Great Britain, he continued. It was America's "Commerce [and] her strength, her Men, that we chiefly wanted." Howe concluded his remarks with a question: "Is there no way of treading back this Step of Independency, and opening the door to a full discussion?"

Franklin was the first to respond. The American people "could not expect Happiness now under the *Domination* of Great Britain. . . . [A]ll former Attachment was obliterated. . . . America could not return again to the Domination of Great Britain." Adams spoke next, saying that "all the Colonies had gone compleately through a Revolution" and that American independence was the wish of "all the Colonies." He added that he personally had no wish "to depart from the Idea of Independency." Rutledge next told Howe that Britain's days of utilizing America's strength for its own ends were over, but that if London formed "an Alliance with her as an independent state," it could reap the advantages of trade with the United States.

If those were America's sentiments, Howe responded, "he could only lament it was not in his Power to bring about the Accommodation he wished." When the envoys pressed Howe about the generous terms that he had mentioned to Sullivan, Howe responded that the general must have misunderstood him. Franklin had very nearly the final word. "[W]ell my Lord," he said, "as America is to expect nothing but unconditional Submission . . . and

Your Lordship has no Proposition to make us," there was no point in continuing the discussion.[24]

Though Independence was declared in July 1776, whether the United States would survive the war and achieve independence was uncertain until the pivotal victory at Yorktown in October 1781. It was a victory made possible by the French alliance that the pro-independence forces had coveted, and had understood was possible only through a declaration of American independence. But whereas Samuel Adams and others had believed that France would ally with the United States immediately after independence was declared, the French proved to be wary. France did not commit to an alliance until early 1778, waiting to be sure that it was not backing a losing cause. The American victory at Saratoga in the autumn of 1777 convinced French leaders that the combination of French naval power and the prowess of the successful Continental army could rapidly bring London to the peace table. France nearly miscalculated. Great Britain held on for forty-two months after the alliance was signed, during which America's economy collapsed and its military capabilities grew steadily more questionable. Had the Franco-American victory at Yorktown not occurred, the odds were considerable that the allies would have had to accept a treaty dictated by a European peace conference.[25]

Lord North remained the British prime minister until a few weeks after word of Yorktown reached London. In 1778, after Saratoga, he at last sought peace and reconciliation by offering bold measures of imperial reform. When North presented his peace plan to Parliament that winter, he did so in a lengthy speech that one observer characterized as the prime minister's "confession and humiliation." North's turnabout was precisely what Dickinson had predicted would happen. Presciently, Dickinson had told Congress in 1775 and 1776 that after a short, brutal war, Great Britain would be willing to give the Americans everything the First Continental Congress had demanded in 1774. In the House of Commons, Charles James Fox bluntly told North that his peace proposals were essentially what the opposition had urged the government to offer rather than rushing to make war. Among other things, North proposed:

repudiation of Parliamentary taxation of the colonies;
recognition of the Continental Congress;
suspension of all American legislation enacted since 1763;
never again keeping a standing army in America during peacetime;
never again changing a colony's charter without the colonists' consent;
assistance to help the colonies retire their war debt; and
consideration of American representation in the House of Commons.[26]

North's proposals were generous, but they came too late. America not only had decided in 1776 that it wanted to be free of Great Britain, but flushed with the great victory at Saratoga, it also knew that its long-coveted alliance with France was at hand. Furthermore, Congress was certain that the Franco-American allies could procure American independence. So the war continued until Yorktown.

It was left to Lord Germain, who, like North, had stayed on through the long war, to bring the prime minister the news of the catastrophe at Yorktown. North, Germain said later, received the tidings "as he would have taken a ball in the breast." Pacing the floor in agitation, North exclaimed: "Oh God, it is all over!"[27] He had never been more correct.

Eight who signed the Declaration of Independence did not live to see the peace treaty that ended the Revolutionary War in 1783. Two were dead within a year of July 4, 1776. John Morton perished of natural causes. Button Gwinnett was killed in a duel. More than half of the signers were gone by the time John Adams was sworn in as president of the United States in 1797. By the time Jefferson's presidency ended in 1809, only sixteen were left. Adams and Jefferson, and Charles Carroll of Carrollton, who had not been in Congress to vote for independence, were the last of the fifty-six signers of the Declaration of Independence still living in America's jubilee year, 1826.

One reason Elbridge Gerry had been so eager to sign the Declaration of Independence was that he anticipated doing so would further his ambition for a long, successful public career and might catapult him to lofty heights.[28] But for the most part, those who had risen to the top in Congress by 1776 continued to predominate in American public life, and those who were lesser congressmen remained secondary figures. To be sure, all who sat in Congress in 1776 were already important figures in their colonies, and most continued to play substantive roles in their states following independence.

The majority of those who sat in Congress on July 2 were gone from that body within a couple of years, but nearly all went on to hold a state office at one time or another after 1776, mostly in the legislature or on the bench. In 1789, Robert R. Livingston gained a minute of national prominence. The chief judicial officer in New York, Chancellor Livingston, as he was called, administered the oath of office to President Washington. Seven signers became state governors. Five sat in the Constitutional Convention in 1787 and three others served in their state's ratification convention that passed on the Constitution. Five sat in Congress after 1789 under the new Constitution, two in the House and three in the Senate. President Washington appointed Samuel Chase to the United States Supreme Court in 1796; he was impeached eight years later but was acquitted in the Senate trial. Seven signers served as soldiers during the Revolutionary War; at least two—Wolcott and Lewis Morris—were on the front lines during major campaigns. Franklin and Adams helped negotiate the Treaty of Paris of 1783, the accord that ended the war and garnered British recognition of American independence. According to legend, Franklin attended the signing ceremony wearing the same suit of spotted Manchester velvet that he had worn on the day of his public humiliation in the Cockpit in January 1774. Subsequently, he, Adams, Jefferson, and Gerry all served as United States ministers to European nations.

Some signers experienced rough going during the War of Independence. Several who lived near the fighting had their homes plundered or destroyed. Four were captured by the British. Rutledge, Heyward, and Middleton endured nearly two years of captivity in Florida. Richard Stockton was taken prisoner late in 1776 and during his few weeks of confinement renounced American independence.

Some in Congress who had opposed independence quickly faded into obscurity, but four flourished politically. George Read, whose opposition made it imperative that Caesar Rodney hurry back to Philadelphia before the vote on July 2, went on to serve as Delaware's chief executive and in the 1790s as its United States senator. Likewise, Rutledge served as governor of South Carolina. Robert Morris and James Wilson were the longtime foes of independence who went on to wield the greatest national influence.

Before July 1776, Morris thought his mercantile company more likely to prosper within the British Empire. Afterward, he reluctantly supported independence and openly acknowledged his hope for peace and the restoration of America's pre-war commerce with the former mother country. Morris played a crucial role in keeping the army supplied in late 1776 and 1777. It was his good fortune to grow steadily wealthier throughout the war, until by its end, he was widely thought to be the richest man in the United States. He was also thought by many to have thrived from insider information and the sale of comestibles to the French armed forces while ignoring the Continental army, which after 1778 increasingly lacked the means of paying for needed items. Morris's business ethics eventually provoked Thomas Paine to publish an attack on his "*low dirty Tricks*," which the essayist thought had introduced a "degree of corruption" into American life. Morris may have acted unethically, but he was wealthy, powerful, and unquestionably shrewd. Those qualities led first to his appointment as the nation's superintendent of finance during the final years of the war and later to his selection as part of Pennsylvania's delegation to the Constitutional Convention in 1787.[29]

Until the last moment, Wilson had resisted independence, fearing the radical political and social change that might be unleashed by the American Revolution. He voted for independence and signed the Declaration, but he spent the Revolution fighting against the Pennsylvania constitution of 1776, which established the most democratic government in America. He and Pennsylvania's other conservatives eventually won their fight, replacing the state's first constitution with a charter that virtually guaranteed control by the elite. Thereafter, Wilson joined the fight to create a strong central government. He, too, sat in the Constitutional Convention, where he played a more substantive role than Morris. Indeed, political scientist Clinton Rossiter concluded that Wilson was second only to James Madison in importance at the Convention, where he worked tirelessly, and ultimately successfully, to fashion a national government under which it would be extremely difficult to bring about meaningful change. He was subsequently nominated for the United States Supreme Court by President Washington and served as an associate justice for nine years.[30]

America's political history has always been filled with unexpected twists and turns. Among the most astonishing was that John Dickinson went on to play a greater role in shaping the new American nation than did Samuel Adams. Even Dickinson, in his final speech against independence, had said that he suspected his political career was over. He left Congress following the vote on independence and commanded his militia battalion for three months. He resigned his commission in September, having lost the confidence of his men and the Pennsylvania government, neither of which thought it right for a foe of independence to lead soldiers in a war that was being waged to set America free of Great Britain. Dickinson took up arms again as a private in a militia company and he was in harm's way during the campaign that was fought after the British army invaded Pennsylvania in 1777. Subsequently, Dickinson served as the chief executive of Delaware, sat on its Supreme Executive Council, and in 1787 was a delegate to the Constitutional Convention, where he worked for the federal system that he had cherished and longed to bring about within the Anglo-American Empire.

Samuel Adams left Congress in 1781. In the years that followed before his death in 1803, he served repeatedly as the moderator of Boston town meetings, sat in the state legislature, and eventually became the governor of Massachusetts, but he never again held a national office. The conservative faction that dominated the state in the 1780s refused to add him to Massachusetts's delegation to the Constitutional Convention. He sought election to the United States House of Representatives in December 1788 from a Boston district, but his fellow Bostonians spurned him in favor of Fisher Ames, a staunch foe of democracy.

No one lost more as a result of the American Revolution than Samuel

Adams's great foe at the First Congress, Joseph Galloway. He had retired from public life and proclaimed himself a neutral in the spring of 1775, but late the following year, as Washington's army retreated across New Jersey, Galloway concluded that a British victory was inevitable. He opportunistically came out of retirement and fled behind British lines, offering the redcoats his help. General Howe subsequently utilized Galloway as an intelligence official, and when Philadelphia fell to the British in September 1777, the former congressman became the police commissioner of the occupied city. Two revolutionaries were executed on Galloway's watch. When the British abandoned Philadelphia in June 1778, Galloway fled with them. In 1779 he went to London, where he wrote countless pamphlets in the hope of keeping British morale from flagging. Following the war, Galloway wished to return to America, but the victorious Pennsylvania authorities threatened him with arrest and trial for his activities in occupied Philadelphia. Galloway might have fared as well as Wilson had he possessed the latter's political sagacity, and especially his uncanny chameleonlike qualities. Instead, he died in exile in England in 1803.

In the long years after 1776, John Adams appears to have given more thought than any other Founder to when and why the colonists embraced the idea of American independence. He was never of one mind on the question. Most famously, he said that the "Revolution was effected before the War commenced. The Revolution was in the Minds and Hearts of the People." The "radical change in the principles, opinions, sentiments, and affections of the People, was the real American Revolution," and those changes occurred "in the course of fifteen Years before a drop of blood was drawn at Lexington."[31] He was suggesting that support for independence evolved slowly in response to a series of British provocations, and that indeed would be an accurate description of the profound changes in outlook that he experienced in the course of nearly a decade after the Stamp Act. But on other occasions Adams said he thought the idea of independence had germinated in the 1740s, when London betrayed American interests in the peace settlement following King George's War; or in the 1750s, when France was driven from Canada as a result of the Seven Years' War; or even as late as 1774, when Parliament enacted the Coercive Acts. In his final years, Adams contended that the idea of independence could be traced back to the first colonists in the seventeenth century. They had been spurred to move to the wilds of America, he said, by a hunger for "Independence [from] English church and state." This led him to conclude: "When we say, that . . . Adams . . . Jefferson, &c., were authors of independence, we ought to say they were only awakeners and revivers of the original fundamental principle of colonization."[32]

Adams did not say that American independence was inevitable, and to be sure, he never suggested that it was certain to occur in his lifetime. No one knew better than Adams how difficult the struggle had been to secure Congress's assent to every defiant step from 1774 onward. The First Congress's statement of American rights had passed by only two or three votes, he subsequently recollected, and he remembered as well that "all the great critical questions" down to the spring of 1776 had been decided by the slimmest of margins. Not infrequently, he recalled, the passage of pivotal measures had hinged on the vote of a single delegate.[33] Adams knew that as late as January 1776 no more than five of the thirteen delegations in Congress, and perhaps not that many, supported American independence.

No one in Congress was more important than Adams in the long struggle for independence. He had rapidly emerged in the Second Congress as the leading figure within the faction of hard-line delegates. Samuel Adams may have initially coached him from behind the curtain, but by sometime in the summer of 1775 John Adams was adroitly managing affairs on his own terms. He wisely understood that Congress could not be pushed toward one truculent stand after another. That would only have created divisions, and it might possibly have driven the more conservative delegates back into the arms of the British government. Instead, John Adams had sought to assuage the reconciliationists, to permit them to play out their hopes, until at long last they discovered what he and Franklin and Jefferson, and all the more radical delegates, had long since come to believe: The mother country would never agree to reconcile with its colonies on fair and just terms. Adams had intuitively understood that time was on his side, for the war would unavoidably radicalize Americans, gradually ripening them for independence.

Adams's greatest virtue was the patience to permit these occurrences to play out, but like any great leader, he understood when the time for final action had arrived. By the late spring and early summer of 1776, Adams knew that the American people were ready for independence, and so too were most congressmen. The time had come, he remarked early in the summer of 1776, to "make thirteen Clocks, strike precisely alike, at the Same Second."[34]

Looking back from the perspective of more than two centuries, it is at first glance astonishing that Great Britain failed to prevent America's independence. Britain's rulers had many opportunities from 1766 onward to make choices that could have peacefully terminated the American protest and restored not only the tranquility that had previously existed within the empire but also the affection that most colonists felt toward their mother country. Had the king and his ministers taken to heart the Virginia Resolves, or

Franklin's warning in 1766 that they risked losing the colonists' respect and admiration, the Stamp Act would never have been followed by an inflammatory pronouncement claiming the unlimited authority of Parliament. The American protests against the Townshend Duties in the late 1760s afforded Britain's rulers with a second opportunity to abandon further provocative taxes. Even as the crisis mounted in the wake of the Boston Tea Party, Britain in 1774, or again in 1775, might have chosen the path of reform rather than stridency. Edmund Burke and a handful of others in Parliament understood that a sincere offer of imperial reform might meet with American approval or, at the very least, it could conceivably so divide the colonists that Congress could be forced into an accommodation. To be sure, Great Britain would have had to grant a greater measure of self-government to the colonists, and the colonists, in turn, would have had to accept a lesser degree of autonomy than their most radical leaders desired. But had London pursued such an enlightened course, it is inconceivable that American independence would have been declared in 1776, or probably even within the lifetimes of those whom we call the Founding Fathers. As Burke charged in one of his first speeches after American independence was declared, the British government "drove them [the colonists] into the declaration of independency; not as a matter of choice, but necessity—and now they have declared it."[35]

On reflection, America's declaration of independence, which at first blush appears to have been avoidable, was in fact nearly inevitable. Time and again throughout history, rulers in the thrall of nationalistic fervor, fearful of appearing weak and indecisive, beholden to the interests of the few that are reaping fortunes from the status quo, and above all spurred by a sense of potency and superiority have been unwilling to bend in the face of changing times. That was the case with Lord North and his king, and with the majority in Parliament. Only forty days before independence was declared, the king in a speech before Parliament made the preposterous claim that Great Britain "can have no safety or security but in that constitutional subordination for which we are contending."[36] Inexorably, myopically, George III and his ministers led Great Britain down a path that they believed would save the British Empire. Instead, the fatal course they chose—that they seemingly could not avoid choosing—led to the loss of most of Britain's Empire in North America.

Today, the best-remembered aspect of the American Revolution may be the Declaration of Independence. However, as historian Pauline Maier has pointed out, the Declaration was quickly "all-but-forgotten" by the Revolutionary generation. The merrymaking in America's cities and hamlets in the summer of 1776 had far more to do with Congress's having declared independence than for the stirring Declaration of Independence itself. Little or nothing was said about the Declaration of Independence during the remainder of the war—or for that matter, until the 1790s. Only then did Americans care enough about the Declaration of Independence even to wonder for the first time who had been its principal author.[37]

It seems odd that a document that came to mean so much to Americans in the centuries that followed could have been so ignored by the Revolutionary generation. It may have been that Jefferson, who had said that his design was to avoid "aiming at originality of principle or sentiment," had succeeded too well.[38] What Jefferson had written about the rights of humankind, as well as the charges he leveled against Britain's leaders, had been broached previously by colonial assemblies, local revolutionary committees, and the Continental Congress. What Jefferson had written was commonplace to his wartime audience.

Only two tracts written during the American Revolution, both penned by Thomas Paine, gained widespread traction with contemporaries. *Common Sense*, the first publication to openly denounce reconciliation and enumerate sound reasons for independence, was fresh and bold, and it electrified the public. In January 1777, in the midst of the despair that flowed from Washington's humbling defeats in New York and his desperate retreat through New Jersey, Paine did it again with the initial essay in *The American Crisis*, a pamphlet that boosted the morale of the the shaken but hopeful Americans.

It was not until the 1790s that the Declaration of Independence first began to be seen as what has been called America's "holy writ" and "sacred text." Speeches or documents that win immediate acclaim are sometimes prized by subsequent generations. That was true of the majestic inaugural addresses of Abraham Lincoln, Franklin D. Roosevelt, and John F. Kennedy and of Martin Luther King Jr.'s inspirational "I have a dream" speech. More frequently, that which is hailed by contemporaries fails the test of time, as was the case with General Douglas MacArthur's "Old soldiers never die" speech in 1951, now a largely forgotten oration. It is extremely rare indeed for something that was initially largely ignored to be exalted by subsequent generations.

Widespread appreciation of the Declaration of Independence initially became evident only when more than half the population was too young to have remembered 1776 or the bitter events leading to it. That, not coincidentally, occurred during the fierce party battles in the 1790s. The Republican Party, largely Jefferson's creation, not only celebrated the Declaration; it also made sure that the public knew the identity of its author.

Starting around 1815, leading Americans, fearful that the memory of the American Revolution was in danger of being lost as the Revolutionary generation passed from the scene, made a concerted effort to preserve as much as possible about America's struggle for independence. Documents and recollections were published, and paintings of events during the Revolution were commissioned. John Trumbull, for instance, painted four scenes commemorating the American Revolution for the new capitol in Washington. His initial work depicted the Committee of Five presenting the draft Declaration of Independence to the Continental Congress.[39]

The striking coincidence of the deaths of Adams and Jefferson on July 4, 1826—the fiftieth anniversary of the Declaration of Independence—additionally helped to reacquaint that generation with the document and to preserve the memory of those two revolutionaries. For that time period, the great triumvirate of the American Revolution, as broadcast by countless orators, came to be Washington, the Revolution's mighty "sword"; Adams, its resounding "tongue"; and Jefferson, its eloquent "pen."[40]

But it was not mere happenstance or politics that caused the Declaration of Independence to become America's most treasured text. The Declaration's content, and Jefferson's felicitous composition, caused those who came after 1776 to embrace and sanctify it. Jefferson wrote about the threats faced by his generation, but he succeeded in penning a timeless message, an affirmation of human liberty and dignity that has captured the hopes of succeeding generations. In time, new generations emerged and faced their own battles against tyranny and injustice, whether the struggle was against slavery or racial oppression, or for the rights of workers or women. In the course of these crusades, people born long after 1776 discovered the Declaration of Independence's ringing passages on equality and natural rights. As they drew sustenance from what Jefferson had said America stood for, the Declaration of Independence at last came to be a living document for Americans, a statement that embodied the national credo and gave an enduring meaning to the American Revolution.

APPENDIX

IN CONGRESS, JULY 4, 1776.
A DECLARATION BY THE
REPRESENTATIVES OF THE
UNITED STATES OF AMERICA,
IN GENERAL CONGRESS
ASSEMBLED.[1]

WHEN in the course of human Events, it becomes necessary for one People to dissolve the Political Bands which have connected them with another, and to assume among the Powers of the Earth, the separate and equal Station to which the Laws of Nature and of Nature's God entitle them, a decent Respect to the Opinions of Mankind requires that they should declare the causes which impel them to the Separation.

WE hold these Truths to be self-evident, that all Men are created equal, that they are endowed by their Creator with certain unalienable Rights, that among these are Life, Liberty, and the pursuit of Happiness—That to secure these Rights, Governments are instituted among Men, deriving their just Powers from the Consent of the Governed, that whenever any Form of Government becomes destructive of these Ends, it is the Right of the People to alter or abolish it, and to institute a new Government, laying its Foundation on such Principles, and organizing its Powers in such Form, as to them shall seem most likely to effect their Safety and Happiness. Prudence, indeed, will dictate that Governments long established should not be changed for light and transient Causes; and accordingly all Experience hath shewn, that Mankind are more disposed to suffer, while Evils are sufferable, than to right themselves by abolishing the Forms to which they are accustomed. But when a long Train of Abuses and Usurpations, pursuing invariably the same Object, evinces a Design to reduce them under absolute Despotism, it is their Right, it is their Duty, to throw off such Government, and to provide new Guards for their future Security. Such has been the patient Sufferance of these Colonies; and such is now the Necessity which constrains them to alter their former Systems of Government. The History of the Present King of Great-Britain is a History of repeated Injuries and Usurpations, all having in direct Object the Establishment of an absolute Tyranny over these States. To prove this, let Facts be submitted to a candid World.

HE has refused his Assent to Laws, the most wholesome and necessary for the public Good.

HE has forbidden his Governors to pass Laws of immediate and pressing Importance, unless suspended in their Operation till his Assent should be obtained; and when so suspended, he has utterly neglected to attend to them.

HE has refused to pass other Laws for the Accommodation of large Districts of People; unless those People would relinquish the Right of Representation in the Legislature, a Right inestimable to them, and formidable to Tyrants only.

HE has called together Legislative Bodies at Places unusual, uncomfortable, and distant from the Depository of their public Records, for the sole Purpose of fatiguing them into Compliance with his Measures.

HE has dissolved Representative Houses repeatedly, for opposing with manly Firmness his Invasions on the Rights of the People.

HE has refused for a long Time, after such Dissolutions, to cause others to be elected; whereby the Legislative Powers, incapable of Annihilation, have returned to the People at large for their exercise; the State remaining in the mean time exposed to all the Dangers of Invasion from without, and Convulsions within.

HE has endeavoured to prevent the Population of these States; for that Purpose obstructing the Laws for Naturalization of Foreigners; refusing to pass others to encourage their Migrations hither, and raising the Conditions of new Appropriations of Lands.

HE has obstructed the Administration of Justice, by refusing his Assent to Laws for establishing Judiciary Powers.

HE has made Judges dependent on his Will alone, for the Tenure of their Offices, and Amount and Payment of their Salaries.

He has erected a Multitude of new Offices, and sent hither Swarms of Officers to harass our People, and eat out their Substance.

He has kept among us, in Times of Peace, Standing Armies, without the consent of our Legislature.

He has affected to render the Military independent of and superior to the Civil Power.

He has combined with others to subject us to a Jurisdiction foreign to our Constitution, and unacknowledged by our Laws; giving his Assent to their Acts of pretended Legislation:

For quartering large Bodies of Armed Troops among us:

For protecting them, by a mock Trial, from Punishment for any Murders which they should commit on the Inhabitants of these States:

For cutting off our Trade with all Parts of the World:

For imposing taxes on us without our Consent:

For depriving us, in many Cases, of the Benefits of Trial by Jury:

For transporting us beyond Seas to be tried for pretended Offences:

For abolishing the free System of English Laws in a neighbouring Province, establishing therein an arbitrary Government, and enlarging its Boundaries, so as to render it at once an Example and fit Instrument for introducing the same absolute Rule in these Colonies:

For taking away our Charters, abolishing our most valuable Laws, and altering fundamentally the Forms of our Governments:

For suspending our own Legislatures, and declaring themselves invested with Powers to legislate for us in all Cases whatsoever.

He has abdicated Government here, by declaring us out of his Protection and waging War against us.

HE has plundered our Seas, ravaged our Coasts, burnt our Towns, and destroyed the Lives of our People.

HE is, at this Time, transporting large Armies of foreign Mercenaries to compleat the Works of Death, Desolation, and Tyranny, already begun with circumstances of Cruelty and Perfidy, scarcely paralleled in the most barbarous Ages, and totally unworthy the Head of a civilized Nation.

HE has constrained our fellow Citizens taken Captive on the high Seas to bear Arms against their Country, to become the Executioners of their Friends and Brethren, or to fall themselves by their Hands.

HE has excited domestic Insurrections among us, and has endeavoured to bring on the Inhabitants of our Frontiers, the merciless Indian Savages, whose known Rule of Warfare, is an undistinguished Destruction, of all Ages, Sexes and Conditions.

IN every stage of these Oppressions we have Petitioned for Redress in the most humble Terms: Our repeated Petitions have been answered only by repeated Injury. A Prince, whose Character is thus marked by every act which may define a Tyrant, is unfit to be the Ruler of a free People.

NOR have we been wanting in Attentions to our British Brethren. We have warned them from Time to Time of Attempts by their Legislature to extend an unwarrantable Jurisdiction over us. We have reminded them of the Circumstances of our Emigration and Settlement here. We have appealed to their native Justice and Magnanimity, and we have conjured them by the Ties of our common Kindred to disavow these Usurpations, which, would inevitably interrupt our Connections and Correspondence. They too have been deaf to the Voice of Justice and of Consanguinity. We must, therefore, acquiesce in the Necessity, which denounces our Separation, and hold them, as we hold the rest of Mankind, Enemies in War, in Peace, Friends.

WE, therefore, the Representatives of the UNITED STATES OF AMERICA, in GENERAL CONGRESS, Assembled, appealing to the Supreme Judge of the World for the Rectitude of our Intentions, do, in the Name, and by the Authority of the good People of these Colonies, solemnly Publish and Declare, That these United Colonies are, and of Right ought to be, FREE AND INDEPENDENT STATES; that they are absolved from all Allegiance to the British Crown, and that all political Connection between them and the State of Great-Britain, is and ought to be totally dissolved; and that as FREE AND INDEPENDENT STATES, they have full Power to levy War, conclude Peace, contract Alliances, establish Commerce, and to do all other Acts and Things which INDEPEN-DENT STATES may of right do. And for the support of this Declaration, with a firm Reliance on the Protection of the divine Providence, we mutually pledge to each other our Lives, our Fortunes, and our sacred Honor.

Signed by ORDER *and in* BEHALF *of the* CONGRESS,
JOHN HANCOCK, PRESIDENT.

ATTEST.
CHARLES THOMSON, SECRETARY.

ABBREVIATIONS

AA	Abigail Adams
AFC	L. H. Butterfield et al., eds. *Adams Family Correspondence.* Cambridge, Mass.: Harvard University Press, 1963–.
Am Archives 4th series	Peter Force, ed. *American Archives.* 4th series. 6 vols. Washington, D.C.: U.S. Government Printing Office, 1837–1846.
Am Archives 5th series	Peter Force, ed. *American Archives*, 5th series. 3 vols. Washington, D.C.: U.S. Government Printing Office, 1847–1853.
BF	Benjamin Franklin
DAJA	L. H. Butterfield et al., eds. *The Diary and Autobiography of John Adams.* 4 vols. Cambridge, Mass.: Harvard University Press, 1961.
DAR	K. G. Davies, ed. *Documents of the American Revolution.* Dublin: Irish University Press, 1972–1981.
DGW	Donald Jackson et al., eds. *The Diaries of George Washington.* Charlottesville: University Press of Virginia, 1976–1979.
EHD	David C. Douglas et al., eds. *English Historical Documents.* London: Eyre & Spottiswoode (Publishers) Ltd.; and New York: Oxford University Press, 1956–.
GW	George Washington
JA	John Adams
JCC	Worthington C. Ford et al., eds. *The Journals of the Continental Congress, 1774–89.* 34 vols. Washington, D.C.: Library of Congress, 1904–1937.
LDC	Paul H. Smith et al., eds. *Letters of Delegates to Congress, 1774–89.* 29 vols. Washington, D.C.: Library of Congress, 1976–2000.
PBF	Leonard W. Labaree et al., eds. *The Papers of Benjamin Franklin.* New Haven, Conn.: Yale University Press, 1959–.
PGWC	W. W. Abbot et al., eds. *The Papers of George Washington: Colonial Series.* Charlottesville: University Press of Virginia, 1983–95.
PGWR	Philander Chase et al., eds. *The Papers of George Washington: Revolutionary War Series.* Charlottesville: University Press of Virginia, 1985–.

PH	T. C. Hansard, ed. *The Parliamentary History of England* . . . *The Parliamentary Debates.* London, 1806–20.
PJA	Robert J. Taylor et al., eds. *Papers of John Adams.* Cambridge, Mass.: Harvard University Press, 1977–.
PTJ	Julian P. Boyd et al., eds. *The Papers of Thomas Jefferson.* Princeton, N. J.: Princeton University Press, 1950–.
SA	Samuel Adams
TJ	Thomas Jefferson
WJA	Charles Francis Adams, ed. *The Works of John Adams, Second President of the United States: With a Life of the Author.* 10 vols. Boston, 1850–56.
WSA	Harry Alonzo Cushing, ed. *The Writings of Samuel Adams.* 4 vols. Reprint, New York: Octagon Books, 1968.

SELECT BIBLIOGRAPHY

The literature on the American Revolution is enormous. What follows is not a comprehensive bibliography but rather a guide to books and articles that I found especially helpful. Many additional works can be found in the notes.

PAPERS AND DOCUMENTARY COLLECTIONS

Adams, John: Charles Francis Adams, ed., *The Works of John Adams, Second President of the United States: With a Life of the Author*, 10 vols. (Boston, 1850–56); L. H. Butterfield et al., eds., *Adams Family Correspondence* (Cambridge, Mass., 1963–); idem, *The Diary and Autobiography of John Adams*, 4 vols. (Cambridge, Mass., 1961); Lestor J. Cappon, ed., *The Adams-Jefferson Letters: The Complete Correspondence Between Thomas Jefferson and Abigail and John Adams*, 2 vols. (Chapel Hill, N.C., 1961); John A. Schutz and Douglass Adair, eds., *The Spur of Fame: Dialogues of John Adams and Benjamin Rush, 1805–1813* (San Marino, Calif., 1966); Robert J. Taylor et al., eds., *Papers of John Adams* (Cambridge, Mass., 1977–).

Adams, Samuel: Harry Alonzo Cushing, ed., *The Writings of Samuel Adams*, 4 vols. (New York, 1904–8).

American Revolution: K. G. Davies, ed., *Documents of the American Revolution, 1770–1783*, 21 vols. (Dublin, 1972–81); Peter Force, *American Archives*, 4th series, 6 vols. (Washington, D.C., 1837–46); idem, *American Archives*, 5th series, 3 vols. (Washington, D.C., 1847–53); Merrill Jensen, ed., *Tracts of the American Revolution, 1763–1776* (Indianapolis, Ind., 1967); idem, ed., *American Colonial Documents to 1776*, vol. 9, in David C. Douglas, ed., *English Historical Documents*, 12 vols. (London, 1956–70).

Continental Congress: Worthington C. Ford et al., eds., *The Journals of the Continental Congress, 1774–1789*, 34 vols. (Washington, D.C., 1904–37); Paul H. Smith et al., eds., *Letters of Delegates to Congress, 1774–1789*, 29 vols. (Washington, D.C., 1976–2000).

Dickinson, John: Paul Leicester Ford, ed., *The Writings of John Dickinson* (Philadelphia, 1895).

Franklin, Benjamin: Verner Crane, ed., *Benjamin Franklin's Letters to the Press* (Chapel Hill, N.C., 1960); Leonard W. Labaree et al., eds., *The Papers of Benjamin Franklin* (New Haven, Conn., 1959–).

Great Britain: [Anon.], *The Manuscripts of the Earl of Dartmouth: Prepared by the Historical Manuscript Commission of Great Britain*, 3 vols. (reprint, Boston, 1972); Clarence Carter, ed., *The Correspondence of General Thomas Gage with the Secretaries of State, and the War Office and the Treasury, 1763–1775* (reprint, New York, 1969); Harry T.

Dickinson, ed., *British Pamphlets on the American Revolution, 1763–1785*, 4 vols. (London, 2007); David C. Douglas, ed., *English Historical Documents*, 12 vols. (London, 1956–1970); John Fortescue, ed., *The Correspondence of George III from 1760 to December 1783* (London, 1927–28); George H. Guttridge et al., eds., *The Correspondence of Edmund Burke*, 10 vols. (Chicago, 1958); T. C. Hansard, ed., *The Parliamentary History of England . . . The Parliamentary Debates*, 36 vols. (London, 1806–20); David Murdoch, *Rebellion in America: A Contemporary British Viewpoint, 1765–1783* (Santa Barbara, Calif., 1979); Lord John Russell, ed., *Memorials and Correspondence of Charles James Fox* (reprint, New York, 1970).

Jefferson, Thomas: Julian P. Boyd et al., eds., *The Papers of Thomas Jefferson* (Princeton, N.J., 1950–); Lestor J. Cappon, ed., *The Adams-Jefferson Letters: The Complete Correspondence Between Thomas Jefferson and Abigail and John Adams*, 2 vols. (Chapel Hill, N.C., 1961); Paul Leicester Ford, ed., *The Writings of Thomas Jefferson*, 10 vols. (New York, 1892–99); A. A. Lipscomb and A. E. Bergh, eds., *The Writings of Thomas Jefferson*, 20 vols. (Washington, D.C., 1900–1904); Saul K. Padover, ed., *The Complete Jefferson* (New York, 1943).

Paine, Thomas: Philip S. Foner, ed., *The Complete Writings of Thomas Paine*, 2 vols. (New York, 1945).

Rodney, Caesar: George Herbert Ryden, ed., *Letters to and from Caesar Rodney* (reprint, New York, 1970).

Washington, George: W. W. Abbot et al., eds., *The Papers of George Washington: Colonial Series*, 10 vols. (Charlottesville, Va., 1983–95); idem, *The Papers of George Washington: Revolutionary War Series* (Charlottesville, Va., 1985–); Donald Jackson et al., eds., *The Diaries of George Washington*, 6 vols. (Charlottesville, Va., 1976–79).

SECONDARY SOURCES

THE AMERICAN REVOLUTION

John Richard Alden, *The American Revolution, 1775–1783* (New York, 1954); David Ammerman, *In the Common Cause: American Response to the Coercive Acts of 1774* (Charlottesville, Va., 1974); Richard Archer, *As If an Enemy's Country* (New York, 2010); Bernard Bailyn, *The Ideological Origins of the American Revolution* (Cambridge, Mass., 1967); idem, *The Ordeal of Thomas Hutchinson* (Cambridge, Mass., 1974); T. H. Breen, *American Insurgents, American Patriots: The Revolution of the People* (New York, 2010); Weldon Brown, *Empire or Independence: A Study in the Failure of Reconciliation, 1774–1783* (Baton Rouge, La., 1941); Benjamin Carp, *Defiance of the Patriots: The Boston Tea Party and the Making of America* (New Haven, Conn., 2010); idem, *Rebels Rising: Cities and the American Revolution* (New York, 2007); Ian Christie and Benjamin Labaree, *Empire or Independence: A British-American Dialogue on the Coming of the American Revolution* (New York, 1976); H. Trevor Colbourne, *The Lamp of Experience: Whig History and the Intellectual Origins of the American Revolution* (Chapel Hill, N.C., 1965); Edward Countryman, *The American Revolution* (New York, 1983); Philip Davidson, *Propaganda and the American Revolution, 1763–1776* (Chapel Hill, N.C., 1941); Jonathan Dull, *A Diplomatic History of the American Revolution* (New Haven, Conn., 1985); John Ferling, *A Leap in the Dark: The Struggle to Create the American Republic* (New York, 2003); Jay Fliegelman, *Prodigals and*

Pilgrims: The American Revolution Against Patriarchal Authority (New York, 1982); Jack P. Greene, "An Uneasy Connection: An Analysis of the Preconditions of the American Revolution," in Stephen G. Kurtz and James H. Hutson, eds., *Essays on the American Revolution* (Chapel Hill, N.C., 1973); William Hogeland, *Declaration: The Nine Tumultuous Weeks When America Became Independent, May 1–July 4, 1776* (New York, 2010); James H. Hutson, "The Partition Treaty and the Declaration of Independence," *Journal of American History* 58 (1972): 877–96; Merrill Jensen, *The Founding of a Nation: A History of the American Revolution* (New York, 1967); Milton Klein, "Failure of a Mission: The Drummond Peace Proposal of 1775," *Huntington Library Quarterly* 35 (1972): 343–80; Benjamin Woods Labaree, *The Boston Tea Party* (New York, 1964); Brendan McConville, *The King's Three Faces: The Rise and Fall of Royal America, 1688–1776* (Chapel Hill, N.C., 2006); Robert Middlekauff, *The Glorious Cause: The American Revolution, 1763–1789* (revised edition, New York, 2007); Pauline Maier, *From Resistance to Revolution: Colonial Radicals and the Development of Opposition to Great Britain, 1765–1776* (New York, 1972); Philip James McFarland, *The Brave Bostonians: Hutchinson, Quincy, Franklin, and the Coming of the American Revolution* (Boulder, Colo., 1998); Jack N. Rakove, *Revolutionaries: A New History of the Invention of America* (Boston, 2010); Ray Raphael, *Founders: The People Who Brought You a Nation* (New York, 2009); idem, *The First American Revolution: Before Lexington and Concord* (New York, 2002); Arthur M. Schlesinger, *Prelude to Independence: The Newspaper War of Britain, 1764–1776* (New York, 1966); Richard van Alstyne, *The Rising American Empire* (Oxford, 1960); Stanley Weintraub, *Iron Tears: America's Battle for Freedom, Britain's Quagmire, 1775–1783* (New York, 2005); Gordon S. Wood, *The Creation of the American Republic, 1776–1787* (New York, 1969); idem, *The Radicalism of the American Revolution* (New York, 1992); Hiller B. Zobel, *The Boston Massacre* (New York, 1970).

THE CONTINENTAL CONGRESS

Edmund C. Burnett, *The Continental Congress* (New York, 1941); H. James Henderson, *Party Politics in the Continental Congress* (New York, 1974); Jerrilyn Greene Marston, *King and Congress: The Transfer of Political Legitimacy, 1774–1776* (Princeton, N.J., 1987); Jack N. Rakove, *The Beginnings of National Politics: An Interpretive History of the Continental Congress* (Baltimore, Md., 1982).

THE DECLARATION OF INDEPENDENCE AND ITS HISTORY

George Anastaplo, "The Declaration of Independence," *Saint Louis University Law Journal* 9 (1964–65): 390–415; Carl Becker, *The Declaration of Independence: A Study in the History of Political Ideas* (New York, 1960); Julian P. Boyd, *The Declaration of Independence: The Evolution of the Text as Shown in Facsimilies of Various Drafts by Its Author* (Washington, D.C., 1943); J. M. Bumstead, "'Things in the Womb of Time': Ideas of American Independence, 1633–1763," *William and Mary Quarterly* 31 (1974): 533–64; Philip F. Detweiler, "The Changing Reputation of the Declaration of Independence: The First Fifty Years," *William and Mary Quarterly*, 3d series, 19 (1962): 558–85; Edward Dumbauld, *The Declaration of Independence and What It Means Today*

(Norman, Okla., 1950); Jay Fliegelman, *Declaring Independence: Jefferson, Natural Language, and the Culture of Performance* (Stanford, Calif., 1993); Herbert Friedenwald, *The Declaration of Independence: An Interpretation and an Analysis* (New York, 1904); Herbert Lawrence Ganter, "Jefferson's 'Pursuit of Happiness' and Some Forgotten Men," *William and Mary Quarterly*, 2d series, 16 (1936): 422–34, 558–85; David Hawke, *Honorable Treason: The Declaration of Independence and the Men Who Signed It* (New York, 1976); idem, *A Transaction of Free Men: The Birth and Course of the Declaration of Independence* (New York, 1964); John Hazleton, *The Declaration of Independence: Its History* (New York, 1906); Stephen E. Lucas, "Justifying America: The Declaration of Independence as a Rhetorical Document," in Thomas W. Benson, ed., *American Rhetoric: Context and Criticism* (Carbondale, Ill., 1989); Pauline Maier, *American Scripture: Making the Declaration of Independence* (New York, 1998); David C. Mearns, *The Declaration of Independence: The Story of a Parchment* (Washington, D.C., 1950); Peter S. Onuf, "A Declaration of Independence for Diplomatic Historians," in Peter S. Onuf, ed., *The Mind of Thomas Jefferson* (Charlottesville, Va., 2007); John Philip Reid, "The Irrelevance of the Declaration," in Hendrik Hartog, ed., *Law in the American Revolution and the Revolution in Law* (New York, 1981); Eric Slauter, "The Declaration of Independence and the New Nation," in Frank Shuffelton, ed., *The Cambridge Companion to Thomas Jefferson* (Cambridge, 2009); Garry Wills, *Inventing America: Jefferson's Declaration of Independence* (Garden City, N.Y., 1978).

GREAT BRITAIN IN THE IMPERIAL CRISIS

Troy Bickham, *Making Headlines: The American Revolution as Seen Through the British Press* (DeKalb, Ill., 2009); Colin Bonwick, *English Radicals and the American Revolution* (Chapel Hill, N.C., 1977); Ian Christie, *Wars and Revolutions: Britain, 1760–1815* (Cambridge, Mass., 1982); Dora Mae Clark, *British Opinion and the American Revolution* (reprint, New York, 1966); Stephen Conway, *The British Isles and the War of Independence* (New York, 2000); idem, *The War of American Independence* (London, 1995); John Derry, *British Politics and the American Revolution* (New York, 1976); H. T. Dickinson, ed., *Britain and the American Revolution* (London, 1998); idem, ed., *A Companion to Eighteenth-Century Britain* (London, 2002); Bernard Donahue, *British Politics and the American Revolution: The Path to War, 1773–1775* (London, 1964); Warren Elofson and John A. Woods, eds., *Party, Parliament, and the American War, 1774–1780* (Oxford, 1996); Eliga H. Gould, *The Persistence of Empire: British Political Culture in the Age of the American Revolution* (Chapel Hill, N.C., 2000); Ira Gruber, *The Howe Brothers and the American Revolution* (New York, 1972); Fred Junkin Hinkhouse, *The Preliminaries of the American Revolution as Seen in the British Press, 1763–1775* (reprint, New York, 1969); Solomon Lutnick, *The American Revolution and the British Press, 1763–1783* (Columbia, Mo., 1967); J. H. Plumb, *England in the Eighteenth Century* (Baltimore, Md., 1950); Jack Sosin, "The Massachusetts Acts of 1774: Coercive or Preventive?" *Huntington Library Quarterly* 26 (1963): 235–52; Peter D. G. Thomas, *British Politics and the Stamp Crisis: The First Phase of the American Revolution, 1763–1767* (New York, 1975); idem, *The Townshend Duty Crisis: The Second Phase of the American Revolution, 1767–1773* (New York, 1987); idem, *Tea Party to Independence: The Third Phase of the American Revolution, 1773–1776* (New York, 1991); Kathleen

Wilson, *Sense of the People: Politics, Culture and Imperialism in England, 1715-1785* (Cambridge, 1995).

THE ANGLO-AMERICAN WAR, 1775-76

Louis Birnbaum, *Red Dawn at Lexington* (Boston, 1986); Thomas A. Desjardin, *Through a Howling Wilderness: Benedict Arnold's March to Quebec, 1775* (New York, 2006); John Ferling, *Almost a Miracle: The American Victory in the War of Independence* (New York, 2007); David Hackett Fischer, *Paul Revere's Ride* (New York, 1994); Richard Frothingham, *History of the Siege of Boston* (Boston, 1849); Richard M. Ketchum, *Decisive Day: The Battle for Bunker Hill* (New York, 1974); Arthur Lefkowitz, *Benedict Arnold's Army: The 1775 Invasion of Canada During the Revolutionary War* (New York and El Dorado Hills, Calif., 2008); James Kirby Martin, *Benedict Arnold: Revolutionary Hero: An American Warrior Reconsidered* (New York, 1977); Piers Mackesy, *The War for America, 1775-1783* (Cambridge, Mass., 1964); David McCullough, *1776* (New York, 2005); Hal Shelton, *General Richard Montgomery and the American Revolution* (New York, 1994); Christopher Ward, *The War of the Revolution*, 2 vols. (New York, 1952).

BIOGRAPHIES

FOREMOST AMERICAN CONGRESSMEN TO 1776 (IN ALPHABETICAL ORDER)

Adams, John: Joseph Ellis, *Passionate Sage: The Character and Legacy of John Adams* (New York, 1993); John Ferling, *John Adams: A Life* (reprint, New York, 2010); John Howe, *The Changing Political Thought of John Adams* (Princeton, N.J., 1966); David McCullough, *John Adams* (New York, 2001).

Adams, Samuel: John K. Alexander, *Samuel Adams: America's Revolutionary Politician* (Lanham, Md., 2002); Cass Canfield, *Samuel Adams's Revolution, 1765-1776* (New York, 1972); William C. Fowler, *Samuel Adams: Radical Puritan* (New York, 1997); Pauline Maier, *The Old Revolutionaries: Political Leaders in the Age of Samuel Adams* (New York, 1982); John C. Miller, *Sam Adams: Pioneer in Propaganda* (Boston, 1936); Ira Stoll, *Samuel Adams: A Life* (New York, 2008).

Dickinson, John: Milton E. Flower, *John Dickinson: Conservative Revolutionary* (Charlottesville, Va., 1983); David L. Jacobson, *John Dickinson and the Revolution in Pennsylvania, 1764-1776* (Berkeley, Calif., 1965).

Franklin, Benjamin: H. W. Brands, *The First American: The Life and Times of Benjamin Franklin* (New York, 2000); David Freeman Hawke, *Franklin* (New York, 1976); J. A. Leo Lemay, *The Life of Benjamin Franklin*, 3 vols. (Philadelphia, 2006-9); Edmund S. Morgan, *Benjamin Franklin* (New Haven, Conn., 2002); Carl Van Doren, *Benjamin Franklin* (New York, 1938); Gordon S. Wood, *The Americanization of Benjamin Franklin* (New York, 2004); Esmond Wright, *Franklin of Philadelphia* (Cambridge, Mass., 1986).

Galloway, Joseph: John Ferling, *The Loyalist Mind: Joseph Galloway and the American Revolution* (University Park, Pa., 1977); Benjamin H. Newcomb, *Franklin and Galloway: A Political Partnership* (New Haven, Conn., 1972).

Gerry, Elbridge: George Athan Billias, *Elbridge Gerry: Founding Father and Republican Statesman* (New York, 1976).

Henry, Patrick: Richard R. Beeman, *Patrick Henry: A Biography* (New York, 1974); Kevin J. Hayes, *The Mind of a Patriot: Patrick Henry and the World of Ideas* (Charlottesville, Va., 2008); Robert D. Meade, *Patrick Henry*, 2 vols. (Philadelphia, 1957–69).

Jefferson, Thomas: Andrew Burstein and Nancy Isenberg, *Madison and Jefferson* (New York, 2010); R. B. Bernstein, *Thomas Jefferson* (New York, 2003); Fawn Brodie, *Thomas Jefferson: An Intimate History* (New York, 1974); Noble E. Cunningham Jr., *In Pursuit of Reason: The Life of Thomas Jefferson* (New York, 1997); Frank J. Dewey, *Thomas Jefferson, Lawyer* (Charlottesville, Va., 1986); Joseph Ellis, *American Sphinx: The Character of Thomas Jefferson* (New York, 1997); John Ferling, *Setting the World Ablaze: Washington, Adams, Jefferson, and the American Revolution* (New York, 2000); Dumas Malone, *Jefferson and His Times*, 6 vols. (Boston, 1948–81); Jack McLoughlin, *Jefferson, and Monticello* (New York, 1988); Peter S. Onuf, ed., *The Mind of Thomas Jefferson* (Charlottesville, Va., 2007); Merrill D. Peterson, *Thomas Jefferson and the New Nation: A Biography* (New York, 1970); Willard Sterne Randall, *Thomas Jefferson: A Life* (New York, 1992); Nathan Schachner, *Thomas Jefferson: A Biography* (New York, 1951).

Lee, Richard Henry: Oliver Perry Chitwood, *Richard Henry Lee: Statesman of the Revolution* (Morgantown, W.Va., 1967); J. Kent McGaughy, *Richard Henry Lee of Virginia: A Portrait of an American Revolutionary* (Lanham, Md., 2004).

Livingston, Robert R.: George Dangerfield, *Chancellor Robert R. Livingston, 1746–1813* (New York, 1960).

Morris, Robert: Clarence L. Ver Steeg, *Robert Morris: Revolutionary Financier* (New York, 1972).

Sherman, Roger: Christopher Collier, *Roger Sherman's Connecticut: Yankee Politicians and the American Revolution* (Middletown, Conn., 1971).

Washington, George: Ron Chernow, *Washington: A Life* (New York, 2010); John Ferling, *The First of Men: A Life of George Washington* (reprint, New York, 2010); James T. Flexner, *George Washington*, 4 vols. (Boston, 1965–72); Douglas Southall Freeman, *George Washington: A Biography*, 7 vols. (New York, 1948–57).

Wilson, James: Mark David Hall, *The Political and Legal Philosophy of James Wilson, 1742–1798* (Columbia, Mo., 1997); Charles Page Smith, *James Wilson: Founding Father, 1742–1798* (Chapel Hill, N.C., 1956).

FOREMOST BRITISH POLITICAL FIGURES TO 1776
(IN ALPHABETICAL ORDER)

Burke, Edmund: Carl B. Cone, *Burke and the Nature of Politics: The Age of the American Revolution* (Lexington, Ky., 1957).

Dartmouth, Earl of: B. D. Bargar, *Lord Dartmouth and the American Revolution* (Columbia, S.C., 1965).

Fox, Charles James: John Derry, *Charles James Fox* (New York, 1972); John Drinkwater, *Charles James Fox* (New York, 1928); Christopher Hobhouse, *Fox* (reprint, London, 1964); L. G. Mitchell, *Charles James Fox* (New York, 1992); Loren Reid, *Charles James Fox: A Man for the People* (Columbia, Mo., 1969).

Gage, General Thomas: John R. Alden, *General Gage in America: Being Principally a History of His Role in the American Revolution* (Baton Rouge, La., 1948); John Shy,

"Thomas Gage: Weak Link of Empire," in George A. Billias, ed., *George Washington's Opponents: British Generals and Admirals in the American Revolution* (New York, 1969).

George III: Stanley Ayling, *George the Third* (New York, 1972); Jeremy Black, *George III: America's Last King* (New Haven, Conn., 2006).

Germain, Lord George: Gerald Saxon Brown, *The American Secretary: The Colonial Policy of Lord George Germain, 1775–1778* (Ann Arbor, Mich., 1963); Alan Valentine, *Lord George Germain* (Oxford, 1962).

Howe, General William and Admiral Richard Howe: Ira D. Gruber, *The Howe Brothers and the American Revolution* (New York, 1972); idem, "Richard Lord Howe: Admiral as Peacemaker," in George A. Billias, ed., *George Washington's Opponents: British Generals and Admirals in the American Revolution* (New York, 1969); Maldwyn A. Jones, "Sir William Howe: Conventional Strategist," in ibid.

North, Frederick Lord: Alan Valentine, *Lord North* (Norman, Okla., 1967); Peter D. G. Thomas, *Lord North* (London, 1967); Peter Whitley, *Lord North: The Prime Minister Who Lost America* (London, 1996).

NOTES

PREFACE

1. TJ to Samuel Kercheval, July 13, 1816, quoted in R. B. Bernstein, *The Founding Fathers Reconsidered* (New York, 2009), 108.

2. JA to AA, April 26, 1777, *AFC* 2:224.

CHAPTER 1: "IN THE VERY MIDST OF A REVOLUTION": THE PROPOSAL TO DECLARE INDEPENDENCE

1. Journal of Lord Adam Gordon, in Howard H. Peckham, ed., *Narratives of Colonial America 1704–1765* (Chicago, 1971), 259–61.

2. Carl and Jessica Bridenbaugh, *Rebels and Gentlemen: Philadelphia in the Age of Franklin* (New York, 1962), 6–21; David Hawke, *In the Midst of a Revolution* (Philadelphia, 1961), 33–57.

3. Charlene Mires, *Independence Hall in American Memory* (Philadelphia, 2002), 6–7.

4. Robert Morris to Silas Deane, June 6, 1776, *LDC* 4:154; Secret Committee to William Hodge, May 30, 1776, ibid., 4:103.

5. Secret Committee to Hodge, May 30, 1776, *LDC* 4:103; Marine Committee to Lambert Wickes, June 10, 1776, ibid., 4:184; Robert Livingston to John Jay, May 21, 1776, ibid., 4:59; JA to Isaac Smith Jr., January 1, 1776, ibid., 4:112; Joseph Hewes to William Tokeley, May 18, 1776, ibid., 4:35; JH to the Colonies, June 7, 1776, ibid., 4:156.

6. David Hawke, *A Transaction of Free Men: The Birth and Course of the Declaration of Independence* (New York, 1964), 6.

7. An officer in Halifax to his friend in Edinburgh, June 8, 1776, in William Bell Clark and William James Morgan, eds., *Naval Documents of the American Revolution* (Washington, D.C., 1964–), 5:421–22; Major Charles Stuart to the Earl of Bute, June 10, 1776, ibid., 5:445.

8. John Hancock to the Massachusetts Assembly, June 14, 1776, *LDC* 4:213; Thomas Stone to James Hollyday[?], May 20, 1776, ibid., 4:50; Josiah Bartlett to Mary Bartlett, June 3, 1776, ibid., 4:124; Commissioners to Canada to Hancock, May 17, 1776, ibid., 4:23; JA to Isaac Smith Sr., June 1, 1776, *AFC* 2:1–2.

9. *JCC* 5:424–26.

10. On Lee's rise, see Oliver Perry Chitwood, *Richard Henry Lee: Statesman of the Revolution* (Morgantown, W.Va., 1967), 7–59, and J. Kent McGaughy, *Richard Henry Lee of Virginia: A Portrait of an American Revolutionary* (Lanham, Md., 2004), 16–78. The "fasten chains of slavery" quotation can be found in McGaughy's biography of Lee, page 78.

11. McGaughy, *Richard Henry Lee of Virginia*, 71–112.

12. James T. Flexner, *George Washington* (Boston, 1965–72), 2:322.

13. JA, Diary, August 29–September 5, October 10, 24, 1774, *DAJA* 2:114–24, 150, 156–57.

14. Silas Deane to Elizabeth Deane, September 10–11, 1774, *LDC* 1:62; JA, Autobiography, *DAJA* 3:308; McGaughy, *Richard Henry Lee of Virginia*, 52.

15. Richard Henry Lee, Draft Address to the People of Britain and Ireland, October 11–18[?], 1774, *LDC* 1:174–79; Silas Deane, Diary, May 23, 1775, ibid., 1:371; Lee to Landon Carter, April 1, June 2, 1776, ibid., 3:470, 4:117.

16. Virginia's Resolution for Independence, June 7, 1776, in Merrill Jensen, ed., *American Colonial Documents to 1776*, 9:867–68, in David C. Douglas, ed., *English Historical Documents*, 12 vols (London, 1956–70); JA, Autobiography, *DAJA* 3:392.

CHAPTER 2: "A SPIRIT OF RIOT AND REBELLION": LORD NORTH, BENJAMIN FRANKLIN, AND THE AMERICAN CRISIS

1. Alan Valentine, *Lord North* (Norman, Okla., 1967), 1:3–189; Peter Whitley, *Lord North: The Prime Minister Who Lost America* (London, 1996), 1–84; Peter D. G. Thomas, *Lord North* (London, 1967), 3–18; Ian Christie, *Wars and Revolutions: Britain, 1760–1815* (Cambridge, Mass., 1982), 74. The description of North's complexion can be found in Valentine, *Lord North*, 1:189.

2. *PH* 16:719–20; Peter D. G. Thomas, *Tea Party to Independence: The Third Phase of the American Revolution, 1773–1776* (Oxford, 1991), 50.

3. Valentine, *Lord North*, 237, 239, 339.

4. Quoted in Thomas, *Tea Party to Independence*, 87.

5. The foregoing draws on J. M. Bumstead, "'Things in the Womb of Time': Ideas of American Independence, 1633 to 1763," *William and Mary Quarterly* 31 (1974): 533–64. On the notion that the Peace of Paris triggered a plot to seek independence, see Julie Flavell, "British Perceptions of New England and the Decision for a Coercive Colonial Policy, 1774–1775," in Julie Flavell and Stephen Conway, eds., *Britain and America Go to War: The Impact of War and Warfare in Anglo-America, 1754–1815* (Gainesville, Fla., 2004), 97.

6. Benjamin Franklin, "Observations concerning the Increase of Mankind, Peopling of Countries, &c." (1751), in *PBF* 4:229. See also Benjamin Franklin, "The Interest of Great Britain Considered with Regard to her Colonies" (1760), ibid., 9:59–100.

7. The king's comment can be found in Eliga H. Gould, *The Persistence of Empire: British Political Culture in the Age of the American Revolution* (Chapel Hill, N.C., 2000), 108. See also John Ferling, *A Leap in the Dark: The Struggle to Create the American Republic* (New York, 2003), 25–29, and Benson Bobrick, *Angel in the Whirlwind: The Triumph of the American Revolution* (New York, 1997), 61.

8. Quoted in Fred Anderson, *The War That Made America: A Short History of the French and Indian War* (New York, 2005), 208.

9. Jack P. Greene, "An Uneasy Connection: An Analysis of the Preconditions of the American Revolution," in Stephen G. Kurtz and James H. Hutson, eds., *Essays on the American Revolution* (Chapel Hill, N.C., 1973), 32–80. See also Keith Mason, "Britain and the Administration of the American Colonies," in H. T. Dickinson, ed., *Britain and the American Revolution* (London, 1998), 21–43.

10. Gould, *Persistence of Empire*, 113–14, 118. The quotation is on page 118.

11. P. D. G. Thomas, *British Politics and the Stamp Act Crisis: The First Phase of the American Revolution, 1763–1767* (Oxford, 1975), 1–39; Merrill Jensen, *The Founding of a Nation: The History of the American Revolution, 1763–1776* (New York, 1967), 41.

12. Richard Archer, *As If an Enemy's Country: The British Occupation of Boston and the Origins of the Revolution* (New York, 2010), 3–7. The quotation can be found on page 7.

13. Jensen, *Founding of a Nation*, 82–87.

14. [Thomas Whately], *The Regulations Lately Made Concerning the Colonies* (1765), in Harry T. Dickinson, ed., *British Pamphlets on the American Revolution, 1763–1785* (London, 2007), 1:115.

15. Anon., *The Justice and Necessity of Taxing the American Colonies Demonstrated* (1766), ibid., 1:236–37.

16. Quoted in Ferling, *A Leap in the Dark*, 31.

17. Archer, *As If an Enemy's Country*, 8–9.

18. Benjamin L. Carp, *Rebels Rising: Cities and the American Revolution* (New York, 2007), 40–41, 81–82, 122, 152, 189–90; Ferling, *A Leap in the Dark*, 38–39; Jensen, *Founding of a Nation*, 113. For the JA quote, see JA, Diary, April 24, 1773, *DAJA* 2:81.

19. Richard R. Beeman, *Patrick Henry: A Biography* (New York, 1974), 1–39; Virginia Stamp Act Resolutions (May 30, 1765), in Merrill Jensen, ed., *American Colonial Documents to 1776*, vol. 9, in David C. Douglas, ed., *English Historical Documents*. (London, 1956–70), 9:669–70; Bernard Bailyn, *The Ideological Origins of the American Revolution* (Cambridge, Mass., 1967), 59–62; Gordon S. Wood, *The Creation of the American Republic, 1776–1787* (Chapel Hill, N.C., 1969), 13–14. Wood demonstrates that the colonists were unaware that their interpretation of the English constitution differed from the prevailing view within the mother country.

20. Jensen, *Founding of a Nation*, 193–97.

21. JA, Diary, December 18, 1765, *DAJA*,1:263.

22. JA to Hezekiah Niles, February 13, 1818, *WJA*, 10:282.

23. H. T. Dickinson, "Britain's Imperial Sovereignty: The Ideological Case Against the American Colonists," in Dickinson, *Britain and the American Revolution*, 64–96. See especially pages 66–67.

24. Quoted in Benjamin Newcomb, *Franklin and Galloway: A Political Partnership* (New Haven, Conn., 1972), 11.

25. James H. Hutson, *Pennsylvania Politics, 1746–1770: The Movement for Royal Government and Its Consequences* (Princeton, N.J., 1972), 6–121; Newcomb, *Franklin and Galloway*, 17–18, 37, 39. The quotation can be found in David Freeman Hawke, *Franklin* (New York, 1976), 157.

26. On BF's life and ascendancy prior to the imperial crisis, see Hawke, *Franklin*; J. A. Leo Lemay, *The Life of Benjamin Franklin* (3 vols., Philadelphia, 2006–9); H. W. Brands, *The First American: The Life and Times of Benjamin Franklin* (New York, 2000); Esmond Wright, *Franklin of Philadelphia* (Cambridge, Mass., 1986); Carl Van Doren, *Benjamin Franklin* (New York, 1938); Edmund S. Morgan, *Benjamin Franklin* (New Haven, Conn., 2002); Walter Isaacson, *Benjamin Franklin: An American Life* (New York, 2003); and Gordon S. Wood, *The Americanization of Benjamin Franklin* (New York, 2004).

27. BF to Galloway, October 11, 1766, *PBF* 12:48n; Brands, *The First American*, 361.

28. BF to Richard Jackson, January 16, 1764, *PBF* 11:19, 13:127n.

29. BF to Galloway, October 11, 1766, *PBF* 12:48n.

30. Galloway to BF, July 18, 1765, *PBF* 12:218.

31. John Hughes to BF, September 8–17, 1765, *PBF* 12:264–66.

32. Deborah Franklin to BF, September 22, 1765, *PBF* 12:271; Samuel Wharton to BF, October 13, 1765, ibid., 12:315–16; Syddon Deed to Franklin's Philadelphia Property, ibid., 283–86n; Brands, *The First American*, 368.

33. Galloway to William Franklin, November 14, 1765, *PBF* 12:374.

34. David Hall to BF, September 6, 1765, *PBF* 12:259.

35. BF, "F.B.: Second Reply to Tom Hunt," December 27, 1765, *PBF* 12:413.

36. Stacy Schiff, *A Great Improvisation: Franklin, France, and the Birth of America* (New York, 2005), 21, 89.

37. *The Examination of Doctor Benjamin Franklin before an August Assembly ...*, February 13, 1766, *PBF* 13:129–59. The quotations can be found on pages 135, 136, 137, 139, and 143.

38. Dickinson, "Britain's Imperial Sovereignty," in Dickinson, *Britain and the American Revolution*, 68.

39. JA, Diary, November 11, 1766, *DAJA* 1:324.

40. John Dickinson, *Letters from a Farmer in Pennsylvania* (1768), in Merrill Jensen, ed., *Tracts of the American Revolution, 1763–1776* (Indianapolis, Ind., 1967), 128–63. The quotation can be found on page 140.

41. BF, "The English Edition of the Reader," May 8, 1768, *PBF* 15:111–12, 110–11n.

42. BF to Mary Stevenson, September 14, 1767, *PBF* 14:253.

43. BF to [?], November 28, 1768, *PBF* 15:272.

44. Morgan, *Benjamin Franklin*, 105–7, 111–12; Brands, *The First American*, 278–79, 341–42, 360, 394, 492; Wood, *The Americanization of Benjamin Franklin*, 83–91, 104, 131–33.

45. Quoted in Brands, *The First American*, 401. See also Morgan, *Benjamin Franklin*, 170–71.

46. BF to Lord Kames, February 25, 1767, *PBF* 14:69–70.

47. BF, "A Horrid Spectacle to Men and Angels," January 17, 1769, *PBF* 16:19; idem., "Purported Letter from Paris," January 17, 1769, ibid., 16:20; idem., "An Account Stated Against GG," January 17, 1769, ibid., 16:22–24.

48. Quoted in Ian R. Christie and Benjamin W. Labaree, *Empire or Independence, 1760–1777* (New York, 1976), 122, 123, 124.

49. BF, "An Account Stated Against GG," January 17, 1769, *PBF* 16:25.

50. Wright, *Franklin of Philadelphia*, 199–200.

51. BF to William Franklin, March 13, 1768, *PBF* 15:75–76.

52. Wood, *Americanization of Benjamin Franklin*, 120–24.

53. BF to Galloway, January 9, 1769, *PBF* 16:17.

54. BF, "Causes of the American Discontents before 1768," January 5–7, 1768, *PBF* 15:12–13.

55. *DGW* 1:338–40.

56. GW to George Mason, April 5, 1769, *PGWC* 8:353, 354n; GW to Bryan Fairfax, August 24, 1774, ibid., 10:155; Arthur Lee to GW, June 15, 1777, *PGWR* 10:43; *DGW* 2:153n.

57. *Boston Gazette*, October 17, 1768, in Harry Alonzo Cushing, ed., *The Writings of Samuel Adams* (reprint, New York, 1968), 1:252; John K. Alexander, *Samuel Adams: America's Revolutionary Politician* (Lanham, Md., 2002), 67; Jensen, *Founding of a Nation*, 351; Ferling, *A Leap in the Dark*, 71–72.

58. Jensen, *Founding of a Nation*, 293, 344.

59. BF to George Whitefield, September 2, 1769, *PBF* 16:192.

60. The best account of the shooting can be found in Archer, *As If an Enemy's Country*, 182–202. See also Hiller B. Zobel, *The Boston Massacre* (New York, 1970), 164–205; William M. Fowler, *Samuel Adams: Radical Puritan* (New York, 1993), 106; John C. Miller, *Sam Adams: Pioneer in Propaganda* (Stanford, Calif., 1936), 186; Thomas, *Townshend Duties*, 180; Robert Middlekauff, *The Glorious Cause: The American Revolution, 1763–1789* (New York, 1982), 203; JA to William Tudor, April 15, 1817, *WJA* 10:251–52. The quotation urging the soldiers to fire can be found in Alexander, *Samuel Adams*, 81.

61. Peter D. G. Thomas, *The Townshend Duty Crisis: The Second Phase of the American Revolution, 1767–1773* (Oxford, 1987), 28–29, 149, 152, 156, 166, 177–78.

62. Thomas, *Townshend Duty Crisis*, 165; Thomas, *Tea Party to Independence*, 2.

63. James H. Hutson, *Pennsylvania Politics, 1746–1770: The Movement for Royal Government and Its Consequences* (Princeton, N.J., 1972), 224–43; Ferling, *A Leap in the Dark*, 78–81; BF to William Franklin, March 13, 1768, *PBF* 15:76.

64. Whitley, *Lord North*, 92–102; Thomas, *Townshend Duty Crisis*, 214–31; Jensen, *Founding of a Nation*, 439; Benjamin Woods Labaree, *The Boston Tea Party* (New York, 1964), 52.

65. Whitley, *Lord North*, 103–14; Valentine, *Lord North*, 1:269–92.

66. BF, "Rules by Which a Great Empire May be Reduced to a Small One," September 11, 1773, *PBF* 20:391–99.

67. BF to Galloway, July 2, 1768, August 22, 1772, *PBF* 15:164, 20:276; "Franklin's Account of His Audience with Hillsborough," ibid., 18:15; BF to Thomas Cushing, June 10, 1771, ibid., 18:122; Van Doren, *Benjamin Franklin*, 383; Morgan, *Benjamin Franklin*, 185.

68. BF to Cushing, December 2, 1772, *PBF* 19:411–12; Wood, *Americanization of Benjamin Franklin*, 141–43; Morgan, *Benjamin Franklin*, 185–87; Brands, *The First American*, 453; Jack Rakove, *Revolutionaries: A New History of the Invention of America* (Boston, 2010), 35–36.

69. Benjamin Carp, *Defiance of the Patriots: The Boston Tea Party and the Making of America* (New Haven, Conn., 2010), 47.

70. SA to Stephen Sayre, November 23, 1770, *WSA* 2:68. For a particularly good treatment of the evolution of American attitudes and political practices, see Pauline Maier, *From Resistance to Revolution: Colonial Radicals and the Development of American Opposition to Britain, 1765–1776* (New York, 1972).

71. Good starting points on the South and the backcountry are Woody Holton, *Forced Founders: Indians, Debtors, Slaves, and the Making of the American Revolution in Virginia* (Chapel Hill, N.C., 1999), and Walter Edgar, *Partisans and Redcoats: The Southern Conflict That Turned the Tide of the American Revolution* (New York, 2001).

72. Oliver Perry Chitwood, *Richard Henry Lee: Statesman of the Revolution* (Morgantown, W.Va., 1967), 54–55; Thomas Jefferson, "Autobiography," in Saul K. Padover, ed., *The Complete Jefferson: Containing His Major Writings, Published and Unpublished, Except His Letters* (reprint, Freeport, N.Y., 1969), 1122.

73. Labaree, *Boston Tea Party*, 77, 79, 118, 130, 133.

74. Rakove, *Revolutionaries*, 37–38.

75. Carp, *Defiance of the Patriots*, 122–38; Jensen, *Founding of a Nation*, 434–60; Labaree, *Boston Tea Party*, 8, 138–45; Arthur Young, "George Robert Twelves Hewes (1742–1840): A Boston Shoemaker and the Memory of the American Revolution," *William and Mary Quarterly* 38 (1981): 562–623; JA, Diary, December 17, 1773, *DAJA* 2:86.

76. BF to the Massachusetts House Committee of Correspondence, February 2, 1774, *PBF* 21:76.

77. Fairfax County Resolves, July 18, 1774, *PGWC* 10:122.

78. On Hancock as the moneybags of the Yankee rebels, see Carp, *Defiance of the Patriots*, 40.

79. For the two paragraphs on the anger sweeping England, see Fred Junkin Hinkhouse, *The Preliminaries of the American Revolution As Seen in the English Press, 1763–1775* (reprint, New York, 1969), 159, 162, 168; Solomon Lutnick, *The American Revolution and the British*

Press, 1775–1783 (Columbia, Mo., 1967), 36–41; Troy Bickham, *Making Headlines: The American Revolution as Seen Through the British Press* (DeKalb, Ill., 2009), 60, 74; William Allen, *The American Crisis: A Letter . . .* (1774); Dickinson, *British Pamphlets on the American Revolution*, 2:354, 405; [Anon.], *A Letter to a Member of Parliament on the Unhappy Dispute between Great-Britain and the Colonies* (1774), ibid., 3:117, 125; David H. Murdoch, ed., *Rebellion in America: A Contemporary British Viewpoint, 1765–1783* (Santa Barbara, Calif., 1979), 129–30.

80. BF to the New Jersey Assembly Committee of Correspondence, February 18, 1774, *PBF* 21:111; BF to Thomas Cushing, March 22, 1774, ibid., 21:152.

81. North had said on the eve of taking power that no minister would "venture to declare open war but upon the last extremity." He never deviated from that view. See *PH* 16:720.

82. Stanley Ayling, *George the Third* (New York, 1972), 243; John Shy, *A People Numerous and Armed* (New York, 1976), 40; Verner Crane, ed., *Benjamin Franklin's Letters to the Press* (Chapel Hill, N.C., 1960), 263n.

83. Bernard Donoughue, *British Politics and the American Revolution: The Path to War, 1773–1775* (London, 1964), 38–42; Valentine, *Lord North*, 1:312–15. The Dartmouth quotation is in *Lord North*, 1:314–15.

84. The quotations can be found in Valentine, *Lord North*, 1:319–20, 314.

85. Thomas, *Tea Party to Independence*, 26–61; Whitley, *Lord North*, 137–41; Valentine, *Lord North*, 1:306–30; Jack Sosin, "The Massachusetts Acts of 1774: Coercive or Preventive," *Huntington Library Quarterly* 26 (1963): 235–52; Dartmouth to John Thornton, February 12, 1774, in *The Manuscripts of the Earl of Dartmouth* (reprint, Boston, 1972), 2:197.

86. The texts of the four Coercive Acts can be found in David C. Douglas et al., eds., *English Historical Documents* (London, 1956–70), 9:779–85.

87. Quoted in Lutnick, *American Revolution and the British Press*, 35.

88. Quoted in Donoughue, *British Politics and the American Revolution*, 77, and Christie and Labaree, *Empire or Independence*, 186.

89. Quoted in Donoughue, *British Politics and the American Revolution*, 79.

90. Holton, *Forced Founders*, 32–36; Henderson, *Party Politics in the Continental Congress*, 41.

91. Donoughue, *British Politics and the American Revolution*, 73–104; Labaree, *Boston Tea Party*, 200–203.

92. Donoughue, *British Politics and the American Revolution*, 89.

93. Carl B. Cone, *Burke and the Nature of Politics: The Age of the American Revolution* (Lexington, Ky., 1957), 1–194.

94. *PH* 17:1184.

95. *PH* 18:1215–70. The quotations are on pages 1224, 1263, 1264, and 1267. On Burke and the Rockinghamite position, see the useful analysis in John Derry, *English Politics and the American Revolution* (New York, 1976), 78–80. For Burke's suggestion that Parliament's policies were driving the colonies to nationhood, see Rakove, *Revolutionaries*, 68.

96. The Preliminary Hearing before the Privy Council Committee . . . the Removal of Hutchinson and Oliver, January 11, 1774, *PBF* 21:19–23; The Final Hearing before the Privy Council Committee . . . , January 29, 1774, ibid., 21:37–70. The text of Webberburn's speech can be found in ibid., 21:43–68. The quotations can be found on pages 47, 48, and 58 and in Van Doren, *Benjamin Franklin*, 469. See also Morgan, *Benjamin Franklin*, 200–3; Brands, *The First American*, 1–2, 4–5, 469–75; and Wright, *Franklin of Philadelphia*, 226–27. For a description of Franklin in the Cockpit, see Van Doren, *Benjamin Franklin*, 467–68.

97. Quoted in editor's note, *PBF* 21:41.

98. Valentine, *Lord North*, 1:311, 319–20.

99. *Examination of Doctor Benjamin Franklin*, February 13, 1766, *PBF* 13:142.

100. BF, "A Letter from London," *Boston Gazette*, April 25, 1774, *PBF* 21:79–83. The "Bull-baiting" quote can be found in BF, "Extract of a Letter from London," *Pennsylvania Gazette*, April 20, 1774, ibid., 21:112.

CHAPTER 3: "DEFENDERS OF AMERICAN LIBERTY": SAMUEL ADAMS, JOSEPH GALLOWAY, AND THE FIRST CONTINENTAL CONGRESS

1. SA to Arthur Lee, January 25, 1774, *WSA* 3:79; Benjamin Woods Labaree, *The Boston Tea Party* (New York, 1964), 147–48; David Hackett Fischer, *Paul Revere's Ride* (New York, 1994), 25–26.

2. Labaree, *Boston Tea Party*, 156–61.

3. BF to Thomas Cushing, February 15[–19], March 22, 1774, *PBF* 21:95, 152; Labaree, *Boston Tea Party*, 218.

4. "The Town of Boston to the Colonies," May 13, 1774, *WSA* 3:107–8; The Committee of Correspondence to the Committee of Correspondence of Philadelphia, May 13, 1774, ibid., 3:110–11; *American Archives*, 1:331, 331n; Joyce Lee Malcolm, *Peter's War: A New England Slave Boy and the American Revolution* (New Haven, Conn., 2009), 37; David Ammerman, *In the Common Cause: American Response to the Coercive Acts of 1774* (Charlottesville, Va., 1974), 19.

5. SA to Arthur Lee, January 25, April 4, May 18, 1774, *WSA* 3:79, 98–102; SA to Elbridge Gerry, March 25, 1774, ibid., 3:84; SA to John Dickinson, April 21, 1774, ibid., 3:104–5; SA to Silas Deane, May 18, 1774, ibid., 3:114–16; SA to Stephen Hopkins, May 18, 1774, ibid., 3:116–17; Labaree, *Boston Tea Party*, 220.

6. Quoted in Ira Stoll, *Samuel Adams: A Life* (New York, 2008), 23.

7. My assessment of Samuel Adams draws in part on several excellent biographies. See John C. Miller, *Sam Adams: Pioneer in Propaganda* (Stanford, Calif., 1936); William M. Fowler, *Samuel Adams: Radical Puritan* (New York, 1997); John K. Alexander, *Samuel Adams: America's Revolutionary Politician* (Lanham, Md., 2002); and Stoll, *Samuel Adams*, 13–78. See also the important essay on SA in Pauline Maier, *The Old Revolutionaries: Political Leaders in the Age of Samuel Adams* (New York, 1982), 3–50. The Jefferson quotation can be found in Miller's biography of SA, page 343. The "nervous eloquence" comment can be found in Cass Canfield, *Samuel Adams's Revolution, 1765–1776* (New York, 1972), 32. The "horned snake" quotation is from Alexander, *Samuel Adams*, page 72. Abigail Adams's comments on SA can be found in AA to Mary Cranch, July 15, 1766, *AFC* 1:54. JA's comments can be found in JA to William Tudor, June 5, 1817, *WJA* 10:263; JA to Jedidiah Morse, December 5, 1815, ibid., 10:190; JA, Diary, December 23, 1765, *DAJA* 1:271; JA to Benjamin Rush, August 1, 1812, in John A. Schutz and Douglass Adair, eds., *The Spur of Fame: Dialogues of John Adams and Benjamin Rush, 1805–1813* (San Marino, Calif., 1966), 253. See also John Ferling, *John Adams: A Life* (reprint, New York, 2010), 448–49. For Hutchinson on SA, see Thomas Hutchinson, *A History of the Colony and Province of Massachusetts-Bay*, ed. Lawrence S. Mayo (Cambridge, Mass., 1936), 2:155–56.

8. [Samuel Adams], *Boston Gazette*, April 4, 11, December 19, 1768, *WSA* 1:202, 205, 270. On the trends in the mother country, see J. H. Plumb, *England in the Eighteenth Century* (Baltimore, Md., 1950), 77–90; John Rule, "Manufacturing and Commerce," in H. T. Dickinson,

ed., *A Companion to Eighteenth-Century Britain* (London, 2002), 127–40; Gordon Mingay, "Agriculture and Rural Life," ibid., 141–57; Peter Borsay, "Urban Life and Culture," ibid., 196–208. The Plumb quotation can be found on page 83 of his book cited above.

9. Miller, *Sam Adams*, 3–47; Maier, *Old Revolutionaries*, 5–11, 17–21; Edmund S. Morgan, "The Puritan Ethic and the American Revolution," *William and Mary Quarterly* 24 (1967): 3–43.

10. The Declarations of the Stamp Act Congress, October 19, 1765, in David C. Douglas et al., eds., *English Historical Documents* (London, 1956–70), 9:672–73.

11. Alexander, *Samuel Adams*, 132–33; Merrill Jensen, *The Founding of a Nation: A History of the American Revolution, 1763–1776* (New York, 1968), 466–67; Ammerman, *In the Common Cause*, 24–25.

12. Jack Rakove, *The Beginnings of National Politics: An Interpretive History of the Continental Congress* (Baltimore, Md., 1979), 23; Labaree, *Boston Tea Party*, 231–32; John Hancock, *An Oration, Delivered March 5, 1774* (Boston, 1774), 17–18.

13. Ammerman, *In the Common Cause*, 5–9.

14. Jensen, *Founding of a Nation*, 474–79; Ammerman, *In the Common Cause*, 31–32; John E. Selby, *The Revolution in Virginia, 1775–1783* (Williamsburg, Va., 1988), 8–9.

15. Jensen, *Founding of a Nation*, 470–73; Ammerman, *In the Common Cause*, 26, 45–47; Labaree, *Boston Tea Party*, 228–29, 240–42.

16. BF to Galloway, August 20, 1768; January 9, 29, 1769; June 11, 1770, *PBF* 15:189–90; 16:15, 30; 17:168.

17. JA, Diary, September 3, October 10, 1775, *DAJA* 2:121, 150; Raymond Werner, ed., "Diary of Grace Growdon Galloway," *Pennsylvania Magazine of History and Biography* 55 (1931): 87, 168; Ernest H. Baldwin, "Joseph Galloway, Loyalist Politician," ibid., 21 (1902): 161–64; Benjamin H. Newcomb, *Franklin and Galloway: A Political Partnership* (New Haven, Conn., 1972), 11, 35, 46, 89, 94, 121.

18. Newcomb, *Franklin and Galloway*, 35–70.

19. Newcomb, *Franklin and Galloway*, 35–104. See also James H. Hutson, *Pennsylvania Politics: The Movement for Royal Government and Its Consequences* (Princeton, N.J., 1972).

20. *PBF* 12:219n; Galloway to BF, July 18, November 16–28, 1765; January 13, February 27, May 23, June 16, 1766, ibid., 12:217–18, 376–77; 13:35–37, 180–81, 285, 317; Galloway to William Franklin, November 14, 1765, ibid., 12:373–74.

21. Galloway to BF, March 10, October 17, 1768, *PBF* 15:71, 231; Newcomb, *Franklin and Galloway*, 216–17.

22. William Nelson, *The American Tory* (Oxford, 1961), 46; Newcomb, *Franklin and Galloway*, 225–26.

23. Janice Potter, *The Liberty We Seek: Loyalist Ideology in Colonial New York and Massachusetts* (Cambridge, Mass., 1983), 112–27. The quotations can be found on page 127.

24. Quoted in Nelson, *American Tory*, 44.

25. Galloway to BF, June 21, 1770; October 12, 1772, *PBF* 17:177–78; 19:331.

26. Richard A. Ryerson, *The Revolution Is Now Begun: The Radical Committees of Philadelphia, 1765–1776* (Philadelphia, 1978), 40–63.

27. Nelson, *American Tory*, 46.

28. Quoted in Rakove, *Beginnings of National Politics*, 23.

29. Galloway to William Franklin, September 3, 1774, *LDC* 1:24: Alexander, *Samuel Adams*, 139.

30. JA, Diary, August 10, 1774, *DAJA* 2:97–98, 97–98n; *DGW*, August 31, 1774, 3:272–74.

31. Silas Deane to Elizabeth Deane, September 23, 1774, *LDC* 1:91.

32. JA, Diary, August 10–25, 1774, *DAJA* 2:97–111.

33. JA, Diary, August 29, 1774, *DAJA* 2:114–15.

34. JA, Diary, September 1, 1774, *DAJA* 2:119; *DGW*, September 4, 1774, 3:274, 275n.

35. JA, Diary, June 20, 1774, *DAJA* 2:96, 97.

36. Silas Deane to Elizabeth Deane, August 31–September 5, 1774, *LDC* 1:15; JA, Diary, August 30, September 7, 22, 1774, *DAJA* 2:116, 127, 136; Carl and Jessica Bridenbaugh, *Rebels and Gentlemen: Philadelphia in the Age of Franklin* (New York, 1965), 1–28.

37. JA, Diary, August 30, 1774, *DAJA* 2:116; Robert Treat Paine, Diary, September 5, 1774, *LDC* 1:13; Deane to Elizabeth Deane, August 31–September 5, 8, 9, 1774, ibid., 1:16, 18, 20, 50, 55.

38. JA to AA, September 14, 18, 29, 1774, *AFC* 1:155, 158, 164; JA, Diary, September 8, 17, 22, 1774, *DAJA* 2:127, 134, 136.

39. H. James Henderson, *Party Politics in the Continental Congress* (New York, 1974), 20–21.

40. JA to AA, September 25, 1774, *AFC* 1:163.

41. JA, Diary, August 23, 1774, *DAJA* 2:109.

42. JA, Diary, September 2, 3, 1774, *DAJA* 2:119, 120, 121.

43. JA, Diary, August 29, September 3, 8, 12, 1774, *DAJA* 2:114–15, 121, 127, 133.

44. Ammerman, *In the Common Cause*, 47–48.

45. JA, Diary, August 30, 1774, *DAJA* 2:115. JA's remark was first noted in Henderson, *Party Politics in the Continental Congress*, 35. Deane to Elizabeth Deane, August 31–September 5, 1774, *LDC* 1:19.

46. Robert Secor and John Pickering, *Pennsylvania 1776* (University Park, Pa., 1975), 274, 281, 301, 304, 322.

47. JA to AA, September 16, 1774, *AFC* 1:156; JA, Diary, September 10, 1774, *DAJA* 2:131.

48. James Duane, Notes of Debate, *LDC* 1:30.

49. Quoted in Richard R. Beeman, *Patrick Henry: A Biography* (New York, 1974), 60.

50. JA, Diary, September 6, 1774, *DAJA* 2:125.

51. JA, Diary, September 6, 1774, *DAJA* 2:124–26.

52. JA to AA, September 8, 14, 1774, *AFC* 1:150, 155.

53. On the colonists' affection for the British monarchy, see the detailed account of the "imperialization of political life" in America in Brendan McConville, *The King's Three Faces: The Rise and Fall of Royal America, 1688–1776* (Chapel Hill, N.C., 2006).

54. Quoted in Robert Douthat Meade, *Patrick Henry* (Philadelphia, 1957), 1:331.

55. Thomas M. Doerflinger, *A Vigorous Spirit of Enterprise: Merchants and Economic Development in Revolutionary Philadelphia* (New York, 1986), 168, 194–95; Jack Rakove, *Revolutionaries: A New History of the Invention of America* (Boston, 2010), 76, 98.

56. *AFC* 1:136n.

57. JA to William Tudor, September 29, 1774, *PJA* 2:177; Joseph Reed to [?], September 4, 1774, Joseph Reed Papers, Historical Society of Pennsylvania; Rakove, *Beginnings of National Politics*, 45; Thomas Lynch to Ralph Izard, October 26, 1774, *LDC* 1:247; SA to Joseph Warren, September 25, 1775, ibid., 1:100; Jerrilyn Greene Marston, *King and Congress: The Transfer of Political Legitimacy, 1774–1776* (Princeton, N.J., 1987), 79; Alexander, *Samuel Adams*, 141.

58. Galloway to William Franklin, September 3, 1774, *LDC* 1:24; Joseph Galloway, *Historical and Political Reflections on the Rise and Progress of the American Revolution* (London,

1780), 67–68. The section containing Galloway's evaluation of SA can also be found in Douglas, *English Historical Documents*, 9:801.

59. Galloway to William Franklin, September 3, 5, 1774, *LDC* 1:24, 27; Alexander, *Samuel Adams*, 138–39.

60. James Duane, Notes of Debates, September 6, 1774, *LDC* 1:32; Deane to Elizabeth Deane, September 6, 1774, ibid., 1:29.

61. *DGW*, September 5–24, 1774, 3:275–79; Robert Treat Paine, Diary, September 9, 1774, *LDC* 1:57, 66; JA Diary, September 7, 8, October 14, 24, 1774, *DAJA* 2:127, 152, 156.

62. *JCC* 1:31–40; JA, Diary, September 17, 1774, *DAJA* 2:134; JA to AA, September 18, 1774, *AFC* 1:157.

63. Jensen, *Founding of a Nation*, 492–96, 503; Samuel Ward, Diary, September 21, 1774, *LDC* 1:90; ibid., 1:94n; *JCC* 1:42; JA, [Notes on Measures to be Taken Up by Congress, September–October, 1774], *DAJA* 2:145; ibid., 2:145–46n.

64. JA, Diary, September 26–27, 1774, *DAJA* 2:137–40; Jensen, *Founding of a Nation*, 496–97.

65. GW, Diary, September 28, 1774, *DGW* 3:282.

66. JA, Diary, September 28, 1774, *DAJA* 2:141–44. Soon after Congress, Galloway elaborated on his September 28 speech in a long pamphlet that was published in New York the following February. See Joseph Galloway, *A Candid Examination of the Mutual Claims of Great Britain and the Colonies* (1775), in Merrill Jensen, ed., *Tracts of the American Revolution, 1763–1776* (Indianapolis, Ind., 1967), 350–99. The bare-bones plan can also be found in Douglas, *English Historical Documents*, 9:811–12.

67. JA is quoted in John Ferling, *The Loyalist Mind: Joseph Galloway and the American Revolution* (University Park, Pa., 1977), 27. See also JA, Diary, September 28, 1774, *DAJA* 2:142–43; Samuel Ward, Diary, October 22, 1774, *LDC* 1:234.

68. JA to Joseph Palmer, September 26, 1774, *PJA* 2:173; JA to William Tudor, October 7, 1774, ibid., 2:188.

69. Samuel Ward, Diary, October 19, 1774, *LDC* 1:221; Jensen, *Founding of a Nation*, 500–507; *JCC* 1:74–81; Douglas, *English Historical Documents*, 9:813–16.

70. The Declaration of Colonial Rights and Grievances, in Douglas, *English Historical Documents*, 9:805–8. The quotation can be found on page 807. The document can also be found in *JCC* 1:63–73. In the most vague terms, the Declaration reminded London that the Ohio Country had been "conquered from France" by Anglo-American soldiery.

71. Thomas M. Doerflinger, *A Vigorous Spirit of Enterprise: Merchants and Economic Development in Revolutionary Philadelphia* (New York, 1986), 70–196; Marston, *King and Congress*, 93–96.

72. Richard Henry Lee's Proposed Resolution, October 3, 1774, *LDC* 1:140; Silas Deane, Diary, October 3, 1774, ibid., 1:138–39.

73. JA to TJ, November 12, 1813, in Lester J. Cappon, ed., *The Adams-Jefferson Letters: The Complete Correspondence Between Thomas Jefferson and Abigail and John Adams* (Chapel Hill, N.C., 1959), 2:392.

74. Samuel Adams's Draft Letter to Thomas Gage, October 7–8, 1774, *LDC* 1:158–60; Samuel Ward, Diary, October 10, 1774, ibid., 1:171; *JCC* 1:60–61; Marston, *King and Congress*, 86–90.

75. Samuel Ward, Diary, October 22, 1774, *LDC* 1:234; ibid., 1:112–17n.

76. *JCC* 1:115–22; JA, Diary, October 24, 1774, *DAJA* 2:156.

77. JA to AA, October 7, 1774, *AFC* 1:164–66; George Read to Gertrude Read, October 24, 1774, *LDC* 1:244.

78. Robert Treat Paine, Diary, October 26, 1774, *LDC* 1:248; Galloway to Thomas Nickleson, November 1, 1774, ibid., 1:255; Galloway to Samuel Verplanck, December 30, 1774, ibid., 1:284; SA to Thomas Young, October [?], 1774, ibid., 1:205.

CHAPTER 4: "IT IS A BILL OF WAR. IT DRAWS THE SWORD": LORD DARTMOUTH, GEORGE WASHINGTON, HOSTILITIES

1. *DGW*, October 27–30, 1774, 3:287–88; GW, Cash Accounts, September and October 1774, *PGWC*: 10:159–60, 166–68.

2. GW to John Connally, February 25, 1775, *PGWC* 10:273; Fairfax Independent Company to GW, October 19, 1774, April 25, 1775, ibid., 10:173, 173–74n, 344; GW to John Augustine Washington, March 25, 1775, ibid., 10:308; GW to Townshend Dade Jr., November 19, 1774, ibid., 10:187; GW to John Tayloe, October 31, 1774, ibid., 10:175; GW to James Cleveland, January 10, [March ?], 1775, ibid., 10:230, 314; GW to William Bronaugh, January 18, 1775, ibid., 10:238; GW to William Stevens, March 6, 1775, ibid., 10:288; GW to Andrew Lewis, March 27, 1775, ibid., 10:310; [GW], Agreement with William Skilling, February 25, 1775, ibid., 10:272–73; William Crawford to GW, March 6, 1775, ibid., 10:292–93; *DGW* 3:291, 302, 303, 309, 321.

3. Milton E. Flower, *John Dickinson: Conservative Revolutionary* (Charlottesville, Va., 1983), 118, 122; Kevin J. Hayes, *The Mind of a Patriot: Patrick Henry and the World of Ideas* (Charlottesville, Va., 2008), 85; Robert D. Meade, *Patrick Henry* (Philadelphia, 1957–69), 2:18–19; John K. Alexander, *Samuel Adams: America's Revolutionary Politician* (Lanham, Md., 2002), 145; Dickinson to Josiah Quincy Jr., October 28, 1774, *LDC* 1:251; William Hooper to Mary Hooper, November 7, 1774, ibid., 1:256; James Duane to Samuel Chase, December 29, 1774, ibid., 1:277; JA to James Warren, January 3, 1775, *PJA* 2:209.

4. John Ferling, *Almost a Miracle: The American Victory in the War of Independence* (New York, 2007), 27; John R. Galvin, *The Minute Men: The First Fight: Myths and Realities of the American Revolution* (Washington, D.C., 1989), 56–57; Joyce Lee Malcolm, *Peter's War: A New England Slave Boy and the American Revolution* (New Haven, Conn., 2009), 43. The two quotations can be found in Ray Raphael, *The First American Revolution: Before Lexington and Concord* (New York, 2002), 162, 182.

5. Bernard Donoughue, *British Politics and the American Revolution: The Path to War, 1773–1775* (London, 1964), 132–33; John Derry, *English Politics and the American Revolution* (New York, 1976), 72–73.

6. Alan Valentine, *Lord North* (Norman, Okla., 1967), 1:260; BF to Cushing, April 3, 1770, *PBF* 20:129; BF to William Franklin, August 17, 1772, ibid., 19:244; Dartmouth to Hutchinson, December 9, 1772, *DAR* 5:239.

7. Quoted in B. D. Bargar, *Lord Dartmouth and the American Revolution* (Columbia, S.C., 1965), 89. The survey of Dartmouth's early life and political career draws on this study, especially pages 1–67.

8. Peter D. G. Thomas, *The Townshend Duty Crisis: The Second Phase of the American Revolution, 1767–1773* (Oxford, 1987), 255–56; BF to William Franklin, July 14, 1773, *PBF* 20:308.

9. JA to Tudor, June 29, 1774, *PJA* 2:104.

10. Valentine, *Lord North*, 1:312–13; Donoughue, *British Politics and the American Revolution*, 38; Bargar, *Lord Dartmouth and the American Revolution*, 109.

11. Peter D. G. Thomas, *Tea Party to Independence: The Third Phase of the American Revolution, 1773–1776* (Oxford, 1991), 60, 61, 67; Bargar, *Lord Dartmouth and the American Revo-*

lution, 107–8; Valentine, *Lord North*, 1:314; Donoughue, *British Politics and the American Revolution*, 37–38, 52–63, 69–70.

12. Bargar, *Lord Dartmouth and the American Revolution*, 115–16; Thomas, *Tea Party to Independence*, 145–46.

13. Thomas, *Tea Party to Independence*, 155, 157.

14. Quoted in Bernard Bailyn, *The Ordeal of Thomas Hutchinson* (Cambridge, Mass., 1974), 304.

15. Jeremy Black, *George III: America's Last King* (New Haven, Conn., 2006), 81–82, 108–43, 209–14. The quotation is on page 209.

16. The two preceding paragraphs draw on BF, Arthur Lee, and William Bollan to the Speaker of the Pennsylvania . . . , December 24, 1775, *PBF* 21:399; King to North, September 11, November 18, December 15, 1774, in Sir John Fortescue, ed., *The Correspondence of George III, 1760–1783* (London, 1927), 3:131, 153, 156; Bargar, *Lord Dartmouth and the American Revolution*, 146–48; Thomas, *Tea Party to Independence*, 166–70; Peter Whiteley, *Lord North: The Prime Minister Who Lost America* (London, 1996), 146–47; Donoughue, *British Politics and the American Revolution*, 217; Black, *George III*, 215–16.

17. Gage to Dartmouth, August 27, September 2, 12, October 3, 17, 30, 1774, in Clarence Carter, ed., *The Correspondence of General Thomas Gage with the Secretaries of State, and the War Office and the Treasury, 1763–1775* (reprint, New York, 1969), 1:366, 367, 370, 371, 374, 378, 380, 383. The figure for the strength of Gage's army is for January 1, 1775. See David Hackett Fischer, *Paul Revere's Ride* (New York, 1994), 309.

18. Penn to Dartmouth, July 5, 1774, *DAR* 8:142; Dunmore to Dartmouth, June 6, 1774, ibid., 8:128; Martin to Dartmouth, September 1, 1774, ibid., 8:172; Bull to Dartmouth, July 31, 1774, ibid., 8:154; Wright to Dartmouth, August 24, 1774, ibid., 8:162.

19. For example, see "The Humble Petition of the Merchants, Traders, and others, of the City of London, concerned in the Commerce of North America" (1775), in Harry T. Dickinson, ed., *British Pamphlets on the American Revolution* (London, 2007), 247–49. See also H. T. Dickinson, "'The Friends of America': British Sympathy with the American Revolution," in Michael T. Davis, ed., *Radicalism and Revolution in Britain, 1775–1848* (New York, 2000), 11; James E. Bradley, "The British Public Opinion and the American Revolution: Ideology, Interest and Opinion," in H. T. Dickinson, ed., *Britain and the American Revolution* (London, 1998), 135; Stephen Conway, *The British Isles and the War of Independence* (New York, 2000), 130–35; and Kathleen Wilson, *The Sense of the People: Politics, Culture and Imperialism in England, 1715–1785* (Cambridge, 1995), 238–40.

20. See [Joseph Cawthorne], *A Plan to Reconcile Great Britain & Her Colonies, and Preserve the Dependency of America* (London, 1774); Dickinson, *British Pamphlets on the American Revolution*, 3:1–58; [Anon.], *A Plan for Conciliating the Jarring Political Interests of Great Britain and Her North American Colonies* (London, 1775), ibid., 183–202. The quotation is on page 56 of *A Plan for Conciliating*.

21. [Anon.], *The Supremacy of the British Legislature Over the Colonies* (London, 1775), ibid., 3:207–44.

22. Dora Mae Clark, *British Opinion and the American Revolution* (reprint, New York, 1966), 76–92; Solomon Lutnick, *The American Revolution and the British Press, 1775–1783* (Columbia, Mo., 1967), 42–45, 42n; H. W. Brands, *The First American: The Life and Times of Benjamin Franklin* (New York, 2000), 481.

23. David Barclay and John Fothergill to BF, December 3, 1774, *PBF* 21:364–65; BF, Hints

for *Conversation* upon the Terms . . . , [December 4–6], 1774, ibid., 21:366–68; editor's notes, ibid., 21:360–66; Carl Van Doren, *Benjamin Franklin* (New York, 1938), 479.

24. BF, Proposals to Lord Howe, [December 31], 1774, ibid., 21:409–11; editor's note, ibid., 21:408–9. Franklin did not learn of Dartmouth's response to his initial hints until February. The American secretary was agreeable to the repeal of the Tea Act, modifying the restraints on American trade, and taxing the colonists only in wartime. However, the repeal of the Coercive Acts "was inadmissible." See "Answers to Franklin's 'Hints,'" [before February 4, 1775], ibid., 21:466–68; editor's note, ibid., 21:465–66. On the ploy to use Franklin in this crisis, see also Van Doren, *Benjamin Franklin*, 495–518, and Philip James McFarland, *The Brave Bostonians: Hutchinson, Quincy, Franklin and the Coming of the American Revolution* (Boulder, Colo., 1998), 143–52, 193–203.

25. BF to Galloway, April 20, 1771, April 6, 1773, February 25, 1774, *PBF* 18:78, 20:149, 21:509.

26. Minute of a Cabinet Meeting, January 21, 1775, in *The Manuscripts of the Earl of Dartmouth, Prepared by the Historical Manuscript Commission of Great Britain* (reprint, Boston, 1972), 1:372.

27. Thomas, *Tea Party to Independence*, 176–81; Ian R. Christie and Benjamin W. Labaree, *Empire or Independence, 1760–1776* (New York, 1976), 231; David Hackett Fischer, *Paul Revere's Ride* (New York, 1994), 51.

28. Dartmouth to Gage, January 27, 1775, in Carter, *Correspondence of General Thomas Gage*, 2:179–81.

29. *PBF* 21:459–61n; BF, "Notes for Discourse with Ld. C. on his Plan," January 31, 1775, ibid., 21:461–62; BF Memorandum on Chatham's Plan of Conciliation, [on or after February 1, 1775], ibid., 21:463–64; BF to JG, February 5[–7], 1775, ibid., 21:469; Peter Douglas Brown, *William Pitt, Earl of Chatham: The Great Commoner* (London, 1978), 380; Stanley Ayling, *The Elder Pitt: Earl of Chatham* (New York, 1976), 411–14.

30. One version of Chatham's speech is in *PH* 18:149–60. A second, based on notes taken by Hugh Boyd that were published in 1779, can also be found in ibid., 18:149–56n. My account draws on both versions. The quotations can be found on pages 150n, 154n, 155n, and 158.

31. *PH* 18:222–24. See also Thomas, *Tea Party to Independence*, 51, 191–97.

32. The quotations can be found in Dickinson, "'The Friends of America,'" in Davis, *Radicalism and Revolution in Britain*, 2.

33. North to the King, February 19, 1775, Fortescue, *Correspondence of George III*, 3:177.

34. *PH* 18:319–20; Thomas, *Tea Party to Independence*, 201. The royal authorities were made aware of North's plan by the American secretary. See Dartmouth, Circular Letter to the Governors, March 3, 1775, *DAR* 9:60–62.

35. *PH* 18:321.

36. Quoted in H. T. Dickinson, "British Imperial Sovereignty: The Ideological Case against the American Colonists," in H. T. Dickinson, ed., *Britain and the American Revolution*, 85. The subminister was William Knox.

37. *PH* 18:438–44; Valentine, *Lord North*, 1:347.

38. *PH* 18:447; Valentine, *Lord North*, 1:347.

39. *PH* 18:478–538. The lengthy quotation can be found in ibid., 18:535–36. Burke's comment about speaking out for honor and conscience can be found in Frank O'Gorman, "The Parliamentary Opposition to the Government's American Policy, 1760–1782," in Dickinson, *Britain and the American Revolution*, 103. For useful analyses of Burke's speech and the na-

ture of the opposition in Parliament, see also John Derry, *English Politics and the American Revolution* (New York, 1976), 129–48.

40. *PH* 18:570.

41. On Hartley's reputation, see *PBF* 21:511.

42. Merrill Jensen, *The Founding of a Nation: A History of the American Revolution, 1763–1776* (New York, 1968), 515–32; Leopold S. Launitz-Schurer, *Loyal Whigs and Revolutionaries: The Making of the Revolution in New York, 1765–1776* (New York, 1980), 145–46.

43. Report of the Braintree Committee of the Continental Association, March 15, 1775, *PJA* 2:396–400.

44. William Nelson, *The American Tory* (Oxford, 1961), 93–94; Ray Raphael, *The First American Revolution: Before Lexington and Concord* (New York, 2002), 59–89; Richard M. Ketchum, *Divided Loyalties: How the American Revolution Came to New York* (New York, 2002), 292.

45. Ketchum, *Divided Loyalties*, 315. On the raising of the Tory military unit, see Dartmouth to Gage, January 27, 1775, in Carter, *Correspondence of General Thomas Gage*, 2:180.

46. On the Tory pamphlets, see [Joseph Galloway], *A Candid Examination of the Mutual Claims of Great Britain and the Colonies* (New York, 1775); [Jonathan Boucher], *A Letter from a Virginian, to the Members of Congress* (New York, 1774); [Samuel Seabury], *The Congress Canvassed . . .* (New York, 1774); [Samuel Seabury], *A View of the Controversy Between Great Britain and her Colonies* (New York, 1775); [Thomas Bradbury Chandler], *A Friendly Address to all Reasonable Americans* (New York, 1774); [Thomas Bradbury Chandler], *What Think Ye of the Congress Now?* (New York, 1775); [Daniel Leonard], *The Origins of the American Contest with Great Britain* (Boston, 1774); Jonathan Sewall, *A Cure for the Spleen; or, Amusements for a Winter's Evening* (Boston, 1775). For extended summaries of the Tory arguments, see John Ferling, *The Loyalist Mind: Joseph Galloway and the American Revolution* (University Park, Pa., 1977), 112–27; Nelson, *American Tory*, 64–84; Jensen, *Founding of a Nation*, 510–13. Galloway's *Candid Examination* is reprinted in Merrill Jensen, ed., *Tracts of the American Revolution, 1763–1776* (Indianapolis, Ind., 1967). The Galloway quotations in this paragraph can be found on pages 375–76 of that source. The "scum will rise" quote can be found in Gordon S. Wood, *The Creation of the American Republic, 1776–1787* (Chapel Hill, N.C., 1969), 476.

47. Galloway, *Candid Examination*, in Jensen, *Tracts of the American Revolution*, 387, 388, 390, 391.

48. John Adams, "The Letters of Novanglus," *PJA* 2:216–387. The quotations are on pages 339 and 374.

49. Alexander Hamilton, *A Full Vindication of the Measures of Congress* (1774), in Harold C. Syrett and Jacob E. Cooke, eds., *Papers of Alexander Hamilton*, (New York, 1961–79), 1:45–78; Alexander Hamilton, *The Farmer Refuted* (1775), ibid., 1:81–165. The quotations can be found on pages 157–58.

50. [Charles Lee], *Strictures on A "Friendly Address to All Reasonable Americans"* (1775), [Early American Imprint Series, no. 13372]; John Alden, *General Charles Lee: Traitor or Patriot?* (Baton Rouge, La., 1951), 62–65.

51. Malcolm, *Peter's War*, 68.

52. Fischer, *Paul Revere's Ride*, 287–88; Ferling, *Almost a Miracle*, 32.

53. The best account of the events on this epic day can be found in Fischer, *Paul Revere's Ride*, 184–260, upon which my description is based. Pitcairn's order to the militiamen to lay

down their arms and Revere's description of the sound of the British musketry can be found in ibid., pages 191 and 195.

54. GW, Diary, February 8, March 31, 1775, *DGW* 3:308, 312, 319.

55. Fairfax County Resolves, July 18, 1774, *PGWC* 10:119–27.

56. GW to George William Fairfax, June 10[–15], 1774, *PGWC* 10:96–97.

57. GW to Fairfax, May 31, 1775, *PGWC* 10:368.

58. GW to Robert McKenzie, October 9, 1774, *PGWC* 10:172.

CHAPTER 5: "A RESCRIPT WRITTEN IN BLOOD": JOHN DICKINSON AND THE APPEAL OF RECONCILIATION

1. Louis Birnbaum, *Red Dawn at Lexington* (Boston, 1986), 196; Richard Frothingham, *History of the Siege of Boston* (Boston, 1849), 101; Allen French, *The Siege of Boston* (New York, 1911), 217.

2. Richard M. Ketchum, *Decisive Day: The Battle for Bunker Hill* (New York, 1974), 64, 75; Birnbaum, *Red Dawn at Lexington*, 71–74. On General Ward, see Charles Martyn, *The Life of Artemas Ward* (New York, 1921).

3. Benjamin Newcomb, *Franklin and Galloway: A Political Partnership* (New Haven, Conn., 1972), 276–78; Joseph Hewes to Samuel Johnston, May 11, 1775, *LDC* 1:342.

4. Robert Livingston to John Stevens, April 23, 1775, *LDC* 1:331.

5. Dickinson to Arthur Lee, April 29, 1775, *LDC* 1:331.

6. Lee to William Lee, May 10, 1775, *LDC* 1:337.

7. JA, Autobiography, *DAJA* 3:314.

8. SA to Richard Henry Lee, March 21, 1775, ibid., 1:321.

9. David Hackett Fischer, *Paul Revere's Ride* (New York, 1994), 267–79. The quotations can be found on pages 269, 270, and 279.

10. Frank L. Mott, "The Newspaper Coverage of Lexington and Concord," *New England Quarterly* 17 (1944): 489–505. The quotations can be found on pages, 496, 499, and 500.

11. Philip Davidson, *Propaganda and the American Revolution, 1763-1776* (Chapel Hill, N.C., 1941), 150–52; Arthur M. Schlesinger, *Prelude to Independence: The Newspaper War on Britain, 1764-1776* (New York, 1966), 232–33.

12. The depositions taken following the fighting can be found in *Am Archives* 4th series, 2:489–502. The quotations are from pages 489, 490, 491, 493, 494, and 495.

13. "Intercepted Letters of the Soldiery in Boston," April 28, 1775, *Am Archives* 4th series, 2:440–41.

14. James Warren, "To the Inhabitants of Great Britain," April 26, 1775, *Am Archives* 4th series, 2:487–88.

15. Robert S. Rantoul, "The Cruise of the 'Quero': How We Carried the News to the King," *Essex Institute Historical Collections* 36 (1900): 5–18; Fred Junkin Hinkhouse, *The Preliminaries of the American Revolution as Seen in the English Press, 1763-1775* (reprint, New York, 1969), 188; Troy Bickham, *Making Headlines: The American Revolution as Seen Through the British Press* (DeKalb, Ill., 2009), 71–72.

16. Lee to Lee, May 10, 1775, *LDC* 1:337; Richard Caswell to William Caswell, May 11, 1775, ibid., 1:339–40; Silas Deane to Elizabeth Deane, May 12, 1775, ibid., 1:345–46; JA to AA, May 8, 1775, *AFC* 1:195; *DGW* 3:329n.

17. JA to AA, May 8, 1775, *AFC* 1:195.

18. Caesar Rodney to Thomas Rodney, May 11, 1775, *LDC* 1:344.

19. *JCC* 2:11–44; GW to Fairfax County Committee, May 16, 1775, *PGWC* 10:364.

20. BF to Galloway, May 8, 1775, *PBF* 22:33; editor's note, ibid., 22:32–33n; Galloway to Joseph Verplanck, June 24, 1775, *Pennsylvania Magazine of History and Biography* 21 (1897), 483; Newcomb, *Franklin and Galloway*, 281–84; Eliphalet Dyer to Joseph Trumbull, May 18, 1775, *LDC* 1:357. Galloway's account of his meeting with BF can be found in Peter O. Hutchinson, ed., *The Diary and Letters of His Excellency Thomas Hutchinson, Esq* . . . (London, 1883–86), 2:237–38.

21. Silas Deane, Diary, May 16, 1775, *LDC* 1:351.

22. Milton E. Flower, *John Dickinson: Conservative Revolutionary* (Charlottesville, Va., 1983), 23; JA, Diary, August 31, September 12, 1774, September 15, 1775, *DAJA* 2:117, 133, 173.

23. Dickinson to Samuel Dickinson, January 18, March 8, April 22, August 15, 1754, January 21, 1755, in H. Trevor Colbourn, ed., "A Pennsylvania Farmer at the Court of King George: John Dickinson's London Letters, 1754–1756," in *Pennsylvania Magazine of History and Biography* 86 (1962): 252, 257, 259, 268, 278, 421; Dickinson to Mary Cadwalader Dickinson, May 25, August 1, 1754, ibid., 86:275, 276.

24. Jack Rakove, *Revolutionaries: A New History of the Invention of America* (Boston, 2010), 6. The quotation can be found in Flower, *John Dickinson*, 38.

25. John Dickinson, *A Speech, Delivered in the House of Assembly of the Province of Pennsylvania, May 24, 1764*, in Paul Leicester Ford, ed., *The Writings of John Dickinson* (Philadelphia, 1895), 1:22–23, 24, 34; Newcomb, *Franklin and Galloway*, 88; editor's note, *PBF* 11:194n; Flower, *John Dickinson*, 38; David L. Jacobson, *John Dickinson and the Revolution in Pennsylvania, 1764–1776* (Berkeley, Calif., 1965), 9.

26. Joseph Galloway, *The Speech of Joseph Galloway* (London, 1765), 28; Newcomb, *Franklin and Galloway*, 89; Jacobson, *John Dickinson and the Revolution in Pennsylvania*, 17–19.

27. Pennsylvania Assembly: Petition to the King, May 23, 26, 1764, *PBF* 11:199–200; Dickinson, *A Speech, Delivered in the House of Assembly*, in Ford, *Writings of John Dickinson*, 1:21–49; Joseph Galloway, *Speech, in Answer to the Speech of John Dickinson, Esq.* (1764), in Charles Evans, *American Bibliography* (Chicago, 1903–59). See the Early American Imprint Series (Readex Microprint, 1955–69), Evans, no. 9671.

28. BF, Preface to The Speech of Joseph Galloway, Esq., [August 1764], *PBF* 11:271–311. BF's quote can be found on page 296.

29. John Dickinson, *A Reply to a Piece called The Speech of Joseph Galloway, Esquire* (1764), in Ford, *Writings of John Dickinson*, 1:77–132; John Dickinson, *An Answer to Joseph Galloway* (1764), ibid., 1:137–40; Joseph Galloway, *To the Public, September 29, 1764*, Early American Imprint Series, Evans, no. 9674. The Dickinson quotes can be found in *A Reply*, pages 78, 81, 94, 102, 110, and 121–22.

30. Quoted in Ernest H. Baldwin, "Joseph Galloway, the Loyalist Politician," *Pennsylvania Magazine of History and Biography* 26 (1902): 186.

31. Newcomb, *Franklin and Galloway*, 90; Flower, *John Dickinson*, 42.

32. Jacobson, *John Dickinson and the Revolution in Pennsylvania*, 23.

33. Newcomb, *Franklin and Galloway*, 94, 98–100.

34. Flower, *John Dickinson*, 43–62; Edmund S. Morgan and Helen M. Morgan, *The Stamp Act Crisis: Prologue to Revolution* (Chapel Hill, N.C., 1953), 108–9, 115.

35. John Dickinson, *An Address to the Committee of Correspondence in Barbados* (Philadelphia, 1766), in Ford, *Writings of John Dickinson*, 1:251–76.

36. Quoted in Flower, *John Dickinson*, 64, and Jacobson, *John Dickinson and the Revolution in Pennsylvania*, 58.

37. Flower, *John Dickinson*, 58, 64–65.

38. See Thomas R. Adams, ed., *American Independence: The Growth of an Idea: A Bibliographical Study of the American Pamphlets Printed Between 1764–1776 Dealing with the Dispute Between Great Britain and Her Colonies* (Providence, R.I., 1965).

39. Flower, *John Dickinson*, 69, 76; Jacobson, *John Dickinson and the Revolution in Pennsylvania*, 43, 69; Adams, *American Independence*, 39; Peter D. G. Thomas, *The Townshend Duty Crisis: The Second Phase of the American Revolution, 1767–1773* (Oxford, 1987), 77; *The Manuscripts of the Earl of Dartmouth: American Papers* (reprint, Boston, 1972), 2:235; Benjamin Franklin, Preface to John Dickinson's *Letters from a Farmer*, May 8, 1768, *PBF* 15:111–12; JA, Diary, August 14, 1769, *DAJA* 1:341–42.

40. Carl F. Kaestle, "The Public Reaction to John Dickinson's 'Farmer's Letters,'" *Proceedings of the American Antiquarian Society* 78 (1968): 323–59. The quotations are from Flower, *John Dickinson*, pages 67 and 70.

41. John Dickinson, "A Song for American Freedom," July 1768, in Ford, *Writings of John Dickinson*, 1:425.

42. [John Dickinson], *Letters from a Farmer in Pennsylvania to the Inhabitants of the British Colonies* (Philadelphia, 1768), in Ford, *Writings of John Dickinson*, 1:406. The quotations can be found on pages 312, 328, 348, 364, 386, 397, 400, and 404.

43. Flower, *John Dickinson*, 76–99. On Josiah Quincy's comments on Fairhill, see "Journal of Josiah Quincy, January 1773," *Proceedings of the Massachusetts Historical Society* 49 (1916): 473.

44. John Dickinson, Two Letters on the Tea Tax, November 1773, in Ford, *Writings of John Dickinson*, 1:457–63. The quotes are on pages 461 and 462.

45. John Dickinson, "Letters to the Inhabitants of the British Colonies" (May 1774), in Ford, *Writings of John Dickinson*, 1:469–501. The quotes are on pages 498–99.

46. Dickinson to Quincy, October 28, 1774, *LDC* 1:251; Dickinson to Arthur Lee, April 29, 1775, ibid., 1:331–32.

47. Dickinson to Arthur Lee, April 29, 1775, *LDC* 1:331–32; Dickinson to Josiah Quincy Jr., October 28, 1774, ibid., 1:251; Dickinson to Cushing, December 11, 1774, ibid., 1:264; Dickinson to Samuel Ward, January 29, 1775, ibid., 1:303; John Dickinson, "Notes for a Speech in Congress," [May 23–25?], 1775, ibid., 1:379.

48. Quoted in Flower, *John Dickinson*, 66.

49. The preceding paragraphs on Dickinson's speech draw on his "Notes for a Speech in Congress," [May 23–25?], 1775, *LDC* 1:371–82.

50. Samuel Ward, Diary, May 15, 1775, *LDC* 1:351; Silas Deane, Diary, May 16, 1775, ibid., 1:351; *JCC* 2:53.

51. Silas Deane, Diary, May 16, 1775, *LDC* 1:352.

52. JA to Warren, May 21, 1775, *PJA* 3:11.

53. Merrill Jensen, *The Founding of a Nation: A History of the American Revolution, 1763–1776* (New York, 1968), 605–6.

54. James Kirby Martin, *Benedict Arnold, Revolutionary Hero: An American Warrior Reconsidered* (New York, 1997), 60–72; Willard Sterne Randall, *Benedict Arnold: Patriot and Traitor* (New York, 1990), 92–108; John Ferling, *Almost a Miracle: The American Victory in the War of Independence* (New York, 2007), 38–39.

55. Connecticut Delegates to Jonathan Trumbull Sr., May 31, 1775, *LDC* 1:422–23; Connecticut Delegates to William Williams, May 31, 1775, ibid., 1:423; Hancock to the New York Provincial Congress, June 1, 1775, ibid., 1:429; *JCC* 2:64–65, 73–75.

56. Silas Deane, Diary, May 23, 1775, *LDC* 1:371.

57. Dickinson, "Notes for a Speech in Congress," [May 23–25], 1775, *LDC* 1:371–82, 386–90; John Dickinson's Notes of Debates, May 23–25, 1775, ibid., 1:390–91; John Dickinson's Proposed Resolutions, [May 23–25], 1775, ibid., 1:383–86.

58. Dickinson's Notes of Debates, [May 23–25], 1775, *LDC* 1:390; JA to James Warren, July 24, 1775, *PJA* 3:89; JA, Autobiography, *DAJA* 3:314.

59. Silas Deane, Diary, May 23, 24, 1775, *LDC* 1:371, 401.

60. *JCC* 2:64–66.

CHAPTER 6: "PROGRESS MUST BE SLOW": JOHN ADAMS AND THE POLITICS OF A DIVIDED CONGRESS

1. JA to AA, July 23, 1775, *AFC* 1:253.

2. JA to Warren, September 30, 1775, *PJA* 3:3:172; William Bradford to James Madison, June 2, 1775, in William T. Hutchinson, William M. E. Rachal, et al., eds., *The Papers of James Madison* (Chicago, 1962–91), 1:149. SA and Lee are quoted in Gordon S. Wood, *The Americanization of Benjamin Franklin* (New York, 2004), 156.

3. BF to Jonathan Shipley, July 7, 1775, *PBF* 22:96; BF to Joseph Priestley, May 16, 1775, ibid., 22:44; BF to Burke, May 15, 1775, ibid., 22:41.

4. BF to Hartley, October 3, 1775, *PBF* 22:217; BF to Shipley, July 7, 1775, ibid., 22:94–95.

5. BF to William Strahan, July 5, 1775, *PBF* 22:85. BF never sent this letter, but there can be no doubt that his harsh tone accurately reflected his outlook in July 1775.

6. Quoted in Wood, *Americanization of Benjamin Franklin*, 159.

7. JA to AA, July 23, 1775, *AFC* 1:253.

8. Esmond Wright, *Franklin of Philadelphia* (Cambridge, Mass., 1986), 238.

9. John Ferling, *A Leap in the Dark: The Struggle to Create the American Republic* (New York, 2003), 10–12, 15.

10. BF, Proposed Articles of Confederation, [on or before July 21, 1775], *PBF* 22:122–25, 120–22n.

11. John Ferling, *Almost a Miracle: The American Victory in the War of Independence* (New York, 2007), 37.

12. James Warren to JA, May 7, June 11, 1775, *PJA* 3:3–4, 24; *DAJA* 3:321; Jerrilyn G. Marston, *King and Congress: The Transfer of Political Legitimacy, 1774–1776* (Princeton, N.J., 1987), 144–45; George Athan Billias, *Elbridge Gerry: Founding Father and Republican Statesman* (New York, 1976), 58; *LDC* 1:432–33n.; Robert Treat Paine to Elbridge Gerry, June 10, 1775, ibid., 1:477; Cushing to Joseph Hawes, June 10, 1775, ibid., 1:470.

13. New York Delegates to the New York Provincial Congress, June 3, 1775, *LDC* 1:442–43; Philip Schuyler to Samuel Springer, June 3, 1775, ibid., 1:444.

14. JA to Moses Gill, June 10, 1775, *PJA* 3:21; SA to Warren, June 10, 1775, *LDC* 1:468.

15. *DAJA* 3:321–23; *JCC* 2:89–93, 96–97.

16. Thomas Cushing to James Bowdoin Sr., June 21, 1775, *LDC* 1:530; Silas Deane to Elizabeth Deane, June 16, 1775, ibid., 1:494; Eliphalet Dyer to Jonathan Trumbull Sr., June 16, 1775, ibid., 1:496; Dyer to Joseph Trumbull, June 17, 1775, ibid., 1:499–500; Hancock to Gerry, June

18, 1775, ibid., 1:507; JA to AA, June 17, 1775, *AFC* 1:215–16; Benjamin Rush to Thomas Rushton, October 29, 1775, in L. H. Butterfield, ed., *Letters of Benjamin Rush* (Princeton, N.J., 1951), 1:92.

17. On Adams's youth and his choices, see, JA, Autobiography, *DAJA* 3:253–61; JA to Jonathan Sewall, February 1760, *PJA* 1:41–42; John Ferling, *John Adams: A Life* (reprint, New York, 2010), 9–17; and John Ferling, *Setting the World Ablaze: George Washington, John Adams, Thomas Jefferson, and the American Revolution* (New York, 2000), 5–7, 20–21.

18. On JA's courtship of AA, and her background, see Edith B. Gelles, *Abigail & John: Portrait of a Marriage* (New York, 2009), 1–19.

19. JA, Autobiography, *DAJA* 3:294; JA to AA, June 29, 1774, *AFC* 1:113. On Adams's struggles and eventual ascent as a lawyer, see Daniel R. Coquillette, "Justinian in Braintree: John Adams, Civilian Learning, and Legal Elitism, 1758–1775," in *Law in Colonial Massachusetts*, Colonial Society of Massachusetts Publications, 62 (1984): 359–418; L. Kinvin Wroth and Hiller Zobel, eds., *Legal Papers of John Adams* (Cambridge, Mass., 1965), 1:lii–xciv; Ferling, *John Adams*, 25–38; Ferling, *Setting the World Ablaze*, 25–27, 54–59.

20. [John Adams], "Instructions to Braintree's Representatives Concerning the Stamp Act," September–October 1765, *PJA* 1:132–43; [John Adams], "Clarendon to Pym," January 13–27, 1766, ibid., 1:155–69; [John Adams], "Replies to Philanthrop, Defender of Governor Bernard," December 9, 1766–February 16, 1767, ibid., 1:174–210.

21. JA, Autobiography, *DAJA* 3:289–91; 1:271, 274, 342, 352; 2:55, 74.

22. JA, Autobiography, *DAJA* 1:342.

23. JA, Autobiography, *DAJA* 3:292–94; *PJA* 1:238n; Hiller B. Zobel, *The Boston Massacre* (New York, 1970), 32, 41, 49, 214, 217–21.

24. JA, Autobiography, *DAJA* 1:339n, 3:294.

25. JA to Hezekiah Niles, February 13, 1818, in *WJA* 10:285–86; JA to William Tudor, June 1, 1817, July 9, 1818, ibid., 10:259, 327; JA to Tudor, November 16, 25, December 7, 1816, Adams Family Papers, Massachusetts Historical Society, Boston, 1954–59, microfilm edition, reel 123; JA to Sheldon Jones, March 11, 1809, ibid., reel 118; JA to TJ, July 15, 1813, July 9, 1818, in Lestor J. Cappon, ed., *The Adams-Jefferson Letters: The Complete Correspondence Between Thomas Jefferson and Abigail and John Adams* (Chapel Hill, N.C., 1961), 2:237, 594; JA, Diary, March 22, 1773, *DAJA* 2:80; JA, Autobiography, ibid., 3:293–94; JA to Benjamin Rush, February 27, 1805, May 1, 21, 1807, in John A. Schutz and Douglass Adair, eds., *The Spur of Fame: Dialogues of John Adams and Benjamin Rush, 1805–1813* (San Marino, Calif., 1966), 35–36, 80, 88; Bernard Bailyn, ed., *Pamphlets of the American Revolution, 1750–1776* (Cambridge, Mass., 1965), 23–30. See also Caroline Robbins, *The Eighteenth-Century Commonwealthmen: Studies in the Transmission, Development, and Circumstance of English Liberal Thought from the Restoration of Charles II Until the War with the Thirteen Colonies* (New York, 1959); John Howe, *The Changing Political Thought of John Adams* (Princeton, N.J., 1966), 15, 17–19, 43; Zoltan Haraszti, *John Adams and the Prophets of Progress* (Cambridge, Mass., 1952), 192; Ferling, *Setting the World Ablaze*, 82–84.

26. JA, Diary, October 19, 1777, *DAJA* 2:64.

27. JA, Diary, October 23, 30, 1772, *DAJA* 2:72, 74.

28. JA to Warren, December 17, 1773, April 9, 1774, *PJA* 2:1–2, 83; JA to James Burgh, December 28, 1773, ibid., 2:206; *DAJA* 2:85–86.

29. JA, Autobiography, *DAJA* 3:282, 307.

30. JA, Autobiography, *DAJA* 3:308–9; 2:156; Ferling, *Setting the World Ablaze*, 95.

31. JA to Shelton Jones, March 11, 1809, in Adams, *Works of John Adams*, 9:612; JA to Wil-

liam Tudor, March 29, 1817, ibid., 10:245; JA to AA, February 9, 1799, Adams Family Papers, Massachusetts Historical Society, Boston, 1954–59, microfilm edition, reel 393; JA to François Adrian Van Der Kemp, April 18, 1815, ibid., reel 322; JA, Diary, April 26, 1779, *DAJA* 2:362–63; TJ to James Madison, January 30, 1787, May 25, 1788, *PTJ* 11:94–95; 13:201–2. On the height of eighteenth-century male colonists, see Kenneth L. Sokoloff and George C. Villaflor, "The Early Achievement of Modern Stature in America," *Social Science History* 6 (1982): 435–81; John Ferling, "Soldiers for Virginia: Who Served in the French and Indian War?" *Virginia Magazine of History and Biography* 94 (1986): 312–23.

32. JA to AA, May 25, 29, June 2, 10, 23, July 8, 12, September 26, 1775, *AFC* 1:206, 207, 208, 213, 226, 243, 285; JA to James Warren, May 21, 1775, *PJA* 3:11.

33. Lewis E. Braverman and Robert D. Utiger, "Introduction to Thyrotoxicosis," in Lewis E. Braverman and Robert D. Utiger, eds., *Werner and Ingbar's The Thyroid: A Fundamental and Clinical Text* (Philadelphia, 1991), 645–57; Sidney Werner, "History of the Thyroid," ibid., 3–5; Robert Volpe, "Graves' Disease," ibid., 648–50; Peter C. Whybrow, "Behavioral and Psychiatric Aspects of Thyrotoxicosis," ibid., 865; Harry B. Burch, "Ophthalmopathy," ibid., 536–52; Vahab Fatourechi, "Localized Myxedema and Thyroid Acropachy," ibid., 553–58; Jeffrey D. Bernhard, "The Skin in Thyrotoxicosis," ibid., 696–700; Leslie J. De Groot et al., *The Thyroid and Its Diseases* (New York, 1984), 2–42, 136–44; Rene Mornex and Jacques L. Orgiazzi, "Hyperthyroidism," in Michael De Visscher, ed., *The Thyroid Gland: Comprehensive Endocrinology* (New York, 1980), 279–91, 306–17; Brita Winsa et al., "Stressful Life Events and Graves' Disease," *Lancet* 338 (December 14, 1991): 1475–79; Paul J. Rosch, "Stressful Life Events and Graves' Disease," ibid., 324 (September 4, 1993): 566–67; A. Horsley, "On the Function of the Thyroid Gland," *Proceedings of the Royal Society of London* 33 (1985): 5; Robert Volpe, "Autoimmune Thyroid Disease," *Hospital Practice* 19 (1984): 141–43; Marjorie Safran and Louis E. Braverman, "Thyrotoxicosis and Graves' Disease," ibid., 20 (1985): 34–36; S. G. Dortman, "Hyperthyroidism: Usual and Unusual Causes," *Archives of Internal Medicine* 137 (1977): 995–96 See also John Ferling and Lewis E. Braverman, "John Adams's Health Reconsidered," *William and Mary Quarterly* 55 (1998): 83–104.

34. JA to Warren, June 27, 1775, *PJA* 3:49.

35. John Ferling, "'Oh that I was a Soldier': John Adams and the Anguish of War," *American Quarterly* 36 (1984): 258–75.

36. JA to AA, May 26, June 10, 1775, *AFC* 1:206, 214.

37. George W. Corner, ed., *The Autobiography of Benjamin Rush: His Travels Through Life Together with His Commonplace Book for 1789–1813* (Princeton, N.J., 1948), 140.

38. Editor's notes, *PJA* 3:7–9, 156–58; 4:17–20.

39. Joseph Ellis, *Passionate Sage: The Character and Legacy of John Adams* (New York, 1993), 42–43; David F. Hawke, *Benjamin Rush: Revolutionary Gadfly* (Indianapolis, Ind., 1971), 164–65; G. S. Rowe, *Thomas McKean: The Shaping of a Republican* (Boulder, Colo., 1978), 164–65; TJ, "Character Sketches," in Saul K. Padover, ed., *The Complete Jefferson* (New York, 1943), 900, 904; Carol Berkin, *Jonathan Sewall: Odyssey of an American Loyalist* (New York, 1974), 142.

40. JA to Warren, June 20, 21, 27, July 6, 1775, *PJA* 3:34, 43, 50, 61; SA to Warren, June 28, 1775, *LDC* 1:553; Matthew Tilghman to Charles Carroll, June 20, 1775, ibid., 1:527.

41. JA to Warren, June 27, July 6, 1775, *PJA* 3:50, 61; JA to Elbridge Gerry, [ante June 11], 1775, ibid., 3:23; JA to Joseph Palmer, July 5, 1775, ibid., 3:54; JA to William Tudor, July 6, 1775, ibid., 3:59–60; New Hampshire Delegates to Matthew Thornton, June 20, 1775, *LDC* 1:524.

42. Commission from the Continental Congress, June 19, 1775, *PGWR* 1:6–7; Instructions from the Continental Congress, June 22, 1775, ibid., 1:21–22. On the Articles of War, see *JCC* 2:122–23 and *PGWR* 1:8n, 64n.

43. JA to AA, June 23, 1775, *AFC* 1:226; Douglas Southall Freeman, *George Washington: A Biography* (New York, 1948–57), 3:458–59; James T. Flexner, *George Washington and the American Revolution* (Boston, 1967), 23.

44. Deane to Elizabeth Deane, June 22, 26–27, 1775, *LDC* 1:532, 542; Connecticut Delegates to Jonathan Trumbull Sr., June 26, 1775, ibid., 1:542; JA to Warren, June 27, 1775, *PJA* 3:50; JA to AA, June 23, 1775, *AFC* 1:227.

45. Samuel Blachley Webb to Joseph Webb, June 19, 1775, in Dennis P. Ryan, ed., *A Salute to Courage: The American Revolution as Seen Through Wartime Writings of Officers of the Continental Army and Navy* (New York, 1979), 7.

46. Account of Adjutant Waller, June 23, 1775, in Samuel Adams Drake, ed., *Bunker Hill: The Story Told in Letters from the Field by British Officers Engaged* (Boston, 1875), 28, 29.

47. Joyce Lee Malcolm, *Peter's War: A New England Slave Boy and the American Revolution* (New Haven, Conn., 2009), 85.

48. Howe [probably to the British adjutant general], June 22, 24, 1775, in Henry Steele Commager and Richard B. Morris, eds., *The Spirit of '76: The Story of the American Revolution as Told by Participants* (Indianapolis, Ind., 1958), 1:132.

49. Recollection of Robert Steele, in George H. Scheer and Hugh F. Rankin, *Rebels and Redcoats* (Cleveland, 1957), 59.

50. The best account of the Battle of Bunker Hill is Richard M. Ketchum, *Decisive Day: The Battle for Bunker Hill* (New York, 1974). My narrative draws heavily on Ketchum. For succinct accounts, see also Richard Frothingham, *History of the Siege of Boston* (Boston, 1849), 133–206; Louis Birnbaum, *Red Dawn at Lexington* (Boston, 1986), 226–54; and Ferling, *Almost a Miracle*, 49–60.

51. Howe is quoted in Maldwyn A. Jones, "Sir William Howe: Conventional Strategist," in George A. Billias, ed., *George Washington's Opponents: British Generals and Admirals in the American Revolution* (New York, 1969), 47. Clinton is quoted in Ketchum, *Decisive Day*, 183. Burgoyne's comments are in John Burgoyne to Lord Stanley, June 25, 1775, *Am Archives* 4th series, 2:1095.

52. Gage to Dartmouth, June 25, 1775, *Am Archives* 4th series, 2:1097.

53. SA to Elizabeth Adams, June 28, 1775, *LDC* 1:552; Henry Middleton to Arthur Middleton, July 6, 1775, ibid., 1:595; TJ to George Gilmer, July 5, 1775, *PTJ* 1:185; BF to Shipley, July 7, 1775, *PBF* 22:94.

54. Samuel Ward, Diary, June 1, 1775, *LDC* 1:431; Hancock to GW, June 28, 1775, ibid., 1:555; ibid., 1:430n; JA to Warren, June 7, 1775, *PJA* 3:17; Jack N. Rakove, *The Beginnings of National Politics: An Interpretive History of the Continental Congress* (Baltimore, Md., 1979), 78, 417.

55. Dartmouth's Circular Letter to the Governors, March 3, 1775, *DAR* 9:60–62.

56. *Am Archives* 4th series, 2:454; Virginia's Resolution on Lord North's Conciliatory Proposal, June 10, 1775, *PTJ* 1:170–74; Marston, *King and Congress*, 207–9.

57. Johnson to Horatio Gates, August 18, 1775, *LDC* 1:704; TJ, Draft Resolution on Lord North's Conciliatory Proposal, July 25, 1775, *PTJ* 1:225–29; The Resolution as Adopted by Congress, July 31, 1775, ibid., 1:230–33.

58. Draft Petition to the King, [June 3–19], 1775, *LDC* 1:440–41; Marston, *King and Congress*, 211–13; Rakove, *Beginnings of National Politics*, 73–79.

59. JA to Warren, July 11, 1775, *PJA* 3:72.

60. JA, Autobiography, *DAJA* 3:318.

61. JA to Warren, July 24, 1775, *PJA* 3:89.

62. For an excellent account of the publication of JA's letter and its impact, see *PJA* 3:90–93n. See also Corner, *Autobiography of Benjamin Rush*, 142.

63. John Dickinson's Notes of Debates, May 23–25, 1775, *LDC* 1:390–91.

64. JA to Warren, July 6, 1775, *PJA* 3:62.

65. Dyer to Joseph Trumbull, July 10, 1775, *LDC* 1:620; JA, Diary, September 28, 1774, *DAJA* 2:140.

66. JA to AA, June 17, 1775, *AFC* 1:216.

67. JA to AA, July 7, October 7, 1775, *AFC* 1:241, 295; JA to Warren, July 6, 1775, *PJA* 3:61; JA to Josiah Quincy, October 6, 1775, ibid., 3:187; JA to Moses Gill, June 10, 1775, ibid., 3:21.

68. Ward to Henry Ward, June 22, 1775, *LDC* 1:535; JA to Timothy Pickering, August 6, 1822, *WJA* 2:512.

69. *PTJ* 1:188n.

70. *PTJ* 1:189n.

71. The Declaration on the Causes and Necessity for Taking Up Arms, July 6, 1775, *PTJ* 1:213–18. For TJ's draft, see ibid., 1:193–98. For Dickinson's draft, see ibid., 1:204–12. The *PTJ* contains an especially useful editorial note on the evolution of the final document. See ibid., 1:187–92. Finally, see *JCC* 2:128–57.

72. JA to Tudor, July 6, 1775, *PJA* 3:59.

CHAPTER 7: "THE KING WILL PRODUCE THE GRANDEST REVOLUTION": GEORGE III AND THE AMERICAN REBELLION

1. Troy Bickham, *Making Headlines: The American Revolution as Seen Through the British Press* (DeKalb, Ill., 2009), 72.

2. Peter D. G. Thomas, *Tea Party to Independence: The Third Phase of the American Revolution, 1773–1776* (Oxford, 1991), 234; Fred Junkin Hinkhouse, *The Preliminaries of the American Revolution as Seen in the English Press, 1763–1775* (reprint, New York, 1969), 185.

3. Gage to Barrington, April 22, 1775, in Clarence E. Carter, ed., *The Correspondence of General Thomas Gage with the Secretaries of State, and the War Office and the Treasury, 1763–1775* (reprint, New York, 1969), 2:674; Gage to Dartmouth, April 22, 1775, ibid., 1:396.

4. Cadwallader Colden to Dartmouth, May 3, 1775, *DAR* 7:317.

5. Gage to Dartmouth, October 20, 1775, in Carter, *Correspondence of General Thomas Gage*, 1:416. Sandwich is quoted in Alan Valentine, *Lord North* (Norman, Okla., 1967), 1:368. Gibbon is quoted in Piers Mackesy, *The War for America, 1775–1783* (Cambridge, Mass., 1965), 38. The secretary at war and the army's adjutant general expressed reservations about the ability of the British army to win the war without considerable naval assistance, with the latter remarking that "attempting to Conquer A[merica] Internally by our L[an]d Force, is as wild an Idea, as ever controverted Comn. Sense." The quote can be found in Stephen Conway, "British Governments and the Conduct of the American War," in H. T. Dickinson, ed., *Britain and the American Revolution* (London, 1998), 159.

6. Thomas, *Tea Party to Independence*, 238–41; B. D. Bargar, *Lord Dartmouth and the American Revolution* (Columbia, S.C., 1965), 170; Dartmouth to Governor Earl of Dunmore, July 5, 1775, *DAR* 10:24; Dartmouth to Carleton, July 24, 1775, ibid., 10:42; Dartmouth to Guy Johnson, July 24, 1775, ibid., 11:56.

7. Louis Birnbaum, *Red Dawn at Lexington* (Boston, 1986), 273–74; Joseph Reed to James Otis Sr., August 14, 1775, *PGWR* 1:307n; Hancock to GW, June 28, 1775, ibid., 1:42–43; GW to Schuyler, August 20, 1775, ibid., 1:332. In October 1775 General Washington finally spurned the offer of the Stockbridge Indians to provide service, telling them that "they would be called when wanted." See Committee of Conference Minutes of Proceedings, October 23–24, 1775, *LDC* 2:236.

8. Mackesy, *War for America*, 524–25; Edward E. Curtis, *The Organization of the British Army in the American Revolution* (New Haven, Conn., 1926), 3.

9. Quoted in Thomas, *Tea Party to Independence*, 254.

10. North to George III, July 26, 1775, in Sir John Fortescue, ed., *The Correspondence of George III from 1760 to December 1783* (London, 1927–28), 3:234; Valentine, *Lord North*, 376–77.

11. Valentine, *Lord North*, 378–79.

12. Stephen Conway, *The War of American Independence, 1775–1783* (London, 1995), 44.

13. Thomas, *Tea Party to Independence*, 254–56.

14. Carleton to Dartmouth, June 7, 1775, *DAR* 9:157–59.

15. Thomas, *Tea Party to Independence*, 259–65.

16. Gage to Barrington, July 18, September 25, November 2, 15, December 14, 1774, in Carter, *Correspondence of General Thomas Gage*, 2:649, 654, 659, 661, 663.

17. Dartmouth to Gage, August 2, 1775, in Carter, *Correspondence of General Thomas Gage*, 1:203.

18. Bargar, *Lord Dartmouth and the American Revolution*, 176–81; Valentine, *Lord North*, 1:389–95, 407–8. The quote can be found in Valentine's biography of North, page 395.

19. Mackesy, *War for America*, 50.

20. Alan Valentine, *Lord George Germain* (Oxford, 1962), 1–94; Gerald Saxon Brown, *The American Secretary: The Colonial Policy of Lord George Germain, 1775–1778* (Ann Arbor, Mich., 1963), 1–25; *PH* 17:1196, 1312.

21. *PH* 17:1162, 1196, 1312–13.

22. *PH* 18:990; Brown, *American Secretary*, 25–30; Valentine, *Lord George Germain*, 93–100.

23. Valentine, *Lord George Germain*, 96; Valentine, *Lord North*, 1:403.

24. George III to North, July 5, 26, 1775, in Fortescue, *Correspondence of George III*, 3:233, 235.

25. Thomas, *Tea Party to Independence*, 260–63; Jeremy Black, *George III: America's Last King* (New Haven, Conn., 2006), 215–22.

26. Proclamation for Suppressing Rebellion and Sedition, August 23, 1775, *EHD* 9:850–51.

27. Gage to Dartmouth, August 20, 1775, in Carter, *Correspondence of General Thomas Gage*, 1:413–14; Dartmouth to Howe, September 5, 1775, *DAR* 11:99, 100. The Germain quote can be found in Ira D. Gruber, *The Howe Brothers and the American Revolution* (New York, 1972), 27.

28. Quoted in Allen French, *The First Year of the American Revolution* (Boston, 1934), 323–24.

29. David McCullough, *1776* (New York, 2005), 3–10.

30. The King's Speech to Parliament, October 26, 1775, *EHD* 9:851–52.

31. Roger Sherman to William Williams, July 28, 1775, *LDC* 1:675; Dyer to Joseph Trumbull, July 28, 1775, ibid., 1:674; Connecticut Delegates to Jonathan Trumbull Sr., July 28, 1775, ibid., 1:672.

32. Jack N. Rakove, *The Beginnings of National Politics: An Interpretive History of the Continental Congress* (Baltimore, Md., 1979), 79.

33. *PJA* 3:9n, 117–18n; BF to Schuyler, August 8, 10, 1775, *PBF* 22:159, 160; New York Provincial Congress to Pennsylvania Committee of Safety, August 16, 19, 1775, ibid., 22:172, 177; BF to Deane, August 27, 1775, ibid., 22:184; BF to Hartley, September 12, 1775, ibid., 22:196; Dumas Malone, *Jefferson and His Time* (Boston, 1948–81), 1:208–9; Duane to Schuyler, August 4, 1775, *LDC* 1:696; Duane to Jonathan Trumbull, August 4, 1775, ibid., 1:697; Deane to Schuyler, August 20, 1775, ibid., 1:704; Chase to Schuyler, August 10, 1775, ibid., 1:700; Ward to BF, August 12, 1775, ibid., 1:701.

34. JA to Warren, September 17, 1775, *PJA* 3:158–59; SA to Gerry, September 26, 1775, ibid., 3:160n.

35. Richard Smith, Diary, September 12, 18, 21, 23, 1775, *LDC* 2:5, 29, 42, 48; Samuel Ward, Diary, September 15, 18, 20, 21, 1775, ibid., 2:29, 39, 42; JA, Diary, September 21, 22, 24, 1775, *DAJA* 2:177, 178–79, 184.

36. William Hooper to Samuel Johnson, May 23, 1775, *LDC* 1:398.

37. JA, Diary, September 16, 1775, *DAJA* 2:173.

38. Harrison to GW, July 21, 1775, *PGWR* 1:145.

39. JA to AA, December 3, 1775, *AFC* 1:332. Joseph Hewes to Samuel Johnston, December 1, 1775, *LDC* 2:421. On JA's relations with Cushing and Paine, see *AFC* 1:333n.

40. Deane to Elizabeth Deane, October 7, 1775, *LDC* 2:138; Josiah Bartlett to Mary Bartlett, October 25, 1775, ibid., 2:252; Ward to Deborah Ward, November 1, 1775, ibid., 2:285; Duane to Cornelius Duane, December 9, 1775, ibid., 2:464; BF to Shipley, September 13, 1775, *PBF* 22:200.

41. BF to Hartley, October 3, 1775, *PBF* 22:216–17; BF to William Strahan, October 3, 1775, ibid., 22:219; BF to Joseph Priestley, October 3, 1775, ibid., 22:218; BF to a Friend in London, October 3, 1775, ibid., 22:215–16.

42. Bartlett to Mary Bartlett, November 6, 1775, *LDC* 2:306–7; Ward to Mary Ward, October 19, 1775, ibid., 2:211; SA to Elizabeth Adams, November 7, 1775, ibid., 2:313.

43. Ward to Deborah Ward, October 12, November 1, 1775, *LDC* 2:172, 283–84; JA to AA, July 16, 1776, *AFC* 2:50; John Ferling, *John Adams: A Life* (reprint, New York, 2010), 175.

44. Francis Lewis to John Alsop, November 19, 1775, *LDC* 2:361; Jay to Sarah Jay, December 23, 1775, ibid., 2:514.

45. GW to Hancock, September 21, 1775, *PGWR* 2:26. With his letter to Congress, GW enclosed a petition from the subalterns concerning a pay increase. See Committee of Second Lieutenants to GW, September 21, 1775, ibid., 2:32–33.

46. Jerrilyn Greene Marston, *King and Congress: The Transfer of Political Legitimacy, 1774–1776* (Princeton, N.J., 1987), 158–64.

47. GW to Hancock, September 21, 1775, *PGWR* 2:26.

48. JA to Warren, October 1, 1775, *PJA* 3:177.

49. Ward to Henry Ward, September 30, 1775, *LDC* 2:84.

50. See the helpful pay table in Marston, *King and Congress*, 160–61.

51. Committee of Conference Minutes of Proceedings, October 23–24, 1775, *LDC* 2:233–38.

52. Ward to Henry Ward, November 21, 1775, *LDC* 2:370; GW to Joseph Reed, November 28, 1775, *PGWR* 2:449; GW to Hancock, December 18, 1775, ibid., 2:574; John Ferling, *Almost a Miracle: The American Victory in the War of Independence* (New York, 2007), 78–80; John Ferling, *The Ascent of George Washington: The Hidden Political Genius of an American Icon*

(New York, 2009), 97–98; Charles Lesser, *The Sinews of Independence: Monthly Strength Reports of the Continental Army* (Chicago, 1976), 8.

53. Hancock to Massachusetts Assembly, December 2, 1775, *LDC* 2:422; Hancock to Jonathan Trumbull, December 2, 1775, ibid., 2:423; Samuel Ward, Diary, October 9, 12, 1775, ibid., 155, 172; Ward to Henry Ward, December 2, 14, 1775, ibid., 2:429, 487; *JCC* 3:340, 393, 408, 448; GW to Hancock, December 4, 18, 25, 31, 1775, *PGWR* 2:484–85, 574, 602, 625; GW to Massachusetts Council, January 10, 1776, ibid., 3:61; GW to Reed, January 4, 14, 1776, ibid., 3:24, 89; Douglas Southall Freeman, *George Washington* (New York, 1948–57), 3:579; Ferling, *Almost a Miracle*, 80, 193. Samuel Adams is quoted in James T. Flexner, *George Washington: The Forge of Experience, 1732–1775* (Boston, 1965), 67. John Adams is quoted in Don Higginbotham, *The War of American Independence: Military Attitudes, Policies, and Practice, 1763–1789* (New York, 1971), 390.

54. JA, Diary, "Notes of Debates," October 3, [4], 1775, *DAJA* 2:189–92.

55. JA, Diary, "Notes of Debates," October 5, 1775, *DAJA* 2:193.

56. JA, Diary, "Notes of Debates," October 5, 12, 1775, *DAJA* 2:194, 204–5.

57. *JCC* 3:308; Jay to Alexander McDougall, October 26, 1775, *LDC* 2:258; JA, Diary, "Notes of Debate," October 27, 1775, *DAJA* 2:219.

58. *JCC* 3:274–75; JA, Diary, "Notes of Debates," October 7, 12, 1775, *DAJA* 2:198–202, 205; JA to Warren, October 19, 1775, *PJA* 3:215; David Freeman Hawke, *Honorable Treason: The Declaration of Independence and the Men Who Signed It* (New York, 1976), 78.

59. Marston, *King and Congress*, 173–74; JA, Diary, October 12, 1775, *DAJA* 2:205; JA to Warren, October 13, 19, 1775, *PJA* 3:205, 215; Silas Deane's Proposals for Establishing a Navy, [October 16?, 1775], *LDC* 2:182–87. The Deane quotation is on page 184.

60. JA, Diary, October 21, 1775, *DAJA* 2:214–15.

61. JA, Diary, October 21, 1775, *DAJA* 2:215–17.

62. David Syrett, *The Royal Navy in American Waters, 1775–1783* (Aldershot, England, 1989), 7–8.

63. BF to Richard Bache, October 24, 1775, *PBF* 22:242–43.

64. GW to Hancock, October 24, 1775, *PGWR* 2:227; SA to Elizabeth Adams, November 7, 1775, *LDC* 2:313; Marston, *King and Congress*, 176–77; Nathan Miller, *Sea of Glory: The Continental Navy Fight for Independence, 1775–1783* (New York, 1974), 52–55; William M. Fowler Jr., *Rebels Under Sail: The American Navy During the American Revolution* (New York, 1976), 42–72.

65. Governor Sir James Wright to Dunmore, July 8, October 14, 1775, *DAR* 11:43, 145; John W. Gordon, *South Carolina and the American Revolution: A Battlefield History* (Columbia, S.C., 2003), 15–36; Hugh T. Lefler and William S. Powell, *Colonial North Carolina: A History* (New York, 1973), 269–77.

66. Dunmore to Dartmouth, June 25, 1775, *DAR* 9:203; John E. Selby, *The Revolution in Virginia, 1775–1783* (Williamsburg, Va., 1988), 14–15, 41–64; Merrill Jensen, *The Founding of a Nation: A History of the American Revolution, 1763–1776* (New York, 1968), 644–45; Michael A. McDonnell, *The Politics of War: Race, Class, and Conflict in Revolutionary Virginia* (Chapel Hill, N.C., 2007), 52–53, 55, 61, 65, 118, 133–34, 135–74.

67. GW to Richard Henry Lee, December 26, 1775, *PGWR* 2:611; Francis Lightfoot Lee to Landon Carter, February 12, 1776, *LDC* 3:237; Thomas Nelson to Mann Page, January 4, 1776, ibid., 3:30; William Hooper to Joseph Hewes and John Penn, February 6, 1776, ibid., 3:208; North Carolina Delegation to North Carolina Council of Safety, February 13, 1776, ibid., 3:250; Edward Rutledge to Ralph Izard, December 8, 1775, ibid., 2:462.

68. Ward to Deborah Ward, November 1, 1775, *LDC* 2:285–86; Ward to Henry Ward, November 2, 1775, ibid., 2:291; SA to Warren, November 4, 1775, ibid., 298.

69. JA to Warren, June 27, 1775, *PJA* 3:49, 50; JA to Joseph Palmer, [July] 5, 1775, ibid., 3:54; *JCC* 2:76–77, 83–84; Samuel Ward, Diary, June 9, 1775, *LDC* 1:463–64; Cushing to Gerry, June 10, 1775, ibid., 2:469; Hancock to the Massachusetts Provincial Congress, ibid., 2:472–73.

70. New Hampshire Delegates to Matthew Thornton, October 2, 1775, *LDC* 2:98–99; Samuel Ward, Diary, October 18, 1775, ibid., 2:200–201; JA, Autobiography, *DAJA* 3:354–55.

71. *JCC* 3:319, 326; New Hampshire Delegates to Thornton, November 3, 1775, *LDC* 2:292–93; SA to Warren, November 4, 1775, ibid., 2:298. On the issue of establishing provincial governments, see Jensen, *Founding of a Nation*, 620–28, 638–41, and Marsten, *King and Congress*, 256–73.

72. Milton E. Flower, *John Dickinson: Conservative Revolutionary* (Charlottesville, Va., 1983), 138–41.

73. Flower, *John Dickinson*, 141–42; *Am Archives* 4th series, 3:1792–93; John Dickinson's Proposed Instructions, November 9, 1775, *LDC* 2:319–20.

74. Robert Morris to [?], December 9, 1775, *LDC* 2:470; John Alsop to Duane, November 29, 1775, ibid., 2:472n; BF to Hartley, October 3, 1775, *PBF* 22:217; TJ to John Randolph, November 29, 1775, *PTJ* 1:269.

CHAPTER 8: "THE FOLLY AND MADNESS OF THE MINISTRY": CHARLES JAMES FOX, THOMAS PAINE, AND THE WAR

1. See John Derry, *English Politics and the American Revolution* (New York, 1976), 131, and John Derry, *Charles James Fox* (New York, 1972), 64. In the former work, Derry provides a useful analysis of the opposition on pages 129–37. For a convenient list of the opposition members in the House of Commons in 1774 and 1775, see Bernard Donoughue, *British Politics and the American Revolution: The Path to War, 1773–1775* (New York, 1964), 291–93.

2. *PH* 18:708, 734–35, 761, 766, 768.

3. *PH* 18:710–11, 907. Peter Whiteley, *Lord North: The Prime Minister Who Lost America* (London, 1996), 158. The quotation is taken from a second speech delivered later by Grafton. On Grafton's entering North's government, see Sir William R. Anson, ed., *Autobiography and Political Correspondence of Augustus Henry Third Duke of Grafton* (London, 1898), xxxv.

4. *PH* 18:722–23.

5. Christopher Hobhouse, *Fox* (reprint, London, 1964), 1–11; John Drinkwater, *Charles James Fox* (New York, 1928), 1–16, 66; Loren Reid, *Charles James Fox: A Man for the People* (Columbia, Mo., 1969), 40; L. G. Mitchell, *Charles James Fox* (New York, 1992), 1, 3, 10, 13, 14.

6. Hobhouse, *Fox*, 23, 69; Mitchell, *Charles James Fox*, 18–19.

7. Hobhouse, *Fox*, 57; Reid, *Charles James Fox*, 43–44; Mitchell, *Charles James Fox*, 22–23, 45; Derry, *Charles James Fox*, 47.

8. Hobhouse, *Fox*, 70; Drinkwater, *Charles James Fox*, 109; *PH* 18:190–93; Mitchell, *Charles James Fox*, 27.

9. Derry, *Charles James Fox*, 69–70.

10. Mitchell, *Charles James Fox*, 33; Hobhouse, *Fox*, 65–69.

11. *PH* 18:769–79.

12. *PH* 18:712–13.

13. *PH* 18:726, 772–73, 796–97.

14. *PH* 18:795–916; Peter D. G. Thomas, *Tea Party to Independence: The Third Phase of the American Revolution, 1773–1776* (Oxford, 1991), 281. The questions asked of Penn, but not his responses, can be found in *PH* 18:911–16.

15. *PH* 18:916–27, 930–34.

16. Thomas, *Tea Party to Independence*, 292.

17. *PH* 18:963–82.

18. Charles James Fox to Lord Ossory, November 5, 1775, in Lord John Russell, ed., *Memorials and Correspondence of Charles James Fox* (reprint, New York, 1970), 1:140.

19. Thomas, *Tea Party to Independence*, 294.

20. *PH* 18:989–91.

21. *PH* 18:991–92.

22. *PH* 18:990; The King's Speech to Parliament, October 26, 1775, *EHD* 9:852.

23. *PH* 18:993–94; Thomas, *Tea Party to Independence*, 298–99; Whiteley, *Lord North*, 161; Ira D. Gruber, *The Howe Brothers and the American Revolution* (New York, 1972), 37–38; The American Prohibitory Act, December 22, 1775, *EHD* 9:853.

24. *PH* 18:995, 999, 1034, 1041, 1058–59; Thomas, *Tea Party to Independence*, 301.

25. BF to John Sargent, June 27, 1775, *PBF* 22:72; BF to Priestley, July 7, 1775, ibid., 22:91; BF to Shipley, July 7, 1775, ibid., 22:95.

26. Orville T. Murphy, *Charles Gravier, Comte de Vergennes: French Diplomacy in the Age of Revolution, 1719–1787* (Albany, N.Y., 1982), 232–33.

27. Richard Van Alstyne, *Empire and Independence: The International History of the American Revolution* (New York, 1967), 89; Weldon A. Brown, *Empire or Independence: A Study in the Failure of Reconciliation, 1774–1783* (Baton Rouge, La., 1941), 169; Samuel Flagg Bemis, *The Diplomacy of the American Revolution* (New York, 1935), 20; Murphy, *Charles Gravier, Comte de Vergennes*, 23, 49, 56, 95, 166, 345; Richard B. Morris, *The Peacemakers: The Great Powers and American Independence* (New York, 1965), 112–13; Jonathan Dull, *A Diplomatic History of the American Revolution* (New Haven, Conn., 1985), 48.

28. Murphy, *Charles Gravier*, Comte de Vergennes, 233; Edward Corwin, *French Policy and the American Alliance of 1788* (reprint, New York, 1970), 74.

29. Jerrilyn Greene Marston, *King and Congress: The Transfer of Political Legitimacy, 1774–1776* (Princeton, N.J., 1987), 220; *PBF* 22:280–81n.

30. Committee of Secret Correspondence to Lee, December 12, 1775, *PBF* 22:296–97; BF to Dumas, December 9, 1775, ibid., 22:288–89; BF to Don Gabriel Antonio de Bourbon, December 12, 1775, ibid., 22:298.

31. Bonvouloir to Guines: Extract, December 28, 1775, *PBF* 22:312–18; Murphy, *Charles Gravier, Comte de Vergennes*, 234.

32. *PGWR* 2:532n; GW to Hancock, December 14, 1775, ibid., 2:548; Hancock to GW, January 6, 1776, *LDC* 3:42. On Penet's and Pliarne's relationship with the French government, see, *PBF* 23:195n; Bemis, *Diplomacy of the American Revolution*, 34n.

33. Richard Smith, Diary, December 30, 1775, *LDC* 2:538; Hancock to Cushing, January 17, 1776, ibid., 3:105.

34. *JCC* 2:109–10; Hancock to GW, June 28, 1775, *LDC* 1:554–55; Don Gerlach, *Proud Patriot: Philip Schuyler and the War of Independence, 1775–1783* (Syracuse, N.Y., 1987), 11, 13, 15.

35. Schuyler to GW, September 20, 26, October 14, November 6[–7], 1775, *PGWR* 2:17, 54, 166, 314; Gerlach, *Proud Patriot*, 60.

36. GW to Schuyler, August 20, 1775, *PGWR* 1:332; Schuyler to GW, August 27, 1775, ibid., 1:368.

37. The best source for Montgomery's troop strength in December is Arthur S. Lefkowitz, *Benedict Arnold's Army: The 1775 American Invasion of Canada During the Revolutionary War* (New York, 2008), 214–15.

38. This narrative of the Canadian invasion draws on John Ferling, *Almost a Miracle: The American Victory in the War of Independence* (New York, 2007), 80–99; Christopher Ward, *The War of the Revolution* (New York, 1952), 1:135–201; James Kirby Martin, *Benedict Arnold, Revolutionary Hero: An American Warrior Reconsidered* (New York, 1977); 104–74; Thomas A. Desjardin, *Through a Howling Wilderness: Benedict Arnold's March to Quebec, 1775* (New York, 2006); Lefkowitz, *Benedict Arnold's Army*; and Hal Shelton, *General Richard Montgomery and the American Revolution* (New York, 1994).

39. Thomas Lynch to Schuyler, January 20, 1776, *LDC* 3:125.

40. Livingston to Thomas Lynch, January [?], 1776, *LDC* 3:178–79; John Dickinson's Draft Address to the Inhabitants of America, January 24[?], 1776, ibid., 3:141–42; William Livingston to Samuel Tucker, January 27, 1776, ibid., 3:158; Robert Morris to Charles Lee, February 17, 1776, ibid., 3:267–68; Bartlett to John Langdon, February 19, 1776, ibid., 3:281; Oliver Wolcott to Laura Wolcott, January 24, 1776, ibid., 3:149; Minutes, Secret Committee, February 14, 1776, ibid., 3:256; Samuel Ward to Henry Ward, February 19, 1776, ibid., 3:286; *JCC* 4:40, 71–76, 99, 106.

41. Ward to Nicholas Cooke, January 7, 1776, *LDC* 3:54; Ward to his Daughter, January 8, 1776, ibid., 3:61; SA to John Pitts, January 12, 1776, ibid., 3:84; Francis L. Lee to Richard Henry Lee, January 8, 1776, ibid., 3:58.

42. [Thomas Paine], "A Dialogue Between General Gage and General Wolfe in a Wood Near Boston" (1775), in Philip S. Foner, ed., *The Complete Writings of Thomas Paine* (New York, 1945), 2:47–48; [Thomas Paine], "An Occasional Letter on the Female Sex" (1775), ibid., 2:34. For a chronological table of Paine's publications in America before *Common Sense*, see ibid., 1:xlvii–xlviii. For biographies and interpretations of his thought and writing, see David Freeman Hawke, *Paine* (New York, 1974); Eric Foner, *Tom Paine and Revolutionary America* (New York, 1976); Alfred Owen Aldridge, *Man of Reason: The Life of Thomas Paine* (Philadelphia, 1959); Jack Fruchtman, *Thomas Paine: Apostle of Freedom* (New York, 1994); Harvey J. Kaye, *Thomas Paine and the Promise of America* (New York, 2005); and Craig Nelson, *Thomas Paine: Enlightenment, Revolution, and the Birth of Modern Nations* (New York, 2006).

43. [Thomas Paine], *Common Sense* (1776), in Foner, *Complete Writings of Thomas Paine*, 1:3–46. The quotations are from pages 6, 8, 15, 16, 18, 20, 21, 22, 26, 35, 39, 45. On English political radicalism, see Colin Bonwick, *English Radicals and the American Revolution* (Chapel Hill, N.C., 1977), 3–26.

44. Bartlett to John Langdon, January 13, 1776, *LDC* 3:88; Wolcott to Laura Wolcott, January 24, 1776, ibid., 3:149; Hancock to Cushing, January 17, 1776, ibid., 3:105; SA to Warren, January 13, 1776, ibid., 3:87; Henry Wisner to John McKesson, January 13[?], 1776, ibid., 3:90–91; Hewes to Samuel Johnston, February 13, 1776, ibid., 3:247; BF to Charles Lee, February 19, 1776, *PBF* 22:357.

45. Paine, *Common Sense*, in Foner, *Complete Writings of Thomas Paine*, 1:17, 46.

CHAPTER 9: "WE MIGHT GET OURSELVES UPON
DANGEROUS GROUND": JAMES WILSON, ROBERT MORRIS,
LORD HOWE, AND THE SEARCH FOR PEACE

1. SA to Samuel Cooper, April 30, 1776, *LDC* 3:601–2.

2. *LDC* 3:63n; Richard Smith, Diary, January 9, 1776, ibid., 3:72.

3. JA to AA, July 23, 1775, *AFC* 1:253. On Wilson, see Charles Page Smith, *James Wilson: Founding Father, 1742–1798* (Chapel Hill, N.C., 1956), 3–77; Geoffrey Seed, *James Wilson* (Millwood, N.Y., 1978), 3–15; Mark David Hall, *The Political and Legal Philosophy of James Wilson, 1742–1798* (Columbia, Mo., 1997), 12–13.

4. Lord Drummond's Notes, [January 3–9?, 1776], *LDC* 3:22.

5. Milton M. Klein, "Failure of a Mission: The Drummond Peace Proposal of 1775," *Huntington Library Quarterly* 35 (1972): 343–80; Hewes to Samuel Johnston, January 6, 1776, *LDC* 3:43; Lord Drummond's Minutes, January 14[?], 1776, ibid., 3:92.

6. On Wilson's appearance, see Smith, *James Wilson*, 3 and 202. The quotation can be found on page 207.

7. SA to JA, January 15, 1776, *LDC* 3:92–93; Milton E. Flower, *John Dickinson: Conservative Revolutionary* (Charlottesville, Va., 1983), 143. George Read to Caesar Rodney, January 19, 1776, *LDC* 3:115n; SA to JA, January 15, 1776, ibid., 3:94; SA to John Sullivan, January 12, 1776, ibid., 3:85. In a letter to Hancock, Cushing spoke of the "Dirty & sly Insinuating Actes & Machinations to destroy my Influence" that had been carried out by the likes of SA and his confederates in Massachusetts politics. See Thomas Cushing to John Hancock, January 30, 1776, ibid., 3:106n. See also John Miller, *Sam Adams: Pioneer in Propaganda* (Stanford, Calif., 1936), 342.

8. George Read to Caesar Rodney, January 19, 1776, *LDC* 3:115n; SA to JA, January 15, 1776, ibid., 3:94; SA to John Sullivan, January 12, 1776, ibid., 3:85; ibid., 3:138n.

9. Flower, *John Dickinson*, 129, 134, 144–46; JA to AA, February [13], 1776, *AFC* 1:347.

10. John Dickinson's Proposed Resolutions on a Petition to the King, [January 9–24, 1776], *LDC* 3:63; John Dickinson's Proposed Resolutions for Negotiating with Great Britain, [January 9–24, 1776], ibid., 3:64–65; John Dickinson's Proposed Instructions for Commissioners to Negotiate with Great Britain, [January 9–24, 1776], ibid., 3:66–68; ibid., 3:145n. Dickinson's notes were undated and, because of congressional secrecy, it is not clear when he spoke. However, it seems likely that Dickinson introduced his ideas in a speech delivered on January 24, the day scheduled for taking up Wilson's proposal regarding Congress's feelings on American independence.

11. Richard Smith, Diary, January 24, 1776, *LDC* 3:148.

12. Hooper and Hewes to John Penn, February 6, 1776, *LDC* 3:208; Penn to Thomas Person, February 14, 1776, ibid., 3:255; Bartlett to Langdon, February 19, 1776, ibid., 3:280; Ward to Henry Ward, February 19, 1776, ibid., 3:285; Wolcott to Samuel Lyman, March 16, 1776, ibid., 3:390.

13. Jerrilyn Greene Marston, *King and Congress: The Transfer of Political Legitimacy, 1774–1776* (Princeton, N.J., 1987), 180.

14. Richard Smith, Diary, January 29, 1776, *LDC* 3:167; Francis Lightfoot Lee to John Page, January 30, 1776, ibid., 3:168–69.

15. JA to AA, February 11, 1776, *AFC* 1:345–46; Lee to Page, January 30, 1776, *LDC* 3:168.

16. *JCC* 4:134–46; Smith, *James Wilson*, 75–76.

17. Richard Smith, Diary, February 13, 1776, *LDC* 3:252.

18. Robert Morris to Robert Herries, February 15, 1776, *LDC* 3:258.

19. Willing has not been the subject of a biography. See Allen Johnson et al., eds., *Dictionary of American Biography* (New York, 1928–37), 20:302–4.

20. The quotes are from Clarence L. Ver Steeg, *Robert Morris: Revolutionary Financier* (New York, 1972), 4.

21. Ray Raphael, *Founders: The People Who Brought You a Nation* (New York, 2009), 66, 102.

22. Willing, Morris & Co. to William Baynes & Co., September 27, 1775, *LDC* 2:75–76. On the business and political activities of Willing and Morris, see Richard A. Ryerson, *The Revolution Is Now Begun: The Radical Committees of Philadelphia, 1765–1776* (Philadelphia, 1978), 50–130; Ver Steeg, *Robert Morris*, 1–8; and Thomas M. Doerflinger, *A Vigorous Spirit of Enterprise: Merchants and Economic Development in Revolutionary Philadelphia* (Chapel Hill, N.C., 1986), 38, 103.

23. JA, Diary, September 25, 1775, *DAJA* 2:183–85; Richard Smith, Diary, December 13, 1775, *LDC* 2:483; Secret Committee Contract, October 9, 1775, ibid., 2:153–54; Secret Committee Minutes of Proceedings, January 11, February 5, 1776, ibid., 3:82, 203; John Alsop, Philip Livingston, Francis Lewis, and Robert Morris to Silas Deane, March 1, 1776, ibid., 3:314; ibid., 2:74n; Morris to Herries, February 15, 1776, ibid., 3:259; Raphael, *Founders*, 207, 257. The Morris quotation can be found in Morris to Deane, August 11, 1776, *LDC* 4:657.

24. Morris to Samuel Inglis, January 30, 1776, *LDC* 3:170; Morris to Charles Lee, February 17, 1776, ibid., 3:270; Morris to Herries, February 15, 1776, ibid., 3:258–59.

25. Morris to [?], December 9, 1775, *LDC* 2:470.

26. Morris to Deane, June 5, 1776, *LDC* 4:147.

27. Morris to Horatio Gates, April 6, 1776, *LDC* 3:495; Morris to Herries, February 15, 1776, ibid., 3:258; Morris to Deane, March 10, 1776, ibid., 3:366.

28. Alan Valentine, *Lord North* (Norman, Okla., 1967), 1:407.

29. The foregoing draws on Ira D. Gruber, *The Howe Brothers and the American Revolution* (New York, 1972), 31–67.

30. *PH* 18:991.

31. William Knox is quoted in Valentine, *Lord North*, 1:408.

32. Walpole is quoted in Gerald Saxon Brown, *The American Secretary: The Colonial Policy of Lord George Germain, 1775–1778* (Ann Arbor, Mich., 1963), 64.

33. *PH* 18:1248–50, 1253, 1255, 1284, 1286.

34. *PH* 18:1144–45, 1154–55, 1156.

35. Brown, *American Secretary*, 66–72.

36. Gruber, *Howe Brothers and the American Revolution*, 72–77; Peter D. G. Thomas, *Tea Party to Independence: The Third Phase of the American Revolution, 1773–1776* (Oxford, 1991), 303–17; Weldon A. Brown, *Empire or Independence: A Study in the Failure of Reconciliation, 1774–1783* (reprint, Port Washington, N.Y., 1966), 82–85.

37. Burke to Richard Champion, May 30, 1776, George H. Guttridge, ed., *The Correspondence of Edmund Burke* (Chicago, Ill., 1958–78), 3:268–69.

38. Hooper to Trumbull, March 13, 1776, *LDC* 3:372.

39. Wolcott to Andrew Adams, March 22, 1776, *LDC* 3:428.

40. JA to AA, April 15, 1776, *AFC* 1:383.

41. SA to Hawley, April 15, 1776, *LDC* 3:528.

CHAPTER 10: "THE FATAL STAB": ABIGAIL ADAMS AND THE REALITIES OF THE STRUGGLE FOR INDEPENDENCE

1. Richard Henry Lee to Landon Carter, April 1, 1776, *LDC* 3:470; Gerry to James Warren, March 26, 1776, ibid., 3:441; JA to Horatio Gates, March 23, 1776, *PJA* 4:59.

2. *DAJA* 2:231–33. Emphasis added by the author.

3. Robert Alexander to the Maryland Council of Safety, February 27, 1776, *LDC* 3:307; Richard Smith, Diary, February 27, 1776, ibid., 3:310.

4. Whipple to Joshua Brackett, March 17, 1776, *LDC* 3:395.

5. Gerry to Warren, March 26, 1776, *LDC* 3:442; Hancock to Certain Colonies, April 12, 1776, ibid., 3:514.

6. Ronald Hoffman, *A Spirit of Dissension: Economics, Politics, and the Revolution in Maryland* (Baltimore, Md., 1973), 157–58; Germain to Robert Eden, December 23, 1775, *Am Archives* 4th series, 4:439–40; Pauline Maier, *American Scripture: Making the Declaration of Independence* (New York, 1997), 80–81.

7. Whipple to Brackett, April 11, 1776, *LDC* 3:509; Joseph Hewes to Samuel Johnston, March 20, 1776, ibid., 3:416.

8. SA to Joseph Hawley, April 15, 1776, *LDC* 3:528; Whipple to Brackett, April 11, 1776, ibid., 3:509; Hewes to Johnston, March 20, 1776, ibid., 3:416; Gerry to Warren, March 26, 1776, ibid., 3:442.

9. JA to Horatio Gates, March 23, 1776, *PJA* 4:59; JA to AA, April 6, 1776, ibid., 3:492; JA to AA, April 12, 1776, *AFC* 1:377.

10. *JCC* 4:214, 229–32. See also James Morgan, "American Privateering in America's War for Independence, 1775–1783," *American Neptune* 36 (April 1976): 80–85, and H. James Henderson, *Party Politics in the Continental Congress* (New York, 1974), 61. Thousands of letters of marquee were issued during the conflict, and according to the best estimate, more than three thousand prizes were captured by American privateers.

11. Eliphalet Dyer to Joseph Trumbull, January 1, 1776, *LDC* 3:5.

12. Committee of Secret Correspondence Minutes of Proceedings, March 2, 1776, *LDC* 3:320–23. See also, Robert Morris to Deane, March 30, 1776, ibid., 3:466–68.

13. Gage to Dartmouth, August 20, 1775, Clarence E. Carter, ed., *The Correspondence of General Thomas Gage with the Secretaries of State, and the War Office and the Treasury, 1763-1775* (reprint, New York, 1969), 1:413–14; Ira Gruber, *The Howe Brothers and the American Revolution* (Chapel Hill, N.C., 1972), 26, 31, 37; Howe to Dartmouth, November 26, 1775, *DAR* 11:191, 193.

14. GW, Circular to the General Officers, September 8, 1775, *PGWR* 1:432–34; Council of War, September 11, 1775, ibid., 1:450–51.

15. GW to Joseph Reed, January 14, 1776, *PGWR* 3:89–90; GW, Instructions to Colonel Henry Knox, November 16, 1775, ibid., 2:384–85; Knox to GW, November 27, December 5, 17, 1775, January 5, 1776, ibid., 2:434, 495–96, 563–66; North Callahan, *Henry Knox: George Washington's General* (New York, 1958), 16–56; John Ferling, *Almost a Miracle: The American Victory in the War of Independence* (New York, 2007), 102–4.

16. Council of War, February 16, 1776, *PGWR* 3:320–22, 323–24n; GW to Reed, February 26[–March 9], 1776, ibid., 3:373.

17. Ferling, *Almost a Miracle*, 105.

18. AA to JA, March 16, 1776, *AFC* 1:358; Christopher Ward, *The War of the Revolution* (New York, 1952), 1:128; Archibald Robinson, *His Diary and Sketches in America, August 1775–April 1776*, in Harry M. Lyndenberg, ed., *New York Public Library Bulletin* (New York,

1933), 73-74. Howe's quote, which Abigail Adams heard and passed on ten days after the event, is likely apocryphal.

19. Hugh Earl Percy to General Harvey, July 28, 1775, in Charles K. Bolton, ed., *Letters of Hugh Earl Percy from Boston and New York, 1774-1776* (Boston, 1902), 58.

20. James Grant to Richard Rigby, October 5, 1775, Papers of James Grant of Ballindaloch, reel 29, Library of Congress.

21. *PGWR* 3:377-78n; GW to Read, February 26[-March 9], 1776, ibid., 3:376.

22. *Am Archives* 4th series, 5:422-23; *PGWR* 4:2n.

23. Francis Lightfoot Lee to Landon Carter, April 9, 1776, *LDC* 3:500.

24. *Am Archives* 4th series, 3:644, 794-95.

25. James Duane, Notes for a Speech in Congress, [May 23-25, 1775], *LDC* 1:392.

26. Quoted in T. H. Breen, *American Insurgents, American Patriots: The Revolution of the People* (New York, 2010), 10.

27. David Hackett Fischer, *Paul Revere's Ride* (New York, 1994), 320-21; Joyce Lee Malcolm, *Peter's War: A New England Slave Boy and the American Revolution* (New Haven, Conn., 2009), 75.

28. BF to Anthony Todd, March 29, 1776, *PBF* 22:393.

29. GW, General Orders, October 26, 31, November 14, 20, 1775, *PGWR* 2:235-36, 269, 369, 443.

30. See David Ammerman, *In the Common Cause: American Response to the Coercive Acts of 1774* (Charlottesville, Va., 1974), 103-24.

31. *Am Archives* 4th series, 3:141-42.

32. *Am Archives* 4th series, 4:858, 1050-51.

33. *Am Archives* 4th series, 4:719.

34. *Am Archives* 4th series, 3:319.

35. *Am Archives* 4th series, 4:713.

36. Breen, *American Insurgents, American Patriots*, 233-34. Breen chronicles the work of these committees in detail and shows how restrained many were in practice. See pages 207-40.

37. *Am Archives* 4th series, 3:218, 692, 462-63, 955, 1072; 4:288; 5:547.

38. *Am Archives* 4th series, 3:133, 322, 682, 692.

39. *Am Archives* 4th series, 3:141-42.

40. Brendan McConville, *The King's Three Faces: The Rise and Fall of Royal America, 1688-1776* (Chapel Hill., N.C., 2006), 63-64, 74, 87, 107, 126, 129-31, 138, 202. The quotations can be found on pages 74 and 202.

41. McConville, *King's Three Faces*, 292, 296-97.

42. Quoted in Merrill Jensen, *The Founding of a Nation: A History of the American Revolution, 1763-1776* (New York, 1968), 669.

43. The literature on republicanism and the American Revolution is voluminous. Good places to start—and on which the foregoing draws—are Bernard Bailyn, *The Ideological Origins of the American Revolution* (Cambridge, Mass., 1967), 48-52, 281-84; Gordon S. Wood, *The Creation of the American Republic, 1776-1787* (Chapel Hill, N.C., 1969), 46-124; Gordon S. Wood, *The Radicalism of the American Revolution* (New York, 1992), 11-189; Robert E. Shalhope, "Republicanism, Liberalism, and Democracy: Political Culture in the Early Republic," in Milton M. Klein et al., eds., *The Republican Synthesis Revisited: Essays in Honor of George Athan Billias* (Worcester, Mass., 1992), 37-90; Robert E. Shalhope, "Republicanism and Early American Historiography," *William and Mary Quarterly* 39 (1982): 334-56; Robert

E. Shalhope, "Toward a Republican Synthesis: The Emergence of an Understanding of Republicanism in American Historiography," ibid., 29 (1972): 49–80; Joyce Appleby, "Republicanism and Ideology," *American Quarterly* 37 (1985): 461–83; Linda K. Kerber, "The Republican Ideology of the Revolutionary Generation," ibid., 37:474–95.

44. Jensen, *Founding of a Nation*, 677–78.

45. *Am Archives* 4th series, 5:608–14.

46. *Am Archives* 4th series, 5:1025–32; Maier, *American Scripture*, 69–72.

47. JA to Warren, April 22, 1776, *PJA* 4:135.

48. *Am Archives* 4th series, 6:1524; *JCC* 5:425; *LDC* 3:417n; Jensen, *Founding of a Nation*, 678.

49. SA to Samuel Cooper, April 30, 1776, *LDC* 3:600–602.

50. Jensen, *Founding of a Nation*, 679.

51. *Am Archives* 4th series, 6:1524; Jensen, *Founding of a Nation*, 680–81.

52. *Am Archives* 4th series, 5:1025–32, 1032–34, 1034–35, 1046–47, 1205–6, 1206–9; 6:514–15. Pauline Maier brought to the attention of all historians what she called "the other declarations of Independence," the local statements adopted between April and July in Virginia, South Carolina, and elsewhere. See Maier, *American Scripture*, 47–96, and see also the convenient log that she provides of these statements, 217–23.

53. Francis Lightfoot Lee to Landon Carter, January 22, March 19, April 9, 1776, *LDC* 3:130, 407, 500.

54. *Am Archives* 4th series, 5:1034–35.

55. [Anon.], "Serious Questions Addressed to the Congress," April [?], 1776, *Am Archives* 4th series, 5:1078.

56. "Salus Populi," March [?], 1776, *Am Archives* 4th series, 5:98–99; [Thomas Paine], "The Forester," [April 1776], ibid., 5:1020; "FA," April 29, 1776, ibid., 5:1134.

57. [Thomas Paine], "A Dialogue between the Ghost of General Montgomery . . . and an American Delegate, in a Wood near Philadelphia," 1776, *Am Archives* 4th series, 5:131; [Anon.], "Plain Hints," March [?], 1776, ibid., 5:214; "Somers," [Williamsburg, Va., March 1776], ibid., 5:122–23; [Anon.], Untitled, March 21, 1776, ibid., 5:450.

58. [Anon.], "Seek Truth," April [?], 1776, *Am Archives* 4th series, 5:1016; [Anon.], "Plain Hints," March [?], 1776, ibid., 5:214; "An American," Untitled, March 15, 1776, ibid., 5:227.

59. Civis, "To the Freeholders . . . of Philadelphia," April 30, 1776, *Am Archives* 4th series, 5:1142; James H. Hutson, "The Partition Treaty and the Declaration of Independence," *Journal of American History* 58 (1972): 351–58.

60. *Pennsylvania Gazette*, May 1, 1776; Cato, "A Letter to the People of Pennsylvania," Letter III and Letter IV [March 1776], *Am Archives* 4th series, 5:445, 514; A Settled Citizen, "On the Present State of Publick Affairs," April 23, 1776, ibid., 5:1037; Civis, "To the Freeholders . . . of Philadelphia," April 30, 1776, ibid., 5:1141–42; Hampden, "Hampden Against Independence," May 1, 1776, ibid., 5:1158–59; CS, "Reply to Remarks of Rationalis on "'Common Sense,'" April 18, 1776, ibid., 5:976; [Anon.], "Reasons for a Declaration of the Independence of the American Colonies," April 20, 1776, ibid., 5:992; Civis, "To the Inhabitants of Philadelphia," [April 1776], ibid., 5:803–4.

61. AB, Untitled, April 12, 1776, *Am Archives* 4th series, 5:861–62.

62. A British American, "To the Inhabitants of the United Colonies," December 28, 1776, *Am Archives* 4th series, 4:473.

63. [Anon.], "To the Inhabitants of New-York," April 11, 1776, *Am Archives* 4th series, 5:856.

64. JA to AA, March 19, 1776, *AFC* 1:363; JA to William Tudor, April 12, 1776, *PJA* 4:118; JA to Warren, May 12, 1776, ibid., 4:182.

65. *PJA* 4:65–68n.

66. [John Adams], *Thoughts on Government* (1776), *PJA* 4:86–93.

67. Robert Treat Paine, Diary, May 5, 1776, *LDC* 3:625–26; Richard Henry Lee to Samuel Purviance Jr., May 6, 1776, ibid., 3:632.

68. Jay to James Jay, January 4, 1776, *LDC* 3:29; Thomas Lynch to GW, January 16, 1776, ibid., 3:101; Morris to Gates, April 6, 1776, ibid., 3:495.

69. *PH* 18:728, 1175, 1181, 1185.

70. Hancock to the Massachusetts Assembly, May, 16, 1776, *LDC* 4:7; Hancock to Certain Colonies, June 4, 1776, ibid., 4:136; William Whipple to Joshua Brackett, June 2, 1776, ibid., 4:119; Wolcott to Laura Wolcott, May 25, 1776, ibid., 4:72; Duane to Robert Livingston, January 5, 1776, ibid., 3:33; Morris to Deane, June 5, 1776, ibid., 4:147; Bartlett to John Langdon, May 19, 1776, ibid., 4:39.

71. Richard Henry Lee to Carter, June 2, 1776, *LDC* 4:117.

72. Wolcott to Laura Wolcott, March 2, 1776, *LDC* 3:325; SA to Elizabeth Adams, February 26, 1776, ibid., 3:303.

73. JA to AA, December 3, 1775, *AFC* 1:331; *AFC* 1; Thomas McKean to George Read, January 19, 1776, *LDC* 3:115; Duane to Alexander McDougall, February 25, 1776, ibid., 3:300; Samuel Ward to Deborah Ward, January 2, 1776, ibid., 3:21; Wolcott to Laura Wolcott, March [8], 19, 1776, ibid., 3:359, 412; Samuel Huntington to Joseph Trumbull, February 20, March 26, 1776, ibid., 3:290; Jay to Robert R. Livingston, March 4, 1776, ibid., 3:328; Bartlett to Mary Bartlett, January 24, 1776, ibid., 3:131; Hancock to Cushing, January 17, 1776, ibid., 3:105; John Rogers to Maryland Council, April 28, 1776, ibid., 3:582n; *JCC* 3:302–3.

74. SA to Warren, March 8, 1776, *LDC* 3:353–54; Paine to Joseph Hawley, January 1, 1776, ibid., 3:6–7; Paine to Joseph Palmer, January 1, 1776, ibid., 3:10–11; Paine to Warren, January 1, 1776, ibid., 3:11–12; JA to AA, April 6, 1776, ibid., 3:493.

75. SA to Elizabeth Adams, February 26, 1776, *LDC* 3:303; Jay to Livingston, March 4, 1776, ibid., 3:328; Ward to His Daughter, February 11, March 8, 1776, ibid., 3:232, 357; Ward to Anna Ward, January 21, 1776, ibid., 3:128; Deane to Elizabeth Deane, January 13, 1776, ibid., 89.

76. AA to JA, May 7, 24, 1775, *AFC* 1:195, 205.

77. AA to JA, June [16], 1775, *AFC* 1:217, 219.

78. AA to JA, November 12, 1775, *AFC* 1:325.

79. Malcolm, *Peter's War*, 80.

80. AA to JA, June [16], 25, July 16, September 8, 25, 29, October 1, 9, November 12, December 10, 1775, *AFC* 1:219, 232, 249, 276–78, 284, 287–88, 288–89, 296, 324–25, 337.

81. AA to JA, October 21, 25, 1775, *AFC* 1:305, 312.

82. AA to JA, June 22, 25, July 5, 1775, March 2, 1776, *AFC* 1:226, 231, 239, 353, 355.

83. JA to AA, June 10, July 7, 1775, *AFC* 1:214, 241–42; AA to JA, July 16, 1775, ibid., 1:247.

84. AA to JA, May 24, 1775, *AFC* 1:205; JA to AA, July 28, September 26, October 1, 2, 7, 13, 19, 1775, ibid., 1:267, 285, 289, 291, 295, 300–301, 303.

85. JA to Abigail Adams, 2d, October 20, 1775, *AFC* 1:304–5; JA to Thomas Boylston Adams, October 20, 1775, ibid., 1:305; JA to AA, October 29, 1775, April 15, 1776, ibid., 1:317–18, 383–84.

86. JA to AA, December 3, 1775, *AFC* 1:331.

87. JA to AA, October 7, 1775, *AFC* 1:295–96. Edith B. Gelles is the recognized authority on Abigail Adams. To understand AA and her relationship with JA, see Gelles's, *Abigail & John: Portrait of a Marriage* (New York, 2009), *Abigail Adams: A Writing Life* (New York, 2002), and *Portia: The World of Abigail Adams* (Bloomington, Ind., 1992). Other biographies of AA include: Woody Holton, *Abigail Adams* (New York, 2009); Charles Akers, *Abigail Adams: A Revolutionary American Woman* (New York, 2007); Lynne Withey, *Dearest Friend: A Life of Abigail Adams* (New York, 1981); and Phyllis Lee Levin, *Abigail Adams: A Biography* (New York, 1987).

88. JA to AA, March 17, April 12, 14, 1776, *AFC* 1:361, 377, 382; AA to JA, March 31, 1776, ibid., 1:369–70.

89. JA to John Winthrop, May 6, 1776, *PJA* 4:175; JA to Warren, May 20, 1776, ibid., 4:195; John Dickinson Sergeant to JA, April 11, 1776, ibid., 4:114; Whipple to Joshua Brackett, April 21, 1776, *LDC* 3:568; SA to Cooper, April 30, 1776, ibid., 3:600–601; Wolcott to Laura Wolcott, April 17, 1776, ibid., 3:555.

90. Whipple to Joseph Whipple, May 6, 1776, *LDC* 3:634; Francis L. Lee to Carter, April 9, 1776, ibid., 3:500; Lee to Charles Lee, May 11, 1776, ibid., 3:655.

91. JA to Joseph Ward, April 16, 1776, *LDC* 3:534; SA to Hawley, April 15, 1776, ibid., 3:528; JA to Warren, April 20, 22, 1776, *PJA* 4:130–31, 136; JA to Winthrop, May 6, 1776, ibid., 4:175; JA to AA, April 28, 1776, *AFC* 1:400–401.

92. JA to Warren, March 21, May 20, 1776, *PJA* 4:56, 195.

93. Richard A. Ryerson, *The Revolution Is Now Begun: The Radical Committees of Philadelphia, 1765–1776* (Philadelphia, 1978), 172–74; William Hogeland, *Declaration: The Nine Tumultuous Weeks When America Became Independent, May 1–July 4, 1776* (New York, 2010), 1–10.

94. JA to Warren, May 15, 1776, *PJA* 4:186; Hogeland, *Declaration*, 11–49, 73–76. On Dickinson's absence, see David Hawke, *A Transaction of Free Men: The Birth and Course of the Declaration of Independence* (New York, 1964), 117–18.

95. Milton E. Flower, *John Dickinson: Conservative Revolutionary* (Charlottesville, Va., 1983), 150.

96. Carter Braxton to Landon Carter, May 17, 1776, *LDC* 4:19; JA, Notes of Debates, [May 13–15, 1776], *DAJA* 2:238–41; *JCC* 4:342, 357–58; Hogeland, *Declaration*, 97–100; Hawke, *A Transaction of Free Men*, 119–20.

97. JA to Warren, May 15, 1776, *PJA* 4:186; JA to AA, May 17, 1776, *AFC* 1:410.

98. Stone to James Hollyday[?], May 20, 1776, *LDC* 4:47.

CHAPTER 11: "NOT CHOICE, BUT NECESSITY THAT CALLS FOR INDEPENDENCE": THE DILEMMA AND STRATEGY OF ROBERT LIVINGSTON

1. Lee to Carter, June 2, 1776, *LDC* 4:117; Carter Braxton to Carter, May 17, 1776, ibid., 4:20; JA to Lee, June 4, 1776, *PJA* 4:239.

2. JA to Lee, June 4, 1776, *PJA* 4:239; *Am Archives* 4th series, 5:1589; Francis L. Lee to Carter, May 21, 1776, *LDC* 4:57.

3. Morris to Deane, June 5, 1776, *LDC* 4:147; Gerry to Warren, June 6, 1776, ibid., 4:152–53; Richard Henry Lee to Thomas Ludwell Lee, May 28, 1776, ibid., 4:90; *Am Archives* 4th series, 6:323; ibid., 5:462–63.

4. *JCC* 4:40, 71, 186; Josiah Bartlett to New Hampshire Committee of Safety, January 20,

1776, *LDC* 3:117–18; Hancock to William Maxwell, January 25, 1776, ibid., 3:153; Hancock to Schuyler, January 24, February 6, 20, 1776, ibid., 3:146, 205, 288.

5. Allen Johnson et al., eds., *Dictionary of American Biography* (New York, 1929–37), 20:525.

6. JA to John Thomas, March 7, 1776, *PJA* 4:43.

7. Hancock to John Thomas, March 6, 1776, *LDC* 3:341.

8. Hancock to the Massachusetts Assembly, January 29, 1776, *LDC* 3:162–63; Caesar Rodney to Thomas Rodney, February 4, 1776, ibid., 3:195; Morris to Charles Lee, February 17, 1776, ibid., 3:268; Resolutions Concerning the Canadian Campaign, March 8, 1776, *PJA* 4:5–6.

9. Richard Smith, Diary, February 14, 1776, LDC 3:257; Instructions to the Commissioners to Canada, March 20, 1776, *PJA* 4:6–9.

10. BF to Josiah Quincy Jr., April 15, 1776, *PBF* 22:400.

11. Thomas to GW, April 7, 27, 1776, *PGWR* 4:49, 151–52; Thomas to Congress, April 8, 1776, *Am Archives* 4th series, 5:822; John Carroll to [?], May 1, 1776, ibid., 5:1167; Commissioners to Canada to Hancock, May 1, 1776, *LDC* 3:611–12.

12. Council of War, April 30, 1776, *Am Archives* 4th series, 5:1166–67; Commissioners to Canada to Hancock, May 8, 1776, *LDC* 3:639.

13. Journal of Thomas Ainslie, May 6, 1776, in Henry Steele Commager and Richard B. Morris, eds., *The Spirit of '76: The Story of the American Revolution as Told by Participants* (New York, 1958), 1:211; John Sullivan to Hancock, June 1, 1776, ibid., 1:212; Commissioners to Canada to Hancock, May 10, 17, 1776, *LDC* 3:645, 4:23; Francis L. Lee to Carter, May 21, 1776, ibid., 4:58; Commissioners to Canada to [William Heath], April 5, 1776, *PBF* 22:398; General Guy Carleton to Germain, *DAR* 12:137–38.

14. Commissioners to Canada to Hancock, May 10, 17, 1776, *LDC* 3:645–46; 4:22; Commissioners to Canada to Schuyler, May 10, 1776, ibid., 3:646–47; Commissioners to Canada to Thomas, May 15, 1776, ibid., 3:680; Chase to Schuyler, ibid., 3:647n.; Commissioners to Canada to BF, May 11, 1776, ibid., 3:649, 650n.

15. Commissioners to Canada to Hancock, May 10, 17, 27, 1776, *LDC* 3:646–47; 4:22–24, 80–82. The two missives were written by Chase and Charles Carroll, as Franklin and Father Carroll had departed.

16. Commissioners to Canada to Hancock, May 27, 1776, *LDC* 4:81.

17. Francis L. Lee to Carter, May 21, 1776, *LDC* 4:58.

18. Chase to Schuyler, May 31, 1776, *LDC* 4:105.

19. Charles P. Whittemore, *A General of the Revolution: John Sullivan of New Hampshire* (New York, 1961), 28; Sullivan to GW, June 7, 8, 1776, Otis G. Hammond, ed., *Letters and Papers of Major-General John Sullivan, Continental Army* (Concord, N.H., 1930–39), 1:226, 228; Paul H. Smith, "Sir Guy Carleton: Soldier-Statesman," in George A. Billias, ed., *George Washington's Opponents: British Generals and Admirals in the American Revolution* (New York, 1969), 120–23; Sullivan to Hancock, June 1, 1776, ibid., 1:212; Sullivan to Schuyler, June 19, 22, July 6, 1776, ibid., 1:250, 258, 280; [Lewis Beebe], "Journal of a Physician on the Expedition Against Canada, 1776," *Pennsylvania Magazine of History and Biography* 59 (1935): 336, 338.

20. Lee to Charles Lee, May 27, 1776, *LDC* 4:86; Lee to Thomas L. Lee, May 28, 1776, ibid., 4:90; Lee to Carter, June 2, 1776, ibid., 4:118.

21. Stone to James Hollyday, May 20, 1776, *LDC* 4:49; Whipple to Langdon, June 2, 1776, ibid., 4:120; Chase to Schuyler, May 31, 1776, ibid., 4:105–6; Hancock to Certain Colonies, June 4, 1776, ibid., 4:136.

22. Hewes to Johnston, June 4, 1776, *LDC* 4:139; Francis L. Lee to Carter, May 21, 1776, ibid., 4:57.

23. Gerry to Warren, May 20, 1776, *LDC* 4:43; Bartlett to Mary Bartlett, June 3, 1776, ibid., 4:124; Richard Henry Lee to Carter, June 2, 1776, ibid., 4:117; JA to Henry, June 3, 1776, *PJA* 4:235.

24. Cynthia A. Kierner, *Traders and Gentlefolk: The Livingstons of New York, 1675-1790* (Ithaca, N.Y., 1992); George Dangerfield, *Chancellor Robert R. Livingston, 1746-1813* (New York, 1960), 3-76. The quotations are from Dangerfield, pages 55 and 66, and New York Delegates to the New York Provincial Congress, July 6, 1775, *LDC* 1:596. On Clermont, Livingston's manor house, see Edward Countryman, *A People in Revolution: The American Revolution and Political Society in New York, 1760-1790* (New York, 1989), 27.

25. JA to AA, July 23, 1775, *AFC* 1:253. JA spoke of the "Timidity" of men of "overgrown Fortunes," a reference to Dickinson and Thomas Willing. See ibid., 253-54n.

26. Quoted in Dangerfield, *Chancellor Robert R. Livingston*, 87.

27. Robert R. Livingston to John Stevens, April 23, 1775, *LDC* 1:331; Robert R. Livingston's Notes for a Speech in Congress, [October 27, 1775], ibid., 2:263-71; Livingston to Thomas Lynch, [January ?, 1776], ibid., 3:179; JA, Notes of Debates, *DAJA* 2:186-87, 188-92, 219-20.

28. *JCC* 3:317, 339-41, 446-52; *LDC* 2:369n, 462n; Livingston to Jay, November 27, December 6, 1775, ibid., 2:397, 451; Committee to the Northward to Hancock, November 23, 1775, ibid., 2:377-79; Committee to the Northward Minutes of Proceedings, November 30, 1775, ibid., 2:411-12; Committee to the Northward to Montgomery, November 30, 1776, ibid., 2:412-13; Robert Treat Paine, Diary, November 8, December 8, 1775, ibid., 2:318, 461.

29. Dangerfield, *Chancellor Robert R. Livingston*, 60.

30. Livingston to Catherine Livingston, May 28, 1776, *LDC* 4:92; Livingston to Jay, May 17, 1776, ibid., 4:29; Livingston to Duane, February 16, 1776, ibid., 3:265. Livingston's "well-timed delays" comment can be found in Merrill Jensen, *The Founding of a Nation: A History of the American Revolution, 1763-1776* (New York, 1968), 697.

31. Jensen, *Founding of a Nation*, 696-97.

32. Quoted in Countryman, *A People in Revolution*, 165. I have drawn on Countryman's excellent analysis of New York politics in writing this section. See Countryman, pages 161-66.

33. Hancock to GW, May 16, 1776, *LDC* 4:8, 9n.

34. Robert R. Livingston to Jay, June 4, 1776, *LDC* 4:140.

35. GW to John A. Washington, July 22, 1776, *PGWR* 5:428-29; GW to Hancock, June 17, July 17, 1776, ibid., 5:21, 356; GW to John Trumbull, June 10, 1776, ibid., 4:496. Lee to Thomas L. Lee, May 28, 1776, *LDC* 4:90-91. See also John Ferling, *Almost a Miracle: The American Victory in the War of Independence* (New York, 2007), 120-24; John Ferling, *The Ascent of George Washington: The Hidden Political Genius of an American Icon* (New York, 2009), 104-9.

36. Hancock to GW, June 7, 1776, *LDC* 4:156. See also Commissioners to Canada to Hancock, May 27, 28, 1776, ibid., 4:84-85, 87-88.

37. *EHD* 9:867-68.

38. *JCC* 5:424-27; TJ, "Notes of Proceedings," [June 7-28, 1776], *PTJ* 1:309; Rhode Island Delegates to Nicholas Cooke, June 21, 1776, *LDC* 4:286; Edward Rutledge to Jay, [June 8, 1776], ibid., 4:174.

39. Rutledge to Jay, [June 8, 1776], *LDC* 4:175; JD to Willing, [June 8?, 1776], ibid., 4:169.

40. JD, Notes for a Speech in Congress, [June 8-10?, 1776], *LDC* 4:165-69.

41. TJ, "Notes of Proceedings," [June 7–28, 1776], *PTJ* 1:309–11; Rutledge to Jay, [June 8, 1776], *LDC* 4:175.

42. Rutledge to Jay, [June 8, 1776], *LDC* 4:174; Gerry to Warren, June 11, 1776, ibid., 4:187.

43. TJ, "Notes of Proceedings," [June 7–28, 1776], *PTJ* 1:311–13.

44. TJ, "Notes of Proceedings," [June 7–28, 1776], *PTJ* 1:313.

45. TJ, "Notes of Proceedings," [June 7–28, 1776], *PTJ* 1:313; *JCC* 5:428–29, 431, 433; *PJA* 342n.

46. Rhode Island Delegates to Nicholas Cooke, June 21, 1776, *LDC* 4:286; Wolcott to Laura Wolcott, June 15, 1776, ibid., 4:226; JA to William Cushing, June 9, 1776, *PJA* 4:245.

CHAPTER 12: "THE CHARACTER OF A FINE WRITER": THOMAS JEFFERSON AND THE DRAFTING OF THE DECLARATION OF INDEPENDENCE

1. Ward to Henry Ward, June 22, 1775, *LDC* 1:535; "Historical and Bibliographical Notes on 'A Summary View of the Rights of British America,'" *PTJ* 1:676.

2. TJ to Thomas Nelson, May 16, 1776, *PTJ* 1:292.

3. J. Kent McGaughy, *Richard Henry Lee of Virginia: A Portrait of an American Revolutionary* (Lanham, Md., 2004), 121–24; Lee to GW, June 13, 1776, *PGWR* 4:514.

4. David Freeman Hawke, *Honorable Treason: The Declaration of Independence and the Men Who Signed It* (New York, 1976), 46–48, 54–57.

5. Christopher Collier, *Roger Sherman's Connecticut: Yankee Politicians and the American Revolution* (Middletown, Conn., 1971), 74, 97, 119–20; JA, Diary, August 17, 1774, *DAJA* 2:100; Roger Sherman to Joseph Trumbull, July 6, 1775, *LDC* 1:600. The sketch of Roger Sherman's activities prior to his service in the Continental Congress draws on Collier's work, pages 3–84. The quotation on his "slender" education is from Collier, page 11.

6. Collier, *Roger Sherman's Connecticut*, 10.

7. JA, Diary, October 10, 1774, September 15, 1775, *DAJA* 2:150, 173; Collier, *Roger Sherman's Connecticut*, 94, 235; Hawke, *Honorable Treason*, 57–58.

8. JA, Diary, September 15, 1775, *DAJA* 2:173; Collier, *Roger Sherman's Connecticut*, 235–36; Hawke, *Honorable Treason*, 59.

9. Roger Sherman to Jonathan Trumbull Sr., June 28, 1775, *LDC* 1:556; ibid., 2:292n; 3:413n.

10. JA, Autobiography, *DAJA* 3:336.

11. JA, Autobiography, *DAJA* 3:336–37; JA to Timothy Pickering, August 6, 1822, *WJA* 2:512–14n; TJ to James Madison, August 30, 1823, in Paul Leicester Ford, ed., *The Writings of Thomas Jefferson* (New York, 1892–99), 10:267–69.

12. JA, Diary, June 23, 1779, *DAJA* 2:391–92.

13. *PBF* 22:442n; BF to GW, June 21, 1776, ibid., 22:484–85; BF to Benjamin Rush, June 26, 1776, ibid., 22:491.

14. Besides, as John Adams remarked, Jefferson had been a congressman for a year, during which time he had spent "a very small part of the time" in Philadelphia. See JA, Autobiography, *DAJA* 3:335.

15. The preceding draws on TJ, Autobiography, in Saul K. Padover, ed., *The Complete Jefferson* (New York, 1943), 1119–20; Sarah N. Randolph, *The Domestic Life of Thomas Jefferson* (New York, 1871), 23; Fawn Brodie, *Thomas Jefferson: An Intimate History* (New York, 1974), 23, 51; Noble E. Cunningham Jr., *In Pursuit of Reason: The Life of Thomas Jefferson* (New York,

1997), 1–4; Dumas Malone, *Jefferson and His Times* (Boston, 1948–81), 1:21–48; R. B. Bernstein, *Thomas Jefferson* (New York, 2003), 1–3.

16. Merrill D. Peterson, *Thomas Jefferson and the New Nation: A Biography* (New York, 1970), 7–8; Willard Sterne Randall, *Thomas Jefferson: A Life* (New York, 1992), 22–24, 37, 41–42; Malone, *Thomas Jefferson*, 1:53–57; Bernstein, *Thomas Jefferson*, 4–5; TJ to Vine Utley, March 21, 1819, in Paul Leicester Ford, ed., *The Writings of Thomas Jefferson* (New York, 1892–99), 9:126; TJ to William Duane, October 1, 1812, in A. A. Lipscomb and A. E. Bergh, eds., *The Writings of Thomas Jefferson* (Washington, D.C., 1900–1904), 2:420–31; TJ to John Page, October 7, 1763, *PTJ* 1:11; Jefferson, Autobiography, in Padover, *Complete Thomas Jefferson*, 1120.

17. Randall, *Thomas Jefferson*, 47, 51, 55–58, 66–68, 98, 109; Malone, *Thomas Jefferson*, 1:122–23; TJ to Ralph Izard, July 17, 1788, *PTJ* 13:372; TJ to Page, December 25, 1762, ibid., 1:5; TJ to William Fleming, [October 1763], ibid., 1:15; TJ to Thomas Jefferson Randolph, June 14, 1806, in Lipscomb and Bergh, *Writings of Thomas Jefferson*, 12:97–98; TJ, Autobiography, in Padover, *Complete Thomas Jefferson*, 1120; Brodie, *Thomas Jefferson*, 61; Frank J. Dewey, *Thomas Jefferson, Lawyer* (Charlottesville, Va., 1986), 83–93.

18. TJ to Page, October 7, 1763, January 19, 1764, *PTJ* 1:11, 13–14; TJ to Fleming, March 20, October [?], 1763, ibid., 1:13, 16. For the best treatment of TJ's tortured relationship with Rebecca Burwell, see Jon Kukla, *Mr. Jefferson's Women* (New York, 2007), 16–40. See also Brodie, *Thomas Jefferson*, 64–67.

19. TJ to Fleming, *PTJ* 1:13; Kukla, *Mr. Jefferson's Women*, 35–37. The most complete elaboration on TJ's possible misogyny can be found in Kenneth A. Lockridge, *On the Sources of Patriarchal Rage: The Commonplace Books of William Byrd and Thomas Jefferson and the Gendering of Power in the Eighteenth Century* (New York, 1992).

20. TJ to Page, February 21, 1770, *PTJ* 1:36.

21. Kukla, *Mr. Jefferson's Women*, 67–70. As for the appeal of Martha's wealth, historian Annette Gordon-Read observed in *The Hemingses of Monticello* (New York, 2008), 98–99, that despite all of her other admirable qualities, it was not likely that TJ would have married her had she been the daughter of a blacksmith.

22. Henry S. Randall, *The Life of Thomas Jefferson* (New York, 1858), 1:34–35, 3:364; Joseph J. Ellis, *American Sphinx: The Character of Thomas Jefferson* (New York, 1997), 120; Peterson, *Thomas Jefferson and the New Nation*, 10; Malone, *Thomas Jefferson*, 1:48; Cunningham, *In Pursuit of Reason*, 22; Randall, *Thomas Jefferson*, 100; Jack McLoughlin, *Jefferson and Monticello* (New York, 1988), 438–39; Edmund Randolph, "Essay on the History of Virginia," *Virginia Magazine of History and Biography* 43 (1953): 115; Noble Cunningham, ed., "The Diary of Frances Few, 1808–1809," *Journal of Southern History* 29 (1963): 350–51; *DAJA* 3:335–36; Gaillard Hunt, ed., *The First Forty Years of Washington Society Portrayed by the Family Letters of Mrs. Samuel Harrison Smith* (New York, 1906), 26; Charles Francis Adams, ed., *Memoirs of John Quincy Adams* (Philadelphia, 1874–77), 1:373; Arthur H. Shaffer, ed., Edmund Randolph, *History of Virginia* (Charlottesville, Va., 1979), 182–83, 213. The quote about TJ's "femininely soft" voice is in David Hawke, *A Transaction of Free Men: The Birth and Course of the Declaration of Independence* (New York, 1964), 21.

23. Charles S. Sydnor, *Gentlemen Freeholders: Political Practices in Washington's Virginia* (Chapel Hill, N.C., 1952), 98–101.

24. TJ, Autobiography, Padover, *Complete Thomas Jefferson*, 1121.

25. TJ to Thomas Adams, February 20, 1771, *PTJ* 1:61; [Thomas Jefferson], *A Summary View of the Rights of British America* (Williamsburg, Va., 1774), ibid., 1:123–24, 133, 135.

26. Woody Holton, *Forced Founders: Indians, Debtors, Slaves, and the Making of the*

American Revolution in Virginia (Chapel Hill, N.C., 1999), 3–73. The Lee and TJ quotations are from this source, page 72.

27. Ellis, *American Sphinx*, 32–34; Peterson, *Thomas Jefferson and the New Nation*, 45–65; Malone, *Thomas Jefferson*, 1:173–79; H. Trevor Colbourn, *The Lamp of Experience: Whig History and the Intellectual Origins of the American Revolution* (Chapel Hill, N.C., 1965), 3–56, 158–60; Bernard Bailyn, *The Ideological Origins of the American Revolution* (Cambridge, Mass., 1967), 55–143; Gordon S. Wood, *The Creation of the American Republic, 1776–1787* (Chapel Hill, N. C., 1969), 10–45; Gordon S. Wood, "Conspiracy and the Paranoid Style: Causality and Deceit in the Eighteenth Century, *William and Mary Quarterly* 39 (1982): 401–2. The quotation is from the Virginia non-importation agreement of 1769, written in part by GW and signed by TJ. See *PGWC* 8:187–89n.

28. TJ, Autobiography, in Padover, *Complete Thomas Jefferson*, 1122; Jefferson, *A Summary View, PTJ* 1:135.

29. Kukla, *Mr. Jefferson's Women*, 35, 39–40. For bibliography on TJ's malady, see the detailed endnotes in Kukla, pages 226–28.

30. JA, Autobiography, *DAJA* 3:335–36. *A Summary View* can be found in *PTJ* 1:121–35. See also the editorial note in ibid., 1:669–76.

31. Malone, *Thomas Jefferson*, 1:202.

32. JA, Autobiography, *DAJA* 3:335; JA to Pickering, August 6, 1822, *WJA* 2:514n.

33. Gordon-Reed, *The Hemingses of Monticello*, 125.

34. Malone, *Thomas Jefferson*, 1:203–17.

35. TJ to Nelson, May 16, 1776, *PTJ* 1:292, 293n; Nathan Schachner, *Thomas Jefferson: A Biography* (New York, 1951), 118.

36. David McCullough, *John Adams* (New York, 2001), 120.

37. JA, Autobiography, *DAJA* 3:336.

38. JA, Autobiography, *DAJA* 3:336; TJ to BF, [June 21, 1776], *PTJ* 1:404. See also *PBF* 22:485. JA said that TJ asked for his suggestions before he showed the draft to Livingston and Sherman.

39. JA to Pickering, August 6, 1822, *WJA* 2:514n; John Ferling, *John Adams: A Life* (reprint, New York, 2010), 148; TJ to Henry Lee, May 8, 1825, in Lipscomb and Bergh, *Writings of Thomas Jefferson*, 7:407.

40. JA to Henry, June 3, 1776, *PJA* 4:235.

41. Committee of Secret Correspondence to Deane, July 8, 1776, *LDC* 4:405; Pauline Maier, *American Scripture: Making the Declaration of Independence* (New York, 1997), 130.

42. Carl Becker, *The Declaration of Independence: A Study in the History of Political Ideas* (reprint, New York, 1960), 151–52; TJ to Madison, August 30, 1823, in Ford, *Writings of Thomas Jefferson*, 10:267–69; "Jefferson's 'original Rough draught' of the Declaration of Independence," *PTJ* 1:423–28, and the editorial note on the evolution of the text, ibid., 1:413–17; "John Adams' Copy of the Declaration of Independence, [ante June 28, 1776], *PJA* 4:341–51; Julian Boyd, *The Declaration of Independence: The Evolution of the Text as Shown in Facsimiles of Various Drafts by Its Author* (Washington, D.C., 1943).

43. Becker, *Declaration of Independence*, 105–14. Becker also thought that TJ's inclusion of "the pursuit of happiness" as a natural right had been derived from a essay published by James Wilson, though subsequent scholarship has shown that was not the case.

44. Maier, *American Scripture*, 124–28; *Am Archives* 4th series, 6:1537. Ironically, the Virginia Convention finally adopted the Declaration of Rights in a slightly modified form on June 12, the very day that the committee's draft—which TJ utilized—appeared in the

Philadelphia newspaper. See John E. Selby, *The Revolution in Virginia, 1775–1783* (Williamsburg, Va., 1988), 100–110.

45. Jay Fliegelman, *Prodigals and Pilgrims: The American Revolution Against Patriarchal Authority* (New York, 1982), 4; Eric Slauter, "The Declaration of Independence and the New Nation," in Frank Shuffelton, ed., *The Cambridge Companion to Thomas Jefferson* (Cambridge, 2009), 18; Peter S. Onuf, "A Declaration of Independence for Diplomatic Historians," in Peter S. Onuf, ed., *The Mind of Thomas Jefferson* (Charlottesville, Va., 2007), 66.

46. Maier, *American Scripture*, 134.

47. See also Herbert Lawrence Ganter, "Jefferson's 'Pursuit of Happiness' and Some Forgotten Men," *William and Mary Quarterly*, 2d series, 16 (1936): 422–34.

48. George Anastaplo, "The Declaration of Independence," *Saint Louis University Law Journal* 9 (1964–65): 401.

49. The term "war criminal" is appropriated from Garry Wills, *Inventing America: Jefferson's Declaration of Independence* (Garden City, N.Y., 1978), 310. Wills wrote that TJ accused the king of "a war crime for his complicity in enslaving Africans."

50. On British attempts to restrict emigration, see Bernard Bailyn, *Voyagers to the West: A Passage in the Peopling of America on the Eve of the Revolution* (New York, 1986), 29–66.

51. For TJ's draft, see "Jefferson's 'original Rough draught' of the Declaration of Independence," *PTJ* 1:423–28.

52. TJ, Notes of Proceedings in the Continental Congress, June 7–August 1, 1776, *PTJ* 1:313–14.

53. Joseph Hawley to Gerry, June 13, 1776, *Am Archives* 4th series, 6:845; Warren to Gerry, June 12, 1776, ibid., 6:829. Warren thought "ninety-nine in a hundred would engage, with their lives and fortunes, to support Congress" should it declare independence. Pauline Maier, *American Scripture*, should be consulted on the foot dragging in Massachusetts, where the upper chamber of the assembly sought to delay or inhibit the break with Great Britain and the lower house did not finally vote for independence until July 3. However, as Maier points out, since January 1776 the Massachusetts congressional delegation had as much authority to concur with the other delegations on a decision for independence as the North Carolina and Delaware congressmen received many months later. See her section on Massachusetts on pages 59–61.

54. *Am Archives* 4th series, 6:867–68, 1029–30, 1628–29, 1491; Maier, *American Scripture*, 59–68; Jonathan Dickinson Sergeant to JA, June 15, 1776, *PJA* 4:316. The "all independent souls" quotation can be found in Larry R. Gerlach, *Prologue to Independence: New Jersey in the Coming of the American Revolution* (New Brunswick, N.J., 1976), 337.

55. Merrill Jensen, *The Founding of a Nation: A History of the American Revolution, 1763–1776* (New York, 1968), 685–87; Maier, *American Scripture*, 65–66; William Hogeland, *Declaration: The Nine Tumultuous Weeks When America Became Independent, May 1–July 4, 1776* (New York, 2010), 143–62; Richard Alan Ryerson, *The Revolution Is Now Begun: The Radical Committees of Philadelphia, 1765–1776* (Philadelphia, 1978), 208–37; *Am Archives* 4th series, 6:755, 962–63; Joseph E. Illick, *Colonial Pennsylvania: A History* (New York, 1976), 301; JA to Warren, May 20, 1776, *PJA* 4:195.

56. Richard Lightfoot Lee to Richard H. Lee, June 30, 1776, *LDC* 4:342–43; Bruce Bliven, *Under the Guns: New York, 1775–1776* (New York, 1972), 318; Barnet Schecter, *The Battle for New York: The City at the Heart of the American Revolution* (New York, 2002), 100; John J. Gallagher, *The Battle of Brooklyn, 1776* (Edison, N.J., 2002), 67.

57. JA to John Sullivan, June 23, 1776, *PJA* 4:330; JA to Nathanael Greene, June 22, 1776, ibid., 4:324.

58. JA to John Winthrop, June 23, 1776, *PJA* 4:331-32; Hewes to James Iredell, June 28, 1776, *LDC* 4:332; Rutledge to Jay, June 29, 1776, ibid., 4:337.

CHAPTER 13: "MAY HEAVEN PROSPER THE NEW BORN REPUBLIC": SETTING AMERICA FREE

1. JA to Archibald Bulloch, July 1, 1776, *PJA* 4:352.

2. JA to AA, April 15, 23, 28, 1776, *AFC* 1:383, 391-92, 401.

3. JA to AA, April 28, May 17, 1776, *AFC* 1:401, 410.

4. TJ to William Fleming, July 1, 1776, *PTJ* 1:411-13.

5. David Hawke, *A Transaction of Free Men: The Birth and Course of the Declaration of Free Men* (New York, 1964), 177.

6. Josiah Bartlett to Nathaniel Folsom, July 1, 1776, *LDC* 4:348; John Penn to Samuel Johnson, June 28, 1776, ibid., 4:333; Penn to [?], June 28, 1776, ibid., 4:334.

7. *DAJA* 2:115n; John Ferling, *Setting the World Ablaze: Washington, Jefferson, Adams, and the American Revolution* (New York, 2000), xviii-xix.

8. *JCC* 5:503; *Am Archives* 4th series, 6:1726-27; GW to Hancock, June 29, 1776, *PGWR* 5:147-49.

9. *JCC* 5:503; Garry Wills, *Inventing America: Jefferson's Declaration of Independence* (Garden City, N.Y., 1978), 4.

10. Milton E. Flower, *John Dickinson: Conservative Revolutionary* (Charlottesville, Va., 1983), 153-57.

11. JA to Zabdiel Adams, June 21, 1776, *AFC* 2:20; JA to Chase, July 1, 1776, *PJA* 4:353; Gerry to Warren, July 2, 1776, *LDC* 4:370.

12. For Dickinson's speech, see John Dickinson's Notes for a Speech in Congress, [July 1, 1776], *LDC* 4:351-56, 356n.

13. JA, Autobiography, *DAJA* 3:395-97; TJ to Samuel Wells, May 12, 1819, Paul Leicester Ford, ed., *The Writings of Thomas Jefferson* (New York, 1892-99), 10:131; Thomas Jefferson, To the Editor of the *Journal de Paris*, August 29, 1787, *PTJ* 12:63.

14. JA to Chase, July 1, 1776, *PJA* 4:354.

15. The quotations can be found in John Hazleton, *The Declaration of Independence: Its History* (New York, 1906), 161-62; John Ferling, *John Adams: A Life* (reprint, New York, 2010), 169.

16. Jefferson, To the Editor of the *Journal de Paris*, August 29, 1787, *PTJ* 12:63.

17. David Freeman Hawke, *Honorable Treason: The Declaration of Independence and the Men Who Signed It* (New York, 1976), 163.

18. JA, Autobiography, *DAJA* 3:379.

19. Jefferson, Notes of Proceedings in the Continental Congress, [June 7-August 1, 1776], *PTJ* 1:314.

20. JA to Chase, July 1, 1776, *PJA* 4:353.

21. *JCC* 5:506-7; *Am Archives* 4th series, 6:1727-28.

22. Peter Stone and Sherman Edwards, *1776: A Musical Play* (New York, 1964), 47.

23. JA, Diary, September 3, 1774, *DAJA* 2:121; Caesar Rodney to John Haslet[?], May 17, 1776, in George Herbert Ryden, ed., *Letters to and from Caesar Rodney*, (reprint, New York,

1970), 80; Rodney to Thomas Rodney, May 8, 1776, ibid., 75; Rodney to Rodney, July 10, 1776, *LDC* 4:433; Hawke, *Honorable Treason*, 155–57. See also William Baskerville Hamilton, *Anglo-American Law on the Frontier: Thomas Rodney and His Territorial Cases* (Durham, N.C., 1953), which discusses the several accounts of Rodney's activities on pages 21–22.

24. John Munroe, *Colonial Delaware* (Millwood, N.Y., 1978), 249–50.

25. Rodney to Rodney, July 4, 1776, *LDC* 4:388; Thomas McKean to Caesar A. Rodney, September 22, 1813, ibid., 4:388n.

26. Hawke, *Honorable Treason*, 106.

27. Merrill Jensen, *The Founding of a Nation: A History of the American Revolution, 1763–1776* (New York, 1968), 383–84, 655–56.

28. JA, Autobiography, *DAJA* 3:360.

29. Jefferson, Notes of Proceedings in the Continental Congress, [June 7–August 1, 1776], *PTJ* 1:314.

30. Quoted in Hawke, *Transaction of Free Men*, 137.

31. Flower, *John Dickinson*, 166.

32. Morris to Joseph Reed, July 21, 1776, *LDC* 4:510–11.

33. Charles Page Smith, *James Wilson: Founding Father, 1742–1798* (Chapel Hill, N.C., 1956), 78–84; *LDC* 4:273–74n.

34. Delegates' Certification of James Wilson's Conduct in Congress, June 20, 1776, *LDC* 4:271–73.

35. JA, Autobiography, *DAJA* 3:350.

36. JA, Diary, September 15, 1775, *DAJA* 2:172; Braxton to Carter, April 14, 1776, *LDC* 3:522–23. Unless otherwise noted, all the profiles of the members of Congress are drawn from Hawke, *Honorable Treason*.

37. Clark to Elias Dayton, July 4, 1776, *LDC* 4:379.

CHAPTER 14: "THIS WILL CEMENT THE UNION": AMERICA IS SET FREE

1. JA wrote two letters to his wife on this day. See JA to AA, July 3, 1776, *AFC* 2:27–28, 30.

2. *JCC* 5:510.

3. *Am Archives* 4th series, 6:1728, 1731–32.

4. GW to Hancock, July 3, 1776, *PGWR* 5:191, 193.

5. Pauline Maier, *American Scripture: Making the Declaration of Independence* (New York, 1997), 144.

6. Maier, *American Scripture*, 145–46.

7. TJ, Notes of Proceedings in the Continental Congress, [June 7–August 1, 1776], *PTJ* 1:314–15. TJ did not specify the Rhode Islanders as among those who wished to strike the section on African slavery, though he wrote in his notes that "our Northern brethren also . . . felt a little tender . . . for tho' their people have very few slaves themselves yet they had been pretty considerable carriers of them to others."

8. This section on Congress's editing of the draft declaration draws on Maier, *American Scripture*, 143–48, which in magnificent detail chronicles each and every alteration made by Congress.

9. The best accounts concerning how Congress edited the draft document are Julian Boyd, *The Declaration of Independence: The Evolution of the Text as Shown in Facsimiles of Various Drafts by Its Author* (Washington, D.C., 1943); Carl Becker, *The Declaration of Inde-*

pendence: A Study in the History of Political Ideas (reprint, New York, 1960), 160–71; and Maier, *American Scripture*, 235–41.

10. See Paul Leicester Ford, ed., *The Writings of Thomas Jefferson* (New York, 1892–99), 10:120n. BF made clear in his prefatory remarks that his parable was also intended to persuade TJ that any work of a "draughtsman . . . to be reviewed by a public body" would inevitably face rough sledding.

11. TJ to Lee, July 8, 1776, *PTJ* 1:456; Lee to TJ, July 21, 1776, ibid., 1:471.

12. JA to Pickering, August 6, 1822, in *WJA* 2:514n.

13. TJ, Notes of Proceedings in the Continental Congress, [June 7–August 1, 1776], *PTJ* 1:315; *LDC* 4:381–82n.

14. Rodney to Thomas Rodney, July 4, 1776, *LDC* 4:388; ibid., 4:390n.

15. Paine, Diary, July 4, 1776, *LDC* 4:386; Paine to Joseph Palmer, July 6, 1776, ibid., 4:399; Ellery to Benjamin Ellery, July 10, 1776, ibid., 4:430; Gerry to Warren, July 5, 1776, ibid., 4:392; SA to Hawley, July 9, 1776, ibid., 4:416; JA to Mary Palmer, July 5, 1776, *AFC* 2:34; JA to AA, July 3, 1776, ibid., 2:30.

EPILOGUE

1. Pauline Maier, *American Scripture: Making the Declaration of Independence* (New York, 1997), 153; David Hawke, *A Transaction of Free Men: The Birth and Course of the Declaration of Independence* (New York, 1964), 186.

2. Hawke, *Transaction of Free Men*, 207–8; John Hazleton, *The Declaration of Independence: Its History* (New York, 1906), 242, 156–57; Gerry to Joseph Trumbull, July 8, 1776, *LDC* 4:406; JA to Chase, July 9, 1776, *PJA* 4:372.

3. Silas Deane to C. W. F. Dumas, August 18, 1776, *Am Archives* 5th series, 1:1021; Claude Crespigny to Ralph Izard, August 25, 1776, ibid., 1:1148; Hazleton, *Declaration of Independence*, 258–81.

4. GW, General Orders, July 9, 1776, *PGWR* 5:246; ibid., 5:247n; GW to Hancock, July 10, 1776, ibid., 5:258; Lt. Col. Thomas Seymour to Gov. Jonathan Trumbull, July 11, 1776, *Am Archives* 5th series, 1:205; Col. Thomas Hartley to Gen. Gates, ibid., 1:630.

5. AA to JA, July 21, 1776, *AFC* 2:56.

6. Jay Fliegelman, *Declaring Independence: Jefferson, Natural Language, and the Culture of Performance* (Stanford, Calif., 1993), 4–28. The quotation can be found on page 10.

7. Andrew Burstein and Nancy Isenberg, *Madison and Jefferson* (New York, 2010), 36–39.

8. Maier, *American Scripture*, 157–59; *Am Archives* 5th series, 1:847.

9. Hazleton, *Declaration of Independence*, 266–71, 561; Maier, *American Scripture*, 157; Stanley Weintraub, *Iron Tears: America's Battle for Freedom, Britain's Quagmire, 1775–1783* (New York, 2005), 70–71.

10. Joseph Barton to Henry Wisner, July 9, 1776, *Am Archives* 5th series, 1:139; Meshech Weare to President of Congress, July 16, 1776, ibid., 1:381; Col. Ogden to Aaron Burr, July 26, 1776, ibid., 1:603; GW, General Orders, July 9, 1776, *PGWR* 5:246; AA to JA, July 21, 1776, *AFC* 2:56.

11. Action of the New York Provincial Convention, July 9, 1776, in Alexander C. Flick, ed., *The American Revolution in New York* (reprint, Port Washington, N.Y., 1967), 325; N.Y. Convention to Congress, July 11, 1776, *Am Archives* 5th series, 1:205; Bartlett to Langdon, July 15, 1776, *LDC* 4:459.

12. *JCC* 5:590–91.

13. Rush to JA, July 20, 1811, in John A. Schutz and Douglass Adair, eds., *The Spur of Fame: Dialogues of John Adams and Benjamin Rush, 1805-1813* (San Marino, Calif., 1966), 183.

14. JA to AA, July 15, 1776, *AFC* 2:49; Gerry to Samuel and John Adams, July 21, 1776, *PJA* 4:402.

15. Hazleton, *Declaration of Independence*, 193-219.

16. *LDC* 3:xvi-xxii, 4:xv-xxi, 5:xvi-xxiii.

17. The Howes' appraisal is quoted in Weintraub, *Iron Tears*, 69.

18. Lord Howe to GW, July 13, 1776, *PGWR* 5:296, 296-97n; Gen. Howe to GW, July 16, 1776, ibid., 341-42, 342n; Memorandum of an Interview with Lieutenant Colonel James Paterson, July 20, 1776, ibid., 5:398-401, 401-3n.

19. Lord Howe to BF, June 20[-July 12], 1776, *PBF*, 22:483-84; BF to Lord Howe, July 20, 1776, 22:519-21. Through BF and other sources, Congress had known for nearly three months that the Howe brothers had been named peace commissioners and were en route to America. See Hartley to BF, March 31, 1776, ibid., 22:396-97.

20. Ira D. Gruber, *The Howe Brothers and the American Revolution* (New York, 1972), 117.

21. JA to Warren, September 4, 1776, *PJA* 5:12; JA to SA, September 14, 1776, *LDC* 5:161; Gruber, *Howe Brothers and the American Revolution*, 117.

22. JA to AA, September 6, 1776, *AFC* 2:120-21.

23. JA, Autobiography, *DAJA* 3:419-20.

24. Henry Strachey's Notes on Lord Howe's Meeting with a Committee of Congress, September 11, 1776, *LDC* 5:137-42; JA to SA, September 14, 1776, ibid., 5:159-62.

25. See John Ferling, *Almost a Miracle: The American Victory in the War of Independence* (New York, 2007), 468-545.

26. Alan Valentine, *Lord North* (Norman, Okla., 1967), 1:509; *PH* 19:762-67; Weldon A. Brown, *Empire or Independence: A Study in the Failure of Reconciliation, 1774-1783* (Baton Rouge, La., 1941), 225-26; Peter D. G. Thomas, *Lord North* (London, 1976), 116; Charles Ritcheson, *British Politics and the American Revolution* (Norman, Okla., 1954), 268-69.

27. Valentine, *Lord North*, 2:274.

28. George Athan Billias, *Elbridge Gerry: Founding Father and Republican Statesman* (New York, 1976), 70.

29. See John Ferling, *A Leap in the Dark: The Struggle to Create the American Republic* (New York, 2003), 222, 238-41.

30. Clinton Rossiter, *1787: The Grand Convention* (New York, 1966), 247.

31. JA to Hezekiah Niles, January 14, February 13, 1818, *WJA* 10:276, 282; JA to TJ, August 14, 1815, in Lestor J. Cappon, ed., *The Adams-Jefferson Letters: The Complete Correspondence Between Thomas Jefferson and Abigail and John Adams* (Chapel Hill, N.C., 1959), 2:455.

32. JA to Mercy Otis Warren, July 20, 27, 1808, in *Warren-Adams Letters: Being Chiefly a Correspondence Among John Adams, Samuel Adams, and James Warren*, Massachussetts Historical Society, *Collections* (Boston, 1917), 4:339-40, 355; JA to Skelton Jones, March 11, 1809, *WJA* 9:611; JA to Tudor, September 18, 1818, ibid., 10:359; JA to TJ, August 24, 1815, in Cappon, *Adams-Jefferson Letters*, 2:455; JA to Benjamin Rush, August 23, 1805, May 21, 1807, in Schutz and Adair, *Spur of Fame*, 34-35, 88.

33. JA to Rush, June 12, 1812, in Schutz and Adair, *Spur of Fame*, 225.

34. JA to Benjamin Kent, June 22, 1776, *PJA* 4:326. In 1818 JA told a publisher that the "accomplishment of it [a Declaration of Independence], in so short a time and by such simple means, was perhaps a singular example in the history of mankind. Thirteen clocks were made to strike together." See JA to Niles, February 13, 1818, *WJA* 10:283.

35. *PH* 18:1442.

36. The King's Speech at the Close of the Session, May 23, 1776, *PH* 18:1365.

37. Maier, *American Scripture*, 160–62.

38. For TJ's intent when drafting the Declaration of Independence, see Chapter 12.

39. The "holy writ" and "sacred text" quotations can be found in Maier, *American Scripture*, 154, 175. This passage on the history of the Declaration of Independence draws on Maier, pages 154–208.

40. L. H. Butterfield, "The Jubilee of Independence, July 4, 1826," *Virginia Magazine of History and Biography* 61 (1953): 135–38; Merrill D. Peterson, *Adams and Jefferson: A Revolutionary Dialogue* (New York, 1976), 3; Andrew Burstein, *American Jubilee* (New York, 2001), 255–86; Daniel Webster, "Adams and Jefferson, August 2, 1826, in *The Writings and Speeches of Daniel Webster* (Boston, 1903), 1:324.

APPENDIX: THE DECLARATION OF INDEPENDENCE

1. The Declaration of Independence bearing the name of John Hancock, and the attestation of Charles Thomson, as it appeared in the broadside ordered by Congress and published on July 5, 1776. See page 342 in the text for mention of the broadside.

INDEX

Note: page numbers in italics refer to figures; those followed by n refer to notes, with note number.

Adams, Abigail Smith, 57, 151, 157, 270–275, 272, 344, 345
Adams, Elihu, 156
Adams, Elizabeth, 184
Adams, John, 299
  and Adams (Samuel), 55, 56, 152, 154–155, 182
  on American Prohibitory Act, 248–249
  appearance of, 155
  on Bartlett, Josiah, 329
  and Boston Massacre, 152–153
  on Boston Tea Party, 41, 154
  on British decadence, 167–168
  on British response to Continental Congress, 89
  on Canadian invasion, 279
  character and deportment, 150–151, 155, 157–158
  on Chase (Samuel), 191
  and Continental Associations, 106
  at Continental Congress, First, 68–72, 74, 77, 79, 80, 83–85, 87, 154–155
  at Continental Congress, Second
    arrival, 122–123
    concerns weighing upon, 156
    and confederation, plan for, 293
    and Continental Army, 146, 148, 150, 158, 187, 190
    correspondence with Abigail, 270–275, 336
    and Declaration of Independence, 246, 293, 294, 298–300, 309–311, 318, 340–342
    and French treaty, drafting of, 293
    inter-session activities, 181
    leadership role, 146, 150, 156–157, 166–167, 269–270
    on mood of Congress, 186
    and Olive Branch Petition, 141, 165–167
    and overtures to France, 210
    on Parliamentary authority, 137
    personal sacrifices, 270, 273–274
    and privateering, 249
    relations with other delegates, 165–166, 182–183, 269–270, 299–300

    on replacement of colonial governments, 194–195
    visits home, 229, 268, 274
  daughter's death, 153
  death of, 357
  Dickinson and, 165–166, 182–183, 230–231, 322
  family life of, 184
  on foreign assistance, need for, 285
  on Franklin, 144, 145
  on Galloway, 62
  health of, 137, 153, 154, 155–156
  on Heyward (Thomas), 325
  on Hopkins (Stephen), 332–333
  on Hutchinson (Thomas), 16
  and independence, drive toward, 276–277, 278, 292
  and independence, vote on, 320, 323–324, 326, 329, 332
  on independence
    difficulty of winning, xi
    early reluctance about, 152
    inevitability of, 167–168, 285
    movement toward, 193–194, 248–249, 259, 318–319, 353–354
    necessity of, 246, 317
  on Jefferson, 307, 309
  on Lee (Richard Henry), 6
  Lexington and Concord battlefields, tour of, 118–119
  life of, 150–151, 350, 351
  on Massachusetts legislature, 68–69
  on Middleton (Arthur), 333
  movement toward radicalism, 153–154
  on Nelson (Thomas), 334
  on Olive Branch Petition, 165–166, 167, 208
  on Paine (Thomas), 264
  as pamphleteer, 108–109
  on Parliament's right to rule colonies, 137, 140
  and peace commission, 245, 347–348
  political career, beginnings of, 152–155
  on public service, 274
  on reconciliationists, 286

Adams, John (*continued*)
　on Revolutionary War, 118–119, 156, 158–159,
　　　293, 317
　on Rodney (Caesar), 327
　on Sherman (Roger), 297
　on Southern delegates, anxiety of, 233
　on Stamp Act, 18–19, 26
　Thoughts on Government, 265–266
　on war fever, after Lexington and Concord
　　　battles, 123
　on Whipple (William), 329
　on Wilson (James), 226
Adams, Samuel, *56*
　Adams (John) and, 55, 56, 152, 154–155, 182
　age of, at time of Revolution, 54
　appearance and demeanor, 57
　and Boston Harbor, closure of, 54
　and Boston Massacre, 152–153
　and Boston Tea Party, 42–43, 46
　on British, 39, 54, 57–58, 192
　and British peace envoy, 228
　on Bunker Hill victory, 163
　centrality to rebellion, 56
　and Continental Congress, First, 58–59,
　　　66–67, 70, 72–73, 77–78, 79, 85–86, 87
　and Continental Congress, Second, 143–144,
　　　148, 182, 187, 268, 269, 278
　family life of, 184
　on Franklin, 144
　Galloway on, 78
　on George III, 217
　and independence, movement toward, 277
　and independence, vote on, 329, 332
　on independence, 248, 260, 340–341
　Jefferson on, 56
　life of, 54–55, 352
　motives for rebellion, 55, 57–58
　Native Americans, negotiations with, 89
　on Paine's *Common Sense*, 222
　on peace commission, 245
　as political agitator, 33, 56–57, 119, 153–155
　political goals of, 143–144
　political militancy of, 55–56, *56*
　and proposed disavowal of independence,
　　　229–230
　response to initiation of hostilities, 119
　on standing armies, 187
　as target of British troops, 110–111
　unified American response as goal of, 58–59
　on war, impact on American attitudes, 224
Adams, Samuel, Sr., 54–55
Adams, Susanna, 153
Address to the Inhabitants of America, 232–234
Administration of Justice Act (1774), 46, 59–60
Admiralty Courts, 15, 84
Albany Plan of Union, 44
Alexander, William, 347
Allen, Andrew, 228
Allen, Ethan, 138, 212

Alsop, John, 196
The American Crisis (Paine), 356
American forces. *See also* Continental Army;
　　　Grand American Army
　British underestimation of, 100
　military preparations, 181–182
　Native Americans in, 172
　shortages, 116–118, 146, 162
American identity, formation of, 254–255,
　　　256, 310
American Prohibitory Act (Capture Act),
　　　207–208, 240, 247–249, 259, 314
American Revolution. *See also* independence;
　　　Revolutionary War
　Adams (John) on, 293
　Declaration of Independence and, 310
　inevitability of, ix, 11–12, 29–31
Anderson, Thomas, 254
Archer, Richard, 14
arms
　efforts to secure, 211, 217, 238, 250, 261
　rifles, American use of, 158
　trade with France, 217, 238, 267
Arnold, Benedict Colonel, 138, *139*, 163, 213–215
Assembly Party, 21–22, 23, 35, 61, 63–64, 86–87,
　　　127–128
Atlantic slave trade
　Declaration of Independence on, 313, 314
　efforts to close, 306

Barclay, David, 96–97
Barré, Isaac, 47, 199, 243, 267
Barrett, James, 112, 113
Barrington, Viscount, 173
Bartlett, Josiah, 4, 268, 316, 329
battle of Brooklyn Heights, 347
Battle of Bunker Hill, *117*, 159–163, *161*
　British casualties, arrival in England, 179
　British response to, 173–178
　impact on Continental Congress, 163–165
battle of Great Bridge, 192
battle of Saratoga, 349, 350
battle of Three Rivers, 283–284
battle of Yorktown, 349, 350
battles of Lexington and Concord, 110–116
　British propaganda on, 170
　British reaction to, 170–173
　impact on Continental Congress delegates,
　　　134–135
　Patriot propaganda on, 119–122
Bernard, Francis, 32–33
Bonvouloir, Achard de, 208–209, 210, 211
Boston
　British bombardment, false reports of
　　　(1774), 79
　British closure of port, 46, 53–54
　British fortification of, 85–86
　British troops deployed to, 32–33
　dysentery outbreak of 1775, 271

Hutchinson Letters and, 37–38
as perceived center of rebellion, 42–43
siege of, *147*, 172, 250–253, 270–273, 274
Stamp Act opposition in, 15–16
Boston Massacre, 33–34, 152
Boston Port Act (1774), 46, 59
Boston Tea Party, 40–41, *42*
   Adams (John) on, 41, 154
   American reactions to, 41–42, 52–53
   British government reactions to, 43–47,
      91–92, 176
   British public's reaction to, 42–43
   compensation for, as issue, 97, 140
   George III's response to, 93–94
   revolutionaries' propaganda on, 52
   as turning point, 355
Boucher, Jonathan, 107
boycotts of British goods, 15, 27, 32, 34, 35,
    58–59. *See also* trade with Britain,
    embargo on
Braxton, Carter, 334–335
British Army, size of, 174. *See also* British forces
    in colonies
British-colonial relations
   after commencement of hostilities, as issue
    in Continental Congress, 140
   Burke on, 49
   in 18th century, 12–13
   Tea Act as turning point in, 39–40
   Townsend Duties as turning point in, 355
British forces in colonies
   British calls for withdrawal of, 95 (*See also*
    Parliament, opponents of war in)
   British confidence in superiority of, 44, 100,
    104, 106, 171, 173–174
   brutality of, 114
   and colonists' suspicion of standing armies,
    32–33, 37–39
   Continental Congress denouncement of, 84
   initiation of hostilities, 99–100
   mercenaries used by, 174, 267–268, 314
   paying for, as issue, 14, 15, 26
   punishment of Americans trading with, 255
   reinforcement of, 99, 110–115, 171–173, 174, 233,
    284–285, 316
   superiority of, 4
British government. *See also* North govern-
    ment; Parliament
   colonists' increased suspicion of, 32, 35, 37–39
   financial problems of, 13, 35, 36
   monopolization of political power by, 18–19
British Navy. *See also* American Prohibitory
    Act
   blockade of colonies, 172, 207, 247
   impressment of seamen, 207
British policy. *See also* North government
   Adams (John) on, 153–154
   colonial apologists for, 64–65
   on colonial land claims, 6

domestic opposition to, 90, 101–106, 198–205,
    207–208, 242–243, 288, 349
   Franklin on, 12, 30–31
   George III's intransigence and, 93–94,
    178–181, 234, 278, 355
   inability to reverse, xi
   lost opportunities in, 354–355
   tightening of colonial control (*See also*
    taxation, British)
    efforts toward, 15, 26–27
    Franklin on, 30–31
    motivations for, 13
Brooklyn Heights, battle of, 347
Bull, William, 95
Bulloch, Archibald, 318
Bunker Hill, battle of, *117*, 159–163, *161*
   British casualties, arrival in England, 179
   British response to, 173–178
   impact on Continental Congress, 163–165
Burgoyne, John, 162–163
Burke, Edmund, *201*
   on British concessions, need for, 104–105,
    205–208, 234, 355
   character and demeanor of, 203
   clear understanding of British-American
    conflict, 244, 355
   Dickinson on, 135
   Fox and, 202, 203
   life of, 48
   on taxation of America, 25, 48–49
Burwell, Rebecca, 303, 307
businessmen, support for British rule, 11, 12, 76
Bute, 3rd Earl of (John Stuart), 14

Camden, Baron (Charles Pratt), 103–105,
    135, 242
Canada campaign, *139*, 212–216, *216*, 278–284
   battle of Three Rivers, 283–284
   British arms shipments, efforts to interrupt,
    189–190
   British defenses, 171–172, 174
   Canadians' support, efforts to obtain,
    280–281
   command of, 279–280, 283
   commissioners delegation and, 280–281,
    282–283
   commissioners' report on, 282–283, 290
   and Committee to the Northward, 287–288
   Continental Congress's reaction to, 215–217,
    232, 316
   disease and, 284
   as impetus toward opening foreign trade,
    217, 222
   Jefferson on, 319
   routing at Quebec, 281–282
   shortages of supplies, 281
*Candid Examination of the Mutual Claims of
    Great Britain and the Colonies*
    (Galloway), 108

Capture Act. *See* American Prohibitory Act
Carleton, Guy, 171–172, 174, 281, 284
Carpenters Hall, 72, *73*
Carroll, Charles, 280, 282, 283, 290, 346, 350
Carroll, John, 280, 282
Charleston, Massachusetts, British burning of,
    161
Chase, Samuel
    activities during congressional hiatus, 182
    on American navy, 189
    appearance of, 189
    and commissioners delegation to Canada,
        280, 282, 283, 290, 295–296
    at Continental Congress, First, 80
    at Continental Congress, Second, 210, 346
    life after independence, 350–351
    privateering and, 249
Chatham, Earl of (William Pitt), 6, 26, 100–102,
    119, 124, 198, 241
checks and balances, Adams (John) on,
    265, 266
City Tavern (Philadelphia), 68, *68*, 70, 72, 133, 140
Clark, Abraham, 329–330, 335
Clinton, Henry, 162
Clymer, George, 346
Coercive Acts (1774)
    and American opinion on monarchy, 257
    British views on, 50, 92, 94
    colonial opposition to, 48, 53–54, 58–60, 133
    Continental Congress rejection of, 84
    Declaration of Independence on, 314
    passage of, 47–48
    provisions of, 46–47
colonial assemblies
    British dissolving of, 26, 60, 307
    extralegal, creation of, 60, 66
    as focus of colonial form of government,
        257–258
colonial governments
    Continental Congress resolution urging
        replacement of, 194–196, 276–277, 310,
        315–316, 319
    intercolonial organization, development of, 39
    political system of, differences from English
        system, 257–258
    replacement of, 194–196, 255, 258–259
colonial governors
    arms sent to, by British government, 172
    flight of, 192
    reports on public unrest, 95
    in Virginia
        campaign against rebels, 192–193, 232
        legislature, dissolution of, 60
        on public unrest, severity of, 95
colonies
    limited contact between, before
        Revolution, 70
    retention of as entities, in Continental
        Congress voting procedures, 74

committee(s) of correspondence, 39, 53, 59, 70,
    107, 119
Committee of Correspondence, congressional,
    212, 217
Committee of Fifty-One, 60–61
Committee of Five, 293, 294–298, 299, 311
Committee of Secret Correspondence, 210–211
Committee on Rights (Grand Committee), 79,
    80, 83–85, 155
committees of safety, intimidation and
    harassment of Tories, 255–256
Committee to the Northward, 287–288
Common Sense (Paine)
    argument of, 219–222
    audience for, 218–219
    form of government advocated in, 264–265
    impact on public opinion, 217, 222–223, 225,
        232, 257, 258, 261, 262, 356
    publication of, 217
    writing of, 218
commonwealth theory of empire, American
    adoption of, 31
Concord, battle of, 110–111, 112–114, 116
    British propaganda on, 170
    British response to, 170–173
    impact on Continental Congress delegates,
        134–135
    Patriot propaganda on, 119–122
confederation, drafting of plan for, 293
Connecticut
    and declaration of independence, 315
    militia, capture of Fort Ticonderoga, 138–140
constitution of United States, calls for, 146,
    230, 232
Continental Army. *See also* American forces;
    Canada campaign
    arms
        efforts to secure, 211, 217, 238, 250, 261
        rifles, use of, 158
        trade with France, 267
    deserters, 214
    discipline of, 186
    enlisted men, retention problems, 185, 186,
        187, 214, 215
    establishment of, 148–149
    hierarchical structure, establishment of,
        185–186
    officers of, 158
    officers pay, raising of, 185–186
    poor performance of, 284–285, 349
    proposals for, 136–137, 141, 146–148, 156–157
    recruitment by, 158–160, 187, 217
    shortages, 188, 351
    and siege of Boston, 250–253
    Washington and
        assumption of command, 147–150, 159
        and Boston, siege of, 250–253
        Declaration of Independence and, 343,
        343, 345

French arms, efforts to obtain, 211
and New York, defense of, 289, 320
officer appointments, 280
officers pay, 185–186
pay as commander, 185
recruitment and retention issues, 187, 337
Continental Associations, 84, 89, 106–107
Continental Congress, First
Adams's (Samuel) goals for, 58–59
address to King, 86, 94
British awareness of proceedings in, 92–93, 206, 227
British government response to, 93–95, 99–100, 101–103, 341
domestic opposition to, 100–101, 102, 103–106
British public's reaction to, 95–96
calls for, 59
Committee on Rights (Grand Committee), 79, 80, 83–85, 155
Connecticut delegation, 76
Declaration of Colonial Rights and Grievances, 84–85, 137, 311
Delaware delegation, 76
delegates
activities after adjournment, 88–89, 114
fear of war, 83–84
first meetings and first impressions among, 70–72
gathering of, 67–68
leisure time pursuits, 69–70, 79
range of political opinions in, 74–77
establishment of, 60–61, 66
first meeting of, 72–74
and independence, debate on, 76, 83–84
lodging for, 68
Maryland delegation, 60, 77
Massachusetts delegation, 67–68, 76, 77–78, 85
meeting site, 72, 73
moderate dominance of, 74, 83–84, 85–86
motives for calling, 59
New Hampshire delegation, 76
New Jersey delegation, 76
New York delegation, 76
North Carolina delegation, 67, 77
pamphlets attacking, 107, 108
Pennsylvania delegation, 76, 87, 133
rancor of debate at, 79–81, 83, 85
resistance to creation of, 60–61, 66–67
Rhode Island delegation, 77, 83
secrecy, policy of, 74
South Carolina delegation, 60, 67, 77
and Suffolk County Resolves, 79–80, 93
Virginia delegation, 60, 67, 71, 77, 80, 85, 307
Continental Congress, Second. See also Declaration of Independence; Olive Branch Petition
accomplishments of, 169

Adams's (John) leadership role at, 146, 150, 156–157, 166–167, 269–270
British government response to, 164
and Bunker Hill battle, 159–160, 163–165
Camp Committee, 186
and colonial governments, replacement of, 194–196, 276–277, 310, 315–316, 319
command of Revolutionary War as issue in, 140
Committee of Correspondence, 212, 217
Committee of Secret Correspondence, 210–211
Connecticut delegation, 327
and Continental Navy, 189–192
Declaration on the Causes and Necessity for Taking Up Arms, 168–169, 295, 311
Delaware delegation, 196, 228, 275, 325, 327–329
delegates
activities during summer hiatus, 181–182
assembly of, 122–123
daily schedules of, 183
families, anxieties of, 270–275
health of, 269, 288
hopes for reunion with Great Britain, 158, 169, 188, 193, 196, 217, 224, 234–235, 245, 288–289, 291, 330, 337, 341
leisure activities, 182, 183–184
liability to treason charges, 156, 169, 327, 345
personal sacrifices of, 184, 268–269, 270, 273–274
relations among, 182–183, 230, 269–270
responses to initiation of hostilities, 118–119
returning and new delegates, 123–124
on Revolutionary War, 124, 316–317
views on British intentions, 124
and France, overtures from, 210–212
George III's October address to Parliament and, 217
Georgia delegation, 228, 329, 338
and independence
debate on, 290–293, 320–325
delegates' views on, 158, 169, 188, 193–194, 196–197, 232, 235, 238–239, 246–247, 248, 317
movement toward, 275–277, 278–279, 284–285, 318
proposed declaration disavowing, 224–225, 228–232
vote on, ix–x, 325–335, 334
and Lexington and Concord battles, impact of, 134–135
Maryland delegation, 196, 329
Massachusetts delegation, 123, 156, 159, 182, 269–270, 329
meeting place, 123
and mercenaries, response to, 267–268

Continental Congress (*continued*)
  national army, proposals for, 136–137, 141,
     146–148, 156–157
  Naval Committee, 190
  New Hampshire delegation, 182, 329
  New Jersey delegation, 196, 228, 324, 329–330
  New York delegation, 228, 275, 288, 325, 330
  North Carolina delegation, 182, 228, 330
  North Peace Plan, consideration of,
     163–164, 295
  overwhelming agenda of, 137–138
  and peace commission, 347–349
  Pennsylvania delegation, 196, 228, 275,
     325–326, 330–332, 346
  procedure in, 3–4
  Rhode Island delegation, 332–333, 338
  Secret Committee, 238
  slow progress of, 136, 140, 148, 167
  South Carolina delegation, 228, 325–326,
     333–334, 338
  summer adjournment, 181
  unity as priority of, 146, 156, 167, 186, 229, 233,
     246, 249, 354
  Virginia delegation, 260–261, 307, 334–335
  voting procedure, 72–73, 83
  warfare, offensive, reluctance to adopt, 189
  wartime business of, 3, 4, 182, 320, 337
  Washington's departure for, 115
Continental Navy
  creation of, 192
  debate on establishment of, 189–192
Conway, Henry, 199
Country Party, 55
Crown Point, American capture of, 138–140
Cushing, Thomas, 46, 67, 72, 77, 80, 91, 183, 229
customs, British efforts to strengthens, 15, 26

Dartmouth, Earl of (William Legge), *45*
  as American secretary, 37, 45, 46, 90–93,
     96–98
  and British response to rebellion, 45, 46, 93,
     96–98, 99–100, 110, 171, 173, 278,
     384n24
  and Bunker Hill, 163
  and Gage, replacement of, 175
  life of, 90
  monitoring of American unrest, 130
  and North Peace Plan, 164
  and peace commission, 239, 240, 243
  resignation of, 175
  and unofficial peace envoy, 227
Davis, Isaac, 113
Dawes, William, 110, 112
Deane, Silas, 181, 183, 189, 190, 249–250
Declaration of Colonial Rights and Grievances
     (1774), 84–85, 137, 311
Declaration of Independence
  Adams (John) on, 246
  British response to, 346–347

  congressional debate on, 320–325
  congressional editing of, 337–340
  congressional responses to, 340–341
  contents of, 309–315
  proposals for, 260–261
  publication of, 336–337, 340, 341–344
  public celebrations of, 342–345
  signers, later life of, 350–353
  signing of, 345–346
  slavery and, 313, 314, 338
  text of, 358–362
  as venerated document, 355–357
  vote on, 325–335, *334*
  writing of
    committee for, 293, 294–298, 299
    congressional editing of, 337–340
    intellectual influences, 311–313
    writing process, 298–301, *308*, 309, 311, 315
Declaration of Rights (Virginia), 312, 313
Declaration on the Causes and Necessity for
     Taking Up Arms, 168–169, 295, 311
Declaratory Act (1766), 26, 49, 103, 104, 205,
     228. *See also* Parliament, right to rule
     colonies
Delaware
  and declaration of independence, 315
  First Continental Congress delegation, 76
  and independence, movement toward,
     278, 292
  Second Continental Congress delegation,
     196, 228, 275, 325, 327–329
democracy, colonial fear of, 82, 107–108, 136,
     186, 194–195, 335, 351–352
Derby, John, 121–122
Dickinson, John, *126*
  Adams (John) and, 165–166, 182–183, 230–231,
     322
  and Address to the Inhabitants of America,
     232–233
  appearance and demeanor, 125
  on British decadence, 125–126, 132
  on British taxation, 61, 64, 140, 231
  and Continental Congress, First, 66, 71,
     86–87, 89, 133
  at Continental Congress, Second
    and confederation, drafting of plan for, 293
    and French treaty, drafting of, 293
    support for reconciliation, 125, 135–136, 137,
     140–141, 145, 164–168, 196, 210, 224,
     230–232, 316, 321–323
  on Tea Act, 133
  evolution in position of, 231–232
  and foreign support, efforts to obtain, 210
  Galloway and, 62, 126–129, 133
  and independence
    debate on, 290–292
    fear of, 135–136
    push toward, 276–277
    vote on, 325, 330–331

Letters from a Farmer in Pennsylvania,
    27–28, 32, 129–132, 222
life of, 125–126, 132, 352
as militia officer, 230–231, 321, 342, 352
movement toward radicalization, 129–130,
    132–134
on negotiations with British, 349
as pamphleteer, 129–132
on Parliament's right to rule colonies, 31, 85,
    129, 131–132, 140, 168–169
political career, 27, 126–129, 132–133, 321–322
public opinion on, 130, 321
response to initiation of hostilities, 118
on Revolutionary War, 134
"A Song for American Freedom," 131
on War, likely difficulties of, 135–136
Wilson (James) and, 224, 225
Dickinson, Mary Norris, 132
Dorchester Heights, American capture of,
    251–252, 274
Drayton, William Henry, 259
Drummond, Lord (Thomas Lundin), 226–230,
    234
Duane, James, 89, 254, 268, 277
Duche, Jacob, 72–73
Dumas, Charles-Guillaume-Frédéric, 210
Dunmore, 4th Earl of (John Murray)
    campaign against rebels, 192–193, 232
    legislature, dissolution of, 60
    on public unrest, severity of, 95

East India Company, 36, 40, 42, 42, 140
economy, American, Revolutionary War and,
    349
Eden, Robert, 248
Eden, William, 173, 176
Ellery, William, 327, 333, 340
English Declaration of Rights, 309–310
Enlightenment rationalism, influence on
    Founding Fathers, 153, 306

Fairfax Independent Company, 88–89
Falmouth (Massachusetts), British bombard-
    ment of, 191–192
Fischer, David Hackett, 119
Fleming, William, 91
foreign assistance. *See also* France, alliance
    with
  Adams (John) on, 123
  Declaration of Independence and, 311
  efforts to obtain, 4, 7, 141, 210–211, 249–250
  fears of not obtaining, 292
  increasing awareness of need for, 232, 248,
    262, 268, 283, 285, 289, 291
  independence necessary for, 4, 7, 246, 253,
    268, 285, 317
  Paine's *Common Sense* on, 221–222
Fort Ticonderoga
  American capture of, 138–140

British plans to recapture, 172
ordnance, transfer to Boston, 251
Fothergill, John, 96–97
Founding Fathers
  enlightenment rationalism and, 153, 306
  fear of democracy, 82, 136
  popular view of, ix
Fox, Charles James, 199–204, *201*, 206–208,
    242–243, 349
France
  alliance with (*See also* foreign assistance)
    American overtures, 210, 249–250
    arms trade, 217, 238, 267
    British concerns about, 204–205
    delay in, 349
    drafting of treaty for, 293
    fears of not obtaining, 292
    increasing awareness of need for, 232, 248,
      262, 268, 283, 285, 289, 291
    as key to victory, 349, 350
    overtures to America, 210–212
  American fear of, 291, 323
  monitoring of revolution by, 208–210
Franklin, Benjamin, 299
  activities during congressional hiatus, 182
  and Albany Plan of Union, 44
  American suspicions about, 144, 145, 146
  Boston Tea Party and, 41–42, 43, 53, 98
  on British decadence, 126
  and British peace commission, 347
  on British rule, 12, 30–31, 51
  British suspicions about, 92, 96
  on British tax policy, 22–23, 24–26
  on British troops in Boston, 33
  on Bunker Hill victory, 163
  character and demeanor, 20–21, 61, 144
  and commissioners delegation to Canada,
    280–281, 282
  concerns about British invasion of
    Philadelphia, 191
  constitution of United States, call for, 146,
    230, 232
  at Continental Congress, Second, 124, 145,
    210–211, 293
  correspondence, 183–184
  on Dartmouth, 91
  and Declaration of Independence, 293, 294,
    300, 309, 311, 339–340
  Dickinson (John) and, 130
  and envoy to France, 249–250
  and foreign support, 210–211
  Galloway and, 21–22, 23, 61, 62–63, 65, 79, 96,
    98–99, 124
  health of, 300
  on Hillsborough, 37
  Hutchinson Letters and, 37–38, 49
  and independence, vote on, 325, 331
  on independence, 98–99, 145, 197, 208
  life of, 20–21, 351

Franklin, Benjamin (*continued*)
  in London, 22–24, 28–29, 49–50, 53, 61
  movement toward radicalization, 24, 31, 50,
    98–99
  on Paine's *Common Sense*, 222
  and peace commission, 248, 348–349
  political career, 21–22, 29, 61, 64, 127, 128–129
  Privy Council public reproach of, 49–50, 351
  on public's growing dislike of England, 254
  reputation of, Stamp Act and, 23–24
  and Revolutionary War
    British efforts to diffuse conflict and,
      96–98, 100
    desire to avoid, 29, 36
    on likelihood of conflict, 29–31, 145,
      354–355
    support for, 144–145
  "Rules by Which a Great Empire May be
    Reduced to a Small One," 36
  and Stamp Act, 20, 22–24
  on Tea Act, 36
  on Townshend Duties, 30
  wife and family of, 28–29
Franklin, William, 28, 62–63, 92, 144
French and Indian War (Seven Years' War)
  American military power and, 44
  and British authority over colonies, 13–14
  and colonists' views on Britain, 12, 75–76
  Franklin and, 22
frontier lands, British closing of, 14, 39, 47–48,
  306

Gadsden, Christopher, 188, 189, 258–259
Gage, Thomas General
  and Bunker Hill, 160, 161, 163
  on Coercive Acts, 94
  initiation of hostilities, 99–100, 110
  on rebellion
    crushing of, 44, 95, 175
    origins of, 171
  recruitment of locals, 107
  replacement as commander, 175
  report on Lexington and Concord battles,
    121–122, 170–171
  reports on militancy of rebels, 90, 94–95
  and siege of Boston, 85–86, 172
Galloway, Grace Growdon, 132
Galloway, Joseph, 63
  on Adams (Samuel), 78
  Adams (John) on, 71
  appearance and demeanor, 62
  and Assembly Party, 21, 61, 63–64, 127–128
  and Continental Congress, First, 66–67, 71,
    72, 75, 78–79, 81–83, 86, 133, 206
  Dickinson and, 62, 126–129, 133
  Franklin and, 21–22, 23, 61, 62–63, 65, 79, 96,
    98–99, 124
  life of, 61–62, 352–353
  pamphleteering by, 107–108

Plan of Union of, 82–83, 86, 92–93, 101, 108
  political career, 118, 124
  political career of, 63, 63–65, 87, 127–129
  response to rebellious unrest, 64–67
  and Stamp Act riots, 23
George II (king of Great Britain), 12
George III (king of Great Britain)
  allegations against, in Declaration of
    Independence, 313–314, 338–339
  American efforts to delegitimize, 259, 260
  and Atlantic slave trade, efforts to close, 306
  and Boston Tea Party, 45–46, 93–94
  character and deportment of, 93
  colonial views on, 12
  declaration of war against colonies, 179, 198
  effigies of, burned after Declaration of
    Independence, 344
  on Fox (Charles James), 202
  on Gage, 175
  intransigence of, 93–94, 178–181, 234, 278, 355
  and Lord North, support for, 8, 9
  opening address to Parliament (1775),
    179–181, 198, 217
  and Parliamentary elections of 1774, 92
  and peace commission, 239–240, 241
  Proclamation for Suppressing Rebellion and
    Sedition, 178–179, 193, 195
  views on colonies, 93–94
Germain, Lord George, 177
  appointment as American Secretary, 175–177
  career of, 176
  character and deportment, 177
  critics of, 243
  intercepted letters of, 248
  and loss of America, 350
  and peace commission, 241–242, 346
  response to rebellion, 206
  and war strategy, 179
Gerry, Elbridge
  at Continental Congress, Second, 229
  and Declaration of Independence, 340,
    345–346
  and independence, 246, 292, 329
  life after independence, 350, 351
Gibbon, Edward, 122, 171, 202
Gordon, Adam, 1
government of United States
  Adams (John) on, 265–266
  Paine on, 264–265
governors, colonial
  arms sent to, by British government, 172
  flight of, 192
  reports on public unrest, 95
  in Virginia
    campaign against rebels, 192–193, 232
    legislature, dissolution of, 60
    on public unrest, severity of, 95
Gower, Earl of, 45
Graff, Jacob, 308, *308*

Grafton, Duke of, 173, 199, 242
Grand American Army, 136, 146–149, 160
Grand Committee (Committee on Rights), 79,
        80, 83–85, 155
Grant, James, 252
Gravier, Charles. *See* Vergennes, Charles
        Gravier, comte de
Great Bridge, battle of, 192
Great Britain
    American opinions on, 75–76, 253–257
    corruption of
        Adams (John) on, 167–168
        Adams (Samuel) on, 54, 57–58, 192
        Dickinson (John) on, 125–126, 132
        as focal point of revolution, 258
        Franklin on, 126
Green Mountain Boys, 138, 212
Grenville, George, 14, 24
Gridley, Jeremiah, 151
Growden, Grace (Galloway), 62
Guines, comte de, 209–210, 211
Gwinnett, Button, 292, 329, 350

Hall, Lyman, 292, 329
Hamilton, Alexander, 108–109
Hancock, John
    and Boston Tea Party, 42–43, 46
    on Canadian invasion, 280
    and Continental Army, 148, 149
    at Continental Congress, Second, 124, 163,
        229, 247, 290–293, 326
    and Declaration of Independence, 342, 345
    and independence, vote on, 320, 329
    on mercenaries, 267
    and negotiations with France, 210
    on Paine's *Common Sense*, 222
    relations with other delegates, 269
    as target of British troops, 110–111
    and wartime business of Congress, 3–4
Harrison, Benjamin
    at Continental Congress, First, 70, 85
    at Continental Congress, Second, 183, 293,
        326, 334
    and France, overtures to, 210
    and independence, vote on, 320
Hart, John, 329–330
Hartley, David, 105–106, 183, 267
Hemings, Robert, 308
Henry, Patrick, 17
    Adams (John) on, 85
    and committees of correspondence, 305
    at Continental Congress, First, 67, 73–74, 77, 85
    at Continental Congress, Second, 141, 143
    Dunmore on, 192
    leadership in Stamp Act opposition, 16–18
    life of, 16
    as militia commander, 181
    Virginia Resolves of, 17–18, 84, 257, 354–355
    wife, death of, 89

Henry, Sarah, 89
Hewes, Joseph, 248, 295, 317, 330
Heyward, Thomas, 325, 333, 351
Hillsborough, Lord (Wills Hill), 27, 36–37
history
    cyclical theory of, 11
    inevitability of, ix
Hooper, William, 89, 232, 244–245, 265, 346
Hopkins, Stephen, 77, 296, 332–333
Hopkinson, Francis, 329
House of Commons, 20, 24, 25
Howe, Richard, Lord, 98
    as commander, North American squadron,
        241
    and peace commission, 240, 241, 242,
        243–244, 346–349
    peace proposal to Franklin, 97–98
Howe, William General
    anticipated strike on New York, 4, 137–138,
        284, 289, 291, 316, 320, 336, 337
    appointment as commander of British
        forces, 175
    and British intelligence, 353
    at Bunker Hill, 160–161, 162
    and peace commission, 241, 242, 244, 252,
        346–349
    redeployment to New York, 179
    and siege of Boston, 250–253
Hughes, John, 23
Humphreys, Charles, 325, 331
Huntington, Samuel, 327
Hutchinson, Thomas
    and Adams (Samuel), 54–55, 57
    as governor, 49
    letters to Whately, exposure of, 37–38, 49,
        153–154
    political career of, 152
    Stamp Act riots and, 16, 57
    Tea Act and, 41
Hutchinson Letters, 37–38, 49

independence. *See also* Declaration of
        Independence
    Adams (John) on
        difficulty of winning, xi
        early reluctance about, 152
        inevitability of, 167–168, 285
        movement toward, 193–194, 248–249, 259,
            318–319, 353–354
        necessity of, 246, 317
    Adams (Samuel) on, 248, 260, 340–341
    American Prohibitory Act as impetus
        toward, 247–249
    British efforts to check drift toward, 13, 20
    consequences of, debate on, 76, 82, 107–108,
        136, 186, 194–195, 263–264, 286, 335,
        351–352
    and Continental Congress, Second
        debate on, 290–293, 320–325

independence (*continued*)
  delegates' views, 158, 169, 188, 193–194,
      196–197, 232, 235, 238–239, 246–247,
      248, 317
  movement toward, 275–277, 278–279,
      284–285, 318
  proposed declaration disavowing,
      224–225, 228–232
  vote on, ix–x, 325–335, *334*
  declaration of, as break from previous policy, 7
  Dickinson's (John) fear of, 135–136
  First Continental Congress on, 76, 83–84
  foreign assistance as goal of, 4, 7, 246, 253,
      268, 285, 317
  Franklin on, 98–99, 145, 197, 208
  inevitability of, 355
  Jefferson on, xi, 197
  Lee's resolution on, 3–5, 7, 278, 284, 289–290,
      314–315, 320, 339
  local declarations of, 258–261
  as model for other nations, 263
  proposed declaration disavowing, 224–225,
      228–232
  public opinion on, evolution of, ix, 219,
      253–264, 271, 275–277, 278–279,
      315–316, 318–319, 353, 354
  Washington on, 253
Independence Hall, 2, 2, 3, 123
Indians. *See* Native Americans
Intolerable Acts. *See* Coercive Acts
Iroquois Confederation, 172, 288

Jay, John
  at Continental Congress, First, 83
  at Continental Congress, Second, 164,
      184, 196
  and Drummond negotiations, 228
  and foreign support, efforts to obtain, 210
  Livingston and, 286
Jefferson, Martha Skelton, 304, 305, 308
Jefferson, Thomas, 299
  activities during congressional hiatus,
      181
  on Adams (John), 155, 157, 324
  on Adams (Samuel), 56
  appearance, 304
  on British policies, 305–306
  on Bunker Hill victory, 163
  character and demeanor, 303–304, 304–305
  on committees of correspondence, 39
  at Continental Congress, Second, 164,
      168–169, 307–308, *308*
  death of, 357
  and Declaration of Independence
    editing of, 339–340
    vote on, 320, 325
    writing of, 293, 295, 299, 309–311, 315, 317,
      344, 356
  health of, 307, 308

  on Hewes (Joseph), 330
  and independence, declaration of, 319, 334
  and independence, vote on, 332
  on independence, xi, 197
  involvement in revolutionary politics,
      306–307
  life of, 301–304, 350, 351
  and North Peace Plan, 164, 295
  on Parliament's right to rule colonies, 168
  reputation as writer, 294–295
  on Sherman (Roger), 298
  and slavery, 305–306, 313, 314
  *A Summary View of the Rights of British
      America*, 307
Johnson, Thomas, 149, 164, 188, 210

Knox, Henry Colonel, 251
Knox, William, 242

Langdon, John, 287
*The Late Regulations Respecting the British
      Colonies* (Dickinson), 129
Lee, Arthur, 122, 167, 178, 210
Lee, Charles General, 109–110, 147, 158, 248
Lee, Francis Lightfoot, 217, 261, 278, 316, 332, 334
Lee, Richard Henry
  Adams (John) on, 71
  and Adams's *Thoughts on Government*, 265
  appearance, 1, 6–7
  on British frontier policies, 6, 48
  on British response to Continental Congress,
      88
  and British threats on Virginia, 248
  character and demeanor of, 5, 6–7
  and committees of correspondence, 39, 305
  at Continental Congress, First, 68, 70, 71, 77,
      80, 86
  at Continental Congress, Second
    on colonial governments, 195
    and Continental military forces, 136, 146,
      191
    and Declaration of Independence, 295,
      340, 346
    and independence, debate and vote on,
      292, 309, 346
    and independence, resolution calling for,
      3–5, 7, 278, 284, 289–290, 314–315,
      320, 339
    on independence, necessity of, 285
    Olive Brance Petition and, 141
    relations with other delegates, 269
  on Franklin, 144
  life of, 5
  movement toward radicalization, 5–7, 18
  on opening of American ports, 188
  and Pitt (William), 100
  on Revolutionary War, 118, 246
Legge, William. *See* Dartmouth, Earl of
      (William Legge)

Leonard, Daniel, 107
Letters from a Farmer in Pennsylvania
(Dickinson), 27–28, 32, 129–132, 222
Lexington, battle of, 110–112, 116
British propaganda on, 170
British reaction to, 170–173
impact on Continental Congress delegates,
134–135
Patriot propaganda on, 119–122
liberty of colonists, direct taxation as assault
on, 18
Livingston, Robert R., 290, 299
on Canadian campaign, 216
at Continental Congress, Second, 270, 287, 288
and Committee to the Northward,
287–288
and confederation, plan for, 293
views on independence, 285, 286–287,
288–289
and Declaration of Independence, 293, 294,
300, 311, 346
on foreign trade, 188
life of, 285–286, 350
support for Patriot cause, 118
Livingston, William, 168
Locke, John, 153, 306
Lundin, Thomas (Lord Drummond), 226–230,
234
Lynch, Thomas, 78, 228, 269, 333
Lynch, Thomas, Jr., 325, 333–334

Mackesy, Piers, 176
Madison, James, 352
Maier, Pauline, 313, 355
Mansfield, Lord (William Murray), 243
Martin, Josiah, 95
Maryland
and declaration of independence, 315, 320
First Continental Congress delegation, 60, 77
and independence, movement toward, 278
legislature, extralegal, creation of, 60
raising of Continental Army companies, 158
Second Continental Congress delegation,
196, 329
Massachusetts. *See also* Boston
British punishment for Boston Tea Party,
46–47
Coercive Acts, solidification of resistance
against, 53–54
Continental Congress's pledge to defend, 86
First Continental Congress delegation,
67–68, 76, 77–78, 85
militia of, 89–90, 138–140
revolutionary government of, 181, 194–195
Second Continental Congress delegation,
123, 156, 159, 182, 269–270, 329
and vote for independence, 412n53
Massachusetts Circular Letter (1768), 27
Massachusetts Committee of Safety, 119–122

Massachusetts Government Act (1774), 46,
59–60, 92
Massachusetts Spy (newspaper), 119–120
Maury, James, 301–302
Mayhew, Jonathan, 12–13
McKean, Thomas, 325, 327–329
mercenaries, British, 174, 267–268, 314
merchants
American
British efforts to regulate, 13, 15, 26
views on independence, 239
British, support for colonial rights, 95, 134
Middleton, Arthur, 325, 333, 351
Mifflin, Thomas, 66, 70, 71
militia
calls for training and arming of, 80, 85, 86, 87
response at Lexington and Concord, 111–113,
116
social equality of, *vs.* Continental Army,
185–186
supplies, lack of, 116–118
suppression of British recruitment, 107
training and arming of, 88–90, 122–123,
181
minutemen, 111
monarchy, changing opinions on, 257
Montesquieu, 153
Montgomery, Richard General, 213–215, 216, 287
Monticello, 304
Montreal, U.S. capture of, 213
Morris, Gouverneur, 65
Morris, Lewis, 351
Morris, Robert, 236
appearance, 235
and boycotts of British goods, 237
character and demeanor, 235
at Continental Congress, Second, 237–238, 293
and independence, 196, 235, 238–239, 330–331,
346
life of, 235–237, 351
political career, 237–238
on Revolutionary War, 238, 267, 268, 280
Morton, John, 325, 331, 350
Murray, John. *See* Dunmore, John Murray, 4th
Earl of
Murray, William. *See* Mansfield, William
Murray, Lord

Native Americans
frontier lands and, 14
Revolutionary War and, 89, 171–172, 174
Nelson, Thomas, 334
New Hampshire
and declaration of independence, 315
First Continental Congress delegation, 76
replacement of colonial governments,
195–196, 258
Second Continental Congress delegation,
182, 329

New Jersey
  and declaration of independence, 315
  First Continental Congress delegation, 76
  and independence, movement toward, 278, 292
  Second Continental Congress delegation,
    196, 228, 324, 329–330
newspapers
  debate on independence in, 261–264
  and wartime propaganda efforts, 119–121, 122
New Ticket. *See* Proprietary Party
New York
  assembly, British dissolving of, 26
  battle of Brooklyn Heights, 347
  and First Continental Congress
    delegation to, 76
    opposition to, 60–61
  Howe's anticipated strike on, 4, 137–138, 284,
    289, 291, 316, 320, 336, 337
  and independence, 292, 345
  Second Continental Congress delegation,
    228, 275, 288, 325, 330
Norfolk, Virginia, Dunmore's shelling of, 193,
  232
North, Frederick, Lord, *10. See also* North
  government
  on American rebellion, 9–11
  appearance of, 9
  on Boston Tea Party, response to, 45, 50
  character and demeanor of, 8–10
  on Coercive Acts, 50
  Dartmouth and, 90
  and Fox (Charles James), 202–203
  and Franklin's public reproach by Privy
    Council, 50
  George III's support for, 8, 9
  intransigence of, 355
  and Lexington and Concord, response to, 171
  and loss of America, 350
  negotiation strategy, 240–241
  North Peace Plan, 102–103, 163–164, 206, 295
  in Parliamentary debates on rebellion,
    206–207
  and Parliamentary elections of 1774, 92
  on Parliament's right to rule colonies, 103, 106
  and peace commission, 239–240, 241–242, 243
  peace envoy, unofficial, 227–230
  peace plan after Saratoga, 349–350
  political career of, 8, 90
  on Revolutionary War, likely outcome of, 173
  unveiling of government response to
    rebellion, 101–102
  unwillingness to challenge king, 178, 234
North Carolina
  and declaration of independence, 315
  First Continental Congress delegation, 67, 77
  royal governor, flight of, 192
  second Continental Congress delegation,
    182, 228, 330
  threat of British invasion, 248

North government
  Boston Tea Party, response to, 43–47
  Bunker Hill, response to, 173–178
  colonial policies, 35
  confidence in swift military victory, 173–174,
    204
  and Continental Congress, response to,
    93–95, 99–100, 101–103, 164, 341
  domestic opposition to, 100–106
  intransigence of, 234–235
  and Lexington and Concord, response to,
    170–173
  missed opportunities for peace, 234–235
  peace commission. *See* peace commission,
    British
  popularity of, 92, 134
  proponents of peaceful settlement in, 173
  and risk of war, awareness of, 43–44
  tax policies, 34–35
North Peace Plan, 102–103, 163–164, 206, 295

Olive Branch Petition
  American hopes for, 188, 208
  British response to, 178–179, 181, 199, 204
  debate on, 140–142, 156, 164–167
  delivery of, 167
  development of, 135–136
  Franklin on, 145
  Howe (William) on, 348
Otis, James, 151, 152, 296

Paca, William, 329
Paine, Robert Treat
  and Committee to the Northward, 287–288
  at Continental Congress, First, 77
  at Continental Congress, Second
  and Adams (John), 183, 269–270
  and independence, 229, 329, 340
Paine, Thomas, 217–218, 219, 262, 276, 324, 351,
  356. *See also Common Sense*
pamphleteering, 107–110, 129–132, 217–223, 256,
  307, 311–312
Parker, John, 111
Parliament
  colonial policy, debate on, x
  confidence of victory in war, 198
  George III opening address to (1775), 179–181,
    198, 217
  intransigence of, 204, 355
  opponents of war in, 198–205, 207–208,
    242–243, 288, 349
  peace commission and, 239, 244
  right to rule colonies (*See also* Declaratory
    Act)
    Adams (John) on, 137, 140
    British insistence upon, 15, 34, 49, 239,
      243–244
    British willingness to retreat from, 99
    Dartmouth on, 91

debate on, at Continental Congress, 75,
  84–85
Dickinson on, 31, 85, 129, 131–132, 140,
  168–169
Franklin on, 30–31, 97
Jefferson on, 168
North on, 103, 106
Stamp Act hearings, 20, 24
Parry, Edward, 255
peace
North government's missed opportunities
  for, 234–235
North Peace Plan, 102–103, 163–164, 206, 295
North's peace plan after Saratoga, 349–350
peace commission
American, 78–79, 165, 231–232
British, 98
North on, 206–207
  American hopes for, 225, 233, 239,
    244–245, 248, 249, 330
  American suspicions about, 347
  authorization of, 239
  debate on, 93, 94, 96, 97, 99
  delay in sending, 234, 239–244
  instructions for, squabble over,
    241–244
  negotiations by, 346–349
peace envoy, British, 227–230
Pendelton, Edmund, 67
Penet, Pierre, 211–212, 217
Penn, John, 95, 265, 316, 330
Penn, Richard, 167, 178, 204
Pennsylvania
Committee of Safety, 228
constitution of, 352
and Continental Congress, establishment of,
  61, 66
and declaration of independence, 315–316
elections of 1776, 275–276, 331
First Continental Congress delegation, 76,
  87, 133
Franklin's efforts to royalize, 22, 27, 35, 37, 61,
  63–64, 127, 144
and independence, movement toward, 278,
  292
legislature, North Peace Plan and, 164
Penn family dominance of, 22
raising of Continental Army companies, 158
Second Continental Congress delegation,
  196, 228, 275, 325–326, 330–332, 346
Tories' political punishment, pre-revolution,
  35, 86–87
Philadelphia, in 1770s, 1–2, 69
Pitcairn, John Colonel, 111, 162
Pitt, William (Earl of Chatham), 6, 26, 100–102,
  119, 124, 198, 241
Plan of Union (Galloway), 82–83, 86, 92–93, 101,
  108
Pliarne, Emmanuel, 211–212, 217

Plumb, J. H., 58
political system of colonies, differences from
  English system, 257–258
Port, Jane, 68
Prescott, Samuel, 112
Prescott, William, 161
privateering, congressional approval of, 249
Privy Council, public reproach of Franklin,
  49–50, 351
Proclamation for Suppressing Rebellion and
  Sedition, 178–179, 193, 195
Proclamation of 1763 (Great Britain), 14
propaganda
on battles of Lexington and Concord,
  119–122, 170
on Boston Tea Party, 52
Proprietary Party, 27, 61, 64, 127, 129
protest infrastructure, as key to effective
  resistance, 38–39
public manipulation strategies. *See also*
  propaganda
Adams (Samuel) and, 153–155
Adams's (John) reaction to, 154
rebels' mastery of, 38–39, 56–57
public officials, motivations of, x
public opinion, American
on Declaration of Independence,
  342–345
on Great Britain, 75–76, 253–257
impact of war on, 122–123, 224, 233, 234, 246,
  248, 253–257, 354
on independence, evolution of, ix, 219,
  253–264, 271, 275–277, 278–279,
  315–316, 318–319, 353, 354
public opinion, British
on proper response to Continental Congress,
  95–96
on war, 122, 171
Putnam, Israel General, 116, 253

Quartering Act, 26, 46, 129
Quebec, 212
American campaign against, 139, 212–216,
  216, 278–284
  battle of Three Rivers, 283–284
  British defenses, 171–172, 174
  Canadians' support, efforts to obtain,
    280–281
  command of, 279–280, 283
  commissioners delegation, 280–281,
    282–283
  commissioners' report on, 282–283, 290
  and Committee to the Northward,
    287–288
  Continental Congress's reaction to,
    215–217, 232, 316
  disease and, 284
  as impetus toward opening foreign trade,
    217, 222

Quebec (*continued*)
    Jefferson on, 319
    routing at Quebec, 281–282
    shortages of supplies, 281
    arms shipments to, American efforts to
        interrupt, 189–190
Quebec Act (1774), 47–48, 84, 314
Quincy, Josiah, 132

Randolph, Edmund, 257, 307
Randolph, Peyton, 72, 123, 183, 269
Read, Deborah, 23, 28–29
Read, George, 230, 325, 327, 346, 351
Reed, Joseph, 71, 78, 92, 172
republicanism
    Adams (John) on, 265–266
    Dickinson on, 291
    as focus of Revolution, 258, 264
Republic Party, Declaration of Independence
    and, 356
Revere, Paul
    and battles of Lexington and Concord,
        110–111, 112
    and Boston Harbor, closure of, 54
    Boston Tea Party and, 52
    and Continental Congress, First, 78, 79, 85
    and wartime propaganda efforts, 119
Revolutionary War
    British public opinion on, 171
    class overtones of, 257–258
    colonial expectations about, 115, 135–136
    command of, as issue, 140
    congressional views on, 124, 316–317
    death toll (1775), 254
    French monitoring of, 208–210
    goals of, 124–125, 134, 135, 137
    impact on American opinions, 224, 233, 234,
        246, 248, 253–257, 354
    moral dimension of, 248
    predictions of outcome
        by Americans, 108–109, 156, 221, 238–239
        by British, 44, 100, 104, 106, 171, 173–174,
            204, 393m5
    victory, key to, 349
Rhode Island
    declaration of independence by, 260
    First Continental Congress delegation, 77, 83
    Second Continental Congress delegation,
        332–333, 338
rights of colonists, direct taxation as assault on,
    17–18
Robbins, Caroline, 153
Rochford, Earl of, 45
Rockingham, Marquis of, 24, 48, 90, 198
Rodney, Caesar, 230, 280, 325, 327–329, 328, 351
Rogers, John, 329
Ross, George, 346
Rossiter, Clinton, 352
Ruggles, Timothy, 257

"Rules by Which a Great Empire May be
    Reduced to a Small One"
    (Franklin), 36
Rush, Benjamin, 71, 218, 253, 346
Rutledge, Edward
    at Continental Congress, First, 83
    at Continental Congress, Second, 290, 292,
        293, 296, 317, 325, 326, 333–334
    on Dunmore, 193
    life after independence, 351
    and peace commission, 348
Rutledge, John
    at Continental Congress, First, 85
    at Continental Congress, Second, 124, 137,
        141, 164, 168, 189, 195–196

St. Johns, Canada, U.S. capture of, 213
Sandwich, Earl of, 44, 46, 99, 104, 171, 204,
    205, 241
Saratoga, battle of, 349, 350
Schuyler, Philip General, 212–213, 282–283, 287
Seabury, Samuel, 108
Sears, Isaac, 60
Secret Committee, 238
Seven Years' War (French and Indian War)
    American military power and, 44
    and British authority over colonies, 13–14
    and colonists' views on Britain, 12, 75–76
    Franklin and, 22
Sewell, Jonathan, 107
Shelburne, Lord, 199, 204–205
Sherman, Roger, 293, 294, 296–298, 299, 300,
    311, 327
Shippen, William, 68, 69
slavery
    Abigail Adams on, 275
    Atlantic slave trade, efforts to close, 306
    Declaration of Independence and, 313, 314,
        338
    Jefferson and, 305–306, 313, 314
slaves of rebels, Virginia governor's threat to
    free, 192–193
Small, William, 302
Smith, Catherine Louisa, 113–114
Smith, Francis, 111–112, 113
Smith, James, 346
Solemn League and Covenant, 58
"A Song for American Freedom" (Dickinson),
    131
Sons of Liberty
    and Boston Tea Party, 40–41
    protest infrastructure of, 38–39
South Carolina
    declaration of independence by, 258–259
    First Continental Congress delegation, 60,
        67, 77
    legislature, extralegal, creation of, 60
    replacement of colonial government, 196,
        258–259

royal governor, flight of, 192
Second Continental Congress delegation,
        228, 325–326, 333–334, 338
threat of British invasion, 248
Spain, American overtures to, 211
Stamp Act (1765), 5–6
    colonial opposition to, 15–18, 20, 23–24, 129,
        151
        politicians' motives, 18
    colonial supporters of, 64
    Parliamentary hearings on, 20, 24
    political dilemma created by, 19–20
    as reminder of colonists' second-class
        citizenship, 18–19
    repeal of, 24–26, 90
Stamp Act Congress, 18, 59, 129
standing armies
    Adams (John) on, 187
    colonists' suspicion of, 32–33, 37–39
    in Declaration of Independence, 314
Stevenson, Margaret, 29
Stockbridge Indians, in American forces, 172
Stockton, Richard, 329–330, 351
Stone, Thomas General, 277, 284–285, 329
Stuart, John (3rd Earl of Bute), 14
Suffolk, Earl of, 44–45, 46, 176
Suffolk County Resolves, 79–80, 93
Sugar Act (1764), 14
Sullivan, John, 283–284, 285, 347
*A Summary View of the Rights of British
        America* (Jefferson), 307

taxation, British. *See also* Stamp Act; Tea Act;
        Tea tax; Townshend Duties
    as assault on colonial rights, 17–18
    British policy on, 15
    British refusal to question right of, 48, 206
    Burke (Edmund) on, 48–49, 104
    colonial opposition to, 15–18, 26–28, 35
    Dickinson on, 61, 64, 140, 231
    direct tax, decision to implement, 14
    Drummond negotiations on, 228
    economic necessity for, 13–14, 35, 36
    Franklin on, 22–23, 24–26
    North government policies on, 34–35, 102–103,
        206 (*See also* North Peace Plan)
    North on, 9
    political dilemma created by, 19–20
    as reminder of colonists' second-class
        citizenship, 18–19, 32
Taylor, George, 346
Tea Act
    British refusal to repeal, 46
    colonial opposition to, 40–41, 42, 52–53,
        65–66, 133
    Dartmouth's opposition to, 91
    purposes of, 36
    as turning point in British-colonial relations,
        39–40

tea tax
    colonists' opposition to, 35, 38–39
    history of, 34
    Tea Act and, 36
Thomas, John, 279–283
Thomson, Charles, 72, 78, 123, 320, 321, 327, 333,
        340
Thornton, Matthew, 346
Thoughts on Government (Adams), 265–266
Three Rivers, battle of, 283–284
Tilghman, Matthew, 295
Tories
    intimidation and harassment of, 106–107, 118,
        255–256, 257
    pamphleteering by, 107–108
    political punishment of, 35
Townshend Duties (1767)
    colonial apologists for, 64–65
    colonial opposition to, 26–28, 31–32, 57, 59,
        129, 131
    Franklin on, 30
    passage of, 26
    repeal of, 34
    as turning point in British-colonial relations,
        355
trade, British Naval blockade, 172
trade with Britain, embargo on. *See also*
        boycotts of British goods; Continen-
        tal Associations
    American hopes for, 133, 191
    calls for, 53, 72, 76, 79–81
    Congress's establishment of, 84, 99
    economic problems created by, 187–188
    effectiveness of, 106
    enforcement of, 255–256
trade with Europe
    arms trade with France, 217, 238, 267
    commencement of, 249
    congressional debate on, 188–189, 287
    as de facto independence, 248, 249
    economic benefits of, 238
    independence as prerequisite for, 246, 261, 262
    necessity of, 248
Treaty of Paris (1763), 12, 13, 14
Treaty of Paris (1783), 351
Trumbull, John, 357

unrest, colonial fear of, 76, 82, 108,
        264, 286

Vergennes, Charles Gravier, comte de,
        208–210, 211
Virginia
    and Atlantic slave trade, efforts to close, 306
    Continental Army companies, raising of, 158
    First Continental Congress delegation, 60,
        67, 71, 77, 80, 85, 307
    and independence, movement toward, 278,
        284, 289–290

Virginia (continued)
 land claims, British denial of, 6
 legislature
  extralegal, creation of, 60
  North Peace Plan and, 164
 local declarations of independence in, 261
 royal governor, flight of, 192
 Second Continental Congress delegation,
  260–261, 307, 334–335
 Stamp Act opposition in, 16–17
 threat of British invasion, 248
Virginia Declaration of Rights, 312, 313
Virginia Resolves, 17–18, 84, 257, 354–355
Voltaire, 153

Walpole, Robert (son), 8
Walpole, Sir Robert (father), 13
Walpole, Thomas, 242
Walton, George, 329
Ward, Artemas, 116–117, 148, 149, 160, 250,
  251, 253
Ward, Samuel, 73, 77, 181, 193, 217, 269, 270
Warren, Joseph, 46, 121–122, 152, 162
Washington, George General
 and American identity, formation of, 254–255
 on Boston Tea Party, 42
 and British peace commission, 347
 on British policies, 88, 114
 and Canada campaign, 213
 character and demeanor, 149–150, 250
 and Continental Army
  assumption of command, 147–150, 159
  and Boston, siege of, 250–253
  Declaration of Independence and, 343,
   343, 345
  French arms, efforts to obtain, 211
  and New York, defense of, 289, 320
  officer appointments, 280
  officers pay, 185–186
  pay as commander, 185
  recruitment and retention issues, 187, 337
 at Continental Congress, First, 67, 68,
  69–70, 88
 at Continental Congress, Second, 115,
  123, 138
 on Dunmore, 193

 on horrors of war, 115
 on independence, 253
 on inevitability of war, 114–115
 life of, after First Continental Congress,
  88–89, 114
 movement toward radicalization, 31–32
 on Native American allies, 172
 as president, 350, 352
Wayne, Anthony, 254
Wedderburn, Alexander, 50, 172, 176, 178
Wells, Elizabeth, 55
West Indies, opening of trade with, 189
Weymouth, Viscount, 45
Whately, Thomas, 37, 49
Whigs, pamphleteering by, 108–110
Whipple, William, 248, 329
White Oaks Company, 23
Wilkes, John, 199
Williams, William, 346
Willing, Morris and Company, 236–239
Willing, Thomas, 188, 189, 236–239, 276,
  325, 331
Wilson, James, 226
 at Continental Congress, Second
  Address to the Inhabitants of America,
   232–234
  and independence, declaration of, 325,
   331–332
  support for reconciliation, 224–233, 235,
   290
 and Drummond peace mission, 227,
  228–229
 life of, 225, 351–352
 political career, 225–226
Witherspoon, John, 329–330
Wolcott, Oliver, 245, 268, 293, 327, 346, 351
women, rights of, Abigail Adams on, 275
Wooster, David General, 279, 281, 283
Wright, Esmond, 145
Wright, James, 95
Wythe, George, 190, 196, 292, 302–303, 309,
  346

Yorktown, battle of, 349, 350

Zubly, John Joachim, 188–189, 190

A Note on the Author

John Ferling is professor emeritus of history at the University of West Georgia. A leading authority on American Revolutionary history, he is the author of ten books, including *Adams vs. Jefferson: The Tumultuous Election of 1800*; *The First of Men: A Life of George Washington*; the award-winning *A Leap in the Dark: The Struggle to Create the American Republic*, and the bestselling *Almost a Miracle: The American Victory in the War of Independence*. His most recent work, *The Ascent of George Washington: The Hidden Political Genius of an American Icon*, was named one of the best books of 2009 by the *Washington Post*. He and his wife, Carol, live in metropolitan Atlanta.

tive View of the **CITY** *of* **PHILADELPHIA**, *in the* **PRO**

3. *Academy* .... 5. *Dutch Calvinist Church* 7. *Quakers Meeting*
4. *Presbyterian Church* 6. *The Court House* 8. *High Street Wh*